OCCUPATIONAL LITERATURE

An Annotated Bibliography

OCCUPATIONAL LITERATURE

1964 Edition

H. W. WILSON COMPANY

An Annotated Bibliography

by

Gertrude Forrester

Formerly, Head Counselor
West Side High School
Newark Public Schools, New Jersey

NEW YORK   1964

Contents

PART I

Introduction

This bibliography has been prepared to assist in acquainting youth with sources of information about occupations—information that has become increasingly important in the complex world of career opportunities. In order that young people may make their career choices wisely, they must be aware of the changing trends in manpower demand. The increasing use of automation and the emergence of new jobs resulting from scientific developments point up the need for current occupational information.

Recent events have indicated that the United States has need of manpower in many occupations, particularly in those requiring exceptional talent and specialized training. To meet this situation in the years ahead, teachers and counselors must be alert to help every young person discover his talents and interests and to encourage him to develop his best capabilities. They must be able to show the student how to relate these capabilities to opportunities in our society and how to relate the occupational information realistically to his needs. It is hoped that this bibliography will provide access to some of the sources of occupational information necessary to the counselor in this task.

In compiling this bibliography, several other purposes have been borne in mind. One is to assist teachers, counselors, and librarians in selecting materials for occupational collections. The second is to serve as a reader's guide to occupational literature, so that an inquirer may determine what to look for in the library or select materials he may wish to purchase. An individual may refer to the descriptions of available material on a specific topic and pursue his examination of the occupational literature with relatively little help. Another purpose is to list the best of the current material on the various subjects so that librarians and counselors may refer students to appropriate sources of information. An obvious aim is to point out the existence of available publications which may be used by research workers.

This bibliography brings together in a central index approximately six thousand selected references to current occupational literature. It includes more than books and pamphlets which simply describe occupations. Since the preparation for a career often involves the selection of a school for training, one section describes the school and college information. Other sections annotate charts, posters, and graphic aids; textbooks for courses in occupations; materials designed to assist youth to evolve a sound vocational plan; references on the techniques of job seeking and job advancement; and publications devoted to the counselors' use of occupational information.

7

Additional sections describe the references to information about scholarships and the publications on studying and working abroad.

Selected titles have been cited in all occupations and fields of work on which useful and authentic material has been found. An attempt has been made to describe as completely as possible all current references which have value and which meet the objectives of vocational and educational guidance.

The fifty-eight series published by forty-five publishers are described in Part II. In the annotated bibliography, Part III, the publications are arranged alphabetically by subject. The data given for each book or pamphlet include the title, author if known, name of publisher, date of publication, number of pages, and price. A reference to a section of a book is indicated by the title of the chapter or section followed by the page reference and the name of the publication. The index then will refer the reader to the page of the full annotation.

Titles of Government publications are followed by the name of the bureau or department which prepared the material. However, if there is a charge for the publication and if the designation "Supt. of Documents" follows, the order should be sent to the Superintendent of Documents, Government Printing Office, Washington 25, D.C.

The references are briefly annotated to indicate the general content of the publication and the major topics included. Most of the publications are prepared for use of students in secondary school and early college years. Otherwise, the annotations point out the age level or special group to which the material is addressed. A limited number of books and pamphlets has been included for graduate students, adult workers, and elementary school pupils.

The prices given are those quoted at the time the publications were examined; because of increasing printing costs, they are subject to change without advance notice. The cost stated is for single copies only; frequently special prices are quoted for large orders. Also there is usually a charge for free publications when ordered in quantity.

Approximately 5,100 pamphlets have been included in this bibliography; there are about 1,500 references to books. The publications have been classified under about 500 occupational titles. For the most part, the headings are the base titles to which code numbers have been assigned in Volume I of the second edition of the *Dictionary of Occupational Titles* and the industry titles given in Volume II of the *Dictionary*. In some cases a general title has been used when it has been convenient to group under one label publications describing a range of occupations, several kinds of work, or related occupations.

For the convenience of users who may wish to arrange their occupational files according to the *Dictionary of Occupational Titles*, the *Dictionary* code numbers have been added to the titles in the annotated bibliography in Part III of this book. The title at the head of each group of entries is the title under which the occupation is defined in the *Dictionary*. Opposite the title, at the right-hand side of the same line, is the code number. This "base" title is the one by which the occupation is most commonly known, or the one which is considered most descriptive of the occupation. Other titles by which the occupation may be designated are given in their proper alphabetical order in the list with a "see" reference to the "basic" title.

The file folders may be arranged in numerical order according to the assigned code numbers. The structure of the United States Employment Service Occupational Classification, as set forth in the second edition of the *Dictionary of Occupational Titles,* is given below. The codes have been assigned in such a manner as to form related categories of occupations, arranged in major groups, divisions, and subdivisions.

MAJOR OCCUPATIONAL GROUPS AND DIVISIONS		NUMBER OF REFERENCES
0. Professional and managerial occupations		
0—0 through 0—3	Professional occupations	2,400
0—4 through 0—6	Semiprofessional occupations	500
0—7 through 0—9	Managerial and official occupations	325
1. Clerical and sales occupations		
1—0 through 1—4	Clerical and kindred occupations	215
1—5 through 1—9	Sales and kindred occupations	50
2. Service occupations		
2—0	Domestic service occupations	10
2—2 through 2—5	Personal service occupations	150
2—6	Protective service occupations	170
2—8 through 2—9	Building service workers and porters	10
3. Agricultural, fishery, forestry, and kindred occupations		
3—0 through 3—4	Agricultural, horticultural, and kindred occupations	65
3—8	Fishery occupations	10
3—9	Forestry (except logging) and hunting and trapping occupations	20
4. 5.	Skilled occupations	700
6. 7.	Semiskilled occupations	175
8. 9.	Unskilled occupations	50
Miscellaneous publications in Sections B through S		1,800
Total number of references		6,650

The number of references to occupations in each of the divisions is indicated to give the user an idea of the distribution of the available literature.

Some counselors and librarians prefer to file their pamphlet collections alphabetically by occupational title. The headings taken from this book may be typed on gummed labels or printed on folders. Thus the file duplicates the arrangement of the pamphlets described in the bibliography.

Whether the pamphlet folders are arranged numerically or alphabetically, either system of filing would require 507 folders and 225 cross-reference cards.

Users who assemble the complete collection may find it advisable to classify further the titles with an unwieldy number of pamphlets. Titles with the largest number of references in this book are as follows:

TITLES	NUMBER OF REFERENCES	TITLES	NUMBER OF REFERENCES
Teacher	90	Journalist	39
Nurse	89	Physicist	37
Scientist	84	Retail manager	37
Librarian	70	Salesperson	36
Physician	69	Religious worker	35
Engineer	63	Forester	34
Social worker	51	Chemist	34
Secretary	46	Lawyer	34
Home economist	45	Medical service worker	33

A star marks the publications recommended for first purchase in small libraries; a double star indicates those most highly recommended.

The criteria given below were used in selecting the literature and in affixing the stars and double stars for special recommendation:

1. *Content*—The topics covered should include those recommended by the National Vocational Guidance Association in its reprints, *Standards for Use in Preparing and Evaluating Occupational Literature* and the 1964 revision, *Guidelines for Preparing and Evaluating Occupational Materials,* listed on page 635.

2. *Authenticity*—Authoritative sources; accurate information; thoroughness of data.

3. *Objectivity*—Unbiased, unprejudiced, and balanced presentation.

4. *Availability of publication.*

5. *Recency of publication*—Date of publication or revision given.

6. *Recency of research or printed sources used.*

7. *Suitability*—Appropriateness for the age, interests, and understanding of individuals who will use them.

8. *Inclusion of information not found elsewhere.*

9. *Style and readability*—Interesting, clear, and concise presentation.

10. *Format and physical features*—Typography and artistic appearance.

11. *Cost*—Effort made to include many free and inexpensive materials.

12. *Motivation for further reading and inquiry*—References for additional information.

13. *Helpfulness in meeting objectives*—Contents aid counselor in meeting goals set forth in many of the authoritative statements listed in the section on "Use of Occupational Information."

Beyond the criteria enumerated above, contents of educational guidance literature, especially, should provide encouragement and assistance to the student in establishing goals commensurate with his abilities, in planning an appropriate course of action to achieve these goals, and in formulating suitable career choices which will mean ultimate satisfaction, success, and increased contributions to society.

This bibliography may be supplemented by the current issues of the *Career Index* (Chronicle Guidance Publications), the *Career Guidance Index* (Careers), the *Counselor's Information Service* (B'naith B'rith Vocational Service), "Current Occupational Literature" in the *Vocational Guidance Quarterly,* the *Guidance Exchange* (Occu-Press), and the *Occupational Index* (Personnel Services, Inc.). These are listed in the section on periodicals.

The 6,650 references annotated and classified in this bibliography are issued by 800 publishers, professional organizations, and government agencies. These sources are all listed in the Publishers' Directory, at the end of the book. Approximately 1,200 publications are available free of charge.

Although an effort has been made to include all materials of unusual merit, some helpful publications have doubtless been omitted. It is inevitable that between the time the manuscript is prepared and the purchase of the book by the user, some publications should go out of print or be repriced. The author and publisher invite users of the bibliography to assist in correcting any shortcomings. Suggestions for improvements in future editions will be appreciated.

For checking and correcting the titles and occupational code numbers, grateful acknowledgment is made to the Branch of Occupational Analysis, United States Employment Service, United States Department of Labor, Washington, D.C. Especial thanks are extended for supplying the code numbers and terminology of titles for many occupations not included in the present edition of the *Dictionary of Occupational Titles.*

PART II

Publications Issued in Series
Arranged According to Publisher of Series

ALUMNAE ADVISORY CENTER, INC., 541 Madison Avenue, New York 22, New York

Mademoiselle College and Career Reprints. 102 reprints. 25c each; 20c each for ten or more

This series consists of reprints of charts and articles which have appeared in *Mademoiselle*, prepared by the College and Careers Department of the magazine. They are available from the Alumnae Advisory Center, a nonprofit organization which publishes some vocational pamphlets and counsels women college graduates on jobs in New York City.

Written in lively style, these four- to ten-page articles are intended to arouse interest in the vocation. Vocational information is often presented through case histories of young women who have succeeded in their specialized fields of work. Because of the attractive illustrations, photographs, and brief biographical sketches of prominent women, these articles are decidedly stimulating in tone. Although the disadvantages of each career are discussed briefly in some of the articles, the approach is intended to create confidence and to encourage further investigation.

Timely information on requirements, opportunities, salaries, and the changing outlook in work for women are considered in many of the series, especially those based on interviews with several young women engaged in the work. However, these reprints are more useful in supplying introductory or supplementary information than in providing complete factual data. The job fields usually are those of interest to college women and high school girls who expect to attend college. Some specialized fields for women such as photo-journalism, puppeteering, wire service reporting, lecture management, and fund raising are included in this series. Some articles contain discussions of job seeking, college information, working abroad, and creative jobs.

The reprints may be ordered either individually or through a subscription of $1 per year for the next five articles as they are issued. There are also two collections, each containing about sixty of the best of the reprints, which are available in loose-leaf hard covers, with indexes and dividers, at a cost of $6 each. The binder entitled File A is designed for the college student or recent college graduate. File B, which includes choosing-a-college features, is for high school students.

A list of the current reprints may be obtained from the Alumnae Advisory Center. About thirty-five titles are described in this bibliography. Typical examples are as follows:

Fashion retailing jobs. 1962	Ten advertising jobs. 1962
Four medical jobs. 1963	Twelve art jobs. 1961
Interior decorator. 1963	Twelve writing jobs. 1963
The job interview. 1962	The woman M.D. 1963
Running a business after marriage. 1963	Your letter is you. 1962

AMERICAN LIBERTY PRESS, 746 West Winnebago Street, Milwaukee 5, Wisconsin

Sextant Series for Exploring Your Future. 12 books; 6 others announced. $5 each hard cover; $4 soft cover; wall chart 60c each. Complete set $75

Each book in this series combines job descriptions with a method of "personal profiling" designed to give each student a more personal relationship with the jobs described. Each book contains a set of fifty personal profile forms for individual pupil use, a series of ninety-five job descriptions, and an organizational chart for the industry showing students "where they can start and where they can go." Additional copies of the profile forms are available at $7.50 per hundred. A teacher's manual accompanies the set.

One page is devoted to each of the ninety-five jobs in each book, presenting the job duties, requirements for entering, promotional outlook, and the pay and skill levels. Each book is 120 pages long, size 8½ by 11 inches. Some users of this series report that they like it because of the personal profiling activity on the part of the student and because of the simplicity of the career information. The available titles are:

EXPLORING YOUR FUTURE IN:

Agriculture. 1962	Insurance. 1961
Banking. 1961	Manufacturing—salaried jobs. 1960
Construction. 1963	Manufacturing—wage or shop jobs. 1960
Graphic arts and publishing. 1963	Professions. 1963
Hospitals. 1961	Public utilities. 1964.
Hotels, motels, restaurants. 1963	Recreation and youth services. 1963

BELLMAN PUBLISHING COMPANY, P.O. Box 172, Cambridge 38, Massachusetts

Vocational and Professional Monographs. $1 each

The seventy-three monographs in this series are designed to provide the essential information a young person needs in considering a field of work as a possible life career. Most of the monographs follow a uniform outline in presenting information about the following basic points:

1. Origin, history and development of the vocation or profession.
2. Personal qualifications needed for entering the vocation or profession.
3. Scholastic training required for engaging in the vocation or profession.
4. Analysis of employment possibilities.
5. Remuneration received.
6. Chances for advancement.
7. Frank statement of advantages and disadvantages.
8. Possibilities for both men and women engaging in the vocation or profession.
9. Professional associations and publications.

Written by authorities in each field, these monographs contain more technical information than some of the other publications. The history, development, and contribution to society of the occupation are unusually well presented. Some monographs contain considerable information about the industry and too few details about the conditions of work, requirements, and qualifications. However, helpful information is usually given about schools for further training, tuition, length of course, and description of the various subjects included in the training sequence.

In each monograph a page is devoted to a biography of the author. The names of outstanding people who are well known in their fields of work establish confidence in the reliability of the text. The pamphlets are bound in heavy paper of varied colors and average from 28 to 36 pages in length. The size is 6 by 9 inches. The number of illustrations varies from one to six.

New titles and revisions of old titles are being added yearly. Of the 113 monographs published in this series, 73 are currently available and are annotated in this bibliography. The publisher allows a discount of 20 per cent on orders of a complete set of titles in print in this series and for all continuation orders to receive new and revised titles as published. A list of the monographs may be obtained from the publisher. Examples of titles are:

Astronomy as a career. 1963
Careers in the railway industry. 1960
Instrument and control engineer. 1958

Medical technologist. 1958
Physical education as a career. 1963
Technical writing as a career. 1961

Other publications of the Bellman Publishing Company described in the appropriate sections of this book are as follows:

Scholarships, fellowships and loans. Volumes III and IV
Scholarships, fellowships and loans news service. (Periodical)

B'NAI B'RITH VOCATIONAL SERVICE, 1640 Rhode Island Ave., N.W., Washington 6, D.C.

B'nai B'rith Occupational Brief Series. 40 briefs. 35c each

The B'nai B'rith Vocational Service conducts occupational and educational research and engages in a broad publications program. It aims to provide up-to-date information for the regional offices conducted in many of the major population centers in cooperation with local Jewish Vocational Service agencies. The service has issued sixty-seven publications on occupations and broad fields of work, college information, job finding, and career planning, as well as charts, research studies, reading lists, and a quarterly bibliography, *Counselor's Information Service.*

The briefs average from four to seventeen pages in length, are written to interest young people, and contain information on outlook, duties, preparation and entry, qualifications, earnings and advancement, physical requirements, working conditions, advantages and disadvantages, and sources of further information. Where information is available, a section is added giving data of interest to Jewish youth.

Most of the briefs are illustrated. They are frequently revised. They are comparatively inexpensive. A B'nai B'rith Guidance Kit is available for $30. This consists of the sixty-seven publications listed in the annual catalog which, if purchased separately, would cost $34.15. Typical titles are:

Careers in memorial counseling. 1959	Latest information on scholarships in the
College guide for Jewish youth. 1963	space age. 1962
Community organization work. 1961	Property management. 1955
Community relations work. 1961	Studying for success. 1961

BOSTON UNIVERSITY, OFFICE OF ADMISSIONS, 705 Commonwealth Avenue, Boston 15, Massachusetts

Career Monographs. 21 titles. Free

This is a series of twenty-one recruiting booklets on subjects for which the university offers training. Considerable information of general interest is included. Each booklet describes the work in various specialized fields and includes discussion of opportunities, qualifications, requirements, advantages, and preparation. The last section pertains to the specific training offered by Boston University.

The booklets have attractive red and white covers with occupational symbols in the center of the page. The average length is 13 pages and the size is 3½ by 7 inches. Examples of titles are as follows:

Accounting as a career. 1962	Finance as a career. 1962
Business management as a career. 1962	Physical education as a career. 1962
Chemistry as a career. 1962	Physics as a career. 1962
Commercial art as a career. 1962	Radio, television, theatre as a career.
Education as a career. 1962	1962

CAREERS. Box 135, Largo, Florida

Career Guidance Service. September through May. $30 per subscription

This publishing company distributes a monthly packet of material to subscribers from September through May. Under the editorship of Raymond

M. Handville, the material is practical and up to date. All of the booklets and posters appearing in the service may be purchased individually or they may be obtained as they are published through an annual subscription. A junior high school service is available for $25. Counselors and librarians may send for a composite sample including one of each of the items listed below. Subscription to one year's service includes the following:

- 40 career briefs. Single copies 25c
- 75 career summaries or thumbnail sketches. Single copies 15c
- 90 reprints of selected career articles. Single copies 15c
- 9 career guidance indexes, listing references to free and inexpensive career materials. Yearly subscription $6
- 14 college guides, listing entrance requirements, costs, etc. $3 per set
- 18 training guides, listing training opportunities for specific careers. $3 per set
- 27 posters, stimulating students to think about their future careers. $10 per set
- 9 book reviews and reprints of timely professional articles
- 3 bonus items: 1 desk-top file, 40 printed tab cards, 1 calendar

Career Briefs. 167 titles. Yearly subscription $9.25. 25c each

These briefs are published at the rate of forty a year and are revised every four years. They contain information on the history and development of the occupation, duties, working conditions, training requirements, training opportunities, personal qualifications, employment prospects, hours and earnings, advancement prospects, measuring one's interests and ability, and a suggested high school program. Most of the briefs contain references to four or more additional readings.

Eight pages in length, the briefs are 5½ by 8½ inches, and are designed to fit the desk-top file. The titles and code numbers are placed on the top in the upper right-hand corner. The information is timely and well presented. Typical titles in this series are:

Auto mechanic. 1962
Bilingual secretary. 1963
Carpenter. 1963
Dental hygienist. 1963

Draftsman. 1963
Forge shop occupations. 1962
Geophysicist. 1960
Programmer. 1962

Career Summaries. 329 summaries. Yearly subscription $9.25. Single copies 15c each

These summaries are distributed at the rate of seventy-five a year and are revised every four years. They contain thumb-nail sketches of duties, working conditions, personal qualifications, training, earnings and hours, recommended high school activities, outlook, places of employment, related careers, measuring one's interests and ability, and sources of further information.

These contain shorter and more concise information than the career briefs, but the filing plan suggested for them makes them convenient to use. They are printed on card stock, both sides, size 5½ by 8½ inches, the same size as the career briefs and career reprints, to fit into the desk-top metal file box. The titles and code numbers are placed on the top in the upper right-hand corner. Because of the large number of titles, this series covers many occupations not found in book-length discussions.

An up-to-date list of titles may be secured from the publisher. Typical titles are:

Advertising manager, store. 1963	Orthoptic technician. 1960
Camera repairman. 1963	Packaging engineer. 1960
Employment interviewer. 1963	Securities salesman. 1963
Fingerprint classifier. 1963	Swimming pool service technician. 1963
Oceanographer. 1961	Traffic manager. 1964

CHANGING TIMES, THE KIPLINGER MAGAZINE, 1729 H Street, N.W., Washington 6, D.C.

Changing Times Reprints. 20 booklets. 15c to 75c each

Collections of related material on careers from *Changing Times* are reprinted in booklet form, size 8½ by 6 inches. Some research bulletins on college and employment information are larger, size 8½ by 11 inches. The style is clear, concise, direct, and convincing, obviously the work of trained writers. The career reprints are three or four pages in length. Examples of titles are:

A business of your own? 1960. 35c	Colleges with room for students. Annually. 75c
Career as an architect. 1960. 15c	
Careers in accounting. 1961. 15c	Commercial loans for college. 1962. 15c
Careers in home economics. 1962. 15c	The job outlook. 1962. 25c
Careers in planning. 1963. 15c	Jobs in journalism. 1959. 15c
Careers in the law. 1960. 15c	Your job and your future. 1963. 35c

CHILDRENS PRESS, INC., and MELMONT PUBLISHERS, INC., Jackson Boulevard and Racine Avenue, Chicago 7, Illinois

"I Want To Be" Series. 35c books. $2 each

This series, designed to encourage independent reading on the beginner level, is prepared for readers with a reading level of upper first grade. They are written by Carla Greene, with the consultation of Dr. Paul Witty of the Psycho-Educational Clinic, Northwestern University. He states that all but about ten to twenty of the approximately two hundred words used in each book are from the first thousand words for children's reading. The books are thirty-two pages in length and are illustrated in color.

These books are used as social studies material to acquaint children in lower elementary grades with services provided in the community. Only a few titles in this series are included in the main bibliography of this book, as examples of available simple materials for young readers:

I want to be a dentist. 1960	I want to be a road builder. 1958
I want to be a doctor. 1958	I want to be a ship captain. 1962
I want to be a librarian. 1960	I want to be a space pilot. 1961
I want to be a musician. 1962	I want to be a zoo keeper. 1961

Primary Social Studies Enrichment Materials. 12 books. $2.50 each

This series is similar to the "I Want To Be" books described above, but is prepared to appeal to grades two through four. It is published by Melmont Publishers, Inc., subsidiary of Childrens Press. Examples of titles are:

About the driver of a bus. 1959	At the bakery. 1953
About the engineer of a train. 1962	At the bank. 1959
About truck farming. 1962	At the dairy. 1958

CHRONICLE GUIDANCE PUBLICATIONS, INC., Moravia, New York

Chronicle "3 in 1" Guidance Service. September through April. $42.50 a year for single subscription; 2-9 subscriptions, $40 each; 10 or more, $37.50 each. For orders entered on a continuing renewal basis there is a 10 per cent discount after the first year.

This service offers a package of occupational, educational, and professional guidance material each month from September through April. The items may be ordered separately or obtained as they are published through an annual subcription. Several of the services are described in this book in the section on "Package Purchases." An annual subscription consists of the following materials:

> 72 job briefs. $17.25 per year. 35c for single copies
> 56 reprints. $6 per year. Set of "150 best" for $12
> 8 career indexes, listing free or inexpensive materials, with attached request post cards, ready to stamp and mail. $8 per year
> 8 posters, suitable for bulletin board use. $6 per year. $1 each
> 5 books such as *Colleges Classified, College Entrance Charts, Student Aid Annual, Student Aid Bulletins,* and *Guide to Majors.* $15 per year
> 12 pieces of professional information. $5 per year

Each year each subscriber receives a bonus package; extra copies are available at reduced prices to subscribers to the service.

Chronicle Occupational Brief Service. 72 briefs a year. $17.25 per subscription per year. Single copies 35c each or 3 for $1. Full set of 285 titles, $41.50 unbound; $43.50 bound in 3 volumes with plastic spine bindings. Cash required with orders totaling less than $2

These briefs are included in the Chronicle "3 in 1" Guidance Service, the Occupational Service, and the Pamphlet Service. They may be purchased separately or on an annual subscription basis. Most of them have been prepared or revised within the last four years; the publishers plan to issue twenty-four new titles each year and to revise about forty-eight. The titles, for the most part, are the base titles to which code numbers have been assigned in the *Dictionary of Occupational Titles* and the code numbers are placed at the top of each brief.

Each four-page brief, size 8½ by 11 inches, contains information on the following topics when possible: duties, working conditions, hours, earnings, personal qualifications, determination of aptitude and interest, training requirements and opportunities, employment outlook, where employed, methods of entry, high school preparation for the job, and references for further reading. Many of the briefs acknowledge the assistance of one to three recognized authorities in the field, whose names are given, and who approve the manuscript.

An up-to-date list of available titles and quantity rates may be secured from the publisher upon request. Examples of titles in this series are:

Athletic coach. 1963	Custodian. 1962
Baker. 1961	Meat cutter. 1960
Barber. 1961	Milliner. 1963
Comparison shopper. 1963	Office machine operator. 1963
Correspondence clerk. 1962	Teacher, nursery school. 1962
County agricultural agent. 1959	Technical illustrator. 1964

COWARD-McCANN, INC., 200 Madison Avenue, New York 16, New York

The Colby Books. 50 titles. $2.50 each; guaranteed library binding, $2.52 net

In this series, written by Carroll B. Colby, numerous photographs and brief text provide an introduction to a wide variety of subjects. Some of the books give a picture of the training, equipment, and nature of the work done in a number of fields. These books are of special interest to boys in grades four through seven and to older, reluctant readers. They average forty-eight pages in length. This series has proved very popular with elementary grades. Some of the titles are:

Air Force Academy. 1962	Park ranger. 1955
Count down: missile bases. 1960	Smoke eaters. 1954
Fish and wildlife. 1955	Snow surveyors. 1959
Night people. 1961	Soil savers. 1957
Our space age Navy. 1962	West Point today. 1963

DODD, MEAD AND COMPANY, 432 Park Avenue South, New York 16, New York

Dodd, Mead Career Books. 74 books. $3 each

The Dodd, Mead career books have numbered over eighty, but many of them are now out of print. All of them are fiction. Whereas the authors of some of the other series are professional writers trained in journalism, the writers of these books are required by the publisher to "have lived the careers they write about and be able to discuss them enthusiastically and with understanding." In addition, the authors of this series must have the special ability to evaluate their personal experiences and to use these to the advantage of readers who want sound advice.

Consequently, many of these books appear to be semiautobiographical. Reading about interviews or discussions of advantages and disadvantages of various types of work, one has the impression that the author is expressing his personal opinions gained from his own experience. The authors are also expressing the opinions of other successful career people in their respective fields, based on actual case records which are woven into the story. The plots may not hold the suspense of the traditional novel, but these books offer considerable occupational information.

The editors of this series have also stipulated that the titles chosen must be careers which offer "plenty of opportunities." As a result, practical rather than glamorous occupations are included in the series. For example, the titles include home economics, librarianship, secretarial work, department store work, and X-ray technician, in addition to nursing and news reporting. The following are examples of these career fiction titles:

> Jeff Carson, young geologist. 1960
> Joan Palmer, policewoman. 1960
> Maggie in fashion. 1961
> Squad room detective. 1960
> Susan, hospital aide. 1964
> Television and teamwork. 1962
> Wendy Scott, secretary. 1961

Juvenile Titles. 10 titles. $2.50; Dodd durable binding $2.57 net

Dodd, Mead and Company also publishes a series of juvenile titles, suitable for grades three to seven. By means of photographs and simple text, each portrays the work done in a variety of fields. The books are approximately sixty-four pages each. Titles are:

What does an astronaut do? 1961	What does a jet pilot do? 1959
What does a civil engineer do? 1960	What does a librarian do? 1963
What does a cowboy do? 1963	What does a parachutist do? 1960
What does a diver do? 1961	What does a policeman do? 1959
What does a forest ranger do? 1964	What does a scientist do? 1959

E. P. DUTTON AND COMPANY, INC. 201 Park Avenue South, New York 3, New York

Dutton Books on Careers. $3.50 to $4.95. Set of 10 Career Books, listed in 1963 brochure, $23.85

These books contain narrative descriptions of various fields of work and the opportunities for careers in them. Although some of the books include biographical sketches of well-known people who have attained prominence in their specialty, the authors do not attempt to dramatize a few incidents in the lives of the workers; rather they aim to present detailed information about the various kinds of work, the qualifications, the promotional steps, and the opportunities.

This series contains thorough and penetrating information, yet is written in simple nontechnical language. It is suitable for the senior high school and the college student. Many of these books are double starred in this bibliography because of the quality and quantity of occupational information presented. The more recent titles in this series include:

CAREERS AND OPPORTUNITIES IN OR FOR:

Advertising. 1964
Astronautics. 1962
Chemistry. 1960
Commercial art. 1963
Electronics. 1963
Engineering. 1959

Fashion. 1964
Music. 1964
Physics. 1961
Science. 1960
Women in business. 1963
How to get into college. 1963

FINNEY COMPANY, 3350 Gorham Avenue, Minneapolis 26, Minnesota

Finding Your Job Series. 3 units of 60 job descriptions each. 2 additional units planned. $20.50 per unit

This series has been developed in response to needs of students in special education classes of slow learners. The publishers state that the materials are prepared for the young people "with limited attention spans, limited comprehensions, and limited vocabularies."

Each unit consists of sixty job descriptions of unskilled or semiskilled occupations, arranged in five "volumes." Each job description is four pages in length, size 8½ by 11 inches. In simple language the following topics are discussed briefly in each: The kind of job this is, What this job pays, What to expect, Working hours, What a worker must be able to do, What a worker must be like, Schooling needed, Money needed before starting work, Good things about this job, Bad things about this job, What's ahead, Helpful subjects in school, Ways to get this job, Things to do at school, Free information, Books to buy, and Movies about this job. A final section considers the question, "Is this the job for you?"

The standardized purchase consists of job descriptions bound in sets of twelve. So many users have been breaking up the sets in order to file the individual titles in folders that arrangements have been made to obtain unbound monographs. The materials are presented in a manner easy to understand and with the purpose of helping potential dropouts, retarded learners, and special education classes consider specific jobs within their capabilities. The descriptions are not arranged according to any classification system, but they represent occupations requiring a limited amount of training; for example:

Bus boy	Night watchman
Cafeteria server	Powder room attendant
Car hop	Redcap
Car washer	Sprayman
Freight elevator operator	Street department worker
Florist's helper	Telegraph messenger
Hospital cleaning lady	Toy stuffer
Hotel maid	Warehouseman
Laundry marker	Window washer

Occupational Guidance Charting Your Course Series. 5 units, 8 volumes in each unit, 20 briefs in each volume. $34.50 per unit

About two thirds of these titles have been prepared for students terminating their education with high school graduation and the other third for students going on for additional training. Each brief is four pages in length, size 8½ by 11 inches. In fairly simple language, the following topics are discussed briefly in each, usually in three or four sentences: Description of work, Earnings, History of occupation, Working conditions, Hours of work, Ability required, Temperament required, Education and training required, Finances required before earning, Attractive features, Disadvantages, Outlook for the future, Licensing, Suggested courses in high school, Methods to enter work, Suggested high school activities, Free information material, Purchasable material, Visual aids, and Ways of testing your interests.

This publication is offered in two different bindings. Each volume is comprised of twenty monographs bound together with a Wir-O (somewhat similar to spiral) binding. The assumption is that users will allow the assembly to remain intact and use one volume at a time. However, unbound material may be ordered at a quantity price of $35 per hundred monographs.

Because each unit contains 160 job briefs, the total number of titles covered is now 800 and includes a wide range of occupational titles. An alphabetical index is available, indicating which unit and volume contains the specific title. A display rack with pockets to accommodate the units is distributed by the publisher to stimulate reading and minimize supervision of the materials. Among the 800 titles are some unusual ones not frequently found in series of career briefs. Examples are:

Baseball umpire	Jail matron
Bridal consultant	Jockey
Circus clown	Moving van driver
Golf professional	Music arranger
Hearing aid fitter	Music critic
House mover	Ship's purser
Information clerk	Trapper
Item control clerk	Weaver

GENERAL MOTORS CORPORATION, Educational Relations Section, Public Relations Staff, Detroit 2, Michigan

Guidance Booklets. 10 booklets. Free

The General Motors Educational Aids catalog lists ten guidance booklets. Single copies are furnished free to educators for instructional purposes. Information concerning price and availability of quantity amounts will be furnished on request. Correspondence should be sent on school stationery to the above address.

These booklets describe the opportunities awaiting young men and women in the various fields and discuss the preparation necessary for employment in these jobs. While booklets on the scientist and engineer encourage college training, some of the others suggest special training. The booklet on the work of the craftsman outlines a typical apprentice training program; the booklets on the draftsman, technician, retail automotive business, and office worker point out opportunities for those without college training. Titles of these booklets include:

Can I be a craftsman? 1961
Can I be a draftsman? 1961
Can I be a scientist? 1961
Can I be a technician? 1961

Can I be an office worker? 1955
Can I get the job? 1954
Career opportunities in the retail automotive business. 1962

THE GUIDANCE CENTRE, Ontario College of Education, University of Toronto, 371 Bloor Street West, Toronto 5, Ontario, Canada

Guidance Centre Occupational Information Monographs. In Canada 15c per copy postpaid; elsewhere 20c per copy postpaid. Special quantity prices

These monographs present information about workers in Canada. Each monograph is prepared by an authority actively associated with the occupation under consideration and checked by the centre's research staff before publication. Each booklet starts with a short definition of the occupational title and gives information under the following headings: history and importance; nature of the work; working conditions; qualifications necessary for entry and success; preparation needed; employment, advancement, outlook; remuneration; advantages; disadvantages; how to get started in or towards the occupation; related occupations; and further readings. Provision is made so that special information concerning the occupation in a particular area may be added.

Four pages in length, containing from 2,500 to 3,500 words, they are printed on heavy, coated stock. One picture is used in each monograph. The information on employment opportunities and wages is based on Canadian statistics; certain sections of many of the monographs apply equally to Canada and the United States.

The monographs are revised about every four years. There are 160 titles included in the following pages. Typical examples are:

Accountant. 1963	Horticulturist. 1960 .
Auto mechanic. 1962	Medical laboratory technologist. 1963
Bricklayer. 1963	Mushroom grower. 1962
Electronic technician. 1962	Oil burner serviceman. 1963

HARPER AND ROW, PUBLISHERS, 49 East 33rd Street, New York 16, New York

"So You Want To Be" Career Books. 13 titles. $3.50 each. Harpercrest library bindings, $3.27 net

This series pays special attention to describing the necessary training, tracing it from the choice of a college, through the first weeks of college preparation, to the beginning of practice. Each book includes a description of the career fields within the profession, desirable scholastic and personal qualifications, rewards, satisfactions, contributions to society, and a look ahead. This series contains less statistical factual information concerning supply, demand, distribution of workers, earnings, and outlook than some of the other publications, although each book is approximately 192 pages in length.

The publishers describe this series as "a practical, lively, readable vocational series." The authors, with one exception, not only have practiced in the fields they cover but are also professional writers. Titles in this series include:

So You Want To Be a (or Go into):

Advertising. 1961	Lawyer. 1959
Chemist. 1963	Librarian. 1963
Dentist. 1963	Nurse. 1961
Doctor. 1963	Physicist. 1963
Engineer. 1962	Scientist. 1960
Industry. 1960	Social worker. 1963
Journalism. 1963	

THE INSTITUTE FOR RESEARCH, 537 South Dearborn Street, Chicago 5, Illinois

Careers Research Monographs. $1 each. $4.75 for 5 titles. On an order for selected titles the following discounts apply: 10 per cent on 25 to 49 titles; 20 per cent on an order for 50 or more titles.

These 274 monographs present detailed information about each career. The monographs follow, in general, a uniform outline. In addition to nature of work, personal qualifications, training, educational requirements, opportunities, earnings, attractive and unattractive features, many monographs contain either a list of schools offering specialized training or the name and address of a professional association from which a list of recommended schools may be obtained. They also give lists of organizations or professional societies, trade journals and periodicals, and suggested readings.

Considerable general information and historical background material are included. A description of a typical day's work constitutes a useful feature of each monograph. The attractive and unattractive features are presented fairly. Some specialized fields such as tax attorney, mineral economist, television and radio writer, and cartoonist are included in this series.

Bound in heavy brown paper covers, they average about 24 pages in length and contain several half-tone illustrations. The covers are sturdy and do not crumple in the folders. The information is not condensed, since the authors are not crowded for space. The pages, size 8½ by 11 inches, contain 2 columns of clearly printed type, averaging about 700 words. In other words, 20 pages are equivalent to twice that amount printed in ordinary book form. Some of the later revisions do not have many changes from the first editions and the references to further reading in the revised editions are not as up to date as one might wish. However, the style is clear, interesting, factual, and nontechnical.

To receive new monographs as published, one may place his name on a continuation order list. Formerly, the monographs were available only in sets of 5, but they may now be ordered by individual titles. Single copies cost $1 each. Typical of the 274 titles in this series are the following:

Air freight and express transportation. 1961

Federal and state fish and wildlife service. 1960

News photographer. 1962

Route and territorial salesman. 1962

State and county highway police departments. 1960

Sports writer. 1961

Truck transportation. 1960

J. B. LIPPINCOTT COMPANY, East Washington Square, Philadelphia 5, Pennsylvania

Informal Vocational Studies by John J. Floherty. 24 books. $3.50 and $3.95 each

Most of these are dramatic stories about the work of men in adventurous and hazardous occupations. The excitement and heroism behind the scenes are described in the daring exploits of the secret service men, policemen, fire fighters, Coast Guardsmen and other sentries of the sea. Mr. Floherty is a good reporter and his accounts are full of human interest stories. For example, to gather the material for books about the Coast Guard, he visited many of the Coast Guard stations and accompanied the men on a number of their expeditions. All facts were taken from the official records of the United States Coast Guard.

These books describe many kinds of work and the daring, danger, and adventure implicit in them. They do not contain discussion of the employment outlook, supply and demand of workers, or training. They seem to be intended for the general reader more than the aspiring career inquirer. However, they are useful because they are well liked by high school boys, especially in grades 8 to 11. Also, they are supplemented by excellent action photographs taken by the authors.

Some of the recent books have been written by or with Mike McGrady. Examples of titles in this series are:

Aviation from the ground up. 1960	Skin-diving adventures. 1962
Behind the silver shield. 1957	Rockets, missiles and space. 1962
Crime scientists. 1961	Whirling wings. 1961
Man against earth. 1961	Youth and the F.B.I. 1960

MACMILLAN COMPANY, 60 Fifth Avenue, New York 11, New York

Macmillan Career Books. 10 titles. $3.50 and $3.95 each

This series contains rather full information as the books average about two hundred pages in length. They have been prepared by authors who have been successful in their careers and who are enthusiastic about helping young people avoid mistakes in choosing a profession. The general editor of the series is Charles W. Cole, former president of Amherst College. Each book includes a description of the history and importance of the career, duties, an average working day, personal characteristics and abilities needed, education and necessary preparation, kinds of work possible, rewards, and possible future developments in the field. Many of the books point to the tremendously varied opportunities open to the person with the necessary training. They are intended for the mature high school student as well as the college student.

This series has been written recently, from 1961 to 1964:

Architect. 1962	Nurse. 1962
Career diplomat. 1964	Physician. 1961
Journalist. 1962	Professor. 1961
Lawyer. 1961	Scientist. 1964
Minister. 1963	Social worker. 1964

JULIAN MESSNER, INC., 8 West 40th St., New York 18, New York

Career Romances for Young Moderns. 59 books. $2.95 each.

These books combine adventurous romance fiction with facts about careers. The information about the kinds of work, qualifications, advantages, disadvantages, promotional steps, and working conditions of a special career is interwoven into the conversations of the main characters. One gets a feeling of the way of life of people engaged in the kind of work described. These fictionalized tales, therefore, may stimulate the reader to search for additional information of a more factual type. The plot and love theme usually are sufficiently strong to lure teen-age readers into reading several of the books, with the result that they receive some information about several fields of work.

In this series of more than fifty books, the occupational information is exceptionally accurate and authentic. About twenty of the books have been written since 1960. For the most part, the authors are professional fiction writers who have had some experience in the various vocations described in the books. They are written for young people of teen age, most of them for girls. The girls read the books for the stories and the romance; incidentally they learn about varied fields of work which they may not have considered previously. A few typical recent titles are:

Brenda becomes a buyer. 1960   Lorna Evans: social worker. 1961
Cheryl Downing: school nurse. 1964   Lynn Pamet: caterer. 1960
Jet stewardess. 1962   Nina Grant: pediatric nurse. 1960
Jinny Williams: library assistant. 1962   Overseas teacher. 1963

Messner Biographies. $3.25 and $3.50 each; Messner certified editions $3.19 and $3.34 net

The Messner biographies number more than 200 books. Uniform in size, $5\frac{5}{8}$ by $8\frac{1}{2}$ inches, clothbound, 192 pages in length, they are attractively printed and written for junior and senior high school boys and girls. They introduce young people to the personalities and achievements of men and women in many fields of endeavor and serve as inspirational reading for teen-agers. Many of them illustrate the triumphs over handicaps and frustrations. Biographies and autobiographies of successful workers have long been recognized as being a rich and stimulating branch of literature for those seeking knowledge about an occupation. Career fiction and inspirational accounts have, as many teachers and counselors will testify, an exceedingly useful function in stimulating the imagination and enthusiasm of the individual who has not seriously considered certain occupations. Many times, the young workers-to-be will learn to approach work as a satisfying way of life and to take courage from the early struggles of people they admire. In the publisher's catalog, each title is followed by symbols indicating recommendations in sources such as the *Booklist, Library Journal, Standard Catalog, Children's Catalog*, etc. Following are examples of these biographies:

America's first woman chemist. 1961
Giant of the atom: Ernest Rutherford. 1962
Inventive wizard: George Westinghouse. 1962
Man against the elements: Adolphus W. Greely. 1960
Pioneer oceanographer: Alexander Agassiz. 1963
Plant explorer: David Fairchild. 1961
She lived for science: Irène-Joliot Curie. 1961

Messner Career Books. $3.50 and $3.95 each; Messner certified edition $3.34 and $3.64 net

Another series of nonfiction career books has been prepared, seven of them under the authorship of Harry Edward Neal. These books are comprehensive and present a well-rounded picture of the careers:

Disease detectives: your career in medical research. 1959
Engineers unlimited: your career in engineering. 1960
Money masters: your career in banking. 1961
Nature's guardians: your career in conservation. 1963

Pathfinders, U.S.A.: your career on land, sea and air. 1963
Skyblazers: your career in aviation. 1963
Stagestruck: your career in theatre. 1963
Your career in electronics. 1963
Your career in chemistry. 1964

MICHIGAN EMPLOYMENT SECURITY COMMISSION, 7310 Woodward Avenue, Detroit 2, Michigan

Michigan Occupational Guide Series. 65 guides. 25c per copy

The objective of the series is the presentation of accurate and authentic job information for the vocational guidance of youth and the placement of workers on jobs better suited to their abilities. In its employment work, the Commission found that one of the greatest weaknesses in vocational guidance programs has been the lack of up-to-date and reliable information about jobs. Consequently, it is trying to supply that need by providing occupational information necessary for wiser occupational choices.

Most of the guides include the history of the occupation, nature of the work, location of jobs, employment outlook, working conditions, organizations, earnings, requirements for entry, advantages, disadvantages, and references for further reading.

The guides are prepared mainly from occupational information collected in Michigan. However, materials and publications from other areas are used in their preparation. Most of the information in each guide is applicable to other areas, especially nature of the work, requirements for entry, training needed, advantages, anad disadvantages. However, the reader should realize that salaries, number of workers, and employment outlook apply chiefly to Michigan.

These guides are objective and contain factual information for the use of employment interviewers as well as counselors. They are the result of careful research. Personal opinion is kept to a minimum.

Averaging about twenty pages, size 5½ by 8½ inches, they have a uniform two-color cover. Because of the low cost of the publications and the vast amount of information contained in them, they are highly recommended. Examples of titles are:

Airplane mechanic. 1961	Plumbing occupations. 1963
Barber. 1963	Sewing machine operators. 1962
Department store occupations. 1963	Supermarket occupations. 1962
Office machine servicemen. 1963	Traffic manager. 1960

NEW YORK LIFE INSURANCE COMPANY, Career Information Service, Box 51, Madison Square Station, New York 10, New York

Booklets on Individual Careers. 60 booklets. Free

Written by prominent authorities in their fields, these booklets are designed to show young people the amount of education and training needed for various careers. The booklets also describe what individual qualifications are necessary for different careers, the cost of training, outlook for future opportunities, and ultimate rewards.

The booklets are reprints of advertisements sponsored by New York Life Insurance Company to encourage parents to prepare for the future education of their children. The last page of each booklet suggests to parents that they formulate an insurance plan. These publications are very readable, and they contain unusually good illustrations.

The reprints are available in booklet form, twelve pages in length, and 4 by 6¼ inches in size. New York Life maintains a mailing list of interested educators, counselors, and librarians and will mail, on request, the booklets as they are published. Examples of titles are:

SHOULD YOU BE A:

Biologist. 1961
Dietitian. 1962
Draftsman. 1962
Electronic computer programmer. 1963
Manufacturing engineer. 1963
Medical technologist. 1961

Newspaperman. 1960
Physicist. 1960
Purchasing agent. 1962
Salesman. 1959
Space scientist. 1963
Veterinarian. 1961

Career opportunities (a paperbound compilation of 54 of the career articles). 1962
Cost of four years of college. 1961

PERSONNEL SERVICES, INC., Box 306, Jaffrey, New Hampshire

Occupational Abstracts. 50c each; 10 or more selected titles, 35c each; special price to students only, 25c cash with order; complete set $30. 100 copies of one title 30c each

These are concise six-page abstracts of available literature on a wide range of occupations. This series was prepared originally under the direction of the National Occupational Conference with a grant provided by the Carnegie Foundation. Under the former editorship of Robert Hoppock and the present editorship of Sydney F. Austin, the abstracts are prepared by a number of authors who "summarize what has appeared in print about the occupations described." From the beginning, the plan has been not to conduct original research or interview workers engaged in the occupation, but to abstract the existing books and pamphlets on the subject. The topics generally summarized are types of work, future prospects, number and distribution of workers, duties, qualifications, preparation, methods of entering, advancement, earnings, advantages, and disadvantages. Each pamphlet also contains a survey and appraisal of the literature, sources of further information, and an annotated bibliography.

Published in a variety of colors, the folders measure 3½ by 8½ inches. Although the information presented is brief, it is to the point. No irrelevant material about the technical aspects of the subject is included. The summaries are presented in a dignified style; there are no overstatements or rash generalities. The reading references are unusually well selected, carefully annotated, and can be depended upon. The recent abstracts contain the *Dictionary of Occupation Titles* code numbers for the convenience of users who file numerically according to the D.O.T. symbols and the titles of the recent abstracts are the base titles to which code numbers are assigned in the *Dictionary.*

Information gathered from available literature on a specific occupation is summarized at the rate of one a month. Subscription to new titles as issued may be ordered at a cost of $3.50 per year; ten titles, one each month except July and August.

Of the 130 occupational abstracts listed in this book, the following are typical examples:

Botanist. 1963	Medical secretary. 1963
Ceramic engineer. 1964	Podiatrist. 1964
Comparison shopper. 1963	Programmer. 1961
Dentist. 1963	Radio repairman. 1961
Florist. 1962	Science teacher. 1963
Mathematics teacher. 1963	Systems analyst. 1963

POPULAR LIBRARY, INC., 355 Lexington Avenue, New York 17, New York
Paperbacks. 50c and 75c each

Some books which other publishers have printed in hard-cover bindings in their original editions have been reprinted in inexpensive paperbacks. The "Your Future" series is published by Richards Rosen Press and is described under its publications. A special discount is available to educators and students who purchase quantity lots of the paperbacks. In most cases, both the original and the paperbound editions are entered in this bibliography, including:

YOUR FUTURE IN OR AS:

Advertising. 50c	Electronic engineering. 50c
Airline stewardess. 50c	Fashion world. 50c
Army. 50c	Foreign service. 50c
Chemical engineering. 50c	Journalism. 50c
Dentistry. 50c	Nuclear energy fields. 50c

How to be accepted by the college of your choice. 75c
U.S. Secret Service. 50c

POPULAR MECHANICS PRESS. Books distributed by Hawthorn Books, Inc., 70 Fifth Avenue, New York 11, New York

Popular Mechanics Career Books. 12 books. $2.95 each

The Popular Mechanics Career Book series is aimed at introducing boys and girls to science careers. The books are prepared for grades 7 to 10.

Through each book runs a story which features Randy Morrow, his younger brother, Sam, and their friends. As the story unfolds, the young people discover the wonderful world of science and learn of the career possibilities in various fields of science.

The books have many illustrations and average about 160 pages. Titles in this series include:

There's adventure in astronautics. 1961	There's adventure in jet aircraft. 1959
There's adventure in atomic energy. 1957	There's adventure in marine science.
There's adventure in chemistry. 1957	1959
There's adventure in electronics. 1957	There's adventure in meteorology. 1958
There's adventure in geology. 1959	There's adventure in rockets. 1958

PRATT INSTITUTE, Office of Information Services, Brooklyn 5, New York

Career Briefs. Bimonthly. Free

These four-page illustrated leaflets are published as an educational service by Pratt Institute. Many of them are devoted to timely information about a particular area of work for which the Institute offers training. Curriculums leading to the bachelor's degree are offered in art teacher education, advertising design, graphic arts and illustration, industrial design, interior design, general home economics, professional foods, fashion, chemistry, chemical engineering, electrical engineering, industrial engineering, mechanical engineering, and architecture. In addition graduate work is offered in library science, architecture, art teacher education, industrial design, and engineering.

The briefs, punched for a ring binder, contain information on personal qualifications, preparation, a typical day's work, and opportunities. The issues go out of print shortly after they are published and the titles are not listed here. However, the career briefs will be sent regularly to any counselor or librarian who requests that his name be added to the mailing list. Requests should be addressed to the Editor, Career Briefs, Office of Information Services, Pratt Institute, Brooklyn 5, New York.

G. P. PUTNAM'S SONS, 200 Madison Avenue, New York 16, New York

Putnam's Career Guides. 13 guides; 5 others in preparation. $2.95 each

These books have been written for grades 6 to 10. They have been prepared by recognized authorities in their fields with the cooperation of a vocational consultant, Martin R. Katz of the Evaluation and Advisory Service Division of the Educational Testing Service. Each book gives an introduction to the various kinds of work within the broad area and pays special attention to suggestions on how to begin obtaining practical experience which will be helpful later and how to prepare for the particular career. Included also are descriptions of the general background and special training necessary, qualifications, and future possibilities.

This series is prepared to have greater appeal for a younger student than some of the other series. The books average 160 pages in length and contain about 15 illustrations. Titles in print are as follows:

FIND A CAREER IN:

Advertising. 1960	Engineering. 1962
Agriculture. 1961	Journalism. 1959
Aviation. 1960	Law enforcement. 1959
Conservation. 1959	Medicine. 1960
Education. 1960	Photography. 1959
Electronics. 1959	Physics. 1963

Choosing a career in a changing world. 1960

Putnam's Sons also publish a series of 55 books designed to make more meaningful the learning experience of classroom trips for grades 1 through 3. They are prepared for reading as preparation before a trip is taken or as an added interest-building exercise after returning to the classroom. Many of these books describe various kinds of work. They are not included in the main bibliography of this book, but typical of the titles are the following:

Let's go to a bakery	Let's go to a post office
Let's go to a bank	Let's go to a supermarket
Let's go to a dairy	Let's go to the telephone company
Let's go to a newspaper	Let's go to a weather station

RESEARCH PUBLISHING COMPANY, Inc., P.O. Box 245, Boston 1, Massachusetts

American Occupations Monographs. 24 booklets. $1 each

Twenty-four monographs have appeared in this series. They are small publications, 4 by 6 inches in size, averaging about thirty-two pages in length. The topics usually included are the history of the occupation, its contribution to society, trends, qualifications, educational requirements, training, salaries and other returns, employment prospects, advantages, and disadvantages.

Each one has been written by an authority in his field. The list of titles available from the publisher contains the affiliation of each author. Some examples of these titles are:

Actuary. 1963	Free-lance writer. 1962
Dental assistant. 1957	Patrol inspector. 1957
Electronic technician. 1958	Public school psychologist. 1963
Fashion designer. 1959	X-ray technician. 1959

American Trades Monographs. 6 booklets. $1.50 each

This series of monographs presents the highlights of trades that do not require college training. The information is condensed in easy-to-read booklets of sixteeen pages each. A series of thirty monographs is announced; the following six are available:

Auto mechanic. 1957
Carpenter. 1957
Electrician. 1957

Machinist. 1957
Mechanical draftsman. 1957
Plasterer. 1957

ROCHESTER INSTITUTE OF TECHNOLOGY, Department of Public Relations, 65 Plymouth Avenue South, Rochester 8, N.Y.

The Vocational Guidance Series. 10 titles. Free

These pamphlets are written to give information to prospective students about some of the fields of work for which the institute offers technological education. Authors of the pamphlets are members of the institute faculty.

There is a minimum amount of recruiting material. Information is given about the various branches of the vocation, the duties performed by persons employed, requirements for employment, wages, promotions, advantages, and disadvantages of employment in that field. An illuminating feature of certain pamphlets is a job chart prepared to aid students in visualizing the kinds of beginning jobs in those fields, as well as the kinds of jobs to which successful persons may be promoted. The chart also lists the training or beginning jobs, the intermediate jobs, and related and supplementary jobs to which persons with demonstrated ability, maturity, and experience may be promoted. The terminal jobs are those toward which college training is specifically directed. The related jobs are those for which the curriculum does not specifically train but which may be attained by demonstrating special aptitudes and by profiting by experience and self-training.

The pamphlets are attractively bound in heavy paper covers, size $5\frac{1}{2}$ by $7\frac{1}{2}$ inches. They average about twenty-four pages. Considerable pertinent information is clearly presented. The titles include:

Careers in business. 1963
Careers in the crafts. 1963
Careers in industrial chemistry. 1958
Careers in food administration. 1961

Careers in interior decoration. 1960
Careers in photography. 1960
Careers in retailing. 1963

RICHARDS ROSEN PRESS, 29 East 21st Street, New York 10, New York

"Careers in Depth" Series. 57 books. $2.95 each; granite library edition, $2.79 net

The "Careers in Depth" series consists of full-book information on each of fifty-seven careers. To help the reader determine whether the career would be a realistic choice, the authors present information to encourage one to weigh his own capabilities and ambitions in light of the requirements, advantages, and drawbacks of such work. A self-evaluation test is part of each book with questions which will lead to an analysis of one's abilities and interests. Each book of 160 pages contains description of the various kinds of work and specializations, desirable personal qualities, training, preparation, earnings, opportunities, related careers, and suggested reading material.

One strong feature of this series is that the books have been written recently, since 1960; and twenty-five were prepared in 1963. Each has been written by a prominent man or woman who has been successful in his field of endeavor. Each stresses what the work requires and what it offers and gives special attention to educational facilities for training and what to expect during the period of preparation. This series contains no photographs.

Examples of the fifty-seven titles annotated in this book are:

YOUR FUTURE IN OR AS:

Aerospace technology. 1962	Electronic computer field. 1962
Credit field. 1963	Hotel management. 1963
Dietitian. 1963	Printing. 1963
Direct selling. 1963	Veterinary medicine. 1963

ROWMAN AND LITTLEFIELD, INC., 84 Fifth Avenue, New York 11, New York

Visual Career Guides. 6 guides; 6 others in preparation. 75c each

Edited by Gail Novak, this series features colored illustrations, numerous charts, diagrams, and other visual aids. About one half of the contents consists of photographs and charts. There are at least 8 full-color and 8 black-and-white illustrations in each book of 64 pages, size 7 by 10 inches. The varnished cover also is in color.

The text provides information on the separate and related areas of the field of work, the nature of activities, location of employment opportunities, future outlook, and lists of institutions offering accredited instruction. Lists of major professional societies and reading lists are included as sources of additional information.

The illustrations are well selected; the books are attractive, as well as inexpensive. The information is addressed to high school youth. The titles in preparation are aerospace, atomic energy, home economics, chemistry, agriculture, and science. Those now available are:

YOUR CAREER OPPORTUNITIES IN:

Engineering. 1962	Nursing. 1962
Journalism. 1962	Printing. 1962
Medicine. 1962	Teaching. 1962

SCIENCE RESEARCH ASSOCIATES, INC., 259 East Erie Street, Chicago 11, Illinois

SRA Guidance Service Subscription Plans. September through April. Plan A: $34.50 for one year; $65 for two years.

Several kits and sets of materials are described in the appropriate sections of this book and in the section on "Package Purchases." Two service plans are available on an annual subscription basis, bringing users monthly packets of guidance materials during the school year. Plan B is a condensed subscription plan providing occupational information by means of briefs, posters, letters, and reports. Plan A is a more comprehensive subscription plan aimed to keep the counselor informed of the latest developments in academic, vocational, and personal guidance. Its components for a school year are as follows:

> 9 books or booklets of varying lengths
> 28 occupational briefs
> 50 job briefs, guidance booklets, professional materials
> 7 guidance newsletters
> 7 research reports
> 7 guidance series posters
> 2 research coupons for individual guidance service
> Special prepublication bonus materials

SRA Occupational Briefs. 360 briefs. Complete set $75. Single copies 35c each. 100 copies 25c each

These illustrated briefs, four pages in length, contain information on 360 major occupations, which the publishers state represent the jobs held by 95 per cent of today's work force. For the most part, the titles are the base titles to which code numbers have been assigned in the *Dictionary of Occupational Titles*. Each brief includes a description of a specific kind of work, qualifications, training required, earnings, future employment outlook, and working conditions. Usually, two authorities in trade associations or professional societies are named who have checked and approved the information.

Most of the briefs contain two illustrations. The occupational title and code number are placed on the side and upper right-hand corner, for convenience in filing. They are of uniform size, 8½ by 11 inches. Titles are being published or revised constantly. Examples of titles are:

Book editors. 1963	Radio operators. 1963
Helicopters pilots. 1961	Railroad dining car waiters. 1961
Physics technicians. 1963	Tape librarians. 1963
Porters. 1963	Variety store workers. 1961

Junior Occupational Briefs. 300 briefs. Complete set $75. Single copies 35c each. 100 copies 25c each

These briefs contain simplified information about selected occupations for younger readers in the junior high school. By encouraging young people to picture themselves in a variety of jobs, the aim is to broaden their occupational interests and orient their estimates of educational needs in terms of the career choices they must make at the appropriate time in later years.

Written in narrative form, the first two pages contain a conversation in which the worker throws some light on the kind of work he is doing and its service to the community. The last page carries in capsule form some important facts about the job, in very simple language under the headings: Required education, High school courses, Training, Location of jobs, Getting started, Getting ahead, Hours of work, Earnings, Number of workers, Future labor requirements, and Other ways of finding out about the job. There are usually two or three sentences under each heading. They are suitable for grades 5 through 9 or for older reluctant readers.

This series is contained in the kit called the *SRA Widening Occupational Roles Kit (WORK)*, which includes student workbooks, junior guidance booklets, a teacher's handbook, and detailed procedures for putting the program into operation at a total cost of $114.50. The three hundred individual briefs are not annotated in the following pages, but the publisher will send a complete list of available titles to those requesting it. Typical brief titles are:

Finding Out About:

Aerospace engineers. 1961	Lathers. 1962
Data-processing machine servicemen. 1962	Mailing service workers. 1962
	Parking attendants. 1962
Dietitian. 1962	Physics technicians. 1962
Divers. 1962	Shipping clerks. 1962

Job Family Series. Set of 16 booklets and 16 charts, $16. Booklets $1 each; charts 35c each

These sixteen booklets and wall charts describe the various job prospects and opportunities within particular fields of work. Each booklet is 32 pages, paperbound, illustrated, and measures 7 by 9½ inches. For each of the specialties within a broad field of work, there is given a description of the nature of work, location of employment opportunities, and potential requirements and rewards. Typical titles in this series are:

Jobs In:

Agriculture. 1960	Performing arts. 1960
Health. 1960	Science. 1958
Mechanical work. 1958	Technical work. 1959
Outdoor work. 1964	Unusual occupations. 1963

SRA Student Guidance Series Booklets. 75 booklets. 50c each

These booklets, prepared for young people by specialists in the various fields, aim to help them solve their problems in many areas—educational, social, personal, and vocational. Recommended especially for group work, they include such topics as adjusting to school, getting along with others, boy-girl relations, understanding and solving personal problems, learning how to study, how to take tests, and how to stay in college.

These 48-page booklets are paperbound and measure 5½ by 8½ inches. They are written in a simple style to appeal to teen-agers, are attractively illustrated, make considerable use of visual aids, and are bound in variously colored bright covers. There is a wide range of titles, including the following:

Finding that part-time job. 1962
Getting along with parents. 1952
Growing up emotionally. 1955
Guide to good leadership. 1956

How to get along with others. 1961
How to increase your self-confidence. 1953
What good is math? 1960

SIMMONS COLLEGE, 300 The Fenway, Boston 15, Massachusetts
Vocational Guidance Series for Young Women. Free

The bulletins in this series, written for high school girls, describe the fields of work for which training is offered at Simmons College. Except for the name of the college, however, there is no specific recruiting material and the information would apply to many other institutions. In general, the contents are: What kind of work is it? What are the rewards? What natural abilities should I have? What should I study in high school? What should I study in college?

The bulletins have been prepared by the various schools and departments of Simmons College. In general, they describe the fields of work in business, education, home economics, library science, nursing, publication, retailing, social work, social science, and science. Four pages in length, they are uniform in size, 6 by 9 inches.

To date the college has prepared more than forty of these. The supply becomes exhausted within a short time after publication. Counselors and librarians wishing to receive the currently available bulletins may request to be placed on the mailing list. Examples of titles are:

The college road to nursing. 1961
Government administration. 1962
Mathematics. 1959
Nursery school teacher. 1960
Nutrition. 1961

Personnel administration. 1963
Physics. 1962
Secretary. 1960
Social worker. 1960
Women in book publishing. 1963

SMALL BUSINESS ADMINISTRATION, U.S. Department of Commerce.
Order from Superintendent of Documents, Washington 25, D.C.

Starting-and-Managing Series. 25c to 60c each

This series consists of publications containing directions on how to establish various small businesses and service establishments in specific fields. The booklets cover opportunities, risks, problems involved, and suggestions to help the prospective owner-manager decide whether he can wisely enter the field. Practical standards are offered by which one can measure his personal qualifications and prospects of success, as well as gain an understanding of the operating problems involved. Considerable technical information is included, with suggestions concerning shop management, equipment, operating costs, capital outlay, location, legal requirements, and management practices whose application is necessary for the attainment of success.

Additional volumes are announced for future publication at irregular intervals. Each will take the viewpoint of the prospective owner-manager and include suggestions for starting and managing a specific kind of small business. Titles included in this bibliography are:

STARTING AND MANAGING A SMALL:

Aviation fixed base operation. 1963. 25c
Business of your own. 1962. 25c
Building business. 1962. 35c
Bookkeeping service. 1962. 30c
Credit bureau and collection service. 1959. 60c
Motel. 1963. 30c
Restaurant. 1964. 45c
Service station. 1961. 35c

STATE OF CALIFORNIA DEPARTMENT OF EMPLOYMENT, 800 Capitol Ave., Sacramento 14, California

Occupational Guide Series. 350 guides. Single copies free

California's occupational guides are designed primarily for vocational counseling in the department's local placement offices and in the state's secondary school system. Each guide is produced according to a prescribed pattern. Questionnaires are mailed to employers. The data secured are then summarized and added to other available information. Wage and other statistical data are the result of a broadly based sampling of employers' returns.

This series contains unusually clear descriptions of the nature of work and duties. Current information also is given on working conditions, employment outlook, wages, hours, promotional and training requirements, and how to find the job. Much of the information is applicable to many states.

Each guide consists of from two to five printed 8½- by 11-inch sheets, stapled and punched for loose-leaf filing. The program is a continuing one. Each guide is revised periodically, usually at two-year intervals.

The department does not send multiple copies outside the state, but an interested enquirer may request a single copy of any one title.

Because the series now covers 350 titles, it includes material on many occupations found in few other publications, such as:

Gunsmith. 1961	Patrolman. 1962
Job analyst. 1961	Plumber apprentice. 1961
Orchard pruner. 1959	Routeman. 1959
Operator of telephone answering service. 1960	Shipping clerk. 1961
	Swimming pool maintenance man. 1962

UNITED STATES CIVIL SERVICE COMMISSION, Washington 25, D.C.

The U.S. Civil Service Commission publishes several booklets describing the opportunities available in the Federal Government. For the most part, they contain information concerning the kinds of work, application procedures, requirements, advantages, and salary ranges. Single copies of publications for which no price is listed may be requested from the commission; others are available at the prices listed from the Superintendent of Documents, Government Printing Office, Washington 25, D.C.

Some of the booklets described in the appropriate annotated sections of this book are as follows:

After college . . . what? 1961. 15c
Federal career directory. 1962. 60c
Federal career service . . . at your service. 1963. 35c
Federal jobs overseas. 1962. 10c
Federal stenographer and typist examination. 1961. 30c
Occupations of Federal white-collar workers. 1963. 50c
Opportunities in trades and crafts with the Federal Government. 1962. Free
Summer employment in Federal agencies. 1963. 15c
The way to a job in Government. 1963. 5c
Working for the U.S.A. 1963. 15c
Your retirement system. 1961. 20c

UNITED STATES DEPARTMENT OF LABOR, BUREAU OF LABOR STATISTICS

Occupational Outlook Handbook. 1963-1964 edition. Bulletin Number 1375. $4.75. Order from Superintendent of Documents, Government Printing Office, Washington 25, D.C.

Concise reports on about seven hundred occupations and thirty-five major industries are contained in the sixth revised edition of this handbook, prepared by the Bureau's Occupational Outlook Service. It is designed for use in counseling young people, veterans, and others in the choice of a career or course of training. Its subtitle is "Employment Information on Major Occupations for Use in Guidance."

The occupations include the professions; skilled trades; clerical, sales, and service occupations; selected agricultural occupations; and occupations in government. Each report describes the employment outlook, the training and qualifications required, earnings, and working conditions. Introductory sections of the book consist of a discussion of population and employment trends as well as industrial and occupational trends as basic information for an understanding of the individual fields of work. An opening chapter on choosing a career is directed toward assisting young people to select, prepare for, and obtain jobs in the right occupations in which they may find the greatest personal satisfaction. An alphabetical index to occupations contains many cross references. The book is illustrated with 225 photographs and 46 charts.

The handbook does not contain the names of schools where training may be secured. However, it often cites a comparison of the number leaving the profession with the estimated number receiving training in it. As the title implies, it is the information on trends and the immediate and long-range employment outlook which is of most value. This is based on extensive research data, of which a considerable amount is available only within the U.S. Department of Labor.

Congress in 1955 provided for a program of regular reappraisal of the employment outlook and for the maintenance of the *Occupational Outlook Handbook* and its related publications on an up-to-date basis. This action made possible the biennial revision of the handbook as well as the initiation of the periodical, the *Occupational Outlook Quarterly,* which is being issued four times annually to provide a flow of current information between editions of the handbook.

Most of the reports are listed and annotated in this bibliography, because the information on employment trends and outlook contained therein is outstanding.

Reprints from the 1963-1964 Occupational Outlook Handbook. 109 reprints. 5c to 20c each

One hundred and nine sections of the *Occupational Outlook Handbook,* separately bound, are available from the Superintendent of Documents. These reprints vary in length from 2 to 26 pages and range in price from 5c to 20c. A complete set of the 109 reprints may be obtained for $9.55 a set.

The reprints of the various chapters are designed for use by the following:

Individuals interested in a particular field of work.
Industry, labor, or professional organizations desiring a supply of the chapters to inform the public about their fields.
Schools and other counseling organizations needing many copies of chapters on industries important in their communities.
Libraries desiring individual sections for their occupational vertical files.
Counselors who want extra copies of chapters to lend to persons interested in various fields.
Teachers who want publications on the career opportunities in fields related to their subjects.

Because of the importance of this series, all of the 109 reprints have been annotated in the appropriate sections of this book and most of them are double starred as being most highly recommended. A 25 per cent discount is given on orders of 100 or more copies of any single publication. A check or money order should be drawn payable to the Superintendent of Documents; no stamps are accepted.

A combination offer including these reprints also is available from the Superintendent of Documents under the title "3-in-1" Occupational Outlook Service. One check every two years buys three services for a cost of $26.35:

2 sets of the 109 reprints
1 copy of *Occupational Outlook Handbook*
2-year subscription of *Occupational Outlook Quarterly*

Occupational Outlook Briefs. 11 briefs. Free

Brief 2- and 4-page multilithed summaries of the outlook for employment in major occupational groups, excerpted from the *Occupational Outlook Handbook*, are available directly from the Occupational Outlook Service, U.S. Bureau of Labor Statistics. The bureau maintains a mailing list of those who wish to receive copies without charge as they are issued. The following are available and may be ordered by title:

Administrative and related occupations
Business administration and related professions
Clerical occupations
Health service occupations
Physical and earth science occupations

Professional and related occupations
Protective service occupations
Sales occupations
Semi-skilled and unskilled workers
Service occupations
Skilled workers

Occupational Outlook Wall Charts. 12 by 17 inches. Free

These charts present graphically the highlights of employment outlook data. They may be obtained from the Occupational Outlook Service free of charge. Available titles include:

Building trades
Clerical workers
Driving occupations
Electronic computer operation
Engineering
Health services
Performing arts
Professional occupations

Science education
Service occupations
Skilled occupations
Social sciences
Teaching
Television and radio broadcasting occupations
Value of an education

UNITED STATES DEPARTMENT OF LABOR, UNITED STATES EMPLOYMENT SERVICE

Occupational Guides. Job Description Section, 5c each; Labor Market Information Section, 5c each. Order from Supt. of Documents, Washington 25, D.C.

The Employment Service publications are the result of many years of personnel research conducted by the U.S. Employment Service in discharging its responsibilities to its affiliated state employment services which operate the 1,800 public employment offices throughout the nation. The materials are designed to help employers, workers, and employment interviewers.

The series of 75 Occupational Guides are synopses of information concerning the duties, requirements, physical demands, and other characteristics of major occupations. They consist of two sections printed on durable 5- by 8-inch stock and identified by occupational title and code: (a) Job Descriptions and (b) Labor Market Information. The Labor Market Information is printed on a separate card so that the Guide may be revised without discarding the relatively stable information in the Job Description. The series may be arranged alphabetically or numerically in a desk file for easy reference.

The Job Descriptions follow a general outline: job summary, work performed, training, occupational tests, related occupations, physical activities, working conditions and hazards, and employment variables. They furnish composite descriptions, based upon analyses of the individual job in a number of different establishments, in various industries. The Labor Market Information sections describe the relative place of the occupation in the economy, the industries in which the job is of importance, the current and near-future job prospects, wages, hours, hiring practices, the extent of unionization in the occupation, and the channels of entry into the job.

Although these occupational guides were prepared some years ago, a number of them are included in this bibliography, because they provide the results of much careful research not easily available elsewhere. Users should be reminded that wage scales, hours, and hiring practices have changed.

The supply of these is low and many of them are now out of print. Many libraries, however, still have these guides in their files and for them it may be a convenience to have the reference to them. They are not starred or double starred in this bibliography, although the job descriptions are excellent, because they are older publications.

Employment Counseling Aids

Other publications of the U.S. Employment Service provide information on training and worker trait requirements pertinent to each job. Still others describe policies, principles, tools, and procedures for counseling and placement of special applicant groups within the employment service, including youth, the handicapped, and older workers. Last but not least, the U.S. Employment Service has prepared the *Dictionary of Occupational Titles*. Some of the booklets which are described in this book in the appropriate sections are as follows:

Career guide for demand occupations. 1959
Counseling and employment service for special worker groups. 1954
Counseling and employment service for youth. 1954
Counseling and employment service for older workers. 1956
Dictionary of Occupational Titles. 1949 edition and 1965 edition

Estimates of worker trait requirements for 4,000 jobs as defined in the *Dictionary of Occupational Titles.* 1956
Guide to local occupational information. 1962
Job guide for young workers. 1963
Occupations in electronic data-processing systems. 1959
Selected occupations concerned with atomic energy. 1961
Technical occupations in research design and development considered directly supporting to engineers and physical scientists. 1961

UNITED STATES DEPARTMENT OF LABOR. WOMEN'S BUREAU

Employment Opportunities for Women. Order from Supt. of Documents, Washington 25, D.C., at prices indicated

The Women's Bureau has prepared almost three hundred bulletins containing current information concerning women's earnings, employment outlook, legal status, labor laws for women, training, and recommended standards for working conditions. Several series on employment opportunities give an account of women's progress and the current and future needs in fields of endeavor such as medical service, home economics, and social work. For the most part these bulletins describe trends in occupations for which training at the college level prepares women, and they are concerned primarily with the changes and developments which affect the outlook for women's employment. They help guide women into fields of work where they are needed and where special opportunities exist. They contain discussions not only of the job outlook and opportunities for advancement, but also of training requirements, qualifications, job duties, conditions of employment, and earnings. Many of them present the minimum requirements for entrance to an approved school for training, for completion of approved courses, and for membership in professional associations.

The bulletins are 6 by 9 inches in size and have many appropriate illustrations. They contain up-to-date information based on extensive research. They are recommended most highly. About forty titles published by the Women's Bureau are described in the following pages, including:

CAREERS FOR WOMEN IN OR AS:

Biological sciences. 1961	Physical sciences. 1959
Federal service. 1962	Retailing. 1963
Legal work. 1958	Technicians. 1961
Life underwriters. 1961	Telephone workers. 1963

Future jobs for high school girls. 1959
Handbook on women workers. 1962
Suggestions to women and girls on training for future employment. 1962
Training opportunities for women and girls. 1960

VETERANS ADMINISTRATION, Department of Medicine and Surgery, Code 135D2, Washington 25, D.C.

Career Pamphlets. 24 pamphlets. Free

The Veterans Administration has prepared a number of pamphlets giving information about the occupations in which they are recruiting workers. These pamphlets describe the opportunities for service, the nature of the work, educational and experience requirements, salaries and promotional possibilities, employment benefits, and procedure for making application.

With attractive colored covers, varying in size and in length from 4 to 20 pages, these pamphlets are generously illustrated. They are addressed primarily to the experienced professional workers and recent college graduates, although some are intended to provide health career information to high school and college students. These pamphlets may be requested from the address given above. Examples of the twenty-four titles included in this book are:

A CAREER FOR YOU AS A VETERANS ADMINISTRATION:

Audiologist and speech pathologist. 1962	Hospital recreation specialist. 1963
Biochemist. 1961	Manual arts therapist. 1963
Dentist. 1962	Medical technology. 1961
Hospital librarian. 1962	Physician. 1962

Educational Requirements for Employment in Selected Professional Fields. 15c each. Order from Superintendent of Documents, Government Printing Office, Washington 25, D.C.

This series of publications, prepared initially for use in the vocational rehabilitation and education program of the Veterans Administration, supplements the brief statements on educational requirements in the *Occupational Outlook Handbook.* They provide information on educational requirements for entry and advancement in the selected professional fields. They also describe, for each field, the functions, fields of specialization, and types of employment in relation to the level of educational preparation acquired. They indicate the types of work for which students can qualify after they have completed training at various levels. Some, however, are now out of print.

These reports were prepared by the Bureau of Labor Statistics in cooperation with the Veterans Administration and published by the Veterans Administration. Number and title are needed when ordering from the Superintendent of Documents.

VA PAMPHLET NUMBER	EDUCATIONAL REQUIREMENTS FOR THE EMPLOYMENT OF:
7-8.2	Biological scientists
7-8.4	Economists
7-8.6	Geophysicists
7-8.7	Physicists

Other publications of the Veterans Administration described in the following pages are as follows:

VA PAMPHLET NUMBER	TITLE
22-7	Careers in business management. 1960
22-1	Employment outlook for technicians. 1958
IS-1	Federal benefits for veterans and dependents. 1962
7-7	Occupations and industries regional series. 1955
22-6	Occupations of epileptic veterans of World War II and Korea. 1960
7-12	Occupations of paraplegic veterans of World War II and Korea. 1957
7-10	Occupations of totally blinded veterans of World War II and Korea. 1956
22-3	War orphans education. 1961

VOCATIONAL GUIDANCE MANUALS, a Division of Universal Publishing and Distributing Corporation, 800 Second Avenue, New York 17, New York

Vocational Guidance Manuals. 53 manuals. $1.45 each, less educational and library discounts. Clothbound library editions, $2.65 each

Averaging 120 pages in length, these manuals present a comprehensive picture of the vocations covered. About half of the space in each manual is devoted to technical information of interest to a beginner in the field, to methods of getting started, and to steps to advancement. In the remaining half, there are descriptions of the types of work, requirements, educational preparation, opportunities, and qualifications for success. In most of them there is a full discussion of the desirable and undesirable aspects and the future prospects. They are complete with glossaries, lists of approved schools, apprentice opportunities, high school and college requirements, names of trade and professional associations, publications, bibliographies, and indexes. For the most part, the bibliographies have been prepared for the reader in quest of technical information and do not include many references to the occupational literature.

In each volume a biographical note about the author establishes his intimate acquaintance with the occupation described. The publishers apparently seek authors who are experienced writers in the fields in which they also have held executive positions. For example, Shepard Henkin, author of the manual on public relations, is a former director of public relations for the Hotel New Yorker; Richard Pack (radio) has been director of publicity of WOR; Dick Moore (acting) is editor of *Equity Magazine;* and John Barry (newspaper careers) is the assistant editor of the *Guild Reporter.*

The variously colored bright covers, containing interesting designs symbolic of the specific careers, add to their attractiveness. Each title is available in both the regular paperbound edition and the clothbound library edition. Many of the earlier books have been revised. Among the fifty-three included in this bibliography are the following titles:

Acting. 1963
Agricultural engineering. 1963
City planning. 1961
Foreign languages. 1964
Free-lance writing. 1964

Interior design and decoration. 1963
Plastics. 1963
Recreation and outdoor education. 1963
Securities business. 1963
Social work. 1963

HENRY Z. WALCK, INC., 19 Union Square West, New York 3, New York

Careers for Tomorrow Series. 17 books; 10 others in preparation. $3.50 each; price to schools and libraries $2.63 net

This series of nonfiction books is about careers of interest to senior high school and college students. Edited by Fon W. Boardman, Jr., the books are written by authorities in their professions. They contain good descriptions of work in the specializations within the broad categories, many case studies of people in the field, and detailed descriptions of a typical day's work. Personality and temperament factors, opportunities, and trends are also given special attention. The books average 108 pages in length and have a uniform grey-blue cover.

This series contains a limited amount of factual career data such as supply and demand, salaries, outlook and disadvantages, but stresses the environment within which the individual works. The descriptions of the major kinds of specializations and the various types of employment potentialities are forthrightly presented. There are about twenty half-pages illustrations in each book. This is one of the more recent series, beginnining in 1961, with fourteen books published since 1962:

Accounting. 1963
Art careers. 1963
Biological sciences. 1963
Building trades. 1964
Business management. 1963
Department store merchandising. 1962
Foreign languages. 1963
Foreign service. 1962

Library careers. 1963
Personnel administration. 1962
Protective services. 1963
Research science. 1961
School teaching. 1962
Secretarial careers. 1961
Social scientists. 1961
Writing as a career. 1963

FRANKLIN WATTS, INC., 575 Lexington Avenue, New York 22, New York
"The Professions and What They Do" Books. 14 books. $3.95 each; Watts guaranteed library bindings, $2.96 net

The purpose of this group of books, as announced by the publisher, is "to give information about the inner workings of a profession as well as the qualities, training, and experience to enter and succeed in that occupation."

They are written with the grades 7 through 10 in mind. They average 196 pages. The words "and what they do" follow the name of the career and indicate the special feature of this series:

Airmen. 1958
Archaeologists. 1960
Clergy. 1961
Conservationists. 1963
Doctors. 1956
Engineers. 1961
Forest fire fighters. 1962

Marines. 1962
Navy men. 1963
News reporters. 1959
Nuclear submarine skippers. 1962
Politicians. 1960
Rocketmen. 1962
Soldiers. 1958

WESTERN PERSONNEL INSTITUTE, Tenth and Dartmouth Streets, Claremont, California

Tomorrow's job. 18 bulletins. 20c to $1 each

The Western Personnel Institute is an association of forty colleges and universities for cooperative research, study, and experimentation in college student personnel administration. It serves as a clearing house of information about occupations and student personnel work. It carries on a continuous program of research and publication on developments in methods of college student personnel work and on occupational information significant for college students.

A series of occupational bulletins includes nature of work, requirements, earnings, opportunities, and outlook. Other publications consist of selected references:

> Atomic energy and automation: forces shaping tomorrow's job. 1955. 20c
> International education bibliography. 1962. $1
> Needed—rehabilitation counselors. 1956. 20c
> Social work—career in the headlines. 1956. 20c
> Student financial aid. (Bibliography). 1963. 75c
> Tomorrow's job in summer camps. 1958. 25c
> Travel while you work. 1955. 20c
> Using your subject major as a special librarian. 1959. 25c

WORLD TRADE ACADEMY PRESS, 50 East 42nd Street, New York 17, New York

Modern Vocational Trends Monographs. 1956-1964. $1.25 each

These 70 monographs contain information about each of several specialties within the fields represented by the titles. For example, the monograph on diplomatic service contains a description of work, training, opportunities, remuneration, and typical places of employment for each of the following: foreign service officer, ambassador, consul general, diplomatic secretary, foreign service reserve and staff officer, diplomatic courier, information and technical specialist, translator and interpreter, radio operator in the foreign service, and nursing in the diplomatic service. Also included in each monograph is a list of educational institutions and private organizations offering scholarships and fellowships in the field.

These monographs are photo-offset with heavy paper binding of various colors, averaging about twenty-four pages in length, and are 7½ by 10½ inches in size. The reading lists usually consist of about twenty-five references. The earlier monographs have been revised. The more recent publications, such as *Careers in the Field of Physics,* contain a full-page illustration on the cover. This series is especially useful for the information concerning scholarships and employment possibilities. Titles of the monographs include:

Air conditioning. 1962	Mechanics, specialized. 1962
Astronautics and space exploration. 1960	Professional agriculture. 1962
Electronics. 1962	Social sciences. 1963
Law enforcement. 1962	Women in science. 1962

Employment and Scholarship Handbooks. $1 to $17.50

Other handbooks and directories, prepared by Juvenal L. Angel, provide detailed information and suggestions on job hunting campaigns. Several of these include practical assistance to persons seeking employment in foreign countries. One offers suggestions to men and women over 45. Two of the directories are compilations of scholarship information.

> Directory of American firms operating in foreign countries. 1964
> How and where to get scholarships and loans. 1964
> Looking for employment in foreign countries. 1961
> Modern vocational trends handbook. 1964
> National and international employment handbook for specialized personnel. 1961
> Register of scholarships and loans. 1964
> Register of fellowships and grants. 1963

PART III

Annotated Bibliography

A. Books and Pamphlets Listed Alphabetically by Occupation

ABLE SEAMAN   5-48.040

Able seaman. Careers. 1961. 2p. 15c
    Career summary for desk-top file. This card, printed on both sides, describes duties, working conditions, personal qualifications, training required, salaries, recommended courses in high school, and employment outlook.

Able seaman. Chronicle Guidance Publications. 1961. 4p. 35c
    Occupational brief summarizing work performed, working conditions, qualifications, determination of aptitudes and interests, opportunities, training, outlook, and methods of entry.

ACCOMPANIST. *See* Instrumental musician

ACCOUNTANT   0-01.

Accountancy: a vocation and profession. Penz, A. J. Bellman Publishing Company. 1958. 44p. $1
    History of accounting, training, employment opportunities, remuneration, working conditions, and personal qualifications.

Accountancy as a career. Institute for Research. 1958. 20p. $1
    Discussion of duties, qualifications, training, typical day's work, salaries, attractive and unattractive sides. Describes opportunities in institutions, governmental bodies, teaching, legal work, and specialized business.

* Accountant. Chronicle Guidance Publications. 1961. 4p. 35c
    Occupational brief containing definition, specialities, history, work performed, working conditions, personal qualifications, determination of aptitudes and interests, training requirements, opportunities, outlook, methods of entry, licensing, and suggested activities.

Accountant. The Guidance Centre. 1963. 4p. 15c in Canada; 20c elsewhere
    Definition, history and importance, nature of work, qualifications, preparation, advancement, outlook, remuneration, advantages, disadvantages, how to get started, and related occupations.

To locate the full entry for a title when only a section or chapter is given, consult the Index of this book.

ACCOUNTANT—*Continued*

Accountants. Careers. 1959. 9p. 25c
> Career brief including duties, working conditions, qualifications, training, earnings, and outlook.

Accountants. Michigan Employment Security Commission. 1962. 20p. 25c
> Introduction, nature of work, location of jobs, working conditions, employment outlook, earnings, requirements for entry, disadvantages, and advantages.

Accountants. Science Research Associates. 1960. 4p. 35c
> Occupational brief describing nature of work, training, qualifications, opportunities, advantages, disadvantages, and future outlook.

**Accountants. One section of *Occupational Outlook Handbook.*
> Nature of work, where employed, training and other qualifications, employment outlook, earnings, and working conditions.

Accounting as a career. Boston University. 1962. 12p. Free
> Recruiting booklet describing qualifications, opportunities, advantages, disadvantages, and preparation. Brief discussion of work in public accounting, private accounting, government accounting, tax specialties, and corporate financing.

Accounting clerk. Careers. 1962. 2p. 15c
> Career summary for desk-top file. Description of duties, working conditions, personal qualifications, training required, salaries, related careers, recommended courses in high school, advantages, disadvantages, and employment outlook.

Accounting for your future. United Business Schools Association. 1961. 20p. Free
> Description of various accounting services, personal qualifications, and opportunities.

**Accounting may be the right field for you. American Institute of Certified Public Accountants. 1961. 25p. 15c
> The nature and limits of accounting, demands of the profession, scope of opportunities, conditions of work, and requirements for success. List of schools of accounting.

Accounting orientation test for high school pupils. American Institute of Certified Public Accountants. 1961. 2p. Free
> For counselors. Brief description of the testing program and directions for ordering.

Auditor. Careers. 1962. 2p. 15c
> Career summary for desk-top file. Duties, qualifications, and outlook.

Bank accountant. The Guidance Centre. 1963. 4p. 15c in Canada; 20c elsewhere
> History and importance, nature of work, qualifications, working conditions, preparation, remuneration, related occupations, and how to get started.

**Careers in accounting. Ashworth, John. Henry Z. Walck, Inc. 1963. 109p. $3.50
> Beginning with descriptions of the nature of work in business, public practice, government, and teaching, this book includes the personal and educational qualifications, employment outlook, rewards, and opportunities.

Careers in accounting. Changing Times. 1961. 3p. 15c
Discussion of preparation, future outlook, and earnings.

Careers in financial management and controllership. Financial Executives Institute. No date. 12p. Free
Description of the kind of work involved, training, advancement, rewards, and how to get started.

Controller. Research Publishing Company. 1963. 32p. $1
Nature of work, history and importance, number engaged in occupation, qualifications, working conditions, trends, training, and promotional opportunities.

Cost accountant. Careers. 1961. 2p. 15c
Career summary for desk-top file. Duties, qualifications, and outlook.

* Cost accounting as a career. Institute for Research. 1957. 24p. $1
Importance of cost accounting, personal qualifications, opportunities, rewards, and requirements for membership in the National Association of Cost Accountants. Description of work in the public accounting field, in government positions, and in the cost accounting department. The latter includes the timekeeper, labor distribution record clerk, payroll records clerk, social security records clerk and distribution cost clerk.

**Employment opportunities for women in professional accounting. Women's Bureau, U.S. Department of Labor. Bulletin Number 258. Supt. of Documents. 1955. 40p. 25c
Definitions of the field of work, survey of women accountants, preparation, opportunities, salaries, outlook, and requirements for the certified public accountant license.

**Employment outlook for accountants. Bureau of Labor Statistics, U.S. Department of Labor. Supt. of Documents. 1964. 8p. 5c
Reprint from the *Occupational Outlook Handbook*.

The field of internal auditing. Institute of Internal Auditors. 1963. 12p. Free
Description of work, qualifications, compensation, advancement, and the difference between internal auditing and public accounting.

Industrial and cost accountant. The Guidance Centre. 1962. 4p. 15c in Canada; 20c elsewhere
History and importance, nature of work, qualifications, working conditions, preparation, remuneration, outlook, related occupations, and how to get started.

Industrial cost accountant. Chronicle Guidance Publications. 1961. 4p. 35c
Occupational brief summarizing work performed, requirements, training, earnings, disadvantages, and outlook.

* Opportunities for you in accounting. International Accountants Society. 1964. 24p. Free
Description of opportunities and outlook in accounting and related fields. The booklet is revised annually.

ACCOUNTANT—*Continued*

Opportunities in accounting. Ankers, Raymond G. Vocational Guidance Manuals. 1958. 96p. $1.45 paper
> Nature of work, qualifications, preparation, opportunities, and employment outlook.

Should you be an accountant? Carey, John L. New York Life Insurance Company. 1961. 12p. Free
> Description of work, demand, qualifications, and training.

* Specialized careers in accounting. Angel, Juvenal. World Trade Academy Press. 1962. 39p. $1.25
> Includes information about each of several specialities within this field.

Young eyes on accounting! American Accounting Association. No date. 8p. Free
> This leaflet presents accounting as an expanding, attractive career field. Describes the variety of duties, opportunities, qualifications, and training. Selected references.

**Your future in accounting. Locklear, Edmund, Jr. Richards Rosen Press. 1963. 159p. $2.95; library edition $2.79 net
> The importance of accounting in modern business is stressed, together with the educational preparation necessary for this career.

See also Bookkeeper; Public accountant

ACOUSTICAL ENGINEER   0-16.01; 0-17.01; 0-35.73

Acoustical contracting, career with a future. Armstrong Cork Company. 1961. 6p. Free
> Description of the growth of the acoustical contracting business and career opportunities.

Acoustics as a career. Acoustical Society of America. 1964. 8p. Free
> A decription of specialized fields in acoustics, training, and occupational opportunities.

ACTOR AND ACTRESS   0-02.

Act one; an autobiography. Hart, Moss. Modern Library. 1959. 444p. $1.95
> This autobiography of a play writer and director gives a picture of work in the theater.

Act one; an autobiography. Hart, Moss. New American Library of World Literature. 1959. 383p. 75c
> A paperback edition of the book described above.

* Actor-actress. Careers. 1962. 8p. 25c
> Career brief describing nature of work, working conditions, qualifications, training, earnings, and outlook.

* Actor and actress. Chronicle Guidance Publications. 1960. 4p. 35c
> Occupational brief summarizing work performed, working conditions, qualifications, training, earnings, methods of entry, related jobs, and outlook.

Actor or actress. The Guidance Centre. 1958. 4p. 15c in Canada; 20c elsewhere
History and importance, nature of work, qualifications, working conditions, preparation, remuneration, related occupations, and how to get started.

**Actors and actresses. One section of *Occupational Outlook Handbook*.
Nature of work, where employed, training, other qualifications, employment outlook, earnings, and working conditions.

Actors and actresses. Science Research Associates. 1959. 4p. 35c
Occupational brief describing nature of work, training, qualifications, opportunities, advantages, disadvantages, and future outlook.

Curtain call for Connie. Anderson, Betty Baxter. Thomas Nelson and Sons. 1953. 192p. $2.50
Career fiction. Story of a girl's career hunting in New York City and her efforts to have a place in the theater.

Curtain going up! The story of Katharine Cornell. Malvern, Gladys. Julian Messner, Inc. 1943. 244p. $3.50. Library binding $3.34 net
Biography which includes information about acting and directing.

Directory of American College Theatre. American Educational Theatre Association. 1963. 6p. Free
List of 1,500 colleges offering courses in theater arts, including a tabulation of undergraduate courses, degrees offered, and student enrollments.

Dusty cloak. Hartwell, Nancy. Henry Holt and Company. 1955. 216p. $3
Career fiction. Story of an aspiring actress during her first year in New York.

**Employment outlook in the performing arts: musicians, singers, actors and actresses, and dancers. Supt. of Documents. 1964. 16p. 10c
Reprint from the *Occupational Outlook Handbook*.

Golden footlights. Jackson, Phyllis Wynn. Holiday House. 1949. 310p. $3.50
The biography of Lotta Crabtree, a comedienne of the American stage.

Hollywood star. Malvern, Gladys. Julian Messner, Inc. 1953. 192p. $2.95
Career fiction. Romance and experiences of a girl who goes to Hollywood to star in "The Pavlova Story."

How to break into the theatre. Harmon, Charlotte. Dial Press. 1961. 127p. $3.50
Includes advice from famous theatrical personalities concerning the work of actor, producer, playwright, director, choreographer, scenic and costume designer, stage manager, company manager, press agent, and the sponsor.

**Jobs in the performing arts. Science Research Associates. 1960. 32p. $1
Describes the variety of job prospects and opportunities for actor, dancer, singer, dramatic arts teacher, and instrumental musician. An accompanying wall chart is available for 35c.

Motion picture extra. Splaver, Sarah. Personnel Services. 1950. 6p. 50c; 25c to students
Occupational abstract. Nature of work, qualifications, preparation, entrance and advancement, supply and demand, earnings, advantages, and disadvantages.

ACTOR AND ACTRESS—*Continued*

Musicians, artists, actresses, and other entertainers. Chapter 6 of *The College Girl Looks Ahead.*

Characteristics of work in the arts, talent needed, trying out, obtaining work, and kinds of work.

On stage, Miss Douglas. Howard, Lisa. Julian Messner, Inc. 1960. 192p. $2.95

Career fiction. The work of an actress is described in this story of a young girl facing a long, hard climb to stardom with courage and imagination.

**Opportunities in acting. Moore, Dick. Vocational Guidance Manuals 1963. 128p. $1.45 paper; library edition $2.65

Description of types of acting positions in the theatre, motion pictures, and television. Discussion of requirements, trends, training, related fields, advantages, and disadvantages.

Radio acting as a career. Institute for Research. 1961. 24p. $1

History of radio acting, qualifications, training, opportunities, outlook and attractive and unattractive features. Also included is a description of a typical week's work in radio.

**Roger Thomas, actor! Ludden, Allen. Dodd, Mead and Company. 1959. 256p. $3

Career fiction. Through the story of training and work experiences, a television star describes work in radio, television, motion pictures, and the stage.

**Stagestruck: your career in theatre. Birschfeld, Burt. Julian Messner, Inc. 1963. 192p. $3.95. Library binding $3.64 net

Presents the variety of theatrical jobs, as well as the arduous work and keen competition involved. Includes actor, business manager, choreographer, dancer, designer, playwright, producer, press agent, stagehand, and talent agent.

Star dust. Belden, Shirley. David McKay Company. 1956. 214p. $3.25

Career fiction. Story of the first year at college and the choosing of a career in the drama workshops rather than on the stage. For younger readers.

**Star on her forehead. Hayes, Helen and Kennedy, Mary. Dodd, Mead and Company. 1949. 256p. $3

Career fiction. Interwoven in this story of two girls who break into the theatre world is information about their training, work, problems, and methods of improving their performances.

Teaching and professional careers in dramatic art. Institute for Research. 1961. 24p. $1

Qualifications, preparation, opportunities, methods of securing a position, advantages, and disadvantages. Also included is information about dramatic criticism and the writing of plays.

The young actress in New York. Moss, Allyn. Alumnae Advisory Center. 1956. 3p. 25c

Advice to those who feel they have the qualifications and abilities necessary to become actresses. Reprint from *Mademoiselle.*

ACTUARY   0-36.55

**Actuarial careers . . . if you have an interest in mathematics. Institute of
Life Insurance. 1961. 16p. Free
Describes an actuarial career in the life insurance business, the required educational training, and the benefits derived.

Actuaries. Science Research Associates. 1958. 4p. 35c
Occupational brief describing nature of work, training, qualifications, opportunities, advantages, disadvantages, and future outlook.

**Actuaries. One section of *Occupational Outlook Handbook*.
Nature of work, training, other qualifications, employment outlook, earnings, and working conditions.

Actuary. Jordan, C. W. Research Publishing Company. 1963. 36p. $1
History, duties, qualifications, preparation, working conditions, outlook, and earnings.

* Actuary. Robinson, H. Alan. Personnel Services. 1958. 6p. 50c; 25c to
students
Occupational abstract describing nature of work, future prospects, qualifications, preparation, entrance and advancement, earnings, number and distribution of workers, advantages, disadvantages, and related occupations.

Actuary. Careers. 1963. 2p. 15c
Career summary for desk-top file. Duties, qualifications, and outlook.

Actuary. The Guidance Centre. 1958. 4p. 15c in Canada; 20c elsewhere
Development of the work, duties, personal qualifications, preparation, employment and advancement, earnings, supply and demand, how to get started, and future prospects.

A career as a casualty actuary. Casualty Actuarial Society. No date. 12p.
Free
Description of work, special abilities needed, training, and future outlook.

Preliminary actuarial examinations. Society of Actuaries. 1962. 54p. Free
Description of examinations, miscellaneous information for candidates, and sample examination questions. The appendix describes the character of actuarial work, qualifications, and opportunities.

Requirements for admission. Society of Actuaries. 1962. 24p. Free
General regulations, description of examinations, and a recommended course of reading.

* Should you be an actuary? Linton, M. Albert. New York Life Insurance
Company. 1962. 12p. Free
Description of work, requirements, salaries, benefits, training, and desirable qualifications.
See also Accountant; Insurance worker; Mathematician; Statistician

ADVERTISING AGENT   0-81.

Advertising as a career. Boston University. 1962. 11p. Free
Recruiting booklet describing opportunities, rewards, and preparation.

ADVERTISING AGENT—*Continued*

* Advertising as a career. Institute for Research. 1963. 24p. $1
 Describes work in various advertising media such as newspaper, national magazine, radio, outdoor advertising, direct mail advertising, business and trade publications, and dealers' helps. Lists qualifications, preparations, earnings, advantages, and disadvantages. Includes duties of advertising manager, advertising agency and association advertising work.

**The advertising business and its career opportunities. American Association of Advertising Agencies. 1961. 21p. 10c; Free to counselors
 The place of advertising in our economy, what attracts young people to careers in advertising, what sort of person succeeds in advertising, getting a start, and kinds of work done in advertising agencies. Ten illustrations.

Advertising manager, store. Careers. 1963. 15c
 Career summary for desk-top file. Duties, qualifications, and outlook.

* Advertising men. Chronicle Guidance Publications. 1960. 4p. 35c
 An occupational brief summarizing work performed, working conditions, personal qualifications, opportunities, methods of entry, and outlook.

Advertising-space salesman. Careers. 1961. 2p. 15c
 Career summary for desk-top file. Duties, qualifications, and outlook.

* Advertising workers. Science Research Associates. 1960. 4p. 35c
 Occupational brief describing kinds of work, preparation, qualifications, opportunities, advantages, disadvantages, and future outlook.

**Advertising workers. One section of *Occupational Outlook Handbook*.
 Nature of work, where employed, training, other qualifications, advancement, employment outlook, earnings, and working conditions.

Books for the advertising and marketing man. Advertising Federation of America. 1957. 38p. $2. Supplement 1958. 16p. 50c
 A classified bibliography on advertising, marketing, selling, and related subjects. One section lists biographies and books on advertising as a vocation.

Career opportunities in advertising-marketing. Benton and Bowles, Inc. 1963. 20p. Free
 Description of work, opportunities, and outlook.

**Careers and opportunities in advertising. Boland, Charles M. Dutton and Company. 1964. 224p. $4.50
 Based on interviews with forty-nine top advertising executives, the author discusses the role of the advertising manager and account executive; the work of the copywriter, artist, production man; and opportunities in television, radio, marketing and research, sales promotion, and public relations.

Careers as advertising copy writers. Institute for Research. 1961. 24p. $1
 Describes the work through the medium of newspapers, radio, magazines, and billboard posters.

Careers in advertising. Angel, Juvenal. World Trade Academy Press. 1959. 34p. $1.25
 Includes description of work, training, opportunities, remuneration, and future outlook.

Careers in industrial advertising. Association of Industrial Advertisers. 1963. 22p. 10c

This booklet defines industrial advertising and gives information on salaries, major fields, qualifications, getting started, and applying for a job.

Confessions of an advertising man. Ogilvy, David. Atheneum Publishers. 1963. 172p. $4.95

Biography of a director of a New York advertising agency who gives a revealing picture of the work of members of a successful advertising staff.

Direct mail advertising workers. Science Research Associates. 1958. 4p. 35c

Occupational brief describing nature of work, training, qualifications, opportunities, advantages, disadvantages, and future outlook.

Directory of advertising, marketing, and public relations education in the United States. Borton, Elon G. Advertising Federation of America. 1960. 90p. $3

Lists degree-credit courses in advertising, marketing, selling, retailing, and public relations offered by 1,043 institutions, arranged alphabetically within states, with titles of courses and credit value. Included also is a list of courses in advertising and distribution offered by university extension correspondence courses and in private home study schools. There is also a partial list of courses offered by advertising clubs.

**Employment outlook for advertising workers, marketing research workers, public relations workers. Bureau of Labor Statistics, U.S. Department of Labor. Supt. of Documents. 1964. 16p. 10c

Reprint from the *Occupational Outlook Handbook.*

**Find a career in advertising. Cogswell, Harry. Putnam's Sons. 1960. 160p. $2.95

An advertising copy writer and account executive draws on his experience to outline career opportunities in advertising for salesmen, photographers, artists, writers, and many other skilled persons. He describes the work in large and small advertising agencies, showing how each department functions. Written for ages 11 to 15.

Jobs in advertising. Advertising Federation of America. 1962. 16p. Single copies free

Description of work in twelve jobs, qualifications, and training.

Madison Avenue, U.S.A. Mayer, M. Harper and Brothers. 1958. 332p. $4.95

Includes discussion of advertising and marketing as a vocation.

Magazine advertising as a career. Institute for Research. 1954. 20p. $1

Description of work, opportunities, qualifications, training, attractive and unattractive features, and list of schools offering the approved sequences in advertising.

Marketing as a career—a bibliography. American Marketing Association. 1964. 4p. Free

Sixteen references most of which pertain to careers in advertising.

ADVERTISING AGENT—*Continued*

Opportunities in advertising. Larison, Ruth H. Vocational Guidance Manuals. 1950. 80p. $1.45 paper

Types of positions in advertising agencies, with manufacturers, service organizations, institutions, magazines, newspapers, retail organizations, and in nonspecialist advertising positions. Educational preparation and how to get started. Describes the examination plan sponsored by the American Association of Advertising Agencies and the high school essay contest sponsored by the Advertising Federation of America.

* Should you go into advertising? West, Paul B. New York Life Insurance Company. 1959. 12p. Free

Description of work, its role in the economy, talents desirable, opportunities, satisfactions, and shortcomings.

**So you want to go into advertising. Ryan, Bernard Jr. Harper and Row. 1961. 178p. $3.50

The nature of work, training, qualifications, and future outlook are followed by a chapter each on creative work, contact work, and service. Under creative aspects, the author explains the work of copy, art, and production. Under contact, he describes the duties of the assistant account executive, the account executive, and the account supervisor. Under service, he covers research, marketing, media, and public relations.

Ten advertising jobs. Alumnae Advisory Center. 1962. 6p. 25c

Reprint from *Mademoiselle* describing ten typical jobs held by women.

What have you done for me lately? Schwimmer, W. Citadel Press. 1957. 256p. $4

Biography of a successful advertising man.

Your career in direct mail advertising. Direct Mail Advertising Association. 1963. 6p. Free

Description of work and opportunities.

**Your future in advertising. Singer, Jules B. Richards Rosen Press. 1960. 160p. $2.95; library edition $2.65 net

Includes the importance of advertising, advantages, kinds of work, and opportunities in an advertising agency, department store, magazine, newspaper, radiotelevision network, and national advertising.

Your future in advertising. Singer, Jules B. Popular Library, Inc. 1961. 160p. 50c

A paperback edition of the book described above.

AERONAUTICAL ENGINEER   0-19.03

Aeronautical-astronautical engineer. The Guidance Centre. 1962. 4p. 15c in Canada; 20c elsewhere

History and importance, nature of the work, qualifications, preparation, advancement, outlook, remuneration, advantages, disadvantages, how to get started, and related occupations.

Aeronautical engineer. Robinson, H. Alan and Wells, Ruth. Personnel Services. 1960. 6p. 50c; 25c to students

Occupational abstract. Nature of work, future prospects, qualifications, preparation, licensure, entrance, advancement, earnings, number and distribution, advantages, disadvantages, and related fields. References for further reading.

Aeronautical engineer. Careers. 1960. 8p. 25c

Career brief describing duties, working conditions, qualifications, training, earnings, and outlook.

Aeronautical engineer. Chronicle Guidance Publications. 1962. 4p. 35c

Occupational brief describing work performed, personal qualifications, training, employment outlook, and related jobs.

Aeronautical engineering. Johnston, S. Paul. Chapter 6 of *Engineering Enrollment in the United States.*

Trends in enrollments and future requirements for specialists in this area.

**Aeronautical engineering as a career. Institute for Research. 1958. 24p. $1

Qualifications, training, salary, and attractive and unattractive features are discussed for each of the major divisions of aeronuatical engineering: aerodynamical engineer, flight test engineer, laboratory and wind tunnel researcher, aircraft designers, engineering designer, weight control engineer, aircraft engine designer, aircraft propeller designer, aircraft instrument designer, airline engineer, flight engineer, and instructor.

Aeronautical engineers. One section of *Occupational Outlook Handbook.*

Nature of work, where employed, and employment outlook.

Aviation engineering as a career. Boston University. 1962. 16p. Free

Recruiting booklet describing outlook, nature of work, qualifications, salary, and preparation.

* Should you be an aeronautical engineer? Sikorsky, Igor. New York Life Insurance Company. 1959. 12p. Free

Includes qualities one should possess, cost of training, advantages, and future prospects.

See also Aerospace industry worker; Air transportation industry; Aviator; Engineer

AERONAUTICAL ENGINEERING TECHNICIAN 0-67.

Aeronautical engineering technician. Careers. 1960. 2p. 15c

Career summary for desk-top file. Duties, qualifications, and outlook.

AEROSPACE INDUSTRY WORKER 0-41; 5, 7-49.000 through 5, 7-49.099

Aerospace (aeronautical) engineers. Science Research Associates. 1961. 4p. 35c

Occupational brief describing nature of work, requirements, opportunities, earnings, and future prospects.

Aerospace highlights. National Aerospace Education Council. 1962. 54p. 50c

Includes selected brief stories and facts in this field.

AEROSPACE INDUSTRY WORKER—*Continued*

Aerospace industries manufacturing workers. Science Research Associates. 1961. 4p. 35c
Occupational brief describing work, requirements, earnings, working conditions, and outlook.

Careers in space. Binder, Otto O. Walker and Company. 1963. 308p. $6.50
Stresses the need for trained scientists, engineers, and technicians and describes the types of positions open to men and women. Of special interest to college students is the listing of industrial firms engaged in astronautical research and construction, with descriptions of the opportunities they offer.

Educational programs and services. National Aeronautics and Space Administration. 1962. 12p. Free
Developments in the peaceful uses of space.

**Employment outlook in aircraft, missile, and spacecraft manufacturing occupations. Bureau of Labor Statistics, U.S. Department of Labor. Supt. of Documents. 1964. 16p. 10c
Reprint from the *Occupational Outlook Handbook*.

From spinning wheel to space craft. Neal, Harry E. Julian Messner, Inc. 1964. 192p. $3.95; library edition $3.64 net
Story of modern man's startling inventions and discoveries that have changed standards of living throughout the world. Includes accounts of many inventors who overcame handicaps to bring their discoveries into existence.

Men, rockets and space rats. Mallan, Lloyd. Julian Messner, Inc. 1961. 368p. $5.95
An account of the men and the research projects concerned with the conquest of outer space. Photographs.

NASA and the universities. National Aeronautics and Space Administration. Supt. of Documents. 1963. 91p. 55c
Description of the program of space exploration and utilization, including the current missions, the development of special skills for research in the space sciences, and the impact of the space program on the universities.

**Occupations in aircraft, missile, and spacecraft manufacturing. One chapter of *Occupational Outlook Handbook*.
Nature and location of the industry, kinds of jobs, training, other qualifications, employment outlook, earnings, and working conditions.

The peaceful uses of space. Bloomfield, Lincoln P. Public Affairs Committee. 1962. 28p. 25c
Sets out some of the peaceful uses of space and analyzes some of the questions of public policy.

Robert Goddard, space pioneer. Dewey, Anne Perkins. Little, Brown and Company. 1962. 154p. $3.50
Biography revealing the hard work and perseverance necessary in the work of the scientist who built and fired the first liquid-fuel rocket.

**Selected aerospace career and scholarship information. Specialist for Aerospace Education, U.S. Office of Education. 1962. 16p. Single copy free
 Bibliography of sources of information in six parts: aerospace career books; military career information; career pamphlets; lists of schools offering certain aviation courses; scholarships, fellowships, and loan information sources; and guidance and counseling.

**Should you be a space scientist? Von Braun, Wernher. New York Life Insurance Company. 1963. 12p. Free
 Description of the various specialists needed in this challenging career, demands, rewards, personal attributes needed, and training.

Space volunteers. Kay, Terrence. Harper and Row. 1960. 136p. $2.50
 Describes work of test pilots and volunteer fliers who attempt to solve problems of manned space flights. For grades 6 to 9.

Step to the stars. Del Rey, Lester. Holt, Rinehart and Winston, Inc. 1954. 211p. $2.92
 Science fiction novel describing the construction of a space station which has the fascination of possible reality.

There's adventure in rockets. May, Julian. Popular Mechanics Press. 1958. 192p. $2.95
 By relating experiences of a boy in this field, the author portrays the various kinds of work. Written for grades 7 to 10.

* A world in space. Newell, Homer E. National Aeronautics and Space Administration. Supt. of Documents. 1963. 20p. 15c
 Briefly discusses geophysics in space, new astronomy, the universe, manned flight through space, engineering in space, environment of space, space measurements, and space phenomena on earth.

**Your career as an aerospace engineer. Institute of the Aerospace Sciences. No date. 24p. Free to counselors and librarians
 Includes a description of the work of engineers and specialists in the air and space sciences. Discusses plans for college years to be made in high school, selection of an engineering college, a typical aeronautical engineering curriculum. Presents list of 162 institutions offering accredited curricula leading to first degrees in engineering. Illustrated.

**Your future in aerospace technology. Ely, Lawrence. Richards Rosen Press. 1962. 153p. $2.95; library edition $2.79 net
 A career study of the aerospace industry and its outlook.
 See also Aeronautical engineer; Air transportation industry worker; Airplane pilot; Astronaut; Missileman

AGRICULTURAL AGENT, COUNTY 0-12.20

* Agricultural and home economics extension workers. Science Research Associates. 1961. 4p. 35c
 Occupational brief describing the work of the agricultural agent, the home demonstration agent, and the 4-H Club agent. Includes requirements, salaries, getting started, advantages, disadvantages, and future outlook.

AGRICULTURAL AGENT, COUNTY—*Continued*

Agricultural extension service workers. One section of *Occupational Outlook Handbook*.
 Nature of work, training, other qualifications, employment outlook, earnings, and working conditions.

Career as a county agricultural agent. Institute for Research. 1957. 24p. $1
 History and development of the career, nature of work, qualifications, training, opportunities, salaries, and attractive and unattractive features. Also included is a description of a day's work with a county agent.

Career as a county home demonstration agent. Institute for Research. 1954. 20p. $1
 Nature and development of work, duties, typical day's work, qualifications, training, salaries, lines of promotion and advancement, outlook, and attractive and unattractive features.

County agricultural agent. Careers. 1960. 2p. 15c
 Career summary for desk-top file. Duties, qualifications, and outlook.

* County agricultural agent. Chronicle Guidance Publications. 1959. 4p. 35c
 Occupational brief summarizing work performed, working conditions, qualifications, training, opportunities, and outlook.

AGRICULTURAL ENGINEER 0-19.10

Agricultural engineer. Careers. 1959. 2p. 15c
 Career summary for desk-top file. Duties, qualifications, and outlook.

Agricultural engineer. Chronicle Guidance Publications. 1964. 4p. 35c
 Occupational brief summarizing work performed, working conditions, training, earnings, and outlook.

Agricultural engineering. Fletcher, L. J. Chapter 7 of *Engineering Enrollment in the United States*.
 Trends in enrollments and future requirements for specialists in this area.

**Agricultural engineering as a career. Institute for Research. 1962. 24p. $1
 Description of work, personal qualifications, preparation, working conditions, attractive and unattractive features, earnings, and securing the first position. Includes a list of schools which offer professional training in agricultural engineering.

**Agricultural engineering: the profession with a future. American Society of Agricultural Engineers. 1962. 6p. Free
 Description of four major areas of agricultural engineering: electric power and processing, farm structures, power and machinery, and soil and water conservation.

Agricultural engineers. One section of *Occupational Outlook Handbook*.
 Nature of work, employment outlook, training and other qualifications.

Agricultural engineers. Science Research Associates. 1962. 4p. 35c
 Occupational brief describing nature of work, requirements, methods of entering, earnings, advantages, disadvantages, and future outlook.

A challenging career in engineering for you. U.S. Department of Agriculture. Supt. of Documents. 1962. 6p. 15c
Describes the scope of and opportunities in rural telephony and electrification.

**Opportunities in agricultural engineering. Stone, Archie A. Vocational Guidance Manuals. 1963. 128p. $1.45 paper; library edition $2.65
Includes discussion of organizations and agencies that employ agricultural engineers, nature of work, employment outlook, training, and opportunities.

See also Engineer

AGRICULTURAL EQUIPMENT INDUSTRY WORKER
4-94.340 through 4-94.399

**Farm equipment industry workers. Science Research Associates. 1958. 4p. 35c
Occupational brief describing nature of work, training, qualifications, opportunities, advantages, disadvantages, and future outlook.

AGRICULTURAL SPECIALIST   0-35.00 through 0-35.49

Agricultural business manager. Chronicle Guidance Publications. 1962. 4p. 35c
Occupational brief summarizing work performed, working conditions, qualifications, training, earnings, related jobs, methods of entry, and outlook.

Agricultural careers. California State Polytechnic College. 1960. 4p. Free
Describes opportunities in production, teaching, government service, and related business.

Agricultural finance workers. One section of *Occupational Outlook Handbook.*
Nature of work, where employed, employment outlook, and sources of additional information.

**Agricultural occupations. One section of *Occupational Outlook Handbook.*
Employment opportunities on farms, significance of agriculture in the economy, farming opportunities, training available, description of the various types of farming, and a discussion of specialized agricultural occupations.

* Agricultural research workers. Careers. 1961. 8p. 25c
Career brief describing specialized work in this field, working conditions, requirements, training, earnings, outlook, and places of employment. Additional readings.

Agricultural research workers. One section of *Occupational Outlook Handbook.*
Nature of work, where employed, employment outlook, and earnings.

Agriculture. Walton, E. V. and Gray, J. D. Bellman Publishing Company. 1958. 32p. $1
Discussion of thirteen kinds of work in farming, fourteen in the industrial field, eight in educational fields of agriculture, three in research, four in regulatory and farm management services. Includes list of forty-eight schools

AGRICULTURAL SPECIALIST—*Continued*

of agriculture and description of courses of study in agricultural economics, agronomy, agricultural engineering, animal husbandry, bacteriology, biochemistry, biology, and dairy technology.

Agriculture: earned degrees, by level, sex, and institution. One section of *Earned Degrees Conferred.*

Useful for judging the extent of a college's program in each of the following specialties: agronomy, animal husbandry, dairy husbandry, dairy technology, farm management, food technology, horticulture, poultry husbandry, soils, and general agriculture.

Agriculture in the Peace Corps. Peace Corps. 1962. 6p. Free

Illustrated leaflet describing needs, qualifications, and experiences.

**Career service opportunities in the U.S. Department of Agriculture. U.S. Department of Agriculture. Agriculture Handbook 45. Supt. of Documents. 1960. 63p. 55c

This publication concerns employment in scientific, technical, professional, and administrative work in the U.S. Department of Agriculture. It describes seventy specialized positions such as entomologist, soil scientist, and plant pathologist. Fifty illustrations.

Careers in professional agriculture. Angel, Juvenal. World Trade Academy Press. 1962. 35p. $1.25

Includes information about each of several specialties within this field.

Careers in specialized occupations in agriculture. World Trade Academy Press. 1961. 28p. $1.25

Includes information about each of several specialties within this field.

**Careers in the U.S. Department of Agriculture. Institute for Research. 1962. 24p. $1

History, types of work, attractive and unattractive features, personal qualifications, training, salaries, and getting a position.

Choose a challenging and rewarding career in the U.S. Department of Agriculture. U.S. Department of Agriculture. Miscellaneous Publication 833. 1960. 8p. Free

Brief statement of opportunities, salaries, and benefits.

**Employment outlook in agricultural occupations. Bureau of Labor Statistics, U.S. Department of Labor. Supt. of Documents. 1964. 24p. 15c

Reprint from the *Occupational Outlook Handbook.*

Enrollment and degrees in agriculture, institutions of higher education. U.S. Office of Education. Supt. of Documents. 1961. 69p. 45c

A survey of enrollments in agricultural colleges and universities and of degrees granted in agricultural curriculums in 1959. Contains tabulations by class, sex, and area of specialization.

The farmer's wings. National Aerospace Education Council. 1955. 44p. 50c

Shows how aviation is used on the farm. For younger readers. Illustrated.

**Find a career in agriculture. Duncan, Clyde H. Putnam's Sons. 1961. 160p. $2.95

Information about careers for specialists in agriculture, including work in farm management, economics, financing, and mechanization. The importance of a college education to the farmer is emphasized. Written for ages 11 to 15.

A future for you in the foreign agricultural service. U.S. Department of Agriculture. 1959. 6p. Free

Description of opportunities and benefits for college graduates in agricultural economics.

**Guidance in agricultural education. Byram, Harold M. Interstate Printers and Publishers. 1959. 238p. $4.50

The purpose of this book is to provide help for the teacher of agriculture for carrying out the guidance activities he finds appropriate in his school. Includes information about occupations in agriculture.

**Handbook of agricultural occupations. Hoover, Norman K. Interstate Printers and Publishers. 1963. 254p. $4.50

Describes the opportunities which exist in the agricultural and agricultural-related fields of employment and gives specific information as to the education needed to get the jobs and the avenues for advancement. Occupational briefs are provided for fifty-five typical off-farm occupations in which farm backgrounds will be an asset. Includes a directory of colleges offering instruction in agriculture.

**Jobs in agriculture. Science Research Associates. 1960. 32p. $1

Describes the variety of job prospects and opportunities within this field. An accompanying wall chart is available for 35c.

Occupations in agriculture. Chapter 10 of *Planning Your Future*.

Includes discussion of our dependence on agricultural workers, farmers' organizations, nature of work, qualifications, advantages, and disadvantages.

Questions and answers on agricultural research in the U.S. Department of Agriculture and the state agricultural experiment stations. U.S. Department of Agriculture. Supt. of Documents. 1960. 28p. 25c

Describes the functions of the several research divisions.

**There's a new challenge in agriculture. American Association of Land-Grant Colleges and State Universities. No date. 22p. 30c. Free from land-grant colleges to students within the state.

Illustrated brochure describing fields of work, opportunities, and outlook.

See also Agricultural agent, county; Agronomist; Soil scientist

AGRONOMIST   0-35.01

Agronomist. Group, Vernard. Personnel Services. 1960. 6p. 50c; 25c to students

Occupational abstract. Nature of work, future prospects, qualifications, preparation, entrance, advancement, and earnings.

Agronomist. California State Department of Employment. 1961. 5p. Single copy free

Description of work, training, promotion, working conditions, and employment outlook.

AGRONOMIST—*Continued*

Agronomist. Careers. 1964. 2p. 15c
> Career summary for desk-top file. Duties, qualifications, and outlook.

Agronomist. Chronicle Guidance Publications. 1964. 4p. 35c
> Occupational brief summarizing work performed, working conditions, qualifications, training, opportunities, and outlook.

Agronomists. Science Research Associates. 1957. 4p. 35c
> Occupational brief describing work, requirements, getting started and advancing, earnings, advantages, disadvantages, and outlook.

Crop scientists. Science Research Associates. 1963. 4p. 35c
> Occupational brief describing nature of work, requirements, training, getting started and advancing, earnings, and future outlook.

What is an agronomist? Bear, Firman. American Society of Agronomy. 1949. 4p. Free
> Discussion of the different phases of agronomy, variety of opportunities, and training required.

**You help to make a better world through your career in agronomy. American Society of Agronomy. 1956. 12p. Free
> Nature of work, opportunities, training, and list of 48 state colleges of agriculture.

> *See also* Agricultural Specialist; Soil scientist

AIR-CONDITIONING ENGINEER. *See* Refrigerating engineer

AIR-CONDITIONING INDUSTRY WORKER   0-19.01; 5-83.941

Careers in air conditioning. Angel, Juvenal. World Trade Academy Press. 1962. 28p. $1.25
> Includes information about each of several specialties within this field.

Your future in the air conditioning and refrigeration industry. Air-Condition and Refrigeration Institute. No date. 20p. 10c
> Explanation of new developments, the various jobs, training, and outlook. Suggested readings.

AIR-CONDITIONING MECHANIC. *See* Refrigeration and air-conditioning mechanic

AIR FORCE AIRMAN   2-68.05

The Air Force. Landis, Lawrence. Viking Press. Revised 1962. 192p. $3
> Details of regulations and opportunities. For grades 7 to 10.

Air Force Academy: cadets, training and equipment. Colby, C. B. Coward-McCann, Inc. 1962. 48p. Library edition $2.52 net
> Photographs and brief text show life while training. Written for grades 4 to 8.

Air Force careers. Careers. 1961. 8p. 25c
Career brief describing the aviation cadet program and the forty-two airmen career fields.

The Air Force: from civilian to airman. Landis, Lawrence C. Viking Press. 1962. 181p. $3
Explains the procedures for entrance, the life of the trainee at Lackland Air Force Base, the specialized training offered in the technical schools, and the opportunities for advancement.

Airman careers—training opportunities. U.S. Air Force. 1962. 4p. Free
Illustrated fact sheet giving requirements for enlistment in the Air Force and information on career opportunities for airmen.

Careers in the United States Air Force. Institute for Research. 1955. 24p. $1
History of air power and the Air Force, peacetime activities of the Air Force, flying jobs in the Air Force for commissioned officers and for enlisted personnel, qualifications, training, attractive and unattractive features, and how to enlist in the Air Force or apply for officer candidate school.

Catalog of information. U.S. Air Force Academy. 1963. 152p. Free
Catalog describing training, eligibility requirements, examining centers, and entrance examinations.

**Current career booklets. U.S. Air Force. 10 booklets. Free
Frequently revised booklets are available from local recruiting offices or the above. Present titles include: Gateway to aerospace, Air Force Officer Training School, Going places, Your daughter in the Air Force, Counsel for prospective candidates, and Educational opportunities in the U.S. Air Force.

Guidance information for counselors. U.S. Air Force. 1962. 4p. Free to counselors.
List of printed sources and films for use of the counselor in advising Air Force candidates.

Pocket guide to Air Force opportunities. U.S. Air Force. 1962. 88p. Free
Emphasis is placed on technical courses and jobs.

Story of the U.S. Air Force Academy. Landis, Lawrence. Holt, Rinehart and Winston. 1960. 224p. $3.95
A portrayal of the academic and military programs, jet pilot training, and first duty and future assignments. Illustrated.

This is the Air Force Academy. Talmadge, Marian and Gilmore, Iris. Dodd, Mead and Company. 1961. 95p. $2.95
Life in the cadet wing of the academy is shown by means of text and numerous photographs.

U.S. Air Force Academy. Engeman, Jack. Lothrop, Lee and Shepard Company. 1962. 128p. $3.50
Story showing the life of a cadet. Two hundred illustrations.

**United States Air Force occupational handbook. U.S. Air Force. 1963. 200p. Free to counselors and librarians
A manual for counselors and Air Force personnel officers. The main body of the book describes the duties performed in each of the forty-five Air Force

AIR FORCE AIRMAN—*Continued*

career fields, suggests educational preparation that can be of value, and explains what training the Air Force provides to prepare airmen for specific assignments. Other sections contain information on pay, requirements for enlistment, opportunities, classification procedures, and a section concerning women in the Air Force.

**Your future in the Air Force. MacCloskey, Monro. Richards Rosen Press. 1963. 160p. $2.95; library edition $2.79 net

An experienced officer describes varied kinds of work, training, qualifications, and opportunities.

* Your son's Air Force life—what you, as parents, should know. U.S. Air Force. 1963. 48p. Free

Illustrated brochure describing training and kinds of career fields.

See also Coastguardsman; Marine; Sailor; Soldier

AIR TRAFFIC CONTROLLER   0-61.60

Air traffic controllers. Careers. 1961. 7p. 25c

Career brief describing duties, working conditions, requirements, training, earnings, and outlook.

* Air traffic controllers. Science Research Associates. 1964. 4p. 35c

Occupational brief describing work, training, qualifications, opportunities, and outlook.

Air traffic controllers. One section of *Occupational Outlook Handbook*.

Outlook summary, duties, qualifications, and earnings.

AIR TRANSPORTATION INDUSTRY WORKER
0-41; 5, 7-49.000 through 5, 7-49.099

**Air transportation occupations. One chapter of *Occupational Outlook Handbook*.

Nature of activities, kinds of work, employment outlook, earnings, and working conditions. Specific information is given concerning pilot, flight engineer, stewardess, airplane mechanic, airline dispatcher, air traffic controller, ground radio operator, and traffic agent. Seven illustrations.

Air transportation workers. Science Research Associates. 1959. 4p. 35c

Occupational brief describing nature of work, preparation, qualifications, opportunities, advantages, disadvantages, and future outlook.

**Career opportunities with the airlines. Air Transport Association of America. 1957. 75p. Free

Includes nature of work, qualifications, and opportunities in flight operations, airline commmunications, airline maintenance, airline office and sales, and professional jobs. The index contains seventy-five airline jobs. Included is a list of the member airlines. Illustrated.

* Careers for women with the airlines. Institute for Research. 1957. 24p. $1
    Basic requirements, training, benefits, salaries, and trends. Describes duties on a typical flight of a stewardess. Information about station positions, traffic positions, dispatcher, meteorologist, teletype operator, and radio telephone operator.

Careers in air freight and express transportation. Institute for Research. 1961. 24p. $1
    Description of various jobs, a typical day's work, attractive and unattractive features, qualifications, training, earnings, and how to get started.

**Employment outlook in air transportation occupations. Bureau of Labor Statistics, U.S. Department of Labor. Supt. of Documents. 1962. 21p. 15c
    Reprint from the *Occupational Outlook Handbook*, 1961 edition.

**Opportunities in airline careers. Mehrens, Harold. Vocational Guidance Manuals. 1959. 96p. $1.45 paper
    Explanation of the scope of aviation occupations; the nature of work and opportunities in flight operations, airline maintenance, airline office and sales jobs, and related fields; and the effects of airline expansion.

Your future in air transportation. United Air Lines, School and College Service. 1962. 18p. Free in quantities of five to teachers and adult leaders.
    Illustrated booklet giving a thumbnail sketch of thirty-eight jobs in air transportation and the qualifications needed.

See also Aerospace industry worker

AIRCRAFT MANUFACTURING INDUSTRY WORKER 0-19.03; 5, 7-03.

Aircraft assemblyman. Careers. 1961. 2p. 15c
    Career summary for desk-top file. Duties, qualifications, and outlook.

Aircraft assemblymen. Group, Vernard. Personnel Services. 1957. 6p. 50c; 25c to students
    Occupational abstract summarizing nature of work, future prospects, qualifications, preparation, entrance and advancement, earnings, advantages, and disadvantages.

**Occupations in aircraft, missile, and spacecraft manufacturing. One chapter of *Occupational Outlook Handbook*.
    Nature and location of the industry, kinds of work, training, other qualifications, advancement, employment outlook, earnings, and working conditions. Four illustrations.

AIRLINE DISPATCHER   0-61.61

Airline dispatcher. Careers. 1961. 7p. 25c
    Career brief describing duties, working conditions, training, qualifications, earnings, outlook, and where employed.

Airline dispatcher. Chronicle Guidance Publications. 1964. 4p. 35c
    Occupational brief describing work, qualifications, opportunities, and outlook.

AIRLINE DISPATCHER—*Continued*

**Airline dispatchers. One section of *Occupational Outlook Handbook*.
Nature of work, qualifications, training, advancement, employment outlook, earnings, and working conditions.

AIRLINE STEWARDESS. *See* Airplane hostess

AIRPLANE HOSTESS   2-25.37

Air line hostess. Splaver, Sarah. Personnel Services. 1959. 6p. 50c; 25c to students
Occupational abstract. Future prospects, nature of work, qualifications, preparation, training, entrance, advancement, earnings, number and distribution of workers, advantages, disadvantages, and sources of additional information.

Air line stewardess. The Guidance Centre. 1963. 4p. 15c in Canada; 20c elsewhere
Definition, history and importance, nature of work, qualifications necessary for entry and success, opportunities for advancement, remuneration, advantages, disadvantages, how to get started, and related occupations.

**Airline hostesses. Science Research Associates. 1959. 4p. 35c
Occupational brief describing nature of work, requirements, education, how to enter and advance, earnings and hours, advantages, disadvantages, and future outlook.

Airline stewardess. California State Department of Employment. 1961. 4p. Single copy free
Job duties, working conditions, entrance requirements, pay, hours, training, promotion, and employment outlook.

**Airline stewardess. Careers. 1963. 8p. 25c
Career brief describing history of the occupation, duties, working conditions, training requirements, training opportunities, personal qualifications, employment prospects, advantages, disadvantages, earnings, advancement prospects, where employed, related careers, suggested high school program, and unionization.

* Airline stewardess. Chronicle Guidance Publications. 1962. 4p. 35c
Occupational brief summarizing work performed, working conditions, personal requirements, training, advantages, disadvantages, and outlook. Selected references.

Airline stewardess: a picture story. Engeman, Jack. Lothrop, Lee and Shepard Company. 1960. 128p. $3.50
On-the-scene photographs, with informative text and captions, show the life of an airline stewardess from her training-school experiences to actual flights aboard modern planes. Many aspects of training are shown: how to apply, requirements for admission, special courses and studies, customs, and traditions.

Goal in the sky. Hill, Margaret. Little, Brown and Company. 1953. 212p. $3
Career fiction. Experiences in training to become an airline hostess.

Happy landings for Ann. O'Malley, Patricia. Dodd, Mead and Company. 1956. 241p. $3
 Career fiction. Story of a girl's training and experiences as an airline hostess.

Hostess in the sky. Hill, Margaret. Little, Brown and Company. 1955. 241p. $3
 Career fiction. Experiences of a junior hostess give an idea of the work and adventure.

Janice: airline hostess. Hager, Alice R. Julian Messner, Inc. 1948. 190p. $2.95
 Career fiction. Describes duties and requirements of airline stewardess.

Jet stewardess, Gerard, Jane. Julian Messner, Inc. 1962. 192p. $2.95
 Career fiction. The romance includes authentic information about work on international jet airlines.

Leslie takes the skyroad. O'Malley, Patricia and McAssey, Mary. Dodd, Mead and Company. 1959. 256p. $3
 Career fiction. Story of a girl's experiences on a small airplane and later on a nonstop jet across country.

* Make travel your career as a United Air Lines stewardess. United Air Lines. 1962. 8p. Free
 Description of work, outlook, training, and qualifications. Illustrated.

Senior hostess. Hill, Margaret. Little, Brown and Company. 1958. 278p. $3
 Career fiction. Conveys a picture of the work and adventure. Written for ages 12 to 15.

**Stewardesses (air transportation). One section of Occupational Outlook Handbook.
 Nature of work, training, other qualifications, advancement, employment outlook, earnings, and working conditions.

**Your future as an airline stewardess. Rudolph, Patricia. Richards Rosen Press. 1961. 158p. $2.95
 Contains description of the life of a stewardess, qualifications, opportunities, pluses and minuses, and how to apply for a stewardess job. Included is a self-evaluation test and a list of twenty-six airlines with the locations of their stewardess bases and cities on their routes.

Your future as an airline stewardess. Rudolph, Patricia. Popular Library, Inc. 1961. 158p. 50c
 A paperback edition of the book described above.

AIRPLANE MECHANIC 5-80.

Aircraft mechanic. The Guidance Centre. 1961. 4p. 15c in Canada; 20c elsewhere
 Definition, importance of the work, qualifications, training, employment and advancement, earnings, advantages, disadvantages, and related occupations.

AIRPLANE MECHANIC—*Continued*

Aircraft mechanics. Chronicle Guidance Publications. 1963. 4p. 35c
Occupational brief summarizing work performed, where employed, qualifications, training, earnings, opportunities, and outlook.

Airplane mechanic. Careers. 1959. 7p. 25c
Career brief describing duties, working conditions, qualifications, training, earnings, places of employment, and outlook.

Airplane mechanics. Michigan Employment Security Commission. 1961. 16p. 25c
Introduction, nature of work, location of jobs, working conditions, employment outlook, earnings, requirements for entry, disadvantages, and advantages.

**Airplane mechanics. Science Research Associates. 1959. 4p. 35c
Occupational brief describing nature of work, qualifications, training, getting started and advancing, earnings and hours, advantages, disadvantages, and future outlook.

**Airplane mechanics. One section of *Occupational Outlook Handbook.*
Nature of work, training, other qualifications, advancement, employment outlook, earnings, and working conditions.

Career as a jet engine technician and mechanic. Institute for Research. 1962. 24p. $1
Description of activities, a typical day's work, qualifications, training, earnings, attractive and unattractive features, and how to get started.

* Career as an aviation mechanic. Institute for Research. 1961. 24p. $1
Describes work of various types of mechanics such as hangar service mechanic, airport ground serviceman, parachute rigger, airline overhaul base mechanic, and airline radio maintenance mechanic. Certification requirements.

Certificated mechanic schools. Federal Aviation Agency. 1963. 8p. Free
Lists alphabetically within Federal Aviation Agency regions the certificated aircraft mechanic schools with rating. Published semiannually.

Civil air regulations for mechanics. Aero Publishers, Inc. 1958. 152p. $4.50; paper $3
Outlines the regulations that are required for aircraft and power plant mechanics, study questions, and examples of questions and answers that are similar to those asked for mechanics' certificates.

Flight engineers. Careers. 1961. 7p. 25c
Career brief describing duties, working conditions, personal requirements, training, earnings, outlook, and ways of measuring one's interest and ability.

Flight engineers. Science Research Associates. 1961. 4p. 35c
Occupational brief describing work, qualifications, working conditions, earnings, how to get started, and outlook. Selected references.

**Flight engineers. One section of *Occupational Outlook Handbook.*
Nature of work, qualifications, training, advancement, employment outlook, earnings, and working conditions.

Ground careers in aviation with air lines and at airports. Institute for Research. 1957. 24p. $1
Qualifications, opportunities, and types of positions.

AIRPLANE PILOT   0-41.10

Aerospace pilot. Coombs, Charles Ira. William Morrow and Company. 1964. 224p. $3.95

Emphasizing the vigorous training required for a career as an aerospace pilot, this book describes the various phases of the preparation from entrance into officer training school to assignment as a test pilot. Illustrated. For grades 6 to 10.

Air line pilot. Robinson, H. Alan. Personnel Services. 1961. 6p. 50c; 25c to students

Occupational abstract. Nature of work, future prospects, qualifications, preparation, licensing, entrance and advancement, earnings, number and distribution, advantages, disadvantages, and related occupations.

Air line pilot. The Guidance Centre. 1960. 4p. 15c in Canada; 20c elsewhere

Definition, nature of work, qualifications, preparation, working conditions, earnings, advantages, disadvantages, and how to get started.

Airmen and what they do. Coombs, Charles. Franklin Watts, Inc. 1958. 192p. $3.95

Description of the work, personal requirements, physical and mental qualifications, specialized training, outlook, and rewards. For grades 7 to 11.

* Airplane pilot. Careers. 1963. 8p. 25c

Career brief describing duties, working conditions, qualifications, training, earnings, and outlook. Additional readings.

Arctic bush pilot. Helmericks, Bud. Little, Brown and Company. 1956. 180p. $3

Career fiction. Experiences in flying over frozen spaces and in rescuing and guiding hunters and fisherman in the Far North. Semiautobiographical story of the author and his experiences with the Arctic bush pilots.

* Aviation from the ground up. Revised edition. Floherty, John J. J. B. Lippincott Company. 1960. 160p. $3.95

Information concerning aerial advertising, helicopters, jet propulsion, crop spraying, and other careers in flying. Thirty-two illustrations.

Civil air regulations and flight standards for pilots. Aero Publishers, Inc. 1962. 169p. $4.50; paper $3

Outlines the requirements to obtain a pilot's license, study questions, and an example of a written examination that is similar to one a student must complete before he can obtain his private pilot's license.

* Commercial airplane pilot. Chronicle Guidance Publications. 1962. 4p. 35c

Occupational brief describing duties, requirements, working hours, pay, training opportunities, and employment outlook.

Commercial pilot examination guide. Federal Aviation Agency. Supt. of Documents. 1962. 20p. 65c

Prepared to aid pilots in their preparation for the commercial pilot written examination. It explains the nature, scope, and content of the examination and recommends basic study materials. Also included is a sample examination.

AIRPLANE PILOT—*Continued*

Daring young men in the flying machines. Thomas Nelson and Sons. 1960. 183p. $3.25

Biographies of nine men who pioneered in over-water flying, showing the grim determination and detailed preparations involved. Illustrated.

A day in the life of a jet test pilot. National Aerospace Education Council. 1954. 34p. 50c

Seventeen full-page illustrations accompanied by text depict the nature of the work of a jet test pilot.

A day in the life of a supersonic project officer. Mallan, Lloyd. David McKay Company. 1958. 192p. $3.95

Includes 127 photographs taken by the author. Describes the work of the airmen at the Air Proving Ground Command in applying exhaustive tests to each new aircraft and piece of equipment.

Educating cadets for the aerospace age. U.S. Air Force Academy. 1962. 17p. Free

Description of the academic program at the academy.

Helicopter pilots. Science Research Associates. 1961. 4p. 35c

Occupational brief describing work, qualifications, training, earnings, ups and downs, and outlook.

I want to be a pilot. Greene, Carla. Childrens Press. 1957. 32p. $2

Prepared for beginning readers with a reading level of upper first grade. Illustrated in color.

Instrument pilot examination guide. Federal Aviation Agency. Supt. of Documents. 1961. 20p. 30c

The purpose of this booklet is to provide the applicant with a list of study materials, a study outline, and sample examination to prepare him to pass the pilot's examination.

Jet flier. Archibald, Joseph. David McKay Company. 1960. 182p. $3.50

Career fiction based on the forced wheels-up landing of a modern jet. Covers many aspects of aviation such as stunt flying, cargoes, the B-24's in World War II, and the big jets.

Jet pilot. DuPre, Flint O. Research Publishing Company. 1959. 32p. $1

Nature of work, history and importance, number engaged in the occupation, qualifications, working conditions, salaries and other returns, training, typical places of employment, and placement channels.

Jet pilot. Lent, Henry. Macmillan Company. 1958. 200p. $3

Career fiction. Story of a jet pilot from the time he joins the U.S. Air Force to the day he receives his overseas flight assignment. For ages 12 to 16.

Jet pilot overseas. Lent, Henry. Macmillan Company. 1959. 183p. $3

Career fiction. Story showing that an assignment to a combat-ready squadron and an overseas tour of duty means constant training. For ages 12 to 16.

Jets away! Montgomery, R. G. Dodd, Mead and Company. 1957. 190p. $3
Career fiction. Story of a volunteer in the Air Force who received training at the Tech School of Amarillo Air Force Base, was assigned as a mechanic crewman on a jet bomber, and became a sergeant crew chief.

Lonely sky. Bridgeman, William B. and Hazard, Jacqueline. Henry Holt and Company. 1955. 316p. $4.95
An account of Bridgeman's experiences as a test pilot for the experimental Douglas supersonic airplane "skyrocket."

Navigator-pilot, airplane. Careers 1959. 2p. 15c
Career summary for desk-top file. Duties, qualifications, and outlook.

Pilot. Le Vier, Anthony as told to John Guenther. Harper and Row. 1954. 263p. $4.50; library binding $3.99 net
Biography of a veteran Lockheed test pilot.

**Pilots and copilots. One section of *Occupational Outlook Handbook*.
Nature of work, where employed, qualifications, training, advancement, employment outlook, earnings, and working conditions.

Sabre pilot. Meader, Stephen W. Harcourt, Brace & World. 1956. 173p. $3.25
Story of the training and experiences of a jet fighter pilot in the Air Force.

There's adventure in jet aircraft. Popular Mechanics Press. 1959. 175p. $2.95
A boy's experiences as a Civil Air Patrol Cadet, in building an operating model jet, and in learning to fly.

United States aircraft, missiles, and spacecraft. National Aerospace Education Council. Published annually. 160p. $1.50
Contains photographs and drawings plus descriptions of current aircraft, missiles, and spacecraft produced in the United States. Ask for latest edition.

What does a jet pilot do? Wells, Robert and Lippman, Harvey. Dodd, Mead and Company. 1959. 58p. $2.50
Simple text and pictures portray various duties. Written for grades 3 to 7.

Women in aeronautics. May, Charles Paul. Nelson and Sons. 1962. 256p. $3.50
An account of women in aviation from the time of Marie Tible's ascent in a fire balloon in 1784 to women working in our space program.

AIRPORT MANAGER   0-98.81

Airport manager. Careers. 1962. 2p. 15c
Career summary for desk-top file. Duties, qualifications, and outlook.

Airport managers. Science Research Associates. 1958. 4p. 35c
Occupational brief describing nature of work, training, qualifications, opportunities, advantages, disadvantages, and future outlook.

Starting and managing an aviation fixed base operation. Small Business Administration. Supt. of Documents. 1963. 52p. 25c
This booklet is published to help prospective small owner-managers decide whether they can wisely enter this business. It describes the advantages and

AIRPORT MANAGER—*Continued*

disadvantages of going into this particular business, the risks involved, the personal characteristics that will contribute to success, and some of the management practices whose application is necessary for the attainment of that success.

ALUMINUM INDUSTRY WORKER   4, 6, 8-94.800 through 4, 6, 8-94.849

Aluminum industry workers. Science Research Associates. 1961. 4p. 35c
Occupational brief describing nature of work, requirements, earnings, employment opportunities, advantages, disadvantages, and future outlook.

ANESTHETIST   0-26.20; 0-33.36

**Anesthetists. Science Research Associates. 1962. 4p. 35c
Occupational brief describing nature of work, training, qualifications, opportunities, advantages, disadvantages, and future outlook.

**Careers in anesthesia. (the physician and the nurse anesthetist). Institute for Research. 1958. 20p. $1
Describes functions of the medical anesthesiologist and the nurse anesthetist. Development and technical progress, typical day's work, educational standards, opportunities, attractive and unattractive features. Requirements for certification and recommended requirements for admission to schools of anesthesia.

See also Nurse anesthetist

ANIMAL HUSBANDMAN   0-35.13

Animal husbandman. Chronicle Guidance Publications. 1962. 4p. 35c
Occupational brief summarizing areas of work, where employed, training, working conditions, entry, and outlook.

A business in pets. Dean, Nell M. Julian Messner, Inc. 1956. 192p. $2.95
Career fiction. A story that combines career interest in a pet shop with light romance.

Fur farmers. Science Research Associates. 1961. 4p. 35c
Occupational brief describing nature of work, training, opportunities, advantages, disadvantages, and future outlook.

Raymond L. Ditmars: his exciting career with reptiles, animals and insects. Wood, Laura N. Julian Messner, Inc. 1944. 256p. $3.50. Library binding $3.34 net
Biography of a boy who turned a hobby into a profession and developed new researches into the habits of animals.

Saddles for breakfast. Randall, Janet. David McKay Company. 1961. 224p. $3.50
Career fiction. Robin's love of horses and willingness to work hard help bring the run-down stables back to their former popularity.

Your career in animal husbandry. Virginia Polytechnic Institute. No date. 4p. Free
An example of a college recruiting brochure pointing out the varied opportunities in this field.

ANTHROPOLOGIST 0-36.01

Anthropologist. Careers. 1960. 2p. 15c
Career summary for desk-top file. Duties, qualifications, and outlook.

**Anthropologists. Science Research Associates. 1964. 4p. 35c
Occupational brief describing nature of work, requirements, earnings, methods of getting started, advantages, disadvantages, and future outlook. Selected references.

Anthropologists. One section of *Occupational Outlook Handbook*.
Nature of work, where employed, training and other qualifications, and employment outlook.

**Anthropology as a career. Sturtevant, William C. Smithsonian Institution. 1963. 20p. 20c
Description of physical and cultural anthropology, training, employment opportunities, outlook, and rewards. Includes list of 116 colleges offering majors in this field. Selected reading list.

Guide to departmental offerings in the field of anthropology. American Anthropological Association. 1963. 44p. Free
A listing of all departments in United States colleges offering the Ph.D. in anthropology, as well as some of the departments conferring only the master's degree. Also included are staff specialities and departmental strengths.

Who are we? Moss, Allyn. Alumnae Advisory Center. 1956. 4p. 25c
Reprint from *Mademoiselle* describing experiences of eight young anthropologists.

APPLIANCE REPAIRMAN. *See* Household appliance serviceman and installer

ARCHAEOLOGIST 0-36.01

Archaeologist. Careers. 1963. 2p. 15c
Career summary for desk-top file. Duties, qualifications, and outlook.

**Archaeologists. Science Research Associates. 1963. 4p. 35c
Occupational brief describing nature of work, requirements, getting started, earnings, advantages, disadvantages, and future outlook.

Archaeologists and what they do. Braidwood, Robert. Franklin Watts, Inc. 1960. 180p. $3.95
Discussion of the varied kinds of work, specialized training, qualifications, and rewards. For grades 7 to 11.

4000 years under the sea: the story of marine archeology. Diole, Philippe. Julian Messner, Inc. 1954. 237p. $4.50
An account of the discovery and exploration of sunken ships on the floor of the Mediterranean which bring to light new aspects of ancient cultural and economic history.

Good digging: the story of archaeology. Samachson, Dorothy and Samachson, Joseph. Rand McNally and Company. 1960. 224p. $3.50
Tales of dramatic "diggings" throughout the world are followed by information on training, preparation for an expedition, and importance to society.

ARCHITECT   0-03.10

American architects directory. R. R. Bowker Company. 1962. 700p. $25
Appendix includes a list of schools of architecture, standards of professional practice, and state registration boards and officers.

**Architect. McLaughlin, Robert W. Macmillan Company. 1962. 201p. $3.50
The author discusses qualifications, registration and licensing, professional schools and apprenticeship, the contributions of renowned men in the field, and a typical week of a practicing architect.

Architect. Shelley, J. M. Research Publishing Company. 1956. 32p. $1
Nature of work, preparation, working conditions, outlook, advantages, disadvantages, and related occupations.

Architect. Splaver, Sarah. Personnel Services. 1962. 6p. 50c; 25c to students
Occupational abstract. Nature of work, qualifications, preparation, outlook, earnings, advantages, and disadvantages.

* Architect. Careers. 1962. 8p. 25c
Career brief describing history and importance of the work, duties, working conditions, training requirements, training opportunities, personal qualifications, employment prospects, advantages, disadvantages, earnings, advancement prospects, related careers, measuring one's interests and ability, suggested high school program, and license requirements.

* Architect. Chronicle Guidance Publications. 1962. 4p. 35c
Occupational brief containing definitions, work performed, working conditions, requirements, determination of aptitudes and interest, employment, opportunities, outlook, methods of entry, and suggested activities.

Architect. The Guidance Centre. 1962. 4p. 15c in Canada; 20c elsewhere
Definition, history and importance, nature of work, qualifications necessary for entry and success, preparation, earnings, advantages, disadvantages, and how to get started.

Architect. Michigan Employment Security Commission. 1959. 16p. 25c
Introduction, nature of work, location of jobs, working conditions, employment outlook, earnings, requirements for entry, disadvantages, and advantages.

Architects. Science Research Associates. 1960. 4p. 35c
Occupational brief describing nature of work, training, qualifications, opportunities, advantages, disadvantages, and future outlook.

**Architects. One section of *Occupational Outlook Handbook.*
Nature of work, where employed, training and other qualifications, employment outlook, earnings, and working conditions.

Architectural engineering. Walter, Ralph. Chapter 8 of *Engineering Enrollments in the United States.*
Trends in enrollments and requirements for specialists in this area.

Architectural technician. Careers. 1961. 2p. 15c
Career summary for desk-top file. Duties, qualifications, and outlook.

Architectural technologist. The Guidance Centre. 1960. 4p. 15c in Canada;
20c elsewhere
> History and importance, nature of work, qualifications. working conditions,
> preparation, remuneration, related occupations, and how to get started.

* Architecture as a career. Institute for Research. 1959. 24p. $1
> Qualifications, training, typical course of study, opportunities, requirements
> for registration, advantages, and disadvantages. List of schools of architecture.

Architecture: earned degrees, by level, sex, and institution. One section of
Earned Degrees Conferred.
> List of seventy-one schools and the number of bachelor's, master's, and
> doctor's degrees conferred by each.

The Bureau of Ships. U.S. Department of the Navy, Bureau of Ships.
1962. 20p. Free
> Description of the work performed by naval architects, electronic and
> mechanical engineers in designing, building, and maintaining the ships of
> the United States Navy.

A career as an architect. Changing Times. 1960. 3p. 15c
> A reprint discussing the preparation and future outlook.

Careers for engineers and architects. New York State Department of Civil
Service. 1962. 4p. Free
> Illustrated leaflet describing opportunities and examination procedures.

* Careers in architecture. Angel, Juvenal. World Trade Academy Press.
1962. 30p. $1.25
> Includes information about each of several specialties within this field.

**Designing a better tomorrow—a career in architecture. American Institute
of Architects. 1959. 20p. Free
> Nature of work, training, specialization, and a list of sixty-one member
> schools of the Association of Collegiate Schools of Architecture.

**Employment outlook for architects. Bureau of Labor Statistics, U.S. De-
partment of Labor. Supt. of Documents. 1964. 4p. 5c
> Reprint from the *Occupational Outlook Handbook.*

Engineering and architectural careers in the Veterans Administration.
Veterans Arministration, Department of Medicine and Surgery. 1958.
4p. Free
> Description of opportunities, training, qualifications, and benefits.

Lady architect. Wyndham, Lee. Julian Messner, Inc. 1957. 187p. $2.95
> Career fiction. Story showing the need for imagination, perseverance, and
> technical skill in this field.

List of accredited schools of architecture. National Architectural Accrediting Board. 1962. 1p. Free
> List of fifty-two schools and the degrees conferred by each upon completion
> of their professional curricula in architecture.

The master builders. Blake, Peter. Knopf, Inc. 1961. 412p. $8
> Biography of three architects who were pioneers in modern building design:
> France's Le Corbusier, Germany's Van der Rohe, and America's Frank Lloyd
> Wright.

ARCHITECT—*Continued*

Member schools. Association of Collegiate Schools of Architecture. 1963. 5p. Free
A directory of sixty-one member schools and fifteen associate member schools and departments of architecture in colleges and universities in the United States and Canada.

Should you be an architect? Belluschi, Pietro. New York Life Insurance Company. 1959. 12p. Free
Nature of work, qualities necessary for success, and training.

**Your future in architecture. Roth, Richard. Richards Rosen Press. 1960. 159p. $2.95
Nature of work, importance to society, qualifications, opportunities, places of employment, preparation, and how to get started. Includes list of schools and state architectural registration boards.

See also Landscape architect; Scientist

ARCHIVIST   0-36.92

Archivist. Careers. 1962. 2p. 15c
Career summary for desk-top file. Duties, qualifications, and outlook.

ARMY OFFICER. *See* Military serviceman; Soldier

ARTIST   0-04.

American art directory. Gilbert, Dorothy, ed. R. R. Bowker Company. 1961. 382p. $22.50
Complete information on education in the fine arts. Lists professional art schools and art departments of colleges and universities in the United States and Canada. Entries indexed by name and interest, such as architecture, archaeology, art, etc. Published triennially for the American Federation of Arts.

**Art as a career. Institute for Research. 1958. 24p. $1
Describes types of work in sculpture, graphic arts, and painting and drawing. Includes training, typical courses of study, qualifications, salaries, related positions, attractive and unattractive features. Chart shows number of established artists in each state classified according to muralists, painters, portrait painters, sculptors, and miniature and water color artists.

Art as a career. National Society of Art Directors. No date. 4p. Free
Brief message directed to the high school student who plans to extend his education by attending a professional art school.

**Art career guide. Holden, Donald. Watson-Guptill Publications. 1961. 280p. $5.75
This book contains sections on planning one's education, choosing a career, finding a job, and schools for preparation. Includes discussions on planning a portfolio, conducting job interviews, and what to expect from school or college. Also, the major art fields are described.

Art, drama, music. Milwaukee-Downer College. 1958. 20p. Free
A college bulletin describing the training and courses of instruction. Illustrated.

**Art professions in the United States. Guitar, Mary Anne and Vaughan, Dana P., ed. Cooper Union, School of Art and Architecture. 1960. 71p. $1. Free to counselors and librarians upon individual request.
This is a revision of the 1950 edition. Study based on questionnaires submitted to alumni of Cooper Union School of Art and Architecture, employers of designers, and administrators of other professional art schools. Discussion of opportunities, attitudes and aptitudes needed, and qualifications. List of fifty-one accredited schools of architecture and thirty-five art schools having membership in the National Association of Schools of Design.

The art school directory. Watson-Guptill Publications. 1961. 52p. $1.50
Names and addresses of art schools in the United States and abroad, with information about course offerings, degrees granted, length of programs, availability of scholarships, and nature of student body.

Artists, general. Careers. 1962. 8p. 25c
Career brief describing duties, working conditions, training, qualifications, salaries, outlook, and places of employment.

Artists, musicians, actresses and others. Chapter 28 of *Vocations for Girls*.
Desirable qualities, kinds of work, and opportunities. Bibliography.

Careers in art. National Art Education Association. No date. 11p. 10c
This booklet describes some of the major art careers and what makes for success in them. Includes art education, advertising design, industrial design, graphic art and illustration, fashion design and illustration, and ceramic design.

* Careers in the arts: fine and applied. McCausland, Elizabeth. John Day Company. 1950. 278p. $4
A survey of the art field to help the beginning artist learn where he can best apply his talents. Discussion of training, opportunities, range of pay, chances for success, and outlook for the future. Includes chapters on architecture, painting, sculpture, graphic art, teaching, advertising, illustration, printing art, textile design, poster art, cartooning, industrial design, interior decoration, costume design, stage design, and other fields. List, alphabetized by states, of art schools and colleges.

Directory of international scholarships in the arts. Institute of International Education. 1958. 120p. 50c
A survey of awards and scholarships available to persons who wish to study or train in foreign countries in the fields of the creative arts.

Directory of member schools. National Association of Schools of Art. 1963. 4p. Free
Information about professional study in art and design in thirty-nine member schools. Includes major programs and degrees or certificates offered.

Famous American painters. McKinney, Roland J. Dodd, Mead and Company. 1955. 125p. $3
Biographies of thirteen American painters. List of art institutions at which the artist's works are located and a reproduction of a typical painting included for each artist.

ARTIST—*Continued*

**The fine and applied arts. Farnum, Royal B. Bellman Publishing Company. 1958. 39p. $1

> Discussion of the kinds of work, qualifications, requirements, and opportunities for the designer and artist. Includes list of forty occupations that require a knowledge of art and design. Also given is a list of ninety-five schools of art and design. Another list contains names of organizations offering scholarship assistance.

Fine and applied arts: earned degrees, by level, sex, and institution. One section of *Earned Degrees Conferred.*

> Useful for judging the extent of a college's program in general art, music, speech and dramatic arts, and fine and applied arts.

Fine arts. Science Research Associates. 1961. 4p. 35c

> Occupational brief describing work, qualifications, training, earnings, and things to consider.

A guide to art studies. National Association of Schools of Design. 1963. 3p. Free

> A statement concerning the objectives of professional education in art and design.

**Jobs in art. Science Research Associates. 1960. 32p. $1

> Describes the variety of job prospects and opportunities within this field, especially for the artist, display worker, industrial designer, interior decorator, and photographer. An acompanying wall chart is available for 35c.

A palette for Ingrid. Hobart, Lois. Julian Messner, Inc. 1956. 192p. $2.95

> Career fiction. Story combines career interest in painting with light romance.

Teaching art as a career. National Art Education Association. No date. 4p. 15c

> Challenges of teaching art, salaries and other benefits, and how to become an art teacher.

Your career in art. Philadelphia Museum College of Art. 1963. 36p. Free

> Facts about careers in art, the futures they offer, and the preparation necessary to enter them.

> *See also* Commercial artist; Industrial designer; Medical illustrator

ASBESTOS and INSULATING WORKER   5-33.110 and 5-33.210

Asbestos and insulating workers. Careers. 1962. 7p. 25c

> Career brief describing duties, working conditions, training, places of employment, earnings, and outlook.

Asbestos and insulating workers. One section of *Occupational Outlook Handbook.*

> Nature of the work, where employed, training, other qualifications, advancement, employment outlook, earnings, and working conditions.

**Employment outlook for painters, paperhangers, glaziers, and asbestos and insulating workers. Bureau of Labor Statistics, U.S. Department of Labor. Supt. of Documents. 1964. 20p. 15c

> Reprint from the *Occupational Outlook Handbook.*

ASTRONAUT 0-41.10

America's space pilots. National Aerospace Education Council. 1963. 12p. 25c

> Illustrated leaflet featuring the photographs and brief biographies of the nine astronaut candidates now in training. The booklet also describes the training of space pilots and discusses the prospects for women in the national space program.

The astronauts: pioneers in space. Golden Press. 1961. 96p. $2.99

> Presented in cooperation with the editors of *Life Magazine* and illustrated with more than one hundred photographs, this is the first book in which the astronauts describe their training in Project Mercury.

**Careers and opportunities in astronautics. Zarem, Lewis. Dutton and Company. 1962. 224p. $3.95

> An engrossing account of the work being done in the exploration of space by men and machines, the qualifications and educational background needed, salaries, and opportunities for advancement. Each of the nineteen specialized fields of astronautics is discussed, including astrodynamics, missiles and space vehicles, nuclear propulsion, propellants and combustion, space law and sociology, and structures and materials. Illustrated.

**Careers in astronautics and rocketry: training and opportunities in the space and missile fields. Adams, Carsbie, C. and Von Braun, Wernher. McGraw-Hill Book Company. 1962. 252p. $6.95

> Written for persons interested in a career in astronautics, the book presents information on the evolution of astronautics and rocketry, astronautics and the natural sciences, astronautics and the engineering disciplines, training, and opportunities. Information is given concerning schools, universities, and technical institutes offering training in astronautics.

* Careers in astronautics and space exploration. Angel, Juvenal. World Trade Academy Press. 1960. 50p. $1.50

> Includes description of the major fields of specialization, education required, opportunities, remuneration, future outlook, and methods of financing an education in astronautics. References for further reading.

I want to be a space pilot. Greene, Carla. Childrens Press. 1961. 32p. $2

> Prepared for beginning readers with a reading level of upper first grade. Illustrated in color.

Results of the third United States manned orbital space flight. National Aeronautics and Space Administration. Supt. of Documents. 1962. 120p. 70c

> Describes the performance of the spaceborne systems, the flight control, recovery operations for the mission, and pilot Walter Schirra's personal account of his flight experiences.

Space volunteers. Key, Terence. Harper and Row. 1960. 136p. $2.95

> Description of the exciting, yet harrowing, experiences of the astronauts, the men who have volunteered to help pave the way to outer space. Illustrated. For younger boys.

ASTRONAUT—*Continued*

There's adventure in astronautics. May, Julian. Popular Mechanics Press. 1961. 160p. $2.95

By relating the experiences of a boy who found a space capsule in the southwestern mountains, the author describes how space scientists are training astronauts and preparing them for adventures in space flight.

What does an astronaut do? Wells, Robert. Dodd, Mead and Company. 1961. 64p. $2.50; library binding $2.57 net

Simple text and pictures portray varied activities, training, and equipment. Written for grades 3 to 7.

See also Aerospace Industry Worker; Airplane pilot; Aviator; Missileman

ASTRONOMER   0-35.61

America's first woman astronomer: Maria Mitchell. Baker, Rachel and Merlen, Joanna. Julian Messner, Inc. 1960. 192p. $3.25. Library binding $3.19 net

Biography of the woman who discovered a comet in 1847 and was the first woman to be elected to the American Academy of Arts and Sciences.

Astronomer. California Department of Employment. 1961. 5p. Single copy free

Duties, working conditions, salaries, training, promotion, and employment outlook in California.

Astronomer. Careers. 1960. 2p. 15c

Career summary for desk-top file. Duties, qualifications, and outlook.

Astronomer. Chronicle Guidance Publications. 1961. 4p. 35c

Occupational brief summarizing work performed, working conditions, qualifications, training, earnings, and outlook.

* Astronomers. Science Research Associates. 1962. 4p. 35c

Occupational brief describing nature of work, requirements, getting started, earnings, advantages, disadvantages, and future outlook.

**Astronomers. One section of *Occupational Outlook Handbook.*

Nature of work, where employed, training, other qualifications, employment outlook, earnings, and working conditions.

Astronomy. The Guidance Centre. 1958. 4p. 15c in Canada; 20c elsewhere

History and importance, nature of work, qualifications, working conditions, preparation, remuneration, related occupations, and how to get started.

**Astronomy as a career. Miller, Freeman D. Bellman Publishing Company. 1962. 32p. $1

History and development, scholastic training, qualifications, employment opportunities, advantages, disadvantages, the organization and work of a large observatory, and names of astronomical organizations.

**A career in astronomy. American Astronomical Society. 1962. 15p. Free
  Discussion of broad general requirements, rewards, opportunities, and some recommendations. List of thirty-eight colleges that offer an undergraduate major in astronomy. Also included is a list of twenty-seven colleges that give the doctor's degree in astronomy, with their major fields of specializations.

Career information on the astronomer. Science Research Associates. 1957. 4p. 25c
  Research report describing nature of work, places of employment, education and qualifications, earnings, and opportunities for the future. Included is a list of twenty-eight colleges offering a major in astronomy.

* Careers in astronomy and related space sciences. Institute for Research. 1962. 24p. $1
  Description of jobs, a typical day's work, qualifications, training, earnings, attractive and unattractive features, and outlook.

Copernicus. Thomas, Henry. Julian Messner, Inc. 1960. 192p. $3.25. Library binding $3.19 net
  Biography of the sixteenth century astronomer who demonstrated that the sun, and not the earth, was the center of the solar system.

**Employment outlook for physical scientists: chemists, physicists, and astronomers. Bureau of Labor Statistics, U.S. Department of Labor. Supt. of Documents. 1964. 16p. 10c
  Reprint from the *Occupational Outlook Handbook.*

Planetary and space science at M.I.T. Massachusetts Institute of Technology. 1962. 20p. Free
  A statement, primarily for prospective students, of educational opportunities and research at M.I.T. in planetary and space science and closely related fields. Includes description of courses offered.

Stars in my pocket. Berry, Erick. John Day Company. 1960. 190p. $3.25
  Career fiction. Story based on occurrences in the life of Maria Mitchell, America's first woman astronomer.

The telescope. Neal, Harry Edward. Julian Messner, Inc. 1958. 192p. $3.95. Library binding $3.64 net
  Includes description of different scientific careers in the brief biographies of the men who invented various parts of the telescope. Sixteen pages of illustration.

ATHLETE   0-57.

**Athletes. Chronicle Guidance Publications. 1962. 4p. 35c
  Occupational brief summarizing work performed, personal qualifications, training, working conditions, earnings, opportunities for advancement, and outlook. Selected references.

**Commercial sports. Science Research Associates. 1960. 4p. 35c
  Occupational brief describing nature of work, training, qualifications, opportunities, advantages, and future outlook.

ATHLETE—*Continued*

Conqueror of Mt. McKinley: Hudson Stuck. Herron, Edward. Julian Messner, Inc. 1964. 192p. $3.25; library edition $3.19 net
Biography of the man whose most gripping adventure was climbing the highest mountain in North America.

Famous American women athletes. Jacobs, Helen Hull. Dodd, Mead and Company. 1964. 160p. $3.25
The author analyzes what each woman contributed to her particular sport and the qualifications that made her a champion in swimming, skating, skiing, golf, bowling, or tennis.

Hockey player. The Guidance Centre. 1960. 4p. 15c in Canada; 20c elsewhere
Nature of work, qualifications, training, earnings, how to enter, advantages. disadvantages, and related occupations.

* Professional athletics as a career. Institute for Research. 1961. 24p. $1
Professional opportunities in baseball, basketball, football, golf, ice hockey. riding, and tennis.

Snow on Blueberry Mountain. Meader, S. T. Harcourt, Brace and World. 1961. 189p. $3.25
Career fiction. Story of a high school boy who dreams of turning a worthless strip of cutover mountainside into a commercial ski slope.

See also Athletic coach; Baseball player; Physical instructor

ATHLETIC COACH   0-57.21

* Athletic coach. Chronicle Guidance Publications. 1962. 4p. 35c
Occupational brief summarizing work performed, working conditions, personal qualifications, training, earnings, opportunities for advancement, advantages, disadvantages, and outlook.

**Athletic coaches. Science Research Associates. 1964. 4p. 35c
Occupational brief describing nature of work, training, qualifications, opportunities, advantages, disadvantages, and future outlook.

Coach. California State Department of Employment. 1960. 4p. Single copy free
Job duties, working conditions, pay, hours, entrance requirements, training, and employment outlook.

Fighting coach. Archibald, Joseph. Macrae Smith Company. 1954. 192p. $2.95
Career fiction. A young coach refuses to compromise the ethics of amateur football for financial gains and public prestige.

You have to pay the price. Blaik, Earl H. and Cohane, Tim. Holt, Rinehart and Winston. 1960. 430p. $4.95
Autobiography of Red Blaik, the famed football coach of Dartmouth and West Point. Interwoven in this portrayal of some of the great football games is information about the work of a college football coach, qualifications, training, hazards, and satisfactions.

See also Athlete; Physical instructor

ATOMIC ENERGY INDUSTRY WORKER
0-35.60 through 0-35.89; 0-66.800; 0-67.000 through 0-67.399; 0-69.850;
4, 6, 8-50.00 through 4, 6, 8-54.99

Atomic energy and automation: forces shaping tomorrow's job. Western Personnel Institute. 1955. 6p. 20c

Analysis of the effects on industry and on the individual wage earner.

Atomic energy engineers and scientists. Careers. 1962. 7p. 25c

Career brief describing nature of work, training, working conditions, personal qualifications, places of employment, related careers, earnings, and outlook. Additional readings.

Atomic energy technicians. Science Research Associates. 1963. 4p. 35c

Occupational brief describing nature of work, requirements, methods of getting started, earnings, and future outlook.

The atomic submarine. Lewellen, John Bryan. Crowell Publishing Company. 1954. 134p. $2.95

Explanation of the harnessing of atomic energy and the development of atomic submarines. Includes description of life and work on the Nautilus. Illustrated.

**A career in the United States Atomic Energy Commission: atomic internships. The Commission, Division of Technical Information. 1963. 18p. Free

Description of atomic internships in management, technical work, health physics, nuclear engineering, construction engineering, legal, and patent attorney training programs. Also included are requirements, selection, employment conditions, and how to apply.

**Careers in atomic energy. Greenleaf, Walter J. U.S. Office of Education. Pamphlet Number 119. Supt. of Documents. 1957. 36p. 25c

Descriptions of atomic energy, government control, occupations in industrial corporations and in offices of the Atomic Energy Commission, training opportunities, and fellowships. Also includes applications of atomic energy in biology, medicine, agriculture, manufacturing, mining, nuclear power, and research and laboratories.

**Careers in atomic energy—planning for scientific and technical professions. U.S. Atomic Energy Commission, Division of Technical Information. 1962. 27p. Free

Discussion of the work of the atomic scientist, college training, scholarships and other financial assistance, location of opportunities, and professional satisfactions. Good reading lists.

* Careers in nuclear science, engineering, and technology. Institute for Research. 1959. 28p. $1

History of atomic power, duties, requirements, precollege educational requirements, undergraduate and graduate school training, and attractive and unattractive features. Also included is a description of types of services needed in atomic power development: metallurgists, chemical engineers, mechanical engineers, electrical engineers, physicists and chemists, health physicists, biologists and research doctors.

ATOMIC ENERGY INDUSTRY WORKER—*Continued*

Careers in the atomic energy industry. Walker, Harold L. Bellman Publishing Company. 1958. 32p. $1

> Development of the industry, nature of work in four major work areas for nuclear scientists and technologists, opportunities for training, personal qualifications, advantages, and disadvantages. Includes list of private companies active in the industry.

Careers in the nuclear field. World Trade Academy Press. 1958. 26p. $1.25

> Includes information about each of several specialities within this field.

**Employment in the atomic energy field—a 1962 occupational survey. Bureau of Labor Statistics, U.S. Department of Labor. Supt. of Documents. 1964. 43p. 35c

> Provides information on employment of workers in selected engineering, scientific, technical, and skilled worker occupations in atomic energy activities. Data are classified by type of facility and function.

**Employment opportunities in the atomic energy field. U.S. Atomic Energy Commission. 1962. 48p. 50c

> Nature of the atomic energy field, occupations in the scientific and engineering fields, opportunities as technicians and skilled workers, and education and training requirements. References for further reading.

**Employment outlook in the atomic energy field. Bureau of Labor Statistics, U.S. Department of Labor. Supt. of Documents. 1964. 20p. 15c

> Reprint from the *Occupational Outlook Handbook*.

**Engineers and scientists opportunities. U.S. Atomic Energy Commission, Division of Technical Information. 1962. 62p. Free

> Information concerning engineering and scientific opportunities in key programs in reactor development, physical research, biology and medicine, regulatory, and other technical work. Included also are salaries, character of work, qualifications, and location of employment of eighty-eight specific jobs.

Giant of the atom: Ernest Rutherford. McKown, Robin. Julian Messner, Inc. 1962. 192p. $3.25. Library binding $3.19 net

> Biography of the man who has a record of major discoveries about the atom and radioactivity, was knighted by the King of England, and won a Nobel prize in chemistry.

J. Robert Oppenheimer and the atomic story. Kugelmass, J. Alvin. Julian Messner, Inc. 1953. 192p. $3.25. Library binding $3.19 net

> Biography of a man who contributed to the development of atomic energy, containing many of the dramatic incidents at the Los Alamos Scientific Laboratory and the Institute for Advanced Study in Princeton, New Jersey.

A memorandum to high school students on careers in the field of atomic energy. U.S. Atomic Energy Commission. 1958. 3p. Free

> Opportunities and need for trained scientists.

The naval nuclear propulsion training program. Supt. of Documents. 1962. 32p. 30c

> Description of the training programs for operators of the propulsion plants of the nuclear powered ships of the U.S. Navy, how to prepare, and how to apply.

Nuclear engineering. Michigan College of Mining and Technology. 1963. 2p. Free
Example of a recruiting leaflet describing work, qualifications, educational requirements, and employment opportunities.

Nuclear engineering at M.I.T. Massachusetts Institute of Technology. 1962. 28p. Free
Illustrated brochure describing the educational opportunities in fission technology and in thermonuclear processes. Includes description of subjects offered and the outlook for professional opportunities in this field.

Nuclear scientists. Science Research Associates. 1960. 4p. 35c
Occupational brief describing uses of atomic energy, types of workers, qualifications, earnings, and outlook. Selected references.

**Occupations in the atomic energy field. One chapter in *Occupational Outlook Handbook.*
Applications and production of atomic energy, nature of the field, kinds of occupations, training, other qualifications, advancement, employment outlook, earnings, and working conditions.

Programs for nuclear educational assistance. U.S. Atomic Energy Commission. 1962. 24p. Free
Includes grants, loans, research opportunities, fellowships, and other assistance to graduate students.

The rocket pioneers on the road to space. Williams, Beryl and Epstein, Samuel. Julian Messner, Inc. 1955. 192p. $3.95
Biographies of several rocket pioneers whose dreams and achievements have contributed to the fulfillment of space travel and rocket transportation.

Rockets and missiles. Bergaust, Erik. G. P. Putnam's Sons. 1957. 48p. $2.50
Includes description of the work of the Army, Navy, and Air Force in the missiles field.

**Selected occupations concerned with atomic energy. U.S. Department of Labor. Supt. of Documents. 1961. 57p. 25c
Presents information for fourteen jobs concerned with the peaceful application of atomic energy, including estimates of the worker trait requirements pertinent to each.

Selected readings on atomic energy. Supt. of Documents. Revised 1958. 74p. 30c
List of references.

Should you be an atomic scientist? Hafstad, Lawrence R. New York Life Insurance Company. 1960. 12p. Free
Illustrated booklet containing nature of work, desirable qualifications, rewards, earnings, and possibilities for advancement.

There's adventure in atomic energy. May, Julian. Popular Mechanics Press. 1957. 174p. $2.95
By relating experiences of a boy in this field, the author portrays the various kinds of work. Written for grades 7 to 10.

ATOMIC ENERGY INDUSTRY WORKER—*Continued*

Union Carbide in nuclear energy. Union Carbide Corporation. 1960. 24p. Free

Lists descriptions of various jobs required for operation of United States Atomic Energy Commission's installations at Oak Ridge and Paducah. Includes opportunities for technical personnel.

**Your future in nuclear energy fields. Thompson, William E., Jr. Richards Rosen Press. 1961. 160p. $2.95

Information and advice concerning the nature of work in government, industry, or teaching are followed by a discussion of training, opportunities, how to look for the first job, and employment information.

Your future in nuclear energy fields. Thompson, William E., Jr. Popular Library, Inc. 1962. 160p. 50c

A paperback edition of the book described above.

ATTORNEY. *See* Lawyer

AUCTIONEER   1-51.10

Auctioneer. Careers. 1959. 2p. 15c

Career summary for desk-top file. Duties, qualifications, and outlook.

**Auctioneer. Chronicle Guidance Publications. 1960. 4p. 35c

Occupational brief summarizing work performed, working conditions, personal qualifications, training requirements, opportunities, employment outlook, and methods of entering the job.

Auctioneer. The Guidance Centre. 1961. 4p. 15c in Canada; 20c elsewhere

Nature of work, qualifications, preparation, working conditions, outlook, advantages, disadvantages, how to get started, and related topics.

AUDITOR. See Accountant

AUTHOR. *See* Writer

AUTOMATIC MERCHANDISING INDUSTRY WORKER
1-15.10; 6-94.653; 7-83.986

Automatic vending routemen. Science Research Associates. 1961. 4p. 35c

Occupational brief describing the work, qualifications, training, and outlook.

Vending machine operator. Careers. 1962. 2p. 15c

Career summary for desk-top file. Duties, qualifications, and outlook.

AUTOMOBILE MANUFACTURING INDUSTRY WORKER   5, 7, 9-02.

The automobile industry. Chapter 4 of *Vocations for Boys*.

Includes brief description of the assembler, technician, craftsman, and maintenance worker.

Automobile manufacturing occupations. One chapter in *Occupational Outlook Handbook*, 1961 edition.

Nature and location of the industry, kinds of work, training, other qualifications, advancement, employment outlook, earnings, and working conditions. Five illustrations.

Automobile manufacturing workers. Science Research Associates. 1961. 4p. 35c

Occupational brief describing various kinds of work, requirements, earnings, and future outlook.

Employment outlook in motor vehicles manufacturing occupations. Bureau of Labor Statistics, U.S. Department of Labor. Supt. of Documents. 1964. 16p. 10c

Reprint from the *Occupational Outlook Handbook*.

Motor vehicles manufacturing occupations. One section of *Occupational Outlook Handbook*.

Nature of work, where employed, training, other qualifications, advancement, employment outlook, earnings, and working conditions.

OK for drive-away. Lent, Henry. Macmillan Company. 1960. 152p. $3

Career fiction. Story showing the steps in manufacturing an automobile from the draftsman's sheet to the assembly line and final testing. For ages 12 to 16.

There's adventure in automobiles. May, Julien. Popular Mechanics Press. 1961. 159p. $2.95

By relating experiences of a boy in this field, the author portrays the various kinds of work. Written for grades 7 to 10.

What it takes to make your car. Automobile Manufacturers Association. 1961. 48p. Free

Booklet, copiously illustrated, showing the various processes of transforming raw materials into the components of an automobile. Good material to illustrate the interdependence of workers.

* Your future in the automotive industry. Taylor, Dawson. Richards Rosen Press. 1963. 160p. $2.95

Various aspects of the automobile industry from manufacture to sales and maintenance are presented.

AUTOMOBILE MECHANIC   5, 7-81.

Automobile-body repairman. Careers. 1959. 2p. 15c

Career summary for desk-top file. Duties, qualifications, and outlook.

Automobile-body repairman. Chronicle Guidance Publications. 1964. 4p. 35c

Occupational brief summarizing work performed, working conditions, personal qualifications, training requirements, opportunities, employment outlook, and entry into the job.

Automobile-body repairman. Michigan Employment Security Commission. 1962. 19p. 25c

Introduction, nature of work, location of jobs, working conditions, earnings, employment outlook, requirements for entry, disadvantages, and advantages.

AUTOMOBILE MECHANIC—*Continued*

* Automobile body repairmen. Science Research Associates. 1961. 4p. 35c
Occupational brief describing work, training, working conditions, getting started, earnings and benefits, things to consider, and future outlook.

Automobile brakeman. Careers. 1960. 2p. 15c
Career summary for desk-top file. Duties, qualifications, and outlook.

Automobile mechanic. Landon, William. Research Publishing Company. 1957. 16p. $1.50
Advantages of working as an automobile mechanic, number engaged in occupation, working conditions, qualifications and special skills required, and chances for promotion.

Automobile mechanic. California State Department of Employment. 1962. 3p. Single copy free
Duties, working conditions, wages, hours, preparation, promotion, and employment prospects.

* Automobile mechanic. Careers. 1962. 8p. 25c
Career brief describing duties, working conditions, training requirements, training opportunities, personal qualifications, employment prospects, earnings, advancement prospects, where employed, measuring one's interest and ability, suggested high school program, and unionization.

Automobile mechanic. Chronicle Guidance Publications. 1962. 4p. 35c
Occupational brief containing definition, history, work performed, working conditions, personal requirements, determination of aptitudes and interests, training requirements, training opportunities, outlook, methods of entry, and related jobs.

Automobile mechanic. The Guidance Centre. 1962. 4p. 15c in Canada; 20c elsewhere
Nature of work, history of the occupation, working conditions, qualifications, preparation, employment and advancement, earnings, how to get started, advantages, and disadvantages.

Automobile mechanic and repair shop owner—careers. Institute for Research. 1961. 24p. $1
Types of jobs, personal qualifications, training, earnings, attractive and unattractive features, typical day's work, and related fields.

Automobile mechanics. Group, Vernard. Personnel Services. 1957. 6p. 50c; 25c to students
Occupational abstract. Nature of the work, future prospects, qualifications, preparation, entrance, advancement, earnings, number and distribution, advantages, and disadvantages.

Automobile mechanics. Michigan Employment Security Commission. 1961. 19p. 25c
Introduction, nature of work, location of jobs, working conditions, employment outlook, earnings, requirements for entry, disadvantages, and advantages.

**Automobile mechanics. One section in *Occupational Outlook Handbook*.
Nature of work, where employed, training, other qualifications, advancement, employment outlook, earnings, and working conditions.

Automobile mechanics. Science Research Associates. 1960. 4p. 35c
Occupational brief describing nature of work, requirements, training, getting started and advancing, earnings, advantages, disadvantages, and future outlook.

**Employment outlook for automobile mechanics and diesel mechanics. Bureau of Labor Statistics, U.S. Department of Labor. Supt. of Documents. 1964. 12p. 10c
Reprint from the *Occupational Outlook Handbook*.

Find a career in auto mechanics. Harrison, C. William. Putnam's Sons. 1964. 160p. $2.95
Emphasizing the broad range of skills needed, this book points out the vital role of the mechanic in safety and public relations. For grades 7 to 11.

Opportunities in automotive service. Automobile Manufacturers Association. 1961. 8p. Free
Includes the wide range of opportunities in this industry and how to train for these jobs.

Tire vulcanizer. Careers. 1962. 2p. 15c
Career summary for desk-top file. Duties, qualifications, and outlook.

Truck mechanic. Careers. 1962. 2p. 15c
Career summary for desk-top file. Duties, qualifications, and outlook.

AUTOMOBILE SALESMAN   1-85.10 through 1-85.19

Automobile salesman. Careers. 1959. 2p. 15c
Career summary for desk-top file. Duties, qualifications, and outlook.

* Automobile salesman. Chronicle Guidance Publications. 1961. 4p. 35c
Occupational brief summarizing work performed, working conditions, earnings, personal qualifications, opportunities, methods of entry, related jobs, and suggested activities.

* Automobile salesmen. Science Research Associates. 1961. 4p. 35c
Occupational brief describing nature of work, qualifications, earnings, getting started and advancing, advantages, disadvantages, and future outlook.

Careers in automobile dealerships. Institute for Research. 1957. 23p. $1
History and types of jobs, a typical dealer's day, attractive and unattractive features, personal qualifications, training, and jobs for women.

Professional profile of an automobile salesman. General Motors Corporation. 1961. 31p. Free
Discussion of requirements, opportunities, and earnings. Indicates that a career in retail automobile selling can mean a good income and life-long security. Includes advice from a number of successful salesmen in this field.

The used car business as a career. Institute for Research. 1956. 24p. $1
Jobs in the used car business, typical day's work, attractive and unattractive features, personal qualifications, training, chances for employment, how to get started, earnings, and related fields.

AUTOMOBILE-SERVICE-STATION ATTENDANT   7-60.500

* Automotive-service-station attendant. Careers. 1963. 8p. 25c
   Career brief describing duties, working conditions, training, qualifications,
   earnings, and outlook.

Automobile service station attendant. Florida State Employment Service.
   1961. 6p. Free to guidance personnel in Florida
   Example of a series prepared to provide information about occupations
   which offer employment opportunities in a specific state. Describes the nature
   of work, opportunities, conditions, and qualifications.

**Employment outlook for gasoline service station attendants. Bureau of
   Labor Statistics, U.S. Department of Labor. Supt. of Documents. 1964.
   4p. 5c
   Reprint from the *Occupational Outlook Handbook.*

**Gasoline service station attendants. One section of *Occupational Outlook
   Handbook.*
   Nature of work, where employed, training, other qualifications, advance-
   ment, employment outlook, earnings, and working conditions.

Opportunities in automotive service. Automobile Manufacturers Association. 1963. 9p. Free
   This leaflet indicates the wide range of opportunities for young men in this
   field, the employment outlook, training, trainee-selection factors, and qualities
   needed for success.

Service station attendant. California State Department of Employment.
   1962. 3p. Single copy free
   Duties, working conditions, pay, training, promotion, and employment
   prospects.

Service station attendant. The Guidance Centre. 1958. 4p. 15c in Canada;
   20c elsewhere
   Nature of work, qualifications, working conditions, outlook, earnings, advantages, disadvantages, how to get started, and related occupations.

Service station management. National Cash Register Company. 1961. 60p.
   Free
   Includes discussion of what the service station business offers, what it
   demands, and ways of getting into service station management.

Service station operation as a career. Institute for Research. 1963. 24p. $1
   Nature of work, duties, training classes conducted by oil companies, qualifications, typical week's work, opportunities, how to build a profitable business,
   and attractive and unattractive features.

**Service-station salesman. Chronicle Guidance Publications. 1962. 4p. 35c
   Occupational brief containing definition, history, work performed, working
   conditions, personal requirements, determination of aptitudes and interests,
   training requirements, training opportunities, outlook, where employed, private
   ownership, methods of entry, related jobs, and suggested activities.

**Service station workers. Science Research Associates. 1960. 4p. 35c
   Occupational brief describing nature of work, opportunities, advantages,
   disadvantages, and future outlook.

Starting and managing a service station. Small Business Administration. Supt. of Documents. 1961. 80p. 35c

This booklet describes the advantages and disadvantages of entering this particular business, the risks involved, the personal characteristics that will contribute to success, and some management practices.

AUTOMOBILE TRANSPORTATION INDUSTRY WORKER. *See* Motor transportation

AUTOMOTIVE ENGINEER 0-19.01

**Automotive engineering as a career. Institute for Research. 1959. 24p. $1

Where automotive engineers find employment, history and development of the work, major divisions of automotive engineering in automobile manufacture, line of advancement, typical day's work, salaries, attractive and unattractive features, personal qualifications, education and experience desirable, getting a job, and future employment prospects.

See also Engineer

AVIATION MECHANIC. *See* Airplane mechanic

AVIATOR 0-41.

Air drop: men, weapons and cargo by parachute. Colby, C. B. Coward-McCann, Inc. 1953. 48p. Library edition $2.52 net

Photographs and brief text reveal work and training. Written for grades 4 to 8.

Aviation as a career. Institute for Research. 1960. 24p. $1

History and development of work, qualifications, and attractive and unattractive features.

Aviation cadet. Archibald, Joseph. David McKay Company. 1955. 167p. $2.95

Fictional account of a cadet in the United States Air Force, giving a picture of the hazards and the satisfactions of the men who earn their wings.

Aviation from the ground up. Revised edition. Floherty, John J. Lippincott Company. 1960. 160p. $3.95

Special attention is given to careers in flying such as aerial advertising, helicopter, jet propulsion, crop spraying, and the Berlin airlift. Replaces the author's *Aviation from shop to sky.* Thirty-two illustrations.

The building of a Marine aviator. U.S. Marine Corps. 1962. 32p. Free

Illustrated brochure containing information about Marine Corps pilot training and the programs available to persons interested in this training.

Careers in aviation. Angel, Juvenal. World Trade Academy Press. 1960. 22p. $1.25

Includes description of work, training required, opportunities, remuneration, and future outlook.

AVIATOR—Continued

**Civil aviation. Bureau of Labor Statistics, U.S. Department of Labor. Supt. of Documents. 1964. 28p. 20c

Reprint from the *Occupational Outlook Handbook.*

Come aboard with the Naval Air Reserve. U.S. Department of the Navy. 1960. 8p. Free

Brief description of the benefits, pay, education, and advancement possible in this branch of service. Also provided is a graph determining how to meet one's military obligation.

**Employment outlook in civil aviation. One section of *Occupational Outlook Handbook.*

Nature of work, training, qualifications, employment outlook, earnings, and working conditions.

Find a career in aviation. Stambler, Irwin. Putnam's Sons. 1960. 160p. $2.95

Information about the many jobs available in this fast-growing field and how to qualify for them. Written for ages 11 to 15.

Flying high with a great team. U.S. Department of the Navy. 1960. 8p. Free

Illustrated booklet describing the eligibility requirements for Naval Aviation Officer Candidates (non-pilot). Also discussed are the three phases of naval aviation officer training and the various categories of flight crew and aviation support assignments.

Helicopters in action. Bergaust, Erik and Foss, William. Putnam's Sons. 1962. 96p. $2.95

An account of the development of this aircraft and information on helicopter flight schools in the United States and Canada. Written for ages 10 to 14.

Helicopters to the rescue: how the amazing whirly-birds do the impossible. Colby, C. B. Coward-McCann, Inc. 1952. 48p. Library edition $2.52 net

Photographs and brief text reveal how the helicopters have come to the rescue in various kinds of situations. Written for grades 4 to 8.

Navy wings of gold. U.S. Department of the Navy. 1962. 52p. Free

A booklet, amply illustrated, describing in story form the development of a naval aviator. The story conveys the general atmosphere of the life of an aviation student and is supported throughout with interesting factual material.

Rocketmen and what they do. Coombs, Charles. Franklin Watts, Inc. 1962. 184p. $3.95

Description of work, personal qualifications, specialized training, outlook, and rewards. For grades 7 to 11.

SAC: men and machines of our Strategic Air Command. Colby, C. B. Coward-McCann, Inc. 1961. 48p. Library binding $2.52 net

Photographs and brief text reveal the work of maintaining a security vigil. Written for grades 4 to 8.

**Skyblazers: your career in aviation. Neal, Harry Edward. Julian Messner, Inc. 1963. 192p. $3.95. Library binding $3.64 net
> Describes the many jobs involved in the aircraft industry, emphasizing the opportunities in military and naval aviation, commercial, and business flying. One chapter is devoted to aviation careers for women.

Story of Amelia Earhart. De Leeuw, Adele. Grosset and Dunlap, Inc. 1955. 181p. $1.95
> Biography of one of America's first women aviators. For younger readers.

Whirling wings. Floherty, John J. and McGrady, Mike. Lippincott Company. 1961. 160p. $3
> Story of the helicopter and the men responsible for its invention and development. Illustrated.

Wider than the sky—aviation as a career. Daugherty, Charles M. Harcourt, Brace and World. 1958. 158p. $2.95
> Beginning with the development of aviation from the time of the Wright brothers to contemporary accomplishments with jets, missiles, and rockets, the author lays stress on current opportunities in aviation. In a final chapter, the various kinds of jobs and their requirements are described.

> *See also* Aerospace industry worker; Air Force airman; Airplane pilot; Astronaut; Atomic energy industry worker

BABY-SITTER   2-07.01

Baby-sitters' handbook. Flander, Judy. Science Research Associates. 1952. 48p. 50c
> Written for teen-age sitters, the booklet includes qualifications for a sitter, the many problems concerning wages and employer-employee relations, duties of a sitter, the care of infants and older children. The book emphasizes that anyone can be a baby-sitter, but it is important to have the required skills and knowledge to be a good one.

A manual for baby sitters: Lowndes, Marion. Little, Brown and Company. 1961. 185p. $3.50
> Description of the skills, desirable qualities needed, and obligations. Includes a list of twelve essentials for baby sitters. Also given are the responsibilities of those who hire sitters. Selected reading lists.

BACTERIOLOGIST   0-35.33

Bacteriologist. Robinson, H. Alan. Personnel Services. 1956. 6p. 50c; 25c to students
> Occupational abstract. Nature of work, future prospects, opportunities, qualifications, preparation, entrance and advancement, earnings, number and distribution of workers, advantages and disadvantages, and related occupations.

Bacteriologist. Careers. 1959. 2p. 15c
> Career summary for desk-top file. Duties, qualifications, and outlook.

Bacteriologist. The Guidance Centre. 1963. 4p. 15c in Canada; 20c elsewhere
> History and importance, nature of work, qualifications, preparation, outlook, remuneration, how to get started, and related occupations.

BACTERIOLOGIST—*Continued*

**Bacteriology as a career. Institute for Research. 1961. 24p. $1
> Discussion of specialites of the field, qualifications, requirements, compensation, and outlook.

* A career for biochemists, bacteriologists, serologists. Veterans Administration, Department of Medicine and Surgery. 1961. 4p. Free
> Description of work, training program, qualifications, and benefits.

Education in bacteriology. Philadelphia College of Pharmacy and Science. 1962. 3p. Free
> One chapter in an illustrated recruiting brochure describing nature of work, opportunities, and training in bacteriology, biology, chemistry and pharmacy.

List of college and university departments offering degree programs in microbiology. American Society for Microbiology. 1962. 6p. 50c
> Revised annually.

Microbiologist. Careers. 1961. 2p. 15c
> Career summary for desk-top file. Duties, qualifications, and outlook.

Microbiologist. Chronicle Guidance Publications. 1961. 4p. 35c
> Occupational brief summarizing work performed, working conditions, earnings, personal qualifications, ways of determining interest and ability, training, opportunities, related occupations, and outlook. Selected references.

* Microbiologists. Science Research Associates. 1963. 4p. 35c
> Occupational brief describing nature of work, requirements, preparation, getting started, advancing, earnings, and outlook.

**Microbiology in your future. American Society for Microbiology. 1962. 20p. 10c. Single copy free
> Attractively illustrated brochure describing scope of microbiology, areas of work, recommended high school program of studies, college preparation, salaries, and employment outlook.

Robert Koch, father of bacteriology. Knight, D. C. Franklin Watts, Inc. 1961. 165p. $1.95
> Biography of the man who first perfected the pure techniques of cultivating and studying bacteria and first isolated the tubercle bacillus, the cause of tuberculosis.

BAKER   4-01.

At the bakery. Colonius, Lillian. Melmont Publishers. 1953. 24p. $2.50
> An account of the processes used in the making of bread in a modern bakery. Reading level grades 2-4.

Baker. Robinson, H. Alan. Personnel Services. 1953. 6p. 50c; 25c to students
> Occupational abstract. Summary of nature of the work, future prospects, opportunities for servicemen, opportunities for women, qualifications, preparation, organizations, entrance and advancement, earnings, number and distribution of workers, advantages, disadvantages, and appraisal of literature.

Baker. Careers. 1959. 2p. 15c
> Career summary for desk-top file. Duties, qualifications, and outlook.

**Baker. Chronicle Guidance Publications. 1961. 4p. 35c

Occupational brief summarizing work performed, working conditions, training, opportunities, employment outlook, related jobs, and suggested activities.

Baker. The Guidance Centre. 1962. 4p. 15c in Canada; 20c elsewhere

History and importance of the work, qualifications, preparation, conditions of work, earnings, employment and advancement, how to get started, and related occupations.

Bakers. Michigan Employment Security Commission. 1963. 2p. Single copy free

Job brief summarizing nature of work, location of jobs, working conditions, employment outlook, earnings, requirements for entry, and suggestions for finding a job.

**Bakers. Science Research Associates. 1959. 4p. 35c

Occupational brief describing nature of work, preparation, qualifications, opportunities, advantages, disadvantages, and future outlook.

**Employment outlook in the baking industry. Bureau of Labor Statistics, U.S. Department of Labor. Supt. of Documents. 1964. 12p. 10c

Reprint from the *Occupational Outlook Handbook*.

Handbook on baking schools and scholarships. Allied Trades of the Baking Industry. 1962. 24p. Free

Stresses the need for more and better trained young bakers and provides information on training opportunities and scholarships.

I want to be a baker. Greene, Carla. Childrens Press. 1956. 32p. $2

Prepared for beginning readers with a reading level of upper first grade. Illustrated in color.

**Occupations in the baking industry. One chapter of *Occupational Outlook Handbook*.

Nature and location of the industry, kinds of jobs, training, other qualifications, advancement, employment outlook, earnings, and working conditions.

Retail bakery operation as a career. Institute for Research. 1958. 24p. $1

Nature of work, qualifications, preparation, list of schools which offer training, apprenticeship jobs, typical day's work, salaries, opportunities, outlook, and attractive and unattractive features.

There's a future for you in the baking industry. American Bakers Association. 1957. 22p. Free

Description of the baking industry, its composition, size, and importance in the economy. Shows the steps in production and marketing, the wide variety of jobs, and the skills required. Distributed through local wholesale bakers who are members of the American Bakers Association.

BALLET DANCER. *See* Dancer

BANK TELLER   1-06.02

Bank teller. Splaver, Sarah. Personnel Services. 1956. 6p. 50c; 25c to
students
Occupational abstract. Nature of the work, qualifications, preparation, entrance and advancement, supply and demand, earnings, advantages, and disadvantages.

* Bank teller. Careers. 1963. 8p. 25c
Career brief describing duties, working conditions, qualifications, training,
earnings, and outlook.

* Bank teller. Chronicle Guidance Publications. 1963. 4p. 35c
Occupational brief summarizing work performed, hours, earnings, personal
requirements, training, methods of entry, promotion, related jobs, and outlook.

Bank teller. The Guidance Centre. 1963. 4p. 15c in Canada; 20c elsewhere
Definition, nature of work, qualifications, preparation, how to get started,
earnings, advantages, and disadvantages.

Tellers. One section of *Occupational Outlook Handbook*.
Nature of work, training, other qualifications, advancement, and employment
outlook.

The work of the bank teller. Beaty, John Y. Bankers Publishing Company.
1952. 77p. $1
Intended as information for the beginning bank teller, the book includes
descriptions of the various tasks and qualifications.

BANK WORKER   0-98.00 through 0-98.19; 1-05. and 1-06.

At the bank. Rees, Elinor. Melmont Publishers. 1959. 32p. $2.50
Elementary functions of a bank described for pupils in grades 3-4.

* Bank careers. Careers. 1963. 8p. 25c
Career brief describing the history and functions of banks, duties of typical
bank workers, training, personal qualifications, earnings, advancement prospects,
measuring one's interest and ability, and hours of work.

Bank clerks and related workers. One section of *Occupational Outlook
Handbook*.
Nature of work, training, other qualifications, advancement, and employment
outlook.

Bank officers. Science Research Associates. 1961. 4p. 35c
Occupational brief containing description of work, qualifications, earnings,
opportunities, things to consider, and outlook. Selected references.

Bank workers. Science Research Associates. 1961. 4p. 35c
Occupational brief describing nature of work, training, qualifications, opportunities, advantages, disadvantages, and future outlook.

**Banking occupations. One chapter in *Occupational Outlook Handbook*.
Nature of work, where employed, employment outlook, earnings, working
conditions, and advancement. Specific information concerning bank clerk, teller,
and bank officer.

Careers in banking. Institute for Research. 1964. 24p. $1
Duties, qualifications, training, lines of promotion, advantages, and disadvantages. Includes description of work of the cashier, teller, bookkeeper, clearing house clerk, central clearing clerk, and file clerk.

**Employment outlook in banking occupuations. Bureau of Labor Statistics, U.S. Department of Labor. Supt. of Documents. 1964. 12p. 10c
Reprint from the *Occupational Outlook Handbook.*

**Future unlimited—career opportunities in banking for high school graduates. American Bankers Association. 1960. 22p. Single copy free
Importance of banks in today's world, wide range of jobs, typical bank positions, opportunities, earnings, and how to apply for a position. Attractively illustrated.

**Money masters: your career in banking. Neal, Harry Edward. Julian Messner, Inc. 1961. 192p. $3.95. Library binding $3.64 net
Training programs bank-paid college educations, fringe benefits and employment opportunities are discussed in this account of the banking structure.

The new look in banking—careers for young women in banking and finance. David McKay Company. 1961. 210p. $3.50
Describes the increasing opportunities for women, nature of work, qualifications, and outlook.

Safe deposit work. Beaty, John Y. Bankers Publishing Company. 1952. 62p. $1
Includes an explanation of the duties and responsibilities involved in safe deposit work.

The Sextant series for exploring your future in banking. American Liberty Press. 1961. 120p. $5; paper $4
One page is devoted to each of ninety-five jobs, presenting the job duties, requirements for entering, promotional outlook, and the pay and skill level. An organizational chart is available for 60c.

Your career in banking. American Bankers Association. 1958. 24p. Single copy free
Written for bank employees and for recruitment of high school students. Describes services offered, advantages, opportunities for women, and suggestions for making a career out of a job.

See also Securities salesman

BANKER   0-98.00 through 0-98.19; 1-65.

Agricultural banker. Chronicle Guidance Publications. 1964. 4p. 35c
Occupational brief summarizing work performed, working conditions, qualifications, training, opportunities, and outlook.

Another look after five years at college men in banking. American Bankers Association. 1962. 4p. Single copy free
Report of a survey concerning recruiting and promoting men graduating from colleges and universities.

BANKER—*Continued*

Bank manager. The Guidance Centre. 1963. 4p. 15c in Canada; 20c elsewhere
Definition, history and importance of work, qualifications, preparation, employment outlook, earnings, and how to get started.

**Bank officers. One section of *Occupational Outlook Handbook*.
Nature of work, training, other qualifications, advancement, and employment outlook.

* Careers in banking. Angel, Juvenal. World Trade Academy Press. 1959. 26p. $1.25
Includes description of the work, education required, opportunities, rewards, future outlook, and methods of financing an education.

Free literature available to educators and vocational counselors. Investment Bankers Association of America. 1963. 2p. Free
Description of available leaflets.

How to achieve success in investment banking. Davis, George W. Investment Bankers Association of America. No date. 5p. Free
Advice given to graduates of a university course in this field.

How to succeed in banking as a career. Beaty, John Y. Bankers Publishing Company. 1950. 71p. $1
Intended to serve beginners in banking as an inspiration for better service, the book stresses qualities desirable in this work.

Should you be a banker? Florence, Fred F. New York Life Insurance Company. 1961. 12p. Free
Discussion of desirable qualities, attractions, and outlook.

To the young man who is interested in everything—a statement on career opportunities in investment banking. Investment Bankers Association of America. 1956. 4p. Single copies free to counselors and librarians.
Reprint from *Career, the Annual Guide to Business Opportunities*.

Want to be a banker? Changing Times. 1959. 3p. 15c
A reprint describing the promising careers in banking.

BARBER   2-32.01

Barber. California State Department of Employment. 1962. 4p. Single copy free
Duties, working conditions, wages, hours, promotion, training, and employment outlook.

Barber. Careers. 1963. 7p. 25c
Career brief describing duties, working conditions, training, personal qualifications, earnings, unionization, and outlook.

Barber. Chronicle Guidance Publications. 1961. 3p. 35c
Occupational brief describing work performed, working conditions, personal qualifications, determination of aptitudes and interests, training requirements, opportunities, outlook, methods of entry, and suggested activities.

Barber. The Guidance Centre. 1961. 4p. 15c in Canada; 20c elsewhere
Nature of work, qualifications necessary for entry and success, employment and advancement, earnings, advantages, disadvantages, and related occupations.

Barber. Michigan Employment Security Commission. 1956. 16p. 25c
Introduction, nature of work, location of jobs, employment prospects, working conditions, earnings, organizations, qualifications for entry, advantages, and disadvantages.

**Barbers. Science Research Associates. 1961. 4p. 35c
Occupational brief describing duties, requirements, training, methods of getting started and advancing, earnings, advantages, disadvantages and future outlook.

**Barbers. One section of *Occupational Outlook Handbook.*
Nature of work where employed, training, other qualifications, advancement, employment outlook, earnings, and working conditions.

**Employment outlook for barbers and beauty operators. Bureau of Labor Statistics, U.S. Department of Labor. Supt. of Documents. 1964. 8p. 5c
Reprint from the *Occupational Outlook Handbook.*

List of accredited schools. Associated Master Barbers and Beauticians of America. 1963. 1p. Free
List of thirty-six schools.

BARTENDER   2-21.10

Job description for bartender. U.S. Employment Service. Supt. of Documents. 1947. 4p. 5c
Occupational guide. Job summary, work performed, training, trainee-selection factors, related occupations, physical activities, working conditions, hazards, and employment variables.

BASEBALL PLAYER   0-57.01

Baseball for everyone; a treasury of baseball lore and instruction for fans and players. DiMaggio, J. McGraw-Hill Whittlesey House. 1948. 224p. $3.95
Includes a discussion of duties and requirements of each position on a team. Illustrated.

**Baseball player. Splaver, Sarah. Personnel Services. 1953. 6p. 50c; 25c to students
Nature of work, future prospects, qualifications, preparation, number and distribution of workers, advantages, and disadvantages.

Baseball's greatest hitters. Meany, Thomas. A. S. Barnes and Company. 1950. 278p. $3.75
Biography of twenty big-league players written by a well-known baseball writer.

Baseball's greatest pitchers. Meany, Thomas. A. S. Barnes and Company. 1951. 325p. $4
As in his *Baseball's Greatest Hitters,* the author uses many anecdotes in the biography of twenty-five outstanding major league pitchers of this century.

BASEBALL PLAYER—*Continued*

Casey Stengel: baseball's greatest manager. Schoor, Gene. Julian Messner, Inc. 1961. 186p. $3.25. Library binding $2.99 net
Biography of the famous former manager of the New York Yankees who began as a baseball player. For grades 6 to 11.

From sandlot to big league: Connie Mack's baseball book. McGillicuddy, Cornelius. Alfred A. Knopf, Inc. 1960. 256p. $2.95
Explains what it takes to be a major league baseball player. Information on the work of the scouts, the various positions on the field, and coaching. Numerous charts of baseball records. Illustrated.

I want to be a baseball player. Greene, Carla. Childrens Press. 1961. 32p. $2
Prepared for beginning readers with a reading level of upper first grade. Illustrated in color.

Jackie Robinson of the Brooklyn Dodgers. Shapiro, Milton J. Julian Messner, Inc. 1957. 192p. $3.25. Library binding $3.19 net
Biography containing information about the struggles and triumphs of the first Negro baseball player in the major leagues.

Joe DiMaggio: the Yankee Clipper. Schoor, Gene. Julian Messner, Inc. 1956. 192p. $3.25. Library binding $3.19 net
Story of the baseball player's rise to a place in baseball's Hall of Fame.

Mickey Mantle: Yankee slugger. Shapiro, Milton J. Julian Messner, Inc. 1962. 192p. $3.25. Library binding $3.19 net
Biography of the baseball player who overcame obstacles to win the Most Valuable Player Award three times.

Phil Rizzuto story. Shapiro, Milton J. Julian Messner, Inc. 1959. 192p. $3.25. Library binding $3.19 net
Biography of a player who overcame the sports handicap of a short stature to become a Yankee shortstop.

The Sal Maglie story. Shapiro, Milton J. Julian Messner, Inc. 1957. 192p. $3.25. Library binding $3.19 net
Biography of a baseball pitcher and his successful comeback in a World Series.

The story of baseball. Rosenburg, John M. Random House, Inc. 1962. 176p. $3.95
Illustrated with many photographs, this book depicts for young readers the growth and development of major league baseball through the past hundred years. Includes descriptions of many of the dramatic highlights that make up baseball's colorful past.

World series thrills. Bell, Joseph N. Julian Messner, Inc. 1962. 192p. $3.95
The author has selected ten of the top thrills in world series play from 1912 to 1960, each followed by a capsule biography of the player and his baseball record. Photographs.

Yogi Berra story. Roswell, Gene. Julian Messner, Inc. 1958. 192p. $3.25. Library binding $3.19 net
Biography of a short, chunky, awkward-looking boy who became the highest-paid catcher in baseball history.
See also Athlete

BEAUTICIAN   2-32.10 through 2-32.29

Beautician. Splaver, Sarah. Personnel Services. 1957. 6p. 50c; 25c to students
Occupational abstract summarizing nature of work, qualifications, preparation, entrance and advancement, opportunities for men, supply and demand, earnings, advantages, and disadvantages.

Beauticians. Chapter 24 of *Vocations for Girls.*
Qualifications, opportunities, and advantages. Bibliography.

Beauty culture. Sinclair, Miriam. Bellman Publishing Company. 1959. 24p. $1
Description of types of positions in the beauty shop and in the cosmetics industry. Includes requirements for license in each of the states.

* Beauty operator. Careers. 1963. 8p. 25c
Career brief describing duties, working conditions, training, personal qualifications, earnings, and outlook.

* Beauty operator. Chronicle Guidance Publications. 1961. 4p. 35c
Occupational brief summarizing work performed, employment conditions, qualifications, training, licensing, opportunities, outlook, and methods of entry.

Beauty operator. Michigan Employment Security Commission. 1961. 19p. 25c
Nature of work, requirements for entry, working conditions, location of jobs, employment outlook, disadvantages, and advantages.

Beauty operators. One section of *Occupational Outlook Handbook.*
Nature of work, where employed, training, other qualifications, advancement, employment outlook, earnings, and working conditions.

* Beauty operators. Science Research Associates. 1960. 4p. 35c
Occupational brief describing nature of work, requirements, getting started and advancing, earnings, advantages, disadvantages, related positions, and future outlook.

Beauty-shop management as a career. Institute for Research. 1962. 20p. $1
History and development of work, qualifications, and attractive and unattractive features.

Careers in beauty—a brief guide to the beauty culture field. Clairol Institute of Haircoloring. 1962. 8p. Free
Some facts about the industry, demands, qualifications, training, earnings, and advantages.

Cosmetology. Chapter 19 of *Vocations for Boys.*
Includes requirements, opportunities, compensations, and disadvantages.

BEAUTICIAN—*Continued*

Cosmetology as a career. National Hairdressers and Cosmetologists Association. 1962. 3p. Free
Leaflet describing work and opportunities.

Electrologist. Shuman, Lionel. Research Publishing Company. 1955. 32p. $1
Personal qualifications, special skills needed, advantages, disadvantages, and list of training centers.

**Employment opportunities for women in beauty service. Women's Bureau, U.S. Department of Labor. Bulletin Number 260. Supt. of Documents. 1956. 51p. 25c
Information on training, entrance requirements, the kind of work done and conditions on the job, earnings, and advancement. Discussion of state wage and hour regulations applying to beauty shop employees and information for the woman who wants to open her own beauty shop. Includes the number of beauty operators in each of the states in 1950 and 1955.

**Employment outlook for barbers and beauty operators. Bureau of Labor Statistics, U.S. Department of Labor. Supt. of Documents. 1964. 8p. 5c
Reprint from the *Occupational Outlook Handbook*.

* Employment outlook for beauty operators. National Association of Cosmetology Schools. No date. 6p. 10c
Nature of work, where employed, training, qualifications, employment outlook, earnings, and working conditions.

Facts about the beauty industry. National Association of Cosmetology Schools. No date. 4p. 10c
Questions and answers concerning the size, growth, and outlook.

The field of cosmetology. Ohio State School of Cosmetology. 1960. 32p. Free
Includes nature of work, preparation, working conditions, earnings, and opportunities for advancement.

Hairdresser. The Guidance Centre. 1962. 4p. 15c in Canada; 20c elsewhere
Nature of work, qualifications, preparation, earnings, how to get started, and related occupations.

**Opportunities in beauty culture. Wall, Florence E. Vocational Guidance Manuals. 1958. 112p. $1.45 paper
Historical background, economic status, prospects of success, general requirements, positions in beauty shops, positions in the cosmetics industry, positions in industrial education, cosmetology in related fields, and organizations and legislation of the trade.

Successful careers in beauty culture. National Association of Cosmetology Schools. No date. 32p. 35c
Stresses beauty culture as a growing field, desirable qualifications, types of jobs in a beauty shop, specializations, advancement, earnings, advantages, and limitations.

You can't tell about love. Olds, Helen Diehl. Julian Messner, Inc. 1950. 183p. $2.95
> Career fiction. The romance contains helpful hints on entrance and progress in the beauty business.

**Your future in beauty culture. Gelb, Richard. Richards Rosen Press. 1963. 160p. $2.95
> Discussion of various phases of beauty culture from manufacturing and selling cosmetics, beauty equipment, and appliances to operating a beauty shop.

BEEKEEPER   3-07.70

Beekeeper. Careers. 1961. 2p. 15c
> Career summary for desk-top file. Duties, qualifications, and outlook.

Beekeeper. The Guidance Centre. 1960. 4p. 15c in Canada; 20c elsewhere
> Definition, history and importance, nature of work, qualifications necessary for entry and success, preparation, employment and advancement, remuneration, advantages, disadvantages, how to get started, and related occupations.

BELLMAN   2-22.01; 2-22.11

Bellmen and bell captains. One section of *Occupational Outlook Handbook*.
> Nature of work, training, other qualifications, advancement, and employment outlook.

BERRY FARMER. *See* Fruit and berry farmer

BIOCHEMIST   0-07.02

Biochemist. Careers. 1960. 8p. 25c
> Career brief describing duties, working conditions, training, personal qualifications, places of employment, earnings, and outlook. Additional readings.

**Biochemist. Chronicle Guidance Publications. 1961. 4p. 35c
> Occupational brief summarizing work performed, working conditions, earnings, personal qualifications, ways of determining interest and ability, training, opportunities, methods of entry, and outlook.

Biochemistry, teaching and research careers. Institute for Research. 1964. 24p. $1
> History, development, and present status of the profession; personal qualifications and attitudes; educational requirements; attractive and unattractive features; and how to get started. Discussion of work of biochemist in medical research, pharmaceutical biochemist, physical chemist, biochemist in the nutrition field, bacteriologist, and the biochemist in industry.

**Careers in biochemistry. Angel, Juvenal. World Trade Academy Press. 1958. 26p. $1.25
> Description of work, historical background, personal qualifications, branches of biochemistry, opportunities, where employment is found, remuneration, advantages, and disadvantages. Also included is a list of colleges offering scholarships and fellowships and a list of corporations and private foundations offering financial aid to students in biochemistry. Bibliography.

BIOCHEMIST—*Continued*

* Careers in biochemistry. American Society of Biological Chemists. 1962.
24p. Single copy free
   Discussion of the nature of work in chemistry of living things, opportunities,
   and training.

The work and education of a biochemist. State University of New York,
College of Forestry. 1962. 4p. Free
   An explanation of biochemistry and how it applies to forestry is followed by
   employment opportunities, salaries, training, and recommended high school
   background.

BIOLOGIST   0-35.22

Begin your career in the biological sciences. Albright College. 1960. 6p.
Free
   Leaflet containing pictures of student activities and various fields of special-
   ization.

Biological science. Michigan College of Mining and Technology. 1963.
2p. Free
   Example of a recruiting leaflet describing work, qualifications, educational
   requirements, and employment opportunities.

**Biological sciences. One chapter of *Occupational Outlook Handbook.*
   Nature of work, where employed, training and other qualifications, employment outlook, earnings and working conditions, and sources of additional information. Specific information is also given for each of the major specialties:
   animal sciences, plant sciences, and microbiology.

Biological sciences: earned degrees, by level, sex, and institution. One
section of *Earned Degrees Conferred.*
   Useful for judging the extent of a college's program in each of the following
   specialties: anatomy, bacteriology, biochemistry, biology, biophysics, botany,
   entomology, genetics, optometry, pathology, pharmacology, physiology, plant
   pathology, plant physiology, premedical sciences, and zoology.

**Biological scientists. Science Research Associates. 1959. 4p. 35c
   Occupational brief describing nature of work, requirements, earnings, advantages, disadvantages, and future outlook.

* Biologist. Careers. 1963. 8p. 25c
   Career brief describing duties, working conditions, training, personal qualifications, outlook, earnings, where employed and measuring one's interests and
   ability.

Biologist. The Guidance Centre. 1960. 4p. 15c in Canada; 20c elsewhere
   Definition, history and importance, nature of work, qualifications necessary
   for entry and success, preparation, employment and advancement, remuneration,
   advantages, disadvantages, how to get started, and related occupations. Further
   readings.

Biologist, assistant. Careers. 1963. 2p. 15c
   Career summary for desk-top file. Duties, qualifications, and outlook.

**Career opportunities in biology: the challenge of the life sciences. Stevens, Russell B. National Academy of Sciences. 1957. 64p. $1
  Description of biology, qualifications, opportunities, rewards, facts, figures, and advice. Twelve pages of reading lists.

Career opportunities in the biological sciences. University of Chicago, Office of Career Counseling and Placement. 1957. 14p. Free
  Suggests vocational outlets for those trained in anatomy, biochemistry, botany, microbiology, pharmacology, physiology, radiology, and zoology.

**Careers for women in the biological sciences. Women's Bureau, U.S. Department of Labor. Supt. of Documents. 1961. 86p. 40c
  Contains information about the types of work activity, nature of the jobs, places of employment, number employed, preparation, earnings and other work factors, ways of finding employment, and a look to the future. Eighteen illustrations.

Careers in anatomy. American Association of Anatomists. 1962. 2p. Free
  Information concerning nature of work, training, and opportunities.

**Careers in animal biology. American Society of Zoologists. 1959. 16p. 25c
  Explains the kind of work available, duties, preparation, earnings, and where employment opportunities may be found.

* Careers in biology. Angel, Juvenal. World Trade Academy Press. 1962. 28p. $1.25
  Career monograph describing the field of biology, training, qualifications, opportunities, compensation, and fields of specialization. Also contains list of colleges offering scholarships in agronomy, bacteriology, biology, biophysics, botany, pharmacology, and zoology.

**Careers in the biological sciences. Fox, William W. Henry Z. Walck, Inc. 1963. 114p. $3.50
  A survey which divides the subject into areas of related professions such as thoughtful sciences, science inside man, and wildlife biology, and then elaborates on one example of each as representative of the area. Discusses educational requirements, compensation, advancement, and outlook. Reading list. Illustrated.

Education in biology. Philadelphia College of Pharmacy and Science. 1962. 4p. Free
  One chapter in an illustrated recruiting brochure describing nature of work, training, and opportunities in biology, bacteriology, chemistry, and pharmacy.

Educational requirements for employment of biological scientists. Veterans Administration in cooperation with Bureau of Labor Statistics. VA Pamphlet Number 7-8.2. Supt. of Documents. 1955. 21p. 15c
  Provides information on educational requirements for entry and advancement. Describes the functions, fields of specialization, and types of employment in relation to the level of educational preparation acquired.

**Employment outlook for biological sciences. Bureau of Labor Statistics, U.S. Department of Labor. Supt. of Documents. 1964. 12p. 10c
  Reprint from the *Occupational Outlook Handbook*.

BIOLOGIST—*Continued*

Job futures for girls in biology. Women's Bureau, U.S. Department of Labor. Supt. of Documents. 1961. 8p. 5c
Concise statements about the work and opportunities.

Manpower resources in the biological sciences. Bureau of Labor Statistics, U.S. Department of Labor. Supt. of Documents. 1955. 53p. 40c
Presents data on the numbers of personnel in the areas of specialization, specialties in which they were employed, functions they were performing, types of employers, income, and such personal characteristics as education, age, and sex.

Should you be a biologist? Glass, Bentley. New York Life Insurance Company. 1961. 12p. Free
Description of work, employment needs, educational requirements, and future outlook.

Source list for careers in the biological sciences. American Institute of Biological Sciences. 1962. 8p. Free
List of 42 publications.

What is a biologist? Upjohn Company. 1962. 4p. Free
Illustrated brochure describing nature of work, opportunities, and rewards.

The work and education of a forest biologist. State University of New York, College of Forestry. 1962. 4p. Free
Description of work, places of employment, salaries, working conditions, qualifications, recommended high school subjects, training, and employment outlook.

BIOPHYSICIST   0-35.49

Biophysicist. Careers. 1963. 2p. 15c
Career summary for desk-top file. Duties, qualifications, and outlook.

* Biophysics, an exciting new frontier science. Biophysical Society. 1963. 4p. Free
An explanation of biophysics, the need for specialists trained in this area, training, opportunities, and qualifications.

BLACKSMITH   4-86.010

Blacksmith. Careers. 1960. 2p. 15c
Career summary for desk-top file. Duties, qualifications, and outlook.

Blacksmiths. Science Research Associates. 1961. 4p. 35c
Occupational brief describing the work of the modern blacksmith, working conditions, training, earnings, and outlook.

**Blacksmiths. One section of *Occupational Outlook Handbook.*
Nature of work, where employed, training, other qualifications, employment outlook, earnings, and working conditions.

**Employment outlook for forge shop occupations and for blacksmiths. Bureau of Labor Statistics, U.S. Department of Labor. Supt. of Documents. 1964. 12p. 10c
Reprint from the *Occupational Outlook Handbook.*

Job brief: blacksmiths, foregemen, and hammermen. Michigan Employment Security Commission. 1962. 2p. Single copy free

> Summary of nature of work performed, training, working conditions, location of jobs, employment outlook, earnings, requirements for entry, and suggestions for finding a job.

BLASTER   5-74.010

Job description for blaster III. U.S. Employment Service. Supt. of Documents. 1948. 5p. 5c

> Occupational guide. Job summary, work performed, training, trainee-selection factors, related occupations, physical activities, working conditions, hazards, and employment variables.

BOILERMAKER   4-83.100

Boilermaker. Careers. 1964. 2p. 15c

> Career summary for desk-top file. Duties, qualifications, and outlook.

* Boilermaker. Chronicle Guidance Publications. 1962. 4p. 35c

> Occupational brief summarizing nature of work, where employed, qualifications, training, earnings, related jobs, and employment outlook.

Boilermakers. Science Research Associates. 1964. 4p. 35c

> Occupational brief describing work, qualifications, training, opportunities, and outlook.

**Boilermaking occupations. One section of *Occupational Outlook Handbook*.

> Nature of work, where employed, training, other qualifications, employment outlook, earnings, and working conditions.

**Employment outlook for welders, oxygen and arc cutters, and boilermakers. Bureau of Labor Statistics, U.S. Department of Labor. Supt. of Documents. 1964. 12p. 10c

> Reprint from the *Occupational Outlook Handbook*.

BOOK ILLUSTRATOR. *See* Artist; Commercial artist; Medical illustrator

BOOKBINDER   4-49.010

Bookbinder. Careers. 1964. 2p. 15c

> Career summary for desk-top file. Duties, qualifications, and outlook.

Bookbinders. Science Research Associates. 1961. 4p. 35c

> Occupational brief describing nature of work, training, qualifications, opportunities, advantages, disadvantages, and future outlook.

**Bookbinding occupations. Michigan Employment Security Commission. 1954. 20p. 25c

> Introduction, nature of work, location of jobs, employment prospects, earnings, working conditions, organizations, qualifications for entry, disadvantages, and advantages.

> *See also* Printing and publishing industry worker

BOOKKEEPER 1-01; 1-02.

Bookkeeper. Splaver, Sarah. Personnel Services. 1959. 6p. 50c; 25c to students

Occupational abstract. Duties, qualifications, training, beginning jobs and possible advancement, earnings, advantages, disadvantages, and prospects.

* Bookkeeper. Careers. 1963. 7p. 25c

Career brief describing duties, working conditions, training, requirements, qualifications, employment prospects, earnings, and related careers.

Bookkeeper. Chronicle Guidance Publications. 1962. 4p. 35c

Occupational brief containing definition, history, work performed, working conditions, determination of aptitudes and interests, training requirements, training opportunities, outlook, methods of entry, advantages and disadvantages, and suggested activities.

Bookkeeper. The Guidance Centre. 1962. 4p. 15c in Canada; 20c elsewhere

Definition, personal qualifications necessary for entry and success, educational requirements, earnings, advantages, disadvantages, and related occupations.

Bookkeeper and bookkeeping machine operator—careers. Institute for Research. 1963. 24p. $1

Duties, typical day's work, personal qualifications, and lines of promotion. Information concerning the bookkeeper, entry clerk, ledger clerk, statement clerk, payroll clerk, bookkeeping machine operator, calculating machine operator, and cashier.

Bookkeepers and cashiers. Science Research Associates. 1958. 4p. 35c

Occupational brief describing nature of work, training, qualifications, opportunities, advantages, disadvantages, and future outlook.

**Bookkeeping workers. One section of *Occupational Outlook Handbook*.

Nature of work, where employed, training, other qualifications, advancement, earnings, and working conditions.

**Employment outlook for bookkeeping workers and office machine operators. Bureau of Labor Statistics, U.S. Department of Labor. Supt. of Documents. 1964. 12p. 10c

Reprint from the *Occupational Outlook Handbook*.

Starting and managing a small bookkeeping service. Small Business Administration. Supt. of Documents. 1962. 64p. 30c

This booklet describes the advantages and disadvantages of this work, the risks involved, the personal characteristics that will contribute to success, and some management practices.

See also Accountant; Public accountant

BOOKKEEPING MACHINE OPERATOR. *See* Office machine operator

BOTANIST   0-35.23

**Botanist. Splaver, Sarah. Personnel Services. 1963. 6p. 50c; 25c to students
Occupational abstract including nature of work, preparation, qualifications, entrance, advancement, earnings, and supply and demand.

* Botanist. Careers. 1960. 8p. 25c
Career brief describing duties, working conditions, training, personal qualifications, places of employment, earnings, and outlook.

Botanist. The Guidance Centre. 1962. 4p. 15c in Canada; 20c elsewhere
History and importance, nature of work, qualifications, working conditions, preparation, remuneration, outlook, related occupations, and how to get started.

Botanists. Science Research Associates. 1961. 4p. 35c
Occupational brief describing work in the special fields of botany, qualifications, places of employment, earnings, and outlook. Selected references.

**Botany as a career. Institute for Research. 1962. 24p. $1
History of botany, types of positions, where botanists are employed, typical day's work, attractive and unattractive features, qualifications, preparation, salaries, how to get started, and outlook.

Careers in botany. Botanical Society of America. No date. 6p. Single copy free
Illustrated booklet describing the work of botanists.

Luther Burbank; plant magician. Beaty, John Y. Julian Messner, Inc. 1943. 251p. $3.50. Library binding $3.34 net
Biography of the man whose amazing achievements in the development of plant varieties enriched the world.

Plant explorer: David Fairchild. Williams, Beryl and Epstein, Samuel. Julian Messner, Inc. 1961. 192p. $3.25. Library binding $3.19 net
Biography of a botanist who brought many plant species into the United States and established the New Crops Research Branch of the U.S. Department of Agriculture.

Plant physiology as a career. American Society of Plant Physiologists. No date. 8p. Free
Nature of work, places of employment, earnings, training, and outlook.

Plant scientist. California State Department of Employment. 1962. 7p. Single copy free
Description of several specialties in this field, entrance requirements, salaries, preparation, and employment outlook in California.

Plants, botany, and you! State University of Iowa, Department of Botany. 1960. 20p. Free
Describes various types of special work requiring training in botany and plant sciences and the courses most useful for each.

BOY SCOUTS PROFESSIONAL WORKER   0-27.99

Boy Scout field executive. Careers. 1963. 2p. 15c
Career summary for desk-top file. Duties, qualifications, and outlook.

BOY SCOUTS PROFESSIONAL WORKER—*Continued*

The happiest man. Boy Scouts of America. 1963. 4p. Free
Description of work, salary, and satisfactions.

Prepare for a career in the Boy Scouts of America. Boy Scouts of America. 1963. 6p. Free
Description of what a career man does in scouting, essential qualities for acceptance, some suggested college courses, and other preparation.

**Your invitation to a career in scouting. Boy Scouts of America. 1963. 8p. Free
Description of qualifications, opportunities, duties of a field scout executive, advancement, compensation, preparation, and how to place an application.

BRICKLAYER   5-24.000 through 5-24.009; 5, 7-24.100

Bricklayer. Careers. 1963. 2p. 15c
Career summary for desk-top file. Duties, qualifications, and outlook.

**Bricklayer. Chronicle Guidance Publications. 1961. 4p. 35c
Occupational brief summarizing work performed, employment conditions, qualifications, determination of aptitudes and interests, training requirements, opportunities, outlook, and related jobs. Selected references.

Bricklayer. The Guidance Centre. 1963. 15c in Canada; 20c elsewhere
History and importance, nature of work, qualifications, preparation, advancement, outlook, remuneration, advantages, disadvantages, how to get started, and related occupations.

Bricklayer, apprentice. Careers. 1962. 2p. 15c
Career summary for desk-top file. Duties, qualifications, and outlook.

Bricklayers. Michigan Employment Security Commission. 1956. 15p. 25c
Introduction, nature of work, distribution of jobs, employment prospects, working conditions, organizations, qualifications for entry, earnings of bricklayers, advantages, and disadvantages.

* Bricklayers. Science Research Associates. 1959. 4p. 35c
Occupational brief describing work, qualifications, training, wages, opportunities, advantages, disadvantages, and outlook. Selected references.

**Bricklayers. One section of *Occupational Outlook Handbook.*
Nature of work, where employed, training, other qualifications, advancement, employment outlook, earnings, and working conditions.

Bricklaying as a vocation. Structural Clay Products Institute. 1962. 4p. Free
Need for bricklayers, employment prospects, nature of work, working conditions, personal requirements, wage rates, and apprenticeship.

**Careers in bricklaying and sheet metal work. B'nai B'rith Vocational Service. 1954. 7p. 35c
Nature of work, qualifications, working conditions, advantages, and disadvantages.

**Employment outlook for bricklayers, stonemasons, marble setters, tile setters, and terrazzo workers. Bureau of Labor Statistics, U.S. Department of Labor. Supt. of Documents. 1964. 20p. 15c
Reprint from the *Occupational Outlook Handbook*.

National bricklayers' apprenticeship program and standards. Bureau of Apprenticeship, U.S. Department of Labor, 1954. 32p. Free
Regulations concerning the employment, training, and instruction of apprentices.

Tile setter. Splaver, Sarah. Personnel Services. 1954. 6p. 50c; 25c to students
Occupational abstract. Nature of work, qualifications, preparation, entrance and advancement, supply and demand of workers, advantages, and disadvantages. Bibliography.

BROADCASTING ENGINEER. *See* Radio operator

BUFFER   6-77.020

Job description for buffer I. U.S. Employment Service. Supt. of Documents. 1948. 4p. 5c
Occupational guide. Job summary, work performed, training, related occupations, physical activities, working conditions, hazards, and employment variables.

BUILDING CONSTRUCTION INDUSTRY WORKER. *See* Construction Industry Worker

BUILDING SERVICE WORKER   2-82.00 through 2-90.99; 2-95

Building service occupations. Chapter 17 in *Occupations and Careers*.
Includes discussion of janitor, charwoman, window cleaner, elevator operator, and porter.

**Building service workers. Science Research Associates. 1961. 4p. 35c
Occupational brief describing duties, requirements, personal qualifications, earnings, advantages, disadvantages, and future outlook. Describes the work of maintenance workers, school custodians, elevator operators, and building superintendents.

Custodian. Chronicle Guidance Publications. 1962. 4p. 35c
Occupational brief summarizing work performed, number of workers and where employed, qualifications, earnings, advantages, disadvantages, and methods of entering.

Janitor. California State Department of Employment. 1962. 4p. Single copy free
Occupational guide summarizing duties, working conditions, employment prospects, earnings, training, requirements for entry, and suggestions for locating a job.

Janitors. Science Research Associates. 1964. 4p. 35c
Occupational brief describing work, qualifications, opportunities, and outlook.

School custodian (janitor). Careers. 1964. 2p. 15c
Career summary for desk-top file. Duties, qualifications, and outlook.

BUS DRIVER 5-36.01

About the driver of a bus. Philips, Eleanor. Melmont Publishers. 1959. 32p. $2.50
   Prepared to give younger readers in grades 1 to 4 an idea of this kind of work and its importance. Illustrated in color.

Bus driver. California State Department of Employment. 1962. 3p. Single copy free
   Duties, working conditions, entrance requirements, and employment prospects.

**Bus driver. Chronicle Guidance Publications. 1962. 4p. 35c
   Occupational brief containing definition, history, work performed, working conditions, requirements, opportunities, outlook, methods of entry, and related jobs.

Bus driver. Michigan Employment Security Commission. 1962. 2p. Single copy free
   Job brief summarizing nature of work, location of jobs, working conditions, employment outlook, earnings, requirements for entry, and suggestions for locating a job.

Bus facts. National Association of Motor Bus Owners. 1962. 52p. Free
   Statistics concerning the motor bus industry, including number of employees and wages.

**Employment outlook in driving occupations. Bureau of Labor Statistics, U.S. Department of Labor. Supt. of Documents. 1964. 24p. 15c
   Reprint from the *Occupational Outlook Handbook*.

I want to be a bus driver. Greene, Carla. Childrens Press. 1957. 32p. $2
   Prepared for beginning readers with a reading level of upper first grade. Illustrated in color.

**Intercity bus drivers. One section of *Occupational Outlook Handbook*.
   Nature of work, where employed, qualifications, employment outlook, earnings, and working conditions.

**Local bus drivers. Science Research Associates. 1963. 4p. 35c
   Occupational brief describing kinds of jobs, requirements, training, getting started, earnings, advantages, and future outlook.

**Local transit bus drivers. One section of *Occupational Outlook Handbook*.
   Nature of work, where employed, qualifications, training, employment outlook, earnings, and working conditions.

Street car operator and bus driver. The Guidance Centre. 1961. 4p. 15c in Canada; 20c elsewhere
   Definition, requirements, entrance and advancement, earnings, working conditions, advantages, disadvantages, and related occupations.

See also Motor transportation worker; Truck driver

BUSINESS OWNER (SELF-EMPLOYED) 0-99.

Big business leaders in America. Atheneum Publishers. 1963. 243p. $1.25
   A discussion of the economic levels, educational backgrounds, geographic locations, marriage status, occupations of parents, and mobility of business leaders.

A business of your own? Changing Times. 1960. 21p. 25c
 Six articles written to guide people who are thinking of starting a business.

**Listen to leaders in business. Love, Albert and Childers, James, editors. Holt, Rinehart and Winston. 1962. 288p. $4.75
 Fourteen leaders in American business give their views on careers in various aspects of this field, the opportunities, and qualifications prerequisite for achievement.

102 ideas for women for a business of her own. New York State Department of Commerce. 1960. 20p. Free
 Description of a home business, personal qualifications, and ideas ranging from the pin-money to the professional class, covering primarily the salable home product and service.

Running a business after marriage. Alumnae Advisory Center. 1963. 6p. 25c
 Reprint from *Mademoiselle* describing the work of several business women.

Should you go into business for yourself? Sontheimer, Morton. New York Life Insurance Company. 1960. 12p. Free
 Discussion of advantages and personality factors needed.

**So you want to go into industry. Hodnett, Edward. Harper and Row. 1960. 160p. $3.50
 A business executive discusses career choice, early years of training and later ones of professional growth, and the way a business is organized. Describes what one can expect from a job in industry and what will be expected in return.

So you're going into business. Domestic Distribution Department, Chamber of Commerce of the United States. 1960. 20p. 25c
 A brief message of information and counsel to individuals contemplating establishment of their own retail business. Includes qualifications and discussion of capital, location, records, and management.

Starting and managing a small business of your own. Small Business Administration. Supt. of Documents. 1962. 50p. 25c
 Advice and questions to consider before establishing one's own business. Describes the common problems of launching small business operations and suggests specific steps to help those interested to arrive at sound decisions.

BUSINESS WORKER   0-70. through 0-99.

Admission test for graduate study in business. Educational Testing Service. Published annually. Free
 Bulletin of information for candidates. Includes list of institutions which require the test, list of examination centers, and sample test questions.

**Business administration and related professions. One section of *Occupational Outlook Handbook*, 1961 edition
 Nature of work, training, advancement, employment outlook, and earnings for each of the following: accountant, advertising worker, industrial traffic manager, marketing research worker, personnel worker, purchasing agent, and public relations worker.

BUSINESS WORKER—*Continued*

Business and commerce: earned degrees, by level, sex, and institution. One section of *Earned Degrees Conferred.*
Useful for judging the extent of a college's program in accounting, secretarial studies, hotel and restaurant administration, and general business and commerce.

Business as a professional career. School of Commerce, Accounts, and Finance, New York University. Revised 1964. 63p. 25c
Information concerning business career opportunities.

Business management as a career. Boston University. 1962. 16p. Free
Recruiting booklet describing qualifications; training; and opportunities in research, distribution, purchasing, personnel finance, production, and management.

**Career opportunities for women in business. King, Alice Gore. Dutton and Company. 1963. 212p. $4.50
Survey of the opportunities in business from a woman's job-hunting perspective. Covers the training needed, the educational and personal attributes most helpful for the jobs, the kinds of advancement within each field, the salary range, and the areas in which the job opportunities are most prevalent.

Careers for women in executive and managerial positions in business organizations. Institute for Research. 1959. 24p. $1
Examples of the work of women executives, qualifications, training, income, attractive and unattractive features, and how to get started.

Careers in business. Scott, Ralston D. Rochester Institute of Technology. Revised 1963. 28p. Free
A general discussion is followed by information about accounting, business administration, marketing and sales, secretarial opportunities, and the job of the medical secretary. Illustrated.

Careers in business. Alpha Kappa Psi Fraternity. 1954. 23p. 10c
A series of articles written by alumni members on the various fields of business in which they are engaged.

Careers in business. Armstrong Cork Company. 1962. 32p. Free
Description of opportunities for college graduates with this company in floor and building products sales, packaging materials sales, industrial specialties sales, insulation sales, research and development, industrial engineering, engineering, accounting, advertising, and production planning. Attractively illustrated.

Careers in business administration. Angel, Juvenal. World Trade Academy Press. 1959. 26p. $1.25
Includes description of work, training required, opportunities, remuneration, and future outlook.

Careers in business administration. St. Francis College. 1957. 4p. Free
Includes a list of 47 careers and the nature of work in each. Bibliography.

**Careers in business management. Mann, Roland. Henry Z. Walck, Inc. 1963. 111p. $3.50
Presenting a picture of the industrial enterprise and modern business management as an expanding career field, this book describes the various management functions, requirements, basic skills needed, opportunities, and outlook.

Careers in business management. VA Pamphlet 22-7. Veterans Administration. Supt. of Documents. 1960. 20p. 20c
Opportunities, qualifications, and outlook.

Careers in financial management and controllership. Financial Executives Institute. 1962. 12p. Free
Describes the work of planning and controlling the financial operations of a business, training, salary, advancement, and how to get started.

Careers in the commercial field with a future. Angel, Juvenal. World Trade Academy Press. 1963. 26p. $1.25
Includes description of the major fields of specialization, training, opportunities, remuneration, and future outlook.

The education of American businessmen. Pierson, Frank C. McGraw-Hill Book Company. 1959. 731p. $7.75
A study of university and college programs in business administration.

Executive careers for women. Maule, Frances. Harper and Row. 1961. 240p. $3.95
Practical suggestions on advancing to executive positions in advertising, finance, government service, fashion, public relations, service industries, travel, and science and technology. Includes examples of many executive positions held by women.

Executives. Science Research Associates. 1961. 4p. 35c
Occupational brief describing the function of management, nature of work, requirements, training, getting started, earnings, advantages, disadvantages, and future outlook.

Junior executive. Group, Vernard. Personnel Services. Revised 1956. 50c; 25c to students
Occupational abstract. Nature of work, future prospects, qualifications, preparation, entrance and advancement, and earnings.

Junior executive. Careers. 1962. 2p. 15c
Career summary for desk-top file. Duties, qualifications, and outlook.

Junior executive. Chronicle Guidance Publications. 1959. 4p. 35c
Occupational brief summarizing work performed, working conditions, earnings, personal qualifications, training requirements, opportunities, and employment outlook.

Manager or executive. The Guidance Centre. 1962. 4p. 15c in Canada; 20c elsewhere
History and importance, nature of work, qualifications, working conditions, preparation, remuneration, advancement, outlook, related occupations, and how to get started.

Managers, general. Careers. 1964. 8p. 25c
Career brief describing advertising, industrial relations, personnel, plant, production, public relations, purchasing, sales, and traffic manager.

My years with General Motors. Sloan, Alfred Pritchard. Doubleday and Company. 1964. 472p. $7.95
The history of a major American business firm by the man who was its chief executive for twenty-three years.

BUSINESS WORKER—*Continued*

Occupational mobility in American business and industry, 1928-1952. University of Minnesota Press. 1955. 315p. $5.50

A study of the effects of various factors on individual success in business and industrial occupations.

**Occupations in business. Chapters 10 and 11 of *The College Girl Looks Ahead*.

Characteristics of work in business, talents needed, trying out, entering, and kinds of work.

Preparing for your career in business: a college guide for junior and senior high school students. Council for Professional Education for Business. 1963. 24p. 25c

Information on preparation for college work leading to careers as business managers, administrators, or specialists such as accountants or financial advisers.

Profile of jobs for women. Harvard-Radcliffe Program in Business Administration. 1963. 9 leaflets. Free

Written in diary form for young women in college who are trying to decide on post-college careers. Includes qualities most needed for success and enjoyment of job. Profiles are entitled: Advertising and publicity, college administration, electronic data processing, executive secretary, financial analysis and counseling, journalism and publishing, marketing, merchandising, and personnel administration.

Service is my business. Rotary International. 1948. 140p. $1

Prepared for employees and youth choosing careers, this book underscores the importance of achieving and maintaining high ethical standards in business and the professions.

Training in business and industry. McGehee, William and Thayer, Paul. Wiley and Sons. 1961. 305p. $6.75

Written for training directors who have staff responsibilities for industrial training as a tool of management.

The world of business and how you fit in. Tri-State College. No date. 12p. Free

An example of a college recruiting leaflet describing opportunities and training.

* Your opportunities in management. National Research Bureau. 1954. 32p. 20c

Functions, duties, responsibilities, career opportunities, and how to become a business manager or executive. Illustrated.

Your tomorrow. New Brunswick Secretarial, Accounting and Prep School. 1963. 16p. Free

An example of an inspirational recruiting bulletin, pointing out the advantages of training for business jobs.

See also Bookkeeper; Clerical worker; Stenographer; Typist

BUTCHER. *See* Meat cutter

BUYER 0-74.; 0-91.

Brenda becomes a buyer. McCarty, Rega Kramer. Julian Messner, Inc. 1960. 192p. $2.95
Career fiction. A realistic story of the challenges and opportunities open to girls who are interested in work in department stores.

**Buyer. Chronicle Guidance Publications. 1964. 4p. 35c
Occupational brief summarizing work performed, working conditions, personal qualifications, training requirements, opportunities, employment outlook, and entry into the job.

Buyer. The Guidance Centre. 1962. 4p. 15c in Canada; 20c elsewhere
Nature of work, duties, qualifications, training, earnings, advantages, disadvantages, and related occupations.

* Buyer (department store). Careers. 1963. 8p. 25c
Career brief describing duties, working conditions, training, personal qualifications, earnings, and outlook.

* Buyers. Science Research Associates. 1960. 4p. 35c
Occupational brief describing work, qualifications, training, earnings, advantages, disadvantages, and outlook. Selected references.

**Careers as a retail merchandise buyer. Institute for Research. 1962. 24p. $1
Duties, typical day's work, personal qualifications, training, attractive and unattractive features. Kind of work, line of promotion, and salary range of the store buyer, assistant buyer, stock clerk, and merchandise manager. Additional information concerning the chain store buyer and mail order buyer.

Department store buyer. Splaver, Sarah. Personnel Service. 1956. 50c; 25c to students
Occupational abstract. Nature of work, qualifications, preparation, entrance and advancement, supply and demand, advantages, and disadvantages.

The resident office buyer. Arcone, Sonia. Alumnae Advisory Center. 1957. 5p. 25c
Reprint from *Mademoiselle* describing the range of work and opportunities of a buyer in the women's apparel industry.

The young American buyer. Small, Verna. Alumnae Advisory Center. 1954. 6p. 10c
Reprint from *Mademoiselle* describing the duties of buyers and containing case histories of several successful women buyers.
See also Merchandise manager; Retail manager

CABINETMAKER 4-32.

Cabinetmaker. Careers. 1962. 2p. 15c
Career summary for desk-top file. Duties, qualifications, and outlook.

* Cabinetmaker. Chronicle Guidance Publications. 1962. 4p. 35c
Occupational brief summarizing duties, working conditions, qualifications, training, earnings, advantages, disadvantages, and outlook.

CAMP COUNSELOR   0-27.40

**Camp counselor. Splaver, Sarah. Personnel Services. 1955. 6p. 50c; 25c to students
> Occupational abstract. Nature of work, qualifications, preparation, entrance and advancement, supply and demand, advantages, and disadvantages.

Camp counselor. California State Department of Employment. 1961. 5p. Single copy free
> Job duties, working conditions, pay, hours, entrance requirements, promotion, training, and employment outlook.

* Camp counselor. Careers. 1962. 2p. 15c
> Career summary for desk-top file. Duties, qualifications, and outlook.

Camp counselors. Science Research Associates. 1960. 4p. 35c
> Occupational brief describing responsibilities, requirements, advancement, earnings, how to find counseling positions, and outlook. Selected references.

Sunny: the new camp counselor. Rosenheim, Lucile G. Julian Messner, Inc. 1952. 179p. $2.95
> Career fiction. An account of experiences in a summer camp for under-privileged children. May inspire young people to work during vacations in low-cost camps.

Tomorrow's job in summer camps. Western Personnel Institute. 1958. 4p. 20c
> Nature of work, requirements, earnings, opportunities, and outlook.

CARPENTER   5-25.

* Career as a carpenter and residential building contractor. Institute for Research. 1961. 24p. $1
> Types of jobs, lines of promotion, earnings and hours, and future outlook.

Carpenter. Townsend, Gilbert. Research Publishing Company. 1957. 16p. $1.50
> Advantages of this trade, working conditions, qualifications and special skills required, how to secure a job, and chances for promotion.

Carpenter. The Guidance Centre. 1961. 4p. 15c in Canada; 20c elsewhere
> Importance of the work, conditions of work, qualifications, preparation, advancement opportunities, and how to get started.

* Carpenter, construction. Careers. 1963. 8p. 25c
> Career brief describing duties, working conditions, personal qualifications, training, earnings, related careers, and outlook.

**Carpenter (construction). Chronicle Guidance Publications. 1963. 4p. 35c
> Occupational brief summarizing work performed, working conditions, personal qualifications, training requirements, opportunities, employment outlook, and methods of entry into the job.

**Carpenters. Bureau of Labor Statistics, U.S. Department of Labor. Supt. of Documents. 1964. 16p. 10c
> Reprint from the *Occupational Outlook Handbook*.

Carpenters. Science Research Associates. 1959. 4p. 35c

Occupational brief describing nature of work, preparation, qualifications, opportunities, advantages, disadvantages, and future outlook.

**Carpenters. One section of *Occupational Outlook Handbook*.

Nature of work, where employed, training, other qualifications, advancement, employment outlook, earnings, and working conditions.

Carpentry. Group, Vernard. Personnel Services. 1950. 6p. 50c; 25c to students

Occupational abstract. Future prospects, nature of work, qualifications, preparation, entrance and advancement, earnings, number and distribution of workers, advantages, disadvantages, and sources of further information.

I want to be a carpenter. Greene, Carla. Childrens Press. 1959. 32p. $2

Prepared for beginning readers with a reading level of upper first grade. Illustrated in color.

CARTOGRAPHER 0-48.15

Careers in cartography and photogrammetry. B'nai B'rith Vocational Service. 1957. 7p. 35c

Employment outlook, kind of jobs, government agencies employing map makers, how jobs are filled, examination requirements, and opportunities.

Cartographer. Careers. 1959. 2p. 15c

Career summary for desk-top file. Duties, qualifications, and outlook.

* Cartographer. Chronicle Guidance Publications. 1960. 4p. 35c

Occupational brief summarizing work performed, qualifications, working conditions, training, earnings, where employed, related jobs, and outlook.

**Cartographers. Science Research Associates. 1962. 4p. 35c

Occupational brief describing nature of work, requirements, getting started, advantages, disadvantages, and future outlook.

**Cartography (map making). Bauer, Hubert A. Bellman Publishing Company. 1957. 32p. $1

Nature and scope of work, qualifications, training, employment opportunities, classification, remuneration, opportunities, advantages, and disadvantages.

Mapping the world: a global project of the Corps of Engineers, U.S. Army. Colby, C. B. Coward-McCann, Inc. 1959. 48p. Library edition $2.52 net

Photographs and brief text reveal the work of mapping the world. Written for grades 4 to 8.

What about a career in photogrammetry? American Society of Photogrammetry. No date. 24p. Free

Illustrated booklet describing the science of obtaining reliable measurements by means of photography. Includes description of what a photogrammetrist does, what instruments he uses, the training needed, where employed, and outlook.

CARTOONIST   0-04.41

* Careers in cartooning. Lariar, Lawrence. Dodd, Mead and Company. 1950. 182p. $3.50

    Information about the various branches of comic art including syndicate cartooning, magazine cartooning advertising cartoons, animated cartoons and comic book cartoons. Illustrated.

Cartooning as a career. Institute for Research. 1962. 24p. $1

    Description of types of cartoon specialization, history of cartooning, general qualifications, training, a typical day's work, attractive and unattractive features, and how to enter the cartooning field.

Cartoonist. Splaver, Sarah. Personnel Services. 1956. 6p. 50c; 25c to students

    Occupational abstract. Nature of work, qualifications, preparation, entrance and advancement, supply and demand, earnings, advantages, and disadvantages.

Cartoonist. Careers. 1960. 8p. 25c

    Career brief describing duties, working conditions, training, personal qualifications, earnings, advancement prospects, and outlook.

* Cartoonist. Chronicle Guidance Publications. 1961. 4p. 35c

    Occupational brief summarizing work performed, working conditions, personal qualifications, training, related jobs, opportunities, outlook, and suggested activities.

* Cartoonists. Science Research Associates. 1961. 4p. 35c

    Occupational brief describing nature of work, qualifications, training, earnings, opportunities, and future outlook.

Comic art, an occupation, information, and career guide. National Cartoonists Society. No date. 5p. Free

    This pamphlet describes the appeal of comic art, the need for more cartoonists, the qualities necessary for success, and training.

    See also Artist; Commercial artist

CASE WORKER. *See* Social worker

CASHIER   1-01.52

Cashier. Careers. 1960. 2p. 15c

    Career summary for desk-top file. Duties, qualifications, and outlook.

Cashiers. One section of *Occupational Outlook Handbook.*

    Nature of work, where employed, training, qualifications, employment outlook, earnings, and working conditions.

**Employment outlook for cashiers. Bureau of Labor Statistics, U.S. Department of Labor. Supt. of Documents. 1964. 4p. 5c

    Reprint from the *Occupational Outlook Handbook.*

CATERER   0-71.01

Caterer. Careers. 1962. 2p. 15c

    Career summary for desk-top file. Duties, qualifications, and outlook.

Lynn Pamet: caterer. Edell, Celeste. Julian Messner, Inc. 1960. 192p. $2.95

Career fiction. After a year of home economics in college, Lynn started her own catering service. However, she learned that she needed to complete her college training to succeed in her chosen field.

So you want to be a caterer. New York State Department of Commerce. No date. 18p. Free

Attractively illustrated booklet describing qualifications, kinds of catering opportunities, how to get started, and how to build a business.

CATTLE FARMER   3-07.10

Cattle farmer. Careers. 1961. 2p. 15c

Career summary for desk-top file. Duties, qualifications, and outlook.

**Cattlemen. Science Research Associates. 1961. 4p. 35c

Occupational brief describing nature of work, qualifications, opportunities, advantages, disadvantages, and future outlook.

Western stock ranching. Saunderson, Mont H. University of Minnesota Press. 1950. 262p. $5

Practical information on the economic problems of ranch management.

See also Animal husbandman; Cowpuncher

CEMENT INDUSTRY WORKER
4, 6, 8-67.000 through 4, 6, 8-67.299; 5, 7-26.

**Careers in mason and cement finishing contracting. B'nai B'rith Vocational Service. 1954. 8p. 35c

Discussion of nature of work, abilities and entry requirements, earnings, advantages, disadvantages, and outlook.

Cement finisher. Careers. 1960. 2p. 15c

Career summary for desk-top file. Duties, qualifications, and outlook.

**Cement manufacturing industry workers. Science Research Associates. 1961. 4p. 35c

Occupational brief describing nature of work, requirements, getting started, earnings, advantages, disadvantages, and future outlook.

* Cement masons. Science Research Associates. 1961. 4p. 35c

Occupational brief describing nature of work, qualifications, opportunities, advantages, disadvantages, and future outlook.

**Cement masons (cement and concrete finishers). One section of Occupational Outlook Handbook.

Nature of work, where employed, training, other qualifications, employment outlook, earnings, and working conditions.

**Employment outlook for plasterers, lathers, and cement masons. Bureau of Labor Statistics, U.S. Department of Labor. Supt. of Documents. 1964. 20p. 15c

Reprint from the Occupational Outlook Handbook.

CEMENT INDUSTRY WORKER—*Continued*

Let's take a trip to a cement plant. Riedman, Sarah. Abelard-Schuman. 1959. 128p. $3

> The processes and machinery are shown that make limestone into concrete in a modern cement plant.

Tile setter. Careers. 1960. 2p. 15c

> Career summary for desk-top file. Duties, qualifications, and outlook.

CEMETERY MANAGER   0-99.73

Cemetery administration and management—a career opportunity for you. American Cemetery Association. 1960. 4p. Free

> Discussion of opportunities, compensation, qualifications, advantages, and disadvantages.

CERAMIC ENGINEER   0-15.11

Ceramic engineer. Splaver, Sarah. Personnel Services. 1964. 6p. 50c; 25c to students

> Occupational abstract. Nature of work, qualifications, preparation, entrance, advancement, earnings, supply and demand, advantages, and disadvantages.

Ceramic engineer. Careers. 1963. 2p. 15c

> Career summary for desk-top file. Duties, qualifications, and outlook.

* Ceramic engineer. Chronicle Guidance Publications. 1963. 4p. 35c

> Occupational brief describing work performed, personal qualifications, working conditions, training, and employment outlook. Includes list of fourteen accredited schools offering a degree in ceramic engineering.

Ceramic engineering. Birch, Raymond E. Chapter 9 of *Engineering Enrollment in the United States.*

> Trends in enrollments and future requirements for specialists in this area.

* Ceramic engineers. Science Research Associates. 1963. 4p. 35c

> Occupational brief describing nature of work, areas of specialization, preparation, opportunities, and outlook.

Ceramic engineers. One section of *Occupational Outlook Handbook.*

> Nature of work, where employed, and employment outlook.

Schools offering degrees in ceramic engineering. Aluminum Company of America. 1963. 1p. Free

> List of fifteen colleges and typical units of study recommended for entrance.

Universities and colleges in the United States offering courses in ceramic engineering or ceramic art. American Ceramic Society. 1962. 3p. Mimeographed. Free

> List of thirty-eight schools.
>
> *See also* Engineer

CERAMICS INDUSTRY WORKER 4, 6, 8-66.

Ceramics—unlimited horizons. Aluminum Company of America. 1962. 16p. Free

Opportunities for skilled ceramic engineers in electronics, missiles, refractories, and in scores of industries.

Clay fingers. De Leeuw, Adele L. Macmillan Company. 1948. 230p. $3.50

Career fiction. While recuperating from an accident, Laura found her interest and talent in ceramics which became her career.

**For career opportunities explore the wonder world of ceramics. American Ceramic Society. No date. 16p. Free

Illustrated brochure describing opportunities in the aircraft industry, structural clay products, refractories, whiteware, glass, porcelain enamels, abrasives, cements, and electronics.

Opportunities in ceramics. Scholes, Samuel Ray. Vocational Guidance Manuals. 1953. 96p. $1.45 paper

Includes the growth and development of ceramics, description of various ceramic raw materials, ceramic industries, various kinds of work, qualifications, training, remuneration, where to seek employment, attributes necessary for success, and getting a job. Contains list of schools offering courses in ceramics.

* Pottery manufacturing industry workers. Science Research Associates. 1961. 4p. 45c

Occupational brief describing nature of work, requirements, getting started and advancing, earnings, advantages, disadvantages, and future outlook.

* Structural clay products manufacturing workers. Science Research Associates. 1961. 4p. 35c

Occupational brief describing work of making brick, tiles, and other clay products. Includes requirements, earnings, getting started and advancing, advantages, disadvantages, and future outlook.

CHAIN STORE MANAGER. See Retail manager

CHAPLAIN. See Clergyman; Priest; Rabbi

CHEF. See Cook

CHEMICAL ENGINEER 0-15.01

* Careers for chemical engineers. Angel, Juvenal. World Trade Academy Press. 1960. 30p. $1.25

Includes description of the major fields of specialization, education required, opportunities, rewards, future outlook, and methods of financing an education in this field.

CHEMICAL ENGINEER—*Continued*

Chemical engineer. Robinson, H. Alan. Personnel Services. 1951. 6p. 50c. 25c to students

Occupational abstract. Nature of work, future prospects, opportunities, qualifications, preparation, entrance and advancement, earnings, advantages, disadvantages, and related occupations.

Chemical engineer. Careers. 1960. 2p. 15c

Career summary for desk-top file. Duties, qualifications, and outlook.

* Chemical engineer. Chronicle Guidance Publications. 1962. 4p. 35c

Occupational brief describing work performed, working conditions, personal qualifications, high school preparation, list of accredited schools, and employment outlook.

Chemical engineer. The Guidance Centre. 1959. 4p. 15c

History and growth of the profession, duties, qualifications, preparation, employment and advancement, earnings, advantages, disadvantages, and related occupations.

Chemical engineering. Michigan College of Mining and Technology. 1963. 2p. Free

Example of a recruiting leaflet describing work, qualifications, educational requirements, and employment possibilities.

* Chemical engineers. Science Research Associates. 1958. 4p. 35c

Occupational brief describing nature of work, qualifications, training, opportunities, advantages, disadvantages, and future outlook.

Chemical engineers. One section of *Occupational Outlook Handbook.*

Nature of work, where employed, and employment outlook.

Chemical engineers at Du Pont. E. I. du Pont de Nemours and Company. 1962. 24p. Free

Illustrated booklet describing work and opportunities.

Chemistry and your career. American Chemical Society. 1964. 20p. Free

Includes a description of a day's work of a chemical engineer on a production job. Illustrated.

* Opportunities in chemical engineering. Katzen, Raphael. Vocational Guidance Manuals. 1957. 83p. $1.45 paper

Description of jobs, related fields, qualifications, training, and opportunities.

School of chemical engineering practice. Massachusetts Institute of Technology. 1959. 16p. Free

Description of the training given for one semester in a chemical industrial enterprise.

**Your future in chemical engineering. Feder, Raymond. Richards Rosen Press. 1961. 155p. $2.95

Includes the importance and development of the work, duties, qualifications, preparation, rewards, opportunities, and related fields. Includes a list of accredited schools.

Your future in chemical engineering. Feder, Raymond. Popular Library, Inc. 1961. 155p. 50c

A paperback edition of the book described above.

See also Chemist; Engineer; Scientist

CHEMICAL LABORATORY TECHNICIAN 0-50.20 through 0-50.99

Assistant chemist. Careers. 1964. 2p. 15c

Career summary for desk-top file. Duties, qualifications, and outlook.

* Chemical technician. Chronicle Guidance Publications. 1961. 4p. 35c

Occupational brief summarizing work performed, working conditions, personal qualifications, training requirements, employment outlook, and methods of entering the job.

**Chemical technicians. Science Research Associates. 1963. 4p. 35c

Occupational brief describing nature of work, qualities leading toward success, training, getting started, and outlook.

CHEMICAL RESEARCH WORKER

0-07.; 0-50.22; 0-50.30 through 0-50.79

**Research careers in chemistry. Institute for Research. 1956. 20p. $1

Definition, history, where research chemists work, types of positions, typical day's work, attractive and unattractive features, qualifications, training, salaries, chances for employment, how to get started, related positions, and positions for women.

CHEMIST 0-07.

America's first woman chemist: Ellen Richards. Douty, E. M. Julian Messner, Inc. 1961. 191p. $3.25; library binding $3.19 net

Biography of a woman who overcame many barriers before her acceptance as the first woman student at Massachusetts Institute of Technology and her later pioneer work in nutrition.

Career and job opportunities in the printing ink industry. National Association of Printing Ink Makers. No date. 20p. Free

Description of the nature of the printing ink industry and the opportunities and rewards it holds for the young man and woman.

A career challenge offering unique rewards. Commercial Chemical Development Association. 1963. 10p. Free

Description of the role of developing new products through chemical research, working conditions, qualifications, and rewards.

**Careers ahead in the chemical industry. Manufacturing Chemists' Association. 1963. 25p. Free

A presentation of the numerous opportunities offered by chemical companies. Featured are the results of recent interviews with industry executives indicating the personal and professional qualifications expected of candidates for employment and the attractions that industry has to offer.

CHEMIST—*Continued*

**Careers and opportunities in chemistry. Pollack, Philip. Dutton and Company. 1960. 147p. $3.50

Included is information about educational requirements, qualifications, opportunities, and rates of pay in different types of chemical work. Given also is a list of colleges granting degrees in chemistry and chemical engineering which are approved by professional organizations. Illustrated.

Careers at Du Pont in chemistry and chemical engineering. E. I. du Pont de Nemours and Company. 1962. 6p. Mimeographed. Free

Description of work and opportunities in research, development, production, and sales.

**Careers in chemistry and chemical engineering. American Chemical Society. 1955. 94p. $1.50

A collection of thirty-one articles that have appeared in *Chemical and Engineering News*. The first section deals with the selection of a career, the training for it, and making a sound start. The second section consists of articles on lifetime pursuits which offer themselves to men with chemical training. First article has bibliography of 123 references.

Careers in industrial chemistry. Van Peursem, Ralph. Rochester Institute of Technology. 1958. 26p. Free

Discussion of kinds of jobs available, qualifications, personal characteristics, education desirable, methods of securing the first job, and job charts. Bibliography.

* Careers in the chemical field. Angel, Juvenal. World Trade Academy Press. 1962. 38p. $1.25

Includes information about the major fields of specialization, opportunities, remuneration, education required, outlook, and how to finance an education in the field of chemistry.

**The chemical profession—an educational and vocational guidance pamphlet. American Chemical Society. 1960. 40p. 25c

Types of work, qualifications, training, development, opportunities, salaries, and minimum standards used as criteria in evaluating undergraduate professional training in chemistry. Twenty-four illustrations.

Chemist. Robinson, H. Alan. Personnel Services. 1959. 6p. 50c; 25c to students

Occupational abstract. Nature of work, future prospects, qualifications, preparation, entrance, advancement, earnings, number and distribution, and related occupations.

Chemist. Careers. 1964. 8p. 25c

Career brief describing duties, working conditions, training, personal qualifications, earnings, related careers, and outlook.

* Chemist. Chronicle Guidance Publications. 1961. 4p. 35c

Occupational brief summarizing work performed, working conditions, qualifications, determination of aptitudes and interests, training, opportunities, outlook and related jobs.

Chemist. The Guidance Centre. 1959. 4p. 15c in Canada; 20c elsewhere
Definition, history and importance, nature of work, working conditions, qualifications necessary for entry and success, preparation, employment and advancement, remuneration, advantages, disadvantages, how to get started toward the occupation, and related occupations.

Chemistry. Michigan College of Mining and Technology. 1963. 2p. Free
Example of a recruiting leaflet describing work, qualifications, educational requirements, working conditions, outlook, and employment opportunities.

Chemistry and chemical engineering as careers. Institute for Research. 1957. 24p. $1
Training, typical course of study, salaries, attractive and unattractive sides. Discussion of opportunities in numerous industries such as textiles, metals, agriculture, glass, explosive, rubber, and synthetic resin compounds.

Chemistry as a profession. Riebsomer, J. L. Bellman Publishing Company. 1959. 20p. $1
History and importance of the work, training, employment opportunities, remuneration, advancement, and trends.

* Chemists. Science Research Associates. 1959. 4p. 35c
Occupational brief describing nature of work, training, qualifications, opportunities, advantages, disadvantages, and future outlook.

**Chemists. One section of *Occupational Outlook Handbook*.
Nature of work, where employed, training and other qualifications, employment outlook, earnings, and working conditions.

Education in chemistry. Philadelphia College of Pharmacy and Science. 1962. 4p. Free
One chapter in a twenty-four-page illustrated recruiting brochure describing nature of work, opportunities, and training in chemistry, biology and pharmacy.

**Employment outlook for physical scientists: chemists, physicists, and astronomers. Bureau of Labor Statistics, U.S. Department of Labor. Supt. of Documents. 1964. 16p. 10c
Reprint from the *Occupational Outlook Handbook*.

**Employment outlook in the industrial chemical industry. Bureau of Labor Statistics, U.S. Department of Labor. Supt. of Documents. 1964. 12p. 10c
Reprint from the *Occupational Outlook Handbook*.

Great discoveries by young chemists. Kendall, James. Thomas Y. Crowell Company. 1954. 231p. $3.95
Describes the lives and struggles of some outstanding young chemists and their epoch-making achievements.

Industrial chemical manufacturing workers. Science Research Associates. 1961. 4p. 35c
Occupational brief describing kinds of work, requirements, training, getting started and advancing, earnings, advantages, disadvantages, and future outlook.

CHEMIST—*Continued*

Joseph Priestley, pioneer chemist. Marcus, R. B. Franklin Watts, Inc. 1961. 145p. $1.95
> Biography of the man who is known as the "father of pneumatic chemistry," because of his pioneer work with gases.

List of institutions the committee deems to be qualified to offer professional training for chemists and chemical engineering. American Chemical Society. 1962. 2p. Free
> List of approved schools for training of chemists and chemical engineers.

**Occupations in the industrial chemical industry. One chapter of *Occupational Outlook Handbook*.
> Nature of the industry, kinds of work, training, other qualifications, advancement, employment outlook, earnings, and working conditions.

Shall I study chemistry? American Chemical Society. 1958. 16p. Free to individuals and nonprofit institutions. 5c per copy to others.
> More simply written than *The Chemical Profession*, described above. Types of work, opportunities, salaries, personal characteristics, and training. Twelve illustrations.

Should you be a chemist? Langmuir, Irving. New York Life Insurance Company. 1961. 12p. Free
> Nature of work, qualifications, and outlook.

**So you want to be a chemist. Nourse, Alan E. Harper and Row. 1963. 192p. $3.50; library binding $3.27 net
> Description of the various kinds of work, training, requirements, demands, and outlook.

There's adventure in chemistry. May, Julian. Popular Mechanics Press. 1957. 156p. $2.95
> By relating experiences of a boy in this field, the author portrays the various kinds of work. Written for grades 7 to 10.

The work and education of a forest and wood chemist. State University of New York, College of Forestry. 1962. 4p. Free
> Description of fields of specialization, opportunities, salaries, recommended high school courses, and training.

**Your career in chemistry. Esterer, Arnulf K. Julian Messner, Inc. 1964. 192p. $3.95; library edition $3.64
> Description of the various branches of chemistry and the anticipated growth in research and developmental activities expected to increase the employment of chemists. Includes information on necessary educational background, training, earnings, rewards, and employment outlook.

Your career in chemistry. Boston University. 1962. 20p. Free
> Recruiting booklet describing what types of careers are available in chemistry and what training is necessary to enter them. Bibliography.

See also Chemical engineer; Scientist

CHIROPODIST. *See* Podiatrist

CHIROPRACTOR   0-39.90

**Chiropractic . . . a career. National Chiropractic Association. 1963. 16p. Free
> Scope of practice, qualifications, compensation, training, and license requirements. An insert folder presents the educational requirements for licensure in each of the states and a list of the eight accredited schools in the United States and Canada.

**Chiropractic as a career. Belleau, Wilfrid. Park Publishing House. 1963. 25p. 75c
> Nature of work, training, qualifications, licensure, entering the field, conditions of work, income, opportunities, advantages, disadvantages, and recognition. Special section on opportunities for women. List of the seven approved colleges for training. Geographical distribution and ratio of chiropractors to population in each of the states.

Chiropractor. Robinson, Ann and Robinson, H. Alan. Personnel Services. 1959. 6p. 50c; 25c to students
> Occupational abstract. Nature of work, future prospects, qualifications, preparation, licensure, entrance, advancement, earnings, number and distribution, advantages, and disadvantages.

Chiropractor. Careers. 1964. 2p. 15c
> Career summary for desk-top file. Duties, qualifications, and outlook.

* Chiropractor. Chronicle Guidance Publications. 1961. 4p. 35c
> Occupational brief summarizing work performed, working conditions, qualifications, determination of aptitudes and interests, training, disadvantages, advantages, outlook, and related jobs. List of the eight accredited chiropractic schools.

Chiropractor. The Guidance Centre. 1962. 4p. 15c in Canada; 20c elsewhere
> Nature of work, qualifications, preparation, working conditions, advantages, disadvantages, how to get started, and related occupations.

Chiropractor. Michigan Employment Security Commission. 1962. 16p. 25c
> Nature of work, location of jobs, working conditions, earnings, requirements, and employment outlook.

* Chiropractors. Science Research Associates. 1961. 4p. 35c
> Occupational brief describing nature of work, training, qualifications, earnings, things to consider, and outlook. Selected references.

**Chiropractors. One section of *Occupational Outlook Handbook.*
> Nature of work, where employed, training, other qualifications, employment outlook, earnings, and working conditions.

Educational standards for chiropractic colleges. National Chiropractic Association. 1961. 24p. Free
> Essentials of an acceptable chiropractic college and courses of training.

**Employment outlook for chiropractors. Bureau of Labor Statistics, U.S. Department of Labor. Supt. of Documents. 1964. 4p. 5c
> Reprint from the *Occupational Outlook Handbook.*

CHIROPRACTOR—*Continued*

**Guidance kit. International Chiropractors Association. 1964. 6 pamphlets. Free

> Brochures containing career information, list of accredited colleges, and scholarship sources.

Vocational guidance manual for counselors. National Chiropractic Association. 1963. 10p. Free

> A folder including several brochures describing work and training.

CIRCUS PERFORMER   0-62.

The fabulous showman—the life and times of P. T. Barnum. Wallace, Irving. Knopf, Inc. 1959. 332p. $5

> Biography of a noted circus owner.

Physical performers. Chronicle Guidance Publications. 1963. 4p. 35c

> Occupational brief summarizing work performed, qualifications, preparation, methods of entry and outlook.

The Ringlings: wizards of the circus. Harlow, Alvin. Julian Messner, Inc. 1951. 181p. $3.25. Library binding $3.19 net

> An account of the career of the Ringling brothers and the ups and downs of creating the spectacle of the circus.

Sawdust in his shoes. McGraw, Eloise Jarvis. Coward-McCann, Inc. 1950. 246p. $3.75

> Career fiction. Story about a circus boy who becomes a star. For younger boys.

CITY MANAGER   0-94.98

City manager. Careers. 1960. 2p. 15c

> Career summary for desk-top file. Duties, qualifications, and outlook.

City managers. Science Research Associates. 1960. 4p. 35c

> Occupational brief describing the administration of local government, requirements, how to get started, advantages, disadvantages, and outlook. Selected references.

Consider a chamber of commerce career. American Chamber of Commerce Executives. No date. 12p. 10c. Free to counselors and librarians

> Challenges of the career, qualifications, opportunities, earnings, related fields, advantages, disadvantages, and how to start.

CITY PLANNER   0-94.912

A career for you in city planning. Georgia Institute of Technology. 1960. 8p. Free

> Value of training for a city planning career, employment opportunities, and outlook.

A career for you in city planning. Southern Regional Education Board. 1957. 6p. Free

Nature of work, need for this service in the South, and information about undergraduate and graduate training for a career in city planning.

A career in urban planning. Michigan State University. 1955. 7p. Free

Description of work, qualifications, training needed, and opportunities.

* Careers in planning. Changing Times. 1963. 4p. 15c

Reprint describing the mounting problems of city growth, traffic, land use, highway locations, and the utilization of natural resources. Includes education, qualifications, and earnings.

City planner. Robinson, H. Alan. Personnel Services. 1956. 6p. 50c; 25c to students

Occupational abstract. Nature of the work, future prospects, opportunities, qualifications, preparation, entrance and advancement, earnings, number and distribution of workers, advantages, and disadvantages.

City planner. California State Department of Employment. 1961. 7p. Single copy free

Duties, working conditions, salaries, hours, entrance requirements, promotion, training, and employment outlook in California.

City planner. Careers. 1960. 2p. 15c

Career summary for desk-top file. Duties, qualifications, and outlook.

**City planner. Chronicle Guidance Publications. 1961. 4p. 35c

Occupational brief summarizing work performed, working conditions, salaries, qualifications, determination of aptitudes and interests, training, opportunities, and employment outlook.

**City planners. Science Research Associates. 1963. 4p. 35c

Occupational brief describing nature of work, requirements, training, methods of getting started, earnings, advantages, disadvantages, and future outlook.

**Employment outlook for urban planners. Bureau of Labor Statistics, U.S. Department of Labor. Supt. of Documents. 1964. 4p. 5c

Reprint from the *Occupational Outlook Handbook.*

**Opportunities in city planning. Berger, Marjorie. Vocational Guidance Manuals. 1961. 100p. $1.45 paper

Discussion of historical development of modern city planning, why planning and planners are needed, nature of work, education, opportunities, future outlook, advantages, and disadvantages. List of schools offering degrees in planning.

Planning jobs and jobs in planning. Ehrlich, Otto H. Bellman Publishing Co. 1945. 40p. $1

Discussion of local, state, and regional planning and of land, water, and energy planning. Information about jobs in social planning, industrial planning, national and international planning, such as industry analyst, marketing specialist, transportation economist, and state planning engineer. Bibliography.

CITY PLANNER—*Continued*

Professional planning education in the United States and Canada. American Institute of Planners. 1963. 2p. Free
> List of colleges offering degrees in planning.

**Professional planning education in the United States and Canada. American Society of Planning Officials. 1962. 8p. Single copy free; additional copies 15c each
> Historical development of professional planning education; list of colleges and universities offering educational programs in planning; programs of study; list of selected readings on planning education and on planning as a career.

Should you be a city and regional planner? Opperman, Paul. New York Life Insurance Company. 1959. 12p. Free
> Nature of work, tasks ahead, preparation, outlook, rewards, and drawbacks.

**Urban planners. One section of *Occupational Outlook Handbook*.
> Nature of work, where employed, training, other qualifications, advancement, employment outlook, earnings, and working conditions.

CIVIL ENGINEER   0-16.01

Brief bibliography on engineering as a career. American Society of Civil Engineers. 1956. 3p. Photo offset. Free
> Prepared for use with high school students. Contains brief statement of qualities essential to prospective engineers.

* Civil engineer. Robinson, H. Alan. Personnel Services. 1956. 6p. 50c; 25c to students
> Occupational abstract. Nature of work, future prospects, opportunities, qualifications, preparation, entrance and advancement, earnings, number and distribution of workers, advantages, disadvantages, and sources of further information.

* Civil engineer. Careers. 1964. 8p. 25c
> Career brief describing duties, working conditions, earnings, personal qualifications, training, suggested high school program, licensing, and outlook. Additional readings.

Civil engineer. Chronicle Guidance Publications. 1962. 4p. 35c
> Occupational brief describing work performed, working conditions, personal qualifications, determination of aptitudes and interests, educational requirements, promotional opportunities, employment outlook, licensing, and where employed.

Civil engineering. Dixon, Howard G. Chapter 11 of *Engineering Enrollment in the United States*.
> Trends in enrollments and future requirements for specialists in this area.

Civil engineering. Michigan College of Mining and Technology. 1963. 2p. Free
> Example of a recruiting leaflet describing work, qualifications, educational requirements, earnings, and employment opportunities.

Civil engineering as a career. Institute for Research. 1957. 24p. $1
Nature of work, qualifications, training, opportunities, earnings, attractive and unattractive features. Describes the various branches of civil engineering and the requirements for registration.

Civil engineering technician. National Council of Technical Schools. 1954. 2p. 5c
Description of work, working conditions, opportunities, advantages, and methods of entering.

Civil engineers. Science Research Associates. 1959. 4p. 35c
Occupational brief describing nature of work, qualifications, preparation, opportunities, advantages, disadvantages, and future outlook.

**Civil engineers. One section of *Occupational Outlook Handbook*.
Nature of work, where employed, and employment outlook.

Educational and research activities in civil engineering at M.I.T. Massachusetts Institute of Technology. 1963. 94p. Free
Illustrated brochure describing significant activities in modern civil engineering education and research. Includes soils research, hydrodynamics, structures research, materials research, civil engineering systems, and experimental studies.

The land divided, the world united—the story of the Panama Canal. Rink, Paul. Julian Messner, Inc. 1963. 189p. $3.95; library edition $3.64 net
Among other things, this book portrays the many problems in a project of this kind.

There's adventure in civil engineering. Ruzic, Neil P. Popular Mechanics Press. 1958. 187p. $2.95
By relating experiences of a boy in this field, the author portrays the various kinds of work. Written for grades 7 to 10.

What does a civil engineer do? Wells, Robert. Dodd, Mead and Company. 1960. 62p. $2.50
Simple text and pictures portray building of bridges, tunnels, dams, and skyscrapers. Written for grades 3 to 7.

Your future in civil engineering. American Society of Civil Engineers. 1960. 16p. Free
This booklet cites examples to show the widespread duties of civil engineers and offers encouragement to start early planning.

CIVIL SERVICE WORKER 0-00. through 9-99.

After college . . . what? U.S. Civil Service Commission. Supt. of Documents. 1961. 24p. 15c
Discussion of how jobs are filled, advantages of working for the Government, and brief information about the Federal-Service Entrance Examination.

Arco civil service exam books. Arco Publishing Company. 1956-63. 50 titles. $3 and $4 each
Study suggestions, questions and answers derived from previous examinations, and review material.

CIVIL SERVICE WORKER—*Continued*

Beginning professional careers with New York State. New York State Department of Civil Service. 1962. 8p. Free
Description of opportunities, requirements, and examination procedures.

Careers for college graduates in New York state government. New York State Department of Civil Service. 1963. 20p. Free to counselors, librarians, and college faculty members
Description of kinds of work and opportunities in various fields of work, such as public administration internships, conservation, economics, social work, statistics, biology, health services, and bank examining.

Civil service: Federal, state, municipal. Chapter 34 of *Vocations for Boys.*
Includes basic qualifications, some of the specialized functions, opportunities, and advantages.

Complete guide to U.S. civil service jobs. Arco Publishing Company. 1962. 128p. $1.50
Describes opportunities with the Government, requirements, and opportunities for advancement. Tells how and where to apply and gives samples of the written examinations.

Current Federal examination announcements. U.S. Civil Service Commission. Revised monthly. 16″ by 21″. Free
List of civil service examinations currently open throughout the country, giving titles, salaries, location of positions, and brief information regarding each examination.

**Federal career directory: a guide for college students. U.S. Civil Service Commission. Supt. of Documents. 1962. 84p. 60c
Includes description of thirty-eight federal agencies and ninety-two job briefs containing nature of work, qualifications required, and career opportunities. One index of job briefs is by position title and another by college major fields of study. For college graduates.

The Federal career service . . . at your service. U.S. Civil Service Commission. Supt. of Documents. 1963. 24p. 35c
Helpful facts about the civil service system and how to prepare for it.

Federal civil service workers. Science Research Associates. 1961. 4p. 35c
Occupational brief describing methods of entering Government service, training, earnings, advantages, and disadvantages. Selected references.

Futures in the Federal Government. U.S. Civil Service Commission. 1961. 36p. Free
Information about opportunities offered through the Federal-Service Entrance Examination and how to apply for them.

Opportunities in civil service. Yarmon, Morton. Vocational Guidance Manuals. 1957. 96p. $1.45 paper
Description of jobs in the civil service, working conditions, how to prepare for them, and how to apply.

Summer employment in federal agencies. U.S. Civil Service Commission. Supt. of Documents. 1963. 31p. 15c
Information about summer employment of student assistants or student trainees in a number of Federal agencies.

Thinking about your first job? Remember Uncle Sam when it comes to choosing an employer. U.S. Civil Service Commission. 1961. 8p. Free
Brief information about opportunities for high school graduates.

The way to a job in government. U.S. Civil Service Commission. Supt. of Documents. 1963. 6p. 5c
Contains general information about steps to be taken in seeking a job in the Federal civil service and lists addresses to which inquiries may be sent.

What's ahead for civil service? Lindsay, David. Public Affairs Committee. 1957. 28p. 25c
Description of the advantages of employment with the civil service, the hiring procedures, pay scales, benefits, and prestige.

**Working for the U.S.A.: applying for a civil service job, what the Government expects of Federal workers. U.S. Civil Service Commission. Supt. of Documents. 1963. 24p. 15c
Explanation of basis of rating, qualifications, opportunities for advancement, incentive awards, employee benefits, and salary scales.

Women in the Federal service, 1939-1959. Women's Bureau. 1962. 21p. 15c
This report gives a comparison of current information with earlier data concerning the types of positions which women hold, and the percentages they comprise of the workers in 117 occupations.

**Your future in the Federal Government. Gould, Stephen. Richards Rosen Press. 1963. 157p. $2.95; library edition $2.79 net
The author explains the civil service programs and discusses overseas job opportunities as well as the multiplicity of Government positions in local communities in the United States.

See also Government service worker

CLEANING AND DYEING INDUSTRY WORKER. *See* Laundry industry worker

CLERGYMAN   0-08.10

Be a rural pastor. National Council of Churches of Christ. No date. 6p. 7c
Description of what a rural ministry involves, duties, advantages, and preparation.

Become a director or minister of Christian education. National Council of Churches, Department of Ministry. No date. 4p. 5c
Discusses the need for persons in the field, the requirements of the job, and the rewards of the work.

CLERGYMAN—*Continued*

Catholic priest: his training and ministry. Lothrop, Lee and Shepard. 1961. 127p. $3.50

Many photographs and simple text prepared for grades seven to ten.

**The clergy. One chapter in *Occupational Outlook Handbook.*

Nature of work, where employed, training, other qualifications, and outlook for Protestant clergymen, Roman Catholic priests, and rabbis.

The clergy and what they do. Spence, Hartzell. Franklin Watts, Inc. 1961. 195p. $3.95

Discussion of the necessary character traits and abilities, training, nature of work, related occupations in religious work, advancement, opportunities for women, and the challenge of the future. For grades 7 to 11.

Clergyman. The Guidance Centre. 1959. 4p. 15c in Canada; 20c elsewhere

Nature of work, qualifications, preparation, working conditions, earnings, advantages, disadvantages, and related occupations.

Clergyman (protestant). Careers. 1963. 8p. 25c

Career brief describing duties, personal qualifications, training, salaries, how to enter, related jobs, and outlook. Includes list of accredited theological schools.

* Clergyman. Chronicle Guidance Publications. 1963. 4p. 35c

Occupational brief describing work performed, personal qualifications, remuneration, training, and employment outlook.

Clergyman. Science Research Associates. 1961. 4p. 35c

Occupational brief describing nature of work, preparation, qualifications, opportunities, advantages, disadvantages, and future outlook.

**Employment outlook for Protestant clergymen. Bureau of Labor Statistics, U.S. Department of Labor. Supt. of Documents. 1964. 8p. 5c

Reprint from the *Occupational Outlook Handbook.*

**Employment outlook for Roman Catholic priests. Bureau of Labor Statistics, U.S. Department of Labor. Supt. of Documents. 1964. 8p. 5c

Reprint from the *Occupational Outlook Handbook.*

An invitation to a pastoral ministry in institutions. National Council of Churches, Department of Ministry. 1963. 6p. 5c

Outlines the opportunities, requirements, and necessary training for the specialized ministry of chaplaincy in hospitals, penitentiaries, and correctional institutions.

**Minister. Coburn, John B. Macmillan Company. 1963. 205p. $3.95

The author discusses schooling, salaries, and the minister's average working day. Primarily for Protestants, though nonsectarian in spirit.

The ministry. Chapter 24 of *Vocations for Boys.*

Includes qualifications, training, opportunities, and recompenses.

The ordained ministry. Board of Christian Education, United Presbyterian
Church. 1962. 4p. Free
Includes duties, personal requirements, education, procedure for entering the
ministry, need, opportunities for development, and disadvantages.

Possibly the ministry. National Council of Churches, Department of
Ministry. No date. 8p. 5c
Need for ministers, qualifications, and rewards.

Preparing for the ministry. Kemp, Charles F. Bethany Press. 1959. 128p.
$1.50
Answers to questions asked by young people who are considering the ministry.

* Should you enter the clergy? Spence, Hartzell. New York Life Insurance
Company. 1959. 12p. Free
Description of challenges, demands, privileges, qualifications for success,
training, opportunities and rewards.

The young minister: his calling, career, and challenge. Wilder, John.
Zondervan Publishing House. 1962. 128p. $1.95
A veteran pastor relates his experiences to help the new minister escape
the mistakes and pitfalls so often encountered.

See also Priest; Rabbi; Religious worker

CLERICAL WORKER   1-01. through 1-49.

Can I be an office worker? General Motors Corporation, Public Relations
Staff. 1955. 32p. Free
Outlines various office positions and discusses duties, preparation, personal
qualities, and chances for advancement. Includes stenography, bookkeeping,
business machine operation, and general clerical work. Available in classroom
sets.

* Careers for women in office work. Institute for Research. 1956. 24p. $1
Duties performed, training, personal qualifications, opportunities, lines of
promotion, and salaries. Discussed under thirty-two occupations: four in the
stenographic group, ten in the accounting group, seven machine operators, and
eleven clerical positions.

Clerical airline jobs. Careers. 1963. 7p. 25c
Career brief describing duties and qualifications of the traffic agent, reserva-
tions agent, ticket agent, passenger agent, station manager, cargo agent, air
freight agent, and personnel director.

**Clerical and related occupations. One section of *Occupational Outlook
Handbook*.
Nature of clerical work, training, other qualifications, advancement, employment outlook, earnings, and working conditions. Specific information is given
concerning secretary, stenographer, typist, bookkeeper, office machine operator,
and electronic computer operator.

* Clerical careers in government service. Institute for Research. 1957. 24p.
$1
Description of the merit system and positions in clerical, administrative,
and accounting work. Duties, opportunities, salary, promotional possibilities,
attractive and unattractive features. Includes description of work of stenog-

CLERICAL WORKER—*Continued*

rapher, typist, junior clerk, senior clerk, statistical clerk, editorial clerk, accounting and auditing clerk, fingerprint classifier, executive positions, and operators of thirteen types of office machines.

Clerical workers. Chapter 8 of *Vocations for Girls.*
Qualifications and opportunities for office workers.

Correspondence clerk. Chronicle Guidance Publications. 1962. 4p. 35c
Occupational brief summarizing work performed, personal qualifications, earnings, methods of entry, advancement, related occupations, and outlook.

Federal office assistant examination, stenographer; typist, clerk, and office machine operator; what it is, and how it is given. U.S. Civil Service Commission. Supt. of Documents. 1963. 61p. 40c
Information about experience, training requirements, and tests for filling a variety of office occupations.

File clerk. Chronicle Guidance Publications. 1963. 4p. 35c
Occupational brief describing duties, qualifications, training, hours, earnings, and future outlook.

File clerks. Science Research Associates. 1963. 4p. 35c
Occupational brief describing nature of work, training, qualifications, opportunities, and outlook.

Finding out about file clerks. Science Research Associates. 1963. 4p. 35c
Junior occupational brief containing concise facts about the job.

Finding out about mailing service workers. Science Research Associates. 1962. 4p. 35c
Junior occupational brief describing work and opportunities.

* General office clerk. Careers. 1964. 8p. 25c
Career brief describing duties, working conditions, training, personal qualifications, earnings, advancement prospects, and ways of measuring one's interest and ability.

**General office clerk. Chronicle Guidance Publications. 1961. 4p. 35c
Occupational brief summarizing work performed, working conditions, qualifications, determination of aptitudes and interests, training, opportunities, outlook, methods of entry, and related jobs.

Information concerning the clerical and clerical-technical positions in the Federal Bureau of Investigation. The Bureau. 1960. 2p. Free
Physical requirements, educational and job qualifications, working hours, and salaries. Positions include translator, fingerprint classifier, stenographer, typist, and clerk.

**Jobs in clerical work. Science Research Associates. 1959. 32p. $1
Describes the variety of job prospects and opportunities within this field. An accompanying wall chart is available for 35c.

Occupations in the clerical group. Chapter 23 of *Planning Your Future.*
Includes discussion of importance and kinds of clerical occupations and specific information about the work of the stenographer.

Office clerk. The Guidance Centre. 1959. 4p. 15c in Canada; 20c elsewhere
> Duties, history and importance of work, qualifications, employment and advancements, remuneration, advantages, disadvantages, how to get started, and related occupations. Further readings.

Office clerks. Science Research Associates. 1959. 4p. 35c
> Occupational brief describing nature of work, qualifications, preparation, opportunities, advantages, disadvantages, and future outlook.

The office occupations. Chapter 14 in *Occupations and Careers.*
> Brief discussion of twenty-five clerical jobs.

**Opportunities in office occupations. Popham, Estelle D. Vocational Guidance Manuals. 1958. 96p. $1.45 paper
> Nature of work, qualifications, preparation, opportunities, and employment outlook.

Reference manual for office employees. Larsen, Lenna and Koebele, Apollonia. South-Western Publishing Company. 1959. 158p. $1.20
> An inexpensive reference guide for the use of stenographers and secretaries indicates the nature of the work.

Secretaries and other clerical workers. Chapter 4 of *The College Girl Looks Ahead.*
> Some characteristics of clerical work, talents needed, trying out and preparing for clerical work, entering, and kinds of work.

See also Bookkeeper; Business worker; Stenographer; Typist

CLINICAL LABORATORY TECHNICIAN. *See* Laboratory technician; Medical technologist

CLOTHES DESIGNER 0-46.

**Careers and opportunities in fashion. Brenner, Barbara. Dutton and Company. 1964. 191p. $3.95
> The nature of work in designing, merchandising, advertising, illustrating, photographing, and modeling for the fashion industry is followed by brief information on qualifications, opportunities, and chances for advancement. Includes list of schools offering training.

* Careers in fashion designing. Institute for Research. 1962. 24p. $1
> Description of work, training recommended, personal qualifications, duties, typical day's work, opportunities, salaries, advantages, and disadvantages. Information about related occupations of fashion illustrator, sketcher or copyist, costume stylist, fashion editor, and designer of accessories.

Clothes designer. The Guidance Centre. 1959. 4p. 15c in Canada; 20c elsewhere
> Definition, nature of work, working conditions, qualifications, preparation, and advancement, remuneration, advantages, disadvantages, how to get started, and related occupations.

Dress designer. Careers. 1959. 2p. 15c
> Career summary for desk-top file. Duties, qualifications, and outlook.

CLOTHES DESIGNER—*Continued*

Dress doctor. Head, Edith and Ardmore, Jane. Little, Brown and Company. 1959. 249p. $4.50

The fashion chief of Paramount Studios tells of her experiences in designing costumes for many famous stars.

Fashion design. Lillard, Marion N. Bellman Publishing Company. 1955. 18p. $1

Description of work in eight fashion careers, training, qualifications, employment opportunities, and remuneration. Brief description of courses usually offered in fashion schools which give instruction in design, patternmaking, fashion fundamentals, sketching, construction, history of costume, economics of fashion, and textiles.

Fashion designer. Fried, Eleanor. Research Publishing Company. 1959. 32p. $1

Nature of work, history and importance, number engaged in occupation, qualifications, salaries, training, placement channels, and promotional opportunities.

Fashion designer. Splaver, Sarah. Personnel Services. 1956. 50c; 25c to students

Occupational abstract. Nature of work, qualifications, preparation, entrance and advancement, supply and demand, earnings, advantages, and disadvantages.

Fashion designer. Chronicle Guidance Publications. 1961. 4p. 35c

Occupational brief containing history, nature of work, working conditions, personal qualifications, determination of aptitudes and interests, training, employment outlook, and methods of entry.

**Fashion designers. Science Research Associates. 1961. 4p. 35c

Occupational brief describing nature of work, qualifications, educational requirements, getting started, pros and cons, and future outlook.

Fashion for Cinderella. Vitray, Laura. Dodd, Mead and Company. 1960. 256p. $3

Career fiction. Story of adventure and problems in dress designing.

Gay design. De Leeuw, Adele L. Macmillan Company. 1942. 279p. $3

Career fiction. Shows Nancy's entry and progress in dress design.

Is the fashion business your business? Fried, Eleanor L. Fairchild Publications. 1958. 270p. $5.50

Case histories show how people of different interests, backgrounds, and training have succeeded as resident buyer, textile designer, comparison shopper, production engineer, department store manager, retail salesperson, fashion director, department buyer, and costume designer.

Job description for hat designer. U.S. Employment Service. Supt. of Documents. 1948. 4p. 5c

Occupational guide. Job summary, work performed, training, trainee-selection factors, related occupations, physical activities, working conditions, and employment variables.

Kit Corelli: TV stylist. Nash, Eleanor Arnett. Julian Messner, Inc. 1955. 192p. $2.95

> Career fiction. The story tells of a girl's experiences as a stylist for a television network.

Lucky Miss Spaulding. Nash, Eleanor Arnett. Julian Messner, Inc. 1952. 182p. $2.95

> Career fiction. The romance gives a glimpse of work in fashion retailing. Gradually the heroine climbs from a position as stock girl to assisting at a fashion show and meeting models, designers and buyers whose business is fashion.

No pattern for love. Williams, Beryl. Julian Messner, Inc. 1951. 178p. $2.95

> Career fiction. The romance contains helpful hints to girls who are thinking of careers in fashion. The heroine is a student at a school for fashion design who explores several aspects of the fashion world before solving her career problems.

Young faces in fashion. Williams, Beryl. J. B. Lippincott Company. 1956. 176p. $3.50

> Biographies of eleven American fashion designers. Descriptions of backgrounds, schooling, early struggles, successes, philosophy, and work give a hint of what one may expect to experience as a fashion designer.

**Your future in the fashion world. The Fashion Group. Richards Rosen Press. 1960. 158p. $2.95

> Twelve leading fashion specialists discuss several facets of the fashion world, including designing of clothing and accessories, fashion buying, advertising and publicity, fashion show and display, fashion reporting, and how to find a job in fashion.

Your future in the fashion world. The Fashion Group. Popular Library, Inc. 1962. 158p. 50c

> A paperback edition of the book described above.

CLOTHING INDUSTRY WORKER   4, 6, 8-21. through 4, 6, 8-27.

**Clothing manufacturing workers. Science Research Associates. 1961. 4p. 35c

> Occupational brief describing some kinds of work, requirements, getting started and advancing, earnings and hours, advantages, disadvantages, and future outlook.

**Employment outlook for the apparel industry. Bureau of Labor Statistics, U.S. Department of Labor. Supt. of Documents. 1964. 12p. 10c

> Reprint from the *Occupational Outlook Handbook*.

Hat manufacturing workers. Science Research Associates. 1961. 4p. 35c

> Occupational brief describing kinds of work, qualifications, getting started, earnings, advantages, disadvantages, and future outlook.

CLOTHING INDUSTRY WORKER—*Continued*

Industry wage survey: women's and misses' dresses. Bureau of Labor Statistics. 1964. 32p. 30c

Survey of wages and supplementary practices in the women's and misses' dress manufacturing industry in twelve important areas. Many tables. Includes cutter, inspector, presser, sewer, sewing machine operator, thread trimmer, and work distributor.

Job descriptions for the garment manufacturing industry. U.S. Employment Service. Supt. of Documents. 1939. 237p. $1.50

One of a series of Volume Job Descriptions. Describes jobs concerned with the manufacture of apparel from woven and knitted fabrics. Illustrated.

**Occupations in the apparel industry. One chapter in *Occupational Outlook Handbook*.

Nature and location of the industry, kinds of jobs, training, other qualifications, advancement, employment outlook, earnings, and working conditions. Four illustrations.

See also Clothes designer; Milliner

COAL INDUSTRY WORKER   5, 7-21.; 6, 8-56.

**Coal industry. Speare, M. Edmund. Bellman Publishing Company. 1957. 32p. $1

Development of the coal industry, future prospects, and kinds of work, preparation, and opportunities for the coal mining engineer and the coal miner.

Coal miner. Careers. 1961. 2p. 15c

Career summary for desk-top file. Duties, qualifications, and outlook.

Mining engineering—a career in coal. National Coal Association. 1959. 13p. Free

Information of interest to those who are preparing for careers in the coal industry.

See also Metallurgist; Mineral industry worker; Mining engineer

COAST GUARDSMAN   2-68.40

A career in the United States Coast Guard. Institute for Research. 1957. 24p. $1

Description of the functions of the Coast Guard and its branches of service. Qualifications, attractive and unattractive features, and salaries of enlisted men and officers and retirement pay.

The coast guard. Paxton, Glenn. Viking Press. Revised 1962. 192p. $3

Details of regulations and opportunities. For grades 7 to 10.

The Coast Guard Academy. Engeman, Jack. Lothrop, Lee and Shepard Company. 1957. 128p. $3.50

Story showing the life of a cadet. Two hundred illustrations.

Coast guard in action. Bergaust, Erik and Foss, William. Putnam's Sons. 1962. 96p. $2.95

The history of the Coast Guard, the story of men who serve in it, and how they carry out their maritime and law enforcement duties. Written for ages 10 to 14.

Coast Guard officer. Careers. 1960. 2p. 15c
Career summary for desk-top file. Duties, qualifications, and outlook.

**Counselor's handbook. U.S. Coast Guard Academy. 1963. 10p. Free to counselors
Handbook of information for advising students applying for appointment to the academy.

Current career booklets. U.S. Coast Guard. Five booklets. Free
Frequently revised materials are available from local recruiting offices or the above. Examples of present titles are: U.S. Coast Guard—a career service; Ships, planes, and stations; Weathermen of the sea, Coast Guard history, and After boot camp.

Danger fighters: men and ships of the U.S. Coast Guard. Colby, C. B. Coward-McCann, Inc. 1953. 48p. Library binding $2.52 net
Photographs and brief text show how men protect life and property at sea and enforce applicable maritime, customs, immigration, and other laws. Written for grades 4 to 8.

Kendall of the Coast Guard. Wyckoff, James. Doubleday and Company. 1961. 142p. $2.50
Career fiction. Story of a boy's experiences on patrol in the North Atlantic reveals the nature of work, training, and gratifications of serving in the Coast Guard.

Let's go to the United States Coast Guard Academy. Butler, Roger. Putnam's Sons. 1964. 48p. Library edition $1.86 net
The cadets are seen in their daily activities as they prepare to be officers. For grades 3 to 6.

Our United States Coast Guard Academy. Crump, Irving. Dodd, Mead and Company. 1961. 242p. $3.50
The author tells of the exploits of the men in war and in peace and describes the development and function of the academy which now trains them.

Search and rescue at sea. Floherty, John J. Lippincott Company. 1953. 160p. $3.95
An account of the adventure, perils, and achievements of the Coast Guardsman. Stories about the service of weather ships, about hurricanes, abandoned ships, salvage, and rescues. Sixteen pages of photographs.

Story of the U.S. Coast Guard. Rachlis, Eugene. Random House. 1961. 176p. $1.95
An account of some of the dramatic incidents in the Coast Guard's past, building up its famous motto, "Always Ready." Includes its service in wartime, the humanitarian work of the Bering Sea Patrol, the scientific research carried on by the International Ice Patrol, and rescue operations effected at sea. Illustrated.

**Take a look at your future. U.S. Coast Guard Academy. 1962. 67p. Free
Description of the four-year curriculum leading to a B.S. degree and a commission in the Coast Guard. Includes scholastic and physical requirements for admission and procedures for application to take entrance examinations. Some sample questions and answers are suggested. Contains application forms. Fully illustrated.

COAST GUARDSMAN—*Continued*

The United States Coast Guard—a career service. U.S. Coast Guard. 1961. 24p. Free
Illustrated booklet telling a young man what to expect as a member of the Coast Guard.
See also Military serviceman

COLLECTOR. *See* Credit and collection manager; Fund raiser; Salesperson

COLLEGE ADMINISTRATOR   0-11.10; 0-11.20

**Careers in college and university administration. Institute for Research. 1962. 24p. $1
Description of the various positions, attractive and unattractive features, salaries, and how to get started.

The college presidency, 1900-1960: an annotated bibliography. Eells, Walter C. and Hollis, Ernest V. U.S. Office of Education. Supt. of Documents. 1961. 143p. 60c
Lists seven hundred publications concerning the duties, qualifications, and responsibilities of the college president.

The academic president—educator or caretaker? Dodds, H. W. McGraw-Hill Book Company. 1962. 294p. $5.95
The former head of Princeton gives brief career descriptions of six outstanding presidents and educes that the president's primary role is educational leadership with the unavoidable accompaniment of public relations and business management.

**College registrar as a career. Harbert, Sylvia. Bellman Publishing Company. 1959. 20p. $1
Origin of the registrar, duties, salaries, training, and preparation. References for further reading.

Dean of women. Careers. 1962. 2p. 15c
Career summary for desk-top file. Duties, qualifications, and outlook.

COLLEGE TEACHER   0-11.50

**College and university teachers. One section of *Occupational Outlook Handbook.*
Nature of work, where employed, training, other qualifications, advancement, employment outlook, earnings, and working conditions.

College teacher. Group, Vernard. Personnel Services. 1956. 6p. 50c; 25c to students
Occupational abstract. Nature of work, future prospects, qualifications, preparation, entrance and advancement, earnings, advantages, and disadvantages.

College teacher. Careers. 1961. 8p. 25c
Career brief describing nature of work, training, advantages, disadvantages, earnings, and outlook.

**College teacher. Chronicle Guidance Publications. 1964. 4p. 35c
    Occupational brief summarizing work performed, personal qualifications, educational requirements, salaries, other benefits, and outlook.

* College teachers. Science Research Associates. 1962. 4p. 35c
    Occupational brief describing nature of work, requirements, methods of securing appointment, earnings, advantages, disadvantages, and future outlook.

College teaching as a career. American Council on Education. 1958. 28p. Free to counselors and librarians
    Prepared to give an impression of the pleasures and satisfactions in the college teaching profession.

**College teaching as a career. Institute for Research. 1957. 24p. $1
    Growth of the profession, qualifications, preparations, salaries, rewards, and drawbacks.

College teaching: perspectives and guidelines. Brown, James and Thornton, James. McGraw-Hill Book Company. 1963. 260p. $5.95
    Part I emphasizes the background of higher education in the United States, the sociological and professional aspects of college teaching, and the goals of the curriculum of higher education in liberal arts colleges. Part II explores the practical aspects of teaching.

The good life: college teaching. National Education Association. No date. 8p. 35 copies $1
    This leaflet describes the kind of life that awaits a young man or woman who plans to teach in college.

Job motivations and satisfactions of college teachers. U.S. Office of Education. Supt. of Documents. 1961. 96p. 35c
    An exploratory study of factors that have influenced faculty members at the University of Minnesota in choosing college teaching as a career, the nature of their background and training, and their present job responsibilities.

A look into the crystal ball. Tickton, Sidney G. Fund for the Advancement of Education. 1962. 2p. Free
    Includes a table showing that faculty salaries at a typical strong college will increase three to four times between 1952 and 1972.

**Professor. Millett, Fred B. Macmillan Company. 1961. 189p. $3.95
    Traces the span of a teaching career from preliminary studies in school and college, through graduate work, early teaching assignments, the importance of tenure, to full professorship and retirement.

The quantity and quality of college teachers. McGrath, Earl J. Bureau of Publications. 1961. 24p. $1
    Recent experiences of 503 liberal arts college presidents in recruiting faculty members are reported together with their opinions on teacher supply and demand in the future. Also includes their proposals for attracting suitable young people into college teaching.

Salaries paid and salary practices in universities, colleges, and junior colleges, 1961-62. National Education Association. 1962. 59p. $1
    The fifth report in this biennial series.

COLLEGE TEACHER—*Continued*

Tomorrow's professors. Diekhoff, John S. Fund for the Advancement of Education. 1959. 91p. Free

A report of the college faculty internship program in eighteen colleges for beginning college teachers.

University teacher. The Guidance Centre. 1963. 4p. 15 in Canada; 20c elsewhere

History and importance, nature of work, qualifications, working conditions, preparation, remuneration, advancement, outlook, related occupations, and how to get started.

See also Teacher

COLUMNIST. *See* Journalist

COMEDIAN. *See* Actor and actress

COMMERCIAL ARTIST   0-44.

**Art careers. Roth, Claire J. and Weiss, Adelle. Henry Z. Walck, Inc. 1963. 116p. $3.50

The authors describe many unique and satisfying careers in advertising, industrial design, interior design, museum work, scenic design, teaching, and illustrating. For each field there is given the nature of work, qualifications, training, and outlook. Good reading list.

Arts and crafts—careers. Institute for Research. 1957. 24p. $1

Information concerning the potter, weaver, basketry and cane worker, woodworker, metalworker, bookbinder, leather worker, maker of jewelry, and maker of novelties.

**Careers and opportunities in commercial art. Biegeleisen, Jacob Israel. Dutton and Company. Revised 1963. 244p. $4.95

Information about the various careers that are related to art in industry such as book covers, caricatures and cartoons, show windows, sign painting, stage setting, and trade-marks. A chapter on art in television is included.

* Careers in advertising art. Institute for Research. 1959. 24p. $1

Describes work of the layout artist, illustrative artist, hand letterer, poster artist, and advertising photographer. Qualifications, training, opportunities, remuneration, attractive and unattractive features. Includes some information on work of fashion illustrator and fashion editor.

* Careers in decorating and design. Angel, Juvenal. World Trade Academy Press. 1961. 26p. $1.25

Includes information about each of several specialties within this field.

Careers in the crafts. Brennan, Harold J. Rochester Institute of Technology. Revised 1963. 30p. Free

Description of the hand arts, abilities needed, training, and vocational opportunities. Illustrated.

Commercial and industrial art as a career. Institute for Research. 1961. 23p. $1

Information concerning work of the advertising artist, costume designer, industrial designer, and art buyer. Qualifications, training, opportunities, salaries, attractive and unattractive features.

Commercial art. Group, Vernard. Personnel Services. 1958. 6p. 50c; 25c to students

Occupational abstract. Nature of work, future prospects, qualifications, preparation, entrance and advancement, earnings, number and distribution of workers, advantages, disadvantages, and sources of further information.

Commercial art as a career. Boston University. 1962. 12p. Free

Recruiting booklet describing opportunities, working conditions, qualifications, and training. Discussion of work in lettering, typography, fashion illustration, package design, interior design, and as art director in an advertising agency.

Commercial artist. California State Department of Employment. 1959. 5p. Single copy free

Duties, working conditions, pay, training, promotion, and employment prospects.

Commercial artist. Careers. 1964. 2p. 15c

Career summary for desk-top file. Duties, qualifications, and outlook.

Commercial artist. The Guidance Centre. 1963. 4p. 15c in Canada; 20c elsewhere

Definition, history and importance, working conditions, qualifications necessary for entry and success, preparation, employment and advancement, remuneration, advantages, disadvantages, and related occupations.

* Commercial artist. One section in *Occupational Outlook Handbook.*

Nature of work, where employed, training, other qualifications, advancement, employment outlook, earnings, and working conditions.

Commercial artists. Science Research Associates. 1960. 4p. 35c

Occupational brief describing nature of work, training, qualifications, opportunities, advantages, disadvantages, and future outlook.

**Employment outlook for commercial artists. Bureau of Labor Statistics, U.S. Department of Labor. Supt. of Documents. 1964. 4p. 5c

Reprint from the *Occupational Outlook Handbook.*

Fashion illustrator. Careers. 1960. 2p. 15c

Career summary for desk-top file. Duties, qualifications, and outlook.

A guide to art studies. National Association of Schools of Design. No date. 3p. Free

A statement concerning the objectives of art studies for different educational purposes.

**Illustrating commercial artist. Chronicle Guidance Publications. 1961. 4p. 35c

Occupational brief summarizing work performed, working conditions, remuneration, qualifications, training, opportunities, methods of entry, and ways of developing talent while in high school.

See also Artist; Industrial designer; Medical illustrator

COMPARISON SHOPPER 1-97.10

Comparison shopper. Robinson, H. Alan and Connors, Ralph. Personnel Services. 1963. 6p. 50c; 25c to students

Occupational abstract. Nature of work, qualifications, preparation, earnings, advantages, and disadvantages.

Comparison shopper. Careers. 1961. 2p. 15c

Career summary for desk-top file. Duties, qualifications, and outlook.

* Comparison shopper. Chronicle Guidance Publications. 1963. 4p. 35c

Occupational brief summarizing duties, personal qualifications, preparation, related occupations, advantages, disadvantages, and outlook.

COMPOSITOR 4-44.

Composing-room occupations. Michigan Employment Security Commission. 1954. 23p. 25c

Introduction, nature of work, distribution of jobs, employment prospects, employer specifications, earnings, working conditions, qualifications for entry, advancement, and transfer.

Compositor. Splaver, Sarah. Personnel Services. 1956. 6p. 50c; 25c to students

Occupational abstract. Nature of the work, qualifications, preparation, entrance and advancement, supply and demand, earnings, advantages, and disadvantages.

Compositor. Chronicle Guidance Publications. 1962. 4p. 35c

Occupational brief summarizing work performed, hours, earnings, requirements, training, where employed, and methods of entry.

Hand compositor. Chronicle Guidance Publications. 1962. 4p. 35c

Occupational brief containing definition, work performed, working conditions, personal requirements, determination of aptitudes and interests, training requirements, training opportunities, advantages and disadvantages, outlook, where employed, methods of entry, related jobs, and suggested activities.

COMPUTER OPERATOR. See Electronic computer operator; Programmer

COMPUTER PROGRAMMER. See Programmer

CONDUCTOR (RAILROAD) 0-92.

**Conductors. One section of *Occupational Outlook Handbook*.

Nature of work, training, other qualifications, advancement, employment outlook, earnings, and working conditions.

Railroad conductor. Careers. 1961. 2p. 15c

Career summary for desk-top file. Duties, qualifications, and outlook.

Railroad conductor. The Guidance Centre. 1960. 4p. 15c in Canada; 20c elsewhere

Nature of work, history and importance, working conditions, qualifications necessary for entry and success, preparation needed, employment and advancement, remuneration, advantages, disadvantages, how to get started, and related occupations.

CONFECTIONERY INDUSTRY WORKER 4, 6, 8-05.

Confectionery industry workers. Science Research Associates. 1960. 4p. 35c

Occupational brief describing types of jobs, requirements, methods of getting started, earnings, advantages, disadvantages, and future outlook.

Job descriptions for the confectionery industry. U.S. Employment Service. Supt. of Documents. 1939. 218p. $1.25

One of a series of Volume Job Descriptions. Describes jobs concerned with the manufacture of hard candies, soft or cream candies, and popcorn confections. Does not include jobs in the manufacture of confections made exclusively of chocolate, or the blanching and roasting of nuts. Illustrated.

CONSERVATION SPECIALIST 0-35.00 through 0-35.49

**Careers in conservation; opportunities in natural resources. Clepper, Henry E., ed. Ronald Press. 1963. 141p. $3.75

Information about opportunities and training in soil conservation, wildlife management, fisheries, forestry, range management, watershed management, and parks and recreational development. Each chapter has been prepared by a specialist.

Careers in wildlife conservation. Madson, John and Kozicky, Edward. Olin Mathieson Chemical Corporation. 1964. 6p. Free

Description of the work of the conservation officer.

Conservation officer. The Guidance Centre. 1963. 4p. 15c in Canada; 20c elsewhere

History and importance, nature of work, qualifications, preparation, advancement, outlook, remuneration, advantages, disadvantages, how to get started, and related occupations.

Conservationists and what they do. Harrison, C. W. Franklin Watts, Inc. 1963. 196p. $3.95

The book states the case for conservation and restoration of natural resources and describes what is being done by foresters, game reserve keepers, and private individuals to stem the losses. Also discussed are the need for conservationists, the many advantages of a career in this field, and the training and qualifications required. For grades 7 to 10.

**Find a career in conservation. Smith, Jean. Putnam's Sons. 1959. 160p. $2.95

Nature of work, qualifications, places of employment, training, how to get started, future outlook, advantages, and disadvantages. Also given are suggestions for the reader who wants to gain practical experience in conservation. Written for ages 11 to 15.

CONSERVATION SPECIALIST—*Continued*

Fish and wildlife. Colby, C. B. Coward-McCann, Inc. 1955. 48p. $2.52 net
Illustrated with photographs portraying the work of the Fish and Wildlife Service. Written for grades 4 to 8.

Gifford Pinchot: the man who saved the forests. White, Dale. Julian Messner, Inc. 1957. 192p. $3.25. Library binding $3.19 net
Biography of the man who instituted a conservation program and alerted the nation to the perils of waste of the forests.

**Nature's guardians: your career in conservation. Neal, Harry Edward. Julian Messner, Inc. 1963. 192p. $3.95. Library binding $3.64 net
Includes explanation of what is expected in each general branch of the U.S. Fish and Wildlife Service, U.S. Forest Service, and the Soil Conservation Service, as well as similar posts with state and commercial institutions. A wide variety of careers described. Bibliography.

* Unusual careers. Munzer, Martha. Alfred A. Knopf, Inc. 1962. 160p. $3
This book emphasizes the opportunities in discovery, conservation, development, and care of the country's natural resources. Includes information about the career of the solar scientist, meteorologist, oceanographer, ecologist, geologist, sanitary engineer, research chemist, and regional and city planner. Good reading lists. For younger readers.

CONSTRUCTION INDUSTRY WORKER
4, 6-84.; 5, 7-23. through 5, 7-33.

Architecture and building construction technology. National Council of Technical Schools. 1954. 2p. 5c
Description of work, working conditions, opportunities, advantages, and methods of entering.

Asbestos and insulating workers. Science Research Associates. 1961. 4p. 35c
Occupational brief describing nature of work, training, earnings, things to consider, and future outlook.

Building construction trades careers. Chronicle Guidance Publications. 1963. 4p. 35c
Occupational brief summarizing work performed in various jobs, working conditions, training, advantages, disadvantages, and methods of entry.

Building contractors. Science Research Associates. 1963. 4p. 35c
Occupational brief describing nature of work, requirements, getting started and advancing, earnings, advantages, disadvantages, and future outlook.

**Building trades. One chapter of *Occupational Outlook Handbook.*
Nature of work, where employed, training, other qualifications, advancement, employment outlook, earnings, and working conditions for each of the following: carpenter, painter and paperhanger, plumber and pipefitter, bricklayer, operating engineer, electrician, rodman, plasterer, roofer, cement mason, sheet-metal worker, asbestos and insulating worker, glazier, marble setter, stonemason, and elevator constructor.

Building your future: careers in construction. National Housing Center. 1963. 4p. Free
Brief statement of the growth of job opportunities in the building crafts.

The building trades. Chapter 6 in *Vocations for Boys*.
Includes brief descriptions of the carpenter, bricklayer, electrician, mason, plumber, painter, and plasterer.

* Careers in the building trades. Kasper, Sydney H. Henry Z. Walck, Inc. 1964. 126p. $3.50
Following a general discussion of the opportunities and outlook for the building trades, specific information is given concerning seventeen occupations.

**Careers in the construction field. Angel, Juvenal. World Trade Academy Press. 1960. 26p. $1.25
Includes information about each of several specialties within this field.

Colleges and universities offering programs and courses in residential building and home construction management. National Association of Home Builders. No date. 6p. Free
List of twenty-two schools.

Construction contracting as a career. Institute for Research. 1958. 24p. $1
History and importance of work, types of jobs, typical day's work, attractive and unattractive features, qualifications, education and training, earnings, and how to get started.

Construction helpers and laborers. Careers. 1961. 8p. 25c
Career brief describing duties, personal requirements, training, earnings, related careers, and outlook.

Construction industry opportunities through apprentice training. Associated General Contractors of America. 1962. 14p. Free
Information concerning opportunities in the construction trades, outlook, wage rates, and choosing the right job.

Construction laborers and hod carriers. One section of *Occupational Outlook Handbook*.
Nature of work, where employed, training and other qualifications, employment outlook, earnings, and working conditions.

Construction machinery operator. Chronicle Guidance Publications. 1963. 4p. 35c
Occupational brief summarizing work performed, earnings, and outlook.

Construction machinery operators. Science Research Associates. 1963. 4p. 35c
Occupational brief describing nature of work, qualifications, training, getting a job, salaries, advantages, disadvantages, and future outlook.

**Employment outlook for construction laborers and hod carriers. Bureau of Labor Statistics, U.S. Department of Labor. Supt. of Documents. 1964. 12p. 10c
Reprint from the *Occupational Outlook Handbook*.

**Employment outlook in the building trades. Bureau of Labor Statistics, U.S. Department of Labor. Supt. of Documents. 1964. 20p. 15c
Reprint from the *Occupational Outlook Handbook*.

CONSTRUCTION INDUSTRY WORKER—*Continued*

Home improvement contracting. B'nai B'rith Vocational Service. 1955. 8p. 35c

> Discussion of services offered, nature of work, preparation, starting one's own business, earnings, outlook, advantages, and disadvantages. Four illustrations.

I want to be a road builder. Greene, Carla. Childrens Press. 1958. 32p. $2

> Prepared for beginning readers with a reading level of upper first grade. Illustrated in color.

**Jobs in building construction trades. Science Research Associates. 1959. 32p. $1

> Describes the variety of job prospects and opportunities within this field. An accompanying wall chart is available for 35c.

Lathers. Careers. 1961. 8p. 25c

> Career brief describing duties, working conditions, training, earnings, and outlook. Additional readings.

Lathers. Science Research Associates. 1964. 4p. 35c

> Occupational brief describing work, qualifications, opportunities, and outlook.

Man against earth: the story of tunnels and tunnel builders. Murray, Don. Lippincott Company. 1961. 192p. $3.95

> Includes description of modern technology and the men who work on tunnels. Railroad and highway tunnels, those through mountains and under rivers, tunnels called mines, and tunnel cities in the Arctic are included.

Occupations in construction. Chapter 13 of *Planning Your Future.*

> Includes kinds of occupations in construction work, nature of work, duties, working conditions, qualifications, organizations available, advantages, and disadvantages.

Should you go into the construction business? Christensen, Allen D. New York Life Insurance Company. 1961. 12p. Free

> Description of work, personal qualifications, educational requirements, and financial rewards.

Starting and managing a small building business. Small Business Administration. Supt. of Documents. 1962. 102p. 35c

> This volume is intended to help prospective builders and those just starting decide whether they can wisely establish themselves in this business. It provides them with some basic management practices which will help them avoid the pitfalls and contribute to success.

Structural steel worker. California State Department of Employment. 1961. 3p. Single copy free

> Occupational guide summarizing duties, working conditions, employment prospects, earnings, and requirements for entry.

Structural-steel workers. Science Research Associates. 1961. 4p. 35c

> Occupational brief describing work, training, earnings, some things to consider, and outlook. Selected references.

COOK   2-26.

* Chef. Splaver, Sarah. Personnel Services. 1955. 6p. 50c; 25c to students
Occupational abstract. Nature of work, qualifications, preparation, earnings, entrance and advancement, supply and demand, opportunities for servicemen, advantages, and disadvantages.

**Chef—cook. Chronicle Guidance Publications. 1963. 4p. 35c
Occupational brief containing definition, work performed, working conditions, personal requirements, training requirements, training opportunities, advantages and disadvantages, outlook, methods of entry and suggested activities.

Cook, domestic. Careers. 1963. 2p. 15c
Career summary for desk-top file. Duties, qualifications, and outlook.

Cook or chef. The Guidance Centre. 1962. 4p. 15c in Canada; 20c elsewhere
History and importance, nature of work, qualifications, preparation, working conditions, earnings, advantages, disadvantages, how to get started and related occupations.

**Cooks and chefs. Careers. 1964. 8p. 25c
Career brief describing duties, working conditions, training, earnings, and outlook.

**Cooks and chefs. Science Research Associates. 1961. 4p. 35c
Occupational brief describing many types of cooks, requirements, training, earnings and hours, how to enter, advantages, disadvantages, and future outlook.

**Cooks and chefs. One section of *Occupational Outlook Handbook.*
Nature of work of cooks and chefs in restaurants, where employed, training, other qualifications, advancement, employment outlook, earnings, and working conditions.

Cooks and chefs in fine restaurants. California State Department of Employment. 1961. 5p. Single copy free
Occupational guide summarizing duties, working conditions, employment prospects, earnings, training, requirements for entry, and suggestions for locating a job.

Cooks and chefs in private households. California State Department of Employment. 1961. 3p. Single copy free
Summary of nature of work, employment outlook, working conditions, earnings, and methods of finding a job.

Dining car cooks. One section of *Occupational Outlook Handbook.*
Nature of work, training, other qualifications, advancement, employment outlook, earnings, and working conditions.

Professional cook and executive chef—careers. Institute for Research. 1962. 24p. $1
Types of eating places, attractive and unattractive features, types of positions, typical day's work, qualifications, earnings, training, chances for employment, and related jobs.

See also Caterer; Food technologist

COPPERSMITH 4-80.010; 4-80.080

Coppersmith. California State Department of Employment. 1962. 4p. Single copy free

Occupational guide summarizing duties, working conditions, employment prospects, earnings, and training.

COPY WRITER 0-06.94

**Advertising copy writer. Splaver, Sarah. Personnel Services. 1957. 6p. 50c; 25c to students

Occupational abstract containing summary, nature of work, qualifications, preparation, entrance and advancement, supply and demand, earnings, advantages, and disadvantages.

Advertising copy writer. The Guidance Centre. 1960. 4p. 15c in Canada; 20c elsewhere

Definitions, history and importance, nature of work, qualifications necessary for entry and success, preparation, employment and advancement remuneration, advantages, disadvantages, how to get started, and related occupations.

* Advertising copywriter. Chronicle Guidance Publications. 1962. 4p. 35c

Occupational brief summarizing work performed, qualifications, preparation, earnings, methods of entry, and outlook.

Careers as advertising copy writers. Institute for Research. 1961. 24p. $1

Describes activities of a copy writer in a small retail store, large department store, advertising agency, and mail order house. Includes qualifications, opportunities, training, salaries, attractive and unattractive features.

Copy writer. Careers. 1964. 2p. 15c

Career summary for desk-top file. Duties, qualifications, and outlook.

Copywriter. California State Department of Employment. 1960. 7p. Single copy free

Description of the work of writing original advertising material, duties, working conditions, pay, hours, finding the job, promotion, and employment outlook.

Lee Devins: copywriter. Mannix, Mary. Julian Messner, Inc. 1957. 164p. $2.95

Career fiction. Lee learns that it takes skill in human relations as well as in writing to succeed as an advertising copywriter.

See also Advertising agent

COUNSELOR 0-36.40

Careers in guidance and student personnel services. Angel, Juvenal L. World Trade Academy Press. 1960. 28p. $1.25

Includes information concerning the school counselor, college counselor, psychologist, school social worker, and placement counselor.

Careers in vocational service in Jewish agencies. B'nai B'rith Vocational Service. 1961. 12p. 35c

This career brief emphasizes the demand for qualified people. Training, opportunities, entry into the field, and occupational outlook are included, as well as a detailed description of demands and duties.

The counselor in a changing world. Wrenn, G. Gilbert. American Personnel and Guidance Association. 1962. 195p. $2.50
> Report of the Commission on Guidance in American Schools, containing discussion of major elements in the school counselor's task. Also contains personal and professional recommendations to the school counselor.

Counselors: school, rehabilitation, and vocational. One section of *Occupational Outlook Handbook.*
> Nature of work, where employed, training, other qualifications, advancement, employment outlook, earnings, and working conditions.

**Employment outlook for counselors: school, rehabilitation, and vocational. Bureau of Labor Statistics, U.S. Department of Labor. Supt. of Documents. 1964. 12p. 10c
> Reprint from the *Occupational Outlook Handbook,* 1963-64 edition.

**Employment outlook for teachers and school counselors. Bureau of Labor Statistics, U.S. Department of Labor. Supt. of Documents. 1962. 14p. 15c
> Reprint from the *Occupational Outlook Handbook,* 1961 edition.

Fellowships, scholarships, and assistantships for guidance and personnel graduate training. McDaniels, Carl. American Personnel and Guidance Association. 1962. 10p. 25c
> Reprint from the *Personnel and Guidance Journal,* reporting on the aid available to graduate students in the fields of guidance and personnel services including counseling and counseling psychology. Data from 236 colleges.

Guidance counselor. Chapman, Leland H. Research Publishing Company. 1954. 32p. $1
> Nature of work, qualifications, training, opportunities, and outlook.

Guidance workers certification requirements. Camp, Dolph. U.S. Office of Education. Supt. of Documents. 1963. 107p. 35c
> Requirements for guidance workers in secondary schools in each of forty-nine states. Certification requirements for school psychologists are also given for twenty-five states which require them.

High school counselor. Careers. 1960. 2p. 15c
> Career summary for desk-top file. Duties, qualifications, and outlook.

**Opportunities in guidance. Splaver, Sarah. Vocational Guidance Manuals. 1961. 138p. $1.45 paper
> Discussion of the counselor's work, requirements, places of employment, state requirements for certification in schools, financial rewards, advantages, and disadvantages. List of colleges offering degrees with majors in guidance.

Opportunities in guidance and personnel work. Michigan State University, College of Education. 1957. 12p. 20c
> Description of typical positions in guidance and personnel work in elementary and secondary school systems, colleges and universities, and government and private agencies.

Orientation to the job of a counselor. Roeber, Edward C. Science Research Associates. 1961. 57p. $1.50
> Prepared for the beginning counselor, this includes nature of the work and duties.

COUNSELOR—*Continued*

Preparation in school and college personnel work; programs and course offerings. U.S. Office of Education. Supt. of Documents. 1963. 196p. $1.25
> Courses offered in the 1963 summer session and the 1963-64 academic year are listed by states and institutions. This directory provides information about opportunities for academic preparation in school and college personnel work, at 308 colleges.

* School counselor. Chronicle Guidance Publications. 1961. 4p. 35c
> Occupational brief summarizing work performed, training, qualifications, earnings, opportunities, advantages, disadvantages, and outlook.

* School counselors. Science Research Associates. 1961. 4p. 35c
> Occupational brief describing nature of work, training, qualifications, opportunities, advantages, disadvantages, and future outlook.

School guidance counselor. Robinson, H. Alan and Connors, Ralph. Personnel Services. 1962. 6p. 50c; 25c to students
> Occupational abstract. Nature of work, future prospects, qualifications, preparation, entrance, earnings, number and distribution of workers, and related occupations.

Should you go into counseling? Wrenn, C. Gilbert. New York Life Insurance Company. 1960. 12p. Free
> Description of work, abilities needed, qualifications, and future outlook.

Status of preparation programs for guidance and student personnel workers. U.S. Office of Education. Supt. of Documents. 1959. 49p. 25c
> Survey of professional preparation in guidance, frequency of programs, type and level of degrees, curriculum for preparation, and supply and demand data.

> *See also* Personnel and employment manager; Vocational rehabilitation counselor

COURT REPORTER   1-37.18

* Career as a court reporter. Institute for Research. 1955. 16p. $1
> Description of work, where court reporters work, typical day's work, attractive and unattractive features, qualifications, training, earnings, chances for employment, related jobs, and opportunities for women.

Court reporter. California State Department of Employment. 1961. 4p. Single copy free
> Duties, working conditions, pay, hours, promotion, training, and employment outlook in California.

Court reporter. Careers. 1960. 8p. 25c
> Career brief describing duties, working conditions, training, qualifications, related careers, earnings, and outlook.

* Court reporter. Chronicle Guidance Publications. 1963. 4p. 35c
> Occupational brief describing work performed, where employed, working conditions, remuneration, personal qualifications, training, methods of entry, and employment outlook.

Court reporter. The Guidance Centre. 1962. 4p. 15c in Canada; 20c elsewhere
Nature of work, qualifications, preparation, advancement, outlook, remuneration, how to get started, and related occupations.

Short hand reporters. Science Research Associates. 1960. 4p. 35c
Occupational brief describing nature of work. requirements, preparation, getting started, earnings, advantages, disadvantages, and future outlook.

See also Stenographer

COWPUNCHER   3-17.20

Book of cowboys. Holling, C. Platt and Munk Company. 1962. 126p. $2.95
Prepared for grades three to five, this gives a picture of the work. In a series of connected stories, the author describes the life and work of cowboys in the West today.

Cowboy-artist: Charles M. Russell. Garst, Shannon. Julian Messner, Inc. 1960. 192p. $3.25. Library binding $3.19 net
Riding herd, living among Indians in the Wild West, Russell raced against time because a historical era was ending and his life's goal was to capture it on canvas and record it in bronze.

Gene Rhodes: cowboy. Day, B. F. Julian Messner, Inc. 1954. 192p. $3.25
Biography of a New Mexico cowboy.

I want to be a cowboy. Greene, Carla. Childrens Press. 1960. 32p. $2
Prepared for beginning readers with a reading level of upper first grade. Illustrated in color.

Stirrup high. Coburn, Walt. Julan Messner, Inc. 1957. 192p. $2.95
Career fiction. Story of a fourteen-year-old boy who spent a summer on a ranch in Montana as a working cowhand.

What does a cowboy do? Hyde, Wayne. Dodd, Mead and Company. 1963. 64p. $2.50; library binding $2.57 net
Simple text and pictures portray calf roping, roundups, stampedes, and rodeo. Written for grades 3 to 7.

CREDIT AND COLLECTION MANAGER   0-85.10

Career as a credit manager. Institute for Research. 1959. 24p. $1
Description of duties, qualifications, and opportunities.

Careers in collection. American Collectors Association. 1960. 12p. 15c
Description of work, employment opportunities, preparation, and qualifications.

Credit collectors. Science Research Associates. 1960. 4p. 35c
Occupational brief describing the role of the collector, related jobs, how and where to start, earnings, promotions, things to consider, and future outlook Selected references.

* Credit manager. Chronicle Guidance Publications. 1963. 4p. 35c
Occupational brief describing work performed, methods of entry, training, personal qualifications, and employment outlook.

CREDIT AND COLLECTION MANAGER—*Continued*

* Credit workers. Science Research Associates. 1960. 4p. 35c
     Occupational brief describing nature of work, qualifications, educational requirements, getting started, earnings, advantages, disadvantages, and outlook.

Starting and managing a small credit bureau and collection service. Small Business Administration. Supt. of Documents. 1959. 187p. 60c
     This booklet describes the advantages and disadvantages of entering this particular business, the risks involved, the personal characteristics that will contribute to success, and some management practices.

* Your future in the credit field. Neifeld, M. R. Richards Rosen Press. 1963. 160p. $2.95
     Description of credit as applied to all business, qualifications, and outlook.

CRIMINOLOGY EXPERT   0-66.30 through 0-66.39

* Criminological work as a career. Institute for Research. 1961. 24p. $1
     Qualifications, requirements, and rewards for police work, penal institution work, probation and parole work, psychological work, preventive work, and crime detection including work with the Federal Bureau of Investigation. Police service includes patrolman, traffic officer, license worker, record worker, and jail worker.

Criminologist. Careers. 1964. 2p. 15c
     Career summary for desk-top file. Duties, qualifications, and outlook.

Finding out about criminologists. Science Research Associates. 1963. 4p. 35c
     Junior occupational brief describing work and opportunities.

CUSTODIAN. *See* Building service worker

CUSTOMS INSPECTOR   0-95.01

Border guard; the story of the United States Customs Service. Whitehead, Don. McGraw-Hill Book Company. 1963. 274p. $5.95
     This account illustrates the ingenuity and courage of the agents who trap smugglers, thieves, saboteurs, and other lawbreakers.
Customs worker. Careers. 1963. 2p. 15c
     Career summary for desk-top file. Duties, qualifications, and outlook.

Finding out about customs inspectors. Science Research Associates. 1963. 4p. 35c
     Junior occupational brief containing brief facts about the job.

Ports of entry, U.S.A. Fribourg, Marjorie. Little, Brown and Company. 1962. 256p. $3.75
     Story of the episodes in the work of men and women in the U.S. Customs Bureau. Describes the nature of their work and the scope of our import and export trade.
     See also Immigration inspector

DAIRY FARMER   3-04.

Dairy farmer. Robinson, H. Alan. Personnel Services. 1958. 6p. 50c; 25c to students

Occupational abstract. Nature of work, future prospects, qualifications, preparation, entrance, advancement, number and distribution, earnings, advantages, and disadvantages.

Dairy farmer. Careers. 1959. 2p. 15c

Career summary for desk-top file. Duties, qualifications, and outlook.

* Dairy farmer. Chronicle Guidance Publications. 1962. 4p. 35c

Occupational brief summarizing work performed, qualifications, training, methods of entry, and outlook.

Dairy farmers. Science Research Associates. 1960. 4p. 35c

Occupational brief describing nature of work, training, qualifications, opportunities, advantages, disadvantages, and future outlook.

* Dairy farming as a career. Institute for Research. 1964. 24p. $1

Attractive and unattractive sides, personal qualifications, training, opportunities, and salaries. Example of a curriculum for a four-year course in dairy husbandry.

Dairy specialist. The Guidance Centre. 1962. 4p. 15c in Canada; 20c elsewhere

History and importance, nature of work, qualifications, working conditions, preparation, remuneration, outlook, related occupations, and how to get started.

I want to be a dairy farmer. Greene, Carla. Childrens Press. 1957. 32p. $2

Prepared for beginning readers with a reading level of upper first grade. Illustrated in color.

DAIRY PRODUCTS INDUSTRY WORKER   4, 6, 8-06.

**Careers in the dairy products industry. Institute for Research. 1958. 24p. $1

Types of positions, qualifications, opportunities, salaries, attractive and unattractive features. Describes work in a creamery plant, ice cream plant, cheese manufacturing plant, large dairy corporation, and a control laboratory of a milk plant and general dairy products plant. Typical day's work of a creamery plant superintendent and control laboratory worker.

The dairy industry. Judkins, H. F. Bellman Publishing Company. 1955. 20p. $1

History, job opportunities, qualifications, chance for advancement, advantages and disadvantages, professional and trade associations.

**Dairy industry jobs. Chronicle Guidance Publications. 1963. 4p. 35c

Occupational brief summarizing work performed, working conditions, training, determination of aptitudes and interests, opportunities, and outlook.

Dairy industry workers. Science Research Associates. 1961. 4p. 35c

Occupational brief describing nature of work, training, qualifications, opportunities, advantages, disadvantages, and future outlook.

DAIRY PRODUCTS INDUSTRY WORKER—*Continued*

Dairy plant operation. Chronicle Guidance Publications. 1963. 4p. 35c
Occupational brief summarizing work performed, working conditions, personal requirements, training, methods of entry, and outlook.

Dairy technologists. Science Research Associates. 1962. 4p. 35c
Occupational brief describing nature of work, requirements, training, getting started, earnings, advantages, disadvantages, and future outlook.

This is the dairy industry. Milk Industry Foundation. No date. 16p. Free
Includes a list of careers in the dairy industry.

Your career in dairy technology. College of Agriculture, Ohio State University. 1954. 3p. Single copies free
Qualifications and training needed. Lists twenty-four jobs in the dairy processing and manufacturing industries.

DANCER   0-45.

Ballet teacher. Wyndham, Lee. Julian Messner, Inc. 1956. 192p. $2.95
Career fiction. Story of a girl who met with an accident on the brink of stardom and became a teacher of ballet.

Dance, study, and work. Alumnae Advisory Center. 1957. 8p. 25c
Reprint from *Mademoiselle* describing work, training, and opportunities.

Dance to my measure. Wyndham, Lee. Julian Messner, Inc. 1958. 192p. $2.95
Career fiction. Experiences of a girl whose interests were in choreography.

Dance to the piper. De Mille, Agnes George. Atlantic-Little, Brown. 1952. 342p. $5.50
Autobiography of a choreographer who introduced a new concept of dance to the American stage.

Dancer. Splaver, Sarah. Personnel Services. 1956. 50c; 25c to students
Occupational abstract. Nature of work, qualifications, preparation, entrance and advancement, supply and demand, earnings, advantages, and disadvantages.

* Dancers. Careers. 1962. 8p. 25c
Career brief describing duties, working conditions, personal qualifications, training, places of employment, earnings, and outlook.

**Dancers. Science Research Associates. 1961. 4p. 35c
Occupational brief describing opportunities, qualifications, education and training, earnings, advantages, disadvantages, and future outlook.

**Dancers. One section of *Occupational Outlook Handbook*.
Nature of work, where employed, training, other qualifications, employment outlook, earnings, and working conditions.

Dancers of the ballet. Atkinson, Margaret and Hillman, May. Alfred A. Knopf, Inc. 1955. 174p. $3.75
Biographical data, including training, career highlights, and personality of forty ballet dancers of today.

Dancer's world. Moss, Allyn. Alumnae Advisory Center. 1957. 7p. 25c

Reprint from *Mademoiselle* describing the glamour, drawbacks, and opportunities. Illustrated.

The dancing heart. Rosenheim, Lucile G. Julian Messner, Inc. 1951. 183p. $2.95

Career fiction. Story of a ballet dancer who overcame obstacles in her career.

**Employment outlook in the performing arts. Bureau of Labor Statistics, U.S. Department of Labor. Supt. of Documents. 1964. 16p. 10c

Reprint from the *Occupational Outlook Handbook*.

Famous ballet dancers. McConnell, Jane. Thomas Y. Crowell Company. 1955. 176p. $2.75

Biographical sketches of fifteen ballet dancers, telling what started them on their careers, how they achieved success, and their unique contributions in ballet.

Gloria: ballet dancer. Malvern, Gladys. Julian Messner, Inc. 1946. 184p. $2.95

Career fiction. Shows the competition, advantages, and drawbacks of entrance into ballet dancing.

I want to be a ballet dancer. Greene, Carla. Childrens Press. 1959. 32p. $2

Prepared for beginning readers with a reading level of upper first grade. Illustrated in color.

* Opportunities in dancing. Denis, Paul. Vocational Guidance Manuals. 1957. 72p. $1.45 paper

Discussion of building a career in the popular fields of dancing, in ballet, in teaching of dancing, and in choreography. Advice to dancers is given by eight well-known dancers.

Prima ballerina. Malvern, Gladys. Julian Messner, Inc. 1951. 179p. $2.95

Career fiction. Story of what goes on behind the scenes with a ballet company on tour, as the heroine rises to stardom.

Student dancer. Woody, Regina. Houghton Mifflin Company. 1951. 276p. $3

Career fiction. Story of a dancer and choreographer, including a glimpse of a variety of careers in the field of dancing. Stresses practice and routine work.

To a young dancer. De Mille, Agnes. Atlantic-Little, Brown. 1962. 175p. $4.50

Description of the exaltation and training of the dancer, the discipline necessary, and the problems which a young choreographer must expect to meet.

Veronica at Sadler's Wells. Hill, Lorna. Henry Holt and Company. 1954. 241p. $2.75

Career fiction. Story built around ballet training. Shows the hard work that must be done before a pupil at the Sadler's Wells Ballet School of London can become part of the ballet company.

DANCER—*Continued*

Young dancer's career book. Woody, R. J. Dutton and Company. 1958. 185p. $3.50

Includes how to evaluate one's talent, education needed, job opportunities, salaries, and how to get a job. One section is devoted to dance therapy.

See also Motion picture industry worker; Television industry worker

DATA-PROCESSING EQUIPMENT SERVICEMAN 5-83.126

****Data-processing equipment servicemen. Brief section in *Occupational Outlook Handbook*.

Nature of work, where employed, and employment outlook.

* Data-processing machine servicemen. Science Research Associates. 1963. 4p. 35c

Occupational brief describing nature of work, training, qualifications, opportunities, and outlook. Selected references.

Finding out about data-processing machine servicemen. Science Research Associates. 1962. 4p. 35c

Junior occupational brief describing work and opportunities.

DATA-PROCESSING EQUIPMENT TECHNICIAN. *See* Electronics technician

DATA-PROCESSING MACHINE OPERATOR. *See* Electronic computer operator

DATA-PROCESSING PROGRAMMER. *See* Programmer

DENTAL ASSISTANT 1-32.10

* Career as a dental assistant. Institute for Research. 1957. 24p. $1

History and importance of work, duties, typical day's work, attractive and unattractive features, personal characteristics, training, earnings, chances for employment, and related positions.

Dear Jill. American Dental Assistants Association. 1963. 8p. Free

An informal letter to a prospective dental assistant, setting forth qualifications, duties, and the attractive features of this work.

Dental assistant. Brauer, John C. and Richardson, Richard E. McGraw-Hill Book Company. 1960. 593p. $8.50

Written for the beginning dental assistant, this book presents information and outlines skills a dental assistant should possess in the modern practice of dentistry.

Dental assistant. Miner, Leroy. Research Publishing Company. 1957. 32p. $1

Nature of work, history and importance, working conditions, salaries and other returns, personal qualifications, training, placement channels, and typical places of employment.

Dental assistant. Splaver, Sarah. Personnel Services. 1950. 50c; 25c to students
Occupational abstract. Nature of work, qualifications, preparation, entrance and advancement, supply and demand, earnings, advantages, and disadvantages.

* Dental assistant. Careers. 1959. 8p. 25c
Career brief describing duties, training, personal qualifications, earnings, how to enter, and outlook. Additional readings.

Dental assistant. Page 67 of *Health Careers Guidebook.*
Description of work, qualifications, and working conditions.

**Dental assistants. Science Research Associates. 1958. 4p. 35c
Occupational brief describing nature of work, training, qualifications, opportunities, advantages, disadvantages, and future outlook.

Dentist's assistant. The Guidance Centre. 1962. 4p. 15c in Canada; 20c elsewhere
History and development of the occupation, nature of work, qualifications, preparation, earnings, how to get started, and related occupations.

The dentist's diplomat. Ritter Company. 1962. 40p. Free
A manual for dental assistants which includes the regular duties, description of a typical day's work, and suggestions for the assistant who would succeed. Illustrated.

In the dentist's office—a guide for auxiliary dental personnel: hygienist, assistant, secretary. Morrison, G. Archanna. Lippincott Company. 1959. 280p. $7.50
Prepared as a reference for members of the dentist's staff, this book gives an idea of the nature of the work.

* Something new in white. Public Health Service, U.S. Department of Health, Education, and Welfare. 1961. 6p. Free
Illustrated brochure stating that today a fascinating career opportunity is opening up for the trained dental assistant. Describes nature of work, job satisfactions, advantages, training, and getting a job.

**The trained dental assistant—facts for counselors. Public Health Service, U.S. Department of Health, Education, and Welfare. Supt. of Documents. 1963. 8p. 15c
Background and importance of the dental assistant, nature of work, number of workers engaged, trends and outlooks, qualifications, licensing requirements, conditions of work, earnings, and nonmonetary rewards. Also included are lists of schools having two-year accredited programs, those having one-year programs, and those with special programs.

**You are invited to be a dental assistant. American Dental Assistants Association. 1963. 6p. Free
Description of duties, qualifications, earnings, training, and need.

DENTAL HYGIENIST   0-50.07

Accredited dental hygiene programs. American Dental Hygienists' Association. 1962. 5p. Mimeographed. Free
List of the forty-three schools approved or provisionally approved by the Council on Dental Education.

DENTAL HYGIENIST—*Continued*

Career as dental hygienist. B'nai B'rith Vocational Service. 1956. 8p. 35c
Discussion of nature of work, training, state licensing, qualifications, entry and advancement, salaries, advantages, and disadvantages.

* Career as a dental hygienist. Institute for Research. 1963. 22p. $1
Typical day's work of dental hygienist in the industrial clinic, school, dentist's office, state or county board of health, and on school staff for student health. Summary of state laws licensing dental hygienists. Number of licensed dental hygienists in each of the states licensing dental hygienists classified according to places of employment.

**Careers in dental hygiene. American Dental Hygienists' Association. 1963. 13p. 10c
Career opportunities, career features, cost of education, examination and licensure requirements, and trends.

Curriculum in dental hygiene. University of Michigan, Publications Distribution Service. 1952. 20p. Free
A recruiting bulletin giving nature of the work and requirements for admission to the curriculum in dental hygiene.

Dental hygiene aptitude testing program. American Dental Hygienists' Association. 1963. 19p. Free
Procedures to be followed by applicants for training in dental hygiene, testing centers, sample test items, and a description of the dental hygiene curriculum.

Dental hygienist. Splaver, Sarah. Personnel Services. 1960. 6p. 50c; 25c to students
Occupational abstract. Nature of work, qualifications, preparation, earnings, number and distribution, advantages, disadvantages, and employment prospects.

Dental hygienist. California State Department of Employment. 1962. 4p. Single copy free
Duties, working conditions, pay, hours, promotion, training, and employment prospects.

* Dental hygienist. Careers. 1963. 8p. 25c
Career brief describing duties, personal qualifications, educational requirements, advantages, disadvantages, and outlook. List of colleges offering approved programs.

The dental hygienist. Columbia University, Courses for Dental Hygienists. 1956. 8p. Free
Includes nature of work, educational preparation, professional education, scope of professional opportunities, and recommended preparatory courses to take in high school.

* Dental hygienist. Chronicle Guidance Publications. 1961. 4p. 35c
Occupational brief summarizing work performed, income, qualifications, training, opportunities, outlook, methods of entry, and suggested activities.

Dental hygienist. The Guidance Centre. 1958. 4p. 15c in Canada; 20c elsewhere
History and importance, nature of work, qualifications, working conditions, preparation, remuneration, outlook, related occupations, and how to get started.

Description of work, personal qualifications, getting started, and future outlook.

Dental hygienist. Pages 68-9 of *Health Careers Guidebook*.

**The dental hygienist, a professional career for women. Dental Hygienists Alumnae Association. 1959. 80p. $2

Discussion of analysis of positions in dental hygiene, characteristics and personal traits necessary, choosing a school for professional education, licensure and registration, and opportunities. Includes list of thirty-three schools offering training. Bibliography.

* Dental hygienists. Science Research Associates. 1959. 4p. 35c

Occupational brief describing nature of work, training, qualifications, opportunities, advantages, disadvantages, and future outlook.

Dental hygienists. Chapter 5 of *Vocations for Girls*.

Includes nature of work, qualifications, training, and opportunities.

**Dental hygienists. One section of *Occupational Outlook Handbook*.

Nature of work, where employed, training and other qualifications, employment outlook, earnings, and working conditions.

Educational qualifications of public health dental hygienists. American Public Health Association. 1956. 8p. Free

Description of duties, present status and future outlook, personal qualities, and educational qualifications.

**Employment outlook for dental hygienists. Bureau of Labor Statistics, U.S. Department of Labor. Supt. of Documents. 1964. 4p. 5c

Reprint from the *Occupational Outlook Handbook*.

**Smart young women are choosing dental hygiene as a career. Miller, Ray A. The author. 1953. 66p. 80c

Importance to society, duties, demand, salaries, opportunities for advancement, how to get started, qualifications, advantages, disadvantages, training, examination and license information, and future outlook.

DENTAL LABORATORY TECHNICIAN 0-50.06

Career as a dental laboratory technician. Institute for Research. 1962. 20p. $1

Description of work, history and development. attractive and unattractive features, qualifications, education and training outlook, and related jobs.

**Dental laboratory technician. Chronicle Guidance Publications. 1963. 4p. 35c

Occupational brief containing definition, history, work performed, working conditions, personal requirements, opportunities, methods of entry, related jobs, suggested activities, determination of aptitudes and interests, training requirements, training opportunities, advantages and disadvantages, and outlook.

Dental laboratory technician. Pages 69-70 of *Health Careers Guidebook*.

Description of work, personal qualifications, education and training, and outlook.

DENTAL HYGIENIST—*Continued*

Dental laboratory technicians. Michigan Employment Security Commission. 1961. 15p. 25c

Introduction, nature of work, location of jobs, working conditions, employment outlook, earnings, requirements for entry, disadvantages, and advantages.

**Dental laboratory technicians. Science Research Associates. 1958. 4p. 35c

Occupational brief describing nature of work, training, qualifications, opportunities, advantages, disadvantages, and future outlook.

**Dental laboratory technicians. One section of *Occupational Outlook Handbook.*

Nature of work, where employed, training, other qualifications, advancement, employment outlook, earnings, and working conditions.

Dental technician. Careers. 1961. 2p. 15c

Career summary for desk-top file. Duties, qualifications, and outlook.

Dental technician. The Guidance Centre. 1960. 4p. 15c in Canada; 20c elsewhere

History and importance, nature of work, qualifications, working conditions, preparation, remuneration, outlook, related occupations, and how to get started.

**Employment outlook for dental laboratory technicians. Bureau of Labor Statistics, U.S. Department of Labor. Supt. of Documents. 1964. 4p. 5c

Reprint from the *Occupational Outlook Handbook.*

* Hands that think—a word about careers in modern dental laboratory technology. National Association of Dental Laboratories. 1963. 6p. Free

Description of work, training, qualifications, earnings, benefits, and opportunities.

DENTIST   0-13.10

Accredited dental schools. American Dental Association, Council on Dental Education. 1963. 2p. Free

Revised list published annually.

**Admission requirements of American dental schools. American Association of Dental Schools. 1964. 128p. $1.50

Presents the admission requirements of forty-nine United States dental schools and seven dental schools in Canada for the 1964-1965 academic year. Useful to help in selecting a school of dentistry or in programming a preprofessional course of study to meet the requirements of the dental schools.

A career as a dentist. Changing Times. 1961. 3p. 15c

Reprint containing opportunities and outlook.

**Careers in dentistry. American Dental Association. 1962. 20p. 15c. Single copy free

Discussion of demand for dentists and dental care, income ranges, qualifications, admission requirements to dental schools, and ways of financing a dental education. List of forty-nine accredited dental schools.

* Careers in dentistry. B'nai B'rith Vocational Service. 1957. 16p. 35c

  Discussion of outlook, nature of work, qualifications, educational requirements, how to apply to a dental school, cost of dental education, licensure, earnings, opportunities for women, advantages, and disadvantages.

* Careers in the dental field. Angel, Juvenal. World Trade Academy Press. 1962. 30p. $1.25

  Includes information about the major fields of specialization, opportunities, education required, remuneration, advantages, disadvantages, and how to finance an education in the field of dentistry.

**The challenge of dentistry. American Association of Dental Schools. 1961. 12p. Free

  Developed specifically as a pamphlet to be given to students after the showing of the film of the same title. Information is given in question and answer form about costs, qualifications, and outlook.

Dental students' register. American Dental Association. 1963. 20p. Free to counselors and librarians

  In tabular form, information is given concerning the enrollment in each of the dental schools in each of the past eight years, admission data, and distribution of undergraduate students by states and other countries. Information is also summarized for schools of dental hygiene.

Dentist. Robinson, H. Alan and Connors, Ralph. Personnel Services. 1963. 6p. 50c; 25c to students

  Occupational abstract. Nature of work, qualifications, preparation, entrance, advancement, earnings, future prospects, advantages, disadvantages, and related occupations.

* Dentist. Careers. 1963. 8p. 25c

  Career brief describing duties, working conditions, training, personal qualifications, earnings, and outlook. List of accredited dental schools. Additional readings.

* Dentist. Chronicle Guidance Publications. 1963. 4p. 35c

  Occupational brief including definition, work performed, working conditions, hours, earnings, requirements, opportunities, advantages, disadvantages, outlook, methods of entry, licensing, and related jobs.

Dentist. The Guidance Centre. 1962. 4p. 15c in Canada; 20c elsewhere

  History and growth of the profession, nature of work, qualifications, training required, earnings, advantages, and disadvantages.

Dentist. Michigan Employment Security Commission. 1955. 22p. 25c

  Introduction, nature of work, location of jobs, prospects in profession, earnings, working conditions, organizations, qualifications for entry, and hiring channels.

Dentistry. Miner, Leroy. Bellman Publishing Company. 1955. 19p. $1

  Qualifications, opportunities, earnings, and license requirements. Includes description of special dental services such as oral surgery, orthodontia, and exodontia. Presents points to be considered in the selection of a dental school and list of approved schools.

DENTIST—*Continued*

Dentistry, a career of service, satisfaction, distinction. American Dental Association. 1961. 8p. Free
This folder points out the advantages of dentistry, the variety of careers, and the nature of the work.

**Dentistry and allied services. Pages 64-7 of *Heath Careers Guidebook.*
Personal qualifications, education, licensing, specialization, and future prospects.

**Dentistry as a career. Belleau, Wilfred. Park Publishing House. 1961. 27p. 75c
History and importance of the work, training, income, qualifications, licensure, entering the field, opportunities, advantages, and disadvantages. Includes a list of forty-seven dental schools.

Dentistry as a career. Institute for Research. 1959. 24p. $1
Qualifications, opportunities, training, typical course of study, duties, license requirements, trends, advantages, and disadvantages. List of thirty-eight dental schools. Some information about the dental technician, dental hygienist, and dental assistant.

Dentists. Science Research Associates. 1960. 4p. 35c
Occupational brief describing nature of work, training, qualifications, opportunities, advantages, disadvantages, and future outlook.

**Dentists. One section of *Occupational Outlook Handbook.*
Nature of work, where employed, training, other qualifications, advancement, employment outlook, earnings, and working conditions.

**Employment outlook for dentists. Bureau of Labor Statistics, U.S. Department of Labor. Supt. of Documents. 1964. 4p. 5c
Reprint from the *Occupational Outlook Handbook.*

Health manpower source book—physicians, dentists, and professional nurses. Public Health Service, U.S. Department of Health, Education, and Welfare. Publication Number 263, Section 9. Supt. of Documents. 1959. 79p. 50c
Data on the numbers, distribution, and characteristics of personnel. Includes information on training, licensure, age, sex, employment status, and income level.

How to decide on dentistry. American Association of Dental Schools. 1961. 8p. Free
Includes a discussion of costs of dental education and minimum requirements for entrance to a dental school.

I want to be a dentist. Greene, Carla. Childrens Press. 1960. 32p. $2
Prepared for beginning readers with a reading level of upper first grade. Illustrated in color.

**New dimensions in dentistry. American Association of Dental Schools. 1961. 8p. Free
Statement of qualifications and opportunities followed by a list of fifty-five dental schools.

Opportunities for dentists in the department of medicine and surgery. Veterans Administration, Department of Medicine and Surgery. 1962. 12p. Free
Description of work, training program, qualifications, and benefits.

* Opportunities in dentistry. Bushel, Arthur. Vocational Guidance Manuals. 1959. 96p. $1.45 paper
History of dentistry, needs, requirements, education, licensure, dental specialties, related fields, opportunities, and establishing a practice. List of accredited dental schools and a list of accredited dental hygiene schools.

Should you be a dentist? Blackerby, Philip E. New York Life Insurance Company. 1960. 12p. Free
Includes qualities one should possess, advantages, and prospects.

**So you want to be a dentist. Greenberg, Saul N. and Greenberg, Joan R. Harper and Row. 1963. 168p. $3.50; library binding $3.27 net
The numerous opportunities in the profession from research to clinical practice are described with the skills and training needed for each. The costs of training and the requirements for dental school are explained. List of forty-seven dental schools.

**Your future in dentistry. Cohen, Raymond. Richards Rosen Press. 1960. 155p. $2.95
The author opens his office to the reader and shares his day as a dentist. He also presents the educational background and aptitudes necessary for a career in dentistry. Several chapters describe work in specialized fields such as oral surgery, orthodontia, periodontia, and oral pathology.

Your future in dentistry. Cohen, Raymond. Popular Library, Inc. 1962. 155p. 50c
A paperback edition of the book described above.

DEPARTMENT STORE WORKER   0-72.; 0-74.; 0-75.; 1-75.; 1-80.; 1-97.

Adventure in store. Swift, Helen Miller. David McKay Company. 1955. 242p. $3.25
Career fiction. Joan refuses further education until her work in a store fashion career shows her its importance. For younger girls.

**Department store occupations. Michigan Employment Security Commission. 1963. 24p. 25c
Description of twenty-six jobs, employment outlook, earnings, advantages, and disadvantages.

Department-store public relations. Lubar, Rea. Alumnae Advisory Center. 1952. 5p. 25c
Reprint from *Mademoiselle* describing jobs and futures in department-store public relations.

Department store receiving, delivering, and related occupations. Careers. 1961. 8p. 25c
Career brief describing duties, working conditions, training, related careers, earnings, and outlook.

DEPARTMENT STORE WORKER—*Continued*

Department store salesclerk. Splaver, Sarah. Personnel Services. 1954. 6p. 50c; 25c to students
> Occupational abstract. Nature of work, qualifications, preparation, entrance and advancement, supply and demand, distribution, earnings, advantages and disadvantages.

Department store salespeople. Science Research Associates. 1961. 4p. 35c
> Occupational brief describing nature of work, requirements, training, getting started, earnings, advantages, disadvantages, and future outlook.

Department stores careers. Seventeen Magazine. 1962. 4p. 10c
> Brief descriptions of the comparison shopper, merchandise manager, fashion coordinator, and mail and phone order takers.

Executive careers for women in department stores. Institute for Research. 1959. 24p. $1
> Types of jobs in the merchandise division, promotion and advertising, service, and operation. Typical day's work, attractive and unattractive features, qualifications, training, chances for employment, securing a position, and related jobs.

Through Charley's door. Kimbrough, Emily. Harper and Row. 1952. 273p. $4.50
> An account of the experiences of a clerk in Marshall Field's store reveals details about department store work.

See also Buyer; Retail manager; Salesperson

DETECTIVE   2-66.11

* Careers in the FBI. Institute for Research. 1957. 24p. $1
> Describes work of the investigative staff. Information about careers in the FBI Technical Laboratory such as identification specialist and fingerprint classifier.

Careers in the United States Secret Services. Institute for Research. 1957. 24p. $1
> Describes the work of the Customs Service, Intelligence Division of the U.S. Coast Guard, Secret Service, Bureau of Internal Revenue, Alcohol Tax Unit, and Bureau of Narcotics. Includes attractive and unattractive features, training, how to secure a position, and allied occupations.

Crime scientists. McGrady, Mike. Lippincott Company. 1961. 160p. $3.25
> True accounts of how criminals have been tracked down in the laboratory with scientific equipment. Describes the roles played by detectives, laboratory technicians, photographers, chemical analysts, biologists, and fingerprint technicians. Illustrated.

Detective, city. Careers. 1961. 2p. 15c
> Career summary for desk-top file. Duties, qualifications, and outlook.

**Detectives. Science Research Associates. 1958. 4p. 35c
> Occupational brief describing nature of work, training, qualifications, opportunities, advantages, disadvantages, and future outlook.

F.B.I.: The "G-Men's" weapons and tactics for combatting crime. Colby, C. B. Coward McCann, Inc. 1954. 48p. Library binding $2.52 net
Photographs and brief text depict the work and training. Written for grades 4 to 8.

**Find a career in law enforcement. Whaley, Henry and MacPherson, Tom. Putnam's Sons. 1961. 160p. $2.95
A former chief of detectives of the Berkeley, California, police force describes careers in private and government law enforcement at various levels. Written for ages 11 to 15.

Men against crime. Floherty, John J. J. B. Lippincott Company. 1946. 255p. $4.50
Describes each branch of the U.S. Treasury Department and the work of the Secret Service in tracking down and prosecuting the smugglers, counterfeiters, income tax dodgers, narcotic traders, and saboteurs within our country.

Secret Service chief. Baughman, U. E. with Robinson, Leonard W. Popular Library. 1962. 192p. 60c. Paperback
The retired chief of the Secret Service describes the behind-the-scenes work of the crime-fighting agency.

The United States Secret Service. Bowen, Walter S. and Neal, Harry Edward. Popular Library. 1960. 238p. 50c. Paperback
Includes description of cases which illustrate the variety of work and the qualifications needed.

What does a secret service agent do? Hyde, Wayne. Dodd, Mead and Company. 1962. 64p. $2.50; library binding $2.57 net
Simple text and pictures portray varied activities. Written for grades 3 to 7.

See also FBI agent; Police officer

DIESEL-ENGINE OPERATOR 5-72.210

**Careers in Diesel engineering and as a Diesel engine technician. Institute for Research. 1958. 24p. $1
History and importance of work, types of positions, typical day's work, attractive and unattractive features, personal qualifications, education and training, earnings, chances for employment, getting started, and related positions.

Your future in the Diesel and gas engine industry. Diesel Engine Manufacturers Association. 1964. 6p. Free
Description of jobs and opportunities.

DIESEL MECHANIC 5-83.931

Diesel electric helper. The Guidance Centre. 1960. 4p. 15c in Canada; 20c elsewhere
History and importance, nature of work, qualifications, working conditions, preparation, remuneration, outlook, related occupations, and how to get started.

Diesel mechanic. Group, Vernard F. Personnel Services. 1961. 6p. 50c; 25c to students
Occupational abstract. Duties, abilities, preparation, entrance and advancement, earnings, distribution of workers, advantages, and disadvantages

DIESEL MECHANIC—*Continued*

Diesel mechanic. California State Department of Employment. 1963. 2p. Single copy free

Occupational guide summarizing duties, working conditions, employment prospects, earnings, preparation, and suggestions for locating a job.

Diesel mechanic. Careers. 1959. 2p. 15c

Career summary for desk-top file. Duties, qualifications, and outlook.

* Diesel mechanic. Chronicle Guidance Publications. 1960. 4p. 35c

Occupational brief summarizing work performed, working conditions, personal qualifications, ways of determining interest and ability, training, wages, licensing, related jobs, and employment outlook.

Diesel mechanic. The Guidance Centre. 1962. 4p. 15c in Canada; 20c elsewhere

Development of the work, qualifications, preparation, employment and advancement, earnings, advantages, disadvantages, and how to get started.

* Diesel mechanics. Science Research Associates. 1961. 4p. 35c

Occupational brief describing nature of work, requirements, training, methods of entering, earnings, advantages, disadvantages, and future outlook.

Diesel mechanics. One section of *Occupational Outlook Handbook*.

Nature of work, where employed, training, other qualifications, advancement, employment outlook, earnings, and working conditions.

* Diesel technician. Chronicle Guidance Publications. 1961. 4p. 35c

Occupational brief summarizing work performed, working conditions, qualifications, training, earnings, related jobs, and outlook.

Diesel technician. National Council of Technical Schools. 1953. 2p. 5c

Description of work, working conditions, opportunities, outlook, advantages, and methods of entering.

**Employment outlook for automobile mechanics and Diesel mechanics. Bureau of Labor Statistics, U.S. Department of Labor. Supt. of Documents. 1964. 12p. 10c

Reprint from the *Occupational Outlook Handbook*.

DIETITIAN   0-39.93

Academic requirements for active membership in the American Dietetic Association and entrance to approved dietetic internships. American Dietetic Association. 1958. 1p. Free

Includes required and recommended additional courses.

* Careers in dietetics. B'nai B'rith Vocational Service. 1957. 12p. 35c

Occupational brief describing duties, outlook, nature of work, education, personal qualifications, earnings, working conditions, advantages, and disadvantages.

Chart your course toward dietetics. American Dietetic Association. 1961. 8p. 5c; single copies free.

Brief information about work of a dietitian and a nutritionist, advantages, and training. Description of the three types of dietetic internships in hospitals, food administration, and food clinics.

A dietetic internship. American Dietetic Association. 1960. 16p. 5c. Single copies free

Answers to questions concerning advantages of internship, duties, requirements, and expenses. Contains brief description of work of a hospital intern, food administration intern, and food clinic intern.

A dietetic internship in the Veterans Administration. Veterans Administration, Department of Medicine and Surgery. 1961. 16p. Free

Description of work, training programs, qualifications, and benefits.

Dietetic internships approved by the American Dietetic Association. American Dietetic Association. 1962. 6p. Single copies free

List of institutions offering administrative, clinic, and hospital courses approved by the American Dietetic Association. Tabulated information includes name of institution, tuition fees, enrollment, and length of course.

**Dietetics as a profession. American Dietetic Association. 1962. 32p. 35c. Free to counselors and librarians.

Employment opportunities in twelve fields of activity, training, conditions of work, salaries, personal qualifications, and methods of securing positions. The association's most complete description of the profession and the career possibilities. Illustrated. Bibliography.

Dietitian. Robinson, H. Alan. Personnel Services. 1958. 6p. 50c; 25c to students

Occupational abstract. Nature of work, future prospects, qualifications, preparation, entrance and advancement, earnings, number and distribution of workers, advantages, disadvantages, and sources of further information.

* Dietitian. Careers. 1963. 8p. 25c

Career brief describing the work of the dietitian and nutritionist, training, personal qualifications, outlook, earnings, where employed, advantages, disadvantages, and opportunities.

Dietitian. Chronicle Guidance Publications. 1963. 4p. 35c

Occupational brief summarizing work performed, working conditions, hours, earnings, personal qualifications, training requirements and opportunities, and employment outlook.

Dietitian. The Guidance Centre. 1962. 4p. 15c in Canada; 20c elsewhere

History and importance, nature of work, qualifications, preparation, advancement, outlook, remuneration, advantages, disadvantages, how to get started, and related occupations.

Dietitian. Pages 70-1 of *Health Careers Guidebook.*

Description of work, opportunities, and prospects.

Dietitians. Science Research Associates. 1959. 4p. 35c

Occupational brief describing the dietitian at work, requirements, earnings, getting started, advantages, disadvantages, and future outlook.

**Dietitians. One section of *Occupational Outlook Handbook.*

Nature of work, where employed, training, other qualifications, advancement, employment outlook, earnings, and working conditions.

DIETITIAN—*Continued*

Dietitians in demand. American Dietetic Association. 1961. 8p. 5c. Single copies free

Illustrated leaflet showing dietitians at work in hospitals, food administration, community nutrition, and research.

**Employment outlook for home economists and dietitians. Bureau of Labor Statistics, U.S. Department of Labor. Supt. of Documents. 1964. 12p. 10c

Reprint from the *Occupational Outlook Handbook*.

* Hospital dietetics as a career. Institute for Research. 1957. 24p. $1

Duties, typical day's work, educational requirements, personal qualifications, opportunities, salaries, attractive and unattractive features, and qualifications for dietetic internship. Also list of hospitals offering courses approved by the American Dietetic Association.

Look ahead—the future is bright. American Dietetic Association. 1962. 12p. 5c. Single copy free

Illustrated booklet pointing out the advantages and opportunities.

Opportunities for the modern dietitian. Veterans Administration, Department of Medicine and Surgery. 1961. 4p. Free

Description of the opportunities and training.

Should you be a dietitian? Beeuwkes, Adelia M. New York Life Insurance Company. 1962. 12p. Free

Description of work, special advantages, training, salaries, and opportunities.

A stimulating career for you as a Veterans Administration dietitian. Veterans Administration, Department of Medicine and Surgery. 1962. 4p. Free

Description of work, training program, qualifications, and benefits.

**Your future as a dietitian. Richards Rosen Press. 1963. 160p. $2.95; library edition $2.79 net

Several dietitians have set down in separate chapters the requirements, talents, education, and interests which are necessary for their particular specialities. Includes list of schools which offer training.

See also Medical service worker; Nutritional chemist

DIPLOMATIC SERVICE WORKER. *See* Foreign service worker

DISPLAY MAN

0-43.30

Display man. California State Department of Employment. 1960. 4p. Single copy free

Duties, pay, hours, training, promotion, and employment outlook.

Display man. Careers. 1960. 2p. 15c

Career summary for desk-top file. Duties, qualifications, and outlook.

* Display man. Chronicle Guidance Publications. 1961. 4p. 35c
  Occupational brief summarizing work performed, working conditions, wages, personal qualifications, training, opportunities, methods of entry, related jobs, outlook, and suggested activities.

* Display workers. Science Research Associates. 1961. 4p. 35c
  Occupational brief describing nature of work, training, qualifications, opportunities, advantages, disadvantages, and future outlook.

Draftsman; poster and display artist. Pages 88-9 of *Health Careers Guidebook.*
  Brief statement of qualifications and opportunities.

Jobs in art. Science Research Associates. 1960. 32p. $1
  Describes the variety of work and opportunities for the display worker.

Sign writer. Chronicle Guidance Publications. 1962. 4p. 35c
  Occupational brief summarizing work performed, number employed, qualifications, preparation, conditions of work, earnings, methods of entering, and advancement.

Window trimmer. Splaver, Sarah. Personnel Services. 1962. 6p. 50c; 25c to students
  Occupational abstract. Nature of work, qualifications, preparation, entrance, advancement, earnings, advantages, and disadvantages. References for further reading.

Window trimmer. California State Department of Employment. 1958. 3p. Single copy free
  Duties, wages, hours, promotion, training, and employment outlook in California.

DIVER   5-89.011

Commercial diver. California State Department of Employment. 1962. 6p. Single copy free
  Description of work, duties, working conditions, hazards, special requirements, training, wages, promotion, and employment opportunities in southern California.

Deep down under. Floherty, John J. J. B. Lippincott Company. 1953. 160p. $3.75
  Stories of all kinds of diving from treasure hunting to building conveyor tubes in the East River. Illustrated.

Diver. The Guidance Centre. 1962. 4p. 15c in Canada; 20c elsewhere
  Definition, importance of work, physical and personal requirements, training, earnings, how to get started, advantages, and disadvantages.

* Divers. Science Research Associates. 1961. 4p. 35c
  Occupational brief describing work, qualifications, earnings, things to consider, and outlook.

Famous underwater adventurers. Wagner, Frederick. Dodd, Mead and Company. 1962. 159p. $3
  Biographical sketches of thirteen scientists, inventors, and explorers who ventured on conquests of the underwater world.

DIVER—*Continued*

Frogmen: training, equipment and operations of our Navy's underseas fighters. Colby, C. B. Coward-McCann, Inc. 1954. 48p. Library binding $2.52 net
Photographs and brief text reveal the work and training of one of the Navy's newest units. Written for grades 4 to 8.

The iron doctor; a story of deep-water diving. Hewes, Agnes D. Houghton Mifflin Company. 1940. 234p. $3.50
Career fiction. Tells how diving is done.

Salvage diver. Zachary, Ball. Holiday House. 1961. 220p. $2.95
Career fiction. Story of two boys who are hired by a salvage master to search for sunken ships off the Florida Keys.

Secret of the undersea bell. Douglas, John Scott. Dodd, Mead and Company. 1951. 242p. $3
Career fiction. Experiences as an abalone diver.

Skin diver. Masters, Kelly Ray. Holiday House. 1956. 251p. $2.95
Career fiction. Story of the thrills, dangers, and rewards of skin diving and underwater exploration on an underwater research expedition in the Bahamas. The author is widely known as Zachary Ball, his pen name.

Skin-diving adventures. Floherty, John J. and McGrady, Mike. Lippincott Company. 1962. 192p. $3.50
Accounts of the men and women who search beneath the sea for knowledge, sport, and excitement. Illustrated.

Ten miles high, two miles deep. Honour, Alan. McGraw-Hill Whittlesey House. 1957. 208p. $3
True story of the twin scientists, Auguste and Jean Piccard, whose ascents into the stratosphere and descent beneath the ocean have revealed new findings in the world of science.

Thirty fathoms deep. Ellsberg, Edward. Dodd, Mead and Company. 1930. 266p. $3
Adventurous tale which describes the work of divers. Other books written by Admiral Ellsberg, specialist in deep-sea diving, are: *On the Bottom, Ocean Gold* and *Treasure Below*.

Underwater adventure. Price, Willard D. John Day Company. 1954. 192p. $3.50
Career fiction. Story of two boys who sail to the South Seas with a scientific expedition, using the latest diving equipment.

What does a diver do? Hyde, Wayne. Dodd, Mead and Company. 1961. 62p. $2.50; library binding $2.57 net
Simple text and pictures portray the various tasks, training, and equipment. Written for grades 3 to 7.
See also Submarine officer

DOCTOR (MEDICAL). *See* Physician

DOMESTIC SERVICE WORKER 2-00. through 2-09.

The domestic service occupations. Chapter 16 in *Occupations and Careers*. Includes earnings, working conditions, and outlook.

* Domestic service occupations. Chronicle Guidance Publications. 1962. 4p. 35c
Occupational brief summarizing nature of work in various jobs, working conditions, earnings, advantages, disadvantages, and outlook.

Finding out about household workers. Science Research Associates. 1963. 4p. 35c
Junior occupational brief containing concise facts about the job.

**Household workers. Science Research Associates. 1958. 4p. 35c
Occupational brief describing nature of work, personal qualifications, opportunities, advantages, disadvantages, and future outlook.

Household workers. Chapter 32 of *Vocations for Girls*.
Desirable characteristics, changed conditions of work, and advantages.

* Job descriptions for domestic service and personal service occupations. U.S. Employment Service. Supt. of Documents. 1939. 261p. $1
One of a series of Volume Job Descriptions. Includes description of occupations concerned with personal services to individuals in and about their homes.

DRAFTSMAN 0-48.

Aeronautical draftsman. Careers. 1963. 2p. 15c
Career summary for desk-top file. Duties, qualifications, and outlook.

Can I be a draftsman? General Motors Corporation. 1961. 16p. Free
Discussion of requirements, opportunities, and earnings.

* Career as a draftsman. Institute for Research. 1957. 20p. $1
Description of work, typical day's duties, attractive and unattractive features, qualifications, training, typical vocational high school courses, salaries, outlook, and related jobs.

Careers in graphic reproductions. Society of Reproduction Engineers. 1963. 6p. Free
Brief statement of duties and required skills.

Drafting as a career. American Institute for Design and Drafting. 1963. 8p. Free
Basic qualifications, preparation, advantages, opportunities for advancement, earnings, and recommended high school subjects.

Drafting as a vocation. American Federation of Technical Engineers. 1963. 2p. Free
Description of work, where employed, qualifications, training, and prospects for employment.

Drafting technology. National Council of Technical Schools. 1958. 2p. 5c
Description of work, qualifications, opportunities, outlook, and critical need.

DRAFTSMAN—*Continued*

Draftsman. Robinson, H. Alan. Personnel Services. 1951. 6p. 50c; 25c to
students
Occupational abstract. Future prospects, nature of work, qualifications,
preparation, entrance and advancement, number and distribution of workers,
earnings, advantages, disadvantages, and sources of further information.

**Draftsman. Careers. 1963. 8p. 25c
Career brief describing duties, kinds of specialization, training, personal
qualifications, outlook, earnings, and measuring one's interest and ability.
Suggested readings.

**Draftsman. Chronicle Guidance Publications. 1962. 4p. 35c
Occupational brief summarizing work performed, types of jobs, working
conditions, qualifications, determination of aptitudes and interest, training,
opportunities, outlook, methods of entry, and related jobs.

Draftsman: architectural, electrical, marine, mechanical, structural. California State Department of Employment. 1962. 4p. Single copy free
Duties, working conditions, pay, finding the job, training, promotion, and
employment prospects.

Draftsmen. Science Research Associates. 1959. 4p. 35c
Occupational brief describing different types of work, how to learn, paths
toward advancement, salary possibilities, where draftsmen work, advantages,
disadvantages, and future prospects.

**Draftsmen. One section of *Occupational Outlook Handbook.*
Nature of work, where employed, training, other qualifications, employment
outlook, and earnings.

**Employment outlook for draftsmen. Bureau of Labor Statistics, U.S. De-
partment of Labor. Supt. of Documents. 1962. 3p. 5c
Reprint from the *Occupational Outlook Handbook,* 1961 edition.

**Employment outlook for technicians: engineering and science technicians,
draftsmen, and surveyors. Bureau of Labor Statistics, U.S. Department of
Labor. Supt. of Documents. 1964. 20p. 15c
Reprint from the *Occupational Outlook Handbook.*

Machine draftsman. The Guidance Centre. 1959. 4p. 15c in Canada; 20c
elsewhere
History and importance, duties, qualifications, preparation, remuneration,
working conditions, employment and advancement, how to get started, and
related occupations.

Mechanical draftsman. Stern, Benjamin. Research Publishing Company.
1957. 16p. $1.50
Advantages of this trade, nature of work, number employed, working conditions, personal qualifications and special skills required, how to secure a
job, and chances for promotion.

Mechanical draftsman. Careers. 1960. 2p. 15c
Career summary for desk-top file. Duties, qualifications, and outlook.

Mechanical draftsman. Florida State Employment Service. 1962. 8p. Single copy free to guidance personnel in Florida

Example of a series prepared to provide information about occupations which offer employment opportunities in a specific state. Describes nature of work, qualifications, opportunities, promotional possibilities, working conditions, wages, and how to find employment.

Mechanical draftsman. Chronicle Guidance Publications. 1962. 4p. 35c

Occupational brief summarizing work performed, working conditions, training, qualifications, where employed, earnings, related jobs, and outlook.

* Should you be a draftsman? Freling, Norman N. New York Life Insurance Company. 1962. 12p. Free

Description of work, abilities needed, training, opportunities, rewards, drawbacks, and future outlook.

DRESS DESIGNER. See Clothes designer

DRESSMAKER 4-25.030

Dressmaker. Careers. 1962. 2p. 15c

Career summary for desk-top file. Duties, qualifications, and outlook.

* Dressmaker. Chronicle Guidance Publications. 1961. 4p. 35c

Occupational brief summarizing work performed, where employed, wages, training, qualifications, advantages, disadvantages, related jobs, and outlook.

Dressmaking occupations. Michigan Employment Security Commission. 1962. 16p. 25c

Introduction, nature of work, location of jobs, employment outlook, working conditions, earnings, requirements for entry, disadvantages, and advantages.

See also Clothes designer

DRIVER 5-36.000 through 5-36.099; 7-35.000 through 7-37.999

**Drivers, motor vehicle. Careers. 1960. 11p. 25c

Career brief describing duties, training requirements, earnings, places of employment, unionization, and outlook for each of the following: truckdrivers, routemen, bus drivers, and taxi drivers.

Driving instructors. Science Research Associates. 1963. 4p. 35c

Occupational brief describing nature of work, training, qualifications, working conditions, earnings, and future outlook.

**Driving occupations. One section of Occupational Outlook Handbook.

Nature of work, qualifications, and employment outlook. Specific information for over-the-road truck driver, local truck driver, routeman, intercity bus driver, local transit bus driver, and taxi driver.

**Employment outlook in driving occupations. Bureau of Labor Statistics, U.S. Department of Labor. Supt. of Documents. 1964. 24p. 15c

Reprint from the Occupational Outlook Handbook.

DRIVER—*Continued*

Men at speed. Rudeen, Kenneth. Holt, Rinehart and Winston. 1961. 137p. $3.75

An account of automobile racing around the world which portrays the challenges the racing drivers must meet, the nature of their work, and the special qualities which they need.

See also Bus driver; Truck driver

DRUG AND COSMETIC INDUSTRY WORKER
4, 6, 8-53.00 through 4, 6, 8-53.149

**Careers in the drug and cosmetic fields. Angel, Juvenal. World Trade Academy Press. 1959. 26p. $1.25

Includes description of the various types of work, education required, opportunities, rewards, future outlook, advantages, and disadvantages.

Drug manufacturing workers. Science Research Associates. 1961. 4p. 35c

Occupational brief describing some jobs in the industry, requirements, methods of getting started, earnings, advantages, disadvantages, and future outlook.

Drugstore workers. Science Research Associates. 1958. 4p. 35c

Occupational brief describing nature of work, training, qualifications, opportunities, advantages, disadvantages, and future outlook.

DRY CLEANING INDUSTRY WORKER. *See* Laundry industry worker

ECONOMIST
0-36.11

Agricultural economists. One section of *Occupational Outlook Handbook*. Brief description of nature of work.

**Career as an economist. Institute for Research. 1962. 24p. $1

Definition of economist, fields of employment, typical day's work, attractive and unattractive features, qualifications, training, opportunities, and related fields.

Economics. Simmons College. 1963. 4p. Free

Discussion of opportunities in business, government, and education; training; compensation; and advantages.

Economist. Robinson, H. Alan. Personnel Services. 1962. 6p. 50c; 25c to students

Occupational abstract. Nature of work, future prospects, qualifications, preparation, entrance, advancement, earnings, number and distribution, advantages, disadvantages, and related occupations. References for further reading.

**Economist. Careers. 1962. 8p. 25c

Career brief describing history and importance of this work, duties, working conditions, earnings, personal qualifications, measuring one's interest and ability, training requirements, promotional prospects, employment outlook, and where employed. Additional references.

* Economist. Chronicle Guidance Publications. 1962. 4p. 35c
  Occupational brief summarizing work performed, preparation, requirements, earnings, methods of entering, and job opportunities.

**Economists. One section of *Occupational Outlook Handbook*.
  Nature of work, where employed, training, other qualifications, and employment outlook.

Educational requirements for employment of economists. Veterans Administration in cooperation with Bureau of Labor Statistics. VA Pamphlet Number 7-8.4. Supt. of Documents. 1955. 11p. 15c
  Provides information on the educational requirements for various fields of specialization, different types of employment, and different functions.

**Employment outlook for advertising, market research, and public relations workers. Bureau of Labor Statistics, U.S. Department of Labor. Supt. of Documents. 1964. 16p. 10c
  Reprint from the *Occupational Outlook Handbook*.

**Employment outlook for social scientists: anthropologists, economists, historians, political scientists, and sociologists. Bureau of Labor Statistics, U.S. Department of Labor. Supt. of Documents. 1964. 16p. 10c
  Reprint from the *Occupational Outlook Handbook*.

Finding out about economists. Science Research Associates. 1963. 4p. 35c
  Junior occupational brief containing brief facts about the job.

Market-research analyst. California State Department of Employment. 1961. 5p. Single copy free
  Job duties, working conditions, pay, hours, entrance requirements, promotion, training, and employment prospects in California.

**Market research workers. Science Research Associates. 1961. 4p. 35c
  Occupational brief describing nature of work, requirements, methods of getting started, earnings, advantages, disadvantages, and future outlook.

**Market research workers. One section of *Occupational Outlook Handbook*.
  Nature of work, where employed, training, other qualifications, employment outlook, earnings, and working conditions.

Marketing and marketing research. Manhattan College. 1963. 6p. Free
  Description of work, opportunities, rewards, and training. One of a series of thirty guidance bulletins.

Marketing research worker. Careers. 1961. 2p. 15c
  Career summary for desk-top file. Duties, qualifications, and outlook.

Opportunities in market research. Platten, John H. Vocational Guidance Manuals. 1951. 112p. $1.45 paper
  Includes consumer and opinion research. Description of market research, educational preparation, training while in other jobs, analysis of jobs in market research, organizing your job-hunting, the path to advancement, and types of research. List of colleges which offer courses in marketing and allied subjects.

ECONOMIST—*Continued*

* The profession of economist. American Economic Association. 1953. 4p. 15c

Occupational summary, major branches, functional activities, educational qualifications, related occupations, and sources of employment.

EDITOR AND EDITORIAL WRITER 0-06.40 through 0-06.59

Book editors. Science Research Associates. 1963. 4p. 35c

Occupational brief describing nature of work, training, qualifications, opportunities, and outlook. Two illustrations. Selected references.

Editor. Schuman, Sylvie. Personnel Services. 1956. 6p. 50c; 25c to students

Occupational abstract. Nature of work, qualifications, preparation, entrance and advancement, number and distribution of workers, earnings, advantages, disadvantages, and sources of further information.

* Editorial work as a career. Institute for Research. 1959. 24p. $1

Describes work of editorial staff in a book publishing house, encyclopedia staff, government position and on newspaper or magazine staff. Qualifications, opportunities, salaries, advantages and disadvantages.

* Editors, general. Careers. 1961. 7p. 25c

Career brief describing duties, personal qualifications, training, related careers, earnings, how to enter, and outlook.

**Find a career in journalism. Parsons, Tom. G. P. Putnam's Sons. 1959. 160p. $2.95

With news gathering as a focal point, the author introduces each principal member of a newspaper editorial staff, with the exploration of several supporting jobs. Written for ages 11 to 15.

Magazine editorial workers. Science Research Associates. 1961. 4p. 35c

Occupational brief describing nature of work, training, qualifications, opportunities, advantages, and future outlook.

Newspaper editor. Careers. 1960. 2p. 15c

Career summary for desk-top file. Duties, qualifications, and outlook.

Newspaper editor. The Guidance Centre. 1962. 4p. 15c in Canada; 20c elsewhere

History and importance, nature of work, qualifications, working conditions, preparation, remunertaion, advancement, outlook, related occupations, and how to get started.

* Newspaper editors and reporters. Science Research Associates. 1959. 4p. 35c

Occupational brief describing kinds of work, training, qualifications, opportunities, advantages, disadvantages, and future outlook.

**Weekly newspaper editor. Chronicle Guidance Publications. 1961. 4p. 35c

Occupational brief summarizing work performed, working conditions, earnings, personal qualifications, how to determine interests and ability, training, methods of entry, opportunities, and outlook.

Women in book publishing. Simmons College. 1963. 4p. Free
Includes description of kinds of work and qualifications.
See also Journalist; Reporter; Writer

ELECTRIC-BRIDGE-CRANE OPERATOR   5-73.010

Job description for electric-bridge-crane operator. U.S. Employment Service. Supt. of Documents. 1948. 5p. 5c
Occupational guide. Job summary, work performed, training, trainee-selection factors, related occupations, physical activities, working conditions, hazards, and employment variables.

ELECTRICAL LIGHT AND POWER UTILITY WORKER. *See* Heat, light, and power industry worker

ELECTRICAL ENGINEER   0-17.01

**Career as a communications engineer and as a technician, in telephone, telegraph, radio, and television work. Institute for Research. 1957. 24p. $1
History and types of positions, typical day's work, attractive and unattractive features, personal qualifications, education and training, earnings, chances for employment, getting started, and related occupations.

The cooperative course in electrical engineering. Massachusetts Institute of Technology. 1961. 8p. Free
Description of opportunity to combine industrial experience with academic work.

Electrical engineer. Robinson, H. Alan. Personnel Services. 1954. 6p. 50c; 25c to students
Occupational abstract. Nature of work, future prospects, opportunities for servicemen, qualifications, preparation, entrance and advancement, earnings, number and distribution of workers, advantages, and disadvantages.

Electrical engineer. Careers. 1960. 2p. 15c
Career summary for desk-top file. Duties, qualifications, and outlook.

* Electrical engineer. Chronicle Guidance Publications. 1963. 4p. 35c
Occupational brief summarizing work performed, employment conditions, salaries, personal qualifications, aptitudes and interests, educational requirements and opportunities, where employed, and outlook.

Electrical engineering. Monteith, A. C. and Moore, G. E. Chapter 12 of *Engineering Enrollment in the United States*.
Trends in enrollments and future requirements for specialists in this area.

Electrical engineering. Michigan College of Mining and Technology. 1963. 2p. Free
Example of a recruiting leaflet describing work, demand, qualifications, educational requirements, and employment opportunities.

ELECTRICAL ENGINEER—*Continued*

* Electrical engineering as a career. Institute for Research. 1962. 24p. $1
   Training, qualifications, compensation, opportunities, advantages, disadvantages, and a typical day's work. Describes work of the operating engineer, designing engineer, and the research engineer and gives the policy of several electrical corporations in selecting and training employees.

* Electrical engineers. Science Research Associates. 1959. 4p. 35c
   Occupational brief describing nature of work, qualifications, preparation, opportunities, advantages, disadvantages, and future outlook.

**Electrical engineers. One section of *Occupational Outlook Handbook*.
   Nature of work, where employed, employment outlook, and earnings.

Opportunities in electrical engineering. Shackleton, S. Paul. Vocational Guidance Manuals. 1953. 128p. $1.45 paper
   Includes description of the branches of electrical engineering: power, communications, electronics, and control systems. Describes qualifications, education and training, requirements for state licenses, getting started, requisites for advancement, opportunities for employment, and related fields. List of schools offering accredited undergraduate engineering curricula.

See also Atom energy industry worker; Engineer; Scientist

ELECTRICAL REPAIRMAN   4-97.420; 5-83.410 through 5-83.449

Electrical engineering technician. Careers. 1962. 2p. 15c
   Career summary for desk-top file. Duties, qualifications, and outlook.

Electrical-household-appliance serviceman. Careers. 1959. 7p. 25c
   Career brief describing duties, working conditions, personal qualifications, training, related careers, and outlook.

Electrical power technician. National Council of Technical Schools. 1954. 2p. 5c
   Description of work, working conditions, opportunities, advantages, outlook, and methods of entering.

* Electrical repairman. Chronicle Guidance Publications. 1963. 4p. 35c
   Occupational brief summarizing work performed, hours, earnings, training, methods of entry, and opportunities.

Electrical technician. Chronicle Guidance Publications. 1960. 4p. 35c
   Occupational brief summarizing work performed, working conditions, requirements, earnings, training, unionization, advantages, disadvantages, and outlook.

The electronic engineering technician. National Council of Technical Schools. 1959. 2p. 5c
   Preparation for the work and methods of entrance.

Electronic technician. The Guidance Centre. 1962. 4p. 15c in Canada; 20c elsewhere
   History and importance, nature of work, qualifications, working conditions, preparation, remuneration, outlook, related occupations, and how to get started.

**Employment outlook for maintenance electricians. Bureau of Labor Statistics, U.S. Department of Labor. Supt. of Documents. 1962. 4p. 5c
Reprint from the *Occupational Outlook Handbook*.

Industrial electronics technician. Careers. 1960. 2p. 15c
Career summary for desk-top file. Duties, qualifications, and outlook.

Maintenance electrician. Careers. 1964. 8p. 25c
Career brief describing duties, working conditions, qualifications, places of employment, earnings, and outlook.

**Maintenance electricians. One section of *Occupational Outlook Handbook*.
Nature of work, where employed, training, other qualifications, advancement, employment outlook, earnings, and working conditions.

ELECTRICIAN   4-97.

Careers in electrical wiring and electrical contracting. Institute for Research. 1957. 24p. $1
Qualifications, training, attractive and unattractive features, opportunities, and related jobs.

Construction electrician. Careers. 1963. 2p. 15c
Career summary for desk-top file. Duties, qualifications, and outlook.

Construction electrician. Chronicle Guidance Publications. 1962. 4p. 35c
Occupational brief summarizing work performed by the construction electrician in installing electrical equipment in new or remodeled buildings. Includes description of working conditions, training, where employed, related jobs, and outlook.

Electrician. Duggan, John. Research Publishing Company. 1957. 16p. $1.50
Advantages of this trade, nature of work, number employed, working conditions, qualifications and special skills required, how to secure a job, and chances for promotion.

Electrician. Group, Vernard F. Personnel Services. 1961. 6p. 50c; 25c to students
Occupational abstract. Nature of work, qualifications, preparation, earnings, number of workers, related occupations, advantages, disadvantages, and prospects.

Electrician. The Guidance Centre. 1959. 4p. 15c in Canada; 20c elsewhere
Development of the occupation, nature of work, conditions of work, qualifications, preparation, earnings, how to get started, and related jobs.

**Electricians. Michigan Employment Security Commission. 1957. 16p. 25c
Description of work of the construction and the maintenance electrician, working conditions, location of jobs, employment outlook, earnings, qualifications for entry, disadvantages, and advantages.

* Electricians and electrical workers. Science Research Associates. 1959. 4p. 35c
Occupational brief describing nature of work, preparation, qualifications, opportunities, advantages, disadvantages, and future outlook.

ELECTRICIAN—Continued

Electricians (construction). One section of Occupational Outlook Handbook.
> Nature of work, where employed, training, other qualifications, advancement, employment outlook, earnings, and working conditions.

**Employment outlook for construction electricians and elevator constructors. Bureau of Labor Statistics, U.S. Department of Labor. Supt. of Documents. 1962. 5p. 5c
> Reprint from the Occupational Outlook Handbook.

Opportunities in electrical trades. Hyman, Joseph S. Vocational Guidance Manuals. 1953. 96p. $1.45 paper
> Duties, salary, training, advancement possibilities, and hazards are given for each of seventy-five types of jobs. In addition to discussion of civilian occupations, there is complete information about career opportunities in the Air Force, Army, and Navy.

ELECTRONIC COMPUTER OPERATOR   1-25.17; 1-25.60

Careers in electronic data processing. Project on Information Processing. 1962. 16p. Free
> Description of the work and stories of some people who are working with computers.

Computer occupations. Michigan Employment Security Commission. 1960. 24p. 25c
> Introduction, nature of work, location of jobs, working conditions, earnings, employment outlook, requirements for entry, disadvantages, and advantages.

Computer operator. California State Department of Employment. 1961. 5p. Single copy free
> Job duties, working conditions, pay, hours, entrance requirements, promotion, training, and employment prospects in California.

Data-processing machine operators. Science Research Associates. 1963. 4p. 35c
> Occupational brief describing nature of work, training, qualifications, opportunities, and outlook. Selected references.

* Electronic computer operating personnel. Careers. 1963. 8p. 25c
> Career brief describing nature of work, duties of various operators, qualifications, training requirements, training opportunities, outlook, earnings, and advancement prospects.

**Electronic computer operating personnel. One section of Occupational Outlook Handbook.
> Nature of work, where employed, training, other qualifications, advancement, employment outlook, earnings, and working conditions.

**Employment outlook for electronic computer operating personnel and programmers. Bureau of Labor Statistics, U.S. Department of Labor. Supt. of Documents. 1964. 12p. 10c
> Reprint from the Occupational Outlook Handbook.

Finding out about data-processing machine operators. Science Research Associates. 1963. 4p. 35c

> Junior occupational brief describing work and opportunities.

A list of publications on careers in electronic data processing. Project on Information Processing. 1962. 2p. Free

> List of nineteen references.

**Occupations in electronic data-processing systems. U.S. Department of Labor. Supt. of Documents. 1959. 44p. 25c

> Presents information for thirteen basic jobs in the field of electronic data processing, including estimates of the worker trait requirements pertinent to each.

Systems analyst. Robinson, H. Alan and Connors, Ralph. Personnel Services. 1963. 6p. 50c; 25c to students

> Occupational abstract. Description of the work of devising computer system requirements and layout, and developing procedures to process data by means of data-processing equipment. Includes future prospects, qualifications, preparation, entrance, advancement, earnings, advantages, disadvantages, and related occupations.

Tape librarians. Science Research Associates. 1963. 4p. 35c

> Occupational brief describing nature of work, training, qualifications, opportunities, and outlook. Selected references.

**Your future in the electronic computer field. Bibby, Dause. Richards Rosen Press. 1962. 159p. $2.95

> The author discusses job opportunities in many aspects of the electronic computer field from manufacturing, programming, and sales.

See also Programmer

ELECTRONIC ENGINEER   0-17.01

Electronic engineering. California State Polytechnic College. 1962. 12p. Free

> Illustrated brochure describing the course of study and opportunities.

Should you be an electronic engineer? Kelly, Mervin J. New York Life Insurance Company. 1959. 12p. Free

> Nature of work, advantages, and qualifications.

**Your future in electronic engineering. Levine, Sol. Richards Rosen Press. 1961. 160p. $2.95

> Includes the development and future outlook of electronics, opportunities, earnings, recommended high school subjects, application for college, and case histories of successful electronic engineers. List of accredited colleges.

Your future in electronic engineering. Levine, Sol. Popular Library, Inc. 1961. 160p. 50c

> A paperback edition of the book described above.

See also Electrical engineer

ELECTRONICS INDUSTRY WORKER

4, 6, 8-98.000 through 4, 6, 8-98.399

Assemblers, electronics manufacturing. Careers. 1961. 8p. 25c

Career brief describing nature of work, training, working conditions, qualifications, earnings, and outlook.

Assemblers in the electronics industry. Science Research Associates. 1964. 4p. 35c

Occupational brief describing work, qualifications, training, opportunities, and outlook.

Career guidance in electronics. DeVry Technical Institute. 1962. 64p. Free

Photographs and reprints showing current activities in television, radio, automation, space and missile electronics, industrial controls, communications, computers, and radar.

**Careers and opportunities in electronics. Carroll, John. Dutton and Company. 1963. 191p. $3.95

This book includes the personal qualifications needed, educational requirements, salary potentials, and employment outlook for many classifications in this field.

* Careers in electronics. Angel, Juvenal L. World Trade Academy Press. 1962. 36p. $1.25

Career monograph containing nature of work, opportunities, training, and remuneration for each of the following: electronics engineer, electronics technician, television and broadcasting technician, television service and repairman, electronics manufacturing technician, and electronics researcher.

Careers in electronics. Institute for Research. 1958. 24p. $1

Kinds of employment, education required, personal qualifications, attractive and unattractive features, suggestions for getting started.

Careers resulting from rural electrification. Institute for Research. 1958. 24p. $1

Information concerning the promotion superintendent, manager of project, electrification adviser, chief engineer, wiring contractor, lineman, and book-keeper. Discussion of opportunities developed as a result of rural electrification such as irrigation and cold storage locker plants.

The challenge of electronics. Institute of Radio Engineers. 1962. 24p. Free

Attractively illustrated brochure containing discussion of the growth of professional employment, the applications of electronics, outlook, and preparation. Included is a list of colleges offering education in electrical engineering and electronics leading to an academic degree.

Electronics in space travel. DeVry Technical Institute. No date. 20p. Free

Ilustrated booklet describing opportunities, need for trained workers, and ways of getting started.

**Electronics manufacturing occupations. One chapter of *Occupational Outlook Handbook*.
> Nature of the industry, kinds of work, training, other qualifications, employment outlook, earnings, and working conditions.

Electronics pioneer: Lee De Forest. Levine, I. E. Julian Messner, Inc. 1964. 192p. $3.25; library edition $3.19 net
> Biography of the famous inventor.

Electronics—your chance to shape the future. Electronic Industries Association. 1962. 16p. 20c. Single copy free to counselors and librarians
> Description of contributions made to electronics progress by the principal scientific investigators, the opportunities offered, and three plans for preparing for careers in electronics. Charts show educational requirements and growth of employment.

**Employment outlook and changing occupational structure in electronics manufacturing. Bureau of Labor Statistics, U.S. Department of Labor. Supt. of Documents. 1963. 61p. 40c
> A detailed report of supply and demand of workers in this area, including projections of manpower requirements by 1970, classified by major product category.

**Employment outlook in electronics manufacturing occupations. Bureau of Labor Statistics, U.S. Department of Labor. Supt. of Documents. 1964. 16p. 10c
> Reprint from the *Occupational Outlook Handbook*.

**Find a career in electronics. West, Wallace. Putnam's Sons. 1959. 160p. $2.95
> Information about the varied opportunities in this fast-moving field, education necessary, and preparation. Written for ages 11 to 15.

There's adventure in electronics. May, Julian. Popular Mechanics Press. 1957. 170p. $2.95
> By relating experiences of a boy in this field, the author portrays the various kinds of work. Written for grades 7 to 10.

**Your career in electronics. Neal, Harry Edward. Julian Messner, Inc. 1963. 192p. $3.95. Library binding $3.64 net
> Challenging career opportunities in space exploration, industrial automation, medicine, and communications are described as part of the fascinating world of electronics.

ELECTRONIC TECHNICIAN 5-83.444

Data processing equipment technician. California State Department of Employment. 1961. 3p. Single copy free
> Job duties, working conditions, wages, hours, entrance requirements, line of promotion, training, and employment outlook.

Data-processing machine servicemen. Science Research Associates. 1963. 4p. 35c
> Occupational brief describing the work of maintaining and repairing electronic computers, conditions of work, preparation, earnings, and future outlook.

ELECTRONIC TECHNICIAN—*Continued*

Electronic technician. Morrison, Louis H. Research Publishing Company. 1958. 24p. $1
> Nature of work, history and importance, working conditions, salaries, qualifications, training, typical places of employment, and promotional opportunities.

Electronic technician. Robinson, H. Alan. Personnel Services. 1956. 6p. 50c; 25c to students
> Occupational abstract. Nature of work, future prospects, qualifications, preparation, entrance and advancement, earnings, number and distribution of workers, advantages, and disadvantages.

* Electronic technician. Chronicle Guidance Publications. 1963. 4p. 35c
> Occupational brief summarizing work performed, working conditions, qualifications, where employed, training, opportunities for advancement, and outlook. Selected references.

Electronic technicians. Science Research Associates. 1960. 4p. 35c
> Occupational brief describing work, qualifications, training, earnings, advantages, disadvantages, and outlook. Selected references.

Electronic technologist. The Guidance Centre. 1962. 4p. 15c in Canada; 20c elsewhere
> History and importance, nature of work, qualifications, working conditions, preparation, remuneration, outlook, related occupations, and how to get started.

See also Instrumentation technician; Programmer

ELECTROPLATER 4-74.010

Electroplaters. Science Research Associates. 1961. 4p. 35c
> Occupational brief describing work, qualifications, points to ponder, and future outlook. Selected references.

**Employment outlook for electroplaters. Bureau of Labor Statistics, U.S. Department of Labor. Supt. of Documents. 1964. 4p. 5c
> Reprint from the *Occupational Outlook Handbook*.

Electroplaters. Careers. 1961. 7p. 25c
> Career brief describing duties, working conditions, training, places of employment, earnings, unionization, and outlook.

**Electroplaters. One section of *Occupational Outlook Handbook*.
> Nature of work, where employed, training, other qualifications, advancement, employment outlook, earnings, and working conditions.

ELECTROTYPER 4-45.010

Electrotyper. Careers. 1962. 2p. 15c
> Career summary for desk-top file. Duties, qualifications, and outlook.

Electrotypers and stereotypers. One section of *Occupational Outlook Handbook*.
> Nature of work, training and other qualifications, employment outlook, earnings, and working conditions.

Stereotypers and electrotypers. Michigan Employment Security Commission. 1955. 15p. 25c
> Introduction, nature of work, location of jobs, employment prospects, earnings, working conditions, qualifications for entry, organizations in field, disadvantages, and advantages.

ELEMENTARY SCHOOL TEACHER   0-30.11

Career as a primary teacher. Institute for Research. 1959. 24p. $1
> Duties, qualifications, requirements, opportunities, and attractive and unattractive features.

Elementary school teacher. Splaver, Sarah. Personnel Services. 1958. 6p. 50c; 25c to students
> Nature of work, future prospects, qualifications, preparation, number and distribution of workers, advantages, and disadvantages.

Elementary school teaching as a career. Institute for Research. 1958. 24p. $1
> History of elementary teaching, duties, typical day's work, lines of promotion, qualifications, training, attractive and unattractive features, salaries, outlook, and related jobs.

Elementary teacher. Careers. 1959. 2p. 15c
> Career summary for desk-top file. Duties, qualifications, and outlook.

* Elementary teacher. Chronicle Guidance Publications. 1961. 4p. 35c
> Occupational brief summarizing work performed, personal requirements, opportunities, salaries, methods of entry, advantages, disadvantages, and outlook.

**Your future in elementary school teaching. Shockley, Robert. Richards Rosen Press. 1961. 159p. $2.95
> Describes the need for well-trained and inspiring teachers, qualifications, and outlook.

ELEVATOR CONSTRUCTOR   5-83.350 through 5-83.359

**Elevator constructors. One section of *Occupational Outlook Handbook*.
> Nature of work, where employed, training, other qualifications, employment outlook, earnings, and working conditions.

**Employment outlook for construction electricians and elevator constructors. Bureau of Labor Statistics, U.S. Department of Labor. Supt. of Documents. 1964. 16p. 10c
> Reprint from the *Occupational Outlook Handbook*.

ELEVATOR OPERATOR   2-95.

Elevator operator. Careers. 1960. 2p. 15c
> Career summary for desk-top file. Duties, qualifications, and outlook.

Finding out about elevator operators. Science Research Associates. 1963. 4p. 35c
> Junior occupational brief containing brief facts about the job.

EMBALMER. *See* Funeral director

EMPLOYMENT INTERVIEWER   0-68.71

Employment interviewer. Group, Vernard. Personnel Services. 1955. 6p. 50c; 25c to students

Occupational abstract. Nature of work, future prospects, qualifications, preparation, entrance, advancement, earnings, and related jobs.

Employment interviewer. Careers. 1963. 2p. 15c

Career summary for desk-top file. Duties, qualifications, and outlook.

* Employment interviewers. Science Research Associates. 1963. 4p. 35c

Occupational brief describing nature of work, training, qualifications, opportunities, and outlook.

See also Personnel and employment manager

ENGINEER   0-14. through 0-21.

**Accredited curricula leading to first degrees in engineering in the United States. Engineers' Council for Professional Development. 1963. 18p. 25c

Reprint from the Council's annual report, made available February each year. Contains list of 162 engineering schools, arranged alphabetically, with indications of the accredited curricula such as civil, electrical, mechanical, and sanitary. A second list names the schools offering accredited undergraduate curricula in each of the major branches of engineering.

After high school, what? Does science or engineering offer a career for you? Engineers' Council for Professional Development. No date. 5p. 3c

Brief summary of nature of work, qualifications, and training. Explains how engineering differs from a career in science.

Annual report. Engineers' Council for Professional Development. 1963. 70p. $1

Contains reports of committees on guidance and selection of engineering students, on professional training, on professional recognition, and on ethics Contains list of accredited undergraduate curricula in each of the major branches of engineering.

The bridge. Gardner, R. M. John Day Company. 1963. 160p. $3.50

A novel for boys about the career of bridge building and the history and lore of great bridges and their builders. Written for ages 12 to 15.

Building an engineering career. Williams, Clement C. and Farber, Erich A. McGraw-Hill Book Company. 1957. 275p. $4.95 cloth; $3.45 paper

This textbook on engineering contains information about the various branches of engineering, qualifications for success, preparation, suggestions on how to study engineering, earnings, historical background of engineering, and achievements in various phases of engineering.

The Bureau of Ships. U.S. Department of the Navy, Bureau of Ships. 1962. 20p. Free

Description of the work performed by naval architects, electronic and mechanical engineers in designing, building, and maintaining the ships of the United States Navy.

**Can I be a scientist or engineer? Let's find out. General Motors, Public Relations Staff. 1961. 24p. Free

Description of work in mathematics, chemistry, physics, and seven main branches of engineering, with typical jobs in each. Includes also opportunities and suggested high school preparation.

A career for you as a Veterans Administration hospital engineer officer. Veterans Administration, Department of Medicine and Surgery. 1963. 4p. Free

Description of work, training program, qualifications, and benefits.

**Careers and opportunities in engineering. Pollack, Philip. Dutton and Company. 1959. 140p. $3.75

This book answers the questions of what one can do in the numerous branches of this expanding profession and stresses as well the enthusiasms, traits, and qualifications one must bring to this field. List of accredited institutions. Illustrated.

* Careers for professional engineers. Angel, Juvenal L. World Trade Academy Press. 1959. 30p. $1.25

Career monograph describing fields of specialization, training, opportunities, remuneration, and where employment is found. One list contains names of colleges offering scholarships in engineering and another list presents names of foundations and private organizations.

Careers in engineering. Purdue University. 1962. 36p. 25c. Single copy free

Information about the different branches of engineering, the qualifications for a successful engineer, and his educational requirements. Special sections on courses to take in high school, difference between the engineer and technician, related careers, and the rewards of an engineer. Bibliography. Illustrated.

**Careers in engineering—requirements, opportunities. Stewart, Lowell O. Iowa State University Press. 2nd edition, 1956. 105p. $1.25

The work of the engineer is discussed under three headings: (1) the degree-granting departments such as agricultural, architectural, ceramic, chemical, civil, electrical, general, and mechanical engineering; (2) functional specialization such as design, development and experiment, construction and manufacturing, sales, commercial, application, service, and operations; (3) opportunities in specific industries such as automotive, radio, refrigeration and air conditioning, telephone, and aviation. Good discussions are included on who should study engineering and the factors determining success. Illustrated.

Definitions of occupational specialties in engineering. American Society of Mechanical Engineers. 1952. 112p. $3.50

This booklet was prepared for the Bureau of Naval Research to define and delineate the terms used for fields of specialization in nineteen branches of engineering. Clear exposition of duties, knowledge needed to work in the field, accessary techniques, and related activities are given for 266 specialties. Fairly technical information.

ENGINEER—*Continued*

Demand for engineers, 1962. Engineering Manpower Commission. 1962. 60p. $2

Summary data on the engineering employment in industry and government, recruiting goals, required employment additions, turnover information, starting salaries, and growth in total employment. All data are broken down by industrial activity, such as chemical, petroleum, electrical machinery, electronics, and research, and by three levels of government. Special sections are included on engineering technicians and physical scientists. Many tables and graphs.

**Do I have engineering aptitude? Johnson, A. Pemberton. Engineers' Council for Professional Development. Revised 1962. 8p. Fifty copies $2

A set of questions, answers, and interpretations of answers for use in self-analysis by young men and women considering careers in engineering. Distributed only in packages of fifty.

Education for engineers. Morgan, Arthur E. Antioch College. 1955. 44p. Free

Includes a discussion of the importance to the engineer of general education, fundamental courses, management courses, and cooperative work experience.

Education in engineering and science. Colorado School of Mines. 1963. 24p. Free

An example of an illustrated college bulletin containing an explanation of the work of the geological, geophysical, metallurgical, mining, petroleum, and petroleum refining engineer.

**Employment opportunities for women in professional engineering. Women's Bureau, U.S. Department of Labor. Bulletin Number 254. Supt. of Documents. 1954. 38p. 20c

A report upon current trends and attitudes relating to women's prospects for the engineering career. Includes the number of women classified as engineers in 1950 census, early indications of aptitude, high school preparation, engineering training, and fields of specialization for women.

**Employment outlook for engineers. Bureau of Labor Statistics, U.S. Department of Labor. Supt. of Documents. 1964. 20p. 15c

Reprint from the *Occupational Outlook Handbook*.

**Engineering. Robie, Edward. Bellman Publishing Company. 1959. 36p. $1

History and nature of work, qualifications, employment opportunities, education, and methods of entry. Contains a list of engineering schools that have one or more accredited curricula, broken down into six geographical areas, with indication of the curricula accredited in each school, and the engineering enrollment of each institution.

**Engineering. One chapter of *Occupational Outlook Handbook*.

Nature of work, where employed, training, qualifications, employment outlook, earnings, and sources of additional information. Specific information is also given for each of ten branches of engineering.

**Engineering, a career of opportunity. National Society of Professional Engineers. 1962. 15p. Free
Growth of the engineering profession, functions, fields of specialization, preparation, women in engineering, earnings, and future prospects. Bibliography.

**Engineering—a creative profession. Engineers' Council for Professional Development. 1962. 32p. 25c
Discussion of kind of work, functions, qualifications, training, and factors to be considered in choosing a college. Branches of engineering described are: aerospace, civil, mining and metallurgical, mechanical, electrical, chemical, and petroleum. Bibliography.

Engineering administration. Michigan College of Mining and Technology. 1963. 2p. Free
Example of a recruiting leaflet describing the need for the engineering graduate who has specialized in business subjects. Includes qualifications, educational requirements, earnings, and employment opportunities.

Engineering as a career, 2nd edition. Smith, Ralph J. McGraw-Hill Book Company. 1962. 394p. $5.95 cloth; $4.50 paper
Designed to acquaint the beginning college student with the functions and branches of engineering, problem-solving, use of mathematical tools, and adjustment to college. Exercises and assignments are given at the end of each chapter.

Engineering at NCE. Newark College of Engineering. 1961. 24p. Free
An example of an illustrated brochure, defining branches taught, and giving qualifications and high school credits required.

An engineering career for you in Soil Conservation Service. U.S. Dept. of Agriculture. Miscellaneous Publication Number 715. Supt. of Documents. 1960. 12p. 10c
An illustrated folder describing the types of work, opportunities, and employment facts such as work locations, training, benefits, and how to apply.

Engineering education on the cooperative plan. General Motors Institute. 1962. 24p. Free
Illustrated brochure describing the plan and the fields for which students prepare through this program.

Engineering enrollments and degrees. Tolliver, Wayne and Armsby, Henry. U.S. Office of Education. Supt. of Documents. 1963. 45p. 35c
Annual analytic report of data relating to both undergraduate and graduate enrollment and degrees, classified in twenty-five fields. Degree data are summarized at the bachelor's, master's, and doctor's level, with indication as to Engineers' Council for Professional Development accreditation, for each of the 245 colleges conferring engineering degrees.

Engineering enrollment in the United States. Barish, Norman N., ed. New York University Press. 1957. 226p. $4
Basic statistics on enrollment trends in engineering education in the United States and trends in future requirements for the different types of engineering specialists. One of the conclusions is that the current shortage of engineering talent is critical with respect to engineers having a high degree of mathematical and scientific orientation and unusual analytic and design creativity.

ENGINEER—*Continued*

The engineering field. Missouri School of Mines and Metallurgy. 1963. 32p. Free

Information concerning various branches of engineering. Includes mining, geological, ceramic, chemical, electrical, mechanical, civil, nuclear, metallurgical, and petroleum engineering. Illustrated.

Engineering is like this. Dodge, Bertha. Little, Brown and Company. 1963. 200p. $3.95

A look at great engineering feats demonstrates that they have been accomplished with human imagination and ingenuity. Written for ages 12 to 15.

Engineering science (engineering mechanics and engineering physics). Goland, Martin. Chapter 13 of *Engineering Enrollment in the United States.*

Trends in enrollments and future requirements for specialists in this area.

* Engineers. Chronicle Guidance Publications. 1962. 8p. 50c

Occupational brief summarizing work performed, qualifications, determination of aptitudes and interests, educational requirements, opportunities, outlook, and related positions.

Engineers. Chapter 26 of *Vocations for Girls.*

Includes a warning of the competition and other obstacles women have encountered.

**Engineers and what they do. Coy, Harold. Franklin Watts, Inc. 1961. 186p. $3.95

Description of the engineering specialties, places of employment, preparation, working conditions, earnings, and future outlook. Includes nuclear engineering and astronautics. Reading lists. For grades 7 to 11.

Engineers at Du Pont. E. I. du Pont de Nemours and Company. 1962. 20p. Free

Illustrated booklet describing work and opportunities in the various branches of engineering.

Engineers did it! Bradley, Duane. Lippincott Company. 1958. 128p. $2.95

Description of some of the world's most spectacular engineering feats and the problems and scientific principles involved.

Engineers, general. Careers. 1960. 10p. 25c

Career brief describing fields of specialization, working conditions, training, places of employment, earnings, licensing, outlook, and measuring one's interest and ability. Additional readings.

**Engineers unlimited: your career in engineering. Neal, Harry Edward. Julian Messner, Inc. 1960. 192p. $3.95. Library binding $3.64 net

Explanation of work in various divisions of engineering and subprofessional jobs which can lead to engineering, such as draftsman, engineering aide, and technician. Information on salaries, training, colleges, and scholarships.

**Find a career in engineering. Stambler, Irwin and Ashmead, Gordon. Putnam's Sons. 1962. 160p. $2.95

Discussion of the activities, preparation, requirements, supply and demand, and future outlook of work as an engineer. Discussions of various branches such as civil, aerospace, mechanical, chemical, mineral, electrical, materials, and nuclear. For younger boys, ages 11 to 15.

The Forest Service engineer: your gateway to the future. U.S. Department of Agriculture. Miscellaneous Publication 841. Supt of Documents. 1961. 32p. 30c

Illustrated brochure depicting the opportunities offered to graduate engineers in the Forest Service.

A guide to engineering education. Eller, Frank. Bureau of Publications. 1958. 56p. $1

Suggestions for identifying potential engineers, descriptions of the major branches in engineering, and typical programs of study for each branch.

How to get into science and engineering. Science Service. No date. 6p. 10c

This pamphlet lists over thirty careers, pointing out the diverse opportunities for well-trained scientists. Many activities are suggested which could help the high school student determine his interests and ability for a scientific or engineering career.

**Jobs in engineering. Science Research Associates. 1959. 32p. $1

Describes the variety of job prospects and opportunities, especially for the aeronautical, ceramic, chemical, civil, electrical, mechanical, metallurgical, and sanitary engineer. An accompanying wall chart is available for 35c.

Man against earth: the story of tunnels and tunnel builders. Murray, Don. Lippincott Company. 1961. 176p. $3.95

The story of man's efforts, from primitive days to the present, to dig his way through the earth. Illustrated

Manual for engineering career advisers. Engineers' Council for Professional Development. 1958. 20p. 20c

Prepared as an aid to engineers who are active as advisers on committees of local engineering clubs and societies. Good list of basic references.

Modern American engineers. Yost, Edna. J. B. Lippincott Company. 1958. 192p. $3.75

Biographical sketches of twelve outstanding engineers representing mechanical, civil, electrical, mining, automotive, research, radio, and television branches of the field. Information covers early education, professional training, and special achievements.

The most desirable personal characteristics. Engineers' Council for Professional Development. 1948. 25p. 25c

Results of a questionnaire in which respondents were asked to rate characteristics in the order of their importance.

ENGINEER—*Continued*

Opportunities for young engineers in the Bureau of Public Roads. U.S. Department of Commerce, Bureau of Public Roads. Supt. of Documents. 1962. 20p. 15c
Provides information for college students interested in highway or highway bridge engineering. Describes opportunities, training programs, and the various fields of activities.

Pre-engineering curricula for junior college students. Michigan College of Mining and Technology. 1963. 2p. Free
Suggestions for selection of courses in a junior college for later transfer to a senior engineering school.

Professional engineer. The Guidance Centre. 1960. 4p. 15c in Canada; 20c elsewhere
Definition, history and importance, nature of work, qualifications necessary for entry and success, preparation, employment and advancement, remuneration, advantages, disadvantages, how to get started, and related occupations. Further readings.

Professional income of engineers, 1962. Engineering Manpower Commission. 1962. 52p. $3
Fifth in a series of reports containing salary information for engineering graduates. Industrial categories, three levels of government, college teachers, technical institutes, and engineering societies are represented. Charts and tables show median, quartile, and decile figures for bachelor's, master's, and doctor's degrees. The sixth survey will be available in December, 1964.

Scientists and engineers in the Federal personnel system. U.S. Civil Service Commission. Supt. of Documents. 1964. 23p. 40c
Information on position classification, selection of staff, and the pay system. Also describes the methods of training for excellence, recognizing achievement, and encouraging a creative environment.

Scientists, engineers, and technicians in the 1960's; requirements and supply. National Science Foundation. Supt. of Documents. 1964. 68p. 45c
A report assessing the supply of personnel and estimating the demand, year by year, to 1970. Following the main text are extensive statistical and technical appendixes.

Should you be an engineer? Glennan T. Keith. New York Life Insurance Company. 1960. 12p. Free
Nature of work, opportunities, salaries, outlook, and considerations to be weighed.

**So you want to be an engineer. Nourse, Alan E. Harper and Row. 1962. 177p. $3.50
Description of the major divisions of engineering, qualifications, basic and specialized training, on-the-job training, opportunities, advancement, choice of a college, and future outlook. List of colleges of engineering.

So you want to be an engineer. Engineers' Council for Professional Development. 1938. 2p. 5c
Reprint presenting qualities necessary for success in engineering pursuits and other factors to be weighed seriously in considering engineering as a life's work,

The three-two plan of engineering education. Armsby, Henry H. U.S. Office of Education. Supt. of Documents. 1961. 32p. 20c

A directory of engineering colleges which conduct this type of program and of the nonengineering colleges cooperating with them in the program.

Trends in engineering education, 1949 to 1959. Armsby, Henry H. U.S. Office of Education. Supt. of Documents. 1961. 67p. 45c

Shows the trends which have been occurring in the number and types of engineering curriculums and degrees offered. Also identifies the curricular fields of engineering education which have enjoyed the most rapid growth. Includes a section on the development of the "three-two" program and the five-year undergraduate program.

Where do you go from here? Allis-Chalmers Manufacturing Company. 1962. 24p. Free

An example of a recruiting booklet describing a graduate training course for graduate engineers.

Why look into engineering? One section of *Three Why's.*

Points out the opportunities and the increasing need for engineers.

Women engineers? Surely! Why not? Society of Women Engineers. 1962. 1p. Free

A brief encouraging memorandum to women.

**Your career as an aerospace engineer. Institute of the Aerospace Sciences. No date. 24p. Free to counselors and librarians

Includes a description of the work of engineers and specialists in the air and space sciences. Discusses plans for college years to be made in high school. Illustrated.

Your career opportunities in engineering. Novak, Gail, ed. Rowman and Littlefield, Inc. 1962. 64p. 75c

One of the Visual Career Guides, about one half of the contents consists of photographs and charts. Includes description of the various kinds of work, training, earnings, and employment outlook. List of accredited schools.

See also

Acoustical engineer
Aeronautical engineer
Agricultural engineer
Automotive engineer
Ceramic engineer
Chemical engineer
City planner
Civil engineer
Electrical engineer
Electronics engineer
Highway engineer
Industrial engineer

Locomotive engineer
Marine engineer
Mechanical engineer
Metallurgist
Mining engineer
Operating engineer
Petroleum engineer
Radio operator
Refrigerating engineer
Safety engineer
Sanitary engineer
Scientist

ENTOMOLOGIST 0-35.30

Entomologist. Careers. 1964. 2p. 15c
Career summary for desk-top file. Duties, qualifications, and outlook.

**Opportunities in professional entomology. Entomological Society of America. 1963. 12p. 25c
Description of nature of work, its value, employment prospects, training, and areas of research specialization.

EVAPORATOR OPERATOR 4-51.755

Job description for evaporator operator II. U.S. Employment Service. Supt. of Documents. 1947. 5p. 5c
Occupational guide. Job summary, work performed, training, related occupations, physical activities, working conditions, hazards, and employment variables.

EXPLORER 0-35.; 0-36.01; 0-36.03; 0-36.93

* Exploring and archaeology as a career. Institute for Research. 1962. 24p. $1
Qualifications, training, opportunities, attractive and unattractive sides. Includes list of twenty-eight types of scientific work in exploratory work and seven positions of a nonscientific nature. List of American museums and types of expeditions.

Roald Amundsen: a saga of the Polar Seas. Kugelmass, J. Alvin. Julian Messner, Inc. 1955. 192p. $3.25. Library binding $3.19 net
Biography of an Arctic explorer, giving experiences in exploring both the North Pole and the South Pole and navigating the Northwest Passage by sailing across the top of the world from ocean to ocean.

EXPORTER AND IMPORTER 0-73.01

Career as an importer. Institute for Research. 1960. 23p. $1
Description of various jobs, a typical day's work, qualifications, training, earnings, attractive and unattractive features, and outlook.

Careers in foreign commerce. Institute for Research. 1962. 24p. $1
Description of work, history, places of employment, typical day's work, attractive and unattractive features, qualifications, training, opportunities, how to get started, and related jobs.

**Careers in the export, import, and foreign operations field. Angel, Juvenal L. World Trade Academy Press. 1961. 28p. Processed. $1.25
Description of work, training, remuneration, and opportunities for several specialties in this field. Includes export manager, traffic manager, air-traffic manager, foreign market analyst, purchasing agent, and consular-export documents assistant. Bibliography.

Export and import workers. Science Research Associates. 1961. 4p. 35c
Occupational brief describing jobs in foreign trade, requirements, earnings, methods of entering, advantages, disadvantages, and future outlook.

FACTORY WORKER   4, 6, 8-01. through 5, 7, 9-18.

**Assemblers. One section of *Occupational Outlook Handbook.*
Nature of work, where employed, employment outlook, earnings, and working conditions. Included with factory occupations not requiring specialized training.

**Employment outlook in factory occupations not requiring specialized training. Bureau of Labor Statistics, U.S. Department of Labor. Supt. of Documents. 1964. 16p. 10c
Reprint from the *Occupational Outlook Handbook.*

The heavy equipment business. Ely, Lloyd. Research Publishing Company. 1957. 40p. $2
Description of a tour through a typical, modern heavy equipment plant is followed by a discussion of employment opportunities and a list of manufacturing occupations.

The Sextant series for exploring your future in manufacturing (wage or shop jobs). American Liberty Press. 1960. 96p. $5; $4 paper
One page is devoted to each of ninety-five jobs, summarizing job duties, requirements for entering, promotional outlook, and pay and skill level.

Shoe manufacturing workers. Science Research Associates. 1961. 4p. 35c
Occupational brief describing nature of work, requirements, earnings, getting started, advantages, disadvantages, and future outlook.

**Some factory occupations not requiring specialized training. One chapter of *Occupational Outlook Handbook.*
Nature of work, employment outlook, and working conditions for each of the following: assembler, inspector, power truck operator, production painter, and stationary firemen (boiler).

FALLER   6-30.140

Job description for faller. U.S. Employment Service. Supt. of Documents. 1947. 6p. 5c
Occupational guide. Job summary, work performed, training, training-selection factors, related occupations, physical activities, working conditions, hazards, and employment variables.

FARM MANAGER   0-97.44; 3-37.

Farm manager. Careers. 1962. 2p. 15c
Career summary for desk-top file. Duties, qualifications, and outlook.

Principles of farm management. Efferson, J. N. McGraw-Hill Book Company. 1953. 425p. $7.50
Presents the basic principles of farm management and the use of these principles in operation of a farm business.

FARM SERVICE WORKER   3-11. through 3-49.

Farm mechanic. Chronicle Guidance Publications. 1962. 4p. 35c
Occupational brief summarizing work performed, where employed, working conditions, methods of entry, promotion, and outlook.

FARM SERVICE WORKER—*Continued*

Farm service jobs. One section of *Occupational Outlook Handbook.*
Brief description of work such as fruit spraying, well drilling, airplane dusting of crops, sheep shearing, fencing, and artificial breeding service.

FARMER   3-01. through 3-09.

Agricultural outlook chartbook. U.S. Department of Agriculture. Supt. of Documents. 1963. 96p. 60c
Charts and maps dealing with the economic situation and trends affecting agriculture.

**Employment outlook in agricultural occupations. Bureau of Labor Statistics, U.S. Department of Labor. Supt. of Documents. 1964. 24p. 15c
Reprint from the *Occupational Outlook Handbook.*

Farm helpers. Payton, Evelyn. Melmont Publishers. 1961. 32p. $2.50
Prepared to give younger readers in grades 1 to 4 an idea of work on a farm. Illustrated in color.

Farm laborers. Science Research Associates. 1960. 4p. 35c
Occupational brief describing nature of work, opportunities, earnings, advantages, disadvantages, and future outlook.

Farmers. Careers. 1960. 8p. 25c
Career brief describing nature of work, types of farms, personal qualifications, advantages, disadvantages, earnings, and outlook.

* General farmer. Chronicle Guidance Publications. 1961. 4p. 35c
Occupational brief summarizing work performed, working conditions, hours, earnings, personal qualifications, training requirements, opportunities, and employment outlook.

General farmer. The Guidance Centre. 1961. 4p. 15c in Canada; 20c elsewhere
Nature of work, qualifications, getting started, earnings, advantages, disadvantages, and related occupations.

I want to be a farmer. Greene, Carla. Childrens Press. 1959. 32p. $2
Prepared for beginning readers with a reading level of upper first grade. Illustrated in color.

Modern agriculture as a career. Institute for Research. 1964. 24p. $1
Description of the life of the farmer, qualifications, opportunities, salary, advantages and disadvantages. Also information concerning the teaching of agriculture.

Opportunities on specific types of farms. One section of *Occupational Outlook Handbook,* 1961 edition.
Discussion of the outlook on dairy, poultry, livestock, corn and wheat, cotton, tobacco, peanut, and crop specialty farms.

Should you be a farmer? Throckmorton, R. I. New York Life Insurance Company. 1960. 12p. Free
Includes qualities one should possess, cost of training, prospects, and advantages.

**Your opportunities in vocational agriculture. Phipps, Lloyd J. Interstate
Printers and Publishers. 1962. 175p. $3.25
  Describes opportunities in farming and nonfarm agricultural occupations for
  high school students.
  See also Agricultural specialist; Animal husbandman; Dairy farmer;
Poultry farmer; Truck farmer

FASHION DESIGNER. *See* Clothes designer

FBI AGENT   2-66.99

**Employment outlook for FBI agents. Bureau of Labor Statistics. U.S.
Department of Labor. Supt. of Documents. 1964. 4p. 5c
  Reprint from the *Occupational Outlook Handbook.*

The F.B.I. Reynolds, Quentin J. Random House, Inc. 1954. 180p. $1.95;
library binding $2.28 net
  Describes the beginnings and functions of the organization, the requirements
  for a career, the training of recruits into skilled investigators, and the methods
  used in solving several well-known cases. For younger readers.

* F.B.I. agent. Chronicle Guidance Publications. 1961. 4p. 35c
  Occupational brief summarizing work performed, personal qualifications,
  training, earnings, where employed, methods of entry, and outlook.

**FBI agents. One section of *Occupational Outlook Handbook.*
  Nature of work, where employed, training, other qualifications, advancement,
  employment outlook, earnings, and working conditions.

* FBI special agents. Careers. 1961. 7p. 25c
  Occupational brief describing nature of work, training, qualifications, opportunities, advantages, disadvantages, and future outlook.

FBI special agents. Careers. 1961. 7p. 25c
  Career brief describing duties, working conditions, training, personal requirements, earnings, outlook, and ways of measuring one's interest and ability.

Facts about a career in the FBI. Federal Bureau of Investigation. 1962.
8p. Free
  Statement of general qualifications, types of jobs, advantages, and how to
  become an FBI agent. Positions include special agent, translator, fingerprint
  technician, stenographer, typist, clerk, and various laboratory positions.

How to become a fingerprint technician with the FBI. Federal Bureau
of Investigation. 1962. 4p. Free
  Brief statement of job qualifications, salary, and advancement.

Information concerning the position of special agent in the Federal Bureau
of Investigation. The Bureau. 1962. 1p. Free
  Brief statement of qualifications.

Jobs for women in the FBI. Federal Bureau of Investigation. 1961. 1p.
Free
  Qualifications for technical and clerical work, including laboratory aides,
  translators, stenographers, typists, and clerks.

FBI AGENT—*Continued*

**Our FBI, an inside story. Floherty, John J. J. B. Lippincott Company. 1951. 192p. $3.75

A book about the organization and activities of the Federal Bureau of Investigation. Includes history, training, and special work of the FBI men. Numerous reports of investigations made by special agents are included to show how they operate and what is required for the job. Illustrated.

Special agent FBI. Robinson, H. Alan and Connors, Ralph. Personnel Services. 1961. 6p. 50c; 25c to students

Occupational abstract. Nature of work, future prospects, qualifications, preparation, entrance, earnings, advantages, disadvantages, and related occupations. References for further reading.

The story of the FBI. By the Editors of *Look.* E. P. Dutton and Company. 1954. 286p. $4.95

With an introduction by J. Edgar Hoover, this book describes how the FBI functions. Describes the training and the importance of the agency in combatting crime. Fully illustrated.

Youth and the F.B.I. Floherty, John J. and McGrady, Mike. Lippincott Company. 1960. 160p. $3.50

A study of law enforcement and how the FBI deals with the problems of youth.

See also Detective; Police officer

FILE CLERK. *See* Clerical worker

FINANCIAL INSTITUTIONS INDUSTRY WORKER
0-98.08; 1-06; 1-65.03

Careers in the consumer finance field. B'nai B'rith Vocational Service. 1953. 8p. 35c

Discussion of outlook, size of industry, kinds of jobs, qualifications, training, advancement, earnings, advantages, and disadvantages.

Careers in the savings and loan business. Institute for Research. 1962. 23p. $1

Description of duties, typical day's work, qualifications, training, earnings, attractive and unattractive features, opportunities, and getting started.

Careers in trust departments of banks and trust companies. Institute for Research. 1962. 23p. $1

Description of the various positions, a typical day's work in a small and large trust company, qualifications, training, earnings, attractive and unattractive features, and getting started.

Employment opportunities for college graduates for the position of financial analyst. U.S. Securities and Exchange Commission. 1962. 2p. Free

Information about the location of positions, duties to be performed, salaries, career opportunities, fringe benefits, training, recruitment policy, and civil service examination.

Finance as a career. Boston University. 1962. 25p. Free

Recruiting booklet describing opportunities, qualifications, advantages, disadvantages, and preparation. Brief discussion of work in a loan department, credit department, foreign department, trust department, investment department, new business department, bank advertising and public relations, investment banking, and stock brokerage.

Jobs in the money. Small, Verna. Alumnae Advisory Center. 1953. 3p. 25c

Reprint from *Mademoiselle* describing jobs and futures in accounting, banking investment, coinage, and credit.

The new look in banking: careers for young women in finance. Paradis, Adrian. David McKay Company. 1961. 203p. $3.50

Description of enticing and varied career opportunities open to women in finance. Suggested readings.

Occupations in finance, insurance, and real estate. Chapter 17 of *Planning Your Future.*

Includes a description of the work of the owner of an insurance agency. Five illustrations.

**Opportunities in the securities business. Shulsky, Sam. Vocational Guidance Manuals. 1963. 128p. $1.45 paper

Discussions of finance yesterday and today, requirements for entering the field, and how to get started. Description of brokerage, banking, investment banking, investment counseling, and related fields. Lists accredited colleges and universities giving degrees in business administration.

Opportunity ahead. Beneficial Management Corporation. No date. 16p. Free

Recruiting booklet describing opportunities in the field of finance. Includes a career quiz for men and one for women.

The small-loan business—saint or sinner? Beneficial Management Corporation. 1954. 8p. Free

Includes a description of the duties and outlook.

Toward careers in finance. Investment Bankers Association of America. 1945. 24p. Free

Description of work, qualifications, outlook, and training.

Your future: careers in consumer finance. National Consumer Finance Associates. 1963. 6p. Free

Nature of work, advantages, potential rewards, qualifications, and training.

See also Bank worker; Securities salesman

FIRE FIGHTER   2-63.

The big fire. Olds, Elizabeth. Houghton Mifflin Company. 1945. 321p. $2.90

Career fiction. Gives a picture of work in a fire department. For sixth or seventh grade boys.

FIRE FIGHTER—*Continued*

Careers in fire protection engineering. Society of Fire Protection Engineers. 1961. 6p. Free
> Description of duties, opportunities, and training.

**Employment outlook for policemen and firemen. Bureau of Labor Statistics, U.S. Department of Labor. Supt. of Documents. 1964. 12p. 10c
> Reprint from the *Occupational Outlook Handbook*.

Fire fighter. The Guidance Centre. 1963. 4p. 15c in Canada; 20c elsewhere
> Nature of work, qualifications, preparation, working conditions, how to get started, earnings, advantages, and disadvantages.

Fire fighter. International Association of Fire Fighters. 1962. 12p. Free
> Duties, requirements, training, and need for skilled technicians.

Fire protection engineers. Science Research Associates. 1963. 4p. 35c
> Occupational brief describing nature of work, requirements, training, places of employment, earnings, and future outlook.

Fireman, Splaver, Sarah. Personnel Services. 1958. 6p. 50c; 25c to students
> Occupational abstract. Duties, qualifications, training, entrance, advancement, earnings, number of workers, advantages, and disadvantages.

Fireman. Careers. 1964. 2p. 15c
> Career summary for desk-top file. Duties, qualifications, and outlook.

* Fireman. Chronicle Guidance Publications. 1964. 4p. 35c
> Occupational brief summarizing work performed, working conditions, hours, earnings, personal qualifications, training requirements and opportunities, and employment outlook.

**Fireman and fire prevention as a career. Institute for Research. 1963. 23p. $1
> Development of fire prevention, opportunities, related jobs, kinds of work, a typical day's work, qualifications, salaries, and attractive and unattractive features. Includes forest fire control and employment by industrial plants and state governments.

* Firemen. Science Research Associates. 1961. 4p. 35c
> Occupational brief describing nature of work, training, qualifications, opportunities, advantages, disadvantages, and future outlook.

**Firemen. One section of *Occupational Outlook Handbook*.
> Nature of work, where employed, training, other qualifications, advancement, employment outlook, earnings, and working conditions.

Forest fire! Judge, Frances. Alfred A. Knopf, Inc. 1962. 152p. $3.29
> History of the fighting of forest fires in America.

Hank Winton, smokechaser. Atwater, Montgomery M. Random House, Inc. 1947. 210p. $2.95. Library binding $3.39 net
> Career fiction. Describes life in the U.S. Forest Service. A sequel, *Smoke Patrol*, describes fighting forest fires by parachute. For younger boys.

I want to be a fireman. Greene, Carla. Childrens Press. 1959. 32p. $2
> Prepared for beginning readers with a reading level of upper first grade.
> Illustrated in color.

Municipal fire fighters. Michigan Employment Security Commission. 1954.
17p. 25c
> Introduction, nature of work, location of jobs, employment prospects, working
> conditions, organizations, earnings, qualification for entry, advantages, and dis-
> advantages.

Smoke eaters; trucks, training and tools of the nation's firemen. Colby,
C. B. Coward-McCann, Inc. 1954. 48p. $2.50
> Photographs and brief text describe the work of firemen.

Smoke patrol. Atwater, Montgomery M. Random House, Inc. 1949. 214p.
$2.95
> Career fiction. Sequel to *Hank Winton, Smokechaser.*

A valiant career: make your career in the fire service. International Association of Fire Chiefs. 1963. 4p. Free
> Description of requirements and rewards.
> *See also* Forest ranger; Police officer

FIREMAN (BOILER)   7-70.040

Job description for stationary boiler fireman. U.S. Employment Service.
Supt. of Documents. 1948. 4p. 5c
> Occupational guide. Job summary, work performed, training, trainee-selection
> factors, related occupations, physical activities, working conditions, hazards, and
> employment variables.

**Stationary fireman (boiler). One section of *Occupational Outlook Hand-
book.*
> Nature of work, where employed, training, employment outlook, earnings, and
> working conditions.

FIREMAN (FIRE DEPARTMENT). *See* Fire fighter

FISH AND GAME WARDEN   0-94.94

Jeff White: young guide. Dietz, Lew. Little, Brown and Company. 1951.
213p. $3.50
> Career fiction. Story of Maine game wardens during the hunting season, with
> accidents, lost hunters, tracking of deer, and a plea for conservation of wild life.

Jeff White, young trapper. Dietz, Lew. Little, Brown and Company. 1951.
191p. $3.50
> Career fiction. This story is a sequel to *Jeff White, Young Woodsman* and
> contains information for a boy who is interested in becoming a trapper or game
> warden.

A nose for trouble. Kjelgaard, Jim. Holiday House. 1949. 250p. $2.95
> Career fiction. An assistant game warden helps locate men who are violating
> game laws. For sixth or seventh grade boys.

FISH AND GAME WARDEN—*Continued*

Start of the trail; the story of a young Maine guide. Rich, Louise. J. B. Lippincott Company. 1949. 224p. $3.50
> Career fiction. Includes experiences of a guide to hunters and fishermen.

Wilderness warden. Janes, Edward C. David McKay Company. 1955. 214p. $3.50
> Career fiction. Conservation story of a young warden who endeavors to stop the illegal slaughter of animals in the Maine wilderness. For younger boys.

See also Wildlife worker

FISHERMAN   0-35.12; 0-35.22; 3-87.

The agricultural, fishery, and forestry occupations. Chapter 19 in *Occupations and Careers*.
> Includes discussion of the sponge gatherer and otter trawler, the lobster and oyster fisherman.

The beautiful ship; a story of the Great Lakes. Prescott, John B. David McKay Company. 1952. 182p. $2.75
> Fictional account of a boy's efforts to become a fisherman on the Great Lakes. For younger boys.

* Careers in fishery science. Chronicle Guidance Publications. 1960. 4p. 35c
> Occupational brief summarizing work performed, where employed, working conditions, qualifications, training, earnings, and outlook.

Careers outdoors. Joseph, James. Nelson and Sons. 1962. 320p. $5.95
> Description of opportunities which combine profitable business careers with life out of doors, many of them in fishing and hunting.

Commercial fisherman. Careers. 1961. 2p. 15c
> Career summary for desk-top file. Duties, qualifications, and outlook.

**Fisheries as a profession: a career guide for the field of fishery science. American Fisheries Society. 1963. 8p. Single copy free
> Description of the work of fishery biologists, the education and training needed to become a fishery manager or fishery researcher, salaries and benefits, avenues of employment, and types of agencies that hire fishery specialists.

Fisherman. The Guidance Centre. 1960. 4p. 15c in Canada; 20c elsewhere
> Definition, nature of work, qualifications, preparation, earnings, advancement opportunities, how to get started, advantages, disadvantages, and related occupations.

**Fishermen. Science Research Associates. 1960. 4p. 35c
> Occupational brief describing nature of work, qualifications, opportunities, advantages, disadvantages, and future outlook.

I want to be a fisherman. Greene, Carla. Childrens Press. 1957. 32p. $2
> Prepared for beginning readers with a reading level of upper first grade. Illustrated in color.

Lady with a spear. Clark, Eugenie. Harper and Row. 1953. 243p. $4.50; library binding $4.43 net

Biography including the author's experiences in search of rare fish, spearing fish, and exploring the underwater world.

Let's take a trip to a fishery. Riedman, Sarah. Abelard-Schuman. 1956. 128p. $2.75

An overview of the fishing industry; how the fish are caught, transported, processed, and distributed to their markets. For ages 8 to 12.

Preparation for positions in fishery research. Fish and Wildlife Service. 1960. 5p. Free

Includes recommended subjects and list of colleges which offer fundamental courses in several specialized fishery subjects.

Sea boots. Du Soe, Robert C. David McKay Company. 1949. 186p. $2.96

Career fiction for junior high school boys. Story of deep sea fishing off the coast of lower California.

The silver fleet. Rydberg, Ernie. David McKay Company. 1955. 150p. $2.75

Fictional account of a boy's experiences on his father's tuna clipper. For younger boys.

Star for a compass. Halacy, D. S., Jr. Macmillan Company. 1956. 172p. $3

Career fiction. Story of the exhilarating, dangerous work of tuna fishing along the coast of Southern California and Mexico, experienced by a young stowaway. Grades six to ten.

Training programs for fishery occupations: program development information. U.S. Office of Education. Supt. of Documents. 1961. 58p. 20c

Includes list of institutions offering degrees or a major in fishery or related sciences.

FLIGHT ENGINEER. *See* Airplane mechanic

FLIGHT STEWARDESS. *See* Airplane hostess

FLOOR LAYER   5-32.752

**Employment outlook for floor covering mechanics. Bureau of Labor Statistics, U.S. Department of Labor. Supt. of Documents. 1964. 16p. 10c

Reprint from the *Occupational Outlook Handbook.*

**Floor covering mechanics. One section of *Occupational Outlook Handbook.*

Nature of work, where employed, training, other qualifications, advancement, employment outlook, earnings, and working conditions.

Floor layer. Careers. 1961. 2p. 15c

Career summary for desk-top file. Duties, qualifications, and outlook.

FLOOR LAYER—*Continued*

Job description for floor layer. U.S. Employment Service. Supt. of Documents. 1945. 5p. 5c
Occupational guide. Job summary, employment variables, physical demands, related occupations, training, trainee-selection factors, work performed, and glossary.

Your opportunity as a professional flooring craftsman. Armstrong Cork Company. 1961. 16p. Free
Points out the need for resilient floor mechanics, ways of learning the trade, earnings, and outlook.

FLORAL DESIGNER   0-43.60

Floral designer. Careers. 1960. 8p. 25c
Career brief describing duties, working conditions, training, personal qualifications, earnings, outlook, and ways of measuring one's interest and ability.

Floral designing as a career. Rittners School. 1963. 5p. Free
Description of work, training, and opportunities.

Florist. Group, Vernard. Personnel Services. 1962. 6p. 50c; 25c to students
Occupational abstract. Nature of work, future prospects, qualifications, preparation, entrance, advancement, advantages, and disadvantages. References for further reading.

* Florist. Chronicle Guidance Publications. 1963. 4p. 35c
Occupational brief describing work performed, qualifications, training, hours, and opportunities. Includes list of twelve schools of floral design.

Florist. The Guidance Centre. 1961. 4p. 15c in Canada; 20c elsewhere
Nature of work, qualifications, preparation, advancement, earnings, how to get started, and related occupations.

**Florists. Science Research Associates. 1962. 4p. 35c
Occupational brief describing the work of the grower, the wholesale florist, and the retail florist. Also includes requirements, training, getting started, earnings, advantages, disadvantages, and future outlook.

**Flower shop operation as a career. Institute for Research. 1962. 24p. $1
History and development of work, qualifications, and attractive and unattractive features.

Opportunities for you in the florist industry. Society of American Florists. 1962. 13p. 10c
Information concerning type of work, training, and future outlook for the grower, the wholesaler, the retailer, and teacher.
See also Horticulturist

FLORIST. *See* Floral designer; Horticulturist

FOOD AND DRUG INSPECTOR   0-95.11

**Food and drug inspector. Careers. 1961. 2p. 15c
Career summary for desk-top file. Duties, qualifications, and outlook.

Food and drug protective services. Pages 72-82 of *Health Careers Guidebook*.
> Information about qualifications, training, and opportunities for the food technologist and the government food and drug inspector and analyst.

Fruitcake and arsenic. Hemphill, Josephine. Little, Brown and Company. 1962. 192p. $3.75
> Story of the episodes in the work of members of the Food and Drug Administration. Describes the nature of their work and the importance of this agency.

FOOD PREPARATION INDUSTRY WORKER
4, 6-01.000 through 4, 6-10.849; 8-01.00 through 8-10.99

Cannery workers. Science Research Associates. 1960. 4p. 35c
> Occupational brief describing kinds of work, working conditions, opportunities, and future outlook.

**The canning industry. Budd, Nelson. Bellman Publishing Company. 1959. 36p. $1
> History and importance of the industry, training, opportunities for employment, and how to seek employment in canning. References for further reading.

Careers in food administration. King, Ferne and Hurley, Elizabeth. Rochester Institute of Technology. Revised 1961. 30p. Free
> Duties of a food manager and hospital dietitian, advantages, difficulties, personal qualifications, income, and positions available in food administration. Also includes a job chart showing training and promotion possibilities.

**Careers in the food industry. Angel, Juvenal. World Trade Academy Press. 1958. 32p. $1.25
> Includes information about each of several specialties within this field.

Soft drink industry workers. Science Research Associates. 1961. 4p. 35c
> Occupational brief describing nature of work, opportunities, advantages, disadvantages, and future outlook.

FOOD STORE WORKER
0-72.21; 1-03.05

Food retailing career opportunities. National Association of Retail Grocers. 1962. 15p. 50c; free to counselors.
> Describes types of food stores, opportunities, and kinds of work. Includes store organization chart and description of positions.

Food store checkers. Science Research Associates. 1963. 4p. 35c
> Occupational brief describing nature of work, requirements, working conditions, training, advancement, earnings, and future outlook.

Food store workers. Science Research Associates. 1961. 4p. 35c
> Occupational brief describing nature of work, requirements, earnings, and future outlook.

Grocery checker. California Department of Employment. 1961. 4p. Free
> Description of work, duties, employment prospects, earnings, working conditions, and how to find a job.

FOOD STORE WORKERS—*Continued*

Grocery checkers. Science Research Associates. 1963. 4p. 35c

Occupational brief describing nature of work, training, qualifications, opportunities, and outlook. Selected references.

Should you go into food retailing? Eberhard, L. V. New York Life Insurance Company. 1960. 12p. Free

Outlook, satisfactions, earnings, qualifications, and training.

See also Retail manager

FOOD TECHNOLOGIST   0-07.02; 0-35.33

Finding out about food technologists. Science Research Associates. 1963. 4p. 35c

Junior occupational brief containing brief facts about the job.

**Food technologists. Science Research Associates. 1963. 4p. 35c

Occupational brief describing nature of work, requirements, training, getting started and advancing, earnings, advantages, disadvantages, and future outlook.

FOOTBALL PLAYER. *See* Athlete

FOREIGN LANGUAGE WORKER. *See* Linguist

FOREIGN SERVICE WORKER   0-94.70 through 0-94.89

Career opportunities as a foreign service officer. U.S. Department of State. Publication 7245. Supt. of Documents. 1961. 32p. 20c

Includes qualifications for employment, regulations, benefits, work and training, information concerning the written, oral, and physical examination, and opportunities. List of cities where the written examination is given.

**Careers in the diplomatic service. Angel, Juvenal. World Trade Academy Press. 1961. 28p. $1.25

Description of work, training, remuneration, opportunities, and places of employment for each of the following: Foreign service officer, ambassador, consul general, diplomatic secretary, foreign service staff employee, translator, and information and technical specialist. Bibliography.

**Careers in the foreign service. Sakell, Achilles. Henry Z. Walck, Inc. 1962. 118p. $3.50

A discussion of the advantages and disadvantages of work in the foreign service, the duties and functions entailed, the qualifications required, benefits, and the type of examinations offered. Reading lists.

* Careers in the U.S. Foreign Service. Institute for Research. 1963. 24p. $1

Discussion of work in the Foreign Service of the United States. Includes duties, qualifications, training, salaries, advantages, disadvantages, and methods of making appointments.

Careers in the U.S. Foreign Service. *Occupational Outlook Quarterly.* May, 1962. Supt. of Documents. 1962. 5p. 35c
This article describes the duties of the consular officer, political officer, and economic officer and includes information on preparation, qualifications, earnings, and advancement.

Foreign service. Chronicle Guidance Publications. 1960. 4p. 35c
Occupational brief summarizing work performed, training, qualifications, salaries, and outlook.

Foreign service careers. Careers. 1960. 11p. 25c
Career brief describing the functions of the service, training, personal qualifications, advantages, disadvantages, salaries, and outlook. Additional readings.

Foreign service girl. McKown, Robin. Putnam's Sons. 1959. 192p. $2.75
Career fiction. A story which gives insight into the work of the State Department overseas.

The foreign service of the United States. U.S. Department of State. Publication 7279. 1962. 55p. 25c
History of the foreign service, description of the work and duty abroad, methods of selection, training, promotion, and service.

Foreign service officer. Connors, Ralph P. and Robinson, H. Alan. Personnel Services. 1962. 6p. 50c; 25c to students.
Nature of the work, qualifications, preparation, entrance, advancement, earnings, advantages, disadvantages, and future prospects.

Foreign service officer. U.S. Department of State. Supt. of Documents. 1963. 36p. 30c
Describes the work and opportunities that exist, how to become an officer in the foreign service, training, pay, promotions, and benefits.

Foreign service secretary. Careers. 1960. 8p. 25c
Career brief describing duties, working conditions, personal qualifications, training, places of employment, earnings, outlook, and ways of measuring one's interest and ability. Additional readings.

Foreign service staff. U.S. Department of State. Supt. of Documents. 1963. 28p. 25c
Discussion of work, opportunities, qualifications, conditions for employment, representative positions, pay, promotions, and benefits.

Foreign service workers. Science Research Associates. 1960. 4p. 35c
Occupational brief describing the nature of the work of the career foreign service officer and the foreign service staff corps, advantages, disadvantages, and future outlook.

**Opportunities in foreign service. Harrigan, Lucille. Vocational Guidance Manuals. 1963. 126p. $1.45 paper; library edition $2.65
Detailed information on the requirements and methods of applying for openings in many areas of foreign service. Includes types of assignments, training, and salaries.

FOREIGN SERVICE WORKER—*Continued*

Sample questions from the foreign service officer examination. U.S. Department of State, Publication Number 7342. Supt. of Documents. 1962. 37p. 15c

> Examples from each general type of question which has been asked in the last few years. Questions from general examinations and special examinations in history and government, economics, and modern languages.

Secretary of State. Price, Don K. Prentice-Hall, Inc. 1960. 200p. $1.95

> Six men who have worked with the State Department contribute their thoughts on the role of the Secretary of State. Portrays the nature of work in the Foreign Service.

Should you go into the foreign service? Henderson, Loy W. New York Life Insurance Company. 1958. 12p. Free

> Description of work, advantages, disadvantages, traits and education needed, opportunities, salaries, and advancement.

Tomorrow's job in the United States foreign service. Western Personnel Institute. 1955. 4p. 20c

> Description of kinds of work, requisites, training, and the four required examinations.

Training of specialists in international relations. Fuller, C. D. American Council on Education. 1957. 136p. $3

> One of the studies in universities and world affairs.

**Your future in the foreign service. Delaney, Robert. Richards Rosen Press. 1961. 161p. $2.95

> Information and advice concerning nature of work, basic training, salaries, other rewards, who can apply, requirements, and a listing of foreign service posts. Also included are examples from the oral and written examination.

Your future in the foreign service. Delaney, Robert. Popular Library, Inc. 1961. 161p. 50c

> A paperback edition of the book described above.

FOREIGN TRADE WORKER. *See* Exporter and importer

FOREST RANGER   0-35.07

Fire in the valley. Hambleton, Jack. David McKay Company. 1960. 156p. $3.75

> The story of an actual forest fire which raged in Sudbury, Ontario, in 1956 reveals the complex operations and dogged bravery of the rangers and fire fighters who guard a nation's forests.

Forest fire fighters. Harrison, C. W. Franklin Watts, Inc. 1962. 143p. $3.95

> An account of men who not only battle fire but also the conditions that encourage fire. For grades 7 to 11.

Forest ranger. Floherty, John J. J. B. Lippincott Company. 1956. 160p. $3.95
> Includes the rigorous training, varied duties, and hazardous adventures of the men who guard our timber from fire, disease, and crime.

Forest ranger. The Guidance Centre. 1962. 4p. 15c in Canada; 20c elsewhere
> History and importance, nature of work, qualifications, preparation, advancement, outlook, remuneration, advantages, disadvantages, how to get started, and related occupations.

In your service—the work of Uncle Sam's forest rangers. U.S. Department of Agriculture. Agriculture Information Bulletin 136. Supt. of Documents. 1955. 24p. 20c
> Illustrated folder describing the various kinds of work.

Jeff White: forest fire fighter. Dietz, Lew. Little, Brown and Company. 1954. 210p. $3.50
> Career fiction. Shows the work of the air forest patrol.

Smoke over Sikanaska—my life as a forest ranger. Gowland, J. S. Ives Washburn, Inc. 1957. 224p. $3.50
> Biographical account of the adventures of a forest ranger in the Canadian Rockies, where he battled fire, the elements, fur poachers, and many other hazards in the course of his patrol.

Tall timber; the work, machines and men of the United States Forest Service. Colby, Carroll B. Coward-McCann, Inc. 1955. 48p. $2.50; library binding $2.52 net
> Includes description of typical events in the day of a forest ranger. Illustrated. Written for grades 4 to 8.

What does a forest ranger do? Hyde, Wayne. Dodd, Mead and Company. 1964. 64p. $2.50; library binding $2.57 net
> Many photographs and simple text describe the work of men who guard and improve our national forests and parks. For grades 3 to 7.

> See also Fire fighter, Park ranger

FORESTER   0-35.07

Avalanche patrol. Atwater, Montgomery M. Random House, Inc. 1951. 247p. $2.95
> Career fiction. Story of a snow ranger in the U.S. Forest Service.

**Careers in forestry. U.S. Department of Agriculture. Miscellaneous Publication 249. Supt. of Documents. 1961. 22p. 20c
> Character of forestry work; qualifications; opportunities in the Federal Government, states, community forests, private forestry, trade and conservation associations, and teaching. Also discussion of future outlook and opportunities for women.

Careers in forestry and related fields. University of Missouri. 1963. 32p. Free
> Fields of employment, undergraduate and graduate training, salaries, where employment may be found, and examples of some typical jobs.

FORESTER—*Continued*

Code of ethics. Society of American Foresters. 1951. 1p. Free
Included in a leaflet describing the purposes of the society.

**Employment outlook for foresters. Bureau of Labor Statistics, U.S. Department of Labor. Supt. of Documents. 1964. 4p. 5c
Reprint from the *Occupational Outlook Handbook.*

The Forest Service engineer: your gateway to the future. U.S. Department of Agriculture. Miscellaneous Publication 841. Supt. of Documents. 1963. 32p. 40c
Description of opportunities offered to graduate engineers. Illustrated.

Forester. Splaver, Sarah. Personnel Services. 1953. 6p. 50c; 25c to students
Occupational abstract. Nature of work, qualifications, preparation, entrance and advancement, supply and demand, advantages and disadvantages.

**Forester. Careers. 1964. 8p. 25c
Career brief describing duties, working conditions, personal qualifications, places of employment, earnings, and outlook. List of accredited schools of forestry.

*Forester. Chronicle Guidance Publications. 1963. 4p. 35c
Occupational brief summarizing work performed, working conditions, hours, earnings, personal qualifications, training requirements and opportunities, employment outlook, and suggested activities.

Forester. The Guidance Centre. 1963. 4p. 15c in Canada; 20c elsewhere
History and importance, nature of work, qualifications, preparation, advancement, outlook, remuneration, advantages, disadvantages, how to get started, and related occupations.

A forester is as a forester does. Southern Regional Education Board. 1962. 12p. Free
Illustrated brochure depicting various kinds of work and listing the six accredited schools of forestry in the South.

Foresters. Science Research Associates. 1959. 4p. 35c
Occupational brief describing nature of work, training, qualifications, opportunities, advantages, disadvantages, and future outlook.

**Foresters. One section of *Occupational Outlook Handbook*
Nature of work, where employed, training and other qualifications, employment outlook, earnings, and working conditions.

**Forestry. Brown, Nelson C. Bellman Publishing Company. 1957. 31p. $1
Historical summary, principal branches of forestry, duties, qualifications, professional training and preparation, organizations employing foresters, remuneration, and opportunities. Includes list of twenty-six accredited schools.

Forestry. Michigan College of Mining and Technology. 1963. 2p. Free
Example of a recruiting leaflet describing work, outlook, earnings, qualifications, educational requirements, and employment opportunities.

**Forestry and its career opportunities. Shirley, Hardy Lomax. McGraw-Hill Book Company. 1952. 492p. $7.95
Presents a broad picture of forestry in relation to its historic development and its place in national and world economy. Emphasizes career opportunities and gives information on study and training for work in forestry.

Forestry as a career. Meyer, Arthur B. Careers. 1959. 4p. 15c
Reprint from *American Forests* describing kinds of work in public, private, and industrial forestry.

*Forestry as a career. Institute for Research. 1962. 24p. $1
Positions in forestry, typical week's work, personal qualifications, training, opportunities, promotional steps, attractive and unattractive features.

Forestry as a profession. Meyer, Arthur B. Mrs. F. G. Brooks. 1953. 18p. 25c
Nature of work, training, and opportunities. Reprint from *Bios, a Journal of Biology.*

**Forestry as a profession. Society of American Foresters. 1956. 16p. 25c
Nature of forestry, types of employment, salaries, requirements and training. List of colleges and universities offering instruction in forestry.

Forestry at Michigan State University. Michigan State University, Department of Forestry. 1961. 4p. Free
Recruiting bulletin describing entrance requirements, curricula, and employment opportunities.

Forestry: earned degrees, by level, sex, and institution. One section of *Earned Degrees Conferred.*
List of forty-six schools and the number of bachelor's, master's, and doctor's degrees conferred by each.

Forestry education in America today and tomorrow. Dana, S. T. and Johnson, E. W. Society of American Foresters. 1963. 402p. $5
Includes discussion of the scope of forestry, related fields, and current programs of professional training.

Forestry schools in the United States. U.S. Department of Agriculture. 1961. 10p. Free to counselors or librarians
List of the institutions, arranged alphabetically by states, which offer professional and technical curricula in forestry. Schools accredited by the Society of American Foresters are so indicated. A brief description of the courses offered by each school is also included.

Forestry technicians. Science Research Associates. 1964. 4p. 35c
Occupational brief describing nature of work, training, qualifications, opportunities, and outlook.

A job with the Forest Service: a guide to nonprofessional employment. U.S. Department of Agriculture. Miscellaneous Publication 843. Supt. of Documents. 1962. 13p. 10c
Includes information about employment as forestry technician, forestry aid, forest and range fire control technician, engineering technician, and other skilled work.

FORESTER—*Continued*

Occupations in forestry and fishing. Chapter 11 of *Planning Your Future*.
Includes discussion of importance to society, types of work, duties, working
conditions, training, qualifications, opportunities for advancement, advantages,
and disadvantages.

*Opportunities in forestry. Demmon, E. L. Vocational Guidance Manuals.
1961. 103p. $1.45 paper
History and importance of forestry developments, future outlook, fields of
forestry work, requirements for entering, education, training, opportunities, and
advancement. List of accredited schools of forestry.

Schools of forestry accredited by the Society of American Foresters. The
Society. 1963. 1p. Free
A directory of accredited schools of forestry.

Science and the forester. Wolff, Leslie. Criterion Books, Inc. 1961. 194p.
$3.95
The reader learns about the work of a forester, especially in maintaining a
healthy forest by careful planting of new trees and felling of the old ones.

*Should you be a forester? Weyerhaeuser, Frederick K. New York Life
Insurance Company. 1960. 12p. Free
Description of the many and varied duties, the demand for qualified foresters,
salaries, special rewards, and college preparation.

What foresters do. State University of New York, College of Forestry.
1954. 4p. Free
Describes work in forest management, research, utilization, and recreation.

The work and education of a forest manager. State University of New
York, College of Forestry. 1962. 4p. Free
Nature of work, duties, places of employment, qualities needed for success,
future outlook, and ways of getting started.

**Your future in forestry. Hanaburgh, David. Richards Rosen Press. 1961.
159p. $2.95
Describes areas of specialization, places of employment, preparation, opportunities, advancement, satisfactions, and drawbacks. List of schools of forestry.

FORGE SHOP WORKER   4-86.

**Employment outlook for forge shop occupations and for blacksmiths.
Bureau of Labor Statistics, U.S. Department of Labor. Supt. of Docu-
ments. 1964. 12p. 10c
Reprint from the *Occupational Outlook Handbook*.

Forge shop occupations. Careers. 1962. 8p. 25c
Career brief describing work, training, working conditions, earnings, unionization, and outlook.

**Forge shop occupations. One chapter of *Occupational Outlook Handbook*.
Nature of work, where employed, training, other qualifications, advancement,
employment outlook, earnings, and working conditions. Includes description of
heater, hammersmith, drop hammer operator, upsetterman, and die sinker.

Heat treater. Chronicle Guidance Publications. 1961. 4p. 35c

Occupational brief summarizing work performed, working conditions, qualifications, earnings, unionization, and outlook.

Job description for forge heater. U.S. Employment Service. Supt. of Documents. 1948. 4p. 5c

Occupational guide. Job summary, work performed, training, related occupations, physical activities, working conditions, hazards, and employment variables.

FOUNDRY WORKER   4, 6-81.; 4, 6, 8-82.

Coremakers. Careers. 1960. 7p. 25c

Career brief describing duties, working conditions, personal qualifications, training, earnings, and outlook.

Coremakers. One section of *Occupational Outlook Handbook.*

Nature of work, training, other qualifications, advancement, employment outlook, earnings, and working conditions.

**Employment outlook in foundry occupations. Bureau of Labor Statistics, U.S. Department of Labor. Supt. of Documents. 1964. 16p. 10c

Reprint from the *Occupational Outlook Handbook.*

Exploring your future in manufacturing (wage and shop jobs). American Liberty Press. 1960. 96p. $5; $4 paper

In this book one page is devoted to each of fifteen foundry jobs, summarizing job duties, requirements for entering, promotional outlook, and pay and skill level. Included are annealer, blacksmith, bench molder, core assembler, coremaker, crucible furnace melter, cupola charger, cupola operator, electric furnace melter, furnace tender, hammerman, machine molder, press operator trimmer, straightening press operator, and wheelabrator operator.

Finding out about foundry workers. Science Research Associates. 1963. 4p. 35c

Junior occupational brief containing simplified information about requirements, training, nature of work, earnings, and opportunities.

Foundry occupations. Careers. 1960. 8p. 25c

Career brief describing work, training, working conditions, unionization, and ways of measuring your interest and ability.

**Foundry occupations. One chapter of *Occupational Outlook Handbook.*

Nature and location of foundry work, kinds of jobs, training, other qualifications, advancement, employment outlook, earnings, and working conditions. Information is given concerning molder, coremaker, and patternmaker.

Foundry workers. Science Research Associates. 1961. 4p. 35c

Occupational brief describing nature of work, requirements, how to enter foundry work, earnings, advantages, disadvantages, and future outlook. Includes work of the patternmaker, molder, coremaker, melter, and inspector.

FOUNDRY WORKER—*Continued*

Job descriptions for job foundries. U.S. Employment Service. Supt. of Documents. 1938. 336p. $1.25
  One of the series of Volume Job Descriptions. Describes occupations in job foundries fitted to undertake any type of work assigned to them. Does not include occupations existing in foundries operating on a production basis. Illustrated.

Molder. Chronicle Guidance Publications. 1960. 4p. 35c
  Occupational brief summarizing work performed, working conditions, wages, ways of determining interest and ability, training, opportunities, unionization, related jobs, methods of entry, and outlook.

Molder and coremaker. California State Department of Employment. 1961. 3p. Single copy free
  Occupational guide summarizing duties, working conditions, employment prospects, earnings, training, requirements for entry, and suggestions for locating a job.

Molders. One section of *Occupational Outlook Handbook*.
  Nature of work, training, other qualifications, advancement, employment outlook, earnings, and working conditions.

Moulder. The Guidance Centre. 1961. 4p. 15c in Canada; 20c elsewhere
  Nature of work, qualifications, preparation, working conditions, advancement opportunities, earnings, advantages, disadvantages, and how to get started.

Your opportunities as a trained technician in the foundry. Crucible Manufacturers' Association. 1964. 4p. Free
  Describes the work of molders, melters, and pourers as well as the casting designer, patternmaker, and the technician engaged in testing and controlling the quality of the product.

FROZEN FOODS INDUSTRY WORKER   4, 6, 8-04.

**Frozen foods industry workers. Science Research Associates. 1961. 4p. 35c
  Occupational brief describing nature of work, requirements, getting started, earnings, advantages, disadvantages, and future outlook.
  See also Food preparation industry worker

FRUIT AND BERRY FARMER   3-05.01

Blueberry mountain. Meader, Stephen W. Harcourt, Brace and World. 1941. 309p. $3.25
  Career fiction. Story of two boys who decided to start a blueberry farm in the mountains in Pennsylvania. For younger readers.

Fruit farmer. Careers. 1963. 2p. 15c
  Career summary for desk-up file. Duties, qualifications, and outlook.

Fruit grower. The Guidance Centre. 1962. 4p. 15c in Canada; 20c elsewhere
  Description of work, importance to society, working conditions, qualifications necessary for entry and success, earnings, how to get started, and related occupations.

**Fruit growers. Science Research Associates. 1960. 4p. 35c
Occupational brief describing nature of work, preparation, opportunities, and future outlook.

I want to be an orange grower. Greene, Carla. Childrens Press. 1956. 32p. $2
Prepared for beginning readers with a reading level of upper first grade. Illustrated in color.

FUEL TECHNOLOGIST. *See* Metallurgist; Mineral industry worker; Oil and gas heating technician

FUND RAISER 1-55.40

Fund raiser. Chronicle Guidance Publications. 1961. 4p. 35c
Occupational brief summarizing work performed, where employed, requirements, earnings, methods of entry, advantages, disadvantages, and outlook.

*Fund raisers. Science Research Associates. 1964. 4p. 35c
Occupational brief describing nature of work, training, qualifications, opportunities, and outlook.

Philanthropic fund-raising as a profession. Church, David M. Bellman Publishing Company. 1957. 32p. $1
Importance and nature of work, qualifications, preparation, entering and advancing, earnings, conditions of work, related occupations, advantages, and disadvantages. Bibliography.

FUNERAL DIRECTOR 0-65.20

Design for Learning. Cincinnati College of Embalming. 1962. 40p. Free
Catalog including admission requirements and procedure, education and training, qualifications, opportunities, and the minimum length of training and apprenticeship required by each of the fifty states.

Funeral director. Careers. 1963. 2p. 15c
Career summary for desk-top file. Duties, qualifications, and outlook.

*Funeral director. Chronicle Guidance Publications. 1963. 4p. 35c
Occupational brief containing definition, working conditions, personal qualifications, determination of aptitudes and interests, training requirements, training opportunities, advantages and disadvantages, outlook, where employed, methods of entry, high school and the job, and suggested activities.

Funeral director and embalmer. The Guidance Centre. 1963. 4p. 15c in Canada; 20c elsewhere
Nature of work, qualifications, preparation, outlook, remuneration, advantages, disadvantages, how to get started, and related occupations.

Funeral directors and embalmers. Science Research Associates. 1959. 4p. 35c
Occupational brief describing nature of work, personal qualifications, training, getting started and advancing, earnings, opportunities, advantages, disadvantages, and future outlook.

FUNERAL DIRECTOR—*Continued*

**Funeral service as a profession. National Funeral Directors Association. 1960. 24p. 35c

> Historical background, functions of funeral service, typical duties of the embalmer-funeral director, opportunities, qualifications, cost of education, list of twenty accredited schools and colleges of embalming and mortuary science, and regulations for license in each of the states.

**Funeral services as a career. Belleau, Wilfrid E. Park Publishing House. 1960. 26p. 75c

> History and importance of occupation, nature of work, training, entering the field, conditions of work, income, opportunities, advantages, disadvantages, and list of the twenty approved schools for training. Also included is a table giving licensing rules and regulations for funeral directors and embalmers in each of the states.

Mortician and embalmer. The Guidance Centre. 1962. 4p. 15c in Canada; 20c elsewhere

> Nature of work, qualifications, preparation, working conditions, earnings, advantages, disadvantages, how to get started, and related occupations.

Morticians. Michigan Employment Security Commission. 1956. 18p. 25c

> Introduction, nature of work, distribution of morticians, employment prospects, earnings of morticians, qualifications for entry, working conditions, professional organizations, advantages, and disadvantages.

Mortuary operation as a career. Institute for Research. 1957. 24p. $1

> Qualifications, training, and rewards. Includes description of types of jobs, typical day's work, attractive and unattractive features, training, earnings, getting started, and related jobs.

* Mortuary science. Merrill, Charles D. Bellman Publishing Company. 1946. 23p. $1

> History of embalming, personal qualifications, apprenticeship, requirements, license requirements in each of the states, remuneration, advantages, disadvantages, and the number of embalmers and funeral directors in each of the states.

**The vocation of funeral service. National Selected Morticians. 1962. 14p. Single copy free

> Contains a brief history of funeral service through the ages, the type of facilities and responsibilities to be found within funeral service today, job classifications, licensing requirements, subjects required in training, and a list of the accredited mortuary training schools.

FUR FARMER. *See* Animal husbandman

FURNITURE INDUSTRY WORKER   4, 6, 8-36.

Furniture manufacturing workers. Science Research Associates. 1961. 4p. 35c

> Occupational brief describing nature of work, requirements, earnings, job prospects, advantages, disadvantages, and future outlook.

FURRIER 4, 6, 8-21.

Careers in the fur industry. Institute for Research. 1958. 24p. $1
Discussion of work of the fur grader, dresser, dyer, estimater, cutter, finisher, designer, buyer, and retailer.

Fur industry workers. Science Research Associates. 1961. 4p. 35c
Occupational brief describing nature of work, training, qualifications, opportunities, advantages, disadvantages, and future outlook. Selected references.

Furrier. Careers. 1961. 2p. 15c
Career summary for desk-top file. Duties, qualifications, and outlook.

Furrier. The Guidance Centre. 1961. 4p. 15c in Canada; 20c elsewhere
Definition, nature of work, qualifications, preparation, working conditions, advantages, disadvantages, how to get started, and related occupations.

GAME WARDEN. See Fish and game warden; Wildlife worker

GARDENER. See Horticulturist

GEM EXPERT 4-71.220

Gem expert. Juergens, H. Paul. Research Publishing Company. 1954. 32p. $1
Nature of work, training, qualifications, earnings, outlook, and how to enter this field.

GEODESIST. See Geophysicist

GENETICIST 0-35.35

Geneticist. Careers. 1963. 2p. 15c
Career summary for desk-top file. Duties, qualifications, and outlook.

GEOGRAPHER 0-36.93
A career in geography. Association of American Geographers. 1962. 24p. 25c. Single copy free
Nature of work, opportunities, training, and outlook.

**A career in geography. Geographical Research Institute. 1962. 24p. 25c
Discussion of nature of work, education, earnings, and opportunities. Includes cartography, political geography, marketing geography, urban geography, and regional geography.

Careers in geography. Institute for Research. 1955. 20p. $1
Types of positions, qualifications, opportunities, salaries, and attractive and unattractive features.

**Employment outlook for geographers. Bureau of Labor Statistics, U.S. Department of Labor. Supt. of Documents. 1964. 4p. 5c
Reprint from the *Occupational Outlook Handbook*.

GEOGRAPHER—*Continued*

Geographer. Careers. 1961. 2p. 15c
Career summary for desk-top file. Duties, qualifications, and outlook.

Geographer. Chronicle Guidance Publications. 1961. 4p. 35c
Occupational brief summarizing work performed, personal qualifications, training, opportunities, earnings, and outlook.

Geographer. The Guidance Centre. 1960. 4p. 15c in Canada; 20c elsewhere
History and importance, nature of work, qualifications, working conditions, preparation, remuneration, outlook, related occupations, and how to get started.

Geographers. Science Research Associates. 1963. 4p. 35c
Occupational brief describing nature of work, requirements, places of employment, earnings, and future outlook.

**Geographers. One section of *Occupational Outlook Handbook.*
Nature of work, where employed, training, other qualifications, employment outlook, earnings, and working conditions.

Geography: earned degrees, by level, sex, and institution. One section of *Earned Degrees Conferred.*
List of 165 schools and the number of bachelor's, master's and doctor's degrees conferred by each.

See also Scientist

GEOLOGIST   0-35.63

Career booklets dealing with the earth sciences. American Geological Institute. 1962. 2p. Free
List of twenty pamphlets.

**Careers in geology. Angel, Juvenal. World Trade Academy Press. 1958. 28p. $1.25
Includes information about each of several specialties within this field.

Careers in geology. B'nai B'rith Vocational Service. 1957. 16p. 35c
Discussion of outlook, nature of work, places of employment, qualifications, training, beginning jobs, earnings, working conditions, number of workers, and advancement.

Directory of geoscience departments in the colleges and universities of the United States and Canada. American Geological Institute. 1964. 150p. $3
Detailed information on faculty, course offerings, degree requirements, and summer field camp programs of 271 degree-granting departments. Also provides geographic listing of 349 colleges offering some geology courses but no degree.

**Employment outlook for geologists, geophysicists, meteorologists, and oceanographers. Bureau of Labor Statistics, U.S. Department of Labor. Supt. of Documents. 1964. 20p. 15c
Reprint from the *Occupational Outlook Handbook.*

From the eagle's wings. Swift, H. H. Morrow and Company. 1962. 287p. $3.95
> Biography of John Muir, the geologist and nature lover, showing his intense dedication to his work.

Geological engineering. Meyerhoff, Howard A. Chapter 14 of *Engineering Enrollment in the United States*.
> Trends in enrollments and future requirements for specialists in this area.

Geological engineering. Colorado School of Mines. No date. 6p. Free
> Description of the work, prospects, training, and requirements for admission for study.

Geologist. Brackett, Warren and Robinson, M. Alan. Personnel Services. 1956. 6p. 50c; 25c to students
> Occupational abstract describing nature of work, future prospects, opportunities, qualifications, preparation, entrance and advancement, earnings, number and distribution, related occupations, advantages, and disadvantages.

Geologist. Careers. 1963. 2p. 15c
> Career summary for desk-top file. Duties, qualifications, and outlook.

* Geologist. Chronicle Guidance Publications. 1961. 8p. 50c
> Occupational brief summarizing work performed, fields of specialization, working conditions, qualifications, training, salaries, opportunities, where employed, and outlook. Selected references.

Geologist. The Guidance Centre. 1963. 4p. 15c in Canada; 20c elsewhere
> Definition, history and importance, nature of work, working conditions, qualifications, preparation, employment and advancement, remuneration, advantages, disadvantages, how to get started, and related occupations.

* Geologists. Science Research Associates. 1963. 4p. 35c
> Occupational brief describing nature of work, requirements, preparation, earnings, and future outlook.

**Geologists. One section of *Occupational Outlook Handbook*.
> Nature of work, where employed, training and other qualifications, employment outlook, earnings, and working conditions.

Geology and geological engineering. Michigan College of Mining and Technology. 1963. 2p. Free
> Example of a recruiting leaflet describing work, qualifications, educational requirements, earnings, and employment opportunities.

Giants of geology. Fenton, Carroll Lane and Fenton, Mildred Adams. Doubleday and Company. 1952. 333p. $4.50
> Biographies of leading geologists.

**Jeff Carson, young geologist. Lemish, John and Lemish, Jane. Dodd, Mead and Company. 1960. 224p. $3
> Career fiction. This story of a summer's experiences as an economic geologist answers the questions of what the field of geology offers and what qualifications and training are necessary. Includes description of work with the United States Geological Survey. During the experiences the geologist encounters former classmates whose descriptions of work in petroleum geology and geophysics demonstrate the diversity of the work of the geologist.

GEOLOGIST—*Continued*

**Opportunities in geology and geological engineering. Snelgrove, Alfred K. Vocational Guidance Manuals. 1960. 86p. $1.45 paper

Explanation of the scope of the earth sciences, nature of work, educational preparation, related fields, and getting started. List of career booklets dealing with the earth sciences. Also included is a list of colleges offering degrees in the geosciences.

Our earth: geology and geologists. Place, Marian. Putnam's Sons. 1961. 192p. $2.95

Story of man's discoveries in geology and their eventual effects, including why geology's possibilities make it a career worth considering. Written for ages 10 to 14.

**Shall I study geological science? American Geological Institute. 1962. 12p. 10c. Single copy free

Nature of work, fields of specialization, employment opportunities, personal traits and interests, and educational preparation required.

**The sphere of the geological scientist. Roy, Chalmer J. American Geological Institute. 1963. 30p. 25c

The author aims to reveal earth science as a way of life which offers challenge and fascination to intellectually alert and competent students. Describes the major career opportunities, personal qualifications, educational requirements, and outlook.

Survey of geology-geophysics students in the colleges and universities of The United States and Canada and of available scholarships, fellowships, and assistantships. American Geological Institute. 1959. 23p. 50c

An annual series of information on enrollments in degree-granting departments of geology-geophysics. At three-year intervals additional information is given on available financial aid.

Technical and teaching careers in geology. Institute for Research. 1961. 24p. $1

Discussion of historical geology, such as astronomic geology; general geology, such as physiography and stratigraphy; and structural geology, such as geophysics and geochemistry. Description of duties, typical day's work, training, typical course of study, advantages, and disadvantages.

There's adventure in geology. May, Julian. Popular Mechanics Press. 1959. 160p. $2.95

By relating experiences of a boy in this field, the author portrays the various kinds of work. Written for grades 7 to 10.

See also Scientist

GEOPHYSICIST   0-35.65

Careers in exploration geophysics. Society of Exploration Geophysicists. 1963. 8p. Free

Illustrated brochure describing what to expect in the field of geophysical exploration.

Careers in geophysics and geochemistry. Institute for Research. 1958. 20p. $1

Types of jobs, requirements, opportunities, and attractive and unattractive features.

Deep sea, high mountain. Roberts, Elliott. Little, Brown and Company. 1961. 288p. $3.75

Story of the episodes in the work of members of the United States Coast and Geodetic Survey. Describes the nature of their work and the importance of this agency.

Educational requirements for employment of geophysicists. Veterans Administration in cooperation with Bureau of Labor Statistics. VA Pamphlet Number 7-9.6. Supt. of Documents. 1955. 10p. 15c

Describes the functions, fields of specialization, and types of employment in relation to the level of educational preparation acquired.

**Employment outlook for geologists, geophysicists, meteorologists, and oceanographers. Bureau of Labor Statistics, U.S. Department of Labor. Supt. of Documents. 1964. 20p. 15c

Reprint from the *Occupational Outlook Handbook*.

Geophysical engineering. Colorado School of Mines. No date. 6p. Free

Description of the work, prospects, training, and requirements for admission for study.

Geophysical engineering. Michigan College of Mining and Technology. 1963. 2p. Free

Example of a recruiting leaflet describing work, qualifications, educational requirements, and employment opportunities.

Geophysicist. Careers. 1960. 8p. 25c

Career brief describing duties, working conditions, training, personal qualifications, earnings, and outlook.

* Geophysicist. Chronicle Guidance Publications. 1962. 4p. 35c

Occupational brief summarizing work performed, working conditions, qualifications, determination of aptitudes and interests, training, opportunities, outlook, and related jobs.

Geophysicist. The Guidance Centre. 1960. 4p. 15c in Canada; 20c elsewhere

History and importance, nature of work, qualifications, working conditions, preparation, remuneration, outlook, and how to get started.

**Geophysicist. One section of *Occupational Outlook Handbook*.

Nature of work, where employed, training and other qualifications, employment outlook, earnings, and working conditions.

* Geophysicists. Science Research Associates. 1963. 4p. 35c

Occupational brief describing nature of work, training, qualifications, opportunities, and outlook.

GEOPHYSICIST—*Continued*

High, wide and deep. Floherty, John J. J. B. Lippincott Company. 1952.
192p. $3.95
> Description of the Coast and Geodetic Survey including interviews with
> officers and engineers. Discussion of the government agency's origin, growth,
> and services. Illustrated.

Information concerning the broad field of geophysics. American Geophysical Union. 1963. 10p. Mimeographed. Free
> Defines and describes geophysics as a whole and the nine specialties.

See also Scientist

GIRL SCOUTS PROFESSIONAL WORKER   0-27.99

* Abbie Higgins, young group work executive. Rittenhouse, Constance and
Vinton, Iris. Dodd, Mead and Company. 1950. 280p. $3
> Career fiction. Story of a harmonica player who becomes a Girl Scout execu-
> tive. Written by two authors with wide Girl Scout and Boys' Clubs group work
> experience.

Girl Scout professional workers. Careers. 1963. 2p. 15c
> Career summary for desk-top file. Duties, qualifications, and outlook.

**Girl scouting as a profession. Adams, Margaret. Bellman Publishing Co.
1949. 24p. $1
> Qualifications, opportunities, remunerations, and description of national staff
> positions and local professional positions such as executive secretary, field, dis-
> trict, and functional secretaries.

**A job, a future, and you. Girl Scouts of the United States of America. 1964.
16p. Free
> An illustrated brochure pointing out the need for trained workers for the
> variety of executive and specialist jobs in Girl Scouting. Includes qualifications,
> benefits, and rewards.

**Professional opportunities in Girl Scouting. Girl Scouts of the United
States of America. 1962. 24p. Free
> Description of qualifications, training, and experience desirable for jobs with
> local units and jobs on the national staff. Also includes a discussion of working
> conditions, chances for the future, international assignments, and how to apply.

Qualifications for local professional positions in Girl Scouting. Girl
Scouts of the United States of America. 1963. 2p. Free
> Brief statement of basic skills and the personal and academic qualifications
> needed.

There is a summer job for you in a Girl Scout camp. Girl Scouts of the
United States of America. 1963. 8p. Free
> List of positions with brief statement of duties.

Why work? Girl Scouts of the United States of America. 1957. 6p. Free
> This brochure points out that a Girl Scout executive's work is varied, stimulat-
> ing, and fun.

GLASS INDUSTRY WORKER   4, 6, 8-65.

Glass manufacturing workers. Science Research Associates. 1961. 4p. 35c
Occupational brief describing nature of work, requirements, methods of getting started, wages, advantages, disadvantages, and future outlook.

GLAZIER   5, 7, 9-77.

**Employment outlook for painters, paperhangers, glaziers, and asbestos and insulating workers. Bureau of Labor Statistics, U.S. Department of Labor. Supt. of Documents. 1964. 20p. 15c
Reprint from the *Occupational Outlook Handbook*.

Glazier. Careers. 1961. 2p. 15c
Career summary for desk-top file. Duties, qualifications, and outlook.

Glaziers. One section of *Occupational Outlook Handbook*.
Nature of work, where employed, training and other qualifications, employment outlook, earnings, and working conditions.

GOLF CADDY   2-40.01

Joey gets the golf bug. Sherman, James W. Little, Brown and Company. 1961. 171p. $2.95
Career fiction. The story reveals some information about the work of a caddy and desirable qualifications.

GOVERNMENT SERVICE WORKER   0-39.99; 0-00. through 9-99.

Administrative positions in city government—careers. Institute for Research. 1957. 24p. $1
History and types of work, description of specialized fields of municipal administration, attractive and unattractive features, personal qualifications, training, salaries, how to get started, and related fields.

Adventures in public service; the careers of eight honored men in the United States Government. Simons, Howard. Vanguard Press. 1964. 272p. $3.95
Biographical sketches of eight men who are serving the Federal Government in important positions and have received the Rockefeller Public Service Award for their achievements.

**Career positions for women in state, county, and city government work. Institute for Research. 1957. 20p. $1
Examples of typical positions, typical day's work, salaries, attractive and unattractive features, personal qualifications, education and training, chances for employment, how to get started, and list of colleges offering a course of study with emphasis on state and local government administration.

Careers in government service. Institute for Research. 1962. 24p. $1
Description of work, qualifications, and attractive and unattractive features.

Careers in the Treasury Department of the United States Government. Institute for Research. 1961. 24p. $1
Description of selected typical positions in different areas, qualifications, earnings, attractive and unattractive features, and how to get started.

GOVERNMENT SERVICE WORKER—*Continued*

Careers in the U.S. Department of Commerce. Institute for Research. 1957. 24p. $1
    Scope and range of work, attractive and unattractive features, salaries, education and experience, and how positions are secured. Includes description of work in the Weather Bureau, Civil Aeronautics Administration, Maritime Administration, National Bureau of Standards, and the Patent Office.

Careers in the United States Department of the Interior. Institute for Research. 1961. 24p. $1
    Description of various positions, attractive and unattractive features, qualifications, training, earnings, and how to secure employment.

Careers in the United States Department of the Interior. U.S. Department of the Interior. Supt. of Documents. 1962. 69p. 35c
    Describes the activities of the department and its thirteen bureaus, the recruitment needs, and minimum qualifications for work in the various categories. Written for college students.

Careers in the U.S. Department of State. Institute for Research. 1959. 24p. $1
    History and importance of work, types of major positions, attractive and unattractive features, qualifications, training, salaries, and how to secure positions.

**Civilian employment in Federal Government. One chapter of *Occupational Outlook Handbook.*
    Employment trends and outlook in work in Federal, state, and local governments; post office occupations; and Armed Forces.

Department of State, a career in Washington, D.C. U.S. Department of State. Supt. of Documents. 1963. 20p. 20c
    This booklet provides information on how men and women may enter the service in the Department of State. It also describes the work and kinds of jobs they may be called upon to do.

**Employment outlook in government occupations. Bureau of Labor Statistics, U.S. Department of Labor. Supt. of Documents. 1964. 20p. 15c
    Reprint from the *Occupational Outlook Handbook.*

**Federal career directory: a guide for college students. U.S. Civil Service Commission. Supt. of Documents. 1963. 84p. 60c
    Written to provide general guidance for the college student who aspires to a Federal public service career, this directory contains information on the method of filling jobs, student trainee programs, pay scales, and promotions. It also describes the work of the various agencies and the career opportunities in each.

Futures in the Federal Government. U.S. Civil Service Commission. 1961. 36p. Free
    Information on entrance requirements and job opportunities in government agencies.

Government administration. Simmons College. 1962. 4p. Free
    Discussion of areas of service, rewards, and preparation.

Government occupations. One section of *Occupational Outlook Handbook*.
Discusses opportunities for civilian employment in the major divisions of
Federal, state, and local government.

Government workers, politicians, and lawyers. Chapter 11 of *The College
Girl Looks Ahead*.
Characteristics of government work, talents needed, trying out, preparation,
and kinds of work.

Graduate study in public administration: a guide to graduate programs.
U.S. Office of Education. Supt. of Documents. 1961. 158p. $1.25
A description of the 145 graduate programs in public administration offered
by 83 institutions in the United States.

Handbook, Office of Education, including career opportunities. U.S. Office
of Education. Supt. of Documents. 1963. 36p. 25c
Brief description of the organization and activities of the office and its one
thousand employees. Explains how positions are filled.

Occupations in government. Chapter 22 of *Planning Your Future*.
Includes discussion of the nature of government occupations, how to enter,
and specific information about the work of the policeman and policewoman.

**Occupations in government. One chapter of *Occupational Outlook Hand-
book*.
Includes civilian employment in Federal, state, and local government; post
office occupations; and career fields for military personnel.

* Professional careers in the Federal Government. Careers. 1962. 8p. 25c
Career brief describing a number of professional careers, how jobs are filled,
earnings, and outlook.

Public service. American Society for Public Administration. 1964. 12p.
Free
Description of careers and opportunities in public service.

Secretary of State. Price, Don. Prentice-Hall, Inc. 1960. 200p. $3.50;
paper $1.95
Six men who have been associated with the work in the State Department
discuss the role of the Secretary of State.

**Six against crime: treasury agencies in action. Neal, Harry Edward.
Julian Messner, Inc. 1959. 192p. $3.95. Library binding $3.64 net
Description of the law-enforcement agencies of the U.S. Treasury Department
and their efficiency and accomplishments. Includes a chapter on the training of
a Treasury agent. Photographs.

Should you become a public servant? Moses, Robert. New York Life
Insurance Company. 1959. 12p. Free
Desirable traits, training costs, prospects, advantages.

Summer employment in Federal agencies. U.S. Civil Service Commission.
Supt. of Documents. 1962. 24p. 15c
Discussion of opportunities for student trainees and student assistants open to
high school and college students.

GOVERNMENT SERVICE WORKER—*Continued*

The United States Department of the Treasury; a story of dollars, customs, and secret agents. Terrell, John Upton. Duell, Sloan and Pearce. 1963. 116p. $2.95

Discussion of the duties carried out by the Bureau of Customs, Bureau of Engraving and Printing, Bureau of the Mint, Secret Service, Coast Guard, Bureau of Narcotics, and Internal Revenue Service.

Way to a job in government. U.S. Civil Service Commission. Supt. of Documents. 1963. 6p. 5c

Steps to take in seeking a job.

What the President does all day. Hoopes, Roy. John Day Company. 1962. 63p. $2.50

This book shows what any President of the United States does in a typical day and is illustrated with photographs of President John F. Kennedy. Gives an idea of the scope and arduousness of the office. For grades 4 to 9.

**Women in the Federal service, 1939-1959. Women's Bureau, U.S. Department of Labor. Supt. of Documents. 1962. 21p. 15c

Highlights of employment trends, job locations, employment standards, grades and salaries, and the variety of occupational opportunity. Includes the number of employees in each of the agencies and the number in each of 125 occupations, with average annual salary.

See also Civil Service worker; Foreign service worker

GREETING CARD INDUSTRY WORKER   4, 6, 8-49.

* Greeting card industry workers. Science Research Associates. 1958. 4p. 35c

Occupational brief describing nature of work, training, qualifications, opportunities, advantages, disadvantages, and future outlook.

GROCERY STORE WORKER. *See* Food store worker; Retail manager

GROUNDS KEEPER. *See* Horticulturist

GROUP WORKER   0-27.40

**Careers in group work. B'nai B'rith Vocational Service. 1955. 8p. 35c

Discussion of outlook, nature of work, beginning jobs, training, qualifications, and salaries. List of organizations conducting group work programs.

Highlighting your future: a professional career in Boys' Club work. Boys' Clubs of America. 1963. 8p. Free

Types of positions, basic characteristics needed, qualifications, salaries, and opportunities.

Manual for group club advisors in Boys' Clubs. Boys' Clubs of America. 1959. 16p. 25c

Includes nature of work, duties, and qualifications.

My sixty years with rural youth. Erickson, T. A. University of Minnesota
Press. 1956. 162p. $2.75
Biography of a pioneer leader in the 4-H club movement for boys and girls.
Illustrated.

Opportunity for you in a challenging career. National Urban League.
1963. 16p. Free
Describes opportunities for trained workers with the National Urban League
to provide professional services to Negro individuals and families faced with
special problems.

Personnel policies and practices for full time professional staff in Boys'
Clubs. Boys' Clubs of America. Revised 1956. 16p. Free
Description of work and duties.

**Professional leadership in Boys' Clubs. Boys' Clubs of America. 1959.
26p. 25c
This booklet sets forth the desirable qualifications for full-time positions in
a boys' club. Duties and educational and experience qualifications are given for
the following: executive director, assistant executive director, program director,
physical director, swimming director, group club supervisor, director of social
program, and membership secretary.

Should you seek a career in youth services? Brunton, Joseph A. New
York Life Insurance Company. 1962. 12p. Free
Description of work, demand for qualified workers, qualifications, training,
and rewards.

You can have a career in Camp Fire Girls. Camp Fire Girls, Inc. No date.
6p. Free
Brief description of work as field director, district director, camp director,
and executive director.

See also Boy Scouts professional worker; Girl Scouts professional
worker; Jewish center worker; Social worker; YMCA secretary; YWCA
professional worker

GUARD AND WATCHMAN   2-61.

Guard (watchman). California State Department of Employment. 1962.
4p. Single copy free
Description of work, pay, hours, how to find work, and employment outlook
in California.

Guard (watchman). Careers. 1963. 2p. 15c
Career summary for desk-top file. Duties, qualifications, and outlook.

**Guards and watchmen. Science Research Associates. 1961. 4p. 35c
Occupational brief describing nature of work, qualifications, training, earnings, and outlook. Selected references.

GUIDANCE AND PERSONNEL WORKER. *See* Counselor; Personnel
and employment manager; Vocational rehabilitation counselor

GUNSMITH   5-83.542

Gunsmith. California State Department of Employment. 1961. 5p. Single copy free

> Job duties, working conditions, pay, hours, entrance requirements, promotion, training, and employment outlook in California.

Gunsmith. Careers. 1962. 2p. 15c

> Career summary for desk-top file. Duties, qualifications, and outlook.

HEALTH EDUCATOR   0-27.20

Educational qualifications and functions of public health educators. American Public Health Association. 1957. 8p. Free

> Scope of work, functions, and educational requirements.

Health education. Pages 82-9 of *Health Careers Guidebook*.

> Information about qualifications, training, and opportunities in public health education, school health education, and health information and communications.

**Health education as your career. American Association for Health, Physical Education, and Recreation. 1963. 8p. 5c. Single copy free

> Nature of work, opportunities, salaries, preparation, advantages, and qualifications.

Health education materials catalog. National Dairy Council. 1963. 35p. Free

> Catalog lists and describes booklets, leaflets, charts, posters, and films. The purchase price of each publication is included. Catalog is issued annually in April.

HEARING THERAPIST. *See* Speech and hearing therapist

HEALTH SERVICE WORKER. *See* Medical service worker

HEAT, LIGHT, AND POWER INDUSTRY WORKER
                              5, 7-51.000 through 5, 7-54.999

Electric power-plant occupations. Careers. 1961. 7p. 25c

> Occupational brief describing duties, working conditions, training earnings, related careers, and outlook.

Electric power plant switchboard operator. Chronicle Guidance Publications. 1960. 4p. 35c

> Occupational brief summarizing work performed, working conditions, qualifications, training, wages, where employed, methods of entry, related jobs, and outlook.

Electrical transmission occupations. Careers. 1962. 8p. 25c

> Career brief describing duties, working conditions, personal qualifications, training, related jobs, unionization, and outlook.

**Employment outlook in electric light and power occupations. Bureau of Labor Statistics, U.S. Department of Labor. Supt. of Documents. 1964. 20p. 15c

Reprint from the *Occupational Outlook Handbook*.

Gas fuel technology. Chronicle Guidance Publications. 1960. 4p. 35c

Occupational brief summarizing work performed, location of work, working conditions, qualifications, training, earnings, opportunities, and outlook.

Lineman (light, heat, and power). Chronicle Guidance Publications. 1960. 4p. 35c

Occupational brief summarizing work performed, working conditions, hours, earnings, personal qualifications, training requirements and opportunities, employment outlook, and entry into the job.

Linemen, cable splicers, and troublemen. One section of *Occupational Outlook Handbook*.

Description of work of installing and repairing electric light and power equipment.

The miracle of light and power. Leyson, B. W. E. P. Dutton and Company. 1955. 186p. $3.50

The last chapter of this account of the Consolidated Edison Company describes the various career opportunities, training, duties, benefits, and advantages. Illustrated.

**Occupations in the electric light and power industry. One chapter of *Occupational Outlook Handbook*.

Nature and location of the industry, kinds of work, employment outlook, earnings, and working conditions. Specific information is given concerning powerplant occupations, transmission and distribution occupations, and customer servicing occupations.

Powerplant occupations. One section of *Occupational Outlook Handbook*.

Description of the work of the boiler, turbine, auxiliary equipment, and switchboard operators.

* Public utility workers. Science Research Associates. 1961. 4p. 35c

Occupational brief describing kinds of work, requirements, getting started, earnings, advantages, disadvantages, and future outlook.

The Sextant series for exploring your future in public utilities. American Liberty Press. 1964. 96p. $5; $4 paper

One page is devoted to each of ninety-five jobs, summarizing job duties, requirements for entering, promotional outlook, and pay and skill level. Accompanying the book is an organizational chart showing the student the beginning jobs and those to which one may be promoted.

Transmission and distribution occupations. One section of *Occupational Outlook Handbook*.

Nature of work, training, employment outlook, earnings, and working conditions.

HERPETOLOGIST   0-35.28

Adventures with reptiles: the story of Ross Allen. Hylander, C. J. Julian
Messner, Inc. 1951. 192p. $3.25. Library binding $3.19 net

> Biography of the naturalist whose interest started with snakes and who be-
> came an authority on reptiles, showing how one man's curiosity about reptiles
> led to a most successful and unusual livelihood.

Ichthyologist. Careers. 1963. 2p. 15c

> Career summary for desk-top file. Describes duties, working conditions, quali-
> fications, training, outlook, where employd, and related careers.

Raymond L. Ditmars: his exciting career with reptiles, animals, and insects. Wood, Laura N. Julian Messner, Inc. 1944. 256p. $3.50. Library
binding $3.34 net

> Entertaining biography of the man whose boyhood hobby of snake collecting
> developed into a career of scientist and curator of reptiles and mammals of the
> New York Zoological Park. Illustrated.

HIGHWAY ENGINEER   0-16.01

Highway engineer. Careers. 1959. 2p. 15c

> Career summary for desk-top file. Duties, qualifications, and outlook.

* Highway engineering as a career. Institute for Research. 1959. 24p. $1

> Requirements and salary range for many professional and subprofessional
> jobs such as chart maker, field tester, and bridge layout man. Discussion of
> outlook and attractive and unattractive features.

HISTORIAN   0-36.91

Historian. Careers. 1963. 7p. 25c

> Career brief describing duties, working conditions, personal qualifications,
> training, places of employment, related careers, earnings, and outlook.

**Historians. One section of *Occupational Outlook Handbook.*

> Nature of work, where employed, training, other qualifications, and employ-
> ment outlook.

**History as a career: to undergraduates choosing a profession. American
Historical Association. 1961. 16p. 6c; single copy free

> Designed to help the undergraduate decide whether he wants to make college
> history teaching a career. Describes what it requires and what it offers. Includes
> brief discussion of the work of historians who are not college teachers.

HOME ECONOMIST   0-12.35; 0-12.36

Begin your career in home economics. Albright College. 1960. 8p. Free

> Leaflet containing pictures of student activities and various fields of specializa-
> tion. Typical of college brochures which provide information and atmosphere
> in a counseling office.

* Career as a home economist in the food field. Institute for Research. 1958. 24p. $1

   Describes duties, qualifications, and opportunities of nutritionist, food service director, journalist, and specialist in foods engaged in advertising or sales promotion work.

A career in home economics extension . . . a diamond in your life. American Home Economics Association. 1959. 6p. 10c

   Nature of work, possible rewards, advantages, and qualifications of work in extension service.

A career in home economics research opens the door to better living. American Home Economics Association. 1957. 12p. 10c

   Opportunities within each of the subject areas of home economics are described. Photographs show the work being done in each area.

Career opportunities in home economics in business. American Home Economics Association. 1959. 20p. 35c

   Discussion of the abilities and personal qualifications needed for jobs in advertising, editorial work, fashion promoting, and equipment and foods merchandising.

**Careers in home economics. Angel, Juvenal L. World Trade Academy Press. 1962. 28p. $1.25

   Description of major fields of specialization: textile and clothing economist, family and child development economist, home economics merchandiser, foods and nutrition economist, and home economics teacher. Discussion of qualifications, training, opportunities for work, opportunities for men, advantages, and disadvantages. Also included is a list of colleges and private organizations offering scholarships in the field of home economics. Bibliography.

Careers in home economics. Changing Times. 1962. 3p. 15c

   Reprint containing discussion of preparation, earnings, and opportunities.

Careers in home economics. U.S. Office of Education, Home Economics Education Branch. 1961. 8p. Free

   Description of professional careers in home economics, preparation, opportunities, salary, and other satisfactions.

**Employment outlook for home economists and dietitians. Bureau of Labor Statistics, U.S. Department of Labor. Supt. of Documents. 1964. 12p. 10c

   Reprint from the *Occupational Outlook Handbook*.

**For you—a double future in home economics. American Home Economics Association. 1957. 34p. 25c

   Gaily illustrated booklet describing the major career areas in home economics. Brief descriptions of duties, qualifications, and opportunities are given for each.

**Futures for home economists. Humphreyville, Theresa. Prentice-Hall, Inc. 1963. 334p. $5.95

   Description of careers open to home economists with bachelor's degrees in schools, social group work, test kitchen research, retailing, journalism, and cooperative extension service.

HOME ECONOMIST—*Continued*

Gay enterprises. Freer, Marjorie Mueller. Julian Messner, Inc. 1952. 176p. $2.95

Career fiction. Gay creates a career for herself in cooking and baking in her own kitchen, and works toward the dream of owning her own restaurant. Includes information about creative baking, marketing, and work in nutrition.

Home demonstration agent. Careers. 1960. 2p. 15c

Career summary for desk-top file. Duties, qualifications, and outlook.

Home demonstration agent. Chronicle Guidance Publications. 1960. 4p. 35c

Occupational brief summarizing work performed, working conditions, qualifications, training, earnings, opportunities, where employed, outlook, and suggested activities.

Home economics. Healey, Katheryne T. Bellman Publishing Co. 1946. 24p. $1

Development, qualifications, educational requirements, and types of positions available for trained home economists.

* Home economics. Careers. 1960. 8p. 25c

Career brief describing duties, working conditions, training, personal qualifications, places of employment, earnings, outlook, and ways of measuring your interest and ability.

Home economics. Milwaukee-Downer College. 1959. 16p. Free

College bulletin giving information about preparation for foods and nutrition, including dietetics and institutional management; textiles and clothing; and home economics education. Illustrated.

Home economics—a guidance aid. American Home Economics Association. 1962. 5p. 25c

Information about nature of work and qualifications. A chart lists a variety of jobs related to home economics.

* Home economics as a career. Institute for Research. 1962. 23p. $1

Qualifications, training opportunities, salaries, advantages and disadvantages. Discussion of work in homemaking, teaching, extension work, food and nutrition, business, institutional management, research, social service, journalism, textile, clothing, and merchandising.

* Home economics as a profession. Tate, Mildred T. McGraw-Hill Book Company. 1961. 432p. $5.50

Presents a comprehensive view of the many professions and vocations open to home economists. Includes the education and training necessary as preparation.

Home economics at Cal Poly leads to. . . . California State Polytechnic College. 1962. 8p. Free

An illustrated brochure depicting four career areas in home economics and outlining the course of study.

* Home economics career for you. Phillips, Velma. Harper and Row. 1957. 278p. $4.50

Designed for a beginning college course for freshman students. Includes opportunities in various areas comprising home economics—housing, equipment, home management, child development, family relations, textiles, clothing, food, nutrition, and art applied to the home. Describes what home economics offers students and what home economics graduates are doing today. Bibliography.

**Home economics career packet. American Home Economics Association. 1962. Fourteen booklets. $2

Attractive folder containing fourteen career booklets available from the association.

Home economics career wheel. American Home Economics Association. 1961. 1p. Free; additional copies 2c each

Colorful wheels depicting opportunities in home economics.

Home economics—careers and homemaking. Hall, Olive A. John Wiley and Sons. 1958. 301p. $4.75

Discussion of the variety of vocational opportunities to which training in this field might lead: homemaking; teaching; working with children, youth, and families; home economics in business; clothing and textiles; food service; dietetics and nutrition; and research.

Home economics: earned degrees, by level, sex, and institution. One section of *Earned Degrees Conferred.*

Useful for judging the extent of a college's program in general home economics, child development, clothing textiles, foods and nutrition, and institution management.

**Home economics has a career for you in textiles and clothing. American Home Economics Association. 1963. 16p. 25c

Discussion of the basic requirements, major duties, qualifications, employment opportunities, salaries, and related work. Includes information about careers in fashion, teaching, research, extension, and communications. Reading list.

Home economics in institutions granting bachelor's or higher degrees. Division of Vocational and Technical Education, U.S. Office of Education. Supt. of Documents. 1964. 81p. 55c

Information about the number of students in each school, the number of home economics students, and the home economics majors offered in each. Published biennially.

Home economics offers you a career in social welfare or public health. American Home Economics Association. 1963. 16p. 25c

Illustrated folder describing opportunities, training, and qualifications.

Home economist. Splaver, Sarah. Personnel Services. 1958. 6p. 50c; 25c to students

Occupational abstract. Nature of work, qualifications, preparation, entrance, advancement, supply and demand, earnings, advantages, and disadvantages.

* Home economist. Chronicle Guidance Publications. 1961. 4p. 35c

Occupational brief summarizing work performed, working conditions, hours, earnings, personal requirements, training requirements, opportunities, and employment outlook.

HOME ECONOMIST—*Continued*

Home economist. The Guidance Centre. 1962. 4p. 15c in Canada; 20c elsewhere
Nature of work, qualifications, preparation, outlook, advancement, earnings, how to get started, and related occupations.

Home economists. Chapter 8 of *The College Girl Looks Ahead.*
Characteristics of work in home economics, talents needed, trying out, preparation, and kinds of work.

Home economists. Chapter 22 of *Vocations for Girls.*
Nature of work, opportunities, and advantages. Bibliography.

**Home economists. One section of *Occupational Outlook Handbook.*
Nature of work, where employed, related fields of work, training, other qualifications, advancement, employment outlook, earnings and working conditions.

Home economists. Science Research Associates. 1958. 4p. 35c
Occupational brief describing nature of work, qualifications, preparation, opportunities, advantages, disadvantages, and future outlook.

Introducing Patti Lewis, home economist. Wells, Helen. Julian Messner, Inc. 1956. 192p. $2.95
Career fiction. Describes the nature of work in the test kitchens of a Midwest flour mill including inventing new recipes, giving parties, traveling to introduce new products, demonstrating, broadcasting, and dealing with women.

Is home economics the career for your daughter? American Home Economics Association. 1960. 4p. 5c. Single copy free
Flier addressed to parents naming the range of positions in home economics.

It's not too early to start thinking about your home economics future. American Home Economics Association. 1960. 6p. 5c. Single copy free
Illustrated folder designed for the junior high school student.

Should you be a home economist? Dennis, Catherine. New York Life Insurance Company. 1960. 12p. Free
Includes nature of work, personal rewards, opportunities, cost of training, earnings, and qualities one should possess.

Teach home economics—a career with a double future. American Home Economics Association. 1959. 6p. 15c
Folder outlining the opportunities and satisfactions awaiting the girl who prepares to teach home economics.

Teaching homemaking as a career in the nation's schools. U.S. Office of Education. Supt. of Documents. 1957. 4p. 5c
Brief discussion of the importance and need for homemaking teachers, salary, and satisfactions.

Unfold your future in home economics. American Home Economics Association. 1959. 10p. 5c
Illustrated folder depicting the career areas in home economics.

Wanted: home economists with advanced degrees. American Home Economics Association. 1956. 8p. 10c
> Illustrated folder encouraging advanced study.

**Your future as a home economist. Paris, Jeanne. Richards Rosen Press. 1963. 160p. $2.95; library edition $2.79 net
> Description of the numerous fields open to a graduate with a degree in home economics. Includes the type of studies to expect and the schools offering such degrees.

HORTICULTURIST 0-35.05

* Gardeners and groundskeepers. Science Research Associates. 1963. 4p. 35c
> Occupational brief describing work, training, qualifications, opportunities, and outlook.

Greenhouse worker. Careers. 1963. 2p. 15c
> Career summary for desk-top file. Duties, qualifications, and outlook.

Groundsman-gardener. California Department of Employment. 1962. 3p. Single copy free
> Description of work, duties, working conditions, requirements, wages, hours, promotion, and employment outlook.

Horticulture a challenging career. American Society for Horticultural Science. 1958. 8p. $3 per 100. Single copy free
> Illustrated brochure describing opportunities in work with fruit, vegetables, and flowers.

Horticulturist. Careers. 1960. 2p. 15c
> Career summary for desk-top file. Duties, qualifications, and training.

* Horticulturist. Chronicle Guidance Publications. 1960. 4p. 35c
> Occupational brief summarizing work performed, working conditions, qualifications, training, earnings, advantages, disadvantages, and outlook.

Horticulturist. The Guidance Centre. 1960. 4p. 15c in Canada; 20c elsewhere
> History and importance, nature of work, qualifications, working conditions, preparation, remuneration, outlook, and how to get started.

**Opportunities in horticulture. Brantley, C. Owen. Vocational Guidance Manuals, Inc. 1953. 96p. $1.45 paper
> Discussion of branches of commercial horticulture, educational requirements, training, how to get started, remuneration, advancement, and basic divisions of the field. Includes list of eighty-six agricultural colleges.

Orchids for April. Freer, Marjorie. Julian Messner, Inc. 1957. 189p. $2.95
> Career fiction. Story of a girl interested in gardening.

See also Floral designer; Landscape architect; Nurseryman; Tree surgeon

HOSPITAL ADMINISTRATOR   0-99.84

**Administration of health services. Pages 43-56 of *Health Careers Guidebook.*
  Description of work, qualifications, training, and future outlook. Also includes information concerning administrative specialties in public health administration and voluntary health agencies.

A career for you as a Veterans Administration hospital housekeeping officer. Veterans Administration, Department of Medicine and Surgery. 1963. 4p. Free
  Description of work, training program, qualifications, and benefits.

* Careers in hospital administration. Angel, Juvenal L. World Trade Academy Press. 1962. 30p. $1.25
  Description of specialized occupations including the general hospital administrator, assistant hospital director, hospital controller, hospital personnel manager, public relations director, and hospital purchasing agent. Also included is a list of fourteen colleges offering courses in hospital administration. Bibliography.

Careers in hospital administration. B'nai B'rith Vocational Service. 1954. 8p. 35c
  Discussion of outlook, development of the field, duties, qualifications, training, opportunities for advancement, earnings, finding a position, working conditions, and a list of schools offering graduate programs in hospital administration.

**Careers in hospitals. American Hospital Association. 1963. 54p. $1.25
  This book contains job descriptions and educational and personal requirements for 130 hospital careers. It estimates earning potentials and opportunities for future advancement in hospital administrative services, plant operation, and paramedical departments. An insert lists approved schools in fifteen hospital professions.

**Employment outlook for hospital administrators. Bureau of Labor Statistics, U.S. Department of Labor. Supt. of Documents. 1964. 4p. 5c
  Reprint from the *Occupational Outlook Handbook.*

* Hospital administration as a career. American College of Hospital Administrators. 1962. 6p. Single copy free
  Description of the work of the administration of hospitals, training, and opportunities. Includes a list of colleges which offer graduate courses in hospital administration.

Hospital administrator. Careers. 1961. 7p. 25c
  Career brief describing duties, working conditions, training, personal requirements, advantages, disadvantages, earnings, and outlook. Additional readings.

Hospital administrator. Chronicle Guidance Publications. 1960. 4p. 35c
  Occupational brief summarizing work performed, working conditions, personal qualifications, training, opportunities, methods of entry, related occupations, and outlook.

**Hospital administrators. Science Research Associates. 1963. 4p. 35c
  Occupational brief describing work, requirements, training, getting started, earnings, advantages, disadvantages, and future outlook.

**Hospital administrators. One section of *Occupational Outlook Handbook*.
Nature of work, where employed, training, other qualifications, advancement, employment outlook, earnings, and working conditions.

Hospital management as a career. Institute for Research. 1959. 22p. $1
Duties, typical day's work, qualifications, training, opportunities, and salaries. Kinds and number of workers, and their salaries are given for small and large hospitals in general administration, nursing department, dietary, housekeeping, and mechanical departments, and accessory professional services.

Hospital with a heart. Wassersug, Joseph. Abelard-Schuman. 1961. 160p. $3
Written for the young person interested in a career in nursing, medicine, science, or social service. Includes discussion of the various hospital departments and the roles of the various specialists.

Job descriptions and organizational analysis for hospitals and related health services. U.S. Employment Service. Supt. of Documents. 1952. 532p. $2.50
One of a series of Volume Job Descriptions. Includes 185 job descriptions covering purpose of the job, performance requirements, physical demands, education, promotion, and other pertinent information. Includes descriptions and organizational charts of the various hospital departments covering such activities as administration, business, professional care, plant operation, and maintenance.

Should you be a hospital administrator? Crosby, Edwin L. New York Life Insurance Company. 1960. 12p. Free
Description of wide range of duties, special demands, abilities needed, educational requirements, and rewards.

Your future in hospital administration. Kirk, Weir Richard. Richards Rosen Press. 1963. 159p. $2.95
Describes the work of a physician from an institutional and administrative point of view.

See also Medical service worker

HOSTESS. *See* Airplane hostess

HOTEL AND RESTAURANT INDUSTRY WORKER 2-24. through 2-29.

Bus boys. Science Research Associates. 1964. 4p. 35c
Occupational brief describing work, qualifications, opportunities, and outlook.

Careers for youth kit. National Restaurant Association. No date. 4 booklets. Free to counselors
Includes an illustrated narration guide for a filmstrip, *New horizons in food service careers.*

Careers in quantity food service. National Restaurant Association. 1958. 20p. Free
Scope of the restaurant industry, advantages, disadvantages, personal qualifications, specialized training, available positions, what is expected from each job, and college training.

HOTEL AND RESTAURANT INDUSTRY WORKER—*Continued*

Directory of schools and colleges offering courses for the training of managers, supervisors, and workers in hotels, restaurants, and institutions. Council on Hotel, Restaurant and Institutional Education. 1961. 36p. 25c
> List of schools arranged by states.

**Employment outlook in hotel occupations. Bureau of Labor Statistics, U.S. Department of Labor. Supt. of Documents. 1964. 16p. 10c
> Reprint from the *Occupational Outlook Handbook.*

**Employment outlook in restaurant occupations. Bureau of Labor Statistics, U.S. Department of Labor. Supt. of Documents. 1964. 16p. 10c
> Reprint from the *Occupational Outlook Handbook.*

Front office clerks (hotel). One section of *Occupational Outlook Handbook.*
> Nature of work, training, other qualifications, advancement, and employment outlook.

Hotel occupations. Michigan Employment Security Commission. 1959. 24p. 25c
> Introduction, nature of work, location of jobs, working conditions, earnings, employment outlook, requirements for entry, disadvantages, and advantages.

**Hotel occupations. One section of *Occupational Outlook Handbook.*
> Nature of business, kinds of work, employment outlook, earnings and working conditions, and sources of additional information. Specific information is given concerning bellman, front-office clerk, hotel housekeeper, hotel manager, and assistants.

Hotel room clerk. Careers. 1963. 8p. 25c
> Career brief describing duties, working conditions, training, personal qualifications, earnings, and outlook.

Hotel service workers. Science Research Associates. 1961. 4p. 35c
> Occupational brief describing nature of work, training, qualifications, opportunities, advantages, disadvantages, and future outlook.

Opportunities in the hotel industry. Henkin, Shepard. Vocational Guidance Manuals. 1953. 96p. $1.45
> Includes the future of the industry, remuneration, personal requirements, educational preparation, opportunities, how to start, and description of various jobs. List of schools offering courses in hotel training.

Restaurant occupations. Michigan Employment Security Commission. 1960. 24p. 25c
> Introduction, nature of work, location of jobs, working conditions, employment outlook, earnings, requirements for entry, disadvantages, and advantages.

**Restaurant occupations. One chapter of *Occupational Outlook Handbook.*
> Nature and location of the restaurant business, kinds of jobs, and employment outlook. Specific information is given for waiter, cook, manager, and assistant.

Room clerk. Chronicle Guidance Publications. 1958. 4p. 35c
  Occupational brief containing definition, history, work performed working conditions, requirements, opportunities, outlook, methods of entry, related jobs, and suggested activities.

Room clerk. The Guidance Centre. 1962. 4p. 15c in Canada; 20c elsewhere
  Nature of work, qualifications, preparation, working conditions, earnings, advantages, disadvantages, and how to get started.

**Vocational guidance manual for the food service industry. National Restaurant Association. 1958. 20p. Free
  Description of the restaurant industry, variety of types of restaurants, kinds of positions available, advantages, and a list of schools offering food service training.

Will hotel work be your career? American Hotel Association. 1958. 21p. Free
  Description of the many and varied jobs that are part of hotel work.

See also Cook; Food preparation industry worker; Food technologist

HOTEL AND RESTAURANT MANAGER   0-71.

**Careers in hotel administration. Angel, Juvenal L. World Trade Academy Press. 1960. 26p. $1.25
  Information concerning several of the careers in this field of work.

**Executive careers in hotel management and motel operation. Institute for Research. 1957. 24p. $1
  Duties, qualifications, opportunities, advantages, disadvantages, and list of schools offering courses in hotel management. Describes work in housing, accounting, food service, and maintenance.

* Hotel manager. Splaver, Sarah. Personnel Services. 1955. 6p. 50c; 25c to students
  Occupational abstract. Nature of work, qualifications, preparation, entrance and advancement, supply and demand of workers, opportunities for servicemen, advantages, and disadvantages.

Hotel manager. California State Department of Employment. 1961. 4p. Single copy free
  Duties, working conditions, pay, hours, entrance requirements, training, promotion, and employment outlook.

**Hotel manager. Careers. 1960. 8p. 25c
  Career brief describing duties, working conditions, personal qualifications, advantages, disadvantages, earnings, advancement prospects, and outlook. Additional readings.

Hotel managers. Science Research Associates. 1964. 4p. 35c
  Occupational brief describing nature of work, training, qualifications, opportunities, and outlook.

Hotel managers and assistants. One section of *Occupational Outlook Handbook*.
  Nature of work, training, other qualifications, advancement, and employment outlook.

HOTEL AND RESTAURANT MANAGER—*Continued*

Welcome to Dunecrest. Williams, Frances Leigh. Julian Messner, Inc. 1955. 192p. $2.95
> Career fiction. A story that combines a career interest in hotel management with light romance.

**Your future in hotel management. Sonnabend, Roger. Richards Rosen Press. 1963. 160p. $2.95; library edition $2.79 net
> Description of varied kinds of work, training, qualifications, and opportunities. Includes list of schools which offer courses and degrees in hotel management.

See also Motel manager

HOUSEHOLD APPLIANCE SERVICEMAN AND INSTALLER
5-83.000 through 5-83.069

Appliance servicemen. Michigan Employment Security Commission. 1963. 24p. 25c
> Occupational guide describing nature of work, location of jobs, working conditions, employment outlook, earnings, requirements for entry, disadvantages, and advantages.

**Appliance servicemen. One section of *Occupational Outlook Handbook*.
> Nature of work, where employed, training, other qualifications, advancement, employment outlook, earnings, and working conditions.

Electrical appliance serviceman. Chronicle Guidance Publications. 1960. 4p. 35c
> Occupational brief including definition, history, work performed, working conditions, hours, wages, requirements, training, opportunities, methods of entry, related jobs, and suggested activities.

Electrical household appliance serviceman. Careers. 1963. 4p. 25c
> Occupational brief describing nature of work, qualifications, training, opportunities, and outlook.

**Employment outlook for appliance servicemen. Bureau of Labor Statistics, U.S. Department of Labor. Supt. of Documents. 1964. 4p. 5c
> Reprint from the *Occupational Outlook Handbook*.

Home appliance servicemen. Science Research Associates. 1963. 4p. 35c
> Occupational brief describing work, training, qualifications, opportunities, earnings, and outlook.

HOUSEKEEPER
2-25.21

Executive housekeeper. Careers. 1964. 2p. 15c
> Career summary for desk-top file. Duties, qualifications, and outlook.

* Executive housekeepers. Science Research Associates. 1963. 4p. 35c
> Occupational brief describing nature of work, training, qualifications, opportunities, and outlook. Selected references.

Executive housekeeping as a career. Institute for Research. 1957. 20p. $1
> Summary of responsibilities, including outline of duties in hotels, hospitals, and other institutions. Opportunities, salaries, and outlook.

Executive housekeeping as a career. National Executive Housekeepers Association. 1959. 4p. Free
   Brief description of work and opportunities.

Housekeepers and assistants (hotel). One section of *Occupational Outlook Handbook.*
   Nature of work, training, other qualifications, and employment outlook.

ICE CREAM INDUSTRY WORKER   4, 6, 8-06.000 through 4, 6, 8-06.299

**Ice cream manufacturing workers. Science Research Associates. 1961. 4p. 35c
   Occupational brief describing types of work, requirements, methods of getting started, earnings, advantages, disadvantages, and future outlook.

ICHTHYOLOGIST.   *See* Herpetologist; Zoologist

ILLUSTRATING COMMERCIAL ARTIST.   *See* Commercial artist; Medical and scientific illustrator

IMMIGRATION INSPECTOR   0-95.91

**A career with the immigration and naturalization service. Immigration and Naturalization Service. 1962. 12p. Free
   Includes answers to the questions most frequently asked about immigration patrol inspection positions in the border patrol. Minimum requirements and physical qualifications are stated.

* Customs and immigration inspectors. Science Research Associates. 1963. 4p. 35c
   Occupational brief describing work, qualifications, training, opportunities, and outlook.

Immigration inspector. Careers. 1962. 2p. 15c
   Career summary for desk-top file. Duties, qualifications, and outlook.

Immigration patrol inspector. California State Department of Employment. 1961. 3p. Free
   Occupational guide describing job duties, employment outlook, working conditions, earnings, entrance requirements, and training.

IMPORTER.   *See* Exporter and importer

INDUSTRIAL DESIGNER   0-46.88

Automobile-body designer. Careers. 1962. 2p. 15c
   Career summary for desk-top file. Duties, qualifications, and outlook.

* Careers and opportunities in industrial design. Angel, Juvenal. World Trade Academy Press. 1960. 22p. $1.25
   Includes description of work, opportunities, rewards, future outlook, advantages, and disadvantages.

INDUSTRIAL DESIGNER—*Continued*

* Careers for specialized designers. Angel, Juvenal L. World Trade Academy Press. 1957. 31p. $1.25
Career monograph describing fields of specialization; and the training, opportunities, and remuneration for each. Lists of colleges and foundations offering scholarships in the field of design.

**Employment outlook for industrial designers. Bureau of Labor Statistics, U.S. Department of Labor. Supt. of Documents. 1964. 4p. 5c
Reprint from the *Occupational Outlook Handbook.*

IDI and you. Industrial Designers Institute. 1962. 6p. Free
Description of work, abilities needed, training and outlook.

Industrial design as a career. American Society of Industrial Designers. 1959. 6p. 50c; 25c to students
Education bulletin describing nature of the work, training, qualifications, outlook, and earnings.

Industrial designer. Splaver, Sarah. Personnel Services. 1962. 6p. 50c; 25c to students
Occupational abstract. Nature of work, qualifications, preparation, entrance and advancement, supply and demand, and earnings.

* Industrial designer. Careers. 1960. 8p. 25c
Career brief describing duties, working conditions, training, personal qualifications, advancement prospects, earnings, and outlook.

**Industrial designer. Chronicle Guidance Publications. 1961. 4p. 35c
Occupational brief summarizing work performed, working conditions, wages, personal qualifications, training, opportunities, and outlook.

Industrial designer. The Guidance Centre. 1963. 4p. 15c in Canada; 20c elsewhere
Definition, history and importance, nature of work, working conditions, qualifications, preparation, employment and advancement, remuneration, advantages, disadvantages, how to get started, and related occupations.

Industrial designers. Science Research Associates. 1958. 4p. 35c
Occupational brief describing nature of work, qualifications, preparation, opportunities, advantages, disadvantages, and future outlook.

**Industrial designers. One section of *Occupational Outlook Handbook.*
Nature of work, where employed, training, other qualifications, advancement, employment outlook, earnings, and working conditions.

Industrial designing as a career. Institute for Research. 1964. 24p. $1
History and development of the work, duties, personal qualifications, training, opportunities, income, attractive and unattractive features. Also describes the work in a design studio.

A list of colleges offering degree programs in industrial design. Industrial Design Education Association. 1962. 2p. Free
List of forty-four schools.
See also Commercial artist

INDUSTRIAL ENGINEER 0-18.01

Careers in industrial engineering. Angel, Juvenal. World Trade Academy Press. 1958. 26p. $1.25
Description of work, training, advantages, disadvantages, opportunities, and future outlook.

The emerging role of industrial engineering. American Institute of Industrial Engineers. 1961. 6p. 25c
Prepared for management, this describes the nature of the work and areas of opportunity for the future.

Have you considered industrial engineering as a profession? American Institute of Industrial Engineers. No date. 6p. Free
Description of work, challenges, and opportunities.

Industrial engineer. Careers. 1961. 2p. 15c
Career summary for desk-top file. Duties, qualifications, and outlook.

Industrial engineering. Bullinger, C. E. Chapter 15 of *Engineering Enrollment in the United States.*
Trends in college enrollments and future requirements for specialists in this area.

* Industrial engineering as a career. Institute for Research. 1962. 20p. $1
Description of work of the engineer concerned with production, history, types of jobs, typical day's work, qualifications, education and training, list of colleges offering training, attractive and unattractive features, salaries, chances for employment, and related jobs.

Industrial engineering technician. National Council of Technical Schools. 1959. 2p. 5c
Description of work, fields of activity, preparation, opportunities ahead, and advantages.

* Industrial engineers. Science Research Associates. 1963. 4p. 35c
Occupational brief describing areas of specialization, requirements, getting started and advancing, earnings, and future outlook.

Industrial engineers. Brief section in *Occupational Outlook Handbook.*
Nature of work, where employed, and employment outlook.

Should you be a manufacturing engineer? Dykstra, John. New York Life Insurance Company. 1963. 10p. Free
Nature of work, qualifications, training, and rewards.
See also Engineer; Scientist

INDUSTRIAL HYGIENIST
0-07.; 0-18.; 0-26.; 0-33.42; 0-33.60 through 0-33.69

Careers in industrial hygiene through Atomic Energy Commission special fellowships. Oak Ridge Institute of Nuclear Studies. 1962. 17p. Free
Description of work, training, programs of study in several universities at the graduate level, and qualifications for fellowships.

INDUSTRIAL HYGIENIST—*Continued*

Educational qualifications of industrial hygiene personnel other than medical, dental, and nursing. American Public Health Association. 1955. 3p. Free
> Describes training requirements and employment outlook.

Industrial hygienist. Pages 110-13 of *Health Careers Guidebook*.
> Personal qualifications, training, opportunities, and prospects.

* Industrial hygienists. Science Research Associates. 1961. 4p. 35c
> Occupational brief describing nature of work, requirements, training, getting started, earnings, advantages, disadvantages, and future outlook. Selected references.

See also Dental hygienist

INDUSTRIAL MACHINERY REPAIRMAN   5-83.300 through 5-83.999

**Employment outlook for millwrights and industrial machinery repairmen. Bureau of Labor Statistics, U.S. Department of Labor. Supt. of Documents. 1964. 8p. 5c
> Reprint from the *Occupational Outlook Handbook*.

**Industrial machinery repairmen. One section of *Occupational Outlook Handbook*.
> Nature of work, where employed, training, other qualifications, employment outlook, earnings, and working conditions.

INSPECTOR   0-50.53; 4, 6-78.670 through 4, 6-78.709; 7-76.

Factory inspectors. Science Research Associates. 1963. 4p. 35c
> Occupational brief describing nature of work, training, working conditions, opportunities, and outlook.

**Inspectors (factory). One section of *Occupational Outlook Handbook*.
> Nature of work, where employed, training, employment outlook, earnings, and working conditions.

Inspectors—metalworking manufacturing occupations. Chronicle Guidance Publications. 1964. 4p. 35c
> Occupational brief summarizing work performed, types of jobs, working conditions, qualifications, training, opportunities, outlook, unionization, and methods of entry.

INSTRUMENT MAKER   4-75.130; 5-00.912; 5-08.066

Instrument maker. Robinson, H. Alan and Connors, Ralph. Personnel Services. 1962. 6p. 50c; 25c to students
> Occupational abstract. Nature of work, future prospects, qualifications, preparation, entrance, earnings, number and distribution of workers, and related occupations. References for further reading.

* Instrument maker. Chronicle Guidance Publications. 1960. 4p. 35c
> Occupational brief summarizing work performed, training, qualifications, and outlook.

* Instrument makers. Science Research Associates. 1960. 4p. 35c
  Occupational brief describing work, qualifications, training, advantages, disadvantages, and outlook.

**Instrument makers. One section of *Occupational Outlook Handbook*.
  Nature of work, where employed, training, other qualifications, advancement, employment outlook, earnings, and working conditions.

  Instrument technologist. The Guidance Centre. 1961. 4p. 15c
  History and importance, nature of work, qualifications, working conditions, preparation, remuneration, outlook, related occupations, and how to get started.

INSTRUMENT REPAIRMAN   5-83.971

**Employment outlook for instrument repairmen. Bureau of Labor Statistics, U.S. Department of Labor. Supt. of Documents. 1964. 4p. 5c
  Reprint from the *Occupational Outlook Handbook*.

  Instrument repairman. Chronicle Guidance Publications. 1960. 4p. 35c
  Occupational brief summarizing work performed, working conditions, qualifications, training, earnings, where employed, and methods of entry.

  Instrument repairmen. Careers. 1960. 8p. 25c
  Career brief describing duties, working conditions, personal qualifications, places of employment, advancement prospects, earnings, and outlook.

* Instrument repairmen. Science Research Associates. 1963. 4p. 35c
  Occupational brief describing nature of work, preparation, qualifications, opportunities, advantages, disadvantages, and future outlook. Selected references.

**Instrument repairmen. One section of *Occupational Outlook Handbook*.
  Nature of work, where employed, training, employment outlook, earnings, and working conditions.

INSTRUMENTAL MUSICIAN   0-24.12

**Employment outlook in the performing arts. Bureau of Labor Statistics, U.S. Department of Labor. Supt. of Documents. 1964. 16p. 10c
  Reprint from the *Occupational Outlook Handbook*.

  Examination booklet. American Guild of Organists. 1952. 45p. $1.25
  Articles and musical examples containing practical helps and explanations of requirements of the Guild examinations for its certificates.

  Examination papers for associateship with solutions. American Guild of Organists. 1962. 6p. $1
  Also available from the same source are examination papers for fellowship and choir master, with solutions.

  Instrumental musician. California State Department of Employment. 1961. 6p. Single copy free
  Description of work, duties, working conditions, employment outlook, training requirements, and how to find work in California.

  Instrumental musician. Careers. 1960. 2p. 15c
  Career summary for desk-top file. Duties, qualifications, and outlook.

INSTRUMENTAL MUSICIAN—*Continued*

Instrumentalist in popular music. Science Research Associates. 1963. 4p. 35c

> Junior occupational brief containing simplified information about requirements, training, location of jobs, and outlook. Another brief is available on the instrumentalist in classical music.

**Musician, instrumental. Chronicle Guidance Publications. 1960. 4p. 35c

> Occupational brief summarizing work performed, working conditions, earnings, personal qualifications, training requirements, opportunities, and employment outlook.

**Musicians and music teachers. One section of *Occupational Outlook Handbook.*

> Nature of work, where employed, training, other qualifications, employment outlook, earnings, and working conditions.

Opportunity keys with organ music. Hammond Organ Company. 1962. 11p. Single copy free

> Brief descriptions of careers open to those having an interest in organ music.

Preparation for the A.G.O. examinations. American Guild of Organists. 1962. 14p. 35c

> Includes description of the tests at the organ and paper work tests. Another statement is available for the choir master examination requirements.

The unashamed accompanist. Moore, Gerald. Macmillan Company. 1945. 84p. $3.50

> Encourages amateur pianists to take up accompanying for their careers and suggests preparation and qualifications. Most useful, however, as advice to the beginning accompanist.

Well-tempered accompanist. Bos, Coenraad Valentyn. Theodore Presser Company. 1950. 162p. $2.50

> Autobiography of a piano accompanist telling of his experiences over fifty years with the famous singers he accompanies.

See also Musician; Music teacher

INSTRUMENTATION TECHNICIAN 0-67.

Customer engineering—opportunity for a lifetime career. International Business Machines Corporation. 1962. 12p. Free

> This booklet is designed to give an insight into the qualifications, training, and duties of a customer engineer who keeps the machines in customers' offices functioning at peak levels of performance.

**Instrument and control engineering. Slater, Lloyd. Bellman Publishing Company. 1958. 46p. $1

> Description of work of designing and building automatic systems, status and importance of work, duties, qualifications, employment opportunities, remuneration, and future outlook. List of schools offering courses in instrumentation and list of manufacturers offering training courses.

Instrumentation technician. Careers. 1960. 2p. 15c

Career summary for desk-top file. Duties, qualifications, and outlook.

Instrumentation technician. One section of *Occupational Outlook Handbook.*

Brief description of work and employment outlook.

See also Electronic technician; Programmer

INSURANCE WORKER 1-08.; 1-57.

**A career for you in a life insurance company. Institute of Life Insurance. 1962. 16p. Free

Describes job qualifications and career opportunities in a life insurance company home office, such as accountants and auditors, home-office underwriters, electronic engineers, claims estimators, actuaries, and investment analysts.

**A career for you in insurance. Insurance Information Institute. 1961. 48p. Free

Subtitle: Career opportunities in casualty and fire insurance and suretyship. Includes the qualifications and opportunities in the property insurance industry. Illustrated with charts and graphs.

A career in marketing life insurance. Institute of Life Insurance. 1962. 12p. Free

Describes the work of a life underwriter and discusses job opportunities, in-service training, and salary possibilities. Opportunities in sales management are pointed out, including positions in local insurance sales agencies and in life insurance company home offices.

Careers in fire and casualty, accident and health insurance. Institute for Research. 1959. 20p. $1

Duties, requirements for state license, opportunities, advantages and disadvantages. Describes work of general agent, survey agent, contract agent, insurance broker, underwriter, rate man, adjuster, and others in the large departmentalized agency.

Careers in life insurance. Institute for Research. 1957. 24p. $1

Duties, responsibilities, requirements for state license, and lines of advancement for salesmen of ordinary, group, and industrial insurance. Description of home-office work of actuary, secretary, underwriter, and advertising workers.

Casualty insurance. Nilan, John. Bellman Publishing Co. 1945. 24p. $1

Origin and growth of casualty insurance, future outlook, training opportunities provided by casualty companies, and vocational opportunities in supervisory, managerial, technical, and clerical work.

College and university courses in insurance. McCahan, David and Hamburg, Morris. Huebner Foundation for Insurance Education. 1958. 46p. $1

Includes information about courses in actuarial science and mathematics, property insurance, insurance law, and general or survey courses in insurance principles. A revised edition is in preparation.

INSURANCE WORKER—*Continued*

**Employment outlook for insurance and real estate agents and brokers. Bureau of Labor Statistics, U.S. Department of Labor. Supt. of Documents. 1964. 12p. 10c
> Reprint from the *Occupational Outlook Handbook.*

**Employment outlook in insurance occupations. Bureau of Labor Statistics, U.S. Department of Labor. Supt. of Documents. 1964. 5p. 5c
> Reprint from the *Occupational Outlook Handbook.*

General insurance agent. The Guidance Centre. 1962. 4p. 15c in Canada; 20c elsewhere
> History and importance, nature of work, qualifications, working conditions, preparation, remuneration, outlook, related occupations, and how to get started.

Insurance adjuster. The Guidance Centre. 1963. 4p. 15c in Canada; 20c elsewhere
> Nature of work, qualifications, advancement, outlook, remuneration, advantages, disadvantages, how to get started, and related occupations.

Insurance adjusters. Science Research Associates. 1963. 4p. 35c
> Occupational brief describing nature of work, qualifications, getting started and advancing, earnings, advantages, disadvantages, and future outlook.

Insurance agent. Splaver, Sarah. Personnel Services. 1959. 6p. 50c; 25c to students
> Occupational abstract. Nature of work, preparation, entrance, training, earnings, advancement, number of workers, advantages, and disadvantages.

Insurance agents. Science Research Associates. 1961. 4p. 35c
> Occupational brief describing nature of work, requirements, education and training, earnings, how to get a job, advantages, disadvantages, and future outlook.

Insurance as a career. Boston University. 1962. 13p. Free
> Recruiting booklet describing the various types of insurance, the kinds of careers in insurance, and preparation.

Insurance underwriter. Splaver, Sarah. Personnel Services. 1963. 6p. 50c; 25c to students
> Occupational abstract. Nature of work, qualifications, preparation, entrance, advancement, advantages, and disadvantages.

Insurance workers. Science Research Associates. 1960. 4p. 35c
> Occupational brief describing nature of work, qualifications, preparation, opportunities, advantages, disadvantages, and future outlook

**Invitation to youth—careers in life insurance. Institute of Life Insurance. 1963. 36p. 20c. Free to counselors and librarians
> Discussion of career opportunities in the life insurance business, advantages, preparation, and the skills called for.

Life insurance. Stone, Mildred F. Bellman Publishing Company. 1955. 32p. $1
> History, job opportunities, how to obtain a job in life insurance, professional and trade publications and organizations.

Life insurance agent. Careers. 1963. 8p. 25c

Career brief describing duties, working conditions, personal qualifications, advantages, disadvantages, advancement prospects, earnings, and outlook.

Life insurance agent. Chronicle Guidance Publications. 1961. 4p. 35c

Occupational brief summarizing work performed, where employed, personal requirements, training, earnings, methods of entry, and outlook. Selected references.

Life insurance agent. The Guidance Centre. 1960. 4p. 15c in Canada; 20c elsewhere

Nature of work, qualifications, preparation needed for entry and success, employment and advancement, earnings, how to get started, and related occupations.

**Life insurance agents. One section of *Occupational Outlook Handbook*.

Nature of work, where employed, training, other qualifications, advancement, employment outlook, earnings, and working conditions.

The life insurance career. Life Insurance Agency Management Association 1962. 20p. Free

This booklet stresses insurance as a social and economic force and points out the advantages of insurance as a career.

Life insurance selling: careers for women as life underwriters. Women's Bureau, U.S. Department of Labor. Supt. of Documents. 1961. 8p. 5c

Leaflet containing brief statement of nature of work, qualities needed, preparation, opportunities, and what the career offers.

**Life insurance selling: careers for women as life underwriters. Women's Bureau, U.S. Department of Labor. Supt. of Documents. 1961. 35p. 20c

This booklet contains a discussion of the types and changing emphasis of life insurance, nature of work, requisites for success, income and methods of compensation, hours of work, outlook, training opportunities, and how to get started. Six illustrations. This is a fuller statement of the leaflet described above.

Life underwriter. Osler, Robert W. Research Publishing Company. 1959. 32p. $1

Nature of work, history and importance, number engaged in occupation, compensation, qualifications, training, methods of securing jobs, and opportunities for promotion.

**Occupations in the insurance business. One chapter in *Occupational Outlook Handbook*.

Nature of the business, kinds of jobs, where employed, training, other qualifications, advancement, employment outlook, earnings, and working conditions.

Property and casualty insurance agent. Careers. 1961. 2p. 15c

Career summary for desk-top file. Duties, qualifications, and outlook.

**Property and casualty insurance agents and brokers. One section of *Occupational Outlook Handbook*.

Nature of work, where employed, training, other qualifications, employment outlook, and earnings.

INSURANCE WORKER—*Continued*

The Sextant series for exploring your future in insurance. American Liberty Press. 1961. 96p. $5; $4 paper
>One page is devoted to each of ninety-five jobs in the insurance field, summarizing job duties, requirements for entering, promotional outlook, and pay and skill level.

Should you seek a career in life insurance. Myers, Clarence J. New York Life Insurance Company. 1958. 12p. Free
>Description of the field today, income, openings, training, and opportunities.

See also Real estate salesman

INTERIOR DECORATOR   0-43.40

Careers in interior decoration. Stampe, Jean M. and Deyo, Mildred. Rochester Institute of Technology. Revised 1960. 32p. Free
>Discussion of jobs in interior decoration, qualifications, and opportunities. List of fifteen questions which may be used as an interest inventory in this field. Job charts. Illustrated.

**Employment outlook for interior designers and decorators. Bureau of Labor Statistics, U.S. Department of Labor. Supt. of Documents. 1964. 4p. 5c
>Reprint from the *Occupational Outlook Handbook*.

Interior decoration. Splaver, Sarah. Personnel Services. 1956. 6p. 50c; 25c to students
>Occupational abstract. Nature of work, qualifications, preparation, entrance and advancement, supply and demand, earnings, advantages, and disadvantages.

Interior decoration. Alumnae Advisory Center. 1963. 6p. 25c
>Reprint from *Mademoiselle* describing the work of several successful women in this field.

Interior decoration as a career. Institute for Research. 1961. 23p. $1
>Nature of work, qualifications, salaries, opportunities, a typical day's work, and attractive and unattractive features.

* Interior decorator. Chronicle Guidance Publications. 1963. 4p. 35c
>Occupational brief containing definition, history, work performed, working conditions, personal requirements, training requirements, training opportunities, advantages and disadvantages, related jobs, outlook, where employed, methods of entry, and suggested activities.

Interior decorator. The Guidance Centre. 1962. 4p. 15c in Canada; 20c elsewhere
>History and importance, duties, working conditions, qualifications necessary for entry and success, preparation, employment and advancement, advantages, disadvantages, how to enter this field, and related occupations.

* Interior decorators. Science Research Associates. 1959. 4p. 35c
>Occupational brief describing nature of work, training, qualifications, preparation, opportunities, advantages, disadvantages, and future outlook.

Interior design and decoration. Pages 194-204 in *Careers in the Arts—Fine and Applied.*
Opportunities, nature of work, and training.

* Interior designer. Careers. 1963. 8p. 25c
Career brief describing duties, where employed, personal qualifications, training requirements, training opportunities, measuring one's interest and ability, opportunities for men, employment outlook, and related jobs. Suggested references.

**Interior designers and decorators. One section of *Occupational Outlook Handbook.*
Nature of work, where employed, training, other qualifications, advancement, employment outlook, earnings, and working conditions.

**Opportunities in interior design and decoration. Ball, Victoria. Vocational Guidance Manuals. 1963. 126p. $1.45 paper; library edition $2.65
Includes discussion of the development of the work, future outlook, qualifications, preparation, opportunities, how to get started, and related fields.

Roberta: interior decorator. Freer, Marjorie Mueller. Julian Messner, Inc. 1947. 209p. $2.95
Career fiction. The romance contains helpful hints to girls who are thinking of careers in interior decorating.

Schools offering courses in interior design and decoration. One section of the *American Art Directory.*
List of schools in the United States, Canada, and Latin America with information concerning courses and costs.

**Your future in interior design. Greer, Michael. Richards Rosen Press. 1963. 157p. $2.95
Stresses the training and knowledge required for skill in participating in this creative field.

INTERNAL REVENUE AGENT   0-94.

**Careers—the Internal Revenue Service, the revenue agent, the revenue officer, the special agent, the estate tax examiner, and tax technician. Internal Revenue Service. 1962. 20p. each. Free
These may be obtained by addressing requests to the College Recruiter at the local District Office of the Internal Revenue Service.

* Internal revenue agent. Careers. 1961. 8p. 25c
Career brief describing duties, working conditions, training, personal qualifications, advantages, disadvantages, advancement prospects, earnings, and outlook.

Internal revenue agents. Science Research Associates. 1963. 4p. 35c
Occupational brief describing nature of work, training, qualifications, opportunities, and outlook.

INTERPRETER AND TRANSLATOR. *See* Linguist

INVENTOR   0-07.; 0-14. through 0-19.

**Career as an inventor. Institute for Research. 1956. 24p. $1
  Discussion of the trend of invention in America, a typical week's work in an experimental laboratory, nature of work, personal characteristics essential to success, education and training, attractive and unattractive features, earnings, chances for employment in industry, and opportunities for women.

Fathers of industries. Fanning, Leonard. Lippincott Company. 1962. 256p. $4.75
  Twenty-four biographies of inventors whose discoveries led to the huge industries of today. Includes accomplishments of men whose inventive genius helped to develop air conditioning, airplane, aluminum, automobile, machine tool, paper, petroleum, radio, rubber, steel, and textile industries. Illustrated.

Inventive wizard: George Westinghouse. Levine, I. E. Julian Messner, Inc. 1962. 192p. $3.25. Library binding $3.19 net
  Biography of the inventor whose air brakes and signal devices changed the railroad industry and whose work on transmitting electricity at low cost brought power and light to millions.

The young inventor's guide. Yates, Raymond. Harper and Row. 1959. 104p. $2.50
  This book describes the importance and rewards of invention as a career. Also explains methods of work, the educational background needed, and the process of securing a patent and financing an invention.

INVESTMENT COUNSELOR. *See* Securities salesman

IRON AND STEEL INDUSTRY WORKER 4, 6, 8-81. through 4, 6, 8-94.

**Employment outlook for structural-, ornamental-, and reinforcing-iron workers and operating engineers. Bureau of Labor Statistics, U.S. Department of Labor. Supt. of Documents. 1964. 20p. 15c
  Reprint from the *Occupational Outlook Handbook.*

**Employment outlook in the iron and steel industry. Bureau of Labor Statistics, U.S. Department of Labor. Supt. of Documents. 1964. 16p. 10c
  Reprint from the *Occupational Outlook Handbook.*

**Iron and steel industry. Campbell, Tom. Bellman Publishing Company. 1957. 40p. $1
  History and development of the industry, job descriptions, suggested educational preparation for jobs in steel, advantages, disadvantages, earnings, and working conditions.

The iron and steel industry. Chapter 29 in *Occupations and Careers.*
  Information concerning preparing pig iron, making castings, making steel, and rolling steel.

Iron and steel workers. Science Research Associates. 1961. 4p. 35c
  Occupational brief describing some kinds of work, requirements, training, earnings, getting started, advantages, disadvantages, and future outlook.

**Occupations in the iron and steel industry. One section of *Occupational Outlook Handbook*.
Description of jobs in the industry, training, other qualifications, advancement, employment outlook, earnings, and working conditions.

**Structural-, ornamental-, and reinforcing-iron (rodmen) workers. One section of *Occupational Outlook Handbook*.
Nature of work, where employed, training, other qualifications, employment outlook, earnings, and working conditions.

Structural-, ornamental-, and reinforcing-iron workers. Careers. 1961. 7p. 25c
Career brief describing duties, working conditions, training, places of employment, earnings, and outlook.

Wage trends in the iron and steel industry. American Iron and Steel Institute. 1962. 4p. Free
Shows the average hourly earnings of production workers for each of the past twenty-one years.

See also Steel industry worker

JANITOR. *See* Building service worker

JEWELER   4, 6-71.

Career as a jeweler and jewelry store management. Institute for Research. 1961. 24p. $1
Description of duties, a typical day's work, attractive and unattractive features, qualifications, training, earnings, and getting started.

**Employment outlook for watch repairmen, jewelers, and jewelry repairmen. Bureau of Labor Statistics, U.S. Department of Labor. Supt. of Documents. 1964. 12p. 10c
Reprint from the *Occupational Outlook Handbook*.

Jeweler. Robinson, H. Alan. Personnel Services. 1956. 6p. 50c; 25c to students
Occupational abstract. Nature of work, future prospects, qualifications, preparation, entrance and advancement, earnings, number and distribution of workers, advantages and disadvantages, and related occupations.

* Jeweler. Careers. 1964. 8p. 25c
Career brief describing duties, working conditions, personal requirements, training, earnings, and outlook.

**Jeweler. Chronicle Guidance Publications. 1962. 4p. 35c
Occupational brief containing definitions, work performed, working conditions, personal requirements, determination of aptitudes and interests, training requirements, training opportunities, outlook, where employed, and suggested activities.

Jeweler. The Guidance Centre. 1963. 4p. 15c in Canada; 20c elsewhere
Duties, working conditions, qualifications, preparation, advancement, outlook, remuneration, how to get started, and related occupations.

JEWELER—*Continued*

* Jewelers. Science Research Associates. 1961. 4p. 35c

    Occupational brief describing the jewelry trades, requirements, training, getting started and advancing, advantages, disadvantages, and future outlook. Selected references.

**Jewelers and jewelry repairmen. One section of *Occupational Outlook Handbook*.

    Nature of work, where employed, training, other qualifications, employment outlook, earnings, and working conditions.

* The jewelry industry. Frankovich, George R. Bellman Publishing Company. 1956. 26p. $1

    History, organization of industry, job opportunities, how to get a jewelry job, advantages, disadvantages, and trade publications and associations.

    See also Watchmaker

JEWISH CENTER WORKER   0-27.99

Career in health and physical education in the Jewish community center. National Jewish Welfare Board. 1962. 15p. Free

    Description of the health and physical education program and placement of qualified personnel. A separate publication describes a work-scholarship program for health and physical education personnel.

**Careers in community organization work. B'nai B'rith Vocational Service. 1961. 12p. 35c

    Discussion of work in Jewish agencies, duties, number of workers, earnings, qualifications, methods of entry, advancement, outlook, advantages, and disadvantages.

Careers in community relations work. B'nai B'rith Vocational Service. 1961. 12p. 35c

    Discussion of work in Jewish agencies, educational requirements, earnings, major functions, number of workers, methods of entry, outlook, advantages, and disadvantages.

Careers in Jewish education. B'nai B'rith Vocational Service. 1961. 8p. 35c

    Discussion of outlook, the nature of work, special fields, earnings, preparation, training, and job opportunities.

Careers in social casework in Jewish agencies. B'nai B'rith Vocational Service. 1961. 12p. 35c

    Discussion of nature of work, number of workers, educational requirements, salaries, advancement, finding a job, advantages, and disadvantages.

Careers in social group work in Jewish agencies. B'nai B'rith Vocational Service. 1961. 8p. 35c

    Discussion of kinds of jobs, requirements, earnings, methods of entry, advancement, outlook, advantages, and disadvantages.

Careers in vocational service in Jewish agencies. B'nai B'rith Vocational Service. 1961. 12p. 35c
Discussion of kinds of work, duties, educational requirements, earnings, opportunities, outlook, advantages, and disadvantages.

Opportunities in Jewish religious vocations. Duckat, Walter. Vocational Guidance Manuals. 1952. 128p. $1.45
Synagogue vocations, Jewish education, religious vocations in Israel, and communal, dietary, mortuary, and miscellaneous vocations.

Scholarships, fellowships, and work-study plans for graduate social work education for individuals interested in Jewish community center work as a career. National Jewish Welfare Board. 1963. 8p. Free
Issued annually.

Your career opportunity in the Jewish community center. National Jewish Welfare Board. 1962. 12p. Free
Nature of work, qualifications, and practices.

Your opportunity for a professional career in Jewish communal service. B'nai B'rith Vocational Service. 1962. 12p. 35c
Description of nature of work, opportunities, and outlook.

JOB ANALYST   0-39.85

Job analyst. Careers. 1962. 2p. 15c
Career summary for desk-top file. Duties, qualifications, and outlook.

Job analyst. Chronicle Guidance Publications. 1964. 4p. 35c
Occupational brief describing nature of work, qualifications, working conditions, opportunities for promotion, and outlook.

JOURNALIST   0-06.

The big story: ten questions and answers about the booming career field of journalism and communications. Sigma Delta Chi. No date. 12p. Free
Discussion of nature of work, opportunities, salaries, incentives besides pay, preparation, and advancement.

**Careers in journalism. Angel, Juvenal L. World Trade Academy Press. 1957. 26p. $1.25
Historical background, qualifications required, training, description of specialized careers in the field of journalism, opportunities, salaries, advantages, and disadvantages. Also included is a list of private organizations and educational institutions offering scholarships and fellowships in journalism.

Careers in journalism. Campbell, Laurence R. Quill and Scroll Society. 1955. 132p. $1.25 paper; $2.20 cloth
Discussion of careers and opportunities open on daily and weekly newspapers and also in press associations and syndicates and on magazine, business papers, and house publications. Consists of a series of forty-seven articles on jobs in journalism prepared by leaders and educators in media of mass communications. Bibliography. Revision in preparation.

JOURNALIST—*Continued*

Careers in journalism—recommended readings. Sigma Delta Chi. 1962. 1p. Free
> List of six books and eleven booklets.

**Choosing a career in journalism. American Council on Education for Journalism. 1960. 32p. 35c
> Description of career opportunities in the various phases of journalism. Suggestions for educational preparation and choosing a school of journalism. Good list of references.

Directory issue. The Journalism Educator. 1963. 32p. $2
> Bulletin of the American Society of Journalism School Administrators containing list of 140 schools and departments offering majors or degrees in journalism. Name of journalism unit is followed by year in which established, association affiliations, student organizations, facilities, and degrees offered.

**Do you belong in journalism? Gemmill, Henry and Kilgore, Bernard. Appleton-Century-Crofts. 1959. 92p. $3
> Eighteen leading newspaper editors give the advice they would give to an interested young man or woman who was considering newspaper work. Carefully considered counsel. The final chapters sum up the requirements: "The first requirement is a college diploma . . . one should like people, reading, travel, and new experience." Illustrated.

English and journalism: earned degrees, by level, sex, and institution. One section of *Earned Degrees Conferred*.
> Useful for judging the extent of a college's program in journalism and in English and literature.

**Find a career in journalism. Parsons, Tom. Putnam's Sons. 1959. 160p. $2.95
> An introduction to the many fields of journalism, the advantages of each, general background and special training necessary, rewards, and tips on how the reader can begin obtaining practical experience. Written for ages 11 to 15.

* Finding a successful career in the daily newspaper business. American Newspaper Publishers Association Foundation. 1962. 48p. 20c Single copy free
> Information about newspaper careers is given under these headings: reporting and editing the news, newspaper business management, newspaper circulation careers, advertising department, newspaper promotion, and production of a daily newspaper.

Foreign correspondents. Science Research Associates. 1957. 4p. 35c
> Occupational brief describing work, requirements, getting started, earnings, advantages, disadvantages, and outlook.

Get that story—journalism, its lore and thrills. Floherty, John J. J. B. Lippincott Company. 1952. 176p. $3.95
> A résumé of the origin and early history of newspapers is followed by an account of reporting, editing, printing, and distribution of a large metropolitan daily. Chapters are included on the work of country newspapers, newspaper photography, and stories of reporters' luck and achievement in journalism. Sixteen pages and photographs.

I wanted to write. Roberts, Kenneth Lewis. Doubleday and Company. 1949. 471p. $4
An author describes his experiences as a roving reporter and his ambition to become a successful writer.

I work on a newspaper. Lent, Henry B. Macmillan Company. 1948. 152p. $3.95
Describing one complete day in a newspaper plant, the author shows how news is received, written, and printed. Fifty illustrations.

Industrial journalist. Menne, Susan. Research Publishing Company. 1956. 31p. $1
Importance of the occupation, personal qualifications, skills needed, salaries, and training. Includes list of sixty-seven approved schools.

Job opportunities for journalism graduates. The Newspaper Fund. 1962. 1p. Free
Survey of forty-one colleges which reported on the number of journalism graduates, number of jobs available in 1962, average beginning salary, and salary range.

Jobs in journalism. Changing Times. 1959. 3p. 15c
Reprint discussing opportunities in newspaper work and related careers.

Joseph Pulitzer: front page pioneer. Noble, Iris. Julian Messner, Inc. 1957. 192p. $3.25. Library binding $3.19 net
Biography of a reporter and newspaper owner, containing considerable inspiring material.

Journalism . . . a key to many doors. Western Personnel Institute. 1955. 4p. 20c
Describes opportunities in many various fields, qualifications, and preparation.

Journalism as a career. Boston University. 1962. 13p. Free
Recruiting booklet describing work on a newspaper, other opportunities, qualifications, advantages, disadvantages, and preparation.

Journalism as a career. Institute for Research. 1955. 24p. $1
Describes work of publisher, editorial staff, business department, and mechanical department. Includes information concerning rewrite man, copy-reader, special writer, critic, correspondent, and columnist. Discusses qualifications, training, opportunities, salaries, attractive and unattractive features.

Journalism as a profession. The Milwaukee Journal. 1951. 40p. Single copies free; $17.50 per hundred
Excerpts from talks by *Milwaukee Journal* staff members highlighting requirements and personal qualifications important in the pursuit of a journalistic career.

Journalism scholarship guide. Newspaper Fund, Inc. 1964. 65p. Free
A listing of scholarships, fellowships, assistantships, and loans at about one hundred universities. Also included is a listing of the approximate number and total value of general scholarships offered at most of these schools.

Journalism; writing; publishing. Chapter 21 of *Vocations for Boys*.
Discussion of factors making for success in journalism, some of the specialized functions, qualifications, and opportunities.

JOURNALIST—*Continued*

**Journalist. Brucker, Herbert. Macmillan Company. 1962. 211p. $3.50
> The author draws upon his experience as a journalist and editor to provide a picture of education and necessary preparation, the different kinds of work available, and the excitement of an average day at a newspaper office.

* Journalist. Careers. 1962. 8p. 25c
> Career brief describing the work of news gathering and writing, working conditions, training requirements, personal qualifications, employment prospects, advantages, disadvantages, earnings, promotional prospects, measuring one's interest and ability, and suggested high school subjects.

* Journalist. Chronicle Guidance Publications. 1962. 4p. 35c
> Occupational brief containing definition, work performed, working conditions, personal requirements, determination of aptitudes and interests, training requirements, training opportunities, outlook, and methods of entry. Selected references.

Journalists. Michigan Employment Security Commission. 1956. 23p. 25c
> Introduction, nature of work, working conditions, location of jobs, employment outlook, earnings, qualifications for entry, organizations, advantages, and disadvantages.

One hundred books for new journalists. Newspaper Fund. 1963. 6p. Free
> Includes many biographies and anecdotal accounts.

Opportunities in business papers. Morrison, Joseph L. Vocational Guidance Manuals. 1955. 96p. $1.45
> Development of business publications, opportunities, training, how to get started, job classifications, and outlook.

Opportunities in journalism. American Press. 1956. 11p. 50c
> Description of kinds of work, qualifications, and opportunities.

**Opportunities in newspaper careers. Barry, John M. Vocational Guidance Manuals. 1960. 128p. $1.45
> Discussion of the newspaper industry, the challenge of the future, intangible rewards, outlook for jobs, training, educational preparation, related fields, and classifications of editorial work. List of schools and departments of journalism.

Printer's devil to publisher; Adolph S. Ochs of the New York *Times*. Faber, Doris. Julian Messner, Inc. 1963. 192p. $3.25. Library binding $3.19 net
> Biography of the man who worked his way up from delivery boy to control of one of the world's greatest newspapers.

Programs in journalism. American Council on Education for Journalism. 1962. 12p. Free
> List of institutions of higher learning accredited by the American Council on Education for Journalism and holding membership in the Association of Accredited Schools and Departments of Journalism. Also lists the schools offering accredited sequences or curricula, such as advertising, radio journalism, news-editorial, etc.

Should you be a newspaperman? Biggers, George C. New York Life Insurance Company. 1960. 12p. Free
> Includes qualities one should possess, cost of training, and advantages.

**So you want to go into journalism. Ryan, Leonard Eames and Ryan, Bernard. Harper and Row. 1963. 192p. $3.50; library binding $3.27 net
>Stressing requirements and opportunities, this book includes vignettes of journalists at work; aerospace reporter, UN correspondent, wire service newsmen, television news photographer, small town stringer, fashion columnist, weekly editor, and managing editor. List of colleges accredited by the American Council on Education for Journalism. Written by an advertising copywriter and a reporter with the New York *Times*.

Your career opportunities in journalism. Novak, Gail, ed. Rowman and Littlefield, Inc. 1962. 64p. 75c
>One of the Visual Career Guides, about one half of which consists of photographs and charts. Includes description of the various kinds of work, qualifications, and employment outlook.

**Your future in journalism. Schaleben, Arville. Richards Rosen Press. 1961. 158p. $2.95
>Describes the work of the editor, news reporter, and some of the specialists such as the photographer and picture editor. Includes also a discussion of requirements, opportunities, salaries, and a self-evaluation test. List of accredited schools.

Your future in journalism. Schaleben, Arville. Popular Library, Inc. 1961. 158p. 50c
>A paperback edition of the book described above.

See also Editor; Reporter; Writer

KINDERGARTEN TEACHER   0-30.02

**Kindergarten and elementary school teachers. One section of *Occupational Outlook Handbook.*
>Nature of work, where employed, training, other qualifications, advancement, employment outlook, earnings, and working conditions.

**Kindergarten and nursery school teachers. Science Research Associates. 1962. 4p. 35c
>Occupational brief describing nature of work, requirements, training, getting started, earnings, advantages, disadvantages, and future outlook.

Kindergarten teacher. Splaver, Sarah. Personnel Services. 1957. 6p. 50c; 25c to students
>Occupational abstract. Nature of the work, qualifications, preparation, entrance, advancement, supply and demand, earnings, advantages, and disadvantages.

Kindergarten teacher. Careers. 1961. 2p. 15c
>Career summary for desk-top file. Duties, qualifications, and outlook.

* Kindergarten teaching as a career. Institute for Research. 1964. 24p. $1
>Development and present status of the kindergarten, a typical day's work, personal qualifications, preparation, opportunities, salaries, attractive and unattractive features.

See also Elementary school teacher: Nursery school teacher; Teacher

LABOR RELATIONS SPECIALIST   0-68.76

Careers in labor relations in industry, unions, government. Institute for Research. 1956. 24p. $1
> History and types of work, attractive and unattractive features, educational preparation, compensation, how to get started, and related positions.

**Industrial and labor relations workers. Science Research Associates. 1961. 4p. 35c
> Occupational brief describing nature of work, training, qualifications, opportunities, advantages, disadvantages, and future outlook.

Jobs in employee relations. Yoder, Dale and Nelson, Roberta. American Management Association. 1959. 52p. $1.50
> Description of the kinds of work in this area.

Labor management as a career. Manhattan College. 1963. 8p. Free
> Description of work, rewards, and training. One of a series of thirty guidance bulletins.

Labor relations man in industry. California State Department of Employment. 1961. 6p. Single copy free
> Job duties, working conditions, pay, hours, entrance requirements, promotion, training, and employment outlook.

* Labor relations specialist. Careers. 1964. 2p. 15c
> Career summary for desk-top file. Duties, qualifications, and outlook.

See also Personnel and employment manager

LABORATORY TECHNICIAN   0-50.

**Basic sciences in the health field. Pages 57-63 of *Health Careers Guidebook.*
> Discussion of some of the interlocking specialties, exploring new health frontiers, getting a start in science, outlook for careers in science, a list of science specialists, and a description of work in laboratory administration and maintenance.

Educational and experience qualifications of public health laboratory workers. American Public Health Association. 1950. 7p. Free
> Includes qualifications for various grades of laboratory workers.

For an age of science: a laboratory career. Ohio Department of Health. No date. 6p. Free
> Description of work and qualifications of public health bacteriologist, public health chemist, clinical laboratory technician, and scientific research worker.

Histology technician. Careers. 1959. 2p. 15c
> Career summary for desk-top file. Duties, qualifications, and outlook.

Industrial laboratory technician. Chronicle Guidance Publications. 1964. 4p. 35c
> Occupational brief summarizing the work performed, working conditions, qualifications, training, earnings, opportunities, advantages, disadvantages, and outlook.

Laboratory technician: materials and soil tester. Chronicle Guidance Publications. 1962. 4p. 35c
Occupational brief summarizing work performed with chemicals, animals, plants, and soil. Includes also training, qualifications, opportunities, and outlook.

Positions of laboratory aide in the laboratory of the Federal Bureau of Investigation. The Bureau. 1960. 1p. Free
Brief statement of nature of work and qualifications.

Technical positions for male applicants in the laboratory of the FBI. Federal Bureau of Investigation. 1960. 3p. Free
Description of work and qualifications.

See also Medical technologist

LANDSCAPE ARCHITECT 0-03.20

**Careers as a landscape architect and landscape nurseryman. Institute for Research. 1961. 24p. $1
History, nature of work, specialties in landscape work, typical day's work, attractive and unattractive features, qualifications, education and training, earnings, opportunities, related positions, and how to get started.

The curriculum in landscape architecture. Michigan State University. 1962. 6p. Free
Description of the work of planning land development and the courses offered.

**Employment outlook for landscape architects. American Society of Landscape Architects. 1961. 4p. 10c
Reprint from the *Occupational Outlook Quarterly* describing nature of work, training, qualifications, earnings, and employment outlook.

**Employment outlook for landscape architects. Bureau of Labor Statistics, U.S. Department of Labor. Supt. of Documents. 1964. 4p. 5c
Reprint from the *Occupational Outlook Handbook.*

Have you ever thought of being a landscape nurseryman? American Association of Nurserymen. 1962. 6p. Free
Description of duties, qualifications, training, and opportunities.

Landscape architect. Careers. 1963. 2p. 15c
Career summary for desk-top file. Describes duties, qualifications, training, working conditions, outlook, and ways of measuring one's interest and ability.

* Landscape architect. Chronicle Guidance Publications. 1963. 4p. 35c
Occupational brief summarizing work performed, working conditions, requirements, training, where employed, methods of entry, related jobs, and outlook. Selected references.

Landscape architect. The Guidance Centre. 1962. 4p. 15c in Canada; 20c elsewhere
History and importance, nature of work, qualifications, working conditions, preparation, remuneration, advancement, outlook, related occupations, and how to get started.

LANDSCAPE ARCHITECT—*Continued*

The landscape architect and land planning. American Society of Landscape Architects. 1962. 4p. 10c
> Illustrated folder describing the character and scope of the work, opportunities,
> and compensation.

* Landscape architects. Science Research Associates. 1961. 4p. 35c
> Occupational brief describing nature of work, requirements, methods of
> getting started, earnings, opportunities, advantages, disadvantages, and future
> outlook.

**Landscape architects. One section of *Occupational Outlook Handbook*.
> Nature of work, where employed, training, other qualifications, advancement,
> employment outlook, earnings, and working conditions.

* Landscape architecture, a professional career in land planning. American
Society of Landscape Architects. 1960. 6p. 5c; free to counselors or
librarians
> Illustrated brochure describing need, training, duties, and opportunities.

List of accredited schools in landscape architecture. American Society
of Landscape Architects. 1962. 1p. Free
> List of sixteen accredited schools and the degrees conferred on completion of
> their professional curricula in landscape architecture.

**Opportunities in landscape architecture. Griswold, Ralph. Vocational
Guidance Manuals. 1961. 80p. $1.45 paper
> Nature of work, preparation, education, rewards, opportunities, and advance-
> ment. List of professional and nonprofessional organizations.

The work and education of a landscape architect. State University of
New York, College of Forestry. 1962. 4p. Free
> Description of kinds of work, places of employment, qualifications, salaries,
> training, and ways of getting started.

See also Architect; Horticulturist; Nurseryman

LATHER   5-32.761

**Employment outlook for plasterers, lathers, and cement masons. Bureau
of Labor Statistics, U.S. Department of Labor. Supt. of Documents.
1964. 20p. 15c
> Reprint from the *Occupational Outlook Handbook*.

Lather. One section of *Occupational Outlook Handbook*.
> Nature of work, where employed, training and other qualifications, employ-
> ment outlook, earnings, and working conditions.

LAUNDRY INDUSTRY WORKER   5, 7, 9-57.

Career as dry cleaner and spotter. B'nai B'rith Vocational Service. 1952.
6p. 35c
> Description of duties, qualifications, working conditions, getting a job, number
> of workers, and employment outlook for both the dry cleaner and the spotter.

* Cleaning and dyeing workers. Science Research Associates. 1961. 4p. 35c
  Occupational brief describing nature of work, conditions of work, opportunities, advantages, disadvantages, and future outlook.

Cleaning and pressing occupations. Michigan Employment Security Commission. 1956. 16p. 25c
  Introduction, nature of work, working conditions, location of jobs, employment outlook, earnings, qualifications for entry, organizations, disadvantages, and advantages.

Dry cleaner spotter. Careers. 1961. 2p. 15c
  Career summary for desk-top file. Duties, qualifications, and outlook.

* Dry cleaning industry jobs. Careers. 1963. 8p. 25c
  Career brief describing kinds of work, training, employment prospects, earnings, advancement prospects, and determination of aptitudes and interest. Suggested references.

Education at NID. National Institute of Drycleaning. No date. 31p. Free
  School catalog describing resident and correspondence courses offered by the institute. Entrance requirements are also explained.

Finding out about dry cleaning workers. Science Research Associates. 1963. 4p. 35c
  Junior occupational brief containing simplified information about nature of work, training, earnings, and opportunities.

Jobs in the dry cleaning industry. Chronicle Guidance Publications. 1963. 4p. 35c
  Occupational brief summarizing work performed, working conditions, hours, wages, qualifications, training, methods of entry, opportunities, and outlook.

* Laundry workers. Science Research Associates. 1961. 4p. 35c
  Occupational brief describing types of work, requirements, getting started and advancing, earnings, pros and cons, and future outlook.

* Opportunity and a future in the drycleaning industry. National Institute of Drycleaning. No date. 16p. Free
  Duties, requirements, and educational courses that are helpful for each of the jobs in the industry. Includes sales, office work, marking, cleaning, spotting, repairing, wetcleaning, finishing, inspection, assembling, bagging, and specialties. Illustrated.

Presser, women's garments. Careers. 1962. 2p. 15c
  Career summary for desk-top file. Duties, qualifications, and outlook.

Shirt presser. Careers. 1963. 2p. 15c
  Career summary for desk-top file. Duties, qualifications, and outlook.

LAWYER   0-22.

Career as a corporation lawyer. Institute for Research. 1960. 24p. $1
  Description of work, attractive and unattractive features, qualifications, training, earnings, getting started, and opportunities in related areas.

LAWYER—*Continued*

Career as a patent attorney. Institute for Research. 1961. 23p. $1

Nature of work, a typical day's activities, attractive and unattractive features, qualifications, training, earnings, and outlook.

Careers for women in the legal profession. Angel, Juvenal. World Trade Academy Press. 1961. 30p. $1.25

Includes description of the major fields of specialization and employment, geographic distribution of women lawyers, where women lawyers work, admission requirements by the law schools, and list of colleges offering scholarships in the field of law. References for further reading.

**Careers in law. American Bar Association. 1961. 30p. 25c

Discussion of prelegal and legal education; law school admission requirements and costs; specialized practice in government, business, and civil service; types of practice; and statistics of the profession.

Careers in law. Washington University. No date. 8p. Free

An example of a recruiting booklet which includes description of law in private practice, government service, business, and military service.

Careers in the law. Changing Times. 1960. 4p. 15c

Report on prospects, pay, and preparation for the legal profession.

**Careers in the legal profession. Angel, Juvenal. World Trade Academy Press. 1960. 28p. $1.25

Description of work, personal qualifications, admission requirements of the law schools, training, opportunities, specializations in the legal profession, remuneration, opportunities for women, advantages, and disadvantages. Also included is a list of colleges and private foundations offering scholarships in the field of law. Bibliography.

Clarence Darrow: defense attorney. Noble, Iris. Julian Messner, Inc. 1958. 192p. $3.25. Library binding $3.19 net

Biography of a man known as a fighter for social progress and a defender of unpopular causes.

Employment opportunities for attorneys. U.S. Securities and Exchange Commission. 1962. 4p. Free

Information about the location of positions, duties to be performed, recruitment policy, salaries, career opportunities, fringe benefits, and examinations.

**Employment opportunities for women in legal work. Women's Bureau, U.S. Department of Labor. Supt. of Documents. 1958. 34p. 20c

Summary of the progress of women in the legal field, the preparation needed, and the prospective opportunities for women as practicing attorneys and in salaried positions where legal training is required. Includes a chart showing the number of lawyers, by sex, in each of the states.

**Employment outlook for lawyers. Bureau of Labor Statistics, U.S. Department of Labor. Supt. of Documents. 1964. 4p. 5c

Reprint from the *Occupational Outlook Handbook.*

How to score high on the law school admission test. Gruber, Edward. Arco Publishing Company. 1962. 364p. $4
Contains questions in law interpretation; nonverbal reasoning; graph, chart, and table interpretation; reading comprehension; writing ability, and cultural background. Included is a sample test resembling the Law School Aptitude Test.

Law. Robinson, H. Alan and Wells, Ruth. Personnel Services. 1961. 6p. 50c; 25c to students
Occupational abstract. Nature of work, qualifications, preparation, entrance, advancement, earnings, number and distribution of lawyers, advantages and disadvantages.

Law as a career. Boston University. 1962. 10p. Free
Recruiting booklet describing the challenge of law, opportunities, qualifications, entering the profession, advancement, rewards, and training.

Law as a career. Institute for Research. 1963. 24p. $1
Discussion of training, opportunities, income, advantages, disadvantages, and legal ethics. Includes description of specialized work of the trial, criminal, tax, real estate, and collection lawyer.

Law: earned degrees, by level, sex, and institution. One section of *Earned Degrees Conferred.*
List of 135 schools and the number of bachelor's, master's, and doctor's degrees conferred by each.

Law school admission test. Educational Testing Service. Published annually. Free.
Bulletin of information for candidates. Includes list of institutions which require the test, list of examination centers, and sample test questions.

* Lawyer. Careers. 1963. 8p. 25c
Career brief describing history, duties, working conditions, training requirements, personal qualifications, employment prospects, advancement prospects, earnings, related careers, measuring one's interest and ability, and suggested high school program.

* Lawyer. Chronicle Guidance Publications. 1960. 4p. 35c
Occupational brief summarizing work performed, working conditions, earnings, personal qualifications, training requirements, opportunities, and employment outlook.

Lawyer. The Guidance Centre. 1961. 4p. 15c in Canada; 20c elsewhere
History and importance of the profession, nature of work, qualifications, preparation, advancement opportunities, earnings, how to get started, and related occupations.

**Lawyer; opportunities for careers in the legal profession. Smith, Talbot. Macmillan Company. 1961. 201p. $3.50
Discussion of the various kinds of specialization open to the young lawyer, the necessary characteristics to achieve success, and the future outlook. Written by a justice of the Supreme Court of Michigan.

Lawyers. Michigan Employment Security Commission. 1958. 16p. 25c
Introduction, nature of work, location of jobs, working conditions, employment outlook, earnings, requirements for entry, disadvantages, and advantages.

LAWYER—*Continued*

* Lawyers. Science Research Associates. 1958. 4p. 35c
    Occupational brief describing nature of work, training, qualifications, opportunities, advantages, disadvantages, and future outlook.

**Lawyers. One section of *Occupational Outlook Handbook*.
    Nature of work, where employed, training, other qualifications, advancement, employment outlook, earnings, and working conditions.

Lawyers. Pages 182-96 of *The College Girl Looks Ahead*.
    Characteristics of work, talents needed, trying out for legal work, and obtaining a start.

Linda Jordan: lawyer. Block, Jean Libman. Julian Messner, Inc. 1953. 173p. $2.95
    Career fiction. Romance and experiences of two law students in their last year of training, showing some of the satisfactions and drudgery in the law profession.

**Listen to leaders in law. Love, Albert and Childers, J. S., editors. Holt, Rinehart and Winston. 1963. 332p. $4.75
    Sixteen lawyers offer advice for young people considering this profession.

Opportunities in law. Elliott, Shelden D. Vocational Guidance Manuals. 1958. 96p. $1.45 paper
    Nature of work, qualifications, preparation, opportunities, and employment outlook.

* Patent law as a profession. Bellman Publishing Co. 1945. 24p. $1
    Duties, qualifications, preliminary education, training, and a description of work in the government, in independent practice, in corporations, and in litigation.

The profession of law. American Bar Association. 1961. 8p. Free
    A concise statement of personal characteristics necessary, education, and rewards.

Should you be a lawyer? Pound, Roscoe. New York Life Insurance Company. 1961. 12p. Free
    Includes qualities one should possess, cost of training, prospects, and advantages.

**So you want to be a lawyer. Nourse, William B. Harper and Row. 1959. 184p. $3.50
    Description of the work of the private practitioner, prelaw education, the choice of a law school, the courses for each year of law school, the bar examination, and the many career fields within the profession.

**So you want to be a lawyer! A vocational guidance manual. Redden, Kenneth R. Bobbs-Merrill Company. 1953. 139p. $3.25
    Discussion of what law is like and what lawyers do, what it takes to be a lawyer, what to study to become a lawyer, how to become a lawyer, number and distribution of lawyers, women lawyers, income, and outlook. Average net income of lawyers is given by years, age, number of years in practice, and type of practice.

Vida Prescott: attorney. Brady, Rita. Abelard-Schuman. 1957. 208p. $2.75
    Career fiction. Story of a girl's first job as a lawyer in her father's office where she unexpectedly finds herself in charge.

LAYOUT MAN (MACHINE TOOLS)   4-75.140

Layout men (machine tools). One section of *Occupational Outlook Handbook*.
    Nature of work, where employed, training, other qualifications, and employment outlook.

LAYOUT MAN (PRINTING)   0-44.25

Lay-out man (printing). Careers. 1962. 2p. 15c
    Career summary for desk-top file. Duties, qualifications, and outlook.

LEATHER INDUSTRY WORKER   4, 6, 8-59. through 4, 6, 8-62.

* Leather manufacturing workers. Science Research Associates. 1961. 4p. 35c
    Occupational brief describing types of work, requirements, methods of getting started, wages, advantages, disadvantages, and future outlook.

The story of leather. Ohio Leather Company. 1949. 80p. Free
    Description of a trip through a modern leather plant, thirty-three of the photographs showing various workers engaged in the processing of leather.

LEGAL SECRETARY   1-33.01

**Career as a legal secretary. Institute for Research. 1957. 20p. $1
    History, duties, typical day's work, attractive and unattractive features, qualifications, training, earnings, chances for employment, how to get started, and related jobs. Includes also a discussion of opportunities for men.

Finding out about legal secretaries. Science Research Associates. 1962. 4p. 35c
    Junior occupational brief containing facts about the job.

* Legal secretaries. Science Research Associates. 1961. 4p. 35c
    Occupational brief describing work, qualifications, training, earnings, things to consider, related jobs, and outlook. Selected references.

Legal secretary. Splaver, Sarah. Personnel Services. 1957. 6p. 50c; 25c to students
    Nature of the work, qualifications, preparation, entrance and advancement, supply and demand, earnings, advantages, and disadvantages. Bibliography.

Legal secretary. California State Department of Employment. 1962. 4p. Single copy free
    Job duties, working conditions, pay, hours, training, promotion, and employment outlook.

LEGAL SECRETARY—*Continued*

Legal secretary. Careers. 1960. 2p. 15c
Career summary for desk-top file. Duties, qualifications, and outlook.

Toby: law stenographer. Bloom, Pauline. Julian Messner, Inc. 1959. 192p. $2.95
Career fiction. Working for a law firm as stenographer, Toby makes mistakes in the first few weeks, but enthusiasm and adaptability help her meet the tests of a difficult job.

LIBRARIAN 0-23.

Accredited graduate library schools. Special Libraries Association. 1962. 1p. Single copy free
List of the currently accredited thirty-two schools.

Accredited library schools. American Library Association. 1963. 2p. Free
List of thirty-three library schools, followed by location, dates of establishment, and names of administrative officers. Issued semiannually in February and August.

Are you telling the library story? American Library Association, Office for Recruitment. 1959. 8p. Free
Checklist devised for the librarian for her use in the "person to person" recruiting program.

At the very center . . . of every area of national emphasis . . . the librarian. American Library Association, Office for Recruitment. No date. 6p. Single copy free
A recruitment leaflet describing the varied types of work and the many kinds of libraries.

Bookmobile librarian. Robinson, H. Alan. Personnel Services. 1957. 6p. 50c; 25c to students
Occupational abstract describing nature of work, future prospects, qualifications, preparation, entrance and advancement, certification, advantages, disadvantages, and related occupations.

Bright particular star. Garthwaite, Marion. Julian Messner, Inc. 1958. 192p. $2.95
Career fiction. Includes description of training in a graduate library school and work as a children's librarian.

Career as a special librarian. Institute for Research. 1958. 20p. $1
Importance and history of the career, nature of work, typical day's work, qualifications, education and training, list of library schools, salaries, attractive and unattractive features, outlook, getting started, and starting a special library.

A career for you as a Veterans Administration hospital librarian. Veterans Administration, Department of Medicine and Surgery. 1962. 4p. Free
Description of work, training program, qualifications, and benefits.

Careers for the professional librarian. Angel, Juvenal L. World Trade Academy Press. 1959. 31p. $1.25

Career monograph describing aptitudes required, training, major fields of specialization, opportunities, supply and demand, positions open, remuneration, advantages, and disadvantages. One list contains names of colleges offering scholarships and another the names of foundations and private organizations.

Careers in librarianship. Graduate Library School, University of Chicago. 1962. 8p. Free

Discussion of opportunities and training.

Certification of school librarians. U.S. Office of Education. Supt. of Documents. 1958. 73p. 30c

A compilation, arranged by states, of current certification regulations and a summary of practices in formulating them.

Children's librarian. Careers. 1963. 2p. 15c

Career summary for desk-top file. Duties, qualifications, and outlook.

Curious missie. Sorensen, Virginia. Harcourt, Brace and World. 1953. 208p. $3

Career fiction. Story of a librarian.

Data sheets on special librarianship. Special Libraries Association. 1962. 8p. Single copies free

One page devoted to special librarianship in each of the following fields: advertising and public relations, biological sciences, business and finance, fine and applied arts, gas and petroleum industry, insurance, publishing and newspapers, and science and technology.

**Employment outlook for librarians. Bureau of Labor Statistics, U.S. Department of Labor. Supt. of Documents. 1964. 5p. 5c

Reprint from the Occupational Outlook Handbook.

Fellowships, scholarships, grants-in-aid, loan funds, and other assistance for library education in the United States and Canada. American Library Association. 1963. 104p. 50c

Includes funds available from library schools and other funds available to residents of specific states or cities.

High school librarian. Careers. 1962. 2p. 15c

Career summary for desk-top file. Duties, qualifications, and outlook.

I want to be a librarian. Greene, Carla. Childrens Press. 1960. 32p. $2

Prepared for beginning readers with a reading level of upper first grade. Illustrated in color.

Jinny Williams: library assistant. Temkin, Sara A. and Hovell, Lucy A. Julian Messner, Inc. 1962. 192p. $2.95

Career fiction. The book suggests that those for whom college is impossible may find rewarding work as a library assistant. The clerical duties, cataloging, mending, sorting, assisting where needed, and volunteering where useful won deserved promotion.

LIBRARIAN—*Continued*

Law librarianship: a profession with a future. Book Publishing Company. No date. 6p. Free
Description of work, where employed, earnings, qualifications, and job prospects.

Librarian. Splaver, Sarah. Personnel Services. 1961. 6p. 50c; 25c to students
Occupational abstract. Nature of work, qualifications, preparation, earnings, number and distribution, advantages, disadvantages, and future prospects.

* Librarian. Careers. 1963. 8p. 25c
Career brief describing duties, working conditions, personal qualifications, advantages, disadvantages, training, earnings, and outlook. List of accredited library schools.

Librarian. Chronicle Guidance Publications. 1960. 4p. 35c
Occupational brief summarizing work performed, working conditions, earnings, personal qualifications, training requirements, opportunities, and employment outlook.

Librarian. The Guidance Centre. 1960. 4p. 15c in Canada; 20c elsewhere
Development and importance of work, duties, qualifications, preparation, working conditions, remuneration, advantages, disadvantages, and related occupations.

The librarian—idea consultant. American Library Association, Office for Recruitment. 1962. 8p. Single copy free
Illustrated booklet describing work, opportunities, and how to begin a library career.

Librarians. Michigan Employment Security Commission. 1960. 19p. 25c
Introduction, nature of work, working conditions, location of jobs, employment outlook, earnings, requirements for entry, disadvantages, and advantages.

Librarians. Science Research Associates. 1959. 4p. 35c
Occupational brief describing nature of work, training, qualifications, opportunities, advantages, disadvantages, and future outlook.

**Librarians. One section of *Occupational Outlook Handbook.*
Nature of work, where employed, training, other qualifications, advancement, employment outlook, earnings, and working conditions.

Librarians. Pages 141-4 of *The College Girl Looks Ahead.*
Some characteristics of the work, talents needed, and preparation.

Librarians endeavor to shed drab image. American Library Association, Office for Recruitment. 1961. 1p. Single copy free
Reprint of an article from the *Wall Street Journal* pointing out the shortage of trained librarians.

Librarians wanted: careers in library service. Paradis, Adrian. David McKay Company. 1959. 288p. $4.50
Opportunities in library work, including numerous special libraries such as legal, newspaper, hospital, etc. Complete list of library science schools.

* Librarianship as a career. Institute for Research. 1962. 24p. $1

Qualifications, opportunities, compensation, advantages, and disadvantages. Describes work of the chief librarian, order librarian, cataloger, reference, circulation, children's, county or regional, school, and special librarian. List of accredited library schools is arranged according to type.

Library assistant. Careers. 1963. 2p. 15c

Career summary for desk-top file. Describes duties, working conditions, training, qualifications, outlook, working conditions, and related careers.

**Library careers. Logsdon, Richard and Logsdon, Irene. Henry Z. Walck, Inc. 1963. 111p. $3.50

This book describes the scope of librarianship, the preparation, requirements, rewards, and the outlook for future developments in libraries. Includes a list of accredited library schools and a good reading list.

Library education directory 1962-63. U.S. Office of Education. Supt. of Documents. 1963. 32p. 30c

In tabular form, information is presented about librarianship programs of twelve or more semester hours in library education in 277 accredited institutions of higher education.

Library profession. Leonard, Ruth and Hazen, Margaret. Bellman Publishing Company. 1955. 20p. $1

Qualifications, training, salaries, advantages, and disadvantages. Includes a list of accredited library schools and a description of basic courses.

Library science: earned degrees, by level, sex, and institution. One section of *Earned Degrees Conferred.*

List of ninety-eight schools and the number of bachelor's, master's, and doctor's degrees conferred by each in library science.

Lois Thornton, librarian. Brady, Rita. Abelard-Schuman. 1959. 192p. $3

Career fiction. Story of a girl who desired to leave college and become a television writer, but who became aware of the deep rewards awaiting the librarian in a small-town library.

Make your career in a special library. Special Libraries Association. 1956. 4p. Free

Illustrated recruiting brochure. Describes the opportunities for library careers in advertising, business, journalism, radio and television, and science.

"Miss library lady." Pfaender, Ann McLelland. Julian Messner, Inc. 1954. 192p. $2.95

Career fiction. The story tells of a girl's experiences in a small branch library and later in a library in Hawaii. Gives an idea of the work, problems, and intangible rewards.

Music librarian. Careers. 1963. 2p. 15c

Career summary for desk-top file. Duties, qualifications, and outlook.

Nancy runs the bookmobile. Johnson, Enid. Julian Messner, Inc. 1956. 192p. $2.95

Career fiction. Experiences of a girl working temporarily with a bookmobile, without library training, followed by her university training for a library science degree and ultimate success. Shows the satisfactions of bringing the right child and the right book together.

LIBRARIAN—*Continued*

Opportunities in library careers. Kingery, Robert E. Vocational Guidance Manuals. 1952. 112p. $1.45 paper

What librarianship is, outlook, remuneration, attributes necessary for success, educational preparation, how to get started and keep going, library careers, and library organizations. Also included is a list of accredited library schools.

Pioneering leaders in librarianship. Danton, Emily M., ed. American Library Association. 1953. 208p. $4.25

Biographies of eighteen men and women who played a strong role in lifting librarianship from a job to a profession.

* Professional education for librarianship—a statement for prospective librarians. American Library Association. Revised annually. 2p. Mimeographed. Free

Discussion of opportunities in library service and the current pattern of education for librarianship.

The professional librarian. Canadian Library Association. 1963. 8p. Free

Describes the library profession, the qualifications, and necessary training. Published by the Britannica Institute in an effort to attract more people to the library field.

The public librarian; with a section on the education of librarians by Robert D. Leigh (a report of the Public Library Inquiry). Bryan, Alice I. Columbia University Press. 1952. 501p. $6

A report on the education, positions, salaries, physical working conditions, library practices with regard to selection, promotion, and in-service training of library personnel in the United States. Also reports on library schools.

Public libraries in the life of the nation. Rossell, Beatrice S. American Library Association. 1943. 116p. $1.50

Describes the work of public, special, and school libraries of various types and sizes. Also includes qualifications and types of positions.

**Putting knowledge to work—the profession of the special librarian. Special Libraries Association. 1960. 18p. Single copies free

Discussion of nature of work, qualifications, opportunities, and outlook. List of thirty-two accredited library schools.

A recruitment primer. Ricking, Myrl. American Library Association, Office of Recruitment. 1960. 15p. Free

Written for practicing librarians. Description of various approaches to interesting young people to prepare for library work. Good bibliography.

A rewarding career is waiting for you—it's in school librarianship. American Library Association, Office for Recruitment. No date. 6p. Single copy free

A folder describing the work and advantages.

Rich the treasure; public library service to children. Long, Harriet G. American Library Association. 1953. 88p. $2

Traces the early beginnings of children's librarianship and the role of the librarian as a guiding influence on the child's reading and cultural development.

Scholarships, fellowships, loans, grants-in-aid for school librarianship. American Association of School Librarians. Available from Office for Recruitment, American Library Association. 1963. 40p. $1
This provides a state-by-state compilation of scholarships and other forms of student aid, in four categories: parent-teacher associations, state school library associations, state departments of education and state teachers associations, and student assistant organizations.

School and college librarianship as a career. Institute for Research. 1959. 24p. $1
Historical development, nature of work, opportunities, salaries, and attractive and unattractive features. Also included is a list of thirty-six accredited library schools in the United States and Canada.

School librarian. Chronicle Guidance Publications. 1960. 4p. 35c
Occupational brief summarizing work performed, qualifications, training, salary, other benefits, and outlook.

Should you be a librarian? Freehafer, Edward. New York Life Insurance Company. 1960. 12p. Free
Description of work, training, qualifications, earnings, and advantages.

**So you want to be a librarian. Wallace, Sarah L. Harper and Row. 1963. 192p. $3.50; library binding $3.27 net
Survey of the work of different kinds of librarians, professional qualifications needed, investment in time and effort, education in college and library school, finding a job, and the returns a librarian may expect. List of thirty-four library schools.

Special librarian. Careers. 1960. 8p. 25c
Career brief describing duties, working conditions, personal qualifications, opportunities, earnings, advancement prospects, and outlook.

Special librarian. Chronicle Guidance Publications. 1960. 4p. 35c
Occupational brief summarizing work performed, working conditions, earnings, qualifications, ways of determining interest and ability, training, opportunities, and outlook.

* Special librarians. Science Research Associates. 1962. 4p. 35c
Occupational brief describing nature of work, requirements, earnings, advantages, disadvantages, and future outlook.

**Special librarianship—information at work. Special Libraries Association. 1964. 16p. 10c. Single copy free
The work of the special librarian is illustrated in eight vignettes, each of which depicts how a qualified man or woman can combine a special subject background and interest with library training for a career of intellectual challenge.

The status of American college and university librarians. American Library Association. 1958. 104p. $3.50
Survey of college and university graduates who became librarians. Includes discussion of the academic status as a factor influencing the choice of a library career.

LIBRARIAN—*Continued*

A study of factors influencing college students to become librarians. American Library Association. 1958. 110p. $2.75

Survey of reasons why college students go on to become librarians.

**To be a librarian. American Library Association. 1957. 20p. Single copy free

Attractive booklet designed for use in the American Library Association person-to-person recruiting program. Includes description of four major types of libraries and kinds of work in each library, personal qualities needed, preparation, salaries and other compensation, qualifications, and opportunities.

The training of the chemical librarian. Shera, J. H. Special Libraries Association. 1956. 12p. 10c. Single copy free

Emphasizes the need, opportunities, and training.

Using your subject major as a special librarian. Western Personnel Institute. 1959. 5p. 25c

Duties, personal requirements, training, working conditions, and opportunities. List of library schools.

Wanted—you, the children's librarian. American Library Association, Office for Recruitment. 1956. 8p. Single copy free

A recruiting leaflet in two colors describing the work of the children's librarian, desirable qualities, preparation, and the rewards of that career.

What does a librarian do? Busby, Edith. Dodd, Mead and Company. 1963. 64p. $2.50; library binding $2.57 net

Varied activities from story hours, bookmobiles, and card catalogs to radio programs, exhibits, books for the blind, and libraries overseas are described. Written for grades 3 to 7.

What is a special librarian? Should you consider becoming a special librarian? Special Libraries Association. 1962. 8p. Single copies free.

Description of the work, where employed, earnings, qualifications, and training.

**What you need to be a librarian. American Library Association. 1963. 10p. Single copy free

Information on qualifications, preparation, cost and length of training, and opportunities. An insert contains the names of accredited library schools.

With a high heart. De Leeuw, Adele L. Macmillan Company. 1945. 207p. $3

Career fiction. Experiences in a rural library, revealing difficulties as well as advantages and rewards. A job in a county library develops into the management of a bookmobile circuit.

**Your future as a librarian. Clarke, Joan Dorn. Richards Rosen, Inc. 1963. 160p. $2.95

Stresses the opportunities in various aspects of library work and the training and education necessary.

LINGUIST 0-68.39

Begin your career in language and literature. Albright College. 1960. 6p. Free
> Leaflet containing pictures of student activities. Typical of college brochures to provide motivation in a counseling office.

* Bilingual secretary. Careers. 1963. 8p. 25c
> Career brief describing duties, working conditions, training, qualifications, places of employment, earnings, and outlook.

Careers in the field of modern foreign languages. Institute for Research. 1960. 24p. $1
> Description of the principal fields for language specialists, a typical day's work, attractive and unattractive features, qualifications, training, earnings, opportunities, and how to get started.

Careers in translating and interpreting. Angel, Juvenal. World Trade Academy Press. 1962. 28p. $1.25
> Includes information about each of several specialties utilizing these skills.

**Careers with foreign languages. Cohn, Angelo. Henry Z. Walck, Inc. 1963. 110p. $3.50
> This book describes the many opportunities, educational requirements, benefits, drawbacks, and the advantage in almost any pursuit of having language skills. Stresses the need for linguists in business, government, teaching, churches, and social agencies.

Discoveries in language and literature. Milwaukee-Downer College. 1960. 16p. Free
> A college bulletin describing opportunities open to students concentrating in the field of language and literature.

Foreign languages and literature: earned degrees, by level, sex, and institution. One section of *Earned Degrees Conferred.*
> Useful for judging the extent of a college's program in each of the languages.

**A handbook for guiding students in modern foreign languages. U.S. Office of Education. Supt. of Documents. 1963. 105p. 45c
> Includes helpful sections on using foreign languages on the job and meeting college foreign language entrance and degree requirements. Good selected references.

A handbook on the teaching of Spanish and Portuguese. Doyle, Henry G. D. C. Heath and Company. 1945. 395p. Paper cover. $4.50
> Three chapters are devoted to vocational opportunities for students of Spanish and Portuguese.

Interpreter. Careers. 1963. 2p. 15c
> Career summary for desk-top file. Duties, qualifications, and outlook.

Interpreter. Chronicle Guidance Publications. 1963. 4p. 35c
> Occupational brief containing definition, work performed, working conditions, personal requirements, determination of aptitudes and interests, training requirements, training opportunities, related jobs, advantages and disadvantages, opportunities for promotion, outlook, where employed, methods of entry, and suggested activities.

LINGUIST—*Continued*

Jobs for language majors. Small, Verna. Alumnae Advisory Center. 1956.
4p. 25c
> Reprint from *Mademoiselle* containing case histories to illustrate types of opportunities for college graduates who have majored in languages.

Linguists. Pages 139-41 of *The College Girl Looks Ahead*.
> Brief information concerning teaching, translating, and interpreting.

Modern foreign language fellowships. U.S. Office of Education. Supt. of
Documents. 1960. 2p. 5c
> Brief explanation of eligibility, duration, stipends and allowances, and application procedures for study of languages approved under the National Defense Education Act.

Occupational opportunities for students majoring in Spanish and Portuguese. Pan American Union. 1959. 5p. Free
> Discussion of types of positions for which mastery of a foreign language is a prime requisite, those in which foreign language is useful as an auxiliary tool, and the teaching of English in Latin America. Bibliography.

**Opportunities in foreign languages. Heubener, Theodore. Vocational
Guidance Manuals. 1964. 144p. $1.45 paper; library binding $2.65 net
> Discussion of opportunities in various vocations, in government positions, and as a teacher of languages. Personal qualifications, training, and methods of securing employment also are included.

Translators and interpreters. Science Research Associates. 1961. 4p. 35c
> Occupational brief describing jobs in business, government, teaching, and miscellaneous agencies.

Vocational opportunities for foreign language students. Third revised
edition. Huebener, Theodore. Modern Language Journal. 1949. 36p.
30c
> Discussion of opportunities and qualifications in business and industry, civil service, teaching, and thirty other vocations. Included are many quotations from employers concerning nature of work and requirements. Bibliography.

LINOTYPE OPERATOR   4-44.110

**Composing room occupations. One section of *Occupational Outlook Handbook*.
> Description of work of the hand compositor and typesetter, imposer, linotype operator, monotype keyboard operator, and phototypesetting operator. Also included is a discussion of training, other qualifications, employment outlook, earnings, and working conditions.

Exploring your future in graphic arts and publishing. American Liberty
Press. 1963. 96p. $5; $4 paper
> One page is devoted to each of ninety-five jobs, summarizing job duties, requirements for entering, promotional outlook, and pay and skill level.

**Linotype operator. Abel, O. L. Bellman Publishing Company. Revised 1956. 32p. $1
History and development, requirements, trade conditions, salaries, advantages, disadvantages, typical preparation, list of schools, and future outlook. Bibliography.

Linotype operator. Careers. 1959. 8p. 25c
Career brief describing duties, working conditions, training, personal qualifications, places of employment, how to enter, earnings, and outlook. Additional readings.

* Linotype operator. Chronicle Guidance Publications. 1962. 4p. 35c
Occupational brief summarizing work performed, working conditions, qualifications, training, opportunities, methods of entry, related jobs, and suggested activities.

Linotyping, the trade with a future. New York Mergenthaler Linotype School. 1962. 12p. Free
A recruiting brochure including nature of work, its importance, advantages, qualifications, and training.

Questions and answers about a linotype course. New York Mergenthaler Linotype School. 1957. 2p. Free
Information about the training, qualifications, and future outlook.

See also Printing and publishing industry worker

LITERARY AGENT   1-48.03

Authors' agent. McKown, Robin. Julian Messner, Inc. 1957. 188p. $2.95
Career fiction. Experiences in placing authors' material with book publishers, magazines, television, radio, and motion picture companies.

**Literary agents. Science Research Associates. 1958. 4p. 35c
Occupational brief describing nature of work, training, qualifications, opportunities, advantages, disadvantages, and future outlook.

LITHOGRAPHER   4-46.

* Lithographic occupations. Michigan Employment Security Commission. 1954. 23p. 25c
Introduction, nature of work, location of jobs, employment prospects, hiring qualifications for experienced workers, earnings, working conditions, qualifications for entry, and advancement.

**Lithographic (offset) occupations. One section of *Occupational Outlook Handbook.*
Nature of work, training and other qualifications, employment outlook, earnings, working conditions, and sources of additional information. Describes the main groups of lithographic workers: cameramen, artists and letterers, platemakers, strippers, and pressmen.

Offset lithographers. Science Research Associates. 1960. 4p. 35c
Occupational brief describing jobs, qualifications, earnings, things to consider and outlook. Selected references.

LOCOMOTIVE ENGINEER   5-41.010

About the engineer of a train. Johnson, Siddie Joe. Melmont Publishers.
 1962. 32p. $2.50
 > Prepared to give younger readers in grades 1 to 4 an idea of this kind of work
 > and its importance. Illustrated in color.

I want to be a train engineer. Greene, Carla. Childrens Press. 1956.
 32p. $2
 > Prepared for beginning readers with a reading level of upper first grade. Illus-
 > trated in color.

Locomotive engineer. Careers. 1961. 2p. 15c
 > Career summary for desk-top file. Duties, qualifications, and outlook.

Locomotive engineer. Chronicle Guidance Publications. 1963. 4p. 35c
 > Occupational brief describing work, qualifications, and outlook.

**Locomotive engineers. One section of *Occupational Outlook Handbook*.
 > Nature of work, training, other qualifications, advancement, employment out-
 > look, earnings, and working conditions.

Locomotive engineman. The Guidance Centre. 1960. 4p. 15c in Canada;
 20c elsewhere
 > Definition, history and importance, nature of work, qualifications necessary
 > for entry and success, preparation, employment and advancement, earnings, ad-
 > vantages, disadvantages, how to get started, and related occupations.

LONGSHOREMAN   9-47.10

Finding out about longshoremen. Science Research Associates. 1962. 4p.
 35c
 > Junior occupational brief containing brief facts about the job.

Longshoremen and stevedores. Science Research Associates. 1960. 4p. 35c
 > Occupational brief describing duties, requirements, wages, getting started,
 > advancing, advantages, disadvantages, and future outlook.

LUMBER INDUSTRY WORKER   4, 6, 8-29. through 4, 6, 8-39.

**Career as a lumber and building materials dealer. Institute for Research.
 1957. 24p. $1
 > History and scope of the business, typical day's work, attractive and unattrac-
 > tive features, personal characteristics, education and training, earnings, getting
 > started, and opportunities.

Gifts from the forest. Wall, Gertrude Wallace. Charles Scribner's Sons.
 1952. 96p. $3.50
 > Photographs and brief explanatory text describe the work involved in convert-
 > ing timber into lumber. For grades 5 to 8.

Job description for grader (lumber) VIII. U.S. Employment Service.
 Supt. of Documents. 1948. 5p. 5c
 > Occupational guide. Job summary, work performed, training, related occupa-
 > tions, physical activities, working conditions, hazards, and employment variables.

Let's go logging. Herman, George. Putnam's Sons. 1962. 48p. $1.95
Readers learn how loggers harvest lumber in the Cascade Range in Oregon. Written for ages 7 to 11.

Logging: the story of an industry. Taylor, Arthur; Sutton, Jack; and Benedict, Bart. Lippincott Company. 1962. 64p. $2.95
The story of the forestry industry from logging to the products that are made from trees. For younger boys.

Lumber in pace with the space age. National Lumber Manufacturers Association. 1960. 8p. Free
Brief history of the lumber industry and its progress. Description of lumber manufacture, distribution, and consumption.

Lumberjack. Meader, Stephen W. Harcourt, Brace and World. 1934. 277p. $3.25
Career fiction. A boy earns the money for college by becoming a lumberjack in the New Hampshire woods. For younger boys.

Lumberjack. Careers. 1961. 2p. 15c
Career summary for desk-top file. Duties, qualifications, and outlook.

**Lumbermen. Science Research Associates. 1961. 4p. 35c
Occupational brief describing nature of work, requirements, getting a job, earnings, advantages, disadvantages, and future outlook. Includes work in the logging camp, in the sawmill, and moving the timber.

This fascinating lumber business. Bobbs-Merrill Company. 1951. 313p. $4.50
Contains an interesting chapter on timber engineering.

LUMBER PRODUCTS INDUSTRY WORKER
4, 6, 8-32. through 4, 6, 8-34.

Opportunities unlimited for careers of prestige and profit in the forest products industries. American Forest Products Industries. 1958. 20p. Free
Description of major career areas, preparation, and opportunities.

Skilled occupations in the production of lumber products. Chronicle Guidance Publications. 1962. 4p. 35c
Occupational brief summarizing work performed, requirements, opportunities, where employed, related jobs, and outlook.

The work and education of a wood products engineer. State University of New York, College of Forestry. 1962. 4p. Free
Kinds of work, places of employment, outlook, training, and ways of getting started.

MACHINE CUTTER
6-27.054

Job description for cutter, machine I. U.S. Employment Service. Supt. of Documents. 1947. 5p. 5c
Occupational guide. Job summary, work performed, training, related occupations, physical activities, working conditions, hazards, and employment variables.

MACHINE TOOL OPERATOR   4, 6-78.000 through 4, 6-78.589

Machine tool operators. Careers. 1962. 8p. 25c
Career brief describing duties, working conditions, training, personal qualifications, advancement prospects, earnings, unionization, and outlook.

**Machine tool operators. One section of *Occupational Outlook Handbook.*
Nature of work, where employed, training, other qualifications, advancement,
employment outlook, earnings, and working conditions.

Semi-skilled machine tool operator. Chronicle Guidance Publications.
1962. 4p. 35c
Occupational brief summarizing work performed, working conditions, training,
earnings, where employed, related jobs, and outlook.

MACHINIST   4-75.; 4, 6, 8-78.

**All-round machinists. One section of *Occupational Outlook Handbook.*
Nature of work, where employed, training, other qualifications, advancement,
employment outlook, earnings, and working conditions.

Boss Ket: a life of Charles F. Kettering. Young, Rosamond. David McKay
Company. 1961. 224p. $3.50
Biography of the energetic Ohioan who invented the automobile self-starter,
knockless gasoline, and hundreds of other products which have changed work
with machines.

Construction machinery operators. Chronicle Guidance Publications. 1959.
4p. 35c
Occupational brief summarizing work performed, working conditions, qualifications, training, opportunities, and outlook.

**Employment outlook in machining occupations. Bureau of Labor Sta-
tistics, U.S. Department of Labor. Supt. of Documents. 1964. 20p. 15c
Reprint from the *Occupational Outlook Handbook.*

Exploring your future in manufacturing (wage and shop jobs). American
Liberty Press. 1960. 96p. $5; $4 paper
In this book one page describes each of twenty machine shop jobs, summarizing job duties, requirements for entering, promotional outlook, and pay and
skill level.

Girls at machines. Chapter 11 of *Vocations for Girls.*
Power machine operation in the garment industry and the needle trades.

Highlights. Allis-Chalmers Manufacturing Company. 1960. 32p. Free
Pictures of the highlights one would see on a tour through the plant. Gives
an idea of the massive machinery and modern machine tools used.

**Machining occupations. One section of *Occupational Outlook Handbook.*
Nature of work, training, other qualifications, advancement, employment outlook, earnings, and working conditions. Information is given concerning all-
around machinist, machine tool operator, tool and die maker, instrument maker,
setup man, and layout man.

Machinist. Group, Vernard F. Personnel Services. 1962. 6p. 50c; 25c to students

> Occupational abstract. Nature of work, qualifications, training, earnings, number and distribution of workers, and employment prospects.

Machinist. Porter, Harold. Research Publishing Company. 1957. 16p. $1.50

> Advantages of this trade, history and development, number engaged in occupation, working conditions, qualifications and special skills required, how to secure a job in the trade, and chances for promotion.

* Machinist. Careers. 1960. 8p. 25c

> Career brief describing duties, working conditions, training, personal qualifications, advancement prospects, places of employment, earnings, and outlook.

* Machinist. Chronicle Guidance Publications. 1962. 6p. 35c

> Occupational brief containing definition, work performed, working conditions, personal requirements, training requirements, where employed, job outlook, related jobs, and suggested activities.

Machinist. The Guidance Centre. 1960. 4p. 15c in Canada; 20c elsewhere

> Nature of work, qualifications, preparation, working conditions, advancement, outlook, earnings, advantages, disadvantages, how to get started, and related occupations.

Machinist and machine-shop operation as a career. Institute for Research. 1962. 24p. $1

> Development and growth of the general machine shop, qualifications, training, wages, opportunities, and attractive and unattractive features. Description of work performed by the bench machinist, engine-lathe operator, milling-machine operator, planer operator, shaper operator, grinding-machine operator, and machine adjuster.

Machinist and tool and die maker apprenticeship standards. Bureau of Apprenticeship. 1956. 28p. Free

> Description of a program established in St. Louis, work processes in which apprentices are trained, qualifications for apprentice training, agreement between employers and apprentices, and functions of the joint apprenticeship committee.

Machinists. Science Research Associates. 1959. 4p. 35c

> Occupational brief describing nature of work, preparation, qualifications, opportunities, advantages, disadvantages, and future outlook.

**Opportunities in machine shop trades. Stern, Benjamin J. Vocational Guidance Manuals. 1953. 95p. $1.45 paper

> Historical sketch, current needs and future outlook, requirements for success, wages, analysis of machine shop occupations, training, getting started, the machinist's progress, and possibilities in related fields. Contains lists of state apprenticeship agencies and field and regional offices of the Bureau of Apprenticeship, U.S. Department of Labor.

MACHINIST—*Continued*

**Setup men (machine tools). One section of *Occupational Outlook Handbook*.

> Nature of work, where employed, training, other qualifications, and employment outlook.

See also Skilled trades worker

MAIL CARRIER 1-28.01

I want to be a postman. Greene, Carla. Childrens Press. 1958. 32p. $2

> Prepared for beginning readers with a reading level of upper first grade. Illustrated in color.

Letter carrier. Careers. 1960. 2p. 15c

> Career summary for desk-top file. Duties, qualifications, and outlook.

Letter carrier. The Guidance Centre. 1961. 4p. 15c in Canada; 20c elsewhere

> Nature of work, qualifications, working conditions, preparation, earnings, advantages, disadvantages, how to get started, and related occupations.

**Mail carriers. One section of *Occupational Outlook Handbook*.

> Nature of work, qualifications, training, advancement, employment outlook, earnings, and working conditions.

Rural mail carrier. Careers. 1962. 2p. 15c

> Career summary for desk-top file. Duties, qualifications, and outlook.

MANAGEMENT ENGINEER. *See* Industrial engineer

MANAGER, CATERER. See Caterer

MANAGER, RETAIL STORE. *See* Retail manager

MANUFACTURER 4, 6, 8-01. through 5, 7, 9-18.

Career as a production manager in manufacturing. Institute for Research. 1960. 20p. $1

> Description of duties, a typical day's work, qualifications, training, earnings, attractive and unattractive features, and getting started. Includes list of colleges which offer training in production management.

* Management and supervisory careers in manufacturing. Institute for Research. 1959. 24p. $1

> Historical background, opportunities, salaries, attractive and unattractive features. Discussion of twenty-four department workers such as planning manager, foreman, shop manager, purchasing agent, and shipping manager.

Occupations in manufacturing. Chapter 14 of *Planning Your Future*.

> Includes discussion of our dependence on the manufacturing occupations, nature of work, major manufacturing industries, working conditions, qualifications, advantages, and disadvantages.

Photographic manufacturing workers. Science Research Associates. 1961. 4p. 35c
>Occupational brief describing nature of the work, requirements, getting started and advancing, earnings, advantages, disadvantages, and future outlook.

The Sextant series for exploring your future in manufacturing (salaried). American Liberty Press. 1961. 96p. $5; $4 paper
>One page is devoted to each of ninety-five jobs, summarizing job duties, requirements for entering, promotional outlook, and pay and skill level. An organizational chart is available for 60c.

MAP MAKER. *See* Cartographer

MARBLE SETTER   5-24.310

**Employment outlook for bricklayers, stonemasons, marble setters, tile setters, and terrazzo workers. Bureau of Labor Statistics, U.S. Department of Labor. Supt. of Documents. 1964. 20p. 15c
>Reprint from the *Occupational Outlook Handbook.*

Marble setters, tile setters and terrazzo workers. Careers. 1962. 8p. 25c
>tions, earnings, advancement prospects, and outlook.

Marble setters, tile setters, and terrazzo workers. One section of *Occupa-*
>Career brief describing duties, working conditions, training, personal qualifica-
tional Outlook Handbook.
>Nature of work, where employed, training, other qualifications, advancement, outlook, earnings, and working conditions.

MARINE   2-68.30

The building of a marine officer. U.S. Marine Corps. 1962. 32p. Free
>Illustrated brochure containing information about Marine Corps Officer Training and various programs for officers.

A career in the United States Marine Corps. Institute for Research. 1959. 24p. $1
>History of the Marine Corps, qualifications, training, and description of service schools. Salaries and retirement pay of officers and enlisted men.

**Current career booklets. U.S. Marine Corps. Six booklets. Free
>Frequently revised materials are available from local recruiting offices or the above. Examples of present titles are: What the Marine Corps offers you, The making of a marine, The building of a marine aviator, A leader among men, and A guide to occupational training.

A guide to occupational training. U.S. Marine Corps. 1959. 44p. Free to counselors
>Handbook of information for advising students concerning career fields in the Marine Corps.

Leatherneck. Colby, C. B. Coward-McCann, Inc. 1957. 48p. $2.50
>Includes description of the training of a U.S. Marine and the methods of combat used. Written for grades 4 to 8.

MARINE—*Continued*

The Marine Corps. Hammond, Cleon. Viking Press. Revised 1962. 192p. $3

Details of regulations and opportunities. For grades 7 to 10.

Marines and what they do. Schuon, Karl and Smith, Earl. Franklin Watts, Inc. 1962. 250p. $3.50

Description of the work, personal requirements, physical and mental qualifications, specialized training, and rewards. For grades 7 to 11.

The story of the U.S. Marines. Hunt, George. Random House, Inc. 1963. 182p. $1.95

Account of the Marine Corps from its founding to its participation in the Korean conflict. Illustrated.

What the Marine Corps offers you. U.S. Marine Corps. 1960. 32p. Free

Basic informational booklet explaining the opportunities available in the Marine Corps.

See also Military serviceman

MARINE ENGINEER 0-19.81

Marine architect. Careers. 1961. 2p. 15c

Career summary for desk-top file. Duties, qualifications, and outlook.

**Marine architects. Science Research Associates. 1958. 4p. 35c

Occupational brief describing the work of preparing plans and designs for construction and repair of ships. Also includes qualifications, opportunities, and future outlook.

Marine engineer. The Guidance Centre. 1958. 4p. 15c in Canada; 20c elsewhere

History and importance, nature of work, qualifications, working conditions, preparation, remuneration, advancement, outlook, related occupations, and how to get started.

Naval architecture and marine engineering. Massachusetts Institute of Technology. 1957. 32p. Free

Illustrated brochure describing the work of the naval architect in designing a ship's hull and the marine engineer in designing its machinery.

Naval architecture and marine engineering. Haeberle, F. E. Chapter 19 of *Engineering Enrollment in the United States.*

Trends in college enrollment and future requirements for specialists in this area.

MARKET RESEARCH ANALYST. *See* Economist

MASON. *See* Cement industry worker

MATERIAL HANDLER 9-88.40

Material handling engineer. Careers. 1961. 2p. 15c

Career summary for desk-top file. Duties, qualifications, and outlook.

Material handling engineer. Chronicle Guidance Publications. 1963. 4p. 35c

Occupational brief summarizing work performed, working conditions, qualifications, where employed, outlook, and list of colleges having accredited industrial engineering departments.

Rigger. Careers. 1962. 2p. 15c

Career summary of the work of moving heavy objects such as structural steel, heavy machinery and equipment, oil drilling equipment, bulk steel, and ship sections.

There are career opportunities for you in material handling. The Material Handling Institute, Inc. 1957. 20p. Free

Description of work opportunities for sales personnel, engineers, and others engaged in moving and storing materials.

Warehouse workers. Science Research Associates. 1961. 4p. 35c

Occupational brief describing nature of work, requirements, getting started and advancing, wages, advantages, disadvantages, and future outlook.

Warehouseman. Careers. 1962. 2p. 15c

Career summary for desk-top file. Duties, qualifications, and outlook.

MATHEMATICIAN   0-35.76

Assistantships and fellowships in mathematics. American Mathematical Society. 1964. 10p. 50c

Special issue of the notices available in January of each year.

* Careers for majors in mathematics. Angel, Juvenal. World Trade Academy Press. 1959. 30p. $1.25

Includes description of the major fields of work requiring special skill in mathematics, opportunities, remuneration, future outlook, and methods of financing a college education.

Careers in mathematics. Institute for Research. 1960. 24p. $1

Types of mathematical work, opportunities for employment, a typical day's work, qualifications, training, earnings, attractive and unattractive features, and outlook.

Careers in mathematics. National Council of Teachers of Mathematics. 1961. 28p. 25c

Short biographies of eight young mathematicians indicate several possible careers. Included is a discussion of jobs that are basically mathematical in nature and other jobs which require training in mathematics.

**Employment in professional mathematical work in industry and government. National Science Foundation. Supt. of Documents. 1962. 82p. 55c

This report presents the findings of a survey of mathematical employment other than teaching. Data collected on the age, education, experience, and other characteristics of these persons, as well as on the nature of their current positions, functions performed, and income received, are discussed. Many statistical tables.

MATHEMATICIAN—*Continued*

**Employment opportunities for women mathematicians and statisticians. Women's Bureau, U.S. Department of Labor. Bulletin Number 262. Supt. of Documents. 1956. 37p. 25c
    Discussion of present and future supply and demand, preparation, personal characteristics needed, methods of obtaining employment, advancement, earnings, and working conditions.

**Employment outlook for mathematicians, statisticians, and actuaries. Bureau of Labor Statistics, U.S. Department of Labor. Supt. of Documents. 1964. 16p. 10c
    Reprint from the *Occupational Outlook Handbook*.

Graduate study in mathematics at M.I.T. Massachusetts Institute of Technology. 1962. 8p. Free
    Includes a table of the proportion of doctor's degrees awarded in mathematics in the last decade in the various areas such as topology and fluid dynamics.

Guide to undergradute programs in mathematics. U.S. Office of Education. Supt. of Documents. 1962. 25p. 25c
    Data on the kinds, requirements, and characteristics of undergraduate degree programs in mathematics in 864 institutions. Good bibliography on careers in mathematics.

Is "math" in the stars for you? Women's Bureau, U.S. Department of Labor. Leaflet Number 28. Supt. of Documents. 1963. 6p. 5c
    Opportunities and outlook in the professions for young women who are qualified in mathematics. Prepared to encourage high school girls to investigate the field of mathematics.

**Jobs in mathematics. Science Research Associates. 1959. 32p. $1
    Describes the variety of job prospects and opportunities within the field of mathematics. An accompanying wall chart is available for 35c.

Manpower resources in mathematics. Bureau of Labor Statistics, U.S. Department of Labor, in cooperation with the National Science Foundation. Supt. of Documents. 1954. 22p. 20c
    Presents data on the numbers of personnel in the areas of specialization, specialties in which they were employed, types of employers, income, and such personal characteristics as age, education, and sex.

Mathematical subjects: earned degrees, by level, sex, and institution. One section of *Earned Degrees Conferred*.
    Useful for judging the extent of a college's program in mathematics and in statistics.

Mathematician. Splaver, Sarah. Personnel Services. 1960. 6p. 50c; 25c to students
    Occupational abstract. Nature of work, qualifications, preparation, entrance and advancement, supply and demand, and earnings. References for further reading.

* Mathematician. Careers. 1963. 8p. 25c
   Career brief describing duties, working conditions, personal qualifications, training, outlook, earnings, where employed, related jobs, and measuring one's interest and ability. Suggested references.

* Mathematician. Chronicle Guidance Publications. 1963. 4p. 35c
   Occupational brief summarizing: work performed in teaching, industry, and government; employment conditions; qualifications; training; opportunities; where employed; and outlook.

* Mathematicians. Science Research Associates. 1962. 4p. 35c
   Occupational brief describing nature of work, training, qualifications, opportunities, advantages, disadvantages, and future outlook.

**Mathematicians. One section of Occupational Outlook Handbook.
   Nature of work, where employed, training, other qualifications, employment outlook, earnings, and working conditions.

Mathematics. Simmons College. 1959. 4p. Free
   Discussion of opportunities for women in the field of mathematics.

Mathematics and your career. Bureau of Labor Statistics, U.S. Department of Labor. Revised 1962. 12p. Free
   Emphasizes the importance of mathematics to successful careers in many fields of work and indicates the amount of mathematics needed for some seventy-five occupations.

Mathematics teachers. Group, Vernard F. Personnel Services. 1963. 6p. 50c; 25c to students
   Nature of work, future prospects, qualifications, preparation, entrance, advancement, earnings, advantages, and disadvantages.

**Mathematics teaching as a career. National Council of Teachers of Mathematics. 1962. 8p. Single copy free
   Discussion of the demand for teachers of mathematics, preparation, salaries, responsibilities, satisfactions, and benefits.

Niels Henrik Abel, mathematician extraordinary. Oystein, Ore. University of Minnesota Press. 1957. 277p. $5.75
   Biography of a Norwegian scientist who made notable contributions to mathematics.

**Opportunities in mathematics. Gehman, Harry M. Vocational Guidance Manuals. 1964. 88p. $1.45 paper; library binding $2.65 net
   Discussion of the nature of work and opportunities for the mathematician in industry, government, high school and college teaching, and research. Also some information about work as a statstician, actuary, and electronic computer programmer. Reading list.

**Professional opportunities in mathematics. Mathematical Association of America. 1961. 32p. 25c
   Includes discussion of opportunities in teaching, mathematical and applied statistics, industry, government, and in the actuarial profession. Includes list of nonacademic organizations employing ten or more mathematicians.

MATHEMATICIAN—*Continued*

Professional training in mathematics. Ficken, F. A. and MacDuffee, C. C. American Mathematical Society. 1963. 9p. 25c
Analysis of current trends in education for the profession.

Should you be a mathematician? Sheppard, Norris E. New York Life Insurance Company. 1958. 12p. Free
Description of specialties, acute shortage in the field, qualifications, education, rewards, and drawbacks.

Why study math? General Electric Company. 1953. 4p. Free
One section of the booklet *Three Whys*. Sets forth the need for the study of more mathematics.

See also Actuary; Scientist; Statistician

MEAT CUTTER 5-58.

Butcher. The Guidance Centre. 1961. 4p. 15c in Canada; 20c elsewhere
Definition, history and importance, nature of work, working conditions, qualifications, preparation, employment and advancement, remuneration, advantages, disadvantages, how to get started, and related occupations. Further readings.

Butchers. Science Research Associates. 1963. 4p. 35c
Occupational brief describing nature of work, requirements, preparation, working conditions, earnings, and future outlook.

Meat cutter. Chronicle Guidance Publications. 1960. 4p. 35c
Occupational brief summarizing work performed, working conditions, personal qualifications, training requirements, opportunities, employment outlook, and methods of entry.

* Meat cutter-butcher. Careers. 1959. 8p. 25c
Career brief describing duties, working conditions, training, earnings, unionization, and outlook.

MEAT PACKING INDUSTRY WORKER 4, 6, 8-09.

Career opportunities in the meat packing industry. American Meat Institute. 1962. 12p. Single copy free
A representative listing of job titles and job descriptions, and the academic requirements for each.

Home-study courses in the meat packing industry. Institute of Meat Packing. 1955. 9p. Free
The description of courses and topics covered give an idea of kinds of work. Some courses are entitled: meat packing science, by-products of the meat packing industry, beef operations, pork operations, and production and marketing of livestock.

The meat packing industry. Heckler, Edwin L. Bellman Publishing Company. 1954. 23p. $1
Includes description of individual jobs and range of income.

Meat packing workers. Science Research Associates. 1960. 4p. 35c
Occupational brief describing work, getting started and advancing, wages, things to consider, and future outlook.

MECHANIC AND REPAIRMAN 5-53.; 5-78. through 5-81.; 5-83.

Camera repairman. Careers. 1963. 2p. 15c
Career summary for desk-top file. Duties, qualifications, and outlook.

**Careers for specialized mechanics. Angel, Juvenal L. World Trade Academy Press. 1962. 28p. $1.25
Description of work, training, opportunities, and remuneration for each of the following: air conditioning, airplane, automobile, business machines, Diesel, electrical appliances, radio and television, industrial machinery, telephone, and typewriter mechanic.

Farm equipment mechanic. Careers. 1963. 2p. 15c
Career summary for desk-top file. Duties, qualifications, and outlook.

I want to be a mechanic. Greene, Carla. Childrens Press. 1959. 32p. $2
Prepared for beginning readers with a reading level of upper first grade. Illustrated in color.

Industrial machinery repairman. Careers. 1962. 8p. 25c
Career brief describing duties, working conditions, training, personal qualifications, where employed, earnings, and outlook.

**Jobs in mechanical work. Science Research Associates. 1963. 48p. $1
Describes the variety of job prospects and opportunities within this field, especially for the auto mechanic, airplane mechanic, machinist, millwright, office machine serviceman, radio and television serviceman, stationary engineer, and tool and die maker.

* Mechanics and repairmen. Chronicle Guidance Publications. 1963. 4p. 35c
Occupational brief describing the work of various kinds of repairmen, qualifications, training, and apprenticeship.

**Mechanics and repairmen. One chapter of *Occupational Outlook Handbook.*
Nature of work, where employed, training, other qualifications, employment outlook, earnings, and working conditions for each of the following: air conditioning and refrigeration mechanic, appliance serviceman, automobile mechanic, business machine serviceman, diesel mechanic, industrial machinery repairman, instrument repairman, jewelry repairman, maintenance electrician, millwright, watch repairman, and television and radio serviceman.

MECHANICAL ENGINEER 0-19.01

Definitions of occupational specialties in engineering. American Society of Mechanical Engineers. 1952. 114p. $3.50
Definitions of about five hundred engineering fields of specialization and the knowledge required to work in each field.

MECHANICAL ENGINEER—*Continued*

Mechanical engineer. Robinson, H. Alan. Personnel Services. 1958. 6p. 50c; 25c to students
Nature of work, future prospects, qualifications, preparation, number and distribution of workers, advantages, disadvantages, earnings, entrance, and advancement.

Mechanical engineer. Careers. 1961. 2p. 15c
Career summary for desk-top file. Duties, qualifications, and outlook.

Mechanical engineering. Barker, Joseph. Chapter 16 of *Engineering Enrollment in the United States.*
Trends in college enrollments and future requirements for specialists in this area.

Mechanical engineering. Michigan College of Mining and Technology. 1963. 2p. Free
Example of a recruiting leaflet describing work, qualifications, educational requirements, earnings, and employment opportunities.

* Mechanical engineering as a career. Institute for Research. 1958. 24p. $1
Types of positions, lines of promotion, working conditions, training, opportunities, income, qualifications, and attractive and unattractive features.

Mechanical engineering at M.I.T. Massachusetts Institute of Technology. 1962. 32p. Free
An illustrated brochure describing especially graduate study and research in mechanical engineering.

* Mechanical engineers. Science Research Associates. 1958. 4p. 35c
Occupational brief describing nature of work, qualifications, preparation, opportunities, advantages, disadvantages, and future outlook.

**Mechanical engineers. One section of *Occupational Outlook Handbook.*
Nature of work, where employed, and employment outlook.

Mechanical engineers at Du Pont. E. I. du Pont de Nemours and Company. 1960. 16p. Free
Illustrated booklet describing work and opportunities.

See also Aeronautical engineer; Air conditioning industry worker; Automotive engineer; Engineer; Refrigeration engineer

MECHANICAL ENGINEERING TECHNICIAN 0-67.

Mechanical engineering technician. Careers. 1961. 2p. 15c
Career summary for desk-top file. Duties, qualifications, and outlook.

Mechanical technician. Chronicle Guidance Publications. 1961. 4p. 35c
Occupational brief summarizing work performed, working conditions, training, qualifications, advantages, disadvantages, and outlook.

MEDICAL AND SCIENTIFIC ILLUSTRATOR 0-44.41

**Medical and scientific illustrators. Science Research Associates. 1961. 4p. 35c
Occupational brief describing nature of work, personal qualifications, training, methods of entrance, earnings, advantages, disadvantages, and future outlook.

Medical artist (illustrator). Careers. 1961. 2p. 15c
Career summary for desk-top file. Duties, qualifications, and outlook.

**Medical illustration. Association of Medical Illustrators. 1963. 7p. Single copy free
Includes description of nature of work, desirable qualifications of applicants, entrance requirements, and training. List of eight teaching departments of medical illustration in medical schools.

Medical illustrator. Pages 87-8 of *Health Careers Guidebook*.
Description of work, qualifications, training, and prospects.

Technical illustrator. Careers. 1962. 2p. 15c
Career summary for desk-top file. Duties, qualifications, and outlook.

See also Commercial artist

MEDICAL LIBRARIAN 0-23.20

Be a medical librarian. Medical Library Association. 1962. 6p. Free
Discussion of the variety and extent of medical libraries, functions of a medical librarian, preparation, job opportunities, and salaries.

**Choose medical librarianship. Medical Library Association. 1962. 6p. Free
Description of a medical library, duties of a medical librarian, education. salaries, and rewards.

Medical librarian. Careers. 1959. 2p. 15c
Career summary for desk-top file. Duties, qualifications, and outlook.

* Medical librarians. Science Research Associates. 1963. 4p. 35c
Occupational brief describing nature of work, requirements, training, getting started, earnings, advantages, disadvantages, and future outlook.

Medical library science. Pages 91-2 of *Health Careers Guidebook*.
Nature of work, training, opportunities for employment, and status and standards.

MEDICAL RECORD LIBRARIAN 0-23.25

About to choose a career? Consider medical record library service. American Association of Medical Record Librarians. 1962. 6p. 10c. 100 copies $6
Description of the position, qualifications, and training needed. An insert provides the list of twenty-nine approved schools for training.

MEDICAL RECORD LIBRARIAN—*Continued*

**Employment outlook for medical technologists, medical X-ray technicians, and medical record librarians. Bureau of Labor Statistics, U.S. Department of Labor. Supt. of Documents. 1964. 12p. 10c
Reprint from the *Occupational Outlook Handbook.*

Essentials of an acceptable school for medical record librarians and list of approved schools. Council on Medical Education and Hospitals of the American Medical Association. 1962. 4p. Free
Includes list of 28 approved schools.

Face the future with security. American Association of Medical Record Librarians. 1963. 1p. Single copy free
List of duties in the course of a work day and a list of twelve schools for training.

Finding out about medical record librarians. American Association of Medical Record Librarians. 1962. 4p. 100 copies $6
Description of work, qualifications, and training needed.

Medical librarian. Careers. 1964. 2p. 15c
Career summary for desk-top file. Duties, qualifications, and outlook.

Medical record librarian. Splaver, Sarah. Personnel Services. 1953. 6p. 50c; 25c to students
Occupational abstract. Nature of work, qualifications, preparation, registration, entrance and advancement, supply and demand, earnings, advantages and disadvantages.

* Medical record librarian. Careers. 1960. 8p. 25c
Career brief describing duties, working conditions, training, personal qualifications, registration requirements, places of employment, earnings, and outlook.

* Medical record librarian. Chronicle Guidance Publications. 1964. 4p. 35c
Occupational brief summarizing work performed, working conditions, earnings, personal qualifications, training requirements, opportunities, employment outlook, and entry into the job.

Medical record librarian. The Guidance Centre. 1963. 4p. 15c in Canada; 20c elsewhere
History and importance, nature of work, qualifications, working conditions, preparation, remuneration, advancement, outlook, related occupations, and how to get started.

* Medical record librarians. Science Research Associates. 1961. 4p. 35c
Occupational brief describing nature of work, personal qualifications, training, opportunities, earnings, advantages, and future outlook.

**Medical record librarians. One section of *Occupational Outlook Handbook.*
Nature of work, where employed, training, other qualifications, advancement, employment outlook, earnings, and working conditions.

Medical record technician. Page 99 of *Health Careers Guidebook.*
Brief statement of training and qualifications.

On the record . . . for your care. American Hospital Association. 1960.
4p. Free
Description of the work of the medical record librarian.

MEDICAL SECRETARY 1-33.01

* Career as a medical secretary. Institute for Research. 1962. 24p. $1
Describes the work of the assistant in a doctor's office who is receptionist and
private secretary, office nurse, and laboratory technician combined. Duties,
typical day's work, qualifications, education and training, list of junior colleges
offering training in medical secretarial work followed by a list of a few vocational schools which offer this course, opportunities, salaries, related positions,
and attractive and unattractive features.

In the doctor's office—the art of the medical assistant. Parsons, Esther
Jane. Lippincott Company. 1956. 326p. $4.75
Prepared as a guide for those who assist the doctor in his office practice, this
book gives an idea of the type of work.

Medical secretary. Splaver, Sarah. Personnel Services. 1963. 6p. 50c;
25c to students
Occupational abstract. Nature of work, qualifications, preparation, entrance,
advancement, earnings, outlook, advantages, and disadvantages.

**Medical secretary. Chronicle Guidance Publications. 1961. 4p. 35c
Occupational brief summarizing work performed, working conditions, qualifications, determination of aptitudes and interests, training, opportunities, employment, and methods of entry.

MEDICAL SERVICE WORKER 0-50. through 0-52.; 2-42.

**Because you like people . . . choose a career in mental health. National
Association for Mental Health. 1960. 16p. $3.95 per 100
Provides general information about the mental health field and specific details about seven mental health jobs: psychiatric aide, recreational therapist,
occupational therapist, psychiatric nurse, psychiatric social worker, clinical psychologist, and psychiatrist.

**Careers in hospitals. American Hospital Association. 1963. 54p. $1.25
This booklet contains job descriptions and educational and personal requirements for 130 hospital careers. It also includes estimates of earning potentials
and opportunities for future advancement in hospital administrative services,
plant operation, and paramedical departments. An insert lists approved schools
in fifteen hospital professions.

Careers in the medical services of the U.S. Armed Forces. U.S. Department of Defense. 1958. 33p. Free
Discussion of requirements for entry and professional opportunities for nurses,
dietitians, occupational therapists, and physical therapists.

MEDICAL SERVICE WORKER—*Continued*

Careers that count. American Hospital Association. 1960. 8p. Free
> Folder opening into a bulletin board chart listing about one hundred hospital careers. Five illustrations.

The challenge of health research. Metropolitan Life Insurance Company. 1962. 36p. Free
> Points out the contribution of specialists, especially the microbiologist, geneticist, mycologist, plant physiologist, and others.

Counselors' kit: mental health careers. National Association for Mental Health. 1960. 12 booklets. $1
> A kit of materials to introduce mental health occupations and provide information about seven basic fields of work.

**Disease detectives: your career in medical research. Neal, Harry Edward. Julian Messner, Inc. 1959. 192p. $3.95. Library binding $3.64 net
> Portrays a picture of scientists at work in modern medical research laboratories.

**Find a career in medicine. Starrett, Robert S. Putnam's Sons. 1960. 160p. $2.95
> Information about the many career opportunities available for would-be doctors, nurses, technicians, researchers, and many others. Written for ages 11 to 15.

For a job in a growing field and an opportunity to serve others. American Heart Association. 1962. 6p. Single copy free from local Heart Associations.
> Leaflet presenting descriptions of work as field representative, program consultant or director, chapter executive, and information and education specialist.

**Four futures—pick a professional career and plan with purpose. U.S. Department of Defense. 1961. 18p. Free
> Discussion of what lies ahead with a professional career, what it takes, and specific information concerning nursing, dietetics, physical therapy, and occupational therapy.

Four medical jobs. Alumnae Advisory Center. 1963. 6p. 25c
> Encouragement to girls who are interested in health work, but not an M.D., to follow their bent as a biologist, psychiatric nurse, medical technologist, or medical secretary. Case histories of young women who have succeeded in these specialized fields.

The healing arts. Chapter 23 of *Vocations for Boys.*
> Includes personal qualifications, training, and opportunities.

Health careers. Careers. 1963. 8p. 25c
> Career brief describing the need for semiprofessional health workers, employment prospects, related careers, and training opportunities. A table presents the number of men and women employed in each of fifteen health careers, normal yearly earnings, and length of training beyond high school.

**Health careers guidebook. National Health Council. 1955. 153p. Free to counselors and librarians
    The first forty pages consist of a preview of health careers, a greeting to future members of the health teams, some cautions, and a health careers calendar showing the time that is required for education or special training for seventy-six health occupations. These sections are followed by health career briefings, containing information about qualifications, training, and future prospects for about forty health career opportunities.

Health manpower source book—hospital house staffs. Public Health Service, U.S. Department of Health, Education, and Welfare. Publications Number 263, Section 13. Supt. of Documents. 1961. 42p. 30c
    Data on the numbers, distribution, and characteristics of personnel. Includes information on training, age, sex, employment status, and income level.

Health manpower source book—industry and occupation data. Public Health Service, U.S. Department of Health, Education, and Welfare. Publications Number 263, Section 17. Supt. of Documents. 1964. 104p. 55c
    Presents basic data on the health services industry and on eighteen occupations as reported in the 1960 Census of Population.

Health professions: earned degrees, by level, sex, and institution. One section of *Earned Degrees Conferred.*
    Useful for judging the extent of a college's program in each of the following specialties: chiropody or podiatry, dental hygiene, hospital administration, medical technology, medicine, nursing, occupational therapy, optometry, osteopathy, pharmacy, physical therapy, public health, radiologic technology, veterinary medicine, and the clinical sciences.

Health professions in the Peace Corps. Peace Corps. 1962. 6p. Free
    Illustrated leaflet describing needs, qualifications, and rewarding experiences.

**Health service occupations. One chapter of *Occupational Outlook Handbook.*
    Outlook summary for medical and other health service occupations. Specific information concerning each of the foremost services. Fifteen illustrations.

Hospital attendants. Science Research Associates. 1963. 4p. 35c
    Occupational brief describing nature of work, requirements, getting started, earnings, advantages, disadvantages, and future outlook.

**Job descriptions and organizational analysis for hospitals and related health services. U.S. Employment Service. Supt. of Documents. 1952. 532p. $2.50
    Describes hospital and related health services occupations. Includes narrative descriptions and organizational charts of the various hospital departments covering such activities as administration, business, professional care, plant operation, and maintenance.

Jobs and futures in mental health work. Ogg, Elizabeth. Public Affairs Committee. 1960. 28p. 25c
    Points out the need for trained workers in psychiatry, clinical psychology, psychiatric social work, psychiatric nursing, and occupational therapy. Also includes costs of training, educational requirements, and areas of practice.

MEDICAL SERVICE WORKER—*Continued*

**Jobs in health. Science Research Associates. 1959. 32p. $1

Describes the variety of job prospects and opportunities within this field. An accompanying wall chart is available for 35c.

**The life you save: your career in health. Burke, Betsy and Paradis, Adrian. David McKay Company. 1962. 256p. $3.95

A practical book about the rewarding opportunities in the health field, pointing up the great need for nurses, aides, therapists and other dedicated people for areas related to health. Suggested readings at the end of each chapter.

Medical and other health service workers. Chapter 5 of *The College Girl Looks Ahead.*

Some characteristics of health occupations, talents needed, entering, and kinds of work.

Medical office services. Pages 99-101 of *Health Careers Guidebook.*

Nature of work, personal qualifications, training, and prospects for the medical secretary and assistant.

**New careers in the health sciences. National Health Council. 1961. 24p. Free to counselors and librarians

Information about the new careers created by the joining of forces of physics, chemistry, mathematics, and engineering with biology and medical research. The opportunities are presented for the biophysicist, biochemist, biometrician, and bioengineer.

One patient at a time—a medical center at work. Zisowitz, Milton. Random House, Inc. 1961. 287p. $5

Describes the work of many medical workers in the New York Hospital of the Cornell Medical Center.

Selected sources of health career information. American Hospital Association. 1961. 3p. Free

Names and addresses of twenty-four national organizations.

Today's hospital . . . career center for America's youth. American Hospital Association. 1963. 8p. Free

A recruiting leaflet pointing out the variety of opportunities and the need for specially trained people in hospital services.

What's in your future—a career in health? Yahraes, Herbert. Public Affairs Committee. 1959. 30p. 25c

Describes the diversification of health careers, demand, prospects, advantages, drawbacks, and training.

Where to get career information on health professions and health related sciences. National Health Council. 1963. 2p. Free

Alphabetical list of national agencies which publish and distribute free on request single copies of career information on health service occupations.

Your future: a career in rehabilitation. National Society for Crippled Children and Adults. No date. 8p. Free
Brief description of rehabilitation and the work of specialists such as physical therapist, occupational therapist, speech pathologist, audiologist, psychologist, social worker, rehabilitation counselor, and special educator.

See also Hospital administrator; Medical technologist; Physician

MEDICAL SOCIAL WORKER 0-27.20

Casework services in public assistance medical care. Bureau of Family Services, U.S. Department of Health, Education, and Welfare. Supt. of Documents. 1962. 110p. 50c
Prepared for in-service training of public assistance caseworkers.

Educational qualifications of medical social workers in public health programs. American Public Health Association. 1962. 7p. Free
Scope of the work, duties performed, types of positions, educational preparation, and qualifications.

Medical social worker. Careers. 1964. 2p. 15c
Career summary for desk-top file. Duties, qualifications, and outlook.

MEDICAL TECHNOLOGIST 0-50.01

Approved schools of medical technology. Council on Medical Education and Hospitals of the American Medical Association. 1963. 16p. Free
For each of the 789 schools there is given the following information: college affiliation, minimum prerequisite college training, length of training in months, maximum enrollment, and tuition. Also included is a statement of essentials of an acceptable school for medical technologists.

** Are you dreaming of a career in medical science—be a medical technologist. American Society of Medical Technologists. 1963. 8 leaflets. Free to counselors and librarians
Folder containing career information.

* Career as a medical technologist. Institute for Research. 1963. 24p. $1
Importance of the medical technologist to the physician, steps necessary to become a technologist, a typical day's work, qualifications, training, salaries, advantages, and disadvantages. Also includes minimum standards for training schools and minimum standards to secure a certificate of registration.

Careers in medical technology. Veterans Administration, Department of Medicine and Surgery. 1961. 12p. Free
Opportunities for medical technologists and medical laboratory technicians, training programs, qualifications, and benefits.

**Careers in the medical laboratory. National Committee for Careers in Medical Technology. Registry of Medical Technologists of the American Society of Clinical Pathologists. 1964. 4p. Free
A fact sheet describing the work of the pathologist, medical technologist, cytotechnologist, and laboratory assistant. Also contains an explanation of the difference between its requirements and certification and those of several registries which are not under medical auspices.

MEDICAL TECHNOLOGIST—*Continued*

Cell examination—new hope in cancer. Public Affairs Committee. 1962. 20p. 25c
> This includes information on cytotechnology as a career.

**Choose medical technology. Registry of Medical Technologists of the American Society of Clinical Pathologists. 1963. 8p. Free
> Illustrated folder giving brief description of work and training for both men and women.

**Employment outlook for medical technologists, medical X-ray technicians, and medical record librarians. Bureau of Labor Statistics, U.S. Department of Labor. Supt. of Documents. 1964. 12p. 10c
> Reprint from the *Occupational Outlook Handbook*.

The girl in the white coat. Wells, Helen. Julian Messner, Inc. 1953. 192p. $2.95
> Career fiction. A story that combines a career interest in science with light romance. Tells of a girl's experiences in college as a science major and in a hospital completing her practical training to become a medical technologist.

The human cell and the cytotechnologist. Registry of Medical Technologists of the American Society of Clinical Pathologists. 1961. 4p. Free
> Describes nature of the work.

List of approved schools of cytotechnology. Registry of Medical Technologists of American Society of Clinical Pathologists. 1961. 4p. Free
> List revised periodically.

Medical laboratory technologist. The Guidance Centre. 1963. 4p. 15c in Canada; 20c elsewhere
> Development and growth of the occupation, working conditions, qualifications, preparation, advancement, earnings, advantages, disadvantages, and how to get started.

Medical technologist. Jackson, Lura. Bellman Publishing Company. 1958. 36p. $1
> Nature and development of work, qualifications, number registered by states, training, opportunities, and future trends. Includes list of approved schools.

Medical technologist. Splaver, Sarah. Personnel Services. 1958. 6p. 50c; 25c to students
> Occupational abstract describing nature of work, qualifications, preparation, certification, entrance and advancement, supply and demand, earnings, advantages, and disadvantages.

* Medical technologist. Careers. 1962. 7p. 25c
> Career brief describing duties, working conditions, training, personal qualifications, places of employment, earnings, and outlook. Additional readings.

* Medical technologist. Chronicle Guidance Publications. 1960. 4p. 35c
> Occupational brief summarizing nature of work, working conditions, qualifications, training, opportunities, outlook, methods of entry, and suggested activities.

Medical technologist, bioanalyst. California State Department of Employment. 1961. 4p. Single copy free
Duties, working conditions, salaries, hours, entrance requirements, training, lines of promotion, and employment outlook.

* Medical technologists. Science Research Associates. 1959. 4p. 35c
Occupational brief describing nature of work, qualifications, opportunities, advantages, disadvantages, and future outlook.

**Medical technologists. One section of *Occupational Outlook Handbook*.
Nature of work, where employed, training, other qualifications, advancement, employment outlook, earnings, and working conditions.

Medical technology. Michigan College of Mining and Technology. 1963. 2p. Free
Example of a recruiting leaflet describing work, qualifications, and employment opportunities.

Medical technology. Pages 101-4 of *Health Careers Guidebook*.
Nature of work, qualifications, and prospects for the medical technologist, cytological technologist, and the blood bank technologist.

**Opportunities in medical technology. Fagelson, Anna P. Vocational Guidance Manuals. 1961. 92p. $1.45 paper
History and progress in medical technology, needs, trends, training, certification requirements, earnings, fringe benefits, and opportunities.

**The profession of medical technology. Registry of Medical Technologists of the American Society of Clinical Pathologists. 1963. 8p. Free
Brief description of work, training, requirements, and opportunities. Twelve illustrations.

Radioactive isotope work. Pages 132-3 of *Health Careers Guidebook*.
Brief statement of work and training.

The registry of medical technologists of the American Society of Clinical Pathologists. The Registry. 1962. 24p. Free
Information about eligibility for registration, technical training requirements, examination of candidates, code of ethics, and brief suggestions for prospective students.

* Should you be a medical technologist? Street, Charlotte. New York Life Insurance Company. 1961. 12p. Free
Description of work, required training, financial rewards, and requirements for success.

What is a medical technologist? Upjohn Company. 1962. 4p. Free
Illustrated brochure describing nature of work, training, and qualifications.

**Your future in medical technology. Paul, Grace. Richards Rosen Press. 1962. 156p. $2.95
Emphasizes that medical technology is an important contributor to the health of the nation and offers opportunities for service, investigation, and many rewards besides financial ones.

See also Laboratory technician; Medical service worker

MERCHANDISE MANAGER 0-74.21

**Careers in department store merchandising. Kaplan, Albert and de Mille, Margaret. Henry Z. Walck, Inc. 1962. 112p. $3.50
   Describes especially the department store buyer who is responsible for the selection, purchase, and selling of one type of merchandise. Includes detailed description of a typical day's work, opportunities and the present-day trend toward the suburban branch store. Reading list. Illustrated.

Careers in marketing. Angel, Juvenal. World Trade Academy Press. 1959. 30p. $1.25
   Includes description of work, training, opportunities, remuneration, and future outlook.

* Careers in merchandising. Angel, Juvenal. World Trade Academy Press. 1963. 26p. $1.25
   Includes description of work, training required, opportunities, advantages, disadvantages, and future outlook.

**Maggie in fashion. Pennoyer, Sara. Dodd, Mead and Company. 1961. 272p. $3
   Career fiction. Story of a girl who used a gift for writing to develop a fashion career. Her first job selling dresses started her promotions through the various phases of work in advertising, display, and promotion.

* Merchandising as a career. Institute for Research. 1958. 24p. $1
   Function of the merchant, description of work of wholesaler, broker, commission merchant, sales agent, importers and exporters, retailer, and auctioneer. Includes department store positions in merchandise, service, publicity, and finance.

   See also Buyer; Retail manager; Salesperson

MERCHANT MARINE 0-88. and 5, 7, 9-48.

Careers in the United States merchant marine (with American steamship lines). Institute for Research. 1957. 24p. $1
   History of the American merchant marine. Description of work of the ship's personnel such as chief steward, deck yeoman, and engine cadet. Types of training available and a discussion of attractive and unattractive sides.

Information booklet. U.S. Merchant Marine Academy. 1963. 6p. Free
   Requirements for appointment, how selections are made, and information about Kings Point training, expenses, and allowances.

Maritime College bulletin. State University of New York Maritime College. 1963. 100p. Free
   Statement of program, admission requirements, and explanation of curriculums offered: Marine transportation, marine engineering, nuclear science, meteorology, and oceanography. Illustrated.

Merchant marine: earned degrees, by level, sex, and institution. One section of *Earned Degrees Conferred.*
   List of five academies and the number of degrees conferred by each.

Merchant seamen. Science Research Associates. 1960. 4p. 35c

Occupational brief describing nature of work, training, qualifications, opportunities, advantages, disadvantages, and future outlook.

Opportunities in the merchant marine. O'Connor, John J. Vocational Guidance Manuals. 1953. 160p. $1.45 paper

Includes an analysis of maritime occupations, both at sea and on shore; working conditions; methods of entering; advancement; advantages; and disadvantages. Lists of American ship owners, operators, and agents; subjects for qualified members of engine department; examination subjects for able seamen; and major legal requirements for deck licenses on ocean vessels.

**Pathfinders U.S.A.: your career on land, sea, and air. Neal, Harry Edward. Julian Messner, Inc. 1963. 192p. $3.95. Library binding $3.64 net

Describes work in the U.S. Merchant Marine Corps, in weather forecasting, industrial meteorology, highway building, coastal surveying, geodetic work, and control of civil aviation. Consideration is given to duties, training, and future prospects.

MESSENGER   1-23.14

Messengers. Chronicle Guidance Publications. 1963. 4p. 35c

Occupational brief describing work, qualifications, and outlook.

Messengers and office boys. Science Research Associates. 1959. 4p. 35c

Occupational brief describing nature of work, training, qualifications, opportunities, advantages, and future outlook.

Office boys and messengers. Science Research Associates. 1962. 4p. 35c

Junior occupational brief describing work and opportunities.

METAL INDUSTRY WORKER   4, 6, 8-71. through 4, 6, 8-95.

Magnesium industry workers. Science Research Associates. 1957. 4p. 35c

Occupational brief describing work, requirements, earnings, getting started, advantages, disadvantages, and future outlook.

The metal trades. Chapter 3 of *Vocations for Boys.*

Information about machine-shop occupations, foundry occupations, forge shop occupations, and welding.

Nonferrous metal industry workers. Science Research Associates. 1961. 4p. 35c

Occupational brief describing nature of work, qualifications, opportunities, advantages, disadvantages, and future outlook.

Prospector. The Guidance Centre. 1962. 4p. 15c in Canada; 20c elsewhere

Nature of work, qualifications, preparation, working conditions, outlook, advantages, disadvantages, how to get started, and related occupations.

METALLURGICAL ENGINEER 0-14.10

Metallurgical engineer. Robinson, H. Alan. Personnel Services. 1955. 6p. 50c; 25c to students
Occupational abstract. Nature of work, future prospects, opportunities for servicemen, qualifications, preparation, entrance and advancement, earnings, number and distribution of workers, advantages, and disadvantages.

Metallurgical engineer. Chronicle Guidance Publications. 1963. 4p. 35c
Occupational brief describing work, qualifications, and training.

Metallurgical engineering. Work, Harold K. and Nielsen, John P. Chapter 17 of *Engineering Enrollment in the United States.*
Trends in college enrollment and future requirements for specialists in this area.

Metallurgical engineering. Colorado School of Mines. No date. 6p. Free
Description of the work, prospects, training, and requirements for admission to the School of Mines.

* Metallurgical engineers. Science Research Associates. 1963. 4p. 35c
Occupational brief describing nature of work, requirements, methods of getting started and advancing, earnings, advantages, disadvantages, and future outlook.

Metallurgical engineers. One section of *Occupational Outlook Handbook.*
Nature of work, where employed, and employment outlook.

METALLURGIST 0-14.20

**Careers in metallurgy and metallurgical engineering. American Institute of Mining, Metallurgical, and Petroleum Engineers. 1960. 16p. Single copy free
Description of work, duties, rewards, qualifications, and training. Includes list of forty-four schools with curricula in metallurgical engineering accredited by the Engineers Council for Professional Development.

**Careers in the mineral industry—opportunities unlimited. American Institute of Mining, Metallurgical, and Petroleum Engineers. 1962. 32p. Single copy free
Discussion of careers in exploration, production, and ore dressing. Sections on desirable high school preparation, college selection, and opportunities.

Metallurgist. Careers. 1961. 2p. 15c
Career summary for desk-top file. Duties, qualifications, and outlook.

* Metallurgist. Chronicle Guidance Publications. 1958. 4p. 35c
Occupational brief summarizing work performed, working conditions, earnings, personal qualifications, training requirements, opportunities, employment outlook, and entry into the job.

Metallurgist. The Guidance Centre. 1963. 4p. 15c in Canada; 20c elsewhere
History and importance, nature of work, qualifications, preparation, advancement, outlook, remuneration, how to get started, and related occupations.

Metallurgy. Cohan, Alvin S. Bellman Publishing Company. 1955. 20p. $1
History and development, training and education, qualifications, and employment opportunities.

Metallurgy. Michigan College of Mining and Technology. 1963. 2p. Free
Example of a recruiting leaflet describing work, qualifications, earnings, and employment opportunities.

Metallurgy and materials science. Massachusetts Institute of Technology. 1961. 30p. Free
Description of opportunities for professional achievement and the training offered.

METEOROLOGIST   0-35.68

Allison Day: weather girl. Dean, Nell M. Julian Messner, Inc. 1958. 192p. $2.95
Career fiction. A girl faces keen competition with men, but she proves she knows her job as a meteorologist.

**Careers in weather forecasting and meteorology. Institute for Research. 1961. 24p. $1
Positions and salaries in the weather bureau. Describes qualifications, training, opportunities, typical day's work, attractive and unattractive features. Also describes work of airways observer, clerk, airline meteorologist, and research-teaching meteorologist.

Colleges and universities for training in meteorology. American Meteorological Society. 1963. 1p. Free
Frequently revised list.

**Employment outlook for geologists, geophysicists, and meteorologists. Bureau of Labor Statistics, U.S. Department of Labor. Supt. of Documents. 1964. 20p. 15c
Reprint from the Occupational Outlook Handbook.

Hurricane fighters. Innis, Pauline B. and Archibald, Joseph. David McKay Company. 1962. 256p. $3.50
Career fiction. Story of a young man who trains to become a member of the Navy's famed Early Warning Squadron, whose business it is to fly into the very eye of hurricanes.

Man against the elements: Adolphus W. Greely. Werstein, Irving. Julian Messner, Inc. 1960. 192p. $3.25
Biography of a versatile pioneer in Signal Corps strategy, military telegraphy, and meteorological expedition experimentation.

Meteorological technician. The Guidance Centre. 1962. 4p. 15c in Canada; 20c elsewhere
History and importance, nature of work, qualifications, working conditions, preparation, remuneration, advancement, outlook, related occupations, and how to get started.

METEOROLOGIST—*Continued*

**Meteorologist. Carlin, A. V. Research Publishing Company. 1955. 39p. $1
> History of meteorology, establishment of U.S. Weather Bureau, subdivisions in meteorology field, typical places of employment, requirements, training, and opportunities.

Meteorologist. Group, Vernard F. Personnel Services. 1962. 6p. 50c; 25c to students
> Nature of work, qualifications, preparation, entrance, advancement, earnings, advantages, and disadvantages. References for further reading.

Meteorologist. California State Department of Employment. 1962. 6p. Single copy free
> Job duties, working conditions, salaries, hours, finding the job, promotion, training, and employment outlook.

Meteorologist. Careers. 1960. 2p. 15c
> Career summary for desk-top file. Duties, qualifications, and outlook.

* Meteorologist. Chronicle Guidance Publications. 1962. 8p. 50c
> Occupational brief summarizing work performed, working conditions, qualifications, determination of aptitudes and interests, training, and employment outlook.

Meteorologist. The Guidance Centre. 1962. 4p. 15c in Canada; 20c elsewhere
> Development and importance of the work, qualifications, preparation, working conditions, opportunities for advancement, advantages, disadvantages, and related occupations.

Meteorologists. Science Research Associates. 1963. 4p. 35c
> Occupational brief describing nature of work, requirements, training, working conditions, how to get started, and future outlook.

**Meteorologists. One section of *Occupational Outlook Handbook*.
> Nature of work, where employed, training, other qualifications, employment outlook, earnings, and working conditions.

Meteorology and oceanography. New York University, Director of Admissions. 1962. 14p. Free
> Example of a recruiting brochure describing nature of work and training.

**Pathfinders, U.S.A.: your career on land, sea, and air. Neal, Harry Edward. Julian Messner, Inc. 1963. 192p. $3.95. Library binding $3.64 net
> An account of behind-the-scenes activities in a variety of jobs in the United States merchant marine, in weather forecasting and industrial meteorology, in highway building, in coastal surveying, geodetic work, and in the control of civil aviation. Includes names of colleges and schools for special training.

Skywatchers: the U.S. Weather Bureau in action. Bixby, William. David McKay Company. 1962. 192p. $3.50
> Stories of individuals at work at their far-flung posts and how their information helps people in many walks of life. Points up the need for trained meteorologists and the steps the Government takes to increase the supply.

There's adventure in meteorology. Ruzic, Neil P. Popular Mechanics Press. 1958. 166p. $2.95
By relating experiences of a boy in this field, the author portrays the various kinds of work. Written for grades 7 to 10.

**Your future in meteorology. Berry, Frederick and Frank, Sidney. Richards Rosen Press. 1962. 155p. $2.95
The authors pinpoint salient facts concerning the applications of meteorological research and development and their appeal. Includes description of activities of the U.S. Weather Bureau and the opportunities in the Navy and Air Force weather services. List of schools offering specialized training.

METERMAN   1-49.94; 5-83.456

Metermen and meter readers. Brief description in *Occupational Outlook Handbook*.
Nature of work and employment outlook.

MICROBIOLOGIST. *See* Bacteriologist

MILITARY SERVICEMAN   2-68.

Armed forces. Science Research Associates. 1961. 4p. 35c
Occupational brief describing opportunities for training and education, advancement in the services, opportunities for women, earnings, and other benefits.

**Basic facts about military service. High School News Service. Published annually in September. 62p. Free
The September issue is a comprehensive military facts survey designed primarily as a yearlong reference source for counselors. Subsequent issues consist of illustrated feature articles on military life, opportunities, and special skills required of men and women in uniform today.

Handbook for conscientious objectors. Central Committee for Conscientious Objectors. 1962. 112p. 50c
Procedures under selective service law to obtain assignment to noncombatant service or to civilian work. Information concerning criminal prosecution if one is not classified as an objector. Also includes a selected, annotated bibliography of conscientious objection to war.

How to choose that career: civilian and military. Feingold, S. Norman. Bellman Publishing Company. 1954. 52p. $1
Helpful hints on planning a high school and college program and the choice of a career.

**It's your choice. U.S. Department of Defense. 1963. 20p. Free
A guide to the opportunities open to volunteers for military service.

Military, naval, air science: earned degrees, by level, sex, and institution. One section of *Earned Degrees Conferred*.
List of sixteen institutions and the number of degrees conferred by each.

Military service as a career. Careers. 1961. 7p. 25c
Career brief describing opportunities and enlistment inducements.

MILITARY SERVICEMAN—*Continued*

Questions and answers on the classification and assignment of conscientious objectors. National Service Board for Religious Objectors. 1963. 40p. 25c
> Procedures for obtaining proper classification and description of the civilian work program in lieu of induction into the armed services.

Selective service: a guide to the draft. Evers, Alf. J. B. Lippincott Company. 1961. 192p. $3.25
> Designed for those about to be eighteen; gives information about registration, classification, questionnaire, volunteers, reserves, mental and physical exams, and other aspects of the draft.

Selective service and you. Careers. 1961. 8p. 25c
> Career brief describing the classification system, appeals, college deferment, other deferments, conscientious objection, and induction into the Armed Forces.

Should you make a career in the Armed Forces? Radford, Arthur W. New York Life Insurance Company. 1960. 12p. Free
> Description of service, possibilities for advancement, advantages, drawbacks, and requirements. Illustrated.

**The student's guide to military service. Harwood, Michael. Channel Press. 1963. 313p. $5.95; paper $2.95
> Suggestions for choosing the method of deferred or present service from among the number of programs offered by the uniformed services. Contains information about obtaining specialized or professional education while fulfilling military obligations. The emphasis is on how to get as much value as possible out of one's tour of duty.

You and the armed services. Gleaves, S. Z. and Wertenbaker, L. T. Simon and Schuster. 1961. 127p. $1.25
> A guide to selective service, the draft, and enlistment. Explains the different types of enlistments and the programs of the Coast Guard, Marines, Navy, Air Force, and Army.

**Your life plans and the Armed Forces. National Association of Secondary-School Principals. 1958. 160p. $1.25
> Prepared under the direction of the Defense Committee of the North Central Association of Colleges and Secondary Schools. Units of study for secondary-school pupils prepared to help them make realistic life plans, to inform them of military obligations and options, and to describe opportunities for continuing their education while in service. Includes the various types of educational and vocational opportunities in the Air Force, Army, Coast Guard, Marine Corps, and Navy.

> *See also* Air force airman; Coastguardsman; Marine; Military servicewoman; Sailor; Soldier

MILITARY SERVICEWOMAN   2-68.

Careers for women in the Armed Forces. U.S. Department of Defense. 1955. 46p. Free
> Information designed to help counselors advise women students about opportunities in the Armed Forces. Describes training and opportunities and discusses major jobs performed by enlisted women.

**Careers for women in the Armed Forces. Women's Bureau, U.S. Department of Labor in cooperation with the U.S. Department of Defense. 1956. 46p. Free
Description of the basic training program, the broad career fields, officer training, off-duty educational opportunities, benefits besides the paycheck, and military job training and experience in relation to civilian careers.

For you an officer's career in the U.S. Armed Forces. U.S. Department of Defense, Defense Advisory Committee on Women in the Services. 1963. 32p. Free
Description of career fields, additional specialties, training, education opportunities, benefits, and eligibility requirements for women officers in Army, Navy, Air Force, and Marine Corps. For college women.

Going places . . . the story of the WAF officer. U.S. Air Force. 1961. 12p. Free
Illustrated brochure depicting opportunities for college women.

**Selected for success. Army Careers, U.S. Continental Army Command. 1963. 44p. Free
Illustrated booklet for the college graduate describing life and opportunities in the Women's Army Corps. Another booklet, *Somebody Special,* is available for the high school graduate.

The women of the United States Marine Corps. U.S. Marine Corps. 1963. 24p. Free
Illustrated brochure describing qualifications and opportunities for college graduates.

Your daughter's role in today's world—what every parent should know about opportunities for women in the Armed Forces. U.S. Department of Defense. 1961. 12p. Free
Descriptions of nine jobs performed by women in the armed services. Other information in question and answer form.

MILLINER   4-23.100

Milliner. Chronicle Guidance Publications. 1963. 4p. 35c
Occupational brief summarizing work performed, working conditions, qualifications, advantages, disadvantages, and outlook.

**Milliners. Science Research Associates. 1961. 4p. 35c
Occupational brief describing kinds of work, qualifications, educational requirements, getting started and advancing, earnings, advantages, disadvantages, and future outlook.

See also Clothing industry worker

MILLING-MACHINE OPERATOR   4, 6-78.031

Job description for milling-machine operator II. U.S. Employment Service. Supt. of Documents. 1947. 5p. 5c
Occupational guide. Job summary, work performed, training, related occupations, physical activities, working conditions, hazards, and employment variables.

MILLMAN 4-33.914

Job description for millman (woodworking). U.S. Employment Service. Supt. of Documents. 1948. 6p. 5c

Occupational guide. Job summary, work performed, training, trainee-selection factors, related occupations, physical activities, working conditions, hazards, and employment variables.

MILLWRIGHT 5-78.100

**Employment outlook for millwrights and industrial machinery repairmen. Bureau of Labor Statistics, U.S. Department of Labor. Supt. of Documents. 1964. 8p. 5c

Reprint from the *Occupational Outlook Handbook.*

Millwright. California State Department of Employment. 1962. 5p. Single copy free

Occupational guide summarizing duties, working conditions, employment prospects, earnings, training, requirements for entry, and suggestions for locating a job.

**Millwright. Careers. 1964. 8p. 25c

Career brief describing duties, working conditions, training, places of employment, earnings, unionization, and outlook.

Millwright. Chronicle Guidance Publications. 1964. 4p. 35c

Occupational brief summarizing work performed, working conditions, hours, earnings, personal qualifications, training requirements, opportunities, employment outlook, and entry into the job.

Millwrights. Science Research Associates. 1963. 4p. 35c

Occupational brief describing nature of work, requirements, training, getting started, earnings, advantages, disadvantages, and future outlook.

**Millwrights. One section of *Occupational Outlook Handbook.*

Nature of work, where employed, training, other qualifications, employment outlook, earnings, and working conditions.

MINER 5, 7-21.000 through 5, 7-22.999; 9-22.

Coal miners. Science Research Associates. 1960. 4p. 35c

Occupational brief describing nature of work, qualifications, working conditions, opportunities, advantages, disadvantages, and future outlook.

I want to be a coal miner. Greene, Carla. Childrens Press. 1957. 32p. $2

Prepared for beginning readers with a reading level of upper first grade. Illustrated in color.

Metal mining workers. Science Research Associates. 1961. 4p. 35c

Occupational brief describing types of work, requirements, methods of getting started, advantages, disadvantages, and future outlook.

Miner (metal). The Guidance Centre. 1960. 4p. 15c in Canada; 20c elsewhere

Nature of work, qualifications, preparation, working conditions, earnings, how to get started, advantages, and disadvantages.

Miners. Chronicle Guidance Publications. 1962. 4p. 35c
Occupational brief summarizing work, requirements, advantages, disadvantages, trends, and outlook.

The mining industry. Chapter 31 in *Occupations and Careers.*
Includes information concerning bituminous coal mining, metal mining, and quarrying and nonmetallic mining.

Occupations in mining. Chapter 12 of *Planning Your Future.*
Includes discussion of extent of mining in the United States, importance of mining, nature of work, working conditions, qualifications, opportunities for advancement, advantages, and disadvantages.

MINERAL INDUSTRY WORKER   5, 7, 9-20. through 5, 7, 9-22.

**Careers in the mineral industry—opportunities unlimited. American Institute of Mining, Metallurgical, and Petroleum Engineers. 1962. 32p. Single copy free.
Discussion of careers in exploration, production, and ore dressing. Sections on desirable high school preparation, college selection, and opportunities.

Men, minerals and midnight oil. Colorado School of Mines. 1963. 96p. Free
College catalog which includes brief descriptions of geological, geophysical, metallurgical, mining, petroleum, and petroleum-refining engineering.

Mineral economics as a career. Institute for Research. 1957. 24p. $1
Types of positions, qualifications, earnings, outlook for employment, lines of promotion, and attractive and unattractive features.

Mineral engineering. Colorado School of Mines. 1962. 34p. Free
A booklet containing information about careers and specific training in the mineral industries. Describes the work of metallurgical, geological, geophysical, petroleum-mining, and petroleum-refining engineer. Also describes the courses in engineering chemistry, mathematics, and physics. Other sections answer questions customarily asked by prospective students about housing, fraternities, and admission.

Mineral industries research. Pennsylvania State University, Mineral Industries Experiment Station. 1950. 32p. Free
Significance of the mineral industries, and description of earth sciences, mineralogy and petrology, geophysics and geochemistry, meteorology, mineral economics, mineral preparation, mineral technology, ceramics, and fuel technology. Illustrated.

Mineral preparation engineering as a career. Institute for Research. 1956. 24p. $1
Types of positions, qualifications, earnings, opportunities, lines of promotion, and attractive and unattractive features.

Should you go into the mineral industry? Vanderwilt, John W. New York Life Insurance Company. 1956. 12p. Free
Description of work, qualifications, training, and future outlook.

MINING ENGINEER   0-20.01

Career opportunities. New Mexico Institute of Mining and Technology.
1962. 8p. Free
> A recruiting brochure which includes brief descriptions of nature of work and
> opportunities. Includes mining, metallurgical, and petroleum engineering;
> physics; geology; geophysics; mathematics; and chemistry.

**The coal industry. Speare, M. Edmund. Bellman Publishing Company.
1957. 32p. $1
> Development of the coal industry, mechanical improvements in underground
> and surface mining, and kinds of work, training, and opportunities for the coal
> mining engineer and the coal miner.

Gil's discovery in the mine. Lee, Rector L. Little, Brown and Company.
1957. 202p. $3
> Career fiction. A summer job in a Colorado mine gives a realistic picture of
> one of the major engineering fields. For younger readers.

Mining engineer. Careers. 1960. 2p. 15c
> Career summary for desk-top file. Duties, qualifications, and outlook.

Mining engineer. Michigan College of Mining and Technology. 1963. 2p.
Free
> Example of a recruiting leaflet describing work, outlook, and opportunities.

Mining engineering. Shaffer, Lysle E. Chapter 18 of *Engineering Enrollment in the United States.*
> Trends in college enrollment and future requirements for specialists in this
> area.

Mining engineering. Colorado School of Mines. No date. 6p. Free
> Description of the work, prospects, training, and requirements for admission
> for study.

Mining engineers. Science Research Associates. 1963. 4p. 35c
> Occupational brief describing nature of work, duties, places of employment,
> training, earnings, and future outlook.

**Mining engineers. One section of *Occupational Outlook Handbook.*
> Nature of work, where employed, and employment outlook.

Opportunities unlimited—careers in the mineral industry. Society of Mining Engineers. 1960. 32p. Single copy free
> Includes history of the mining industry, training, college costs, opportunities,
> and salaries.

See also Engineer; Petroleum engineer

MINISTER. *See* Clergyman

MISSILEMAN   0-41.10.; 5-03.599

Count down: behind the scenes at our missile bases. Colby, C. B. Coward-
McCann, Inc. 1960. 48p. Library binding $2.52 net
> Photographs and brief text reveal the work and training. Written for grades
> 4 to 8.

The mighty Thor: missile in readiness. Hart, Julian. Duell, Sloan and Pearce, Inc. 1961. 271p. $4.50
Describes the work of the civilian and military personnel involved in the construction of the Thor, the intermediate-range ballistic missile.

The missile technician. Careers. 1957. 2p. 15c
Reprint from *Air Force Magazine,* describing kinds of work, requirements, training, and outlook.

Missileman. DuPre, Flint O. Research Publishing Company. 1959. 24p. $1
Nature of work, history and importance, number engaged in occupation, qualifications, working conditions, salaries and other returns, training, placement channels, and promotional opportunities.

Operation watchdog: rockets, guided missiles, aircraft and radar of our defenses. Colby, C. B. Coward-McCann, Inc. 1956. 48p. Library edition $2.52 net
Photographs and brief text reveal the work of the Continental Air Defense Command. Written for grades 4 to 8.

Rockets, missiles and space. Pizer, Vernon. Lippincott Company. 1962. 160p. $3.95
Explanations of how rockets, missiles, and space vehicles work and a history of man's efforts to conquer space. Illustrated.

See also Aerospace industry worker; Air Force airman; Airplane pilot; Astronaut

MODEL   2-43.40 through 2-43.49

Beth Hilton: model. Wyndham, Lee. Julian Messner, Inc. 1961. 192p. $2.95
Career fiction. Because Beth is tall and gawky, she enrolls in a charm school, becomes interested in modeling, and learns the realistic side of a competitive work that requires effort and dedication.

A career in modeling. Fraser, Helen. Barbizon School of Modeling. 1961. 28p. 25c
A recruiting bulletin which includes a description of photographic and fashion modeling, types of models used, employment opportunities, general requirements, and the training program.

Careers in modeling. Angel, Juvenal. World Trade Academy Press. 1958. 18p. $1.25
Description of work, training, advantages, disadvantages, opportunities, and future outlook.

Fashion model. Splaver, Sarah. Personnel Services. 1960. 6p. 50c; 25c to students
Occupational abstract. Nature of work, qualifications, preparation, entrance and advancement, supply and demand, distribution of workers, earnings, disadvantages, and appraisal of the literature.

MODEL—*Continued*

**Fashion, photographic, and television modeling as a career. Institute for Research. 1958. 24p. $1
    Types of work, related opportunities, attractive and unattractive features, and suggestions for evaluating schools for training.

Kate Brennan, model. Daly, Maggie. Dodd, Mead and Company. 1956. 250p. $3
    Career fiction. Experiences of a model pointing out that the work is hard and the competition keen in this glamorous field.

Make your name in modeling and television. Jones, Candy. Harper and Row. 1960. 134p. $3.95
    This book describes the difficult as well as pleasant aspects of a model's work.

Model. Careers. 1964. 8p. 25c
    Career brief describing duties, working conditions, training, personal qualifications, advantages, disadvantages, earnings, and outlook. Additional readings.

* Model. Chronicle Guidance Publications. 1964. 4p. 35c
    Occupational brief summarizing work performed, working conditions, hours, earnings, personal qualifications, training requirements, opportunities, employment outlook, and entry into the job.

**Modeling. Conover, Harry. Bellman Publishing Company. 1955. 22p. $1
    Characteristics a model must have, preparations for becoming a model, and description of work in photographic and life modeling. Bibliography.

* Models. Science Research Associates. 1961. 4p. 35c
    Occupational brief describing kinds of modeling, qualifications, training, methods of getting started, earnings, advantages, disadvantages, and future outlook.

What it takes to be a model. Burke, Betsy. Seventeen Magazine. 1956. 4p. 10c
    Reprint describing the demands of the work and the requirements for a modeling career.

**Your future in modeling. MacGil, Gillis. Richards Rosen Press. 1963. 160p. $2.95; library edition $2.79 net
    The founder of a fashion model agency describes qualifications, opportunities, and the varied kinds of work.

MORTICIAN. *See* Funeral director

MOTEL MANAGER   0-71.

Hawthorne house. De Leeuw, Adele. Macmillan Company. 1950. 220p. $3.50
    Career fiction. When fortunes run low, a big rambling house is turned into a tourist's home and the whole family enjoys the responsibilities as well as the rewards of the business. Written for ages 12 to 16.

**Hotel-motel education kit. American Hotel Association. 1962. Six leaflets. Free
  A number of helpful career pamphlets about this work.

Motel manager. Chronicle Guidance Publications. 1961. 4p. 35c
  Occupational brief summarizing work performed, where employed, working conditions, qualifications, earnings, advantages, disadvantages, and outlook.

Starting and managing a small motel. Small Business Administration. Supt. of Documents. 1963. 70p. 30c
  This booklet describes the advantages and disadvantages of entering this particular business, the risks involved, the personal characteristics that will contribute to success, and some management practices.

Will hotel-motel work be your career? American Hotel Association. 1963. 6p. Free
  Description of the work of the various divisions of the hotel-motel and the training necessary for each.

  See also Hotel manager

MOTION PICTURE INDUSTRY WORKER
0-02.; 0-06.20 through 0-06.39; 5, 7, 9-56.

Film editors. Science Research Associates. 1963. 4p. 35c
  Occupational brief describing nature of work, training, qualifications, opportunities, and outlook.

Motion picture producers and directors. Science Research Associates. 1961. 4p. 35c
  Occupational brief describing nature of work, training, qualifications, opportunities, advantages, disadvantages, and future outlook. Selected references.

MOTION-PICTURE PROJECTIONIST
5-55.010

Finding out about motion-picture projectionists. Science Research Associates. 1963. 4p. 35c
  Junior occupational brief containing simplified information about requirements, training, earnings, and opportunities.

Motion picture projectionist. Careers. 1964. 2p. 15c
  Career summary for desk-top file. Duties, qualifications, and outlook.

Motion picture projectionist. Chronicle Guidance Publications. 1960. 4p. 35c
  Occupational brief summarizing work performed, working conditions, hours, earnings, personal qualifications, training requirements, opportunities, employment outlook, and entry into the job.

Motion-picture projectionists. Michigan Employment Security Commission. 1958. 16p. 25c
  Introduction, nature of work, location of jobs, employment outlook, working conditions, earnings, requirements for entry, disadvantages, and advantages.

MOTION-PICTURE PROJECTIONIST—*Continued*

**Motion picture projectionists. Science Research Associates. 1958. 4p. 35c
Occupational brief describing nature of work, training, qualifications, opportunities, advantages, disadvantages, and future outlook.

MOTOR TRANSPORTATION INDUSTRY WORKER   5, 7, 9-49.200

American motor transport industry. Curry, Neil J. Bellman Publishing Company. 1956. 40p. $1
History and importance of the industry, employment opportunities, preparation, related occupations, and trade organizations.

**Careers in truck transportation. Institute for Research. 1960. 24p. $1
Description of positions within the trucking industry including driver, sales manager, traffic manager, dispatcher, terminal manager, freight accountant, and claims adjuster. Also included is discussion of qualifications, training, establishing a local trucking business, and attractive and unattractive features.

Opportunities in motor transportation. Rawson, Charles B. Vocational Guidance Manuals. 1951. 112p. $1.45
Contents: scope of motor transportation, the truck driver, bus driver, truck and bus mechanic, other jobs in the industry, educational opportunities, opportunities for self-employment, and opportunities in related fields.

Scholarship programs of motor carriers. American Trucking Associations. 1962. 11p. Free
List of scholarships offered by motor carriers and allied companies. Includes contributors, eligibility, number, value, field of study, and source of additional information.

Transportation courses in United States colleges and universities. American Trucking Associations. 1961. 10p. Free
A listing, by state, of 308 colleges and the courses they offer in transportation, traffic management, highway engineering, and related subjects.

Unlimited opportunities in America's fastest growing industry—motor transportation. Tri-State College. No date. 6p. Free
An example of a college recruiting leaflet describing training and opportunities.

**Your future in the trucking industry. Eskow, Gerald. Richards Rosen Press. 1964. 160p. $2.95; library edition $2.79 net
Description of the various jobs including business administration, traffic control, engineering, and personnel management.

See also Transportation worker; Truck driver

MUSEUM WORKER   0-39.00 through 0-39.09

Careers in archive and museum management. Bishop, C. N. Careers. 1959. 1p. 15c
Reprint describing nature of work and advantages.

Finding out about museum curators. Science Research Associates. 1962. 4p. 35c
> Junior occupational brief describing work and opportunities.

**Museum workers. Science Research Associates. 1961. 4p. 35c
> Occupational brief describing nature of work, requirements, getting started, rewards, and future outlook.

Treasures by the millions: the story of the Smithsonian Institution. Neal, Harry Edward. Julian Messner, Inc. 1961. 192p. $3.95 Library binding $3.64 net
> The author leads the reader on a tour through the various departments of the Smithsonian Institution, describing the activities of the curators and miscellaneous other museum experts.

MUSIC TEACHER   0-24.31

**A career in music education. Music Educators National Conference. 1962. 24p. 50c
> Information for high school students interested in teaching music. Includes qualifications, training, and opportunities. Good list of references.

Music teacher. Careers. 1964. 2p. 15c
> Career summary for desk top file. Duties, qualifications, and outlook.

Music teacher. Chronicle Guidance Publications. 1962. 4p. 35c
> Occupational brief summarizing work performed, qualifications, training, opportunities, earnings, and outlook.

* School music as a career. Institute for Research. 1962. 24p. $1
> Qualifications, preparation, salaries, and typical state requirements for certification. Includes description of a typical day's work as a small and large city school supervisor.

Song for Julie. Porter, Ella B. Macmillan Company. 1951. 160p. $3
> Career fiction. Story of a young music teacher's first position in New Mexico.

**Your future as a teacher of music in the schools. Sur, William. Music Educators National Conference. 1959. 8p. 30c
> Description of various positions, personal qualifications, training, salaries, and opportunities. Includes advice from experienced teachers.

> *See also* Instrumental musician; Musician; Singer

MUSICAL INSTRUMENT MANUFACTURING WORKER
5, 7-13.350 through 5, 7-13.399

**Musical instrument manufacturing workers. Science Research Associates. 1961. 4p. 35c
> Occupational brief describing nature of work, requirements, getting started, earnings, advantages, disadvantages, and future outlook.

MUSICIAN   0-24.

Associates and fellowship examination requirements. American Guild of
Organists. 1962. 2p. Free
    Includes description of the tests at the organ and paper work tests. Another
    statement is available for the choir master examinations requirements.

Career as cantor. B'nai B'rith Vocational Service. 1960. 8p. 35c
    Discussion of nature of work, requirements, training, cantorial certification,
    advantages, and disadvantages.

A career for Carol. Drury, Maxine and John P. David McKay Company.
1958. 216p. $3
    Career fiction. Sleuthing for a lobster thief and a first romance lend excite-
    ment to Carol's summer project for earning money toward a musical career.

**Careers and opportunities in music. Rich, Alan. Dutton and Company.
1964. 224p. $4.50
    Includes the opportunities and qualifications needed for the solo performer,
    the ensemble musician, the operatic specialist, the composer, teacher, and music
    critic.

Careers in music. Angel, Juvenal. World Trade Academy Press. 1960.
22p. $1.25
    Includes description of major fields of specialization, opportunities, rewards,
    future outlook, advantages, and disadvantages.

**Careers in music. Music Educators National Conference. 1961. 4p. 10c
    Brochure prepared for music educators and counselors calling attention to
    opportunities. The inside is a chart containing career information on teacher,
    music therapist, instrumentalist, vocalist, church musician, composer, conductor,
    and music librarian.

**Employment outlook for the performing arts: musicians, singers, actors and
actresses, and dancers. Bureau of Labor Statistics, U.S. Department of
Labor. Supt. of Documents. 1964. 16p. 10c
    Reprint from the *Occupational Outlook Handbook*.

I want to be a musician. Greene, Carla. Childrens Press. 1962. 32p. $2
    Prepared for beginning readers with a reading level of upper first grade.
    Illustrated in color.

Leonard Bernstein. Ewen, David. Chilton Company. 1960. 174p. $3.50
    Biography of one of the world's foremost symphony conductors and com-
    posers which shows not only his accolades and triumphs but also the frustra-
    tions and despair that preceded his success.

Leonard Bernstein, the man, his work, and his world. Briggs, John. Popular Library. 1961. 156p. 50c. Paperback
    Biography originally published by the World Publishing Company.

Music. Helm, Everett. Bellman Publishing Co. 1940. 44p. $1
    Description of work in radio, cinema, and recording, and as concert artist,
    orchestra player, conductor, organist, composer, music critic, teacher, and music
    librarian. Requirements, opportunities, a list of schools of music, and descrip-
    tion of courses usually offered.

Music as a career. Boston University. 1962. 10p. Free
Recruiting booklet describing opportunities, qualifications, and training. Discussion of work in teaching music, concert work, and in musical composition.

* Music as a career. Institute for Research. 1957. 24p. $1
Qualifications, preparation, opportunities, advantages, and disadvantages. Information concerning work of the pianist, accompanist, vocalist, orchestra player, orchestra conductor, organist, composer, music critic, piano teacher, radio musician, musicologist, music therapist, and school music supervisor.

Music therapist. Careers. 1960. 2p. 15c
Career summary for desk-top file. Duties, qualifications, and outlook.

Musician. Splaver, Sarah. Personnel Services. 1951. 6p. 50c; 25c to students
Occupational abstract. Nature of work, qualifications, preparation, entrance and advancement, supply and demand, earnings, advantages, and disadvantages.

Musician. The Guidance Centre. 1961. 4p. 15c in Canada; 20c elsewhere
Nature of work, qualifications, preparation, working conditions, remuneration, advantages, disadvantages, how to get started, and related occupations.

Musicians, general. Careers. 1962. 8p. 25c
Career brief describing duties, working conditions, training, personal qualifications, earnings, and outlook. Additional readings.

**Opportunities in music. Spaeth, Sigmund. Vocational Guidance Manuals. 1950. 128p. $1.45 paper
Discussion of individual fields of performance, and qualifications and opportunities in vocal music, conducting, composing and arranging, and teaching. Also opportunities for musical amateurs, music criticism, lecturing, research, selling, and management. A section presents excerpts from experts giving well-considered opinions as to opportunities in music.

**The performing arts. One chapter of *Occupational Outlook Handbook.*
Nature of work, where employed, training, other qualifications, employment outlook, earnings, and working conditions for each of the following: musicians and music teachers, singers and singing teachers, actors and actresses, and dancers.

Performing musicians. Science Research Associates. 1961. 4p. 35c
Occupational brief describing nature of work, requirements, earnings, getting started, advantages, disadvantages, and future outlook. Selected references.

* Popular music as a career. Institute for Research. 1958. 24p. $1
Types of positions, qualifications, training, typical day's work, salaries, favorable and unfavorable features.

Professional musicians. Michigan Employment Security Commission. 1955. 20p. 25c
Introduction, nature of work, location of musicians, employment outlook, working conditions, earnings, organizations, qualifications for entry, advantages, and disadvantages.

MUSICIAN—*Continued*

**Your future in music. Curtis, Robert. Richards Rosen Press. 1962. 160p. $2.95

 Includes discussion of many job opportunities in the field of music that are not generally known to the student.

 See also Instrumental musician; Music teacher; Singer

NAVIGATOR   0-41.60

Navigator. Chronicle Guidance Publications. 1963. 4p. 35c

 Occupational brief including definition, history, work performed, working conditions, hours, wages, requirements, opportunities, outlook, methods of entry, related jobs, and suggested activities.

NUCLEAR PHYSICIST. *See* Atomic energy industry worker; Physicist

NUMISMATIST   0-68.81

Numismatics. (Coin collecting). Regan, Lewis M. Bellman Publishing Company. 1955. 16p. $1

 How to become a professional numismatist, job opportunities, and professional organization. Bibliography. Illustrated.

NURSE (REGISTERED PROFESSIONAL)   0-33.

American women of nursing. Yost, Edna. Lippincott Company. 1955. 224p. $3.50

 Biographies of ten nurses who were outstanding in their special fields: pediatrics, physiotherapy, public health, nursing education, and visiting nursing.

America's first trained nurse: Linda Richards. Baker, Rachel. Julian Messner, Inc. 1959. 192p. $3.25. Library binding $3.19 net

 Biography of a nurse who revolutionized hospital care.

Books on careers in nursing. Committee on Careers, National League for Nursing. 1962. 16p. 5c

 An annotated list of selected books about nursing as a profession. Includes career guides, fiction, personal narratives, biographies, history, and general information.

A cap for Corrine. Macdonald, Zillah K. Julian Messner, Inc. 1952. 184p. $2.95

 Career fiction. Romance of a registered nurse during her year of graduate training, told against the background of a New York hospital. Includes experiences in various situations such as nursing victims of an explosion.

A cap for Mary Ellis. Newell, Hope. Harper and Row. 1953. 200p. $3.50; library binding $3.27 net

 Career fiction. Story of the training of two Negro girls for the nursing profession.

* Career as an industrial nurse. Institute for Research. 1963. 24p. $1
  Duties, requirements, opportunities, and training. Includes description of work in some typical places such as the factory, large office, bank, department store, and chemical plant.

**Careers for nurses. Deming, Dorothy. McGraw-Hill Book Company. 2d ed. 1952. 351p. $6
  Description of fifteen branches of nursing, with information on the duties, working conditions, salaries, preparation, advancement, and future prospects. Considerable information about the fields of specialty and the personal qualities needed to succeed in nursing.

**Careers in professional nursing. Angel, Juvenal L. World Trade Academy Press. 1962. 30p. $1.25
  Description of the field of nursing, aptitudes, training, licensure, status and standards, employment opportunities, salaries, opportunities for male nurses, and prospects for specialized professional nurses. Also included is a list of colleges, foundations, and private organizations offering scholarships in the field of nursing. Bibliography.

Catholic schools of nursing. Conference of Catholic Schools of Nursing. 1961. 6p. Free
  List of schools.

Cheryl Downing: school nurse. MacLeod, Ruth. Julian Messner, Inc. 1964. 192p. $2.95
  Career fiction. Story of a young school nurse and her efforts to cope with the challenges in her job.

The college road to nursing. Simmons College. 1961. 4p. Free
  Future outlook, preparation, qualifications, and courses that should be taken in high school.

The college way to a nursing career. Committee on Careers, National League for Nursing. 1962. 16p. 20c
  Information about the widening opportunities for graduates of the college nursing program leading to a baccalaureate degree. Includes qualifications, costs, and suggestions for choosing a college program.

Curious calamity in ward 8. Deming, Dorothy. Dodd, Mead and Company. 1954. 184p. $3
  Career fiction written by a registered nurse. A mystery story for girls, laid in a realistic hospital setting, making one understand why it is so exciting to be a nurse.

Current career booklets. U.S. Department of the Navy, Bureau of Medicine and Surgery. Four booklets. Free
  Frequently revised booklets are available in local recruiting offices or at the above. Present titles include: Navy nurse corps, Join a skillful team, Opportunities for education in the nurse corps, and Navy nurse corps candidate program.

* Do you want to be a nurse? Committee on Careers, National League for Nursing. 1963. 24p. 10c
  Illustrated booklet describing the many careers within nursing, requirements, future outlook, and four types of nursing schools.

NURSE (REGISTERED PROFESSIONAL)—*Continued*

**Employment outlook for registered professional nurses and licensed practical nurses. Bureau of Labor Statistics, U.S. Department of Labor. Supt. of Documents. 1964. 12p. 10c
Reprint from the *Occupational Outlook Handbook.*

Facts about nursing, 1961. American Nurses' Association. 1961. 255p. $2.75
A compilation of current statistics concerning number and distribution of professional nurses, education, economic status, placement, licensure, practical nurses and auxiliary workers, health facilities, and personnel. An annual publication.

Facts about the Army Nurse Corps. U.S. Army Medical Service. 1962. 6p. Free
Brief summary of the requirements for and opportunities in the Army Nurse Corps.

Facts and figures about nursing personnel. Committee on Careers, National League for Nursing. 1963. 4p. 3c
Fact sheet, published annually, giving up-to-date figures on supply and demand for nursing personnel, factors contributing to the need for nurses, and facts about career opportunities in professional and practical nursing.

Flight nurse. Dean, Nell M. Julian Messner, Inc. 1963. 192p. $2.95
Career fiction. The romance includes a description of the duties, responsibilities, and crises that must be faced by nurses in the U.S. Air Force.

Functions, standards and qualifications for occupational health nurses. American Nurses' Association, Occupational Health Nurses Section. 1960. 32p. Single copy free
Written for the trained nurse, this booklet sets forth the functions and standards for the practice of nurses, including a one-nurse service, nurses in supervisory positions, and occupational health nurse directors.

Functions, standards and qualifications for the practice of office nursing. American Nurses' Association, Office Nurses Section. 1962. 12p. Single copy free
Written for the trained nurse whose activities are concerned with medical and nursing services in a clinic or office.

Great day in the morning. Means, Florence C. Houghton Mifflin Company. 1946. 182p. $3
Career fiction. A Negro student at Tuskegee Institute realizes the need for nurses and decides to train for the profession. For grades 7 to 10.

Health manpower source book—physicians, dentists, and professional nurses. Public Health Service, U.S. Department of Health, Education, and Welfare. Publication Number 263, Section 9. Supt. of Documents. 1959. 79p. 50c
Data on the numbers, distribution, and characteristics of workers. Includes information on training, licensure, age, sex, and income level.

Hilda Baker: school nurse. Deming, Dorothy. Dodd, Mead and Company. 1955. 244p. $3
>Career fiction. Story of a year in a high school nurse's life, showing what the work requires and offers.

I want to be a nurse. Greene, Carla. Childrens Press. 1957. 32p. $2
>Prepared for beginning readers with a reading level of upper first grade. Illustrated in color.

Industrial nurse. California State Department of Employment. 1962. 4p. Single copy free
>Job duties, working conditions, employment outlook, wages, hours, entrance requirements, lines of promotion, and training.

Jane Arden, space nurse. Harris, Kathleen. Popular Library. 1962. 126p. 40c. Paperback
>Career fiction. Story of exciting adventures at Cape Canaveral.

A lamp is heavy. Russell, Sheila MacKay. J. B. Lippincott Company. 1950. 257p. $3.95
>Career fiction. Story of the period of nurse's training, stressing the ideals of the profession and dispelling some of the glamour described in many books. The background is that of a Canadian school of nursing.

Linda Kent, student nurse. Deming, Dorothy. Dodd, Mead and Company. 1952. 274p. $3
>Career novel written by a registered nurse, following a student nurse through her training two years in college, thirty months of hospital training, and a tour of duty in Labrador. Depicts the modern trend in nursing education toward the five-year training program including college work. Includes information on requirements, duties, and opportunities.

Look to your future in hospital nursing. Committee on Careers, National League for Nursing. 1962. 6p. 8c
>Nature of work, preparation, qualifications, rewards, and choice of a hospital.

Look to your future in mental health and psychiatric nursing. Committee on Careers, National League for Nursing. 1962. 6p. 8c
>Nature of work, preparation, personal qualifications, and new horizons ahead.

Man nurse. Careers. 1964. 2p. 15c
>Career summary for desk-top file. Duties, qualifications, and outlook.

Man nurse. Chronicle Guidance Publications. 1961. 8p. 50c
>Occupational brief summarizing work performed, working conditions, qualifications, training, earnings, opportunities, where employed, licensing, and outlook.

Materials about nursing as a career. Committee on Careers, National League for Nursing. 1962. 8p. Free
>Annotated price list of available pamphlets and posters.

Men working for a career in nursing. Committee on Careers, National League for Nursing. 1958. 6p. 4c
>Picture folder depicting opportunities and preparation for careers in professional nursing for men.

NURSE (REGISTERED PROFESSIONAL)—*Continued*

**Modern nursing. Ducas, Dorothy. Henry Z. Walck, Inc. 1962. 111p. $3.50
    Emphasizes the larger scope of present nursing duties, the place of the
    nurse in hospitals and related institutions, and the many new opportunities
    offered by the recent growth of nursing specialties. Reading list. Illustrated.

Nina Grant: pediatric nurse. Stone, Patti. Julian Messner, Inc. 1960. 192p.
    $2.95
    Career fiction. Nina's sympathy interfered with her efficiency, but when an
    epidemic struck testing her courage and nursing skill, she proved herself the
    good nurse she longed to be.

Now you can be a nurse in two years. Seventeen Magazine. 1956. 4p. 10c
    Includes names of eleven colleges that offer a two-year nurse-training
    program. Illustrated.

**Nurse. Lewis, Edith Patton. Macmillan Company. 1962. 178p. $3.50
    The author describes the qualities desirable in the successful nurse and the
    opportunities and fields of practice open to her.

Nurse. The Guidance Centre. 1962. 4p. 15c in Canada; 20c elsewhere
    History and importance, nature of work, qualifications, preparation, advance-
    ment, outlook, remuneration, advantages, disadvantages, how to get started,
    and related occupations.

The nurse everyone needs. Public Affairs Committee. 1963. 28p. 25c
    Explains the relationship between the registered nurse and the licensed
    practical nurse as well as the nurse's aides.

Nurse, general. Careers. 1960. 8p. 25c
    Career brief describing duties, working conditions, training, personal quali-
    fications, licensing, earnings, advancement prospects, outlook, and ways of
    measuring one's interest and ability.

Nurse Todd's strange summer. Macdonald, Zillah K. and Ahl, Vivian J.
    Julian Messner, Inc. 1960. 192p. $2.95
    Career fiction. Experiences in private duty and skillful surgical nursing
    combined with mystery and romance.

Nurses and other hospital personnel. Women's Bureau, U.S. Department of
    Labor. Supt. of Documents. 1961. 44p. 25c
    Information about the need for nurses, employment conditions, and earnings.

Nursing and related services for patients. Pages 104-10 of *Health Careers
    Guidebook.*
    Qualifications, opportunities, and prospects for the professional nurse, prac-
    tical nurse, nursing aide, orderlies, inhalation therapist, and the ward clerk.

Nursing as a career. Institute for Research. 1962. 24p. $1
    Description of work, qualifications, and attractive and unattractive features.

Nursing assignment in El Salvador. Deming, Dorothy. Dodd, Mead and
    Company. 1954. 244p. $3
    Career fiction written by a registered nurse. Experiences of two nursing
    instructors who go to El Salvador, where under the auspices of one of the
    departments of the United States Government they serve as consultants and
    teachers.

Nursing careers in mental health. Public Health Service, U.S. Department of Health, Education, and Welfare. Supt. of Documents. 1964. 10p. 15c
This booklet points out the need for psychiatric nurses, preparation, opportunities for service, and earnings.

Nursing education programs today. Committee on Careers, National League for Nursing. 1961. 16p. 20c
Booklet describing and interpreting five types of educational programs in nursing: practical nursing, associate degree program, diploma program, baccalaureate degree program, and graduate education.

Nursing with a college degree. Weaver, Polly and Lynch, Nancy. Alumnae Advisory Center. Revised 1956. 7p. 25c
Reprint from *Mademoiselle* describing training and compensation. A mimeographed supplement contains opportunities for registered professional nurses in foreign service.

Organdy cupcakes. Stolz, Mary S. Harper and Row. 1951. 213p. $3.50
Career fiction. Story of three nurses in their senior year of training.

Orientation to nursing. Chamberlain, Edith M. McGraw-Hill Book Company. 1962. 196p. $4.95
Orients the student not only to the nursing education program that lies ahead but to nursing itself, providing the new student with skills and techniques for her personal and professional development and adjustment to nursing.

**Penny Marsh, R. N., director of nurses. Deming, Dorothy. Dodd, Mead and Company. 1960. 320p. $3
Career fiction. Interwoven in this story of a nurse's successes and failures is a picture of preparation for nursing and other career information.

Professional nurse. Chronicle Guidance Publications. 1963. 4p. 35c
Occupational brief summarizing work performed, working conditions, personal qualifications, training requirements, earnings, opportunities, and employment outlook.

Professional nursing as a career. Schulz, Cecilia. Bellman Publishing Company. 1963. 24p. $1
Includes the history of nursing, requirements, training, opportunities, and advantages. Also describes the kinds of nursing courses.

Professional nursing as a career. Boston University. 1962. 11p. Free
Recruiting booklet describing preparation and opportunities in hospital work, private nursing, public health work, and other openings.

Professional nursing—trends, responsibilities, and relationships. Spalding, Eugenia Kennedy. Lippincott Company. 1959. 694p. $6
A discussion of major trends and problems affecting nursing. One section is devoted to choosing, preparing and succeeding in a field of nursing.

Psychiatric nurse. Careers. 1961. 2p. 15c
Career summary for desk-top file. Duties, qualifications, and outlook.

NURSE (REGISTERED PROFESSIONAL)—*Continued*

The psychiatric nurse. National Association for Mental Health. 1962. 4p.
10c
> Duties, training, earnings, and future outlook. Selected references.

Recommended job responsibilities. American Association of Industrial
Nurses. 1962. 7 reprints. $1
> Duties of consultant, administrator of a health service, administrator of
> nursing services, charge nurse, staff nurse, supervisor, and junior supervisor.

Registered nurse. Splaver, Sarah. Personnel Services. 1954. 6p. 50c; 25c to
students
> Occupational abstract. Nature of work, qualifications, preparation, registra-
> tion, entrance and advancement, opportunities for servicemen, supply and
> demand of workers, earnings, advantages, and disadvantages.

Registered professional nurses. Science Research Associates. 1959. 4p. 35c
> Occupational brief describing nature of work, training, qualifications, op-
> portunities, advantages, and future outlook.

**Registered professional nurses. One section of *Occupational Outlook Hand-
book*.
> Nature of work, where employed, training, other qualifications, advancement,
> employment outlook, and earnings.

Registered professional nurses . . . your skills are needed. American National Red Cross. 1961. 9p. Free
> Description of qualifications and jobs available for nurses in the Red Cross
> national blood program.

Resort nurse. Dean, Nell M. Popular Library. 1960. 125p. 40c. Paperback
> Career fiction. Story of adventures as a nurse at Squaw Valley, site of the
> 1960 Winter Olympics.

A rewarding career for you as a Veterans Administration nurse. Veterans
Administration, Department of Medicine and Surgery. 1962. 4p. Free
> Description of work, training program, qualifications, and benefits.

Rosemary wins her cap. Macdonald, Zillah K. Julian Messner, Inc. 1955.
192p. $2.95
> Career fiction. Against the background of a busy hospital, the story gives
> an idea of work in a hospital.

Roxanne: industrial nurse. Macdonald, Zillah K. Julian Messner, Inc.
1957. 192p. $2.95
> Career fiction. Roxanne leaves a hospital to become an industrial nurse
> in a sugar refinery.

Sandra: surgical nurse. Stone, Patti. Julian Messner, Inc. 1961. 192p.
$2.95
> Career fiction. Story shows the rigorous training and discipline necessary.
> Gives a clear picture of this specialized field.

Scholarships, fellowships, educational grants and loans available on a national or regional level to graduate nurses. Committee on Careers, National League for Nursing. 1961. 6p. 5c

For graduate nurses. List of sixteen organizations with the type of financial aid they offer.

Schools of professional nursing in the United States. Committee on Careers, National League for Nursing. 1963. 40p. 10c

List of state-approved schools of professional nursing, coded for national accreditation, type of program, admission of men, and other information.

**Sharon's nursing diary. Deming, Dorothy. Dodd, Mead and Company. 1949. 272p. $3

Diary entries of Sharon's adventures into hospitals, homes, industry, towns, cities, and an island off the cosat of Maine. Besides showing a variety of nursing services, the book depicts many of the rewarding opportunities open to nurses.

Should you be a nurse? Sleeper, Ruth. New York Life Insurance Company. 1960. 12p. Free

Attractive features of the career, training, earnings, qualifications, and outlook.

**So you want to be a nurse. Nourse, Alan E. Harper and Row. 1961. 186p. $3.50; library binding $3.27 net

The various approaches to an R.N. degree are described, along with the scholastic, personal, training, and examination qualifications needed. Also included is a discussion of the future of nursing with its contributions and satisfactions.

Sources of scholarships and loans suggested for students entering schools of nursing. Committee on Careers, National League for Nursing. 1964. 2p. 5c

List of student aids available for beginning students.

Story of Clara Barton. Price, Olive. Grosset and Dunlap, Inc. 1954. 178p. $1.95

Biography of the woman who served as a nurse on Civil War battlefields and founded the American Red Cross. For younger readers.

The story of nursing. Dodge, Bertha S. Little, Brown and Company. 1954. 256p. $3.50

Part one tells about the heritage of the profession through persons like Florence Nightingale and those who followed her. Part two describes the opportunities in private, hospital, and public health nursing. Illustrated.

Strange disappearance from ward 2. Deming, Dorothy. Dodd, Mead and Company. 1956. 243p. $3

A mystery story with a hospital background, showing some of the human drama and satisfactions which nursing holds. Written by a registered nurse.

NURSE (REGISTERED PROFESSIONAL)—*Continued*

Student nurse: her life in pictures. Engeman, Jack. Lothrop, Lee and Shepard Company. 1958. 128p. $3.50
   More than 250 photographs, with informative text and captions, show activities of a student nurse from orientation week to graduation.

Sue Barton, student nurse. Boylston, Helen. Atlantic-Little, Brown. 1936. 244p. $3
   Career fiction. This book describes the training with its dormitory life, hospital life, and life in the hospital wards. This series is popular with pupils of junior high school age. Other titles in the series, written by the same author, deal with later experiences in a nurse's progress, such as:
   Sue Barton, senior nurse
   Sue Barton, rural nurse
   Sue Barton, visiting nurse
   Sue Barton, superintendent of nurses
   Sue Barton, neighborhood nurse
   Sue Barton, staff nurse

Sue Morris, sky nurse. Deming, Dorothy. Dodd, Mead and Company. 1953. 256p. $3
   Career Fiction. Adventures of an aviation nurse first with a commercial airline flying the ocean and then as an air ambulance nurse in the Northwest. Explains requirements to enter this field of work and some of the specialties which await the present-day graduate of schools of nursing.

There's a star in your future in Veterans Administration nursing service. Veterans Administration, Department of Medicine and Surgery. 1963. 12p. Free
   Illustrated brochure describing opportunities, qualifications, and benefits.

Trudy Wells, R.N., pediatric nurse. Deming, Dorothy. Dodd, Mead and Company. 1957. 244p. $3
   Career fiction written by an R.N. Story of the experiences of a supervising nurse for an infirmary in a modern children's home of 150 girls and boys.

Under this emblem. American National Red Cross. 1961. 11p. Free
   Information about qualifications and jobs available for nurses in Red Cross nursing services.

Walk proudly into the future as an Air Force nurse. U.S. Air Force. 1962. 16p. Free
   Illustrated brochure depicting opportunities.

Your career opportunities in nursing. Novak, Gail, ed. Rowman and Littlefield, Inc. 1962. 64p. 75c
   One of the Visual Career Guides, about one half of the contents consists of photographs and charts. Includes description of the various kinds of work, training, earnings, and employment outlook.

**Your future in nursing. McDonnell, Virginia. Richards Rosen Press. 1963. 157p. $2.95
   Various areas of nursing are presented with the preparation and qualifications necessary for entrance into this field.

Your nursing services today and tomorrow. Ogg, Elizabeth. Public Affairs Committee. 1961. 30p. 25c
Explanation of new approaches to nursing services, educational requirements, and ways of channeling resources toward improvement of nursing in the community.

See also Practical nurse; Public health nurse

NURSE AID 2-42.20

Candy stripers. Wyndham, Lee. Julian Messner, Inc. 1958. 192p. $2.95
Career fiction. As a junior volunteer aide in a medical center, wearing a pink-striped uniform, Bonnie realized that her work could lead to other scientific careers.

Love's golden circle. Hager, Alice Rogers. Julian Messner, Inc. 1962. 192p. $2.95
Career fiction. Lisa becomes a "grandma sitter" for the elderly to earn money for college and decides to major in social service.

Nurse aide. Careers. 1960. 2p. 15c
Career summary for desk-top file. Duties qualifications, and outlook.

Nursing assistant. The Guidance Centre. 1961. 4p. 15c in Canada; 20c elsewhere
Definition, history and importance, nature of work, working conditions, qualifications necessary for entry and success, preparation, employment and advancement, remuneration, advantages, disadvantages, how to get started toward the occupation, and related occupations.

Psychiatric aide. Careers. 1961. 2p. 15c
Career summary for desk-top file. Duties qualifications, and outlook.

The psychiatric aide. National Association for Mental Health. 1962. 4p. 10c
Nature of work, training, earnings, and future outlook.

Susan, hospital aide. Colver, Alice Ross. Dodd, Mead and Company. 1964. 256p. $3.25
Career fiction. Story of a college undergraduate who spent a summer working in a New York City hospital.

NURSE ANESTHETIST 0-33.36

Anesthesia, a special type of nursing. American Association of Nurse Anesthetists. 1962. 8p. Free
A booklet designed for nurses describing the work, outlook, and requirements for becoming a certified registered nurse anesthetist.

Anesthesia, an art, a science. American Association of Nurse Anesthetists. 1962. 16p. Free
An illustrated booklet prepared for use with a film strip available from the same source.

NURSE ANESTHETIST—*Continued*

Approved schools for nurse anesthetists. American Association of Nurse Anesthetists. 1962. 8p. Free
> List designed for nurses, arranged alphabetically by states. Revised semiannually.

* Nurse anesthetist. Careers. 1959. 2p. 15c
> Career summary for desk-top file. Duties qualifications, and outlook.

**Nurse anesthetist career. American Association of Nurse Anesthetists. 1962. 8p. Free
> Kind of work, where services are used, what to study in high school, professional training, and advantages.

NURSERY SCHOOL TEACHER   0-30.02

Karen's nursery school project. Harris, Betty K. Julian Messner, Inc. 1955. 192p. $2.95
> Career fiction. The story shows nature of work in a nursery school, requirements, and satisfactions.

**Nursery school operation as a career. Institute for Research. 1962. 20p. $1
> History of the nursery schools, duties of nursery school teacher, work of the nursery school director, attractive and unattractive features, personal qualifications, training, earnings, outlook, and related jobs.

* Nursery school teacher. Careers. 1964. 2p. 15c
> Career summary for desk-top file. Duties, qualifications, and outlook.

* Nursery school teacher. Chronicle Guidance Publications. 1962. 4p. 35c
> Occupational brief summarizing work performed, personal qualifications, educational requirements, earnings, and outlook.

Nursery-school teacher. The Guidance Centre. 1959. 3p. 15c in Canada; 20c elsewhere
> Definition, history and importance, nature of work, working conditions, qualifications, preparation, employment and advancement, remuneration, advantages, disadvantages, how to get started, and related occupations.

Nursery school teacher. Simmons College. 1960. 4p. Free
> Discussion of the variety of opportunities, duties, personal characteristics needed, and courses that should be taken in high school and college.

See also Kindergarten teacher

NURSERYMAN   3-38.20

Career opportunities in the nursery business. American Association of Nurserymen. 1963. 5p. Free
> Description of nursery work, career opportunities, and training. Includes a list of schools which offer preparation for the work.

* Have you ever thought of being a landscape nurseryman? National Landscape Nurserymen's Association. 1962. 6p. Free
> Description of duties, qualifications, training, and opportunities.

* The nursery business. American Association of Nurserymen. 1963. 14p. Free

> Description of the types of work, qualifications, opportunities, and outlook. Lists several publications which are available from state agricultural experiment stations.

Nurseryman. Careers. 1964. 2p. 15c

> Career summary for desk-top file. Duties, qualifications, and outlook.

**Nurseryman. Chronicle Guidance Publications. 1960. 4p. 35c

> Occupational brief summarizing work performed, working conditions, earnings, personal qualifications, training requirements, opportunities, employment outlook, and entry into the job.

Nurserymen and landscapers. Science Research Associates. 1961. 4p. 35c

> Occupational brief describing nature of work, qualifications, training, earnings, methods of getting started, advantages, disadvantages, and future outlook. Selected references.

Training program for landscape nurserymen. National Landscape Nurserymen's Association. 1962. 2p. Free to counselors

> Includes a list of schools for training.

See also Horticulturist; Landscape architect

NUTRITIONAL CHEMIST 0-07.02

Career as a food chemist. Institute for Research. 1953. 20p. $1

> Description of work, types of jobs, jobs in the Federal Government and in state and city health departments, typical day's work, qualifications, attractive and unattractive features, training, chances for employment, and related jobs.

Career opportunities in nutrition. American Institute of Nutrition. 1963. 4p. Free

> Brief description of the growing opportunities in this field.

Educational qualifications of nutritionists in health agencies. American Public Health Association. 1962. 6p. Free

> Scope of work, duties, educational qualifications, and experience recommended for each of three types of work: staff nutritionist, nutritionist consultant, and director of nutrition service in a health agency.

Nutrition. Simmons College. 1961. 4p. Free

> Discussion of the areas of specialization and preparation for careers as dietitian, nutritionist, college teacher, and research nutritionist.

Nutritionist. Careers. 1963. 2p. 15c

> Career summary for desk-top file. Duties, qualifications, and outlook.

**Nutritionist. Pages 71-4 of *Health Careers Guidebook.*

> Description of work, training, opportunities, and prospects.

See also Dietitian

NUTRITIONIST. *See* Nutritional chemist

OCCUPATIONAL THERAPIST   0-32.04

Before you enter an occupational therapy course. American Occupational
Therapy Association. 1964. 6p. Single copy free; 50 copies 75c
   A check list of admission requirements for the high school student, beginning
   college student, and the college graduate.

Colleges and universities offering courses in occupational therapy. American Occupational Therapy Association. 1964. 1p. Single copy free;
50 copies 50c
   A one-page list.

Colleges and universities offering courses in occupational therapy. American Occupational Therapy Association. 1964. 12p. Single copy free;
50 copies $1.25
   For each of the thirty-two schools approved by the Council on Medical
   Education and Hospitals of the American Medical Association there is given
   the name and address of director, amount of tuition, type of course, entrance
   requirements, length of course, month classes start, and whether men, women
   or both are accepted.

**Employment outlook for physical therapists and occupational therapists.
Bureau of Labor Statistics, U.S. Department of Labor. Supt. of Docu-
ments. 1964. 8p. 5c
   Reprint from the *Occupational Outlook Handbook.*

Facts about occupational therapy. American Occupational Therapy Association. 1964. 1p. Free
   Facts about the number of occupational therapists, the projected need,
   education, tuition, and salaries.

The healing heart: the story of Ora Ruggles, pioneer in occupational therapy. Carlove, John with Ruggles, Ora. Julian Messner, Inc. 1961. 260p.
$3.95
   Biography of a woman whose work contributed greatly to the establishment
   of occupational therapy as a profession and its widespread use in hospitals.

**Join the recovery team . . . be an occupational therapist. American Occu-
pational Therapy Association. 1964. 12p. Single copy free; 50 copies
$1.25
   An illustrated leaflet describing the field of work, types of therapy, educational requirements, personal qualifications, and opportunities. An insert page
   lists the thirty-two approved schools offering courses in occupational therapy.

* Occupational therapist. Careers. 1963. 8p. 25c
   Career brief describing duties, working conditions, salaries, personal qualifications, training requirements, list of accredited schools, outlook, opportunities
   for men, related jobs, measuring one's interest and ability, and suggested high
   school program.

Occupational therapist. Chronicle Guidance Publications. 1964. 4p. 35c
   Occupational brief summarizing work performed, working conditions, earnings, personal qualifications, training requirements, opportunities, and employment outlook.

Occupational therapist. The Guidance Centre. 1962. 4p. 15c in Canada;
20c elsewhere

> Importance of growth of the profession, nature of work, qualifications,
> preparation, opportunities, outlook, earnings, advantages, disadvantages, how
> to get started, and related occupations.

The occupational therapist. National Association for Mental Health. 1962.
4p. 10c

> Describes duties of the occupational therapist in the mental health field,
> training, earnings, and future outlook. Selected references.

Occupational therapists. Science Research Associates. 1959. 4p. 35c

> Occupational brief describing nature of work, personal qualifications, edu-
> cational requirements, getting started, earnings, advantages, disadvantages, and
> future outlook.

**Occupational therapists. One section of *Occupational Outlook Handbook*.

> Nature of work, where employed, training, other qualifications, advancement,
> employment outlook, earnings, and working conditions.

Occupational therapy. Milwaukee-Downer College. 1962. 24p. Free

> A college bulletin describing what is expected of an occupational therapist
> and the required courses. Illustrated.

* Occupational therapy. Pages 114-18 of *Health Careers Guidebook*.

> Nature of work, types of therapy, personal qualifications, opportunities, and
> educational requirements. Also information is given about the homemaking
> counselor.

* Occupational therapy as a career. Institute for Research. 1957. 24p. $1

> Types of institutions which employ occupational therapists, personal quali-
> fications, duties, typical day's work, advantages, disadvantages, educational re-
> quirements and description of recommended courses. List of accredited schools.

Occupational therapy—publications and other materials. American Occupational Therapy Association. 1964. 12p. Free

> A listing of professional literature and other materials available from the
> association. Prices are given for items for which a charge is made and are
> subject to change without notice.

Opportunities in occupational therapy. Franciscus, Marie Louise. Vocational Guidance Manuals, Inc. 1952. 112p. $1.45 paper

> Description of occupational therapy, tools of the profession, scope of the
> field, development and growth, requirements to enter the profession, job
> descriptions, personal expectations and limitations, present trends and future
> outlook, related fields, and professional organizations. Also included is a list
> of schools offering courses in occupational therapy.

A stimulating career for you as a Veterans Administration occupational
therapist. Veterans Administration, Department of Medicine and Surgery.
1963. 4p. Free

> Description of work, training program, qualifications, and benefits.

OCCUPATIONAL THERAPIST—*Continued*

**Where to look for financial help. American Occupational Therapy Association. 1964. 16p. Single copy free; 50 copies $1.35
  Lists sources of scholarships for professional education in occupational therapy, funds available for higher education, organizations with local chapters or member agencies awarding funds for general education, sources of loans, and a reference list of further sources of information.

**Your future in occupational therapy. Shuff, Frances. Richards Rosen Press. 1963. 160p. $2.95; library edition $2.79 net
  Description of the work, training, qualifications, and opportunities. Includes list of schools offering training.

  See also Medical service worker; Physical therapist

OCEANOGRAPHER   0-35.65

A career in oceanography. Interagency Committee on Oceanography. 1964. 60p. 50c
  Information concerning training, opportunities, and the need for trained manpower in marine science.

Education and recruitment of oceanographers in the United States. American Society of Limnology and Oceanography. 1960. 24p. 20c. Single copy free
  A report explaining opportunities in oceanography, educational training and field experience needed, supply and demand of marine scientists, and employment data.

**Employment outlook for earth scientists: geologists, geophysicists, meteorologists, and oceanographers. Bureau of Labor Statistics, U.S. Department of Labor. Supt. of Documents. 1964. 20p. 15c
  Reprint from the *Occupational Outlook Handbook.*

Employment outlook for oceanographers. Careers. 1963. 4p. 25c
  Reprint from the *Occupational Outlook Quarterly* describing nature of work, training, qualifications, advancement, where employed, outlook, and earnings.

**Employment outlook for oceanographers. *Occupational Outlook Quarterly.* May, 1963. 4p. 30c
  Nature of work, where employed, training, other qualifications, earnings, working conditions, and employment outlook.

Ocean harvest: the future of oceanography. Vogel, Helen and Caruso, Mary. Alfred A. Knopf, Inc. 1961. 147p. $3
  Focuses attention on the fact that only one per cent of mankind's food comes from the sea and that scientists are needed to take more interest in the potential food and minerals from the ocean.

Oceanographer. California State Department of Employment. 1962. 4p. Single copy free
  Description of work, entrance requirements, salaries, promotion, preparation, and employment outlook.

Oceanographer. Careers. 1961. 2p. 15c
Career summary for desk-top file. Duties, qualifications, and outlook.

Oceanographer. Chronicle Guidance Publications. 1960. 4p. 35c
Occupational brief summarizing work performed, working conditions, qualifications, training, opportunities, where employed, related jobs, and outlook.

Oceanographer. The Guidance Centre. 1962. 4p. 15c in Canada; 20c
elsewhere
History and importance, nature of work, qualifications, working conditions,
preparation, remuneration, advancement, outlook, related occupations, and how
to get started.

**Oceanographers. Science Research Associates. 1963. 4p. 35c
Occupational brief describing nature of work, requirements, training,
methods of entering, advantages, disadvantages, and future outlook.

**Oceanographers. One section of *Occupational Outlook Handbook*.
Nature of work, where employed, training, other qualifications, advancement,
employment outlook, earnings, and working conditions.

Pioneer oceanographer: Alexander Agassiz. Williams, Beryl and Epstein,
Samuel. Julian Messner, Inc. 1963. 192p. $3.25. Library binding $3.19
net
Biography of the man whose work contributed to marine zoological information and techniques.

There's adventure in marine science. May, Julian. Popular Mechanics
Press. 1959. 160p. $2.95
By relating experiences of a boy in this field, the author portrays the
various kinds of work. Written for grades 7 to 10.

University curricula in oceanography 1963-64. Interagency Committee on
Oceanography. 1963. 162p. Free to counselors
Description of courses offered in the marine sciences in each of forty-five
American colleges. Aimed to present information about existing training in the
application of science to the study of the sea.

See also Scientist

OFFICE MACHINE OPERATOR   1-25.

Addressing machine operator. Careers. 1961. 2p. 15c
Career summary for desk-top file. Duties, qualifications, and outlook.

Bookkeeping machine operator. Careers. 1960. 8p. 25c
Career brief describing duties, working conditions, training, earnings, related careers, and outlook.

Business machine operators. Splaver, Sarah. Personnel Services. 1962. 6p.
50c; 25c to students
Occupational abstract. Nature of work, qualifications, preparation, entrance,
advancement, supply and demand, earnings, advantages, and disadvantages.

OFFICE MACHINE OPERATOR—*Continued*

**Employment opportunities for women as secretaries, stenographers, typists, office-machine operators and cashiers. Women's Bureau, U.S. Department of Labor. Bulletin Number 263. Supt. of Documents. 1957. 30p. 20c
  Includes qualifications and training necessary, earnings and hours, advancement, and need for trained workers.

**Employment outlook for bookkeeping workers and office machine operators. Bureau of Labor Statistics, U.S. Department of Labor. Supt. of Documents. 1964. 12p. 10c
  Reprint from the *Occupational Outlook Handbook*.

Key punch operators. Science Research Associates. 1958. 4p. 35c
  Occupational brief describing nature of work, training, qualifications, opportunities, advantages, disadvantages, and future outlook.

Office-machine operator. Careers. 1960. 2p. 15c
  Career summary for desk-top file. Duties, qualifications, and outlook.

Office machine operator. The Guidance Centre. 1961. 4p. 15c in Canada; 20c elsewhere
  History and importance, nature of work, qualifications, working conditions, preparation, remuneration, advancement, outlook, related occupations, and how to get started.

**Office-machine operators. Chronicle Guidance Publications. 1963. 4p. 35c
  Occupational brief summarizing work performed, working conditions, hours, earnings, personal qualifications, training requirements and opportunities, and employment outlook.

Office machine operators. Science Research Associates. 1958. 4p. 35c
  Occupational brief describing nature of work, preparation, qualifications, advantages, disadvantages, and future outlook.

**Office machine operators. One section of *Occupational Outlook Handbook*.
  Nature of work, where employed, training, other qualifications, advancement, employment outlook, earnings, and working conditions.

OFFICE-MACHINE SERVICEMAN   5-83.100 through 5-83.149

Business machine serviceman. Careers. 1958. 8p. 25c
  Career brief describing duties, working conditions, training, personal qualifications, outlook, earnings, how to enter, advancement prospects, and related careers.

**Business machine servicemen. One section of *Occupational Outlook Handbook*.
  Nature of work, where employed, qualifications, training, advancement, employment outlook, earnings, and working conditions. Brief information about the servicemen who repair the typewriter, adding machine, calculating machine, cash register, bookkeeping machine, dictating machine, duplicating machine, and data-processing equipment.

Business machines sales and service as a career. Institute for Research. 1961. 24p. $1
    Description of duties, a typical day's work, attractive and unattractive features, qualifications, training, earnings, and outlook.

**Employment outlook for business machine servicemen. Bureau of Labor Statistics, U.S. Department of Labor. Supt. of Documents. 1964. 12p. 10c
    Reprint from the *Occupational Outlook Handbook*.

Finding out about office machine servicemen. Science Research Associates. 1963. 4p. 35c
    Junior occupational brief summarizing requirements, training, earnings, and opportunities.

Occupations in business services and repair services. Chapter 18 of *Planning Your Future*.
    Includes discussion of kinds of work included in business services, repair services, and in the business service of advertising. Five illustrations.

Office machine repairman. Robinson, H. Alan. Personnel Services. 1950. 6p. 50c; 25c to students
    Occupational abstract. Future prospects, nature of work, qualifications, preparation, entrance and advancement, earnings, number and distribution of workers, advantages, and disadvantages.

Office machine serviceman. Careers. 1963. 8p. 25c
    Career brief describing duties, working conditions, training, training opportunities, personal qualifications, earnings, advancement prospects, and outlook.

* Office-machine serviceman. Chronicle Guidance Publications. 1963. 4p. 35c
    Occupational brief summarizing work performed, working conditions, earnings, hours, personal qualifications, training requirements and opportunities, employment outlook, and entry into the job.

Office-machine servicemen. Michigan Employment Security Commission. 1962. 16p. 25c
    Introduction, nature of work, location of jobs, working conditions, employment outlook, earnings, requirements for entry, disadvantages, and advantages.

* Office machine servicemen. Science Research Associates. 1961. 4p. 35c
    Occupational brief describing duties, qualifications, training, earnings, getting started and advancing, advantages, disadvantages, and future outlook.

OFFICE MANAGER   0-97.12

**Careers in office management. B'nai B'rith Vocational Service. 1956. 12p. 35c
    Employment opportunities, duties, qualifications, preparation, working conditions, and earnings.

Office management as a career. Institute for Research. 1962. 24p. $1
    Scope of the work, duties, typical day's work, personal qualifications, training, opportunities, salaries, attractive and unattractive features. Also routes of promotion to office management.

OFFICE MANAGER—*Continued*

Office manager. Careers. 1962. 8p. 25c
> Career brief describing duties, personal qualifications, working conditions, training, earnings, advancement prospects, and outlook. Additional readings.

Office managers. Science Research Associates. 1964. 4p. 35c
> Occupational brief describing work, qualifications, training, opportunities, and outlook.

**Opportunities in office management. Place, Irene and Hicks, Charles. Vocational Guidance Manuals. 1959. 92p. $1.45 paper
> Explanation of patterns of organization, duties, compensation, how to get started, related fields, personal attributes necesary, advantages and disadvantages. List of courses offering courses in office management.

OFFSET PRESSMAN 4-48.050

Job description for offset-press man. U.S. Employment Service. Supt. of Documents. 1948. 6p. 5c
> Occupational guide Job summary, work performed, training, trainee-selection factors, related occupations, physical activities, working conditions, hazards, and employment variables.

Offset pressman. Careers. 1963. 8p. 25c
> Career brief describing duties, working conditions, training, earnings, advancement prospects, places of employment, and outlook.

Offset pressman. Chronicle Guidance Publications. 1962. 4p. 35c
> Occupational brief containing definition, history, work performed, working conditions, personal requirements, determination of aptitudes and interests, training requirements, training opportunities, outlook, methods of entry, related jobs, and suggested activities.

OIL AND GAS HEATING TECHNICIAN 5-83.024 and 5-83.033

**Oil burner service and installation technician. Burkhardt, Charles H. Research Publishing Company. 1956. 32p. $1
> Nature of work, personal qualifications, training, promotional opportunities, and methods of securing jobs.

Oil-burner serviceman. The Guidance Centre. 1963. 4p. 15c in Canada; 20c elsewhere
> Nature of work, qualifications, and outlook.

Opportunities are unlimited as a gas fuel technician. Southern Technical Institute. 1957. 4p. Free
> A recruiting leaflet describing the training program.

OPERATING ENGINEER (CONSTRUCTION MACHINERY OPERATOR) 5, 7-23.000 through 5, 7-23.999

**Employment outlook for structural-, and ornamental-, and reinforcing-iron workers and operating engineers. Bureau of Labor Statistics, U.S. Department of Labor. Supt. of Documents. 1964. 20p. 15c
> Reprint from the *Occupational Outlook Handbook*.

**Operating engineers (construction machinery operators). Careers. 1960. 8p. 25c
Career brief describing duties, working conditions, training, personal qualifications, places of employment, earnings, and outlook. Additional readings.

**Operating engineers (construction machinery operators). One section of *Occupational Outlook Handbook.*
Nature of work, where employed, training, other qualifications, advancement, employment outlook, earnings, and working conditions.

See also Engineer

OPHTHALMOLOGIST 0-26.10

* Ophthalmologist. Brackett, Warren and Robinson, H. Alan. Personnel Services. 1956. 6p. 50c; 25c to students
Occupational abstract describing nature of work, qualifications, preparation, certification, entrance and advancement, earnings, number and distribution, future prospects, related occupations, advantages and disadvantages.

Ophthalmologist. Careers. 1963. 2p. 15c
Career summary for desk-top file. Duties, qualifications, and outlook.

* Ophthalmologists. Science Research Associates. 1961. 4p. 35c
Occupational brief describing nature of work, requirements, methods of entrance, related occupations, advantages, disadvantages, and future outlook.

OPTICIAN 5-08.010

**Dispensing opticians and optical laboratory mechanics. One section of *Occupational Outlook Handbook.*
Nature of work, where employed, training, other qualifications, advancement, and employment outlook.

**Employment outlook for dispensing opticians and optical laboratory mechanics. Bureau of Labor Statistics, U.S. Department of Labor. Supt. of Documents. 1964. 8p. 5c
Reprint from the *Occupational Outlook Handbook.*

Optician. Robinson, H. Alan. Personnel Services. 1950. 6p. 50c; 25c to students
Occupational abstract. Nature of work, future prospects, qualifications, preparation, entrance and advancement, earnings, number and distribution of workers, advantages, disadvantages, and related occupations.

* Optician. Careers. 1963. 7p. 25c
Career brief describing duties, working conditions, training, earnings, advancement opportunities and outlook.

* Optician. Chronicle Guidance Publications. 1960. 4p. 35c
Occupational brief summarizing work performed, working conditions, personal qualifications, ways of determining interest and ability, training, opportunities, methods of entry, licensing, related jobs, and outlook.

OPTICIAN—*Continued*

Optician. Pages 119-20 of *Health Careers Guidebook.*
Nature of work, aptitudes, training, and outlook.

Optician and optical mechanic—careers. Institute for Research. 1959. 24p. $1
Nature of work, qualifications, salary, and outlook.

Opticians. Michigan Employment Security Commission. 1955. 15p. 25c
Introduction, nature of work, location of jobs, employment outlook, working conditions, organizations, earnings, qualifications for entry, disadvantages, and advantages.

* Opticians. Science Research Associates. 1961. 4p. 35c
Occupational brief describing nature of work, requirements, training, entrance and advancement, earnings, opportunities, related occupations, advantages, disadvantages, and future outlook.

OPTOMETRIST   0-39.92

**Employment outlook for optometrists. Bureau of Labor Statistics, U.S. Department of Labor. Supt. of Documents. 1964. 4p. 5c
Reprint from the *Occupational Outlook Handbook.*

**Monograph on optometry. American Optometric Association. 1962. 32p. Free
Includes discussion of the need for optometrists, educational requirements, cost of education, distribution of optometrists by states, license requirements, and admission regulations for each of the twelve accredited colleges. Good reading list.

* Opportunities in optometry and optics. Pollack, Philip. Vocational Guidance Manuals. 1955. 95p. $1.45 paper
Discussion of the history and importance of the work, qualifications, earnings, and outlook. The training required to be an optometrist, optician, or an optical engineer is given.

Optometrist. Splaver, Sarah. Personnel Services. 1950. 50c; 25c to students
Occupational abstract. Nature of work, qualifications, preparation, licensing, entrance and advancement, supply and demand, earnings, advantages, disadvantages, and appraisal of literature.

Optometrist. Careers. 1963. 2p. 15c
Career summary for desk-top file. Duties, qualifications, and outlook.

Optometrist. Chronicle Guidance Publications. 1962. 4p. 35c
Occupational brief summarizing work performed, working conditions, earnings, personal qualifications, training requirements and opportunities, and employment outlook.

Optometrist. The Guidance Centre. 1963. 15c in Canada; 20c elsewhere
Definition, history and importance, nature of work, qualifications, preparation, outlook, remuneration, advantages, disadvantages, how to get started, and related occupations.

Optometrist. Michigan Employment Security Commission. 1955. 18p. 25c
  Introduction, nature of work, location of optometrists, prospects in this profession, working conditions, organizations, earnings, qualifications for entry, disadvantages, and advantages.

Optometrist. Pages 118-19 of *Health Careers Guidebook*.
  Nature of work, aptitudes, training, licensing, and how to get started.

Optometrists. Science Research Associates. 1959. 4p. 35c
  Occupational brief describing nature of work, training, qualifications, opportunities, advantages, disadvantages, and future outlook.

**Optometrists. One section of *Occupational Outlook Handbook*.
  Nature of work, where employed, training, other qualifications, advancement, employment outlook, earnings, and working conditions.

Optometry as a career. Institute for Research. 1964. 24p. $1
  History and development, typical day's work, personal qualifications, educational requirements, types of positions, salaries, and license requirements.

**Planning your professional career in optometry. American Optometric Association. 1960. 20p. Free
  This booklet gives the prospective student of optometry the highlights of information concerning the profession—what optometry is, opportunities in optometry, education needed, and requirements for a successful practice.

**Prospective optometrist. American Optometric Association. 1963. Eight booklets. Free to counselors and librarians
  Brochure containing several booklets designed to give a picture of optometry as a career.

Requirements for admission to the schools and colleges of optometry. American Optometric Association. 1962. 14p. Free
  A compilation of the entrance requirements for the ten approved schools and colleges of optometry in the United States and two in Canada.

Scholarships in optometry. American Optometric Association. 1962. 20p. Free
  Scholarships and loan funds available from the association's state organizations and women's auxiliaries.

What is an optometrist? American Optometric Association. No date. 8p. Free
  Service rendered by the optometrist, education required, and list of colleges offering training.

**Your future in optometry. Gregg, James R. Richards Rosen Press. 1960. 160p. $2.95
  Describes the functions of optometrists, preparation, specialized training, licensure, employment opportunities, qualifications for success, and future outlook. Includes a list of schools of optometry.

Your opportunity as a lady O.D. American Optometric Association. 1960. 16p. Free
  Description of opportunities for women in optometry.

ORTHOPEDIC TECHNICIAN 5-09.410

Orthopedic and prosthetic appliance work. Pages 121-2 of *Health Careers Guidebook*.
> Personal qualifications, training, opportunities, and prospects for the prosthetist and orthotist.

Orthotist. Careers. 1962. 2p. 15c
> Career summary for desk-top file. Duties, qualifications, and outlook.

Professional preparation in prosthetics and orthotics. New York University, School of Education. 1963. 6p. Free
> Growing need, requirements, and training for the prosthetist in work with the design, fabrication, and fitting of artificial limbs, and for the orthotist in work with braces.

Prosthetist (orthopedic appliance and limb technician). Careers. 1961. 2p. 15c
> Career summary for desk-top file. Duties, qualifications, and outlook.

ORTHOPTIC TECHNICIAN 0-52.85

**Career as orthoptic technician. Chronicle Guidance Publications. 1962. 4p. 35c
> Occupational brief describing nature of the work, working conditions, personal qualifications, determination of aptitudes and interest, training requirements, outlook, methods of entry, and certification. Also included is a list of training centers. Selected references.

Orthoptic technician. Brackett, Warren and Robinson, H. Alan. Personnel Services. 1953. 6p. 50c; 25c to students
> Occupational abstract describing nature of the work, future prospects, qualifications, preparation, certification, entrance and advancement, earnings, number and distribution of workers, advantages, and disadvantages.

Orthoptic technician. Careers. 1960. 2p. 15c
> Career summary for desk-top file. Duties, qualifications, and outlook.

Orthoptic technician. Page 120 of *Health Careers Guidebook*.
> Brief statement of nature of work and training.

A profession in orthoptics. American Orthoptic Council. No date. 6p. Free
> Description of work, qualifications, prospects, earnings, training, and costs. List of centers offering training.

OSTEOPATHIC PHYSICIAN 0-39.96

Careers in osteopathy. Brewster, Royce E. American Osteopathic Association. Revised 1961. 9p. Free
> Revision of the leaflet originally prepared by the U.S. Office of Education. Includes history and progress of the profession, census data, training, licensure, and compensation.

Doctor of osteopathy. Pages 122-3 of *Health Careers Guidebook.*
Nature of work, training requirements, licensure, and outlook.

**Employment outlook for osteopathic physicians. Bureau of Labor Statistics, U.S. Department of Labor. Supt. of Documents. 1964. 4p. 5c
Reprint from the *Occupational Outlook Handbook.*

Osteopath. Splaver, Sarah. Personnel Services. 1961. 6p. 50c; 25c to students
Occupational abstract. Nature of work, future prospects, qualifications, preparation, entrance and advancement, women in the field, earnings, advantages, disadvantages, licensing, number and distribution of workers, and sources of further information.

Osteopathic physician. Careers. 1964. 8p. 25c
Career brief describing duties, working conditions, training, personal qualifications, advantages, disadvantages, earnings, advancement prospects, and outlook.

Osteopathic physician. Chronicle Guidance Publications. 1963. 4p. 35c
Occupational brief summarizing work performed, working conditions, earnings, personal qualifications, training requirements and opportunities, and employment outlook.

Osteopathic physician. The Guidance Centre. 1961. 4p. 15c in Canada; 20c elsewhere
Nature of work, qualifications, preparation, outlook, remuneration, advantages, disadvantages, how to get started, and related occupations.

Osteopathic physician. Michigan Employment Security Commission. 1961. 20p. 25c
Introduction, nature of work, location of jobs, working conditions, earnings, employment outlook, requirements for entry, disadvantages, and advantages.

**The osteopathic physician and surgeon. Belleau, Wilfrid. Park Publishing House. 1962. 27p. 75c
Nature of work, training, qualifications, licensure, entering the field, conditions of work, a typical day's work, income, opportunities, advantages, disadvantages, and salaries. Geographical distribution and ratio of osteopathic physicians to population in each of the states. Discussion of opportunities for women. Bibliography.

Osteopathic physicians. Science Research Associates. 1961. 4p. 35c
Occupatonal brief describing nature of work, personal qualifications, training, licensing, earnings, how to get started, advantages, disadvantages, and future outlook.

**Osteopathic physicians. One section of *Occupational Outlook Handbook.*
Nature of work, where employed, training, other qualifications, employment outlook, earnings, and working conditions.

The osteopathic profession. American Osteopathic Association. No date. 8p. Free
Description of work, license requirements, and admission requirements to the five approved osteopathic colleges.

OSTEOPATHIC PHYSICIAN—*Continued*

**The osteopathic profession and its colleges. Mills, Lawrence. **American Osteopathic Association. 1963. 36p. Free
Growth of osteopathy, qualifications, preprofessional requirements, professional training, and distribution of osteopathic physicians in each of the states. Information concerning each of the five colleges approved by the American Osteopathic Association. Good bibliography.

PACKAGING ENGINEER 0-68.60

**Package manufacturing workers. Science Research Associates. 1961. 4p. 35c
Occupational brief describing nature of work, requirements, wages, advantages, disadvantages, and future outlook.

Packaging engineer. Group, Vernard. Personnel Services. 1954. 6p. 50c; 25c to students
Occupational abstract. Nature of work, future prospects, qualifications, preparation, entrance, earnings, advantages, and disadvantages.

* Packaging engineer. Careers. 1960. 2p. 15c
Career summary for desk-top file. Duties, qualifications, and outlook.

PAINT AND VARNISH INDUSTRY WORKER 4, 6, 8-50.

Paint, varnish, and lacquer industry workers. National Paint, Varnish and Lacquer Association. 1961. 4p. Free
Describes the industry as creative and expanding with a challenging future.

Paint, varnish, and lacquer industry workers. Science Research Associates. 1961. 4p. 35c
Occupational brief describing kinds of work, requirements, getting started, earnings, advantages, disadvantages, and future outlook.

Your brightest tomorrow is in the paint, varnish, and lacquer industry. National Paint, Varnish and Lacquer Association. No date. 16p. Free
Points out job prospects and requirements.

PAINTER 5, 7-27.

Construction painter. Careers. 1959. 8p. 25c
Career brief describing duties, working conditions, training, personal qualifications, places of employment, earnings, and outlook.

* Construction painter. Chronicle Guidance Publications. 1962. 4p. 35c
Occupational brief summarazing duties, working conditions, wages, qualifications, apprenticeship training, opportunities, related jobs, and outlook.

**Employment outlook for painters, paperhangers, glaziers, and asbestos and insulating workers. Bureau of Labor Statistics, U.S. Department of Labor. Supt. of Documents. 1964. 20p. 15c
Reprint from the *Occupational Outlook Handbook*.

Painter. Group, Vernard. Personnel Services. 1953. 6p. 50c; 25c to students
Nature of work, future prospects, qualifications, preparation, entrance, advancement, earnings, advantages, and disadvantages.

Painter. The Guidance Centre. 1962. 4p. 15c in Canada; 20c elsewhere
Nature of work, qualifications, preparation, earnings, advancement opportunities, how to get started, advantages, disadvantages, and related occupations.

Painter, construction. Chronicle Guidance Publications. 1962. 4p. 35c
Occupational brief summarizing work performed, training, qualifications, wages, related jobs, opportunities, and outlook.

Painters. Michigan Employment Security Commission. 1955. 16p. 25c
Introduction, nature of work, location of jobs, employment outlook, working conditions, earnings, qualifications for entry, organizations, disadvantages, and advantages.

Painters and paper hangers. Science Research Associates. 1960. 4p. 35c
Occupational brief describing nature of work, training, requirements, earnings, getting started and advancing, advantages, disadvantages, and future outlook.

**Painters and paperhangers. One section of *Occupational Outlook Handbook.*
Nature of work, where employed, training, other qualifications, advancement, employment outlook, earnings, and working conditions.

Painters, decorators and paperhangers. Brotherhood of Painters, Decorators and Paperhangers of America. 1960. 4p. Free
Occupational brief describing nature of work, advantages of learning a trade, opportunities, qualifications, apprenticeship requirements, advancement, and employment outlook.

* Painting and decorating contracting as a career. Institute for Research. 1955. 24p. $1
Description of work, attractive and unattractive features, qualifications, training, prospects, typical day's work, earnings, and methods of establishing a painting and decorating contracting business.

Painting contractor. B'nai B'rith Vocational Service. 1954. 8p. 35c
Discussion of qualifications, starting one's own business, earnings, advantages, and disadvantages.

Production painter. Careers. 1962. 2p. 15c
Career summary for desk-top file. Duties, qualifications, and outlook.

**Production painters. One section of *Occupational Outlook Handbook.*
Description of painting metal or wood products in factories, where employed, training, employment outlook, earnings, and working conditions.

PALEONTOLOGIST   0-36.03

Paleontologist. Careers. 1963. 2p. 15c
Career summary for desk-top file. Duties, qualifications, and outlook.

PAPER INDUSTRY WORKER 4, 6, 8-41. through 4, 6, 8-42.

The dynamic fibre box industry. Fibre Box Association. No date. 8p. Free
Information about the growth of this industry and its future.

**Employment outlook in the pulp, paper, and paper products industry.
Bureau of Labor Statistics, U.S. Department of Labor. Supt. of Documents. 1964. 12p. 10c
Reprint from the *Occupational Outlook Handbook.*

From trees to paper. Lent, Henry B. Macmillan Company. 1952. 149p.
$3.95
Description of the work involved in converting trees in the Quebec north
woods to newsprint. For grades 6 to 8.

Grow with an exciting business. American Paper and Pulp Association.
1961. 24p. 15c
Includes description of technical and managerial jobs in the paper industry. Lists colleges which offer specialized courses in paper technology and
the member companies which offer scholarships or financial aid to students.

**Occupations in the pulp, paper, and paper products industry. One section
of *Occupational Outlook Handbook.*
Nature and location of the industry, kinds of jobs, training, other qualifications, employment outlook, earnings, and working conditions.

**Paper and pulp industry workers. Science Research Associates. 1961. 4p.
35c
Occupational brief describing kinds of work, requirements, getting started
and advancing, earnings, advantages, disadvantages, and future outlook.

Pulp and paper, a rewarding career. Syracuse Pulp and Paper Foundation.
1961. 10p. Free
Description of the industry, opportunities, training, and some available
financial student aids.

What you should know about career opportunities offered by the pulp
and paper industry. Technical Association of the Pulp and Paper Industry. No date. 32p. Free
Discussion of the progress and future outlook of opportunities, especially
basic research, process and product development, and process and production
control.

The work and education of a pulp and paper engineer. State University
of New York, College of Forestry. 1962. 4p. Free
Description of work, places of employment, salaries, working conditions,
future outlook, recommended high school subjects, and training.

PAPERHANGER 5-28.100

Paperhanger. Careers. 1963. 2p. 15c
Career summary for desk-top file. Duties, qualifications, and outlook.

**Paperhanger. Chronicle Guidance Publications. 1959. 4p. 35c
Occupational brief summarizing work performed, working conditions, hours, earnings, personal qualifications, training requirements, opportunities, employment outlook, and entry into the job.

See also Painter

PARACHUTIST 0-62.30

The space age sport: sky diving. Darby, Ray. Julian Messner, Inc. 1964. 192p. $3.95
Includes information about the parachutist.

What does a parachutist do? Hyde, Wayne. Dodd, Mead and Company. 1960. 64p. $2.50; library binding $2.57 net
An account of the thrills and dangers encountered, the vigorous training, the exciting first descent, and work done with the aid of parachutes. Illustrated. Written for grades 4 to 7.

PARK RANGER 0-68.10

Avalanche patrol. Atwater, Montgomery. Random House Inc. 1951. 247p. $2.95
Adventure story of an avalanche patrolman who keeps a treacherous region safe for skiers.

Career employment in the National Park Service. National Park Service, U.S. Department of the Interior. 1962. 31p. Free
Information concerning permanent full-time employment in the National Park Service. Description of types of positions, qualifications, and how positions are filled.

Park ranger. Careers. 1960. 2p. 15c
Career summary for desk-top file. Duties, qualifications, and outlook.

**Park ranger. Chronicle Guidance Publications. 1961. 4p. 35c
Occupational brief summarizing work performed, working conditions, personal qualifications, training, how to determine aptitudes and interests, opportunities, methods of entry, related jobs, and outlook.

Park rangers; the work, thrills and equipment of the National Park Rangers. Colby, Carroll Burleigh. Coward-McCann, Inc. 1955. 48p. $2.50. Library binding $2.52 net
Describes what life is like for a ranger in a national park where he must serve as guide, surveyor, policeman, fire fighter, and rescuer of wildlife. For younger readers, grades 4 to 8.

Recommended preparation for the position of park ranger. National Park Service, U.S. Department of the Interior. 1961. 7p. Mimeographed. Free
Qualifications for entrance to park ranger examinations and recommended college courses in preparation.

PARK RANGER—*Continued*

Sledge patrol. Howarth, David. Macmillan Company. 1957. 239p. $5.50
  Story of the wartime assignment of seven hunters to patrol a stretch of
  coast and to protect Greenland's weather stations from German invasion. A
  true story of one of the Allied victories.

See also Forest ranger; Forester

PARKING-LOT ATTENDENT   7-60.100

Finding out about parking attendants. Science Research Associates. 1962.
  4p. 35c
  Junior occupational brief describing work and opportunities.

Parking attendants. Science Research Associates. 1964. 4p. 35c
  Occupational brief describing work, qualifications, opportunities, and outlook.

Parking-lot attendant. Careers. 1964. 2p. 15c
  Career summary for desk-top file. Duties, qualifications, and outlook.

PAROLE OFFICER. *See* Probation officer

PASTOR. *See* Clergyman

PATHOLOGIST   0-26.40

A career in medical science: pathology. Herzog, Milan. Intersociety Committee for Research Potential in Pathology, Inc. No date. 32p. Free
  How pathology relates to other medical disciplines, nature of work, why
  research in pathology is exciting and satisfying, training, growing demand,
  satisfactions, and rewards.

Pathologist. Splaver, Sarah. Personnel Services. 1953. 6p. 50c; 25c to
  students
  Occupational abstract. Nature of work, qualifications, preparation, entrance
  and advancement, certification, distribution, supply and demand, earnings,
  advantages and disadvantages.

Should you be a pathologist? Moritz, Alan R. New York Life Insurance
  Company. 1962. 12p. Free
  Nature of work, financial rewards, opportunities, and abilities needed.

PATROLMAN   2-66.20 through 2-66.29

Patrol inspector. Kelly, Willard F. Research Publishing Company. 1957.
  48p. $1
  Nature of work, history and importance, personal qualifications, working
  conditions, benefits, training, promotional opportunities, and methods of
  securing jobs.

State highway patrolman (trooper). Careers. 1963. 2p. 15c
  Career summary for desk-top file. Duties, qualifications, and outlook.

State traffic officer and highway patrolman. California State Department of Employment. 1962. 3p. Single copy free
Duties of the job, working conditions, wages, hours, entrance requirements, promotion, training, and employment outlook.

White terror; adventures with the Ice Patrol. Floherty, John J. Lippincott Company. 1947. 182p. $3.50
Interesting stories of actual incidents in effecting rescues at sea and on the Greenland ice cap. Good illustrations.

See also Military serviceman; Police officer

PATTERNMAKER   5-17.

Aircraft plaster patternmaker. California State Department of Employment. 1961. 3p. Single copy free
Occupational guide summarizing duties, employment prospects, earnings, requirements for entry, and suggestions for locating a job.

Metal patternmaker. Careers. 1963. 2p. 15c
Career summary for desk-top file. Duties, qualifications, and outlook.

Model maker. Careers. 1963. 2p. 15c
Career summary for desk-top file. Duties, qualifications, and outlook.

* Patternmaker. Chronicle Guidance Publications. 1963. 4p. 35c
Occupational brief summarizing work performed, working conditions, where employed, requirements, training, methods of entry, and outlook.

Patternmaker. The Guidance Centre. 1962. 4p. 15c in Canada; 20c elsewhere
Definition, history and importance, nature of work, qualifications, preparation, advancement opportunities, advantages, disadvantages, how to get started, and related occupations.

Patternmaker (foundry). California State Department of Employment. 1964. 4p. Single copy free
Occupational guide summarizing duties, working conditions, employment prospects, earnings, training, requirements for entry, and suggestions for locating a job.

**Patternmakers. Michigan Employment Security Commission. 1956. 16p. 25c
Introduction, nature of work, working conditions, location of jobs, employment outlook, earnings, qualifications for entry, organizations, disadvantages, and advantages.

* Patternmakers. Science Research Associates. 1964. 4p. 35c
Occupational brief describing nature of work, training, qualifications, opportunities, and outlook.

**Patternmakers. One section of Occupational Outlook Handbook.
Nature of work, training, other qualifications, and employment outlook.

PEACE CORPS VOLUNTEER   0-00. through 9-99.

Complete Peace Corps guide. Hoopes, Roy. Dial Press. 1961. 180p. $3.50
   Aimed to give the prospective volunteer authoritative answers to questions
   now being asked about the Peace Corps.

High school students and the Peace Corps. Peace Corps. 1962. 8p. Free
   Suggestions for high school students who wish to prepare for Peace Corps
   service and answers to nine most common questions about the Peace Corps.

**Peace Corps factbook. Peace Corps. 1963. 25p. Free
   Illustrated booklet explaining how the volunteers are selected, trained, assigned, paid, classified for draft status, and examples of services being rendered.

U.S. Peace Corps: the challenge of good will. Whittlesey, Susan. Coward-
   McCann, Inc. 1963. 128p. $2.95
   A book to challenge young people to find a career with the Peace Corps.

Women in the Peace Corps. Peace Corps. 1962. 8p. Free
   Illustrated leaflet describing qualifications, opportunities for women, and
   examples of services being rendered.

PEN AND PENCIL INDUSTRY WORKER   7-13.110 through 7-13.169

The pen industry. Parker, Daniel. Bellman Publishing Company. 1955.
   16p. $1
   History, distribution of pens, type of work available, employment opportunities, educational requirements, and professional publications.

PERSONAL SERVICE WORKER   2-20.00 through 2-59.99

Job descriptions for domestic service and personal service occupations.
   U.S. Employment Service. Supt. of Documents. 1939. 261p. $1
   One of a series of Volume Job Descriptions. Describes occupations found
   in barber shops, beauty shops, garment alteration and repair shops, glove
   repair shop, hosiery repair shops, public baths, shoe shining shops, textile
   weaving and mending shops, and undertaking establishments; also includes
   jobs, such as hat checker and doorman, that occur in a large number of
   establishments and involve services to or for a person.

Occupations in personal services. Chapter 19 of *Planning Your Future.*
   Includes discussion of the nature of personal service, kinds of occupations
   included, and the work of the waitress.

One golden summer. Noble, Iris. Julian Messner, Inc. 1959. 192p. $2.95
   Career fiction. Story of a girl's first job away from home as a maid at a
   sophisticated summer camp.

   See also Barber; Beautician; Domestic service worker

PERSONNEL AND EMPLOYMENT MANAGER
                                   0-39.800 through 0-39.899

Applied psychology for employees. Lawshe, Charles H. and Thomas,
   Leon L. American Technical Society. 1954. 30p. 75c
   Directed to employees and potential employees, this booklet guides the way
   to better relations through knowledge that comes from understanding the employer and the fellow worker.

**Careers in personnel administration. Splaver, Sarah. Henry Z. Walck, Inc. 1962. 107p. $3.50
  Description of the work; opportunities in industry, schools, and labor unions; preparation; responsibilities of various positions; personal qualities needed; and the satisfactions and disadvantages of the field. Reading list.

Careers in personnel management. Angel, Juvenal. World Trade Academy Press. 1957. 28p. $1.25
  Includes information concerning each of the following; industrial relations director, personnel manager, job analyst, employment agency manager, labor relations conciliator, and personnel assistant.

* Employment manager. Chronicle Guidance Publications. 1963. 4p. 35c
  Occupational brief summarizing work performed, training, qualifications, earnings, and outlook.

**Employment outlook for personnel workers. Bureau of Labor Statistics, U.S. Department of Labor. Supt. of Documents. 1964. 4p. 5c
  Reprint from the *Occupational Outlook Handbook.*

Industrial counseling. Arbuckle, D. S. and Gordon, Thomas. Bellman Publishing Company. 1949. 47p. $1.25
  Description of management counseling, union counseling, and community services counseling. Also explanation of techniques and results and a chapter on the future of industrial counseling.

Industrial personnel work. Western Personnel Institute. 1954. 4p. 20c
  Nature of work, types of positions, preparation, and outlook.

Jobs in employee relations. American Management Association. 1959. 52p. $1.50
  Career trends and opportunities in personnel administration.

The legal basis for college student personnel work. Bakken, Clarence J. American College Personnel Association. Order from American Personnel and Guidance Association. 1961. 55p. $2
  Purpose is to provide legal information pertaining to guidance for those working in college personnel services. Selected court decisions illustrate the legal basis for authority for services, admissions, records, housing and food services, scholarships, loans, and student discipline.

Personnel administration. Sorensen, Clark C. Bellman Publishing Company. 1955. 18p. $1
  History and development, qualifications, training, opportunities, remuneration, advantages, and disadvantages.

Personnel administration. Simmons College. 1963. 4p. Free
  Discussion of preparation, qualifications, salaries, and nature of work in industry, government, education, and social service.

Personnel administration occupations. Careers. 1960. 8p. 25c
  Career brief describing duties, working conditions, training, personal requirements, earnings, advancement prospects, and outlook.

PERSONNEL AND EMPLOYMENT MANAGER—*Continued*

Personnel manager. California State Department of Employment. 1960. 4p. Single copy free
Duties, working conditions, wages, entrance requirements, promotion, training, and employment outlook.

Personnel manager. Chronicle Guidance Publications. 1963. 4p. 35c
Occupational brief summarizing duties, qualifications, training, salary, and outlook.

**Personnel specialist. Chronicle Guidance Publications. 1963. 4p. 35c
Occupational brief including definition, history, work performed, working conditions, requirements, training, methods of entry, outlook, related jobs, and earnings.

Personnel work as a career. Boston University. 1962. 16p. Free
Recruiting booklet describing opportunities, qualifications, advantages, disadvantages, and preparation. Discussion of work as personnel manager, employment manager, director of training, health supervisor, psychologist, and research assistant.

* Personnel work in commerce and industry as a career. Institute for Research. 1957. 24p. $1
Duties, typical day's work, personal qualifications, training, salaries, favorable and unfavorable features. Describes the activities of personnel director, employment manager, supervisor of training, supervisor of apprenticeship, vocational counselor, safety engineer, supervisor of research, supervisor of insurance and benefits, and supervisor of compensation.

Personnel work; industrial relations; public relations. Chapter 17 of *Vocations for Boys*.
Includes description of duties, preparation, and some of the specialized functions.

Personnel workers. Science Research Associates. 1961. 4p. 35c
Occupational brief describing work in labor relations, in a personnel department, and in industrial personnel. Includes requirements, getting started, salaries, advantages, disadvantages, and future outlook.

Personnel workers. Chapter 13 of *Vocations for Girls*.
Discussion of work, qualifications, and opportunities.

**Personnel workers. One section of *Occupational Outlook Handbook*.
Nature of work, where employed, training, other qualifications, advancement, employment outlook, earnings, and working conditions.

* Promising careers in personnel. Moore, Paul L. American Society for Personnel Administration. 1962. 2p. Free
Brief discussion of the duties and responsibilities of the personnel worker, educational and training requirements, salaries, and outlook for the future.

Public-school personnel administrator. National Education Association. 1962. 80p. 75c
A study of the origin, administrative status, duties and responsibilities, and trends of the position.

Should you go into personnel work? Ching, Cyrus S. New York Life Insurance Company. 1959. 12p. Free
Nature of work, opportunities, desirable characteristics, earnings, and advantages.

Your career in public personnel administration. Public Personnel Association. 1963. 13p. Free
Description of work, functions, training, opportunities, earnings, and advantages.

**Your future in personnel work. Pond, John. Richards Rosen Press. 1962. 159p. $2.95
Various areas of personnel work are described with the qualifications necessary.

See also Counselor; Vocational rehabilitation counselor

PERSONNEL WORKER
0-39.800 through 0-39.899; 0-68.70 through 0-68.79

A flair for people. Wells, Helen. Julian Messner, Inc. 1955. 192p. $2.95
Career fiction. The story tells of a girl's experiences in personnel work in a doll factory and later in a large department store.

Preparation in school and college personnel work. U.S. Office of Education. Supt. of Documents. 1963. 196p. $1.25
Directory of programs and course offerings for preparation for personnel work. Courses offered in the 1963 summer session and the 1963-1964 academic year are listed by states and institutions.

See also Counselor; Personnel and employment manager; Vocational rehabilitation counselor

PETROLEUM ENGINEER
0-20.11

**Careers in petroleum engineering. American Institute of Mining, Metallurgical, and Petroleum Engineers. 1961. 16p. Single copy free
Discussion of the work in exploration, drilling, production, transportation, refining, and marketing. Includes growth, trends, high school preparation, and college training.

Petroleum engineer. Careers. 1961. 2p. 15c
Career summary for desk-top file. Duties, qualifications, and outlook.

Petroleum engineer. Chronicle Guidance Publications. 1960. 4p. 35c
Occupational brief summarizing work performed, working conditions, qualifications, training, earnings, and outlook.

Petroleum engineering. Carpenter, M. T. Chapter 20 of Engineering Enrollment in the United States.
Trends in college enrollment and future requirements for specialists in this area.

Petroleum engineering. Kirkpatrick, C. V. Bellman Publishing Company. 1958. 24p. $1
History and development of work, training, employment opportunities, advancement, and trends. Selected references.

Petroleum engineering. Colorado School of Mines. No date. 6p. Free
Description of the work, prospects, training, and requirements for admission for study.

**Petroleum engineers. Science Research Associates. 1963. 4p. 35c
Occupational brief describing nature of work, requirements, training, methods of getting started, earnings, advantages, disadvantages, and future outlook.

Petroleum-refining engineering. Colorado School of Mines. No date. 6p. Free
Description of the work, prospects, training, and requirements for admission for study.

PETROLEUM INDUSTRY WORKER   5, 7, 9-20. and 4, 6, 8-55.

Careers in the oil industry. American Petroleum Institute. 1962. 16p. Free to school guidance personnel
Describes job opportunities in several major groups: science-math, mechanical, operational-control, meet-the-public, and administrative. Also contains a section on college, career, and scholarship information.

**Employment outlook in petroleum production and refining occupations. Bureau of Labor Statistics, U.S. Department of Labor. Supt. of Documents. 1964. 16p. 10c
Reprint from the *Occupational Outlook Handbook.*

Flowing gold; the romance of oil. Floherty, John J. Lippincott Company. 1957. 224p. $3.95
Description of the oil industry with dramatic glimpses behind the scenes. Includes history, exploration, refineries, laboratories where new products are developed, and distribution by pipe lines and tank ships. Illustrated.

Oil driller. The Guidance Centre. 1959. 4p. 15c in Canada; 20c elsewhere
History and importance, nature of work, qualifications, working conditions, preparation, remuneration, advancement, outlook, related occupations, and how to get started.

Oil in the service of man. Rathbone, M. J. Standard Oil Company of New Jersey. 1963. 14p. Free
This pamphlet describes the contributions and future roles of petroleum.

Opportunities in the petroleum industry. Patrick, Gene. Vocational Guidance Manuals. 1952. 95p. $1.45 paper
Scope of the industry and opportunities in exploration and production, refining and processing, transportation and communication, distribution and marketing, administration, research, and petroleum engineering.

Petroleum exploration and production workers. Science Research Associates. 1961. 4p. 35c
Occupational brief describing nature of work, requirements, training, earnings, methods of getting started, advantages, disadvantages, and future outlook.

**Petroleum production and refining occupations. One chapter of *Occupational Outlook Handbook.*
Nature and location of the industry, training, earnings, and employment outlook in petroleum production and in petroleum refining.

Petroleum products occupations (production occupations). Careers. 1961. 8p. 25c
Career brief describing duties, working conditions, training, earnings, and outlook. Additional readings.

* Petroleum refinery workers. Science Research Associates. 1961. 4p. 35c
Occupational brief describing duties, requirements, training, methods of getting started, earnings, advantages, disadvantages, and future outlook.

Petroleum refining occupations. Careers. 1962. 8p. 35c
Career brief describing duties, working conditions, training, personal qualifications, earnings, and outlook.

There's a job for you in the liquefied petroleum gas industry. Liquefied Petroleum Gas Association, Inc. No date. 8p. Free
Description of job opportunities and training at Southern Technical Institute.

PHARMACEUTICAL SALES REPRESENTATIVE   1-85.33

A career in pharmaceutical sales? Burroughs Williams and Company. 1961. 4p. Free
Duties, qualifications, training, earnings, and advancement.

Is your future in pharmaceutical sales? Squibb and Sons. 1962. 8p. Free
Nature of assignments, training, earnings, benefits, and advancement.

Pharmaceutical sales representative. Robinson, H. Alan and Connors, Ralph P. Personnel Services. 1963. 6p. 50c; 25c to students
Occupational abstract. Nature of work, future prospects, qualifications, preparation, earnings, entrance, and advancement.

PHARMACIST   0-25.

Accredited colleges of pharmacy. American Council on Pharmaceutical Education. 1963. 10p. Single copy free
List of accredited colleges of pharmacy in the United States.

* Careers in pharmacy. Angel, Juvenal L. World Trade Academy Press. 1962. 28p. $1.25
Description of work, training, opportunities, remuneration; and where employment is found for each of the following: pharmacist, hospital pharmacist, industrial pharmacist, teacher of pharmacy, and pharmaceutical salesman. Also included is a list of organizations and colleges offering scholarships in the field of pharmacy.

Careers in pharmacy. B'nai B'rith Vocational Service. 1957. 16p. 35c
Discussion of nature of work, educational requirements, training, employment, qualifications, earnings, working conditions, licensing, advantages, and disadvantages.

A challenging career for you as a Veterans Administration pharmacist. Veterans Administration, Department of Medicine and Surgery. 1962. 4p. Free
Description of work, training program, qualifications, and benefits.

PHARMACIST—*Continued*

Drug store operation as a career. Institute for Research. 1959. 24p. $1
Description of work, a typical day, personal qualifications, opportunities, attractive and unattractive features. In addition to information concerning owning and operating a drugstore, data are given about the work of the pharmacist and fountain manager.

Education in pharmacy. Philadelphia College of Pharmacy and Science. 1962. 6p. Free
One chapter in an illustrated recruiting brochure describing nature of work, opportunities, and training in pharmacy, bacteriology, biology, and chemistry.

**Employment outlook for pharmacists. Bureau of Labor Statistics, U.S. Department of Labor. Supt. of Documents. 1964. 4p. 5c
Reprint from the *Occupational Outlook Handbook*.

**Health manpower source book, section 15, pharmacists. Public Health Service, U.S. Department of Health, Education, and Welfare. Supt. of Documents. 1963. 66p. 40c
Presents basic data on the numbers, location, and characteristics of pharmacists in the United States. The appendix contains statistics on undergraduate enrollments and graduates of the United States schools of pharmacy.

**Opportunities in pharmacy careers. Gable, Fred B. Vocational Guidance Manuals. 1964. 144p. $1.45 paper; library edition $2.65
Includes the development of pharmacy, educational requirements, training, duties, rewards, employment, and kinds of specialization within the profession.

Orientation to pharmacy. Burlage, Henry; Lee, Charles; and Rising, L. Wait. McGraw-Hill Book Company. 1959. 306p. $6.95
A guide for beginning pharmacy students, this book contains a discussion of the professional aspects, requirements, and opportunities of the pharmacist.

* Pharmaceutical industry. Closs, John O'Neill. Bellman Publishing Company. 1956. 28p. $1
Development and size of the industry, opportunities, compensation, advantages, and disadvantages.

Pharmacist. Splaver, Sarah. Personnel Services. 1960. 6p. 50c; 25c to students
Occupational abstract. Nature of work, qualifications, preparation, entrance and advancement, earnings, number and distribution, licensing, future prospects, advantages, and disadvantages.

Pharmacist. Careers. 1963. 8p. 25c
Career brief describing duties, working conditions, earnings, personal qualifications, licensure, opportunities, and outlook. List of accredited colleges of pharmacy.

* Pharmacist. Chronicle Guidance Publications. 1963. 4p. 35c
Occupational brief summarizing work performed, working conditions, hours, earnings, personal qualifications, training requirements, opportunities, employment outlook, and entry into the job.

Pharmacist. The Guidance Centre. 1962. 4p. 15c in Canada; 20c elsewhere
Definition, nature of work, qualifications, training, working conditions, remuneration, outlook, advantages, disadvantages, how to get started, and related occupations.

Pharmacists. Michigan Employment Security Commission. 1963. 20p. 25c
Introduction, nature of work, employment prospects, earnings, qualifications for entry, working conditions, organizations, disadvantages, and advantages.

* Pharmacists. Science Research Associates. 1960. 4p. 35c
Occupational brief describing nature of work, requirements, salaries, getting started, advantages, disadvantages, and future outlook.

**Pharmacists. One section of *Occupational Outlook Handbook.*
Nature of work, where employed, training, other qualifications, advancement, employment outlook, earnings, and working conditions.

Pharmacy. Guth, Earl P. Bellman Publishing Company. 1959. 24p. $1
History and development of pharmacy, future outlook, qualifications, training, and remuneration. Includes vocational opportunities for pharmacist, pharmacologist, pharmaceutical chemist, pharmacognosist, teacher of pharmacy, and pharmacist apprentice.

**Pharmacy. Pages 124-7 of *Health Careers Guidebook.*
Personal qualifications, education, licensing and registration, opportunities, and prospects. Also a discussion of retail pharmacy and hospital pharmacy.

Pharmacy as a career. Institute for Research. 1964. 24p. $1
History and development, kinds of work, qualifications, licensing, earnings, and outlook.

Pharmacy—get ready for tomorrow. National Association of Chain Drug Stores. 1962. 8p. Free
Outlook, opportunities, earnings, and qualifications for pharmacy, the bridge between scientific knowledge and health. Included is a list of the colleges which offer training in pharmacy.

**See your future in pharmacy. American Pharmaceutical Association. 1962. 16p. Free
Nature of the work, personal qualifications, education, opportunities, and prospects. Included is a list of the accredited colleges of pharmacy.

**Shall I study pharmacy? National Advisory Commission on Careers in Pharmacy. 1962. 32p. 35c
Discussion of nature of work, earnings, conditions of work, advancement, opportunities, qualifications, and training. Includes list of seventy-five accredited colleges of pharmacy. Illustrated.

She is a pharmacist. Kappa Epsilon Career Guidance Committee. 1958. 30p. 20c
General information about women pharmacists is followed by interviews with several women practicing in various fields of pharmacy.

Should you be a pharmacist? Briggs, W. Paul. New York Life Insurance Company. 1961. 12p. Free
Description of work, personal requisites for success, training, and outlook.

PHARMACIST—*Continued*

What is a pharmacist? Upjohn Company. No date. 6p. Free
An illustrated brochure describing opportunities for the pharmacist in several areas other than retail pharmacy.

**Your future in pharmacy. Kraemer, James. Richards Rosen Press. 1963. 160p. $2.95; library edition $2.79 net
Stresses the various aspects of work in this field in addition to the retail pharmacy, preparation, and opportunities. Includes list of schools offering training.

PHARMACOLOGIST 0-35.34

A career in pharmacology. American Society for Pharmacology and Experimental Therapeutics. 1961. 32p. Free
Applications of pharmacology in research, teaching, industry, and public health; opportunities, outlook, and training. Twelve illustrations.

Pharmacologist. Chronicle Guidance Publications. 1964. 4p. 35c
Occupational brief summarizing work performed, qualifications, training, earnings, opportunities, and outlook.

Pharmacology. Careers. 1963. 2p. 15c
Career summary for desk-top file. Duties, qualifications, and outlook.

PHOTOENGRAVER 4-47.100

Photoengraver. Flader, Louis. Research Publishing Company. 1954. 44p. $1
Nature of work, qualifications, preparation, opportunities, and related occupations.

* Photoengraver. Chronicle Guidance Publications. 1962. 4p. 35c
Occupational brief summarizing work performed, working conditions, qualifications, training, opportunities, outlook and methods of entry.

Photoengraver. The Guidance Centre. 1960. 4p. 15c in Canada; 20c elsewhere
History and importance, nature of work, qualifications, working conditions, preparation, remuneration, advancement, outlook, related occupations, and how to get started.

Photoengraver (relief printing). Careers. 1960. 2p. 15c
Career summary for desk-top file. Duties, qualifications, and outlook.

**Photoengravers. One section of *Occupational Outlook Handbook*.
Nature of work, where employed, training, other qualifications, employment outlook, earnings, and working conditions.

Photoengravers and lithographers. Science Research Associates. 1960. 4p. 35c
Occupational brief describing nature of work, preparation, qualifications, opportunities, advantages, disadvantages, and future outlook.

Photoengraving occupations. Michigan Employment Security Commission. 1954. 24p. 25c

Introduction, nature of work, distribution of jobs, employment prospects, qualifications for entry, earnings, working conditions, guides for vocational selection, and advancement.

PHOTOGRAPHER 0-56.

Career for Jennifer. De Leeuw, Adele. Macmillan Company. 1941. 280p. $3.95

Career fiction. Photography becomes a profitable business.

Careers in photography. Neblette, C. B. Rochester Institute of Technology. Revised 1960. 28p. Free

Includes a description of the various kinds of photography, such as advertising, industrial, portrait, newspaper, documentary, and motion picture; information on the manufacture and sale of photographic equipment and materials; photofinishing; applied photography; and preparation for a career. Job charts.

Commercial photographer. Careers. 1963. 2p. 15c

Career summary for desk-top file. Duties, qualifications, and outlook.

Darkroom technician. Careers. 1963. 2p. 15c

Career summary for desk-top file. Duties, qualifications, and outlook.

**Employment outlook for photographers. Bureau of Labor Statistics, U.S. Department of Labor. Supt. of Documents. 1964. 4p. 5c

Reprint from the *Occupational Outlook Handbook*.

**Find a career in photography. Hood, Robert E. Putnam's Sons. 1959. 160p. $2.95

A magazine photographer draws on his own experience and that of some industrial, portrait, advertising, and fashion photographers to introduce young readers to the field. Written for ages 11 to 15.

Katie and her camera. Hobart, Lois. Julian Messner, Inc. 1955. 192p. $2.95

Career fiction. A story that combines career interest in photography with light romance.

News photography as a career. Institute for Research. 1962. 24p. $1

Description of work, types of jobs, typical day's work, attractive and unattractive features, personal qualifications, training, salaries and remuneration, chances for employment, and related jobs.

Opportunities in photography. Deschin, Jacob. Vocational Guidance Manuals. 1950. 112p. $1.45 paper

Contents: The new photographer, photography grows up, learning photography, getting started, occupations in photography, organizations and honors, related fields, and places where career photography is taught.

Photographer. Splaver, Sarah. Personnel Services. 1951. 6p. 50c; 25c to students

Occupational abstract. Nature of work, qualifications, preparation, entrance and advancement, distribution of workers, supply and demand, earnings, advantages and disadvantages, and professional associations.

PHOTOGRAPHER—*Continued*

Photographer. Careers. 1961. 8p. 25c
> Career brief describing duties, working conditions, training, personal require-
> ments, earnings, advancement opportunities, and outlook. Additional readings.

Photographer. The Guidance Centre. 1962. 4p. 15c in Canada; 20c elsewhere
> Nature of work, specialized areas in this field, working conditions, qualifica-
> tions, training, earnings, how to get started, advantages, and disadvantages.

Photographer as a career. Professional Photographers of America. 1959. 4p.
Free
> Description of the various kinds of photography, preparation, professional
> background needed, and list of schools offering instruction in photography.

* Photographers. Science Research Associates. 1959. 4p. 35c
> Occupational brief describing nature of work, preparation, qualifications,
> opportunities, advantages, disadvantages, and future outlook.

**Photographers. One section of *Occupational Outlook Handbook.*
> Nature of work, where employed, training, other qualifications, advancement,
> employment outlook, earnings, and working conditions.

Photographic manufacturing workers. Science Research Associates. 1961.
4p. 35c
> Occupational bricf describing nature of the work, requirements, earnings, and
> future outlook.

Photography as a career. Institute for Research. 1964. 24p. $1
> Branches of photography, types of positions, qualifications, earnings, attractive
> and unattractive features.

* Professional photographer. Chronicle Guidance Publications. 1961. 4p.
35c
> Occupational brief summarizing work performed, working conditions, earn-
> ings, determination of aptitudes and interests, opportunities, and outlook.

* Record photography in industry. Cornwell, Wallace. Bellman Publishing
Co. 1945. 24p. $1
> Qualifications, training, opportunities, and description of work of the micro-
> film camera operator, record copying camera and contact printer operator.

PHOTOLITHOGRAPHER   4-46.200

Photolithographer. Chronicle Guidance Publications. 1961. 4p. 35c
> Occupational brief summarizing work performed, working conditions, train-
> ing, qualifications, earnings, advantages, disadvantages, where employed, and
> methods of entry.

PHYSICAL INSTRUCTOR   0-57.41

**Career as an athletic coach. Institute for Research. 1958. 24p. $1
> Pioneer coaches, where coaches are employed, types of positions, duties,
> typical day's work, attractive and unattractive features, qualifications, education
> and training, suggested program for four years of college, salaries, outlook, and
> related fields.

A challenging career for you as a Veterans Administration corrective therapist. Veterans Administration, Department of Medicine and Surgery. 1963. 4p. Free
Description of work, training program, qualifications, and benefits.

Physical education—a career that puts play to work. Metzner, Romola. Careers. 1963. 4p. 25c
Reprint from the *American Girl*, describing nature of work, training, requirements, and desirable aspects.

**Physical education as a career. Makechnie, George. Bellman Publishing Company. 1963. 32p. $1
Personal qualifications, training, outline of standard curricula, analysis of employment opportunities, remuneration, opportunities for advancement, advantages and disadvantages. Includes list of institutions giving professional training in health and physical education.

* Physical education as a career. Institute for Research. 1962. 24p. $1
Qualifications, training, opportunities, salaries, advantages, and disadvantages. Includes description of recent developments in recreational activities, private camps, and physical therapy.

Physical education as your career. American Association for Health, Physical Education, and Recreation. 1963. 8p. 5c. Single copy free
Nature of work, employment prospects, salaries, advantages, preparation, and qualifications.

Physical education for high school students. American Association for Health, Physical Education, and Recreation. 1960. 416p. $3
This book of sports, athletics, and recreational activities for teen-age boys and girls contains a chapter on physical education as a career.

Physical education or physical therapy as a career. Boston University. 1962. 11p. Free
Recruiting booklet describing qualifications, opportunities, work of the physical director and the physical therapist, advantages, disadvantages, and preparation.

* Physical education teacher. Careers. 1961. 8p. 25c
Career brief describing the importance of the work, duties, working conditions, training, personal requirements, earnings, advancement prospects, and outlook. Additional readings.

* Physical education teacher. Chronicle Guidance Publications. 1962. 4p. 35c
Occupational brief describing work performed, working conditions, personal qualifications, training requirements, promotional opportunities, employment outlook, and where employed. Selected references.

Physical education teachers. Science Research Associates. 1961. 4p. 35c
Occupational brief describing kinds of work, requirements, earnings, getting started, advantages, disadvantages, and future outlook. Two illustrations.

Physical educator. The Guidance Centre. 1958. 4p. 15c in Canada; 20c elsewhere
History and importance, nature of work, qualifications, working conditions, preparation, remuneration, advancement, outlook, related occupations, and how to get started.

PHYSICAL INSTRUCTOR—*Continued*

Your career in physical education. Johnson, Granville; Johnson, Warren; and Humphrey, James. Harper and Row. 1957. 275p. $3.75
Designed for an introduction to physical education course for freshman and sophomore classes in college to introduce both young men and young women to the scope, requirements, and opportunities of physical education as a career.

See also Athlete; Athletic coach; Baseball player

PHYSICAL SCIENTIST. *See* Scientist

PHYSICAL THERAPIST 0-52.80

A challenging career for you as a Veterans Administration physical therapist. Veterans Administration, Department of Medicine and Surgery. 1962. 4p. Free
Description of work, training program, qualifications, and benefits.

Educational and experience qualifications of physical therapists in public health agencies. American Public Health Association. 1954. 7p. Free
General scope of the field, duties, types of positions, educational preparation, and qualifications for different types of positions.

**Employment outlook for physical therapists and occupational therapists. Bureau of Labor Statistics, U.S. Department of Labor. Supt. of Documents. 1964. 8p. 5c
Reprint from the *Occupational Outlook Handbook*.

Laurie: physical therapist. Hobart, Lois. Julian Messner, Inc. 1957. 192p. $2.95
Career fiction. Laurie encounters daily challenges as she helps patients.

Physical education or physical therapy as a career. Boston University. 1962. 11p. Free
Recruiting booklet describing qualifications, opportunities, work of the physical director and the physical therapist, advantages, disadvantages, and preparation.

Physical therapist. Careers. 1960. 8p. 25c
Career brief describing duties, working conditions, training, personal qualifications, earnings, advancement prospects, and outlook.

* Physical therapist. Chronicle Guidance Publications. 1962. 4p. 35c
Occupational brief summarizing work performed, working conditions, qualifications, training, opportunities, outlook, methods of entry, related jobs, and suggested activities.

Physical therapist. The Guidance Centre. 1961. 4p. 15c in Canada; 20c elsewhere
Development and growth of the profession, working conditions, preparation, opportunities for advancement, earnings, advantages, disadvantages, how to get started, and related occupations.

* Physical therapists. Science Research Associates. 1961. 4p. 35c

Occupational brief describing nature of work, requirements, college courses, getting started, salaries, working hours, advantages, disadvantages, and future outlook.

**Physical therapists. One section of *Occupational Outlook Handbook*.

Nature of work, where employed, training, other qualifications, employment outlook, and earnings.

Physical therapists . . . where to? American Physical Therapy Association. 1962. 10p. 7c. Single copy free

Written for adults, especially counselors. Explains opportunities for experienced and capable physical therapists.

Physical therapy. Pages 127-9 of *Health Careers Guidebook*.

Nature of work, qualifications, education, opportunities, and salary.

* Physical therapy as a career. Institute for Research. 1958. 24p. $1

History and development of work, types of institutions which employ physical therapy technicians, duties and a typical day's work, personal qualifications, training and usual course of instruction, opportunities, salaries, attractive and unattractive features. Also requirements for membership in the American Physiotherapy Association.

Physical therapy is the right answer for many. American Physical Therapy Association. 1964. 2p. 4c. Single copy free

Designed especially for counselors. Brief statement of need and preparation.

Physical therapy sampler. American Physical Therapy Association. 1962. 12p. 6c. Single copy free

Illustrated brochure explaining work, contribution, and satisfactions.

Schools offering courses in physical therapy. American Physical Therapy Association. 1964. 2p. 4c. Single copy free

List of forty-two schools, arranged by states.

Sources of financial assistance for physical therapy students. American Physical Therapy Association. 1963. 8p. 5c. Single copy free

Sources available to prospective students, arranged by states.

**There's work to be done . . . a career to be built in physical therapy. American Physical Therapy Association. 1961. 2p. 5c. Single copy free

Nature of work, the current needs and opportunities for physical therapists, professional requirements, educational requirements, and how to begin. Included is a list of forty-two schools with programs approved by the Council on Medical Education and Hospitals of the American Medical Association.

Your dream of tomorrow can begin now. American Physical Therapy Association. 1962. 8p. 8c. Single copy free

Brief explanation of career opportunities and requirements, prepared for junior high school level.

PHYSICIAN 0-26.

**Admission requirements of American medical colleges, including Canada. Association of American Medical Colleges. 1963. 252p. $3

Information concerning the admission requirements and admission procedures of each of the eighty-eight medical schools in the United States, the twelve medical schools in Canada, and one in the Philippines. Contains recommendations on early preparation for medical education and how to go about the details of filing applications to medical schools. Estimated expenses and information about financial aid also are included. Good reading lists.

The appraisal of applicants to medical schools. Gee, Helen H. and Cowles, John T., ed. Association of American Medical Schools. 1957. 228p. $3 cloth; $2 paper

This book presents the results of a survey and analysis of the methods of selecting from increasing numbers of qualified young men and women those who will fill society's medical needs most effectively. Discusses the problem of identifying students of superior intellect who have, in addition, the capacity to work persistently. Bibliography.

Cancer, cocaine and courage: the story of Dr. William Halsted. Beckhard, Arthur J. and Crane, William D. Julian Messner, Inc. 1960. 192p. $3.25. Library binding $3.19 net

Biography of a surgeon who unwittingly became a drug addict, overcame the habit, and went on to perform miracles of surgery.

Careers in industrial medicine and hygiene. Institute for Research. 1957. 24p. $1

History and development, a typical week's work, attractive and unattractive features, personal qualifications, education and training, earnings, and getting started. Includes a list of universities offering graduate training in industrial medicine to graduates of medical schools.

Careers in medicine. Angel, Juvenal. World Trade Academy Press. 1960. 26p. $1.25

Includes description of the major fields of specialization, education required, opportunities, remuneration, future outlook, and methods of financing an education.

Careers in medicine. B'nai B'rith Vocational Service. 1957. 20p. 35c

Discussion of outlook, qualifications, training, licensure, cost of a medical education, earnings, advantages, disadvantages, and related careers.

The choice of a medical career. Garland, Joseph and Stokes, Joseph, editors. Lippincott Company. 1961. 244p. $5.50

Twenty-two specialists describe their fields for the medical student and young physician. Includes preparation, roles, responsibilities, opportunities, and rewards. For the advanced student, this is a guide to the various medical specialties.

Clinical pathologist. Careers. 1960. 2p. 15c

Career summary for desk-top file. Duties, qualifications, and outlook.

A doctor alone: biography of Elizabeth Blackwell, first woman doctor. Chambers, Peggy. Abelard-Schuman. 1958. 184p. $2.75

Biography of the woman who, in 1849 after many hardships, became the first woman medical practitioner.

Doctor Ellen. De Leeuw, Adele L. Macmillan Company. 1944. 210p. $3.50

Career fiction. Ellen is beginning her third year at medical school and the story gives glimpses of the various critical tests she must meet.

Doctor: his education and training. Engeman, Jack. Lothrop, Lee and Shepard. 1964. 152p. $3.95

More than 250 photographs and informative text present the day-to-day life of a medical student from the start of his studies until he is a practicing physician. For grades 7 to 11.

Dr. Kay Winthrop, intern. Chandler, Caroline A. Dodd, Mead and Company. 1947. 195p. $2.25

Career fiction. Story of the experiences of a young woman intern. The author bases her writing on some of her own experiences.

Doctor of medicine. Michigan Employment Security Commission. 1961. 16p. 25c

Introduction, nature of work, location of jobs, earnings, working conditions, employment outlook, requirements for entry, disadvantages, and advantages.

The doctor who dared: William Osler. Nobel, Iris. Julian Messner, Inc. 1959. 192p. $3.25. Library binding $3.19 net

An inspirational biography with insight into the medical profession.

Doctors and what they do. Coy, Harold. Franklin Watts, Inc. 1956. 183p. $3.95

The reader is taken behind the scenes to watch doctors at work. For grades 7 to 11.

The Doctors Mayo. Clapesattle, Helen. University of Minnesota Press. 1941. Second edition, condensed. 426p. $4.75

Biography of the Mayo brothers and the Mayo Clinic. Illustrated.

Educational qualifications of school physicians. American Public Health Association. 1953. 8p. Free

General scope of the field, duties, and classification of school physicians are included.

Elizabeth Garrett, M.D. Manton, Jo. Abelard-Schuman. 1960. 160p. $3

Biography of England's first woman doctor, and the story of her overcoming countless discouragements and rebuffs.

**Employment outlook for physicians. Bureau of Labor Statistics, U.S. Department of Labor. Supt. of Documents. 1964. 4p. 5c

Reprint from the *Occupational Outlook Handbook.*

Eye, ear, nose, and throat specialists—careers. Institute for Research. 1961. 24p. $1

History, development, and present status of work, typical day's work, personal qualifications, educational requirements, special training and certification, opportunities, attractive and unattractive features. Requirements for fellowship in the American College of Surgeons.

PHYSICIAN—*Continued*

Famous men of medicine. Chandler, Caroline. Dodd, Mead and Company. 1950. 140p. $3
> Biographies of men and women whose works represent the milestones in medical progress from antiquity until the present time.

Find a career in medicine. Starrett, Robert. Putnam's Sons. 1960. 160p. $2.95
> Introduction to the various kinds of work in this broad area, special training necessary, and future possibilities. Stresses the importance of a liberal education.

First woman ambulance surgeon: Emily Barringer. Noble, Iris. Julian Messner, Inc. 1962. 192p. $3.25. Library binding $3.19 net
> Biography of the first woman who was allowed to intern in a hospital, illustrating the courage and talent to enter a profession reserved for men.

The first woman doctor. Baker, Rachel. Scholastic Book Services. 1961. 192p. 35c
> Paperback edition of biography of Elizabeth Blackwell.

General practice physician. Robinson, Ann and Robinson, H. Alan. Personnel Services. 1959. 6p. 50c; 25c to students
> Occupational abstract. Nature of work, future prospects, qualifications, preparation, licensure, entrance, earnings, number and distribution, advantages, and disadvantages.

Great men of medicine. Hume, Ruth Fox. Random House, Inc. 1961. 192p. $1.95
> Biographies of ten men who were pioneers in modern medical science. The final chapter concerns the future outlook of medical research.

A guide to vocations in the medical and related areas. Ralya, Lynn and Ralya, Lillian. The authors. 1955. 36p. $1
> A brief discussion of each of twenty-two fields and references to selected publications which contain additional information.

Happy life of a doctor. Lee, Roger Irving. Little, Brown and Company. 1956. 278p. $4
> Biography of a doctor who found contentment in public and private service.

Health manpower source book—medical specialists. Public Health Service, U.S. Department of Health, Education, and Welfare. Publication Number 263, Section 14. Supt. of Documents. 1962. 234p. $1.25
> This source book presents basic data on the numbers, distribution, and characteristics of physicians engaged in medical specialties. Information on physicians by type of practice and by type of specialty is shown for selected years, 1931-1962. For each of twenty-six specialties there are given findings on certification, age, sex, state location, and medical school from which graduated.

How to score high on the medical college admission test. Groff, Morris and Gruber, Edward. Arco Publishing Company. 1963. 240p. $4
> Practice questions and answers in addition to study suggestions.

I want to be a doctor. Greene, Carla. Childrens Press. 1961. 32p. $2
Prepared for beginning readers with a reading level of upper first grade. Illustrated in color.

Intern or internist? American Society of Internal Medicine. No date. 6p. Free
Differentiates between the hospital apprenticeship and the work of the specialist in internal medicine.

Internist. Splaver, Sarah. Personnel Services. 1963. 6p. 50c; 25c to students
Occupational abstract. Description of the work of experienced physicians who specialize in internal medicine or the diagnosis and treatment of problems involving the internal organs and functions of the body. Includes qualifications, preparation, certification, advantages, and disadvantages.

Is your future in medicine or dentistry? Union College. No date. 10p. Free
Discussion of premedical training, discouraging factors, and a sampling of college courses required by some medical schools.

Jungle doctors. McGrady, Mike. Lippincott Company. 1962. 160p. $3.25
Short biographies of the heroic men and women who take medical help to people in distant lands. Illustrated.

Junior intern. Nourse, Alan. Harper and Row. 1955. 210p. $3.50; library binding $3.27 net
Career fiction. Story of an intern and the consideration he gives to the question of why a person enters the medical profession.

**Listen to leaders in medicine. Love, Albert and Childers, J. S., editors. Tupper and Love, Inc. 1963. 340p. $4.75
Seventeen medical authorities tell their personal experiences and offer advice concerning the opportunities open to young doctors.

Man alive in outer space—our space surgeons' greatest challenge. Lent, Henry B. Macmillan Company. 1961. 147p. $3.50
Depicts the importance of the men behind the men who will be going out into space. Story of the U.S. Air Force aerospace surgeon's work in testing and solving the problems of manned space flight. For ages 12 to 16.

Master surgeon: a biography of Joseph Lister. Farmer, Laurence. Harper and Row. 1962. 141p. $2.95
Biography of the famous surgeon.

The Mayo brothers. Clapesattle, Helen. Houghton Mifflin Company. 1962. 180p. $1.95
Biography of William and Charles Mayo and a picture of the growth and improvement of medical services.

The Mayos: pioneers in medicine. Regli, Adolph. Julian Messner, Inc. 1942. 256p. $3.50. Library binding $3.34 net
Biography recommended for boys considering the medical field as a career.

PHYSICIAN—*Continued*

**Medical professions. Pages 92-8 of *Health Careers Guidebook*.
    Qualifications, training, licensing, advantages, and disadvantages of a career as a physician. Also included is a list of twenty recognized fields of medical specialization.

Medical scholarship and loan fund programs sponsored or administered by medical societies. Council on Rural Health. 1961. 34p. Free
    Programs sponsored by state and county medical societies in twenty-eight states.

Medicine. O'Hara, Dwight. Bellman Publishing Co. 1946. 24p. $1
    Includes discussion of choice of college and medical school and the cost of medical education. List of recognized medical schools.

**Medicine as a career. American Medical Association. 1963. 24p. Free
    This booklet answers many of the questions which students ask when exploring the challenges, demands, and opportunities of a career in medicine. Includes suggested high school preparation, desirable qualities, choice of a college of arts and sciences, how to get into medical school, licensure, and list of eighty-three medical schools and three schools of basic medical sciences.

Medicine as a career. Boston University. 1962. 10p. Free
    Recruiting booklet describing the demands of medicine, need for doctors, opportunities, income, and training.

* Medicine as a career. Institute for Research. 1962. 24p. $1
    Qualifications, training, advantages, disadvantages, and distribution of physicians by states. Describes work of the general practitioner and of many of the thirty-one specialists listed.

Medicine in action today and tomorrow. Hyde, Margaret. McGraw-Hill Whittlesey House. 1956. 144p. $3
    Presents opportunities in 150 areas in medicine or allied fields and cites the need for more workers. Charts furnish information concerning educational requirements and length of training needed for the various careers.

Men against death. De Kruif, Paul. Harcourt, Brace and World. 1936. 363p. $4.50
    Biographies of scientists who made discoveries in the field of medicine.

Occupations in professional services. Chapter 21 of *Planning Your Future*.
    Includes description of the nature of professional service and specific information about the work of the physician.

**The opportunities and rewards of medicine can be yours. American Medical Association. No date. 8p. Free
    Discussion of the versatility of the practice of medicine, rewards, suggested prerequisite high school courses, and ways of preparing for medical school.

* Physician. Careers. 1964. 8p. 25c
    Career brief describing duties, working conditions, training, personal qualifications, earnings, outlook, and ways of measuring one's interest and ability.

* Physician. Chronicle Guidance Publications. 1960. 4p. 35c
  Occupational brief summarizing work performed, working conditions, earnings, personal qualifications, training requirements, opportunities, employment outlook, and entry into the job.

Physician. The Guidance Centre. 1963. 4p. 15c in Canada; 20c elsewhere
  History and growth of the profession, duties, working conditions, qualifications, preparation, remuneration, advantages, disadvantages, how to get started, and related occupations.

**Physician: healer and scientist. Atchley, Dana W. Macmillan Company. 1961. 129p. $3.50
  Discussion of the varieties of specialization, premedical education, medical school training, internship, residency, recompense, and responsibilities of the physician. Lists of medical colleges included.

Physicians. Science Research Associates. 1961. 4p. 35c
  Occupational brief describing nature of work, qualifications needed, training requirements, entering, earnings, advantages, disadvantages, and future outlook.

**Physicians. One section of *Occupational Outlook Handbook*.
  Nature of work, where employed, training, other qualifications, employment outlook, earnings, and working conditions.

Physicians in the department of medicine and surgery. Veterans Administration, Department of Medicine and Surgery. 1962. 4p. Free
  Description of opportunities, training programs, and benefits.

Preparation for medical education: a restudy. Severinghaus, Aura E.; Carman, Harry J.; and Cadbury, William E. McGraw-Hill Book Company. 1961. 404p. $7.95
  An evaluation of the role of the liberal arts college in preparing students for medical school, the book reports the results of the second National Buck Hill Falls Conference on this subject. The five major topics considered are: The total education span, The gifted student, The culminating year, Problems on medical school admissions, and The place of science in premedical education.

**Program materials on medical careers. American Medical Association. 1963. Six leaflets. Free to counselors and librarians
  A kit of materials planned to help the counselor or local medical society provide students with information on the field of medicine. Includes program suggestions, speeches, handbook, and brochures.

Should you be a doctor? Alvarez, Walter C. New York Life Insurance Company. 1959. 12p. Free
  Aimed to encourage parents to prepare for their children's future education. Includes qualities one should possess, cost of training, and advantages.

**So you want to be a doctor. Nourse, Alan E. Harper and Row. Revised 1963. 189p. $3.50; library binding $3.27 net
  A young doctor unravels for high school and college students the details of training for a medical career: costs, courses required, procedure for application to medical schools, courses for each year of medical school, and outlook. Also describes specialized medical careers.

PHYSICIAN—*Continued*

So you want to be a doctor. Changing Times. 1960. 4p. 15c
Reprint surveying prospects, opportunities, training, and preparation for a medical career.

Story behind great medical discoveries. Montgomery, Elizabeth R. Dodd, Mead and Company. 1945. 247p. $3
Biographies of individuals who made medical discoveries such as penicillin, radium, insulin, vaccination, and sulfonamides. Illustrated.

The story of America's medical schools. American Medical Association. No date. 33p. Free
Includes information on preparation for medical study, hospital training and specialization, licensure, and cost of education. List of eighty-three approved medical schools and three schools of basic medical sciences, arranged alphabetically by states.

The woman M.D. Alumnae Advisory Center. 1963. 6p. 25c
Reprint from *Mademoiselle* containing case histories of some successful women physicians.

Your career opportunities in medicine. Novak, Gail, ed. Rowman and Littlefield, Inc. 1962. 64p. 75c
One of the Visual Career Guides, about one half of the contents consists of photographs and charts. Includes description of the various kinds of work, training, and employment outlook. List of medical schools.

Your career opportunities in medicine. Charles Pfizer and Company. 1962. 32p. Free
Illustrated brochure describing qualifications, training, specialization, opportunities, licensure, and what to plan for in high school. Includes list of medical schools.

**Your future as a physician. Kalb, S. William. Richards Rosen Press. 1963. 158p. $2.95
This book contains a discussion of desirable personal qualifications, required high school courses, cost of a medical education, training, internship, license eligibility, and future outlook. Includes a list of eighty approved medical schools in the United States and fifteen outside the country. Suggested reading list.

See *also* Chiropractor; Medical service worker; Ophthalmologist; Optometrist; Osteopathic physician; Pathologist; Podiatrist; Veterinarian

PHYSICIAN'S ASSISTANT 1-32.20

* Medical assistant. Chronicle Guidance Publications. 1961. 4p. 35c
Occupational brief summarizing work performed, working conditions, qualifications, determination of interest and ability, training, opportunities, outlook, methods of entry, and related jobs.

Medical assistants. Science Research Associates. 1961. 4p. 35c
Occupational brief describing work, qualifications, training, earnings, things to consider, related jobs, and outlook. Selected references.

**Physician's assistant. Careers. 1963. 2p. 15c
Career summary for desk-top file. Duties, qualifications, and outlook.

See also Medical secretary

PHYSICIST 0-35.73

Albert A. Michelson: America's first Nobel prize physicist. Wilson, John H., Jr. Julian Messner, Inc. 1958. 192p. $3.25; library binding $3.19 net
Biography of an experimental physicist who proved Einstein's theory of relativity which paved the way for nuclear development.

* Career as a physicist. Institute for Research. 1958. 24p. $1
Duties, qualifications, requirements, and trends. Discusses fields of physics and the nature of research in physics. Illustrated.

**Careers and opportunities in physics. Pollack, Philip. Dutton and Company. 1961. 159p. $3.75
Some chapter headings are: Physics designs the modern world, Electronics, Atomic energy, Optical engineering, Aeronautical research, Power production, Meteorology, and Physics invades other fields. Includes lists of schools and qualifications for a career in physics.

Careers in college physics teaching. American Institute of Physics. 1962. 26p. Free
Five teachers have set forth their views about teaching physics in various types of institutions. Included also is a discussion of need, supply, demand, salaries, supplementary earnings, and preparation.

Careers in health physics through Atomic Energy Commission special fellowships. Oak Ridge Institute of Nuclear Studies. 1962. 26p. Free
Description of the work, training, programs of study at the graduate level, and qualifications for fellowships.

Careers in high-school physics teaching. American Institute of Physics. 1962. 20p. Free
Discussion of duties, education required, demand and supply, salaries, and obtaining a teaching position.

Careers in nuclear science, engineering, and technology in industry. Institute for Research. 1959. 24p. $1
Development of work opportunitites, requirements, training, and attractive and unattractive features.

**Careers in physics. Smith, Alpheus W. and Hole, Winston L. Long's College Book Company. Revised 1960. 310p. $5.95
Discussion of the nature and scope of physics, the opportunities it offers for service to mankind and for a satisfying way of life, and the variety of activities in which physicists may engage. Describes the fields of specialization in fundamental and applied physics as well as interdisciplinary fields of specialization. Includes list of research laboratories having major programs in physics. Selected references.

PHYSICIST—*Continued*

Careers in the field of physics. Angel, Juvenal. World Trade Academy Press. 1962. 30p. $1.25
Includes information about the major fields of specialization, employment opportunities, remuneration, education required, future outlook, and how to finance an education in the field of physics. References for further reading.

Educational requirements for employment of physicists. Veterans Administration in cooperation with Bureau of Labor Statistics. VA Pamphlet Number 7-8.7. Supt. of Documents. 1955. 11p. 15c
Describes the functions, fields of specialization, and types of employment in relation to the level of educational preparation acquired.

**Employment outlook for physical scientists: chemists, physicists, and astronomers. Bureau of Labor Statistics, U.S. Department of Labor. Supt. of Documents. 1964. 16p. 10c
Reprint from the *Occupational Outlook Handbook*.

Explorer of sound: Michael Pupin. Markey, Dorothy. Julian Messner, Inc. 1964. 192p. $3.25; library edition $3.19 net
Biography of the well-known inventor.

Find a career in physics. Schussler, Eileen and Schussler, Ray. Putnam's Sons. 1963. 160p. $2.95
Information about the varied opportunities in this field, special training necessary, rewards, and future outlook. Written for ages 11 to 15.

Health physicist. Careers. 1959. 8p. 25c
Career brief describing work, training, personal qualifications, working conditions, related careers, earnings, outlook, and ways of measuring one's interest and ability.

Health physicist. Chronicle Guidance Publications. 1959. 4p. 35c
Occupational brief summarizing work performed, where employed, qualifications, training, working conditions, earnings, and outlook.

Health physics technician. Careers. 1962. 2p. 15c
Career summary for desk-top file. Duties, qualifications, and outlook.

Health physics technician. Chronicle Guidance Publications. 1959. 4p. 35c
Occupational brief summarizing work performed, where employed, working conditions, qualifications, training, earnings, how to enter, and outlook.

List of colleges and universities offering physics majors. American Institute of Physics. 1962. 4p. Free
List of 695 schools, arranged alphabetically by states, with symbols indicating those offering bachelors, masters, and doctorate degrees.

Michael Faraday: from errand boy to master physicist. Sootin, Harry. Julian Messner, Inc. 1954. 192p. $3.25. Library binding $3.19 net
Biography of the scientist whose experiments led to the development of the dynamo and the electric motor.

Physicist. Group, Vernard. Personnel Services. 1958. 6p. 50c; 25c to students
Occupational abstract describing nature of work, future prospects, qualifications, preparation, entrance and advancement, earnings, number and distribution of workers, and related occupations. Selected references.

* Physicist. Careers. 1963. 8p. 25c
Career brief describing duties, major branches, working conditions, training requirements, personal qualifications, employment prospects, earnings, related careers, measuring one's interest and ability, and suggested high school program.

* Physicist. Chronicle Guidance Publications. 1962. 4p. 35c
Occupational brief summarizing work performed, working conditions, qualifications, training, salaries, opportunities, outlook, methods of entry, and suggested activities. Selected references.

Physicist. The Guidance Centre. 1961. 4p. 15c in Canada; 20c elsewhere
History and importance of the work, qualifications necessary for entry and success, preparation, outlook, remuneration, advantages, disadvantages, and related occupations.

Physicist, assistant. Careers. 1963. 2p. 15c
Career summary for desk-top file. Duties, qualifications, and outlook.

* Physicists. Science Research Associates. 1959. 4p. 35c
Occupational brief describing nature of work, requirements, earnings, where physicists work, advantages, disadvantages, and future outlook.

**Physicists. One section of *Occupational Outlook Handbook.*
Nature of work, where employed, training and other qualifications, employment outlook, earnings and working conditions.

Physics. Manhattan College. No date. 16p. Free
Description of nature and scope of physics, recent advances, training, opportunities, and rewards. One of a series of thirty guidance bulletins.

Physics. Simmons College. 1962. 4p. Free
Discussion of work in research, teaching, and applied research or development; requirements; and opportunities.

Physics and applied physics. Michigan College of Mining and Technology. 1963. 2p. Free
Example of a recruiting leaflet describing work, qualifications, educational requirements, and employment opportunities.

**Physics as a career. American Institute of Physics. 1960. 24p. Free
Includes nature of work, training, and opportunities in industry, in teaching, and in the Federal Government. Explains opportunities in such newer specializations as nuclear physics, solid-state physics, and the electronics and communications areas of applied physics.

Physics as a career. Boston University. 1962. 22p. Free
Recruiting booklet describing opportunities, training, and current research in physics.

PHYSICIST—*Continued*

Physics technicians. Science Research Associates. 1963. 4p. 35c
> Occupational brief describing nature of work, training, qualifications, opportunities, and outlook. Selected references.

Planning for graduate study in physics. American Institute of Physics. 1960. 16p. Free
> Discussion of choice of an undergraduate program which will provide the background for graduate study, selection of college, applying for admission and for financial aid, and some procedures in graduate study.

Rewarding careers for women in physics. American Institute of Physics. 1962. 20p. Free
> Includes discussion of opportunities that are offered to women and the problems they face in becoming physicists. Descriptions of biophysics, astrophysics, and communications suggest areas of work. Includes a distribution of salary by type of employer and level of education.

Should you be a physicist? Compton, Arthur H. New York Life Insurance Company. 1960. 12p. Free
> Description of the challenges ahead, ned for advanced education, rewards, and satisfactions.

**So you want to be a physicist. Nourse, Alan E. Harper and Row. 1963. 183p. $3.50; library binding $3.27 net
> Considers the expanding areas in experimental work and applied physics, training, responsibilities, and rewards. Describes the qualities of personality needed and the education of the modern physicist.

Why should you study physics in high school? American Institute of Physics. 1962. 16p. Free
> Case histories showing that physics is a help in many careers.

See also Atom energy industry worker; Scientist

PHYSIOLOGIST   0-35.13; 0-35.27

**A career in physiology—your challenge and opportunity. American Physiological Society. 1960. 36p. Free
> An illustrated brochure describing nature of work, the specialization within the profession, places of employment, training, opportunities, rewards, and outlook.

PIPE FITTER   5-30.000 through 5-30.499

Finding out about pipe fitters. Science Research Associates. 1964. 4p. 35c
> Junior occupational brief containing some concise facts about the job and listing ways of finding out about the nature of the work.

Steamfitter. Chronicle Guidance Publications. 1964. 4p. 35c
> Occupational brief describing nature of work, qualifications, working conditions, opportunities for promotion, and outlook.

Steam fitters and pipe fitters. Michigan Employment Security Commission. 1956. 16p. 25c

> Introduction, nature of work, working conditions, location of jobs, employment outlook, earnings, qualifications for entry, organizations, advantages, and disadvantages.

See also Plumber

PLANER OPERATOR 4-33.461

Job description for planer operator IV. U.S. Employment Service, U.S. Department of Labor. Supt. of Documents. 1948. 5p. 5c

> Occupational guide. Job summary, work performed, training, trainee-selection factors, related occupations, physical activities, working conditions, hazards, and employment variables.

PLANT PATHOLOGIST 0-35.26

Agriculture. Pages 243-7 of *The College Girl Looks Ahead.*

> Opportunities for women in work with plants and animals.

* Careers in plant pathology. American Phytopathological Society. 1959. 12p. Free

> Description of fields of work, preparation, getting started, and rewards.

* Plant pathologist. Careers. 1959. 2p. 15c

> Career summary for desk-top file. Duties, qualifications, and outlook.

Plant science as a profession. Zuck, Robert K. Mrs. F. G. Brooks. 1949. 5p. 25c

> Nature of work and opportunities. Reprint from *Bios, A Journal of Biology.*

PLASTERER 5-29.

Careers in plastering and cement finishing. B'nai B'rith Vocational Service. 1954. 8p. 35c

> Nature of work, preparation, advantages, and disadvantages.

**Employment outlook for plasterers, lathers, and cement masons. Bureau of Labor Statistics, U.S. Department of Labor. Supt. of Documents. 1964. 20p. 15c

> Reprint from the *Occupational Outlook Handbook.*

Finding out about plasterers. Science Research Associates. 1963. 4p. 35c

> Junior occupational brief containing some concise facts about the job and listing ways of finding out about the nature of the work. Includes suggestions for reading and a list of other occupational briefs on related topics.

Plasterer. Van Den Branden, F. Research Publishing Company. 1957. 16p. $1.50

> Advantages of plastering as a trade, number engaged in occupation, working conditions, qualifications, how to secure an apprenticeship, and chances for promotion.

PLASTERER—*Continued*

Plasterer. Careers. 1959. 2p. 15c
Career summary for desk-top file. Duties, qualifications, and outlook.

* Plasterer. Chronicle Guidance Publications. 1964. 4p. 35c
Occupational brief summarizing work performed, working conditions, hours, earnings, personal qualifications, training requirements, opportunities, employment outlook, and entry into the job.

Plasterer. The Guidance Centre. 1962. 4p. 15c in Canada; 20c elsewhere
History and nature of work, conditions of work, preparation, qualifications, advancement, advantages, disadvantages, how to get started, and related occupations.

Plasterer. Michigan Employment Security Commission. 1956. 18p. 25c
Introduction, nature of work, distribution of jobs, employment prospects, working conditions, organizations, qualifications for entry, earnings, advantages, and disadvantages.

* Plasterers. Science Research Associates. 1963. 4p. 35c
Occupational brief describing nature of work, training, wages, getting started and advancing, advantages, disadvantages, and future outlook.

* Plasterers. One section of *Occupational Outlook Handbook.*
Nature of work, where employed, training, other qualifications, advancement, employment outlook, earnings, and working conditions.

Plastering contractor. B'nai B'rith Vocational Service. 1955. 8p. 35c
Discussion of nature of work, abilities and entry requirements, starting one's own business, earnings, outlook, advantages, and disadvantages.

PLASTICS INDUSTRY WORKER   4, 6, 8-51.400 through 4, 6, 8-51.599

Engineering education in plastics. Society of Plastics Engineers. 1961. 10p. Free
Description of specialized training desirable for an engineering career in the plastics industry, including two introductory courses to supply broad coverage of the field and four more highly specialized courses.

**Opportunities in plastics. Dearle, Denis A. Vocational Guidance Manuals. 1963. 128p. $1.45 paper
Includes a history of plastic materials, description of the plastics industry and jobs in its various branches, qualifications, outlook for jobs, the future of the industry, getting started, and wage rates and salaries. Contains lists of plastic material manufacturers, custom molders and extruders, and colleges offering plastics study.

Plastics as an engineering career. Society of Plastics Engineers. 1961. 8p. Free
History and development of the plastics industry, training, opportunities, and outlook.

* Plastics industry workers. Science Research Associates. 1961. 4p. 35c
Occupational brief describing kinds of work, requirements, training, getting started, earnings, advantages, disadvantages, and future outlook.

Plastics—the story of an industry. Society of the Plastics Industry, Inc. 1962. 40p. Free
Includes a list of colleges offering instruction in plastics.

PLAYWRIGHT 0-06.05

* Playwright. Careers. 1963. 2p. 15c
Career summary for desk-top file. Duties, qualifications, and outlook.

* Playwrights. Science Research Associates. 1961. 4p. 35c
Occupational brief describing the work, training, getting started, rewards, and outlook. Selected references.

See also Writer

PLUMBER 5-30.200 through 5-30.299

Careers in plumbing and heating contracting. B'nai B'rith Vocational Service. 1954. 8p. 35c
Discussion of training, qualifications, getting an apprenticeship, and types of contractors.

* Careers in plumbing and plumbing contracting. Institute for Research. 1961. 24p. $1
History and development, personal qualifications, opportunities, earnings, apprenticeship, union training, and training in the nonunion field. Includes work of journeyman and contractor.

**Employment outlook for plumbers and pipefitters. Bureau of Labor Statistics, U.S. Department of Labor. Supt. of Documents. 1964. 16p. 10c
Reprint from the *Occupational Outlook Handbook*.

Plumber apprentice. California State Department of Employment. 1961. 4p. Single copy free
Nature of apprenticeship, duties, working conditions, wages, hours, entrance requirements, promotion, training, and employment outlook in California.

* Plumber (construction). Chronicle Guidance Publications. 1962. 4p. 35c
Occupational brief containing definition, history, work performed, working conditions, personal requirements, training requirements, training opportunities, outlook, where employed, methods of entry, related jobs, and suggested activities.

Plumber. The Guidance Centre. 1959. 4p. 15c in Canada; 20c elsewhere
Nature of work, qualifications, training, working conditions, outlook, earnings, advantages, disadvantages, and related occupations.

* Plumbers and pipe fitters. Science Research Associates. 1959. 4p. 35c
Occupational brief describing nature of work, requirements, training, earnings, advantages, disadvantages, and future outlook.

**Plumbers and pipefitters. One section of *Occupational Outlook Handbook*.
Nature of work, where employed, training, other qualifications, advancement, employment outlook, earnings, and working conditions.

PLUMBER—*Continued*

Plumbers and pipefitters (construction). Careers. 1959. 8p. 25c
    Career brief describing duties, working conditions, training, personal quali-
fications, earnings, unionization, and outlook. Additional readings.

Plumbing. Group, Vernard. Personnel Services. 1950. 6p. 50c; 25c to
    students
    Occupational abstract. Nature of work, future prospects, qualifications,
preparation, earnings, number and distribution of workers, unions, advantages,
disadvantages, and related occupations.

Plumbing occupations. Michigan Employment Security Commission. 1954.
    17p. 25c
    Introduction, nature of work, distribution of jobs, employment prospects,
working conditions, organizations, earnings, qualifications for entry, disadvantages, and advantages.

PODIATRIST   0-39.901

A career in health—podiatry (chiropody). American Podiatry Association.
    1959. 5p. Single copies free
    Reprint from *Health* containing history of chiropody, opportunities, quali-
fications, training, specialties, earnings, and satisfactions.

Chiropodist (podiatrist). Careers. 1958. 2p. 15c
    Career summary for desk-top file. Duties, qualifications, and outlook.

**Employment outlook for podiatrists. Bureau of Labor Statistics, U.S. De-
    partment of Labor. Supt. of Documents. 1964. 4p. 5c
    Reprint from the *Occupational Outlook Handbook*.

If you're planning a professional career. American Podiatry Association.
    No date. 4p. Single copies free
    Why podiatrists are needed, earnings, hours, satisfactions, opportunities, and
requirements for a degree. Includes list of five approved schools for training.

Podiatrist. Splaver, Sarah. Personnel Services. 1964. 6p. 50c; 25c to stu-
    dents
    Occupational abstract. Nature of work, qualifications, preparation, entrance,
advancement, earnings, supply and demand, advantages, and disadvantages.

Podiatrist. California State Department of Employment. 1961. 6p. Single
    copy free
    Nature of work, duties, working conditions, income, hours, entrance require-
ments, promotion, training, and employment outlook in California.

Podiatrist. Chronicle Guidance Publications. 1960. 4p. 35c
    Occupational brief summarizing work performed, working conditions, per-
sonal qualifications, training requirements, opportunities, employment outlook,
and suggested activities.

Podiatrist (chiropodist). Careers. 1963. 2p. 15c
    Career summary for desk-top file. Describes duties, working conditions,
qualifications, training, and outlook.

Podiatrist (chiropodist). The Guidance Centre. 1958. 4p. 15c in Canada; 20c elsewhere

History and importance, nature of work, qualifications, working conditions, preparation, remuneration, advancement, outlook, related occupations, and how to get started.

Podiatrist-chiropodist. Michigan Employment Security Commission. 1962. 12p. 25c

Introduction, nature of work, location of jobs, working conditions, earnings, employment outlook, requirements for entry, disadvantages, and advantages.

Podiatrists. Science Research Associates. 1963. 4p. 35c

Occupational brief describing nature of work, training, qualifications, opportunities, advantages, disadvantages, and future outlook. Two illustrations. Selected references.

**Podiatrists. One section of *Occupational Outlook Handbook*.

Nature of work, where employed, training, other qualificattions, advancement, employment outlook, earnings, and working conditions.

**Podiatry (chiropody) as a career. Belleau, Wilfrid. Park Publishing House. 1963. 27p. 75c

Nature of work, types of practice, training, qualifications, licensure, entering the field, conditions of work, a typical day's work, income, opportunities, and disadvantages. Discussion of opportunities for women. Geographical distribution and ratio of chiropodists to population by states and large cities. Bibliography.

POLICE OFFICER   2-66.01

Behind the silver shield. Floherty, John J. J. B. Lippincott Company. Revised 1957. 208p. $4

Description of work of police officer, detective, and patrolman. Includes qualifications, training, and advancement. Sixteen illustrations.

Careers in law enforcement. Angel, Juvenal. World Trade Academy Press. 1962. 26p. $1.25

Includes information about each of several specialties within this field.

**Careers in the protective services. Chamberlin, Jo Hubbard. Henry Z. Walck, Inc. 1963. 100p. $3.50

Presenting a view of this growing career field, this book describes the range of work in the various services, the qualifications, and training required. The field includes police and detectives; fire fighters; guards, watchmen, and doorkeepers; the investigative agents of the Treasury, the Department of Justice, and other Government agencies; and county sheriffs, marshals, constables, and bailiffs.

Careers with state and county highway police departments. Institute for Research. 1960. 23p. $1

Description of various positions, a typical day's work, qualifications, training, earnings, attractive and unattractive features, and getting started.

POLICE OFFICER—*Continued*

Colleges offering training for policemen. International Association of Chiefs of Police. 1962. 5p. Free

List of eighty colleges with indications of departments offering training, degrees, and majors in law enforcement, corrections, or criminalistics.

The delinquent and the law. Brecher, Ruth and Brecher, Edward. Public Affairs Committee. 1962. 28p. 25c

A discussion of the role of the police, the court, and the community in dealing with the problem of juvenile delinquency. Contains a description of the varied ways in which the police carry out their job.

**Employment outlook for policemen and firemen. Bureau of Labor Statistics, U.S. Department of Labor. Supt. of Documents. 1964. 12p. 10c

Reprint from the *Occupational Outlook Handbook*.

Fingerprint classifier. Careers. 1963. 2p. 15c

Career summary for desk-top file. Duties, qualifications, and outlook.

I want to be a policeman. Greene, Carla. Childrens Press. 1958. 32p. $2

Prepared for beginning readers with a reading level of upper first grade. Illustrated in color.

**Joan Palmer, policewoman. Schimmel, Gertrude. Dodd, Mead and Company. 1960. 256p. $3

Career fiction. Interwoven in this story is a picture of the work, adventure, opportunities, and rewarding service of a policewoman.

**John Benton, rookie policeman. Connors, Thomas and Glaser, Paul. Dodd, Mead and Company. 1957. 288p. $3

Career fiction. Interwoven in this story of the experiences of a policeman are descriptions of the grueling training period and other career information. Both authors are members of the New York City Police Department.

Opportunities in law enforcement (municipal). O'Connor, John J. Vocational Guidance Manuals. 1955. 96p. $1.45

Description of duties of city policemen, conditions of employment, salary ranges, qualifications, and women in law enforcement.

Police. Science Research Associates. 1960. 4p. 35c

Occupational brief describing nature of work, training, qualifications, opportunities, advantages, disadvantages, and future outlook.

**Police and crime prevention work as a career. Institute for Research. 1957. 32p. $1

History, job opportunities, number of workers, qualifications, training, and attractive and unattractive features.

Police officer. Personnel Services. 1958. 6p. 50c; 25c to students

Occupational abstract. Nature of work, qualifications, preparation, advancement, earnings, number and distribution of workers, advantages, disadvantages, and prospects. Also qualifications for position of policewoman.

Police officers. Michigan Employment Security Commission. 1955. 24p. 25c
Introduction, nature of work, location of jobs, employment prospects, working conditions, earnings, qualifications for entry, disadvantages, and advantages.

Police: the work, equipment and training. Colby, C. B. Coward-McCann, Inc. 1954. 48p. Library edition $2.52 net
Photographs and brief text reveal the work of law-enforcement officers. Written for grades 4 to 8.

* Policeman. Careers. 1964. 2p. 15c
Career summary for desk-top file. Duties, qualifications, and outlook.

Policeman (municipal). The Guidance Centre. 1958. 4p. 15c in Canada; 20c elsewhere
History and importance, nature of work, qualifications, working conditions, preparation, remuneration, advancement, outlook, related occupations, and how to get started.

**Policeman-policewoman. Chronicle Guidance Publications. 1961. 4p. 35c
Occupational brief summarizing work performed, employment conditions, determination of aptitudes and interests, training, opportunities, and employment outlook.

Policeman-policewoman. International Association of Chiefs of Police. No date. 4p. Free
Statement of duties and responsibilities, employment conditions, requirements, education needed, personal attributes, and residency requirements.

Policeman (Provincial police). The Guidance Centre. 1960. 4p. 15c in Canada; 20c elsewhere
History and importance, nature of work, qualifications for entry and success, working conditions, preparation, earnings, advancement, outlook, related occupations, and how to get started.

Policeman (Royal Canadian Mounted Police). The Guidance Centre. 1962. 4p. 15c in Canada; 20c elsewhere
Nature of work, qualifications, preparation, opportunities for advancement, how to get started, advantages, and disadvantages.

**Policemen. One section of *Occupational Outlook Handbook*.
Nature of work, where employed, training, other qualifications, advancement, employment outlook, earnings, and working conditions.

Policewoman. Science Research Associates. 1961. 4p. 35c
Occupational brief describing work, qualifications, training, earnings, advancement, and outlook. Selected references.

Policewoman; a young woman's initiation into the realities of justice. Uhnak, Dorothy. Simon and Schuster, Inc. 1964. 251p. $4.50
Includes typical episodes based on ten years of experience with the New York City Transit Police Department. Describes police work as a social service and pays respect to dedicated officers.

POLICE OFFICER—*Continued*

Royal Canadian mounted police. Neuberger, Richard L. Random House, Inc. 1953. 182p. $1.95
This book includes the varied character of duties and the differences in training from that of regular policemen. Illustrated.

Should you go into law enforcement? Hoover, J. Edgar. New York Life Insurance Company. 1961. 12p. Free
Nature of work, demands, rewards, character requirements, salary, and outlook.

**Squad room detective. Glaser, Paul. Dodd, Mead and Company. 1960. 288p. $3
Career fiction. Story of the experiences of a police officer whose capable work in law enforcement earned for him appointment as a detective. The author writes from twenty years' experience as a policeman in New York City and is co-author of *John Benton, Rookie Policeman.*

The story of the Secret Service. Kuhn, Ferdinand. Random House, Inc. 1957. 188p. $1.95
An account of the origin of the service, what it does, and a collection of case histories illustrating its accomplishments.

Troopers all. Floherty, John J. Lippincott Company. 1954. 160p. $3.95
Accounts of the state police and the many facets of their activities. Illustrated.

What does a policeman do? Johnston, Johanna and Harris, Martin. Dodd, Mead and Company. 1959. 56p. $2.50
Simple text and pictures portray varied activities of the police force. Written for grades 3 to 7.

**Your future in law enforcement. Gammage, Allen. Richards Rosen Press. 1961. 159p. $2.95
Police work is described as not only an exciting career but one that challenges those who want to make tomorrow's world a better one.

See also Detective; FBI agent

POLITICAL SCIENTIST 0-36.96

Political science at M.I.T. Massachusetts Institute of Technology. 1962. 24p. Free
Illustrated brochure describing graduate and undergraduate study at M.I.T. and the outlook for professional opportunities for graduates.

**Political scientist. Careers. 1962. 8p. 25c
Career brief describing history, work performed, working conditions, salaries, personal qualifications, determination of aptitudes and interest, training requirements, promotional opportunities, outlook, and possibilities for women. Additional references.

* Political scientist. Chronicle Guidance Publications. 1961. 4p. 35c
Occupational brief summarizing work performed, requirements, training, opportunities, where employed, related jobs, and outlook.

**Political scientists. One section of *Occupational Outlook Handbook*.
  Nature of work, where employed, training, other qualifications, and employment outlook.

  See also Politician

POLITICIAN   0-36.; 0-83.; 0-94.

Breaking into politics. Charles, Barbara B. Alumnae Advisory Center. 1956. 6p. 25c
  Mademoiselle reprint describing jobs and futures for women in politics.

Diary of democracy: the story of political parties in America. Neal, Harry Edward. Julian Messner, Inc. 1962. 192p. $3.95. Library binding $3.64 net
  Account of the rise and fall of political parties in terms of important persons, issues, and events in American political history. Has relevance for those interested in seeking political office.

**Employment outlook for social scientists. Bureau of Labor Statistics, U.S. Department of Labor. Supt. of Documents. 1964. 15p. 10c
  Reprint from the *Occupational Outlook Handbook*.

Herbert Hoover, engineer, humanitarian, statesman. McGee, D. H. Dodd, Mead and Company. 1959. 308p. $3.50
  Biography revealing many fascinating events and achievements in the life of Herbert Hoover.

Jobs in politics. Alumnae Advisory Center. 1964. 8p. 25c
  Reprint from *Mademoiselle* containing case histories of several successful women in politics.

Law and politics. Pages 178-82 of *Vocations for Boys*.
  Includes qualities necessary, training, and opportunities.

Political scientist. Careers. 1962. 4p. 35c
  Occupational brief describing nature of work, training, qualifications, opportunities, and outlook.

* Political workers. Science Research Associates. 1961. 4p. 35c
  Occupational brief describing nature of work, methods of getting started, requirements, advantages, disadvantages, and future outlook.

Politicians and what they do. Botter, David. Franklin Watts, Inc. 1960. 213p. $3.95
  Includes duties of persons holding varied political jobs, personal qualifications, and training. For grades 7 to 11.

Politics as a career. Institute for Research. 1962. 24p. $1
  Describes work in public office and with political parties.

What it means to be a politician. Bullitt, Stimson. Doubleday and Company. 1961. 215p. 95c
  An experienced lawyer who has been active in politics describes the nature of the work as a politician and the many involvements forced upon him.

POLITICIAN—*Continued*

Women of the 88th Congress. Women's Bureau, U.S. Department of Labor. 1963. 29p. Free
Biographical sketches of the thirteen women of the Eighty-eighth Congress of the United States, of whom two are in the Senate and eleven are in the House of Representatives.

Young John Kennedy. Schoor, Gene. Harcourt, Brace and World. 1963. 253p. $3.95
Biography from boyhood to his election, including excerpts from letters and journals. Illustrated. Written for grades 6 to 10.

See also Political Scientist

PORTER   2-86.; 2-91.

Porters. Science Research Associates. 1963. 4p. 35c
Occupational brief describing nature of work, training, qualifications, opportunities, and outlook.

**Pullman porters and passenger attendants. One section of *Occupational Outlook Handbook*.
Nature of work, training, other qualifications, advancement, employment outlook, earnings, and working conditions.

Redcaps. One section of *Occupational Outlook Handbook*.
Nature of work, training, other qualifications, advancement, employment outlook, earnings, and working conditions.

POST OFFICE CLERK   1-27.

* Careers in the United States Postal Service. Institute for Research. 1964. 24p. $1
Origin and history of the postal service, types of positions, and how to get started. Duties, earnings, opportunities, typical day's work, and attractive and unattractive features are given for each of the following: post office clerk, mail carrier, rural mail carrier, post office inspector, postmaster of various grades, railway postal clerk, and clerk of sea post or ocean mail service.

**Employment outlook in post office occupations. Bureau of Labor Statistics, U.S. Department of Labor. Supt. of Documents. 1964. 16p. 10c
Reprint from the *Occupational Outlook Handbook*.

Post office clerk. Chronicle Guidance Publications. 1963. 4p. 35c
Occupational brief summarizing work performed, working conditions, hours, earnings, personal qualifications, training requirements, opportunities, employment outlook, and entry into the job.

**Post office occupations. One section of *Occupational Outlook Handbook*.
Occupations in the postal service, employment outlook, earnings, and working conditions. Specific information is given concerning mail carrier and postal clerk.

Postal clerk. Careers. 1963. 2p. 15c
Career summary for desk-top file. Duties, qualifications, and outlook.

**Postal clerks. One section of *Occupational Outlook Handbook*.
  Nature of work, qualifications, training, advancement, employment outlook,
  earnings, and working conditions.

Postal employees. Chronicle Guidance Publications. 1961. 8p. 50c
  Occupational brief describing various jobs, hours, earnings, requirements,
  opportunities, advantages, disadvantages, and outlook.

Postal workers. Science Research Associates. 1959. 4p. 35c
  Occupational brief describing nature of work, training, qualifications, opportunities, advantages, disadvantages, and future outlook.

POULTRY FARMER   3-08.

Find your career in the poultry industry. Interstate Printers and Publishers.
  No date. 47p. 25c
  Discussion of personnel needed, preparation, opportunities, and nature of
  work in various branches of poultry husbandry.

* Opportunities in the poultry industry. Hough, John W. Vocational Guidance Manuals. 1960. 100p. $1.45 paper
  Discussion of the size and importance of the industry, job prospects, job
  classifications, training, earnings, and future outlook.

* Poultry farm manager. Chronicle Guidance Publications. 1963. 4p. 35c
  Occupational brief summarizing work performed, requirements, earnings,
  methods of entry, and outlook.

Poultry farmer. Robinson, H. Alan. Personnel Services. 1955. 6p. 50c; 25c
  to students
  Occupational abstract. Nature of work, future prospects, qualifications,
  preparation, entrance and advancement, number and distribution of workers,
  earnings, advantages, and disadvantages.

Poultry farmer. Careers. 1960. 2p. 15c
  Career summary for desk-top file. Duties, qualifications, and outlook.

Poultry farming as a career. Institute for Research. 1958. 20p. $1
  History, typical day's work, earnings, how to get started, attractive and unattractive features, and factors that make for success.

The poultry industry. Jasper, A. William. Bellman Publishing Company.
  1958. 36p. $1
  Scope of the poultry industry, capsule job descriptions, opportunities, qualifications, remuneration, advantages, disadvantages, and outlook for the future.
  Bibliography.

Poultryman. The Guidance Centre. 1961. 15c in Canada; 20c elsewhere
  Definition, requirements, employment and advancement, earnings, and related
  occupations.

* Poultrymen. Science Research Associates. 1960. 4p. 35c
  Occupational brief describing nature of work, preparation, opportunities,
  advantages, disadvantages, and future outlook.

POWER-SHOVEL OPERATOR　　　5-73.210

Job description for power-shovel operator. U.S. Employment Service, U.S.
Department of Labor. Supt. of Documents. 1948. 6p. 5c
　　Occupational guide. Job summary, work performed, training, related occupa-
　　tions, physical activities, working conditions and hazards.

POWER TRUCK OPERATOR　　　7-88.410; 7-88.412

Electric-truck operator. Careers. 1962. 2p. 15c
　　Career summary for desk-top file. Duties, qualifications, and outlook.

Finding out about power truck operators. Science Research Associates. 1963.
4p. 35c
　　Junior occupational brief containing brief facts about the job.

Power truck operators. Science Research Associates. 1964. 4p. 35c
　　Occupational brief describing work, qualifications, opportunities, and outlook.

**Power truck operators. One section of *Occupational Outlook Handbook.*
　　Nature of work, where employed, training, employment outlook, earnings,
　　and working conditions.

PRACTICAL NURSE　　　2-38.20

Career as a practical nurse. Institute for Research. 1962. 24p. $1
　　Description of work, personal qualifications, education and training, typical
　　day's work, attractive and unattractive features, earnings, opportunities, chances
　　for advancement, and list of schools approved by state boards of nurse examin-
　　ers or other accrediting authorities.

**Employment outlook for registered professional nurses and licensed prac-
　　tical nurses. Bureau of Labor Statistics, U.S. Department of Labor. Supt.
　　of Documents. 1962. 8p. 10c
　　Reprint from the *Occupational Outlook Handbook.*

Guides for developing curricula for the education of practical nurses. Vo-
　　cational and Technical Education Division, U.S. Office of Education.
　　Supt. of Documents. 1959. 165p. 60c
　　Prepared for instructors and supervisors of training courses. Includes the role
　　of the practical nurse, qualifications, and training.

Let's be practical about a nursing career. Committee on Careers, National
　　League for Nursing. 1963. 40p. 10c
　　Describes how to become a licensed practical nurse. Lists all state-approved
　　schools of practical nursing, together with prenursing academic requirements
　　for licensure in each state and admission policies of individual schools on men,
　　married students, and nonwhite students. Published annually.

* Licensed practical nurses. Science Research Associates. 1961. 4p. 35c
　　Occupational brief describing nature of work, requirements, training, getting
　　started, salaries, advantages, disadvantages, and future outlook.

The nurse everyone needs. Clark, Marguerite. Public Affairs Committee. 1963. 28p. 25c

Tracing the development of the practical nurse from an untrained low-paid attendant to one who today is trained and licensed, the author describes the current training program, requirements, and the increasing professional recognition.

Practical nurse. Splaver, Sarah. Personnel Services. 1955. 6p. 50c; 25c to students

Occupational abstract. Nature of work, qualifications, preparation, entrance, supply and demand, opportunities for servicemen, earnings, advantages, and disadvantages.

Practical nurse. Careers. 1960. 8p. 25c

Career brief describing duties, working conditions, training, personal qualifications, places of employment, earnings, and advancement prospects.

* Practical nurse. Chronicle Guidance Publications. 1961. 4p. 35c

Occupational brief summarizing work performed, employment conditions, earnings, qualifications, determination of aptitudes and interests, training requirements, opportunities, outlook, opportunities for men, and related jobs.

The practical nurse. National Association for Practical Nurse Education and Service. 1963. 2p. Free

Information on duties, qualifications, preparation, opportunities and salaries.

**Practical nurses and auxiliary nursing workers. One section of Occupational Handbook.

Nature of work, where employed, training, other qualifications, employment outlook, and earnings.

Practical nursing in the Veterans Administration. Veterans Administration, Department of Medicine and Surgery. 1963. 12p. Free

Description of work, training program, qualifications, and benefits.

Team mates—what is the difference between professional and practical nursing? Which should I choose? Committee on Careers in Nursing, National League for Nursing. 1960. 4p. 1c

Describes the work and training of both.

Trained practical nurse. Torrop, H. M. Research Publishing Company. 1954. 32p. $1

Nature of work, preparation, qualifications, licensing, opportunities, and typical places of employment.

PRIEST   0-08.10

The Catholic priest: his training and ministry. Engeman, Jack. Lothrop, Lee and Shepard Company. 1961. 128p. $3.50

More than 250 photographs, with informative text and captions, describe the training for the priesthood and the way of life in a Catholic seminary.

**Employment outlook for Roman Catholic priests. Bureau of Labor Statistics, U.S. Department of Labor. Supt. of Documents. 1964. 8p. 5c

Reprint from the Occupational Outlook Handbook.

PRIEST—*Continued*

**Roman Catholic priests. One section of *Occupational Outlook Handbook*.
Nature of work, where employed, training, other qualifications, advancement,
employment outlook, earnings, and working conditions.

See also Clergyman; Religious worker

PRINCIPAL   0-31.10

Secondary school principal. Chronicle Guidance Publications. 1963. 4p.
35c
Occupational brief summarizing duties, requirements, entrance, advancement,
and outlook.

PRINTING AND PUBLISHING INDUSTRY WORKER
0-06.40 through 0-06.99; 4, 6-44. through 4, 6-49.

Anna-Marie. Dehkes, Evelyn. Abelard-Schuman. 1960. 192p. $3
Career fiction. Set in Norway at the turn of the century, this is a story of
a girl whose father wanted her to be a maid but who learned typesetting and
helped a friend become a journalist.

Bibliography of guidance publications in the field of graphic arts. Graphic
Arts Industry. 1959. 4p. Free
List of thirty publications.

Book publishing. Bechtold, Grace. Bellman Publishing Co. 1946. 24p. $1
Kinds of publishing, qualifications, remuneration, opportunities, chances of
advancement, allied fields, and future outlook.

Bookbinders and related workers. One section of *Occupational Outlook
Handbook*.
Nature of work, training and other qualifications, employment outlook, earn-
ings, and working conditions.

Bowker lectures on book publishing. R. R. Bowker Company. 1957. 389p.
$5
Seventeen lectures on various phases of book publishing. One chapter by
Edward Weeks traces his publishing career from first reader to editor-in-chief.

Business careers in newspaper publishing. Institute for Research. 1962. 24p.
$1
Development of modern newspaper business; description of work in circulation, promotion, advertising, and research; qualifications; training; list of
thirty-four schools offering professional training in journalism, typical day's
work, and attractive and unattractive features.

* Career as a printer—the printing business. Institute for Research. 1958.
24p. $1
Types of jobs, requirements, training, earnings, and attractive and unattractive features.

* Career opportunities in the printing industry. Graphic Arts Industry. 1962. 32p. Free
  Illustrated brochure including importance of the printing industry, kinds of work, advantages, and opportunities.

Careers in printing. Angel, Juvenal. World Trade Academy Press. 1957. 26p. $1.25
  Includes description of work, training, opportunities, remuneration, and future outlook.

* Careers in publishing. Angel, Juvenal L. World Trade Academy Press. 1957. 25p. $1.25
  Description of duties, responsibilities, working conditions, training, salary, and employment opportunities. Occupations included are editor, book designer, publicity and promotion head, proofreader, typesetter, linotype operator, photo-engraver, bookbinder, and others.

Careers in the publishing field. Institute for Research. 1957. 24p. $1
  Qualifications, training, salaries, advantages, and disadvantages. Describes work in a book publishing firm and on a newspaper. Information concerning workers in the business management, correspondence, editorial, art, accounting, advertising, sales, manufacturing, and shipping departments.

Careers with magazine and periodical publishing companies. Institute for Research. 1961. 24p. $1
  Description of various positions, a typical week's work, qualifications, training, earnings, outlook, and how to get started.

Compositors, typesetters and printing pressmen. Science Research Associates. 1961. 4p. 35c
  Occupational brief describing various kinds of work, requirements, earnings, getting started and advancing, advantages, disadvantages, and future outlook.

**Employment outlook in printing occupations. Bureau of Labor Statistics, U.S. Department of Labor. Supt. of Documents. 1964. 20p. 15c
  Reprint from the *Occupational Outlook Handbook*.

Exploring your future in graphic arts and publishing. American Liberty Press. 1963. 120p. $5; paper $4
  One page is devoted to each of ninety-five jobs, presenting the duties, requirements for entering, promotional outlook, and the pay and skill level. An organizational chart for the industry also is available.

Job descriptions for compositor, linotype operator, lithographer, photo-engraver, and pressman. California State Department of Employment. 1962. 4p. Single copy free
  Occupational guide summarizing duties, employment prospects, earnings, requirements for entry, and suggestions for locating a job.

Jobs and futures in book publishing. Melcher, Daniel. Alumnae Advisory Center. 1952. 5p. 25c
  Reprint from *Mademoiselle* describing typical jobs, how to begin, salaries, warnings, and case histories of three women who succeeded in the publishing business.

PRINTING AND PUBLISHING INDUSTRY WORKER—*Continued*

**Jobs in publishing. Science Research Associates. 1960. 32p. $1
> Describes the variety of job prospects and opportunities within this field. An accompanying wall chart is available for 35c.

Jobs in the printing trade. Careers. 1960. 8p. 25c
> Career brief describing nature of work, working conditions, training, personal qualifications, earnings, and outlook.

Management career opportunities in the graphic arts. American Book-Stratford Press. No date. 5p. Free
> One of a series of articles about printing and the graphic arts industry.

Manual for use by local Graphic Arts Industry Education Advisory Committees. Graphic Arts Industry, Inc. 1955. 20p. Free
> Suggestions for cooperation between schools and local committees.

Opportunities in the printing trade. Boughal, Patrick. Vocational Guidance Manuals. 1950. 112p. $1.45 paper
> History of printing, opportunities in the trade, educational preparation, and a description of work.

Printer. The Guidance Centre. 1961. 4p. 15c in Canada; 20c elsewhere
> Nature of work, qualifications, training, working conditions, opportunities for advancement, wages, how to get started, advantages and disadvantages.

**Printing (graphic arts) occupations. One chapter of *Occupational Outlook Handbook.*
> Discussion of nature and location of the industry, kinds of jobs, training, other qualifications, employment outlook, earnings, and working conditions. Specific information is given for each of the following: composing room occupations, photoengraver, electrotyper, printing pressman, lithographer, and bookbinder.

The printing industry. Chapter 30 in *Occupations and Careers.*
> Information concerning jobs in the composing room, pressroom, and bindery.

Scholarships offered by the graphic arts industry. Graphic Arts Industry. 1962. 15p. Free
> Information arranged by states.

Should you go into the printing industry? Walling, William H. New York Life Insurance Company. 1960. 12p. Free
> Importance of printing, kinds of work, outlook, opportunities, earnings, and advantages.

**So you want to get into book publishing—the jobs, the pay, and how to start. Melcher, Daniel. R. R. Bowker Company. Revised 1962. 16p. 25c
> Advice about preparation, getting facts about book publishing, opportunities, job hunting, getting ahead on the job, and description of editorial and non-editorial work. List of books for further reading.

The truth about publishing. Unwin, Sir Stanley. Macmillan Company. Revised 1960. 350p. $3.50
> Basic and readable information, written from the British point of view.

What happens in book publishing. Grannis, Chandler B., ed. Columbia University Press. 1957. 414p. $6.50

> A detailed account of the process of publishing a book.

Your career in printing. Printing Industries of Metropolitan New York, Inc. 1957. 26p. $1

> Illustrated booklet describing nature of work, qualifications, and opportunities in the printing industry. Excellent pictures of people at work and excellent typography.

Your career in printing and the graphic arts. Graphic Arts Industry. 1963. 28p. Free

> A compilation of twelve articles from the official publication of the Milwaukee Advertising Club describing twelve jobs. Includes a list of colleges offering graphic arts courses and a list of technical institutes offering a two-year program.

Your career opportunities in printing. Novak, Gail, ed. Rowman and Littlefield, Inc. 1962. 64p. 75c

> One of the Visual Career Guides, about one half of the contents consists of photographs and charts. Includes description of the various kinds of work, training, earnings, and employment outlook.

* Your future in printing. Geinfeld, George, Jr. Richards Rosen Press. 1963. 159p. $2.95

> A descriptive view of various career opportunities in the printing industry.

PRINTING PRESSMAN 4-48.

* Job-printing pressman. Chronicle Guidance Publications. 1960. 4p. 35c

> Occupational brief summarizing work performed, working conditions, hours, earnings, personal qualifications, training requirements, opportunities, employment outlook, and entry into the job.

Pressman. Robinson, H. Alan. Personnel Services. Revised 1956. 6p. 50c; 25c to students

> Occupational abstract. Nature of work, future prospects, qualifications, preparation, entrance and advancement, earnings, number and distribution of workers, advantages, disadvantages, and sources of further information.

* Printing pressmen. Michigan Employment Security Commission. 1954. 19p. 25c

> Introduction, nature of work, location of jobs, employment prospects, working conditions, organizations, earnings, qualifications for entry, disadvantages, and advantages.

**Printing pressmen and assistants. One section of *Occupational Outlook Handbook*.

> Nature of work, training, other qualifications, employment outlook, earnings, and working conditions.

PROBATION OFFICER   0-27.20

Conscience of the court. Porter, Edward S. Prentice-Hall, Inc. 1962. 203p. $3.95

The author draws upon his experiences as a probation officer to explain the importance of the work and its gratifications.

**Help wanted in probation and parole. National Council on Crime and Delinquency. 1963. 10p. Free

Explanation of nature of work, special assignments, preparation, qualifications, returns, and how to get started.

* Parole and probation officer. Chronicle Guidance Publications. 1963. 4p. 35c

Occupational brief describing work performed, working conditions, remuneration, personal qualifications, training required, and employment outlook.

* Probation and parole workers. Science Research Associates. 1961. 4p. 35c

Occupational brief describing work, qualifications, how to get started, things to consider, and outlook. Selected references.

Probation officer. Careers. 1960. 2p. 15c

Career summary for desk-top file. Duties, qualifications, and outlook.

Probation officer and parole agent. California State Department of Employment. 1962. 8p. Single copy free

Duties, working conditions, wages, hours, entrance requirements, promotion, training, and employment outlook in California.

Standards for selection of probation and parole officers. National Council on Crime and Delinquency. 1962. 6p. Free

Duties, qualifications, requirements, and methods of selection.

Training for juvenile probation officers. Children's Bureau, Social Security Administration. Supt. of Documents. 1962. 78p. 30c

A report of a workshop concerned with the necessity for providing adequate training for the people who work with delinquent youth. One section is a discussion of the role of the probation officer and another summarizes the knowledge, skills, and attitudes necessary for effective performance.

PROGRAMMER   0-69.981

Computer programming: a new profession for you. Electronic Computer Programming Institute. 1961. 16p. Free

Explanation of the development of office automation, the nature of work of the programmers to utilize the electronic data processing equipment, requirements, and training.

The data processing programmer. Chronicle Guidance Publications. 1959. 4p. 35c

Occupational brief summarizing work performed, personal qualifications, training, where employed, promotional opportunities, related jobs, advantages, disadvantages, and outlook.

Electronic data processing—a suggested two-year post high school curriculum for computer programmers and business applications analysts. Office of Education. Supt. of Documents. 1963. 49p. 40c
This curriculum guide outlines a sequence of courses designed to give experience with techniques and methods of handling business data.

**Employment outlook for electronic computer operating personnel and programers. Bureau of Labor Statistics, U.S. Department of Labor. Supt. of Documents. 1962. 9p. 10c
Reprint from the *Occupational Outlook Handbook*.

**Programers. One section of *Occupational Outlook Handbook*.
Nature of work of preparing the step-by-step directions for the electronic computer, where employed, training, other qualifications, advancement, employment outlook, earnings, and working conditions.

Programmer. Connors, Ralph and Robinson, H. Alan. Personnel Services. 1961. 6p. 50c; 25c to students
Occupational abstract. Nature of work, future prospects, qualifications, preparation, entrance, advancement, earnings, advantages, disadvantages, and related occupations. References for further reading.

Programmer. Careers. 1962. 4p. 25c
Occupational brief describing nature of work, qualifications, training, opportunities, and outlook.

Programmer (electronic data processing equipment). Careers. 1962. 8p. 25c
Career brief describing duties, working conditions, training, personal qualifications, earnings, and outlook.

Programmers. Science Research Associates. 1960. 4p. 35c
Occupational brief describing nature of work, training, qualifications, opportunities, and outlook. Selected references.

Programming, a new profession for you. UNIVAC Division of Remington Rand, Inc. 1959. 28p. Free
Description of work, opportunities, and training.

Should you go into electronic computer programming? McCracken, Daniel D. New York Life Insurance Company. 1963. 10p. Free
Description of nature of work, duties, qualifications, training, rewards, and satisfactions.

Sources of information on career opportunities in mathematics, programming, and in electronic data processing occupations. Association for Computing Machinery. 1962. 1p. Free
List of nine reading materials.

See also Electronic Computer Operator

PROOFREADER 1-10.07

Finding out about proofreaders. Science Research Associates. 1962. 4p. 35c
Junior occupational brief containing concise facts about the job.

PROOFREADER—*Continued*

Proofreader. Careers. 1963. 2p. 15c
Career summary for desk-top file. Duties, qualifications, and outlook.

Proof-reader. The Guidance Centre. 1962. 4p. 15c in Canada; 20c elsewhere
Nature of work, qualifications, preparation, working conditions, advancement, outlook, earnings, and related occupations.

PSYCHIATRIC SOCIAL WORKER 0-27.20

Health manpower source book—medical and psychiatric social workers. Public Health Service, U.S. Department of Health, Education, and Welfare. Publication Number 263, Section 12. Supt. of Documents. 1961. 71p. 40c
Data on the numbers, distribution, and characteristics of personnel. Includes information on training, age, sex, employment status, and income level.

Psychiatric social work as a career. Institute for Research. 1962. 24p. $1
History and development, description of work, lines of promotion, qualifications, training, salaries, attractive and unattractive features, typical day's work, outlook, and related jobs.

Psychiatric social worker. Robinson, H. Alan. Personnel Services. 1955. 6p. 50c; 25c to students
Occupational abstract. Nature of work, future prospects, opportunities for servicemen, opportunities for men, qualifications, preparation, entrance and advancement, earnings, number and distribution of workers, advantages, and disadvantages.

Psychiatric social worker. Careers. 1960. 2p. 15c
Career summary for desk-top file. Duties, qualifications, and outlook.

* The psychiatric social worker. National Association for Mental Health. 1962. 4p. 10c
Duties, training, earnings, and future outlook. Selected references.

Psychiatric social worker. Pages 135-6 of *Health Careers Guidebook*.
Nature of work, training, opportunities, personal qualifications, and salaries.

Psychiatric social workers. Science Research Associates. 1963. 4p. 35c
Occupational brief describing nature of work, qualifications, training, earnings, advantages, disadvantages, and future outlook.

PSYCHIATRIST 0-26.10

A descriptive directory of psychiatric training in the United States and Canada. American Psychiatric Association. 1960. 116p. $3
Third edition compiled by the Committee on Medical Education of the American Psychiatric Association.

Psychiatrist. Careers. 1963. 2p. 15c
Career summary for desk-top file. Duties, qualifications, and outlook.

* The psychiatrist. National Association for Mental Health. 1962. 4p. 10c
>What the psychiatrist does, professional training, earnings, and future outlook. Selected references.

* Psychiatrists. Science Research Associates. 1963. 4p. 35c
>Occupational brief describing nature of work, training, earnings, and future outlook.

**Psychiatry as a career. Terhume, William B. American Psychiatric Association. 1957. 6p. Single copy free
>Description of nature of work, essential personality traits, types of practice, earnings, and professional development.

Psychiatry as a career. Institute for Research. 1957. 24p. $1
>Personal qualifications, educational requirements, advantages, disadvantages, typical day's work in private practice, institutional work, and government services. Some information about the related fields of psychologist, occupational therapist, psychiatric social worker, and supervisor of recreation. Requirements for internship and certificate of the American Board of Psychiatry and Neurology.

PSYCHOLOGIST 0-36.21

Career as a psychologist. Hirt, Michael. Bellman Publishing Company. 1962. 26p. $1
>Nature of work, outlook, personal requirements, preparation, economic returns, occupational relationships, distribution of workers, advantages, and disadvantages. Selected references.

A career for you as a Veterans Administration psychologist. Veterans Administration, Department of Medicine and Surgery. 1963. 4p. Free
>Description of work, training program, qualifications, and benefits.

**A career in psychology. American Psychological Association. 1963. 32p. Single copy free
>Explanation of what psychologists do, where they work, necessary training, employment future, and lists of the universities with APA approved doctoral programs in counseling psychology and in clinical psychology.

Careers and opportunities in psychology. Angel, Juvenal. World Trade Academy Press. 1960. 30p. $1.25
>Includes description of work, opportunities, rewards, future outlook, advantages, disadvantages, and methods of financing an education in this field.

Careers in psychology. B'nai B'rith Vocational Service. 1957. 16p. 35c
>Nature of work, qualifications, preparation, training, outlook, opportunities, earnings, and rewards.

Clinical psychologist. Dudycha, George. Personnel Services. 1956. 6p. 50c; 25c to students
>Occupational abstract. Future prospects, nature of work, qualifications, training, certification, entrance, salaries, number and distribution of workers, advantages, disadvantages, and sources of further information.

Clinical psychologist. Careers. 1961. 2p. 15c
>Career summary for desk-top file. Duties, qualifications, and outlook.

PSYCHOLOGIST—*Continued*

The clinical psychologist. National Association for Mental Health. 1962. 4p. 10c
Duties, training, earnings, and future outlook. Selected references.

Educational facilities and financial assistance for graduate students in psychology. American Psychological Association. 1963. 23p. 25c. Single copy free
Requirements for admission to graduate programs in psychology are given for each of 190 institutions. Also included are the tuition, financial aid, and assistantships available at each school.

Educational psychologist. Careers. 1961. 2p. 15c
Career summary for desk-top file. Duties, qualifications, and outlook.

**Employment outlook for psychologists. Bureau of Labor Statistics, U.S. Department of Labor. Supt. of Documents. 1964. 4p. 5c
Reprint from the *Occupational Outlook Handbook*.

General psychologist. Careers. 1964. 2p. 15c
Career summary for desk-top file. Duties, qualifications, and outlook.

**Jobs in psychology. Science Research Associates. 1962. 43p. $1
Describes the variety of job prospects and opportunities within this field. Each area is introduced through a case study approach of a psychologist engaged in the work of that area. An accompanying wall chart is available for 35c.

**Opportunities in psychology. Super, Donald E. Vocational Guidance Manuals. 1955. 96p. $1.45 paper
Nature of the psychologist's work in each of the special branches, status and employment prospects, education and training, tangible and intangible rewards, advantages and disadvantages, and how to get started and get ahead.

Psychologist. Chronicle Guidance Publications. 1963. 4p. 35c
Occupational brief summarizing work performed, working conditions, qualifications, training, outlook, and licensing.

Psychologists. Science Research Associates. 1961. 4p. 35c
Occupational brief describing nature of work, requirements, earnings, getting started, advantages, disadvantages, and future outlook.

**Psychologists. One section of *Occupational Outlook Handbook*.
Nature of work, where employed, training and other qualifications, employment outlook, earnings, and working conditions.

Psychologists in action. Ogg, Elizabeth. Public Affairs Committee. 1955. 28p. 25c
Discussion of work in helping individuals, working with groups, psychological testing in schools, and laboratory experimentation. Aims to describe fields of work in which psychologists function.

Psychology. Pages 129-32 of *Health Careers Guidebook*.
Brief discussion of the clinical psychologist, counseling psychologist, social psychologist, and the psychometrist.

* Psychology as a career. Institute for Research. 1962. 24p. $1
   Development of the work in industry, welfare agencies, and educational institutions. Includes training, personal qualifications, attractive and unattractive features, how to get started, and outlook for employment.

Psychology: earned degrees, by level, sex, and institution. One section of *Earned Degrees Conferred.*
   List of 553 schools and the number of bachelor's, master's, and doctor's degrees conferred by each in psychology.

Public school psychologist. Mullen, Frances A. Research Publishing Company. 1963. 24p. $1
   History and importance of the work, personal qualifications, outlook, working conditions, remuneration, training, opportunities, advantages, and disadvantages.

School psychologist. Dudycha, George. Personnel Services. 1956. 6p. 50c; 25c to students
   Occupational abstract. Future prospects, nature of work, qualifications, training, certification, entrance, salaries, number and distribution of workers, advantages, disadvantages, and sources of further information.

School psychologist. Chronicle Guidance Publications. 1962. 4p. 35c
   Occupational brief summarizing duties, qualifications, preparation, methods of entering, advancement, and outlook.

The woman psychoanalyst. Lynch, Nancy. Alumnae Advisory Center. 1957. 5p. 25c
   Reprint from *Mademoiselle* reporting on interviews with sixteen women psychoanalysts about their work.

PUBLIC ACCOUNTANT   0-01.30

CPA—a day in the life of a certified public accountant. American Institute of Certified Public Accountants. 1960. 2p. Free
   A film brochure describing a 29-minute 16mm film designed to show the work of accountants. The film is distributed on free loan by Association Films, Inc.

* Careers as a public accountant (C.P.A.). Institute for Research. 1958. 24p. $1
   Development and growth of public accounting, duties, a typical day's work in six types of positions, personal qualifications, training, salaries, opportunities, attractive and unattractive features, and requirements for C.P.A. certificate and state license. Description of services such as auditing, system installation, special investigation, tax reports, cost accounting, consultation and interpretation.

Certified public accountant. Robinson, H. Alan. Personnel Services. 1957. 6p. 50c; 25c to students
   Occupational abstract summarizing nature of work, future prospects, opportunities for women, qualifications, preparation, certification, entrance and advancement, earnings, advantages, and disadvantages.

The profession of accounting. Stans, Maurice H. American Institute of Certified Public Accountants. 1958. 16p. 5c
   A former U.S. Budget Director outlines the history of accounting and the future outlook and discusses the legal, ethical, and social responsibilities of certified public accountants.

PUBLIC ACCOUNTANT—*Continued*

Standards of education and experience for certified public accountants—summary pamphlet. American Institute of Accountants. 1956. 146p. 25c
   A report summarizing professional practice, legal regulations, educational facilities, experience requirements, and the CPA examination.

To be or not to be a certified public accountant. American Woman's Society of Certified Public Accountants. 1963. 9p. Free
   Discussion of the demands and requisites of the work, educational background, personal characteristics, mental and emotional attitudes needed, and the value of the CPA certificate.

**Which way young lady? American Woman's Society of Certified Public Accountants. 1962. 16p. 15c
   Description of accounting work and specialties, need for accountants, opportunities for women, personal characteristics needed, training, earnings, and advancement patterns. Reading list.

   See also Accountant; bookkeeper

PUBLIC ADMINISTRATION WORKER. *See* Government service worker

PUBLIC HEALTH NURSE   0-33.50 through 0-33.59

**Anne Snow, mountain nurse. Deming, Dorothy. Dodd, Mead and Company. 1947. 272p. $3
   Career fiction. Story of rural nursing services and how public health nurses serve the people of a rugged country area. Written by a registered nurse.

Career as a public health nurse. Institute for Research. 1958. 24p. $1
   Types of service, training, related jobs, opportunities, and attractive and unattractive features.

Educational qualifications of public health nurses. American Public Health Association. 1962. 5p. Free
   Scope of work, functions, and educational qualifications.

Educational programs accredited for public health nursing preparation by the National League for Nursing. 1962. 6p. 25c
   Annual list of universities and colleges offering programs approved for the preparation of public health nurses.

Elaine Forrest: visiting nurse. Hobart, Lois. Julian Messner, Inc. 1959. 192p. $2.95
   Career fiction. The story shows that public health nursing duties and responsibilities include a warm, sympathetic approach to patients.

**Look to your future in public health nursing. Committee on Careers, National League for Nursing. 1962. 6p. 8c
   Nature of work, preparation, personal qualifications, rewards, opportunities, and outlook.

Nurses in public health. Public Health Service, U.S. Department of Health, Education, and Welfare. Supt. of Documents. 1962. 59p. 40c
This is a report of the number and educational preparation of nurses employed for public health work by national agencies, schools of nursing, state and local health agencies, and boards of education. Contains many statistical tables.

**Penny Marsh, public health nurse. Deming, Dorothy. Dodd, Mead and Company. 1938. 266p. $3
Career fiction. Story of varied experiences with a flood and a blizzard, and routine work in her profession. The Penny Marsh series is distinguished because the stories, written by a registered nurse, center around the romance of nursing rather than on personal anecdotes about the heroines. Other novels by the same author which contain authentic information are:
Penny Marsh, Supervisor of Public Health Nurses
Penny Marsh Finds Adventure in Public Health Nursing
Penny and Pam, Nurse and Cadet
Pam Wilson, Registered Nurse
Penny Marsh, Director of Nurses

Public health nurse. Splaver, Sarah. Personnel Services. 1960. 6p. 50c; 25c to students
Occupational abstract. Nature of work, qualifications, preparation, licensing, entrance, advancement, earnings, supply, and demand.

Public health nurse. Careers. 1963. 2p. 15c
Career summary for desk-top file. Duties, qualifications, and outlook.

See also Nurse (registered professional); Practical nurse

PUBLIC HEALTH NUTRITIONIST. *See* Nutritional chemist

PUBLIC HEALTH OFFICER 0-26.10

**Careers for professionals in public health. Angel, Juvenal L. World Trade Academy Press. 1962. 36p. $1.25
Description of work, training, opportunities, and remuneration for each of the following: physician, psychiatrist, public health nurse, public health dentist, social worker, public health engineer, optometrist, food technologist, food and drug inspector, and pharmacist. Also included is a list of schools offering training and scholarships in public health.

**Careers in public health work. Institute for Research. 1959. 24p. $1
Types of public health services and positions, employment opportunities, number of persons engaged in public health work, and types of positions in the U.S. public health service.

Educational qualifications of directors of public health departments. American Public Health Association. 1955. 8p. Free
Scope of work, functions, and eductional requirements.

Educational qualifications of executives of voluntary health organizations and health councils. American Public Health Association. 1959. 5p. Free
Description of functions of voluntary health organizations, duties of their executives, and educational preparation and experience.

PUBLIC HEALTH OFFICER—*Continued*

Specialized occupations in public health. Angel, Juvenal. World Trade
Academy Press. 1962. 42p. $1.25
> Includes information about each of several specialties within this field.

William Crawford Gorgas: tropic fever fighter. Williams, Beryl and
Epstein, Samuel. Julian Messner, Inc. 1953. 192p. $3.25. Library bind-
ing $3.19 net
> Biography of a health officer who launched a sanitary campaign and freed
> the area of yellow fever and malaria so American workers could build the
> Panama Canal.

PUBLIC RELATIONS MAN   0-06.97

Careers in public relations. Angel, Juvenal. World Trade Academy Press.
1959. 26p. $1.25
> Includes description of work, training, opportunities, remuneration, and future
> outlook.

Careers in public relations work. Institute for Research. 1961. 24p. $1
> Describes work of a public relations director and a publicity assistant in a
> national trade association, hospital, public library, youth organization, farm co-
> operative, dental society, public utility, medical association, air line, and public
> relations agency. Includes qualifications, training, and salaries.

For immediate release. Paradis, Adrian. David McKay Company. 1955.
209p. $3
> Discussion of public relations in business, government, social agencies, edu-
> cation, entertainment, and publishing.

**Employment outlook for advertising workers, marketing research workers,
public relations workers. Bureau of Labor Statistics, U.S. Department
of Labor. Supt. of Documents. 1964. 16p. 10c
> Reprint from the *Occupational Outlook Handbook*.

**Let's consider public relations; an occupational guide. Public Relations
Society of America. 1963. 24p. Free
> This booklet describes the role of public relations, qualifications, preparation,
> employment opportunities, kinds of organizations using public relations, salaries,
> how to get started, advantages, and drawbacks. Suggested readings.

List of colleges reporting courses of instruction in public relations. Public
Relations Society of America. 1963. 4p. Free
> List of 19 colleges offering a major, 35 reporting a sequence, and 120 teaching
> one or two elective courses.

Opportunities in public relations. Henkin, Shepard. Vocational Guidance
Manuals. 1964. 144p. $1.45 paper
> Description of public relations, educational preparation, chances for success,
> general returns, personal attributes, how to get started, and fields of public re-
> lations and publicity such as political, government, social service agencies, hotels
> and institutions, house organ, industrial, entertainment, and public relations
> for personalities. List of colleges offering courses in public relations.

Public relations. Bernays, Edward L. Bellman Publishing Co. 1945. 24p. $1
Historical development, duties, personal qualifications, scholastic training, opportunities, remuneration, and ethics of the profession.

Public relations. Guitar, Mary Anne. Alumnae Advisory Center. 1956. 4p. 25c
Reprint from *Mademoiselle* describing duties, educational requirements, and methods of entrance.

Public relations. Schwartz, Jane. Aluminae Advisory Center. 1956. 11p. 50c
Nature of work, requirements, and opportunities.

**Public relations man. Careers. 1962. 8p. 25c
Career brief describing duties, media used, training requirements, training opportunities, personal qualifications, employment prospects, earnings, promotional prospects, where employed, related careers, measuring one's interest and ability, and suggested high school courses. Additional references.

Public relations man. Chronicle Guidance Publications. 1959. 4p. 35c
Occupational brief summarizing work performed, where employed, personal qualifications, training, earnings, and outlook.

Public relations secretary. Careers. 1959. 2p. 15c
Career summary for desk-top file. Duties, qualifications, training, and outlook.

* Public relations workers. Science Research Associates. 1960. 4p. 35c
Occupational brief describing nature of work, requirements, how to get started, incomes, advantages, disadvantages, and future outlook.

**Public relations workers. One section of *Occupational Outlook Handbook*.
Nature of work, where employed, training, other qualifications, advancement, employment outlook, earnings, and working conditions.

Publicity girl. McKown, Robin. Putnam's Sons. 1959. 160p. $2.75
Career fiction. Story of a girl who found a rewarding career in the publicity field in New York City.

Publicity work as a career. Institute for Research. 1961. 24p. $1
Description of a typical day's work, qualifications, earnings, possibilities of advancement, and attractive and unattractive features.

Should you go into public relations? Hill, John W. New York Life Insurance Company. 1960. 12p. Free
Description of duties, qualities needed, how to get a start, advantages, and disadvantages.

**Your future in public relations. Bernays, Edward L. Richards Rosen Press. 1961. 158p. $2.95
A picture of public relations as a rapidly expanding field offering a wide variety of opportunity in the complex area of communications.

PULP AND PAPER INDUSTRY WORKER. *See* Paper industry worker

PURCHASING AGENT									0-91.60

Careers in purchasing—industry, commerce, government. Institute for Research. 1959. 24p. $1
Includes a description of the work of the industrial, public utility, government, school, and institutional purchasing agent.

**Employment outlook for purchasing agents and industrial traffic managers. Bureau of Labor Statistics, U.S. Department of Labor. Supt. of Documents. 1964. 8p. 5c
Reprint from the *Occupational Outlook Handbook*.

Purchasing agent. Group, Vernard. Personnel Services. 1954. 6p. 50c; 25c to students
Occupational abstract. Nature of work, future prospects, qualifications, preparation, entrance and advancement, earnings, number and distribution of workers.

* Purchasing agent. Careers. 1960. 8p. 25c
Career brief describing duties, working conditions, training, personal qualifications, earnings, advancement prospects, and outlook.

Purchasing agent. Careers. 1961. 2p. 15c
Career summary for desk-top file. Duties, qualifications, and outlook.

* Purchasing agent. Chronicle Guidance Publications. 1963. 4p. 35c
Occupational brief summarizing work performed, working conditions, qualifications, training, earnings, opportunities, and outlook.

* Purchasing agents. Science Research Associates. 1959. 4p. 35c
Occupational brief describing nature of work, requirements, training, earnings, getting started, advantages, disadvantages, and future outlook.

**Purchasing agents. One section of *Occupational Outlook Handbook*.
Nature of work, where employed, training, other qualifications, advancement, employment outlook, earnings, and working conditions.

**Purchasing as a career. National Association of Purchasing Agents. 1961. 26p. 50c
Description of the purchasing function and its importance, types of positions, types of training, compensation, and opportunities for qualified college graduates.

Should you be a purchasing agent? Affleck, Gordon Burt. New York Life Insurance Company. 1962. 12p. Free
Description of responsibilities; duties of the purchasing agent, buyer, and purchasing clerk; and financial rewards.

Your career in purchasing. National Association of Purchasing Agents. No date. 4p. Free
Description of specific jobs in purchasing, preparation, salaries, and intangible rewards.

RABBI   0-08.99

**Careers in the rabbinate. B'nai B'rith Vocational Service. 1960. 12p. 35c
    Description of duties, salary ranges, educational requirements, qualifications, method of entering, outlook, advantages, disadvantages, and opportunities.

**Employment outlook for rabbis. Bureau of Labor Statistics, U.S. Department of Labor. Supt. of Documents. 1964. 8p. 5c
    Reprint from the *Occupational Outlook Handbook*.

Rabbis of the United States. Linfield, H. S. Jewish Statistical Bureau. 1957. 23p. Free
    Survey of the number of rabbis, rabbinical training facilities, secular education, areas of service, and the number of rabbis in the United States for three centuries.

What makes a Reform rabbi? Hebrew Union College and Jewish Institute of Religion. 1959. 16p. Free
    Illustrated brochure describing the responsibilities of a rabbi.

RADIO AND TELEVISION ANNOUNCER   0-69.21

Announcers' qualifications. National Broadcasting Company, Department of Information. 1953. 3p. Mimeographed. Free
    Personal requisites, education, duties, experience, and opportunities for advancement.

Broadcasting. Pages 237-43 of *The College Girl Looks Ahead*.
    Characteristics of broadcasting, talents needed, trying out, preparing for and obtaining a job.

Disc jockey. California State Department of Employment. 1960. 3p. Single copy free
    Description of the work of conducting a program of musical recordings, interspersed with comments and advertising material. Includes working conditions, training, salary, hours, promotion, and employment outlook.

Disc jockey. Chronicle Guidance Publications. 1963. 4p. 35c
    Occupational brief describing nature of work, qualifications, working conditions, opportunities for promotion, and outlook.

Disk jockeys. Science Research Associates. 1961. 4p. 35c
    Occupational brief describing work, qualifications, training, ways to get started, advantages, disadvantages, and outlook. Selected references.

Finding out about disk jockeys. Science Research Associates. 1961. 4p. 35c
    Junior occupational brief containing concise facts about the job.

* Radio and television announcer. Chronicle Guidance Publications. 1963. 4p. 35c
    Occupational brief including definition, history, work performed, working conditions, personal requirements, determination of aptitudes and interests, requirements, opportunities, outlook, methods of entry, and related jobs.

RADIO AND TELEVISION ANNOUNCER—*Continued*

**Radio and television announcers. Careers. 1962. 8p. 25c
Career brief describing duties, working conditions, training requirements, personal qualifications, employment prospects, advantages, disadvantages, earnings, advancement prospects, how to enter, measuring one's interest and ability, and suggested high school program.

Radio and television announcers. Science Research Associates. 1961. 4p. 35c
Occupational brief describing nature of work, training, qualifications, opportunities, advantages, disadvantages, and future outlook.

* Radio and television announcers. One section of *Occupational Outlook Handbook.*
Nature of work, training, other qualifications, advancement, employment outlook, earnings, and working conditions.

Radio announcer. Splaver, Sarah. Personnel Services. 1959. 6p. 50c; 25c to students
Occupational abstract. Nature of work, qualifications, preparation, entrance, advancement, earnings, supply and demand.

Radio announcing and news broadcasting—careers. Institute for Research. 1958. 24p. $1
History, job descriptions, qualifications, training, compensation, opportunities, outlook, and related fields.

Sports announcer. Splaver, Sarah. Personnel Services. 1957. 6p. 50c; 25c to students
Occupational abstract containing summary, nature of work, qualifications, preparation, entrance and advancement, supply and demand, earnings, advantages, and disadvantages.

RADIO AND TELEVISION BROADCASTING INDUSTRY WORKER
0-17.01; 0-61.; 0-97.70 through 0-97.89; 4, 6, 8-98.

**Broadcasting occupations. Michigan Employment Security Commission. 1958. 20p. 25c
Information concerning programming and engineering in radio and television broadcasting. Includes nature of work, location of jobs, working conditions, employment outlook, earnings, qualifications for entry, disadvantages, and advantages.

**Careers in broadcasting. Lerch, John, editor. Appleton-Century-Crofts. 1962. 113p. $3.95
Twenty-six of radio and television's leading performers give advice on the career opportunities in broadcasting. A penetrating inside view is given concerning what radio and television offer and what they demand. The reader will also find reasoned advice from executives in the industry. Illustrated.

Careers in radio. Institute for Research. 1962. 24p. $1
Nature of work, qualifications, and attractive and unattractive features.

Careers in radio. National Association of Broadcasters. 1963. 6p. Free
Brief history of the field, training, specific operations, getting a job, and opportunities for women.

Careers in television and radio. Angel, Juvenal. World Trade Academy Press. 1959. 28p. $1.25
Includes information about each of several specialties within this field.

Directory of college courses in radio and television. U.S. Office of Education. 1962. 65p. Free
Alphabetical list by state and by institutions with brief description of nature of courses. Of the 300 institutions offering radio-television courses, 113 confer undergraduate and graduate degrees.

**Employment outlook in radio and television broadcasting occupations. Bureau of Labor Statistics, U.S. Department of Labor. Supt. of Documents. 1964. 16p. 10c
Reprint from the *Occupational Outlook Handbook.*

Job inventory. National Broadcasting Company, Department of Information. No date. 33p. Mimeographed Free
Description of many of the jobs existing within the company and the minimum qualifications for each job. Prepared as an aid to all persons who seek employment with the company.

Marconi: pioneer of radio. Coe, Douglas, pseud. Julian Messner, Inc. 1943. 256p. $3.50. Library binding $3.34 net
Biography which includes the story of the development of wireless telegraphy.

Opportunities in radio. Ranson, Jo and Pack, Richard. Vocational Guidance Manuals, Inc. 1949. 104p. $1.45 paper
Includes description of work, requirements, and opportunities in the following: announcing, acting, radio writing, production, publicity, news reporting, sales, sales promotion, research, engineering, and electronics. Selections from civil service tests for a dramatic director, a publicity director, and a continuity writer for WNYC.

Program for Christine. Bentel, Pearl Bucklen. David McKay Company. 1953. 249p. $3
Career fiction. The story follows Christine's activities while she works toward her goal of writing for radio.

Radio and television as a career. Boston University. 1962. 12p. Free
Recruiting booklet describing opportunities, salaries, and preparation.

**Radio and television broadcasting occupations. One chapter of *Occupational Outlook Handbook.*
Nature and location of the industry, kinds of jobs, training, other qualifications, advancement, employment outlook, earnings, and working conditions. Specific information is given concerning the announcer, broadcast technician, and personnel in the programing department, sales, and business management.

Radio-TV, not New York. Alumnae Advisory Center. 1953. 4p. 25c
Information indicating that the smaller towns have the best opportunities for beginners. Reprint from *Mademoiselle.*

RADIO AND TELEVISION BROADCAST-TIME SALESMAN   1-87.11

Radio and television broadcast-time salesman. Careers. 1962. 2p. 15c
Career summary for desk-top file. Duties, qualifications, and outlook.

Radio-television time salesmen. Science Research Associates. 1963. 4p.
35c
Occupational brief describing nature of work, growth of the media, requirements, earnings, and future outlook.

RADIO AND TELEVISION PROGRAM DIRECTOR   0-97.74

Radio and television program director. Chronicle Guidance Publications.
1962. 4p. 35c
Occupational brief summarizing duties, number of workers, qualifications,
preparation, methods of entry, and working conditions.

RADIO BROADCASTING TECHNICIAN   0-66.00 through 0-66.09

Broadcast technician. Careers. 1960. 2p. 15c
Career summary for desk-top file. Duties, qualifications, and outlook.

**Broadcast technicians. One section of *Occupational Outlook Handbook*.
Nature of work. training, other qualifications, employment outlook, earnings, and working conditions.

Broadcasting technicians. Science Research Associates. 1961. 4p. 35c
Occupational brief describing nature of work, training, qualifications,
getting started, earnings, advantages, disadvantages, and future outlook. Selected references.

* Radio and TV broadcasting technicians. Chronicle Guidance Publications. 1962. 4p. 35c
Occupational brief containing definitions, work performed, personal requirements, determination of aptitudes and interests, amateur license requirements, training and commercial license requirments, training opportunities,
outlook, and suggested activities.

Radio and television technician. Careers. 1960. 2p. 15c
Career summary for desk-top file. Duties, qualifications, and outlook.

Radio and television technician. The Guidance Centre. 1959. 4p. 15c
in Canada; 20c elsewhere
Work performed, qualifications, training, advancement opportunities, how
to get started, advantages, and disadvantages.

**Television and radio technician, serviceman, and service manager—
careers. Institute for Research. 1959. 24p. $1
History and development of work, size of the industry, where television
and radio technicians and servicemen work, types of positions, typical day's
work, attractive and unattractive features, personal characteristics, education
and training, list of technical schools which offer training, salaries and earnings, chances for employment, and getting started.

See also Television and radio serviceman

RADIO OPERATOR 0-61.

Ground radio operators and teletypists. One section of *Occupational Outlook Handbook*.

Description of work of transmitting messages between ground station and flight personnel, where employed, training, and employment outlook.

Radio operator. Careers. 1960. 7p. 25c

Career brief describing duties, working conditions, training, personal qualifications, earnings, advancement prospects, and outlook.

Sea Hawk calling! Henriksen, Hild. Harcourt, Brace and World. 1962. 157p. $2.95

Career fiction. Story of the experiences of a woman ship-radio operator.

RADIO REPAIRMAN. *See* Television and radio serviceman

RAILROAD CONDUCTOR. *See* Conductor (railroad)

RAILROAD INDUSTRY WORKER U-98.7 and 5, 7, 9-38. through 9-44.

American railroads: their growth and development. Association of American Railroads. 1960. 32p. Free

Contains illustrations and maps showing the expansion of our railroad system by decades.

Brakemen. One section of *Occupational Outlook Handbook*.

Nature of work, employment outlook, earnings, and working conditions.

**Bridge and building workers. One section of *Occupational Outlook Handbook*.

Nature of work, training, other qualifications, advancement, earnings, and working conditions. Pertains to the work of constructing, maintaining, and repairing structures owned by the railroads.

Careers as engineers, conductors, and trainmen. Institute for Research. 1953. 24p. $1

Description of work in railway train and engine service: conductors, engineers, firemen, trainmen, and yardmen. Wages, qualifications, attractive and unattractive features, employment conditions, and how to get started.

Careers in railroading. Institute for Research. 1961. 24p. $1

Brief history of American railroad development, description of representative positions, typical day's work of a general agent, attractive and unattractive features, qualifications, education and training, earnings, chances for employment, and methods of getting started. Also included is a list of colleges offering courses in railroad engineering, transportation, and traffic management.

Careers in the American railroad industry. Morgret, Charles. Bellman Publishing Company. 1960. 32p. $1

Development and importance of the railroad industry, variety of employment, qualifications, advancement, advantages, disadvantages, and how to seek a railroad job. Selected readings.

RAILROAD INDUSTRY WORKER—*Continued*

College courses in railroad subjects. Association of American Railroads. 1958. 48p. Free

A list of colleges and universities offering courses in engineering, transportation, and traffic management with special reference to the railroad field. Technical schools and home study courses also included.

Employment and changing occupational patterns in the railroad industry, 1947-1960. Bureau of Labor Statistics, U.S. Department of Labor. Supt. of Documents. 1963. 32p. 30c

Analysis of employment trends and occupational changes in the railroad industry during this period.

**Employment outlook in railroad occupations. Bureau of Labor Statistics, U.S. Department of Labor. Supt. of Documents. 1964. 28p. 20c

Reprint from the *Occupational Outlook Handbook.*

The human side of railroading. Association of American Railroads. 1961. 16p. Free

A discussion of the railroad organization, payroll, opportunities in the railway field, and how to seek employment. Illustrated.

**Locomotive fireman (helpers). One section of *Occupational Outlook Handbook.*

Nature of work, training, other qualifications, advancement, employment outlook, earnings, and working conditions.

New frontiers in transportation. New York Central System. 1964. 8p. Free

Brochure directed to graduates in industrial, mechanical, electrical, and civil engineering, and transportation, accounting, and business administration.

Operating railroad workers. Science Research Associates. 1961. 4p. 35c

Occupational brief describing kinds of work, requirements, how to enter and advance, earnings, and future outlook.

Quiz on railroads and railroading. Association of American Railroads. 1958. 64p. Free

Contains more than three hundred questions and answers on many phases of railroading.

The railroad. Atchison, Topeka and Santa Fe Railway System. 1962. 36p. Free

History and development of railway transportation and its part in the unification and growth of our nation.

Railroad brakeman. Careers. 1962. 2p. 15c

Career summary for desk-top file. Duties, qualifications, and outlook.

Railroad brakeman. Science Research Associates. 1964. 4p. 35c

Occupational brief describing work, qualifications, training, opportunities, and outlook.

Railroad clerks. One section of *Occupational Outlook Handbook.*

Nature of work, training, other qualifications, advancement, employment outlook, earnings, and working conditions.

Railroad diesel locomotive fireman (helper). Careers. 1962. 2p. 15c
Career summary for desk-top file. Duties, qualifications, and outlook.

**Railroad occupations. One chapter of *Occupational Outlook Handbook*.
Nature and location of the industry, kinds of jobs, training, other qualifications, advancement, employment outlook, earnings, and working conditions. Specific information is given concerning locomotive engineer, fireman, conductor, brakeman, and pullman porters and passenger attendants. Seven illustrations.

Railroad track workers. Science Research Associates. 1964. 4p. 35c
Occupational brief describing nature of work, training, qualifications, opportunities, and outlook.

Railroads at work. Association of American Railroads. 1960. 48p. Free
Subtitle: A picture book of the American railroads in action. About sixty photographs with explanatory captions showing many workers in action.

Railway brakeman. The Guidance Centre. 1960. 15c in Canada; 20c elsewhere
Nature of work of train, freight, and yard brakeman, working conditions, qualifications, outlook, earnings, advantages, disadvantages, and related occupations.

**Shop trades (railroad). One section of *Occupational Outlook Handbook*.
Nature of work in building, maintaining, and repairing railroad cars and locomotives. Also included is description of training, other qualifications, advancement, employment outlook, earnings, and working conditions.

**Signal department workers (railroad). One section of *Occupational Outlook Handbook*.
Nature of work, training, other qualifications, advancement, employment outlook, earnings, and working conditions.

**Station agents. One section of *Occupational Outlook Handbook*.
Nature of work, training, other qualifications, employment outlook, earnings, and working conditions.

Track workers (railroad). One section of *Occupational Outlook Handbook*.
Nature of work, training, other qualifications, advancement, employment outlook, earnings, and working conditions.

READING SPECIALIST. *See* Remedial reading specialist

REAL ESTATE SALESMAN 1-63.10

Careers in property management. B'nai B'rith Vocational Service. 1955. 8p. 35c
Discussion of outlook, nature of work, qualifications, how to get started, earnings, opportunities for women, and advancement. Also description of public housing management careers.

REAL ESTATE SALESMAN—*Continued*

The challenge of real estate—your chances for service and profit in a dynamic field. National Association of Real Estate Boards. 1959. 24p. Single copy free.
Career horizons, preparation, and rewards. Discussion of work in brokerage, property management, farm brokerage, land development, financing, appraisal, counseling, and research.

**Employment outlook for insurance and real estate agents and brokers. Bureau of Labor Statistics, U.S. Department of Labor. Supt. of Documents. 1964. 12p. 10c
Reprint from the *Occupational Outlook Handbook*.

List of universities and colleges offering courses in real estate. National Association of Real Estate Boards. 1963. 2p. Single copy free
List of schools offering one or more courses in real estate, including those which offer real estate as a major field and those where graduate study is available. Another list contains names of universities offering correspondence courses in real estate.

Preparing for the real estate business. National Association of Real Estate Boards. 1950. 4p. Single copy free.
Description of the principal fields of activity, educational preparation, license requirements, how to go about entering the business, and rewards.

* Real estate: a career with a bright future. Davis, John G. National Association of Real Estate Boards. 1962. 5p. Single copy free.
Reprint describing nature of work, opportunities, and outlook.

Real estate agent. The Guidance Centre. 1958. 4p. 15c in Canada; 20c elsewhere
Nature of work, qualifications, preparation, earnings, advancement opportunities, advantages, disadvantages, how to get started, and related occupations.

**Real estate agents. Science Research Associates. 1961. 4p. 35c
Occupational brief describing real estate specialties, requirements, training, methods of getting started, earnings, advantages, disadvantages, and future outlook.

Real estate and insurance business as a career. Institute for Research. 1961. 24p. $1
Description of jobs in real estate, typical day's work, attractive and unattractive features, qualifications, list of twenty-seven schools offering a four-year course leading to a degree with real estate as a major or specialization, getting a license, and opportunities for women.

Real estate appraiser. Careers. 1962. 2p. 15c
Career summary for desk-top file. Duties, qualifications, and outlook.

Real estate broker. Splaver, Sarah. Personnel Services. 1961. 6p. 50c; 25c to students
Occupational abstract. Nature of work, qualifications, preparation, entrance, advancement, earnings, supply, and demand.

* Real estate management as a career. Institute for Research. 1958. 24p. $1
Qualifications, typical day's work, earnings, trends, advantages, and disadvantages. List of twelve universities offering courses in real estate.

* Real estate salesman. Careers. 1964. 2p. 15c
Career summary for desk-top file. Duties, qualifications, and outlook.

* Real estate salesman. Chronicle Guidance Publications. 1962. 4p. 35c
Occupational brief including definition, history, work performed, working conditions, hours, earnings, personal requirements, training, opportunities, outlook, methods of entry, related jobs, and suggested activities.

**Real estate salesmen and brokers. One section of *Occupational Outlook Handbook*.
Nature of work, where employed, training, employment outlook, earnings, and working conditions.

Sally's real estate venture. Johnson, Enid and Margaret. Julian Messner, Inc. 1954. 192p. $2.95
Career fiction. Story of a girl's experiences as a general assistant to a real estate agent.

Successful real estate selling. Krueger, Cliff W. McGraw-Hill Book Company. 1960. 285p. $7
A practical guide to profitable real estate selling, this book contains information for both the beginning salesman and the experienced realtor.

Title to happiness. De Leeuw, Adele. Macmillan Company. 1947. 222p. $3.50
Career fiction. Story of a girl who advances from secretary to sales work in a real estate office.

**Your future in real estate. Durst, Seymour and Stern, Walter. Richards Rosen Press. 1960. 159p. $2.95
The authors describe the requirements, opportunities, and methods of entering the field. Information is given about residential brokerage, commercial brokerage, realty management, building, realty finance, and other related opportunities.

RECEPTIONIST 1-18.43

Receptionist. Splaver, Sarah. Personnel Services. 1954. 6p. 50c; 25c to students
Occupational abstract. Nature of work, qualifications, preparation, entrance and advancement, supply and demand of workers, earnings, advantages, and disadvantages.

Receptionist. California State Department of Employment. 1959. 2p. Single copy free
Duties, preparation, how to start, promotion, and employment prospects.

Receptionist. Careers. 1963. 2p. 15c
Career summary for desk-top file. Duties, qualifications, and outlook.

RECEPTIONIST—*Continued*

* Receptionist. Chronicle Guidance Publications. 1961. 4p. 35c

    Occupational brief summarizing work performed, working conditions, hours, earnings, personal qualifications, training requirements, opportunities, employment outlook, and entry into the job.

  Receptionists. Science Research Associates. 1958. 4p. 35c

    Occupational brief describing nature of work, training, qualifications, opportunities, advantages, disadvantages, and future outlook.

* Restaurant hostess. Careers. 1959. 8p. 25c

    Career brief describing duties, working conditions, training, personal qualifications, earnings, and outlook.

RECORD INDUSTRY WORKER   4, 6, 8-98.

**Jobs in the record industry. Sachs, Dorothy. Alumnae Advisory Center. 1956. 4p. 25c

    Reprint from *Mademoiselle* which describes the many kinds of jobs in the industry and methods of entering this field.

RECREATION LEADER   0-27.06; 0-27.40; and 0-98.57

Colleges and universities reporting major curricula in recreation. National Recreation Association. 1963. 2p. Single copy free

    List of schools with indication of whether graduate or undergraduate degrees are offered.

A future for you . . . in recreation. American National Red Cross. 1961. 12p. Free

    Description of positions and qualifications for women recreation workers and recreation aides assigned to Red Cross programs in military hospitals.

* The future is yours—a career in recreation leadership. National Recreation Association. 1963. 6p. $3 per 100. Single copy free

    Types of leadership positions, professional preparation, qualifications, and demand.

Occupations in the amusement and recreation group. Chapter 20 of *Planning Your Future.*

    Includes discussion of occupations in amusement and recreation and the work of the motion-picture-theater manager.

**Opportunities in recreation and outdoor education. Nash, Jay B. Vocational Guidance Manuals. 1963. 112p. $1.45 paper; library binding $2.65

    Includes discussion of opportunities, qualifications, personal satisfaction, historical background, future outlook, and pathways to advancement. List of institutions offering professional training.

Playground director. Splaver, Sarah. Personnel Services. 1955. 6p. 50c; 25c to students

    Occupational abstract. Nature of work, qualifications, preparation, entrance and advancement, supply and demand of workers, opportunities for servicemen, advantages, and disadvantages.

Recreation as your career. American Association for Health, Physical Education, and Recreation. 1963. 8p. 5c. Single copy free
　Discussion of services, evidence of growth, opportunities for placement, salaries, preparation, and qualifications.

* Recreation director. Careers. 1962. 8p. 25c
　Career brief describing duties, working conditions, training requirements, lists of colleges offering major curriculums in recreation, personal qualifications, employment prospects, earnings, where employed, measuring one's interest and ability, and suggested high school program.

* Recreation director. Chronicle Guidance Publications. 1963. 4p. 35c
　Occupational brief summarizing work performed, working conditions, hours, earnings, personal qualifications, training requirements, opportunities, employment outlook, entry into the job, and suggested activities.

Recreation director. The Guidance Centre. 1961. 4p. 15c in Canada; 20c elsewhere
　History and importance, nature of work, qualifications for entry and success, working conditions, preparation, earnings, advancement, outlook, related occupations, and how to get started.

Recreation leadership. Sutherland, W. C. Bellman Publishing Company. 1957. 36p. $1
　History and importance of recreation, types of positions, professional preparation, advancement, salaries, qualifications, satisfactions, and unfavorable features.

* Recreation leadership as a career. Institute for Research. 1963. 24p. $1
　Types of positions and compensation, qualifications, requirements, opportunities, trends, attractive and unattractive features. Includes list of schools and colleges offering courses with sequences in recreation leading to a bachelor's degree.

Recreation leadership with the ill and the handicapped. National Recreation Association. 1959. 10p. Single copy free
　Brief description of the expanding field of hospital recreation.

The recreation specialist. National Association for Mental Health. 1962. 4p. 10c
　Describes the duties of the recreation specialist in the mental health field, training, earnings, and future outlook. Selected references.

Recreation therapist. Careers. 1961. 2p. 15c
　Career summary for desk-top file. Duties, qualifications, and outlook.

* Recreation workers. Science Research Associates. 1960. 4p. 35c
　Occupational brief describing nature of work in youth-serving organizations, community recreation, hospital recreation, armed services, and industrial recreation. Also includes requirements, getting started, salaries, advantages, disadvantages, and future outlook.

A rewarding career for you as a Veterans' Administration hospital recreation specialist. Veterans Administration, Department of Medicine and Surgery. 1963. 4p. Free
　Description of work, training program, qualifications, and benefits.

　See also Physical instructor

RED CROSS WORKER 0-27.

Be a disaster representative. American National Red Cross. 1961. 6p. Free
Description of work and qualifications of a field representative of the Red Cross Disaster Services.

**Careers in Red Cross. American National Red Cross. 1963. 40p. Distribution restricted to counselors and placement officers
This booklet describes the organization and its functions, and provides information about professional and technical positions.

Employment information. American National Red Cross. 1959. 4p. Free
Discussion of positions in which openings occur most frequently in the national organization. Gives information on how to apply, special regulations regarding overseas assignments, and service for volunteers.

Employment opportunities. American National Red Cross. 1962. 6p. Free
Mimeographed sheet giving spectrum of entry positions for professional workers.

Go places . . . careers for men. American National Red Cross. 1958. 6p. Free
Information about qualifications and work as an assistant field director in the Red Cross program of service at military installations.

Here's the experience for you. American National Red Cross. 1961. 12p. Free
Description of positions and qualifications for women recreation workers assigned to the Red Cross clubmobile program in Korea.

* Looking for a future. American National Red Cross. 1954. 20p. Free
Description of work and opportunities in eight major fields: community organization, social casework, disaster service, recreation, nursing, first aid and water safety instruction, secretarial and clerical, and special professional and technical positions. Directed toward high school students.

REFRIGERATING ENGINEER 5-72.310

**Air conditioning and refrigeration engineers. Science Research Associates. 1962. 4p. 35c
Occupational brief describing nature of work, training, qualifications, opportunities, advantages, disadvantages, and outlook.

**Career as an air conditioning engineer and as an air conditioning technician. Institute for Research. 1962. 24p. $1
History and development of work, types of positions, typical day's work, attractive and unattractive features, qualifications, training, earnings, chances for employment, getting started, and allied positions.

Refrigerating engineering as a career. Institute for Research. 1959. 16p. $1
Definition, history, where the refrigerating engineer works, types of jobs, typical day's work, attractive and unattractive features, qualifications, training, earnings, opportunities, and related jobs.

REFRIGERATION AND AIR-CONDITIONING MECHANIC 5-83.941

Air conditioning and heating technology. Chronicle Guidance Publications. 1963. 4p. 35c
Occupational brief summarizing work performed, working conditions, qualifications, training, earnings, and outlook.

**Air-conditioning and refrigeration mechanics. One section of *Occupational Outlook Handbook*.
Nature of work, where employed, training, other qualifications, advancement, employment outlook, earnings, and working conditions.

Air conditioning technician. Careers. 1961. 2p. 15c
Career summary for desk-top file. Duties, qualifications, and outlook.

Air-conditioning technician. One section of *Occupational Outlook Handbook*.
Brief description of nature of work and employment outlook.

* Air conditioning technicians. Science Research Associates. 1961. 4p. 35c
Occupational brief describing nature of work, requirements, methods of getting started and advancing, earnings, advantages, disadvantages, and future outlook.

Career as refrigeration and air conditioning contractor. B'nai B'rith Vocational Service. 1954. 8p. 35c
Discussion of nature of work, qualifications, preparation, starting one's own business, earnings, advantages, disadvantages, and outlook.

Electric refrigerator serviceman. Chronicle Guidance Publications. 1963. 4p. 35c
Occupational brief summarizing work performed, training, qualifications, opportunities, and outlook.

**Employment outlook for aid-conditioning and refrigeration mechanics. Bureau of Labor Statistics, U.S. Department of Labor. Supt. of Documents. 1964. 4p. 5c
Reprint from the *Occupational Outlook Handbook*.

Finding out about refrigeration and air-conditioning mechanics. Science Research Associates. 1964. 4p. 35c
Junior occupational brief containing some concise facts about the job and listing ways of finding out about the nature of the work. Includes suggestions for reading and the titles of other occupational briefs on related topics.

Heating, air-conditioning and refrigeration mechanic and serviceman. Chronicle Guidance Publications. 1962. 4p. 35c
Occupational brief summarizing work performed, working conditions, qualifications, training, earnings, where employed, unionization, and outlook.

Job description for electric-refrigerator serviceman. U.S. Employment Service, U.S. Department of Labor. Supt. of Documents. 1948. 5p. 5c
Occupational guide. Job summary, work performed, training, related occupations, physical activities, working conditions, hazards, and employment variables.

REFRIGERATION AND AIR-CONDITIONING MECHANIC—*Continued*

The refrigeration, heating and air conditioning technician. National Council of Technical Schools. 1956. 2p. 5c
The development of the industry, areas of work, need, outlook, opportunities, advantages, and how to enter.

Refrigeration mechanic. California State Department of Employment. 1962. 3p. Single copy free
Duties, working conditions, finding the job, wages, hours, training, promotion, and employment prospects.

Refrigeration mechanic. Careers. 1960. 2p. 15c
Career summary for desk-top file. Duties, qualifications, and outlook.

* Refrigeration mechanic. Chronicle Guidance Publications. 1963. 4p. 35c
Occupational brief summarizing work performed, working conditions, hours, earnings, personal qualifications, training requirements, opportunities, employment outlook, and entry into the job.

REHABILITATION OFFICER. *See* Vocational rehabilitation counselor; Vocational rehabilitation worker

RELIGIOUS WORKER   0-08.10; 0-32.86

Called to missions. Board of Missions of The Methodist Church. 1962. 6p. Free
Demands of and qualifications for missionary service.

Career leaflets. Evangelical United Brethren Church, Board of Christian Education. 1962. 9 leaflets. Free
Titles include: A church career in missions, Vocations for women within the local church, The call to the ministry, and Would I make a good minister?

Careers in synagogue and temple administration. B'nai B'rith Vocational Service. 1960. 8p. 35c
Discussion of duties, qualifications, training, and future outlook.

Christian horizons: current openings. Commission on World Mission. 1961. 20p. 10c
A listing of the kinds of vocations for which there is a need by forty Protestant missions.

Christian vocation and church vocations packet. United Presbyterian Church. 1963. 15 leaflets. $1
Includes career leaflets, reading lists, and information about scholarships and educational loans available from the United Presbyterian Church.

The church and vocation. United Presbyterian Church. Order from Westminster Book Store. 1962. 48p. 50c
Information about the opportunities and needs in the church vocations, such as ordained ministry, Christian education, music, church social work, and national missions.

Church vocation monographs and pamphlets. United Christian Missionary Society. 1962. 14 pamphlets. Free
Nature of work, opportunities, qualifications, preparation, advancement, rewards, vocational planning, and selected references. The titles include: Campus ministry, Church music, Home Mission, Institutional chaplaincy, Military chaplaincy, Pastoral ministry, and World mission.

College majors and church careers. National Council of Churches, Department of Ministry. 1962. 4p. 10c
List of church vocations that particular college majors can lead to. Chart form.

Director of Christian education. Careers. 1963. 2p. 15c
Career summary for desk-top file. Duties, qualifications, and outlook.

Directory of theological schools in the United States and Canada. American Association of Theological Schools. 1963. 44p. Free
List of schools which are members of the Association.

Journey into mission. Williams, Philip. Friendship Press. 1957. 190p. $1
This is the diary of a young missionary who spent five years in Japan. It reveals opportunities and problems a Christian missionary faces in lands abroad.

Listing of church vocations. Nelson, John Oliver. National Council of Churches of Christ. No date. 6p. 10c
In tabular form, information is presented for forty-eight occupations, including estimated number of present workers, activities involved, and training requirements. Bibliography.

Manual on enlistment for church vocations. National Council of Churches, Department of Ministry. 1951. 36p. 75c
Description of vocations, training, opportunities.

Men and women overseas. Board of Missions of the Methodist Church. 1962. 6p. Free
Description of career missionary service and the qualifications.

Methodist service projects. Interboard Committee on Christian Vocations. 1963. 64p. 15c
Annual directory of Methodist church-related vocations and short-term service opportunities, with explanation of qualifications and training required for each. Contains sections on summer service projects, selective service law, and Methodist student loan and scholarship funds.

The missionary task. Commission on World Mission. 1960. Five booklets. 15c each
Kinds of jobs and qualifications in communications, teaching, and medical service.

On call: deaconesses across the world. Herzel, Catherine. Holt, Rinehart and Winston, Inc. 1961. 121p. $2.75
Description of the nature of work, training, personal qualifications, rewards, and the growth of the deaconess movement. For younger girls.

RELIGIOUS WORKER—*Continued*

Opportunities for vocations. United Church of Christ. 1962. 20p. Free
> Discussion of the possibilities of service in Christian education, the pastoral ministry, chaplaincies, overseas service, and homeland frontiers.

**Opportunities in Catholic religious vocations. Poage, Godfrey. Vocational Guidance Manuals. 1952. 144p. $1.45 paper
> Survey of the field, qualifications, how to get started, opportunities in the priesthood, opportunities in the brotherhood, opportunities in the sisterhood, conclusion, and directory of communities.

Packet of career materials. Lutheran Church in America. Three booklets. 1963. Free
> Discussions of the continuing need and expanding opportunities in religious occupations.

Religion. Nichols, James A. Bellman Publishing Company. Revised 1955. 24p. $1
> Types of positions, description of training, and list of religious schools and seminaries.

Religion as an occupation: a study in the sociology of professions. Fichter, Joseph H. University of Notre Dame Press. 1961. 295p. $6.50
> Material presented in a course in sociology of vocations at Notre Dame. Includes discussion of selection of candidates, their professional training and education, the roles they perform, and problems they meet during their careers.

Religion: earned degrees, by level, sex, and institution. One section of *Earned Degrees Conferred*.
> Useful for judging the extent of a college's program in religion, theology, and religious education.

Religious education director. Chronicle Guidance Publications. 1963. 4p. 35c
> Occupational brief summarizing work performed, training, qualifications, methods of entering, advancement, earnings, and outlook.

Religious vocations. Science Research Associates. 1961. 4p. 35c
> Occupational brief describing nature of work, training, qualifications, opportunities, advantages, disadvantages, and future outlook.

Social and religious workers and counselors. Chapter 7 of *The College Girl Looks Ahead*.
> Characteristics of religious work, talents needed, trying out and preparing for religious work, entering, and kinds of work.

Sources of information on church careers for women. National Council of Churches, Department of Ministry. No date. 7p. 20c
> A bibliography on many types of church careers open to women.

Statement on pre-seminary studies. American Association of Theological Schools. 1963. 4p. Free
> Defines function of preseminary education and recommends course of study for college students who plan to become ministers.

Suggested readings on church vocations. United Christian Missionary Society. 1962. 7p. Mimeographed. Free
Suggestions for students and adult advisers.

**Vocation and Protestant religious occupations. Nelson, John Oliver. Vocational Guidance Manuals. 1963. 160p. $1.45; paper; library binding $2.65
Describes opportunities in church vocations, the pastorate, the church's world mission, Christian education, chaplaincies, campus work, church music, social work, and interchurch work. Also discusses preparation in high school and college, choosing a seminary, and how to begin.

Vocations for women. United Church of Christ. 1960. 8p. Free
For sixteen church vocations, there is a brief description and suggestions as to necessary preparation.

Vocations packet. Interboard Committee on Christian Vocations. 1963. 30 leaflets. 50c
Leaflets on specific church vocations. Some contain discussions on selecting a college, planning a career, and investigating Church related vocations.

We have these ministries. Church of the Brethren. 1960. 4p. Free
Typical activities and recommended training for thirty-four church vocations.

Women's church vocations. National Council of Churches, Department of Ministry. No date. 8p. 5c
Brief description of church secretary, parish music director, church journalist or publicist, college religion teacher, minister, and missionary. Also suggestions to consider before reaching a decision.

Your faith and your life. Million, Elmer. Friendship Press. 1960. 80p. $1
Presentation of a variety of church occupations.

See also Clergyman; Priest; Rabbi

REMEDIAL READING SPECIALIST 0-32.

Positions in the field of reading. Dever, Kathryn. Bureau of Publications. 1956. 165p. $4.25
Report of the role and extent of responsibility of the reading specialist in 3,000 schools. Includes description of jobs and the major functions performed.

**Reading specialist. Robinson, H. Alan. Personnel Services. 1958. 6p. 50c; 25c to students
Occupational abstract. Nature of work, future prospects, qualifications, preparation, entrance, advancement, earnings, advantages, and disadvantages. References for further reading.

REPAIR MECHANIC. See Maintenance mechanic

REPORTER 0-06.71

Better than working. Catling, Patrick Skene. Macmillan Company. 1960. 212p. $3.95
A thoughtful account of the author's first ten years as a reporter.

REPORTER—*Continued*

Career as a news correspondent. Institute for Research. 1960. 24p. $1
> Description of various positions, a typical week's work, qualifications, training, earnings, attractive and unattractive features, and how to get started.

**Career as a newspaper reporter. Institute for Research. 1957. 24p. $1
> Qualifications, earnings, attractive and unattractive features, and outlook. Types of work as a general reporter, foreign correspondent, financial reporter, police reporter, political reporter, and sports writer.

**David White, crime reporter. Lewis, Milton. Dodd, Mead and Company. 1958. 256p. $3
> Career fiction. Story of the adventures in covering criminal cases, requiring curiosity, integrity, and ability.

**Employment outlook for newspaper reporters and technical writers. Bureau of Labor Statistics, U.S. Department of Labor. Supt. of Documents. 1964. 12p. 10c
> Reprint from the *Occupational Outlook Handbook*.

I want to be a news reporter. Greene, Carla. Childrens Press. 1958. 32p. $2
> Prepared for beginning readers with a reading level of upper first grade. Illustrated in color.

The making of the President 1960. White, T. H. Atheneum Publishers. 1961. 400p. $6.95
> Reporting on the workings of American politics, this book gives insight into political reporting.

Nellie Bly: first woman reporter. Noble, Iris. Julian Messner, Inc. 1956. 192p. $3.25. Library binding $3.19 net
> Biography of a reporter who pioneered the way for today's newspaperwomen in exposing crime and corruption.

News reporters and what they do. Botter, David. Franklin Watts, Inc. 1959. 214p. $3.95
> An experienced newspaperman describes the work of reporters, the variety of assignments, and specialized reporting from newspaper-magazine work to radio and television. Many anecdotes about well-known reporters are included. For grades 7 to 11.

Newspaper reporter. Splaver, Sarah. Personnel Services. 1958. 6p. 50c; 25c to students
> Nature of work, qualifications, preparation, entrance and advancement, earnings, advantages, and disadvantages.

Newspaper reporter. Careers. 1960. 2p. 15c
> Career summary for desk-top file. Duties, qualifications, and outlook.

Newspaper reporter. Chronicle Guidance Publications. 1960. 4p. 35c
> Occupational brief summarizing work performed, working conditions, qualifications, training, earnings, opportunities, methods of entry, related jobs, and outlook.

**Newspaper reporters. One section of *Occupational Outlook Handbook*.
Nature of work, where employed, training, other qualifications, advancement, employment outlook, earnings, and working conditions.

Reporter. California State Department of Employment. 1960. 4p. Single copy free
Duties, working conditions, finding the work, pay, hours, training, promotion, and employment outlook.

Reporter. The Guidance Centre. 1962. 4p. 15c in Canada; 20c elsewhere
History and importance, nature of work, qualifications, working conditions, preparation, remuneration, advancement, outlook, related occupations, and how to get started.

Reporter for the *Sentinel*. Butler, Albert. Abelard-Schuman. 1961. 192p. $3.50
Career fiction. A boy's summer job as a reporter teaches him much about newspaper work.

* Reporters. Science Research Associates. 1963. 4p. 35c
Occupational brief describing nature of work, requirements, earnings, and future outlook.

Reporters around the world. Kelly, Frank K. Little, Brown and Company. 1957. 242p. $3.50
Seventeen adventures of famous newspapermen and women participating in events that shook the world. For younger readers.

Wire service reporting. Greene, Gael. Alumnae Advisory Center. 1957. 4p. 25c
Reprint from *Mademoiselle* describing this work for a woman.
See also Editor; Journalist; Writer

RESEARCH WORKER 0-68.40 through 0-68.49

Armstrong research. Armstrong Cork Company. 1962. 10p. Free
Illustrated booklet describing basic areas of research.

Basic research, a national resource. National Science Foundation. Supt. of Documents. 1957. 64p. 45c
The booklet presents the case for basic research in science as an activity so indispensable to the nation that the Federal Government cannot avoid responsibility for its encouragement and support. Describes some basic research in action.

**Careers in research science. Wachs, Theodore, Jr. Henry Z. Walck, Inc. 1961. 96p. $3.50
Describes scientific research in each of the major divisions of physical science: physics, chemistry, mathematics, and astronomy. Contains discussion of work in government, universities, and industry with the advantages and disadvantages of each. Reading list. Illustrated.

* Careers in scientific research and development work in industry. Institute for Research. 1960. 24p. $1
Extent of research and development in industry, duties, typical day's work, attractive and unattractive features, qualifications, earnings, opportunities, and how to get started.

RESEARCH WORKER—*Continued*

Decision for research. American Heart Association. 1962. 12p. Single copy free from local Heart Associations
Booklet for high school and college students describing research opportunities and steps to be taken by students interested in research careers. Illustrated.

**Disease detectives: your career in medical research. Neal, Harry E. Julian Messner, Inc. 1959. 192p. $3.50
Information on nature of work, qualifications, and preparation of a wide variety of research workers. Includes bacteriologist, biochemist, medical artist, pharmacist, physiologist, psychiatrist, and radiation specialist.

Du Pont research. E. I. du Pont de Nemours and Company. 1962. 8p. Free
An illustrated reprint describing applied research opportunities.

Manpower for medical research requirements and resources, 1965-1970. Public Health Service, U.S. Department of Health, Education, and Welfare. Supt. of Documents. 1963. 72p. 55c
Describes the growth of medical research and the outlook for the future. Emphasizes the manpower requirements to meet the future growth of medical research.

Research careers in agriculture. Institute for Research. 1962. 24p. $1
Some outstanding research achievements, places of employment, attractive and unattractive features, qualifications, training, salaries, getting started, and outlook.

Research careers in the medical field. Institute for Research. 1958. 24p. $1
Kinds of work, qualifications, educational requirements, earnings, attractive and unattractive features, and outlook for employment. Includes a list of foundations, organizations, and pharmaceutical manufacturers which employ medical research workers.

Title examiner. Careers. 1963. 2p. 15c
Career summary for desk-top file. Duties, qualifications, and outlook.

Unusual careers. Munzer, Martha E. Alfred A. Knopf, Inc. 1962. 160p. $3
The careers described are solar scientist, geologist, meteorologist, oceanographer, ecologist, sanitary engineer, research chemist, and city and regional planner. This book emphasizes the opportunities in the conservation of natural resources.

The work of the United States cotton ginning research laboratories. U.S. Department of Agriculture. Miscellaneous Publication Number 731. Supt. of Documents. 1956. 20p. 15c
Describes the research accomplishments, nature of work, and the need for continuing research.

See also Scientist

RESTAURANT MANAGER 0-71.

I want to be a restaurant owner. Greene, Carla. Childrens Press. 1959. 32p. $2
> Prepared for beginning readers with a reading level of upper first grade. Illustrated in color.

The restaurant business. Voegele, Walter O. Bellman Publishing Company. 1956. 36p. $1
> Characteristics and size of the business, outlook and trends, kinds of jobs, compensation, how to get started, and qualifications needed to succeed.

Restaurant manager. Careers. 1961. 2p. 15c
> Career summary for desk-top file. Duties, qualifications, and outlook.

Restaurant manager. Chronicle Guidance Publications. 1961. 4p. 35c
> Occupational brief summarizing work performed, where employed, requirements, training, methods of entry, advantages, disadvantages and outlook.

Restaurant managers. Science Research Associates 1964. 4p. 35c
> Occupational brief describing nature of work, training, qualifications, opportunities, and outlook.

**Restaurant managers and assistants. One section of *Occupational Outlook Handbook*.
> Nature of work, where employed, training, other qualifications, employment outlook, earnings, and working conditions.

* Restaurant, tea room and cafeteria operation as a career. Institute for Research. 1959. 24p. $1
> Advantages, disadvantages, typical day's work, training, and earnings. List of eighteen routine positions in restaurant work.

School lunch director. Careers. 1960. 2p. 15c
> Career summary for desk-top file. Duties, qualifications, and outlook.

Snack shop restaurant operation as a career. Institute for Research. 1963. 24p. $1
> Kinds of snack shops, qualifications, training, duties, factors necessary for success, and attractive and unattractive features. Also described is a typical day's work in a snack shop restaurant.

Starting and managing a small restaurant. Small Business Administration. Supt. of Documents. 1964. 116p. 45c
> Published to help prospective restaurant owners decide whether they have the basic qualifications, financing, and experience for success.

See also Hotel and restaurant manager; Motel manager

RETAIL MANAGER 0-72.

The A&P way. Editors of Supermarket News. Fairchild Publications. 1957. 36p. $1
> The merchandising methods described give an idea of the nature of work in a supermarket.

RETAIL MANAGER—*Continued*

Antique shop operation as a career. Institute for Research. 1962. 20p. $1
 Personal qualifications, training, related jobs, attractive and unattractive features, earnings, and what the antique shop owner needs to know.

Auto accessories and parts retailing as a career. Institute for Research. 1961. 20p. $1
 Description of various positions, a typical day's work, attractive and unattractive features, qualifications, training, earnings, and how to get started.

Business proprietor, retail. Chronicle Guidance Publications. 1961. 4p. 35c
 Occupational brief summarizing work performed, personal qualifications, opportunities, and employment outlook.

Camera and photo supply shop management as a career. Institute for Research. 1961. 20p. $1
 Types of camera and photo supply shops, size of the business, opportunities in this field, personal qualifications, education and training, typical day's work, attractive and unattractive features, salaries and earnings, kinds of jobs, and how to get started.

Candy store operation as a career. Institute for Research. 1962. 24p. $1
 Discussion of types of candy stores, opportunities, and requirements.

Career opportunities in national general merchandise chains. Institute of Distribution. 1963. 6p. Free
 Description of careers in retailing including the managerial and executive training offered by some chain stores.

**Careers for women in retailing. Women's Bureau, U.S. Dept. of Labor. Supt. of Labor. 1963. 52p. 25c
 Describes nature of work and requirements for positions in merchandising other than selling in personnel, sales promotion, and other divisions found in department and specialty stores.

Careers in furniture stores and furniture store management. Institute for Research. 1962. 23p. $1
 Description of jobs, typical day's work, qualifications, training, earnings, attractive and unattractive features, and getting started.

Careers in hardware retailing. Institute for Research. 1961. 22p. $1
 Description of jobs, a typical day's work, attractive and unattractive features, qualifications, training, earnings, and how to get started.

Careers in household appliance retailing. Institute for Research. 1961. 19p. $1
 Description of various positions, typical day's work, attractive and unattractive features, qualifications, training, earnings, and getting started.

* Careers in retailing. Hogadone, Edwina. Rochester Institute of Technology. Revised 1963. 28p. Free
 Description of jobs in selling, buying, personnel, and advertising. Discussion of advantages, problems, and training. Includes a chart showing the individual abilities and interests and the retail positions generally matching these.

Careers in the athletic and sporting goods shop. Institute for Research. 1956. 24p. $1

Nature of the business, a typical day's work, job opportunities, potential earnings, attractive and unattractive features, personal qualifications, education, training, and opportunities for women.

Directory of colleges and universities with specializations in retailing. American Collegiate Retailing Association. 1961. 20p. 15c. Single copy free

Includes list of sixty-four degree-granting institutions offering a major in retailing or marketing. Detailed information about the sixteen schools which are members of the American Collegiate Retailing Association.

Employee earnings in retail trade, June 1961. Bureau of Labor Statistics, U.S. Department of Labor. Supt. of Documents. 1963. 67p. 45c

Presents estimates of employment, average hourly earnings, and weekly hours of work of nonsupervisory employees in retail trade.

F. W. Woolworth: five and ten boy. Myers, Elisabeth P. Bobbs-Merrill Company. 1962. 200p. $2.25

Biography prepared for third to seventh grades, showing how the founder of the five and ten cent stores got started.

Farm equipment dealers. Science Research Associates. 1961. 4p. 35c

Occupational brief describing nature of work, requirements, ways of getting started, earnings, advantages, disadvantages, and future outlook.

Farm equipment dealership sales and service—careers. Institute for Research. 1956. 24p. $1

History and types of jobs, typical day's work, attractive and unattractive features, qualifications, education and training, earnings, opportunities, and how to get a dealership.

Gift and art shop operation as a career. Institute for Research. 1964. 24p. $1

Types of positions, typical day's work, qualifications, opportunities, attractive and unattractive features.

Gift shop owners and managers. Science Research Associates. 1961. 4p. 35c

Occupational brief describing nature of work, requirements, getting started, income possibilities, advantages, disadvantages, and future outlook.

The girl from Boothill. Randall, Janet. David McKay Company. 1962. 192p. $3.50

Career fiction. Working in a curio shop, a girl's knowledge of historical lore is useful in the semi-ghost town in Nevada.

Grocery store operation and supermarket management careers. Institute for Research. 1958. 24p. $1

Opportunities, how to get started, earnings, and attractive and unattractive features.

The hardware business. National Retail Hardware Association. 1962. 24p. Free

Discussion of where and how to start, capital needed, requirements, and operating problems.

RETAIL MANAGER—*Continued*

I want to be a storekeeper. Greene, Carla. Childrens Press. 1958. 32p. $2
> Prepared for beginning readers with a reading level of upper first grade. Illustrated in color.

Job descriptions for the retail trade. U.S. Employment Service, U.S. Department of Labor. Supt. of Documents. 1938. 743p. 3 volumes. $3.75
> One of a series of Volume Job Descriptions. Describes occupations in retail store establishments, including both department stores and specialty shops. Volume I includes merchandise handling, management and personnel jobs, maintenance and operation jobs, and accommodation services such as credit and adjustment. Volume II includes merchandising jobs and merchandise services. Volume III includes selling and sales promotion such as advertising and display. Illustrated.

Mail order workers. Science Research Associates. 1958. 4p. 35c
> Occupational brief describing nature of work, qualifications, opportunities, advantages, and future outlook.

Men's clothing store operation as a career. Institute for Research. 1961. 23p. $1
> Qualifications, training, typical day's work, attractive and unattractive features, and opportunities for operating an independent store and a chain store.

* Opportunities in retailing. American Collegiate Retailing Association. 1962. 22p. Free
> Description of positions available to graduates of a specialized retailing program, education, salary, outlook, and opportunities. Included also is information about the sixteen colleges offering major study programs in retailing.

Pointing the way toward merchandising today. National Cash Register Company. 1961. 24p. Free
> Contains a comparison of past and present retailing. The ten principles of modern retailing give an idea of the scope of work involved.

**Retail business proprietor. Chronicle Guidance Publications. 1961. 4p. 35c
> Occupational brief summarizing work performed, working conditions, personal qualifications, earnings, training, factors in success and failure, methods of entry, advantages, disadvantages, and ways of determining interest and ability.

Retailing as a career. Dakins, J. Gordon. Bellman Publishing Company. 1959. 52p. $1
> History and importance of retailing, kinds of jobs, qualifications, preparation, opportunity for advancement, earnings, conditions of work, advantages, and disadvantages. Includes list of schools offering special courses in retailing.

Retailing as a career. Boston University. 1962. 15p. Free
> Recruiting booklet describing opportunities in the field of retail trade such as merchandising, sales promotion, store management, finance and control, and retailing department of a manufacturing concern. Also discussion of qualities needed and training.

**Retailing has a career for you. National Retail Dry Goods Association. No date. 24p. 35c
  Discussion of the opportunities and rewards retailing offers as well as the qualities needed to enter and succeed in retailing. Includes merchandising, store operation, sales promotion, personnel, and control.

Sand in my castle. Belden, Shirley. David McKay Company. 1958. 174p. $2.95
  Career fiction. Story of girl who acquires self-reliance through photography, and gift shop and tearoom management.

Should you go into food retailing? Eberhard, L. V. New York Life Insurance Company. 1960. 12p. Free
  Outlook, satisfactions, earnings, qualifications, and training.

Should you go into retailing? Lazarus, Fred, Jr. New York Life Insurance Company. 1960. 12p. Free
  Opportunities, advantages, disadvantages, salaries, preparation, and qualities necessary for success.

Television, radio, records, and Hi Fi retailing as a career. Institute for Research. 1962. 24p. $1
  Qualifications, opportunities, typical day's work, and attractive and unattractive features. Information about work of owner, television and radio salesman, record clerk, and radio and television serviceman.

Your future in retailing. Scott, George. Richards Rosen Press. 1961. 160p. $2.95
  Presents the field of retailing from the specialty shop to the department store as rich in opportunity and interest.

See also Department store worker; Food store worker; Salesperson

ROOFER   5-25.220 and 7-31.

**Employment outlook for sheet-metal workers and roofers. Bureau of Labor Statistics, U.S. Department of Labor. Supt. of Documents. 1964. 16p. 10c
  Reprint from the *Occupational Outlook Handbook.*

Roofer. Careers. 1960. 2p. 15c
  Career summary for desk-top file. Duties, qualifications, and outlook.

Roofers. Science Research Associates. 1961. 4p. 35c
  Occupational brief describing work, qualifications, working conditions, earnings, and outlook.

**Roofers. One section of *Occupational Outlook Handbook.*
  Nature of work, where employed, training, other qualifications, advancement, employment outlook, earnings, and working conditions.

ROPE MAKER   4-19.731

The cordage business. Scherff, William A. Research Publishing Company. 1951. 32p. $2
  Description of a tour through a typical, modern cordage plant is followed by a discussion of employment opportunities, stability of the industry, advantages, and disadvantages of work in the making of ropes and cords.

ROUTEMAN   7-35.100

Career as a route and territorial salesman. Institute for Research. 1962. 24p. $1
   Description of duties, a typical week's work, personal qualifications, training, earnings, attractive and unattractive features, opportunities, and how to get started. Includes a list of members of the National Association of Direct Selling Companies.

* Delivery route salesmen. Science Research Associates. 1961. 4p. 35c
   Occupational brief describing work, qualifications, earnings, things to consider, and outlook. Selected references.

Routeman. California State Department of Employment. 1959. 4p. Single copy free
   Duties, pay, hours, promotion, training, and employment prospects in California.

Routeman. Careers. 1963. 2p. 15c
   Career summary for desk-top file. Duties, qualifications, and outlook.

Routeman. Chronicle Guidance Publications. 1960. 4p. 35c
   Occupational brief summarizing work performed, working conditions, hours, earnings, personal qualifications, training requirements, opportunities, employment outlook, and entry into the job.

**Routemen. One section of *Occupational Outlook Handbook*.
   Nature of work, where employed, qualifications, earnings, employment outlook, and working conditions.

RUBBER INDUSTRY WORKER   4, 6, 8-57.

**Rubber industry workers. Science Research Associates. 1961. 4p. 35c
   Occupational brief describing kinds of work, requirements, training, earnings, advantages, disadvantages, and future outlook.

SAFETY ENGINEER   0-18.01

Careers in fire protection engineering. Illinois Institute of Technology. No date. 6p. Free
   Description of work, opportunities, salaries, and training. The sequence of college courses required to earn a degree in fire protection and safety engineering is listed for eight semesters.

Safety engineer. Group, Vernard. Personnel Services. 1958. 6p. 50c; 25c to students
   Occupational abstract. Nature of work, future prospects, qualifications, preparation, entrance, earnings, related occupations, number, and distribution of workers.

Safety engineer. Careers. 1961. 2p. 15c
   Career summary for desk-top file. Duties, qualifications, and outlook.

Safety engineer. Pages 113-14 of *Health Careers Guidebook*.
   Personal qualifications, training, opportunities, and prospects.

**Safety engineering. American Society of Safety Engineers. 1961. 7p. Free
  Description of the work of removing physical hazards from a plant and devising safe practices to prevent accidents and injuries. Includes duties, training, earnings, and a list of colleges offering preparation.

* Safety engineers. Science Research Associates. 1961. 4p. 35c
  Occupational brief describing work, qualifications, how to get started, and outlook.

SAILOR   2-68.20

All about the U.S. Navy. Castillo, Commander Edmund. Random House, Inc. 1961. 144p. $1.95
  Admiral Nimitz states in the Foreword that this book is about the Navy today—the excitement of a carrier task force launching a strike against an "enemy" base on land, frogmen creeping ashore to lay the groundwork for a massive amphibious assault, the men who hide beneath the sea in submarines carrying missiles, and the constant struggle for supremacy between the surface ship and the submarine. Illustrated.

Annapolis; the life of a midshipman. Engeman, John T. Lothrop, Lee and Shepard Company. 1956. 152p. $3.50
  Photographs and brief text depicting life at Annapolis from plebe year through graduation.

Annapolis today. United States Naval Institute. 1963. 329p. $6
  The preface to this sixth edition states that the text has been revised, additional chapters included, and a new selection of photographs used. Includes description of customs, traditions, and way of life at the Naval Academy.

Careers in the naval services of the United States. Institute for Research. 1958. 24p. $1
  History of the Navy and description of work in its various branches. Qualifications, attractive and unattractive features, and salaries and allowances for officers and enlisted men.

**Current career booklets. U.S. Department of the Navy. Fifteen booklets. Free
  Frequently revised booklets are available from local recruiting offices or from the above. Present materials include: High school seaman recruit, Nuclear field seaman recruit, and Sub-venture in the atomic Navy.

Go, Navy, go. Archibald, Joseph. Macrae Smith Company. 1956. 192p. $2.95
  Fictional account of an Annapolis cadet who learns to participate in football and other activities with true Navy spirit.

Midshipman Lee of the Naval Academy. White, Robb. Random House, Inc. 1954. 216p. $2.95
  Career fiction. Describes the life of a midshipman preparing for a career as a naval officer. For junior high school boys.

Naval officer. The Guidance Centre. 1961. 4p. 15c in Canada; 20c elsewhere
  History and importance, nature of work, qualifications, working conditions, preparation, remuneration, advancement, outlook, related occupations, and how to get started.

SAILOR—*Continued*

The Naval Reserve Officers Training Corps. U.S. Department of the Navy. Revised annually. 38p. Free

Opportunities offered, obligations involved, eligibility requirements, and the selection procedures of the NROTC program. Includes names and locations of the colleges which are recognized as training centers. Information concerning the test which all applicants are required to take, including physical requirements and the physical defects for which they may be disqualified. Deadline dates and the list of documents required for interviews.

Naval seaman. The Guidance Centre. 1962. 4p. 15c in Canada; 20c elsewhere

History and importance, nature of work, qualifications, working conditions, preparation, remuneration, advancement, outlook, related occupations, and how to get started.

The navy. Robertson, Keith. Viking Press. Revised 1962. 192p. $3

Details of regulations and opportunities. For grades 7 to 10.

Navy career opportunities. Careers. 1961. 8p. 25c

Career brief describing opportunities and requirements for enlistment.

Navy men and what they do. Gimpel, Herbert J. Franklin Watts, Inc. 1963. 196p. $3.95

Discussion of the mission and importance of the navy; the variety of occupations on land, sea, and in the air; duties; and training. For grades 7 to 11.

Our space age navy. Colby, Carroll B. Coward-McCann, Inc. 1962. 48p. $2.50. Library edition $2.52 net

Illustrated with many photographs of carriers, aircraft, submarines, and missiles. Written for ages 8 to 12.

Regulations governing the admission of candidates into the U.S. Naval Academy as midshipmen. Bureau of Naval Personnel, U.S. Department of the Navy. 1963. 46p. Free

Description of the life of a career naval officer, sources of nomination, general requirements for admission, physical and scholastic qualifications, nomination procedures, and entrance procedures.

United States Naval Academy. The Academy. 1963. 106p. Free

Catalogue of information describing the courses of study, the midshipman's routine, the basic curriculum, and regulations at the academy.

**United States Navy occupational handbook. U.S. Department of the Navy. 1960. 166p. Free to counselors and librarians

This handbook contains 72 vocational information briefs containing information about related civilian jobs. This book also includes the Navy's "stay in school" policy for schools, with information on education, classification, enlistment requirements, promotions, pay and retirement, a school subject index for educational guidance, career pattern, and suggestions for use. The briefs may be obtained separately. Each of the briefs describes the nature of work, duties, work assignment, qualifications, preparation, training given, related civilian jobs, and emergency service ratings. Suitable for boys and girls. Generously illustrated.

See also Military serviceman; Submarine officer

SALES ENGINEER   0-15. through 0-20.

Job description for sales engineer I. U.S. Employment Service, U.S. Department of Labor. Supt. of Documents. 1947. 4p. 5c
  Occupational guide. Job summary, work performed, training, related occupations, physical activities, working conditions, and employment variables.

SALESPERSON   1-70.; 1-75.; 1-80.; 1-85. through 1-87.; 1-96.

Bookshop and bookstore sales clerks. Science Research Associates. 1961. 4p. 35c
  Occupational brief describing nature of work, requirements, getting started, income, advantages, disadvantages, and future outlook. Selected references.

A career for you in direct selling. National Association of Direct Selling Companies. 1960. 16p. Free
  A recruiting brochure describing nature of work and its advantages.

Careers in retail selling. Institute for Research. 1956. 24p. $1
  Development of retail selling, attractive and unattractive features, personal qualifications, training, earnings, chances for employment, how to get started, and opportunities for advancement.

Clothing store salespeople. Science Research Associates. 1963. 4p. 35c
  Occupational brief describing work, qualifications, training, opportunities, and outlook.

Demonstrators. Science Research Associates. 1963. 4p. 35c
  Occupational brief describing nature of work, training, qualifications, opportunities, and outlook. Selected references.

Drugstore salesperson. Careers. 1962. 2p. 15c
  Career summary for desk-top file. Duties, qualifications, and outlook.

**Employment outlook for sales workers in retail stores, wholesale trade, and manufacturing. Bureau of Labor Statistics, U.S. Department of Labor. Supt. of Documents. 1964. 16p. 10c
  Reprint from the *Occupational Outlook Handbook*.

Grocery products salesman. Careers. 1963. 2p. 15c
  Career summary for desk-top file. Describes duties, working conditions, qualifications, training, working conditions, and outlook.

House-to-house salesman. Careers. 1964. 8p. 25c
  Career brief describing work performed, personal qualifications, training, working conditions, earnings, and outlook.

House-to-house salespeople. Science Research Associates. 1963. 4p. 35c
  Occupational brief describing the nature of work, requirements, entering the field and advancing, earnings, advantages, disadvantages, and future outlook.

House-to-house salesperson. Chronicle Guidance Publications. 1961. 4p. 35c
  Occupational brief summarizing work performed, working conditions, earnings, personal qualifications, ways of determining interest and ability, training, opportunities, methods of entry, and outlook.

SALESPERSON—*Continued*

**Jobs in selling. Science Research Associates. 1959. 32p. $1
Describes the variety of job prospects and opportunities within the field, especially for the selling of automobiles, travel, real estate, insurance, or merchandise in department stores.

Manufacturer's representative. Careers. 1961. 8p. 25c
Career brief describing duties, working conditions, training, personal requirements, places of employment, earnings, and outlook.

**Manufacturers' salesmen. One section of *Occupational Outlook Handbook*.
Nature of work, where employed, training, employment outlook, earnings, and working conditions.

**Opportunities in selling. Haas, Kenneth B. Vocational Guidance Manuals. 1960. 96p. $1.45 paper
This manual explains the meaning and scope of salesmanship, describes the various kinds of selling, suggests a pathway for advancement, summarizes opportunities and rewards, and tells what is required of a person who wants to be a success in the selling field.

Opportunities in selling. Council on Opportunities in Selling, Inc. 1963. 23p. 25c. Free to counselors
Includes qualifications, training, and opportunities in sales work.

Retail clothing salespeople. Science Research Associates. 1963. 4p. 35c
Occupational brief describing nature of work, requirements, preparation, working conditions, earnings, and future outlook.

Retail salespeople. Science Research Associates. 1963. 4p. 35c
Occupational brief describing nature of work, requirements, getting started and advancing, earnings, advantages, disadvantages, and future outlook. Selected references.

* Retail salespersons. Chronicle Guidance Publications. 1962. 4p. 35c
Occupational brief describing work performed, working conditions, personal qualifications, determination of aptitudes and interests, training requirements, promotional opportunities, employment outlook, methods of entry, and related jobs.

Sales manager. Careers. 1961. 2p. 15c
Career summary for desk-top file. Duties, qualifications, and outlook.

**Sales occupations. One chapter of *Occupational Outlook Handbook*.
Nature of work, where employed, training, other qualifications, advancement, employment outlook, earnings, and working conditions for each of the following: salesmen and saleswomen in retail stores, salesmen in wholesale trade, manufacturers' salesmen, life insurance agents, property and casualty insurance agents and brokers, and real estate salesmen and brokers.

* Salesman. Chronicle Guidance Publications. 1962. 4p. 35c
Occupational brief explaining the difference and similarities between the work of the wholesale, retail, and the manufacturer's salesmen. Also description of qualifications, working conditions, earnings, methods of entry, opportunities, and outlook.

Salesman. The Guidance Centre. 1963. 4p. 15c in Canada; 20c elsewhere
History and importance, nature of work, qualifications, preparation, advancement, outlook, remuneration, advantages, disadvantages, how to get started, and related occupations.

* Salesmanship as a career. Institute for Research. 1957. 24p. $1
Importance of salesmanship, typical day's work, salaries, ways of getting started, advantages and disadvantages. Duties and qualifications for retail salesman and traveling specialty and commodity salesmen.

**Salesmen and saleswomen in retail stores. One section of *Occupational Outlook Handbook*.
Nature of work, where employed, training, other qualifications, advancement, employment outlook, earnings, and working conditions.

**Salesmen in wholesale trade. One section of *Occupational Outlook Handbook*.
Nature of work, where employed, training, employment outlook, earnings, and working conditions.

Salesmen—manufacturers' and wholesalers'. Science Research Associates. 1961. 4p. 35c
Occupational brief describing duties, requirements, getting started and advancing, earnings, advantages, disadvantages, and future outlook.

Salesperson. Careers. 1960. 2p. 15c
Career summary for desk-top file. Duties, qualifications, and outlook.

Scientist salesman. Careers. 1964. 2p. 15c
Career summary for desk-top file. Duties, qualifications, and outlook.

* Selling as a career. Changing Times. 1959. 3p. 15c
Reprint discussing the preparation and future of a career in sales.

Selling as a career. Sales and Marketing Executives-International. No date. 5p. Free
Discussion of opportunities for promotion, advantages, and challenges in the field of selling.

Should you be a salesman? Whitney, Robert A. New York Life Insurance Company. 1959. 12p. Free
Discussion of qualities one should possess.

Super market occupations. Michigan Employment Security Commission. 1962. 19p. 25c
Introduction, nature of work, working conditions, location of jobs, employment outlook, earnings, requirements for entry, disadvantages, and advantages.

Variety store salesclerks. Science Research Associates. 1961. 4p. 35c
Occupational brief describing jobs for young women, jobs for young men, requirements, training, getting started and advancing, earnings, advantages, disadvantages, and future outlook.

Your future in direct selling. Goodrich, Foster. Richards Rosen Press. 1963. 158p. $2.95
Describes the qualifications, training programs, and the increase in direct selling with the suburban trend.

SALESPERSON—*Continued*

Your marketing career in industry. National Research Bureau. 1957. 32p.
20c
 Discussion of the many kinds of jobs in distribution, its varied career opportunities, and how to prepare for them. Illustrated.

 See also Automobile salesman; Department store worker; Retail manager

SALT INDUSTRY WORKER   4, 6, 8-52.30 through 4, 6, 8-52.39

The salt industry. Wilcox, Wendell. Bellman Publishing Company. 1958.
31p. $1
 Methods of salt production, characteristics of the industry, and employment.

SANITARY ENGINEER   0-16.01

Educational and other qualifications of public health sanitarians. American Public Health Association. 1957. 8p. Free
 General scope of the work, functions, and educational requirements.

Educational qualifications of sanitary engineers engaged in the field of
public health. American Public Health Association. 1955. 9p. Free
 Scope of work and educational requirements.

Environmental health services. Pages 74-9 of *Health Careers Guidebook.*
 Information about qualifications, training, and opportunities for the sanitary
engineer and the sanitarian.

Health manpower source book, Section 16, sanitarians. Public Health
Service, U.S. Department of Health, Education, and Welfare. Supt. of
Documents. 1963. 52p. 35c
 Basic data on the employment, salaries, education, location, and character-
istics of sanitarians. Many statistical summaries.

* Public health sanitarians. Science Research Associates. 1963. 4p. 35c
 Occupational brief describing nature of work, training, qualifications, opportunities, advantages, disadvantages, and future outlook. Selected references.

Sanitary engineer. Careers. 1960. 2p. 15c
 Career summary for desk-top file. Duties, qualifications, and outlook.

Sanitary engineer. The Guidance Centre. 1961. 4p. 15c in Canada; 20c
elsewhere
 History and importance, nature of work, qualifications, working conditions,
preparation, earnings, advancement, outlook, related occupations, and how to
get started.

Sanitary engineering. Hollis, Mark D. and Ludwig, Harvey F. Chapter 21
of *Engineering Enrollment in the United States.*
 Trends in enrollments and future requirements for specialists in this area.

Sanitary engineering as a career. Institute for Research. 1948. 20p. $1
 Advantages, disadvantages, qualifications, training, opportunities, and salaries.
Typical work in government service, industry, manufacturing plant, and private
office of a consulting engineer

* Sanitary engineers. Science Research Associates. 1963. 4p. 35c
Occupational brief describing nature of work, duties, requirements, training, earnings, advantages, disadvantages, and future outlook.

SCIENTIST 0-35.; 0-36.

**American science manpower. National Science Foundation. Supt. of Documents. 1962. 105p. 65c
A report of the National Register of Scientific and Technical Personnel, presenting information on economic and professional characteristics of over two hundred thousand scientists. Includes number in each of ninety-five subfields by type of employer. The median annual salaries are reported for each of ninety-five subfields, also.

American women of science. Revised edition. Yost, Edna. J. B. Lippincott Company. 1955. 256p. $3.75
Biographies of twelve women scientists.

Begin your career in science or mathematics. Albright College. 1960. 8p. Free
Leaflet containing pictures of student activities and various fields of specialization.

Can I be a scientist or engineer? Let's find out. General Motors, Public Relations Staff. 1961. 24p. Free
Description of work in mathematics, chemistry, physics, and seven main branches of engineering, with typical jobs in each. Includes also opportunities and suggested high school preparation.

Career opportunities in the physical sciences. University of Chicago, Office of Career Counseling and Placement. 1957. 20p. Free
Suggestions for vocational outlets for those trained in astronomy, chemistry, geography, geology, mathematics, physics, and meteorology.

**Careers and opportunities in science. Pollack, Philip. Dutton and Company. 1960. 194p. $3.95
Revised edition providing information about work in chemistry, physics, atomic power production, geology, biology, conservation, and medical research. For each special field the author discusses the ever-growing opportunities, the personal and educational qualifications, working conditions, prospects for advancement, and further rewards. This book communicates to the reader a sense of the creative excitement that a career in science has to offer, while at the same time imparting the requirements of hard work and adequate training.

Careers for women in science. Angel, Juvenal. World Trade Academy Press. 1962. 42p. $1.25
Includes information about the major fields of specializaiton, opportunities, education required, remuneration, outlook, and how to finance an education in the field of science. References for further reading.

Careers for women in scientific fields. Institute for Research. 1961. 24p. $1
History of women in science, where women scientists work, types of jobs, a typical day's work in an experimental laboratory, attractive and unattractive features, personal characteristics, training, earnings, chances for employment, how to get started, and related positions.

SCIENTIST—*Continued*

**Careers for women in the physical sciences. Women's Bureau, U.S. Department of Labor. Supt. of Documents. 1959. 83p. 35c

This booklet describes the basic preparation recommended for a scientific career, kinds of work, rewards, and outlook. It also analyzes data on the employment, education, type of work, and characteristics of women scientists.

Careers in engineering, mathematics, science, and related fields: a selected bibliography. U.S. Office of Education. Supt. of Documents. 1961. 39p. 25c

Lists of 385 free or inexpensive publications about careers in the sciences: agriculture, biological sciences, engineering, forestry, the health professions, mathematics, and the various physical sciences.

Careers in science. St. Francis College. 1958. 8p. Free

Includes a list of eighty-three careers and the nature of work in each. Bibliography.

Careers in science: a selected bibliography for high school students. American Association for the Advancement of Science. 1961. 23p. 15c

A listing of 236 publications classified under 24 headings. A very useful compilation.

Careers in science at the National Bureau of Standards. National Bureau of Standards, U.S. Department of Commerce. 1962. 32p. Free

Discussion of the types of scientific and technical research and development projects in progress, positions available, and opportunities for promotion. Illustrated.

Careers in science teaching. Future Scientists of America. 1955. 16p. Single copy free; 10 copies, $1

A series of photographs shows the science teacher at work and encourages young people with the necessary qualifications to enter this field.

Careers in the scientific fields. Angel, Juvenal. World Trade Academy Press. 1959. 46p. $1.25

Includes description of the major fields of specialization, education required, opportunities, rewards, future outlook, and methods of financing an education in science.

Degrees in the biological and physical sciences, mathematics, and engineering. U.S. Office of Education. Supt. of Documents. 1963. 35p. 35c

Information about earned degrees in the broad areas as well as in the various specific disciplines within these areas. Data are presented on an annual basis in order to show trends, totals are given for the eleven-year period prior to 1960, and doctorate production by individual institution is given for a ten-year period.

Demand for engineers, 1962. Engineering Manpower Commission. 1962. 60p. $2

A special section is included on employment data for physical scientists.

Dr. George Washington Carver: scientist. Graham, Shirley and Lipscomb, George. Julian Messner, Inc. 1944. 192p. $3.25. Library binding $3.19 net

Biography of the Negro scientist whose research and experiments helped to change agriculture in the South.

* Earth sciences. Massachusetts Institute of Technology. 1963. 32p. Free
    Illustrated brochure describing what the earth sciences are about, what earth scientists do, and how students at M.I.T. prepare themselves for careers as meteorologists, oceanographers, geologists, geophysicists, and geochemists.

Earth sciences: earned degrees, by level, sex, and institution. One section of *Earned Degrees Conferred.*
    Useful for judging the extent of a college's program in each of the following specialties: geology, geophysics, oceanography, and other earth sciences.

Education in the sciences. Philadelphia College of Pharmacy and Science. 1962. 24p. Free
    Illustrated recruiting leaflet describing nature of work, training, and opportunities in pharmacy, chemistry, biology, and bacteriology.

Educational programs and facilities in nuclear science and engineering. Oak Ridge Institute of Nuclear Studies. 1962. 119p. Free to counselors
    Information about the degrees, courses, and facilities for nuclear education in 236 institutions.

**Employment outlook for earth scientists. Bureau of Labor Statistics, U.S. Department of Labor. Supt. of Documents. 1964. 20p. 15c
    Reprint from the *Occupational Outlook Handbook.*

**Employment outlook for physical scientists. Bureau of Labor Statistics, U.S. Department of Labor. Supt. of Documents. 1964. 16p. 10c
    Reprint from the *Occupational Outlook Handbook.*

**Employment outlook for social scientists. Bureau of Labor Statistics, U.S. Department of Labor. Supt. of Documents. 1964. 16p. 10c
    Reprint from the *Occupational Outlook Handbook.*

**Engineers and scientists opportunities. U.S. Atomic Energy Commission, Division of Technical Information. 1962. 62p. Free
    Information concerning engineering and scientific opportunities in key programs in reactor development, regulatory, physical research, biology and medicine, and other technical work. Included also are salaries, character of work, qualifications, and location of employment of eighty-eight specific jobs.

Famous scientists. Stevens, William O. Dodd, Mead and Company. 1952. 164p. $3
    Short biographies of twenty-one pioneers in varied scientific fields—astronomy, botany, physics, and geology Subjects were chosen to show the gradual progress of science.

Federal funds for science X. National Science Foundation. Supt. of Documents. 1962. 145p. 75c
    Yearly report concerning funds for conduct of research and development and recent trends in Federal research.

George Washington Carver: an American biography. Holt, Rackham. Doubleday and Company. 1963. 360p. $4.95
    Biography of the Negro scientist.

SCIENTIST—*Continued*

How to get into science and engineering. Science Clubs of America. 1962. 2p. 10c
   A leaflet to inspire and inform students interested in scientific careers. Includes career possibilities.

I want to be a scientist. Greene, Carla. Childrens Press. 1961. 32p. $2
   Prepared for beginning readers with a reading level of upper first grade. Illustrated in color.

Information on science scholarships and student loans. National Science Foundation. 1960. 9p. Free
   Encouragement for future scientists.

Investing in scientific progress. National Science Foundation. 1961. 30p. Free
   Discussion of how scientific progress affects the nation's future and a plea for further investment in science, engineering education, and basic research.

Is there a future scientist or engineer in your home? Battelle Memorial Institute. 1960. 32p. Free
   Designed to help parents and leaders of young people in the discovery and encouragement of future scientists and engineers. Includes such topics as: Some characteristics which may indicate an embryo scientist or engineer, traits observed in the scientifically talented, what future scientists-engineers must complete in high school, and how to direct the young scientist.

**Jobs in science. Science Research Associates. 1963. 48p. $1
   Describes the variety of job prospects and opportunities within this field, especially for the agronomist, astronomer, chemist, meteorologist, biologist, and physicist. An accompanying wall chart is available for 35c.

The limitless frontiers of science. Indiana University. 1950. 64p. Free
   Description of scope and possibilities in each of twelve natural sciences.

The long-range demand for scientific and technical personnel—a methodological study. National Science Foundation. Supt. of Documents. 1961. 70p. 50c
   Describes methods of projecting employment of scientists, engineers, and technicians; gives illustrative projections, in occupational and industry detail, of the demand for scientists and engineers in 1970 and the implications for education and training.

Madame Curie, a biography. Curie, Eve. Doubleday and Company. 1949. 393p. $5
   Biography which unmistakably points out the value of effort and persistence.

Manpower resources in the earth sciences. Bureau of Labor Statistics, U.S. Department of Labor in cooperation with the National Science Foundation. 1955. 75p. 45c
   Presents data on the numbers of personnel in the areas of specialization, specialties in which they were employed, functions they were performing, types of employers, income, and such personal characteristics as education, age, and sex.

Marie Curie. McKown, Robin. Coward-McCann, Inc. 1959. 128p. $2.95
This biography conveys the spirit of perseverance and devotion to science of the woman who discovered radium. Written for ages 10 to 14.

Meeting manpower needs in science and technology, report number one: graduate training in engineering, mathematics, and physical sciences. The President's Science Advisory Committee. Supt. of Documents. 1963. 45p. 20c
Discussion of the supply of new manpower, ways for expanding that supply to meet increasing needs, and means for producing engineers, mathematicians, and physical scientists of high quality. For administrators.

National science youth program. Science Clubs of America. 1962. 8p. Free
Brief descriptions of science service activities to encourage science talent.

Natural scientists, engineers, and architects. Chapter 13 of *The College Girl Looks Ahead.*
Some characteristics of work in the sciences, talents needed, preparation, and kinds of work.

**New careers in the health sciences. National Health Council. 1962. 25p. Single copy free
Aimed to show high school students the relationship of biology, physics, chemistry, mathematics, and engineering to careers in the health sciences.

**Physical and earth sciences. One section of *Occupational Outlook Handbook.*
Summary of trends and outlook in natural sciences. Specific information is given for each of the major branches: chemistry, astronomy, geology, geophysics, physics, and meteorology. Six illustrations.

Physical science in the Federal Government. U.S. Civil Service Commission. 1955. 12p. Free
Description of career opportunities, qualifications, salary, advantages, and how to apply. Bibliography. Illustrated.

Physical sciences: earned degrees, by level, sex, and institution. One section of *Earned Degrees Conferred.*
Useful for judging the extent of a college's program in each of the following specialties: astronomy, chemistry, metallurgy, meteorology, physics, and general physical science.

* Physical scientist. Chronicle Guidance Publications. 1962. 8p. 50c
Occupational brief summarizing duties, working conditions, opportunities, and outlook for each of the following: astronomer, geographer, geologist, geophysicist, meteorologist, oceanographer, and physicist. Selected references.

Projects: space. Science Clubs of America. 1962. 221p. 50c
The story of U.S. space exploration with reports on fourteen student science projects in space-age science. Written with the technical assistance of the National Aeronautics and Space Administration.

Publications of the National Science Foundation. National Science Foundation. 1962. 8p. Free
Price list of annual reports, brochures, bulletins, studies, and announcements.

SCIENTIST—*Continued*

Publications on scientific and technical manpower. Bureau of Labor Statistics, U.S. Department of Labor. 1962. 8p. Free
> List of about forty publications describing current employment, outlook, and salary information in scientific and technical fields.

Salaries and characteristics of scientists in the National Register of Scientific and Technical Personnel. National Science Foundation. Supt. of Documents. 1962. 10p. 15c
> Information updated every two years on the supply and professional characteristics of scientific personnel in important science fields.

Science. Milwaukee-Downer College. 1959. 16p. Free
> A college bulletin describing opportunities open to the person trained in science.

Science and engineering in American industry. Bureau of Labor Statistics, U.S. Department of Labor. Supt. of Documents. 1960. 117p. 70c
> Prepared for the National Science Foundation. Gives estimates of the number and types of scientists and engineers employed in research and other activities, by industry. Also gives estimates of the total cost of industrial research and development and of the numbers of companies conducting research. Discusses the extent of basic research in private industry and the scientific fields in which the research is conducted.

Science and your career. Bureau of Labor Statistics, U.S. Department of Labor. Revised 1962. 13p. Free
> Emphasizes the importance of science to successful careers in many fields of work and indicates the amount of scientific training needed for some seventy occupations.

Science futures for girls. Women's Bureau, U.S. Department of Labor. Supt. of Documents. 1959. 7p. 5c
> An encouraging brochure stressing that tomorrow's scientists will find rewarding opportunities in industry, teaching, and government.

Science projects handbook. Science Clubs of America. 1961. 254p. 55c
> Includes a discussion on how to become a scientist. Describes a variety of successful projects done by winners in the Science Talent Search and the National Science Fair.

Science teacher. Group, Vernard. Personnel Services. 1963. 6p. 50c; 25c to students
> Occupational abstract. Nature of work, qualifications, preparation, entrance, advancement, earnings, future prospects, and related occupations.

Science teacher. Chronicle Guidance Publications. 1962. 4p. 35c
> Occupational brief summarizing work performed, earnings, benefits, personal requirements, educational qualifications, opportunities, and outlook. Selected references.

Scientific and technical personnel in industry. National Science Foundation. Supt. of Documents. 1961. 58p. 45c
> A survey of employment of scientific and technical personnel in private industry. Includes discussion of trends and distribution by function, industry, and size of employing company.

Scientific and technical personnel in state government agencies. National Science Foundation. Supt. of Documents. 1961. 67p. 45c
Gives information on the number of persons employed by state agencies in the major scientific and engineering occupations. Data are classified by state, type of agency, and function.

Scientific careers and vocational development theory. Super, Donald and Bachrach, Paul B. Bureau of Publications. 1957. 135p. $1
Includes summary of the characteristics of natural scientists, mathematicians, and engineers.

Scientific research and development in American industry—a study of manpower and costs. Bureau of Labor Statistics, U.S. Department of Labor. Supt. of Documents. 1953. 106p. 50c
Provides information on the numbers and types of scientists and engineers employed in research and other activities, by industry; also on employment of supporting personnel and cost of industrial research and development.

**Scientist. Morison, Robert S. Macmillan Company. 1964. 200p. $3.95
The author draws upon his experience as a physician to provide a picture of education and necessary preparation, the various opportunities, and the excitement of achievements in modern science.

Scientists and engineers in the Federal Government. National Science Foundation. Supt. of Documents. 1961. 44p. 35c
Report on the fields of employment of scientific and technical personnel in Federal agencies. Shows the numbers of those persons engaged in research and development. Many tables show trends, occupational distribution, agency employment, and geographical distribution.

Scientists who changed the world. Poole, Lynn and Poole, Gray. Dodd, Mead and Company. 1960. 164p. $3
Biographies of seventeen pioneers who have opened up new frontiers in their various fields of science.

Scientists who work with astronauts. Poole, Lynn and Poole, Gray. Dodd, Mead and Company. 1964. 192p. $3.50
Biographies of key men and women in twelve areas of science that are essential to the success of the space program.

She lived for science: Irene Joliot-Curie. McKown, Robin. Julian Messner, Inc. 1961. 192p. $3.25. Library binding $3.19 net
Biography of the oldest daughter of the noted Marie and Pierre Curie, who with her husband, discovered artificial radioactivity and won a Nobel prize in chemistry. For grades 7 to 11.

The shortage of scientists and engineers. McGraw-Hill Book Company. 1957. 12p. Free
A series of articles to increase public knowledge and understanding of this problem.

Should you be a scientist? Teller, Edward. New York Life Insurance Company. 1958. 12p. Free
Description of recent achievements in science, need for trained scientists, requisites necessary for success, advantages, and disadvantages.

SCIENTIST—*Continued*

**So you want to be a scientist. Nourse, Alan. Harper and Row. 1960. 182p. $3.50

For those who are interested in becoming creative scientists, the disciplines, demands, rewards, educational and training requirements, variety of work, and future outlook are described. Separate chapters are included on mathematics, physics, chemistry, biology, and earth sciences.

Some new technologies and their promise for the life sciences. President's Science Advisory Committee. Supt. of Documents. 1963. 22p. 15c

This report attempts to clarify the relations between some of the life sciences and technological change, and to evaluate their significance.

Statistical handbook of science education. National Science Foundation. Supt. of Documents. 1960. 94p. 55c

This publication is a compilation of pertinent statistical material on the education and training of scientists and engineers. Of interest to those concerned with the training of scientific and engineering manpower and those concerned with program administration and policy formation in scientific matters.

The story of Madame Curie. Thorne, Alice. Scholastic Book Services. 1961. 160p. 35c

Paperback edition of biography of the scientist.

Summer science training programs for high-ability secondary school students. National Science Foundation. Published annually. 20p. Free

Explanation of the types of training offered, qualifications, and financial aid for participants. List of colleges which offer these programs and the number of students accepted in each.

Thousands of science projects. Science Clubs of America. 1955. 46p. 25c; 10 for $1

Suggestions for projects from the Science Talent Search Scholarship contest and the National Science Fair may be found in this listing of projects prepared by students during the past several years.

Today's scientists. Gourlay, Walter E. Sterling Publishing Company. 1962. 64p. $1.10 paper

This book presents the biographies and discoveries of twenty-eight leading modern scientists.

Twelve pioneers of science. Sootin, Harry. Vanguard Press. 1960. 254p. $3

Inspiring biographies of twelve scientists from various countries, each a pioneer in his field. All of them persisted through years of failure and disappointment but continued to explore frontier areas of human knowledge such as radioactivity, chlorine, electric battery, barometric pressure, potassium, and electromagnetic waves.

Unusual careers. Munzer, Martha E. Alfred A. Knopf, Inc. 1962. 160p. $3

The author emphasizes the opportunities in the conservation of natural resources. The careers described are solar scientist, geologist, meteorologist, oceanographer, ecologist, sanitary engineer, research chemist, and city and regional planner.

What does a scientist do? Zarchy, Harry. Dodd, Mead and Company. 1959. 64p. $2.50
Simple text and pictures portray varied activities of scientists. Written for grades 3 to 7.

Why study science? One section of *Three Why's.*
Points out the need for the study of science.

**Women in scientific careers. National Science Foundation. Supt. of Documents. 1961. 18p. 20c
An effort to acquaint women students with the career opportunities and intellectual satisfactions of work in science and engineering. Included is a table giving the distribution of employed women scientists by field and work activity.

Women of modern science. Yost, Edna. Dodd, Mead and Company. 1959. 176p. $3
Biographies of eleven women who have made contributions to research in the science to which they were dedicated.

Your career in industry as a scientist or engineer. National Research Bureau. 1958. 32p. 20c
Encourages student interest in science studies. Discussion of the crucial importance of science and engineering, the numerous opportunities, and how to prepare for them. Good section on testing one's interest in science. Illustrated.

See also Engineer; Research worker

SECRETARY   1-33.

Announcement of the CPS examination. National Secretaries Association. 1963. 6p. 5c
Information about the examination content and qualifications which must be met to become a certified professional secretary.

Applied secretarial practice. Fifth edition. Gregg, John Robert; Fries, Albert; Rowe, Margaret; and Travis, Dorothy. Gregg Publishing Company, McGraw-Hill Book Company. 1962. 512p. $4.64
Textbook for use with classes in secretarial practice. Includes skills and personal qualities needed, duties, finding a job, and how to succeed on the job.

Calling professional secretaries. National Secretaries Association. 1961. 6p. 8c
Description of duties, qualifications, opportunities, and how to meet the standards of the title, "certified professional secretary."

**Careers for specialized secretaries. Angel, Juvenal L. World Trade Academy Press. 1958. 27p. $1.25
Description of work, training, remuneration, opportunities, and where employment is found for each of the following: Diplomatic secretary, public relations secretary, foreign trade secretary, bilingual secretary, medical secretary, legal secretary, and executive secretary.

College secretarial procedures. Third edition. Place, Irene and Hicks, Charles. Gregg Publishing Division, McGraw-Hill Book Company. 1964. 536p. $5.25
This college textbook includes discussion of many secretarial duties.

SECRETARY—*Continued*

Confidential secretary. Carr, Harriett H. Macmillan Company. 1958. 212p. $2.95
> Career fiction. As confidential secretary to a business executive, Joyce finds excitement in her job and in the nation's capital. Written for ages 12 to 16.

**Employment opportunities for women as secretaries, stenographers, typists, and as office-machine operators and cashiers. Women's Bureau, U.S. Department of Labor. Bulletin Number 263. Supt. of Documents. 1957. 30p. 20c
> Description of typical jobs, qualifications, training, earnings, working conditions, advantages, and employment outlook.

**Employment outlook for secretaries, stenographers, and typists. Bureau of Labor Statistics, U.S. Department of Labor. Supt. of Documents. 1964. 8p. 5c
> Reprint from the *Occupational Outlook Handbook*.

Executive secretary. Careers. 1960. 8p. 25c
> Career brief describing duties, working conditions, personal qualifications, training, earnings, places of employment, opportunities for men, outlook, and ways of measuring one's interest and ability.

**Executive secretary. Chronicle Guidance Publications. 1964. 4p. 35c
> Occupational brief describing nature of work, qualifications, working conditions, opportunities for promotion, and outlook.

Forty-seven keys. Berry, Erick. Macmillan Company. 1949. 200p. $2.75
> Career fiction. A high school girl with ambition to write finds an interesting and provocative summer job as an author's secretary. Written for ages 12 to 16.

The girl with the halo. Underwood Corporation. 1962. 24p. 50c
> A cross section of opinion from executives throughout the country on what is needed to become an ideal secretary. Also contains "Twenty tips for tiptop typing."

Male secretary. Careers. 1963. 8p. 25c
> Career brief describing duties, working conditions, training, personal qualifications, employment prospects, and earnings.

Male secretary. Chronicle Guidance Publications. 1960. 4p. 35c
> Occupational brief summarizing work performed, working conditions, personal requirements, training, opportunities, outlook, methods of entry, and related jobs.

Marcia: private secretary. MacDonald, Zillah K. Julian Messner, Inc. 1949. 216p. $2.95
> Career fiction. Includes helpful hints to the would-be secretary and a glimpse of the variety of duties and problems.

The personal secretary. Place, Irene. University of Michigan. 1946. 33p. Mimeographed. $1
> A study of duties, factors that determine success, criteria for personal secretaries, education, salary, and experiences of personal secretaries in sixteen communities in Michigan.

Private and social secretaryship as a career. Institute for Research. 1962. 24p. $1
> History and development of work, qualifications, and attractive and unattractive features.

Roman candle. Baldridge, Letitia. Houghton Mifflin Company. 1956. 308p. $3.75
> Biography of a secretary of the American Embassy in Rome, under Clare Booth Luce.

**Secretarial careers. Anderson, Ruth I. Henry Z. Walck, Inc. 1961. 106p. $3.50
> Presentation of the responsibilities, opportunities, qualifications, and personality and temperament factors to be considered. Includes discussion of specialized secretarial work such as legal, medical, foreign service, bilingual positions, public stenography, social secretary, and civil service. Reading list. Illustrated.

Secretarial futures. Bryant College. 1962. 26p. Free
> Includes personal qualifications, tips for promotion, and what the employer expects of the employee.

**Secretarial science. Langston, Mildred. Bellman Publishing Company. 1959. 29p. $1
> Description of duties, training, personal qualifications, salaries, benefits other than wages, and advancement opportunities. Includes types of organizations employing secretaries. Selected references.

Secretarial work as a career. Boston University. 1962. 7p. Free
> Recruiting booklet describing qualifications, opportunities, and preparation.

Secretaries, stenographers, and typists. Science Research Associates. 1958. 4p. 35c
> Occupational brief describing nature of work, qualifications, preparation, opportunities, advantages, disadvantages, and future outlook.

**Secretaries, stenographers, and typists. One section of *Occupational Outlook Handbook*.
> Nature of work, where employed, training, other qualifications, advancement, employment outlook, earnings, and working conditions.

Secretaries who succeed. Becker, Esther R. Harper and Row. 1947. 121p. $2.95
> Describes qualifications needed to progress in secretarial work. Partial contents: Adapt your attitude to your job; Protect your boss's prestige; Relieve your boss of details; Be "photogenic"; Daily "do's and don'ts"; Personality and poise.

Secretary. Splaver, Sarah. Personnel Services. 1950. 6p. 50c; 25c to students
> Occupational abstract. Nature of work, qualifications, preparation, entrance and advancement, supply and demand, earnings, advantages, disadvantages, and appraisal of literature.

* Secretary. Careers. 1963. 8p. 25c
> Career brief summarizing duties, working conditions, training requirements, personal qualifications, employment prospects, earnings, related careers, measuring one's interest and ability, and suggested high school program. Additional references.

SECRETARY—*Continued*

**Secretary. Chronicle Guidance Publications. 1962. 4p. 35c
Occupational brief summarizing work performed, types of secretaries, working conditions, qualifications, training, opportunities, outlook, and suggested activities. Includes discussion of opportunities for men.

Secretary. The Guidance Centre. 1963. 4p. 15c in Canada; 20c elsewhere
Definition, importance of work, qualifications, preparation, advancement, outlook, remuneration, advantages, disadvantages, how to get started, and related occupations.

The secretary. Simmons College. 1960. 4p. Free
Qualifications, skills needed, opportunities for advancement, and preparation.

The secretary at work. Strony, Madeline and Greenaway, M. Emily. Gregg Publishing Division, McGraw-Hill Book Company. 1958. 224p. $2.75
A textbook for secretarial office practice classes that shows the importance of personality and proper work habits for success in secretarial work. Emphasizes proper grooming and public relations as well as skills. Illustrated with case histories.

The secretary's handbook. 8th edition. Taintor, Sarah A. and Monro, Kate M. Macmillan Company. 1958. 573p. $5.95
Secretarial procedures, especially for the writing of letters and other business forms.

Should you be a secretary? Jennings, Clare H. New York Life Insurance Company. 1958. 12p. Free
Description of work, qualifications, earnings, training, and opportunities.

Should you be a secretary? Changing Times. 1959. 3p. 15c
Report on earnings, training, jobs, advancement, and limitations in secretarial work.

Strictly for secretaries. Whitcomb, Helen and Whitcomb, John. McGraw-Hill Whittlesey House. 1957. 167p. $3
A reference book for secretaries including discussion of the most effective way to apply for the position one wants and preparation for the top secretarial position.

The successful secretary. Gilmore, Sybil Lee. Dartnell Corporation. 1951. 60p. 50c
Includes the requirements of a good secretary and a secretary's self-evaluation chart. Written for the secretary who wishes to progress.

The successful secretary. Royal McBee Corporation. 1963. 32p. Free
Included are the personal qualities of a good secretary and brief hints for transcription and correct telephone techniques.

Technical secretary. Careers. 1964. 2p. 15c
Career summary for desk-top file. Duties, qualifications, and outlook.

Technical secretaries. Careers. 1959. 2p. 15c
Career summary of the work of relieving the scientist or engineer of many clerical jobs.

Washington secretary. Hager, Alice Roger. Julian Messner, Inc. 1958. 192p. $2.95
Career fiction. Experiences as secretary for a congresswoman show an atmosphere of party political intrigue.

Wendy Scott, secretary. Mayo, Lucy Graves. Dodd, Mead and Company. 1961. 352p. $3.50
Career fiction. Interwoven in this story of a secretary is picture of the training, qualifications, and opportunities offered.

White collar girl. Hall, Marjory. Funk and Wagnalls Company. 1959. 248p. $2.95
Career fiction. Experiences of a girl in secretarial school and her first year of work.

* You . . . as a secretary. Royal McBee Corporation. 1961. 16p. Free
Nature of work, duties, opportunities, training, qualities necessary for promotion, and advantages of secretarial work. Prepared under the sponsorship of Delta Pi Epsilon, Alpha Chapter.

Your career as a secretary. United Business Schools Association. 1964. 24p. Free
Includes description of various specialties such as court reporter, executive secretary, and engineering-scientific secretary.

**Your future as a secretary. Noyes, Nell Braly. Richards Rosen Press. 1963. 158p. $2.95
An experienced secretary describes various positions open to a skilled secretary and the qualifications.

See also Legal secretary; Medical secretary; Stenographer

SECURITIES SALESMAN   1-65.03

Baruch: my own story. Baruch, B. M. Henry Holt and Company. 1957. 351p. $5
Biographical account of many of the author's financial coups and failures, speculations, investments, and activities in public life as chairman of the War Industries Board.

Bond trader. The Guidance Centre. 1962. 4p. 15c in Canada; 20c elsewhere
Definition, nature of work, qualifications, training, advancement, earnings, working conditions, advantages, disadvantages, and how to get started.

**Careers in the stock and bond business and investment banking. Institute for Research. 1956. 24p. $1
History and importance of work, types of positions, attractive and unattractive features, qualifications, education and training, earnings, chances for employment, and how to get started.

Employment opportunities for college graduates for the position of trainee investigator. U.S. Securities and Exchange Commission. 1962. 2p. Free
Information about the location of positions, duties to be performed, salaries, career opportunities, fringe benefits, training, recruitment policy, and civil service examination.

SECURITIES SALESMAN—*Continued*

Financial analyst. California State Department of Employment. 1962. 5p. Single copy free

Duties, working conditions, pay, hours, entrance requirements, training, and employment prospects.

**Opportunities in the securities business. Shulsky, Sam. Vocational Guidance Manuals. 1963. 126p. $1.45 paper; library edition $2.65

Description of the world of finance, requirements for entering, personal attributes, how to get started, and opportunities in brokerage, investment banking, investment counseling, and mutual funds.

* Securities salesman. Careers. 1963. 2p. 15c

Career summary for desk-top file. Duties, qualifications, and outlook.

Securities salesmen. Science Research Associates. 1961. 4p. 35c

Occupational brief describing nature of work, requirements, methods of entering and advancing, earnings, advantages, disadvantages, and future outlook.

* Stock brokerage business. Fowler, Elizabeth M. Bellman Publishing Company. 1955. 31p. $1

Definition of terms, job opportunities, and requirements.

Woman stock broker. Moss, Allyn. Alumnae Advisory Center. 1955. 2p. 25c

Reprint from *Mademoiselle* describing opportunities for women.

See also Financial institutions industry worker

SERVICE-STATION ATTENDANT. *See* Automobile-service-station attendant

SEWING-MACHINE OPERATOR   6-27.460 through 6-27.639

Drapery seamstress. Careers. 1962. 2p. 15c

Career summary for desk-top file. Duties, qualifications, and outlook.

Sewing-machine operator. Careers. 1961. 8p. 25c

Career brief describing duties, working conditions, training, personal qualifications, earnings, advancement opportunities, and outlook.

Sewing-machine operators. Michigan Employment Security Commission. 1962. 11p. 25c

Introduction, nature of work, location of jobs, working conditions, employment outlook, earnings, requirements for entry, disadvantages, and advantages.

Sewing machine operators. Science Research Associates. 1964. 4p. 35c

Occupational brief describing nature of work, training, qualifications, opportunities, and outlook.

SHEEP HERDER   3-17.50

Sheep herder. California State Department of Employment. 1962. 4p. Single copy free

Nature of work, duties, working conditions, employment outlook, wages, hours, training requirements, and how to find employment.

Sheep: life on the South Dakota range. Gilfillan, Archer B. University of Minnesota Press. 1957. 272p. $4
One of the few books on sheepherding.

SHEET-METAL WORKER   4-80.

Careers in bricklaying and sheet metal work. B'nai B'rith Vocational Service. 1954. 7p. 35c
Nature of work, qualifications, working conditions, advantages, and disadvantages.

**Employment outlook for sheet-metal workers and roofers. Bureau of Labor Statistics, U.S. Department of Labor. Supt. of Documents. 1962. 6p. 10c
Reprint from the *Occupational Outlook Handbook*.

Finding out about sheet-metal workers. Science Research Associates. 1964. 4p. 35c
Junior occupational brief containing some concise facts about the job and listing ways of finding out about the nature of the work.

Sheet metal worker. Careers. 1964. 2p. 15c
Career summary for desk-top file. Duties, qualifications, and outlook.

* Sheet metal worker. Chronicle Guidance Publications. 1962. 4p. 35c
Occupational brief summarizing work performed, where employed, qualifications, training, earnings, advancement, and outlook.

Sheet metal worker. The Guidance Centre. 1962. 4p. 15c in Canada; 20c elsewhere
Definition, importance of the work, qualifications, preparation, earnings, working conditions, how to get started, advantages, and disadvantages.

Sheet metal workers. Michigan Employment Security Commission. 1956. 18p. 25c
Introduction, nature of work, employment outlook, working conditions, organizations, earnings, qualifications for entry, advantages, and disadvantages.

* Sheet metal workers. Science Research Associates. 1961. 4p. 35c
Occupational brief describing nature of work, requirements, apprenticeship training, paths of advancement, earnings, advantages, disadvantages, and future outlook.

**Sheet-metal workers. One section of *Occupational Outlook Handbook*.
Nature of work, where employed, training, other qualifications, advancement, employment outlook, earnings, and working conditions.

SHIPBUILDER   5, 7, 9-05.500 through 5, 7, 9-05.799

**Shipbuilders. Science Research Associates. 1961. 4p. 35c
Occupational brief describing various kinds of work, qualifications, training, earnings, advantages, disadvantages, and future outlook.

SHIPPING CLERK   1-34.

**Employment outlook for shipping and receiving clerks. Bureau of Labor Statistics, U.S. Department of Labor. Supt. of Documents. 1964. 4p. 5c
Reprint from the *Occupational Outlook Handbook*.

SHIPPING CLERK—*Continued*

Finding out about shipping clerks. Science Research Associates. 1962. 4p. 35c

> Junior occupational brief describing work and opportunities.

* Shipping and receiving clerks. Chronicle Guidance Publications. 1963. 4p. 35c

> Occupational brief describing nature of work, qualifications, working conditions, opportunities for promotion, and outlook.

**Shipping and receiving clerks. One section of *Occupational Outlook Handbook*.

> Nature of work, where employed, training, other qualifications, advancement, employment outlook, earnings, and working conditions.

Shipping clerk. California State Department of Employment. 1961. 2p. Single copy free

> Duties, pay, hours, finding the job. training, promotion, and employment prospects.

* Shipping clerks. Science Research Associates. 1964. 4p. 35c

> Occupational brief describing nature of work, training, qualifications, opportunities, and outlook.

SHOE REPAIRMAN   4-60.100

Finding out about shoe repairmen. Science Research Associates. 1964. 4p. 35c

> Junior occupational brief containing some concise facts about the job and listing ways of finding out about the nature of the work. Includes suggestions for reading.

Shoe repairman. Splaver, Sarah. Personnel Services. 1956. 6p. 50c; 25c to students

> Occupational abstract. Includes description of nature of work, qualifications, preparation, entrance and advancement, supply and demand, earnings, advantages, and disadvantages.

Shoe repairman. Careers. 1963. 8p. 25c

> Career brief describing duties, working conditions, training, personal qualifications, earnings, and outlook.

**Shoe repairman. Chronicle Guidance Publications. 1960. 4p. 35c

> Occupational brief summarizing work performed, working conditions, hours, earnings, personal qualifications, training requirements, opportunities, employment outlook, and entry into the job.

Shoe repairman. The Guidance Centre. 1961. 4p. 15c in Canada; 20c elsewhere

> Nature of work, qualifications, working conditions, outlook, earnings, advantages, disadvantages, and related occupations.

Shoe repairman. Michigan Employment Security Commission. 1955. 23p. 25c

> Introduction, nature of work, location of jobs, employment prospects, working conditions, earnings, qualifications for entry, advantages, and organizations.

**Shoe repairmen. Science Research Associates. 1961. 4p. 35c
Occupational brief describing nature of work, requirements, getting started, earnings, advantages, disadvantages, and future outlook.

SINGER 0-24.00 through 0-24.09

Awards for singers. Central Opera Service. 1963. 4p. 25c
A list, arranged alphabetically by states, of colleges and other organizations that offer scholarships and awards to singers.

Career as a popular singer and entertainer in show business. Institute for Research. 1962. 8p. $1
Description of typical jobs in show business, qualifications, attractive and unattractive features, training, earnings, and getting started.

**Employment outlook in the performing arts. Bureau of Labor Statistics, U.S. Department of Labor. Supt. of Documents. 1964. 16p. 10c
Reprint from the *Occupational Outlook Handbook.*

Singer. Splaver, Sarah. Personnel Services. 1952. 6p. 50c; 25c to students
Occupational abstract. Nature of work, qualifications, preparation, entrance and advancement, distribution, supply and demand, unions, earnings, advantages, and disadvantages.

**Singer and singing teachers. One section of *Occupational Outlook Handbook.*
Nature of work, where employed, training, other qualifications, employment outlook, earnings, and working conditions.

Singers. Science Research Associates. 1961. 4p. 35c
Occupational brief describing work, qualifications, training, earnings, getting started, and things to consider. Selected references.

Upon my lips a song. Smith, Kate. Funk and Wagnalls Company. 1960. 213p. $3.95
In this autobiography, Kate Smith traces her musical career, pointing out the difficulties encountered in her early struggles.

See also Musician; Music teacher

SKILLED TRADES WORKER 4-01. through 5-99.

Can I be a craftsman? Let's find out. General Motors, Public Relations Staff. 1961. 24p. Free
Description of work of machinist, die maker, tool maker, pattern maker, sheet metal worker, millwright, machine repairman, and electrician. Includes a check list for self-inventory of interests and abilities and explanation of the apprentice program.

Clay fingers. De Leeuw, Adele Louise. Macmillan Company. 1948. 230p. $3.50
Career fiction. Facing a year of limited activity after an injury, Laura becomes interested in ceramics and develops a career from a hobby as she becomes a skilled craftsman.

SKILLED TRADES WORKER—*Continued*

Opportunities in trades and crafts with the Federal Government. U.S. Civil Service Commission. 1962. 8p. Free
  Describes opportunities for skilled and semiskilled workers and explains how to locate and apply for jobs.

The outlook for the skilled worker. Wolfbein, Seymour. Chronicle Guidance Publications. 1962. 3p. 35c
  A reprint pointing out the need for the skilled craftsmen, training requirements, and the implications for guidance and counseling.

**Skilled trades and other industrial occupations. One section of *Occupational Outlook Handbook.*
  Nature of work, training, qualifications, employment trends, and outlook.

Trade and industrial training: earned degrees, by level, sex, and institution. One section of *Earned Degrees Conferred.*
  List of seventy-four colleges and number of bachelor's degrees conferred by each in trade and industrial training.

Woodworker. Chronicle Guidance Publications. 1962. 4p. 35c
  Occupational brief summarizing work performed, working conditions, qualifications, training, opportunities, and outlook.

Your opportunities in industry as a skilled craftsman. National Research Bureau. 1956. 32p. 20c
  Standards which apply to the apprenticeable occupations, list of the key crafts in manufacturing and the average length of apprentice training, and specific information about the millwright, tool maker, die maker, maintenance electrician, machinist, and wood pattern maker.

SOAP AND GLYCERIN INDUSTRY WORKER
4-53.150 through 4-53.249

Soap and detergent industry. Gale, Oliver M. Bellman Publishing Company. 1955. 19p. $1
  History, importance of the industry, employment opportunities, and professional and trade organizations. Bibliography. Illustrated.

Soap manufacturing workers. Science Research Associates. 1956. 4p. 35c
  Occupational brief describing jobs in the soap industry, requirements, methods of getting started and advancing, earnings, advantages, disadvantages, and future outlook.

SOCIAL SCIENTIST   0-36.

Applied social sciences: earned degrees, by level, sex, and institution. One section of *Earned Degrees Conferred.*
  Useful for judging the extent of a college's program in each of the following specialties: agricultural economics, foreign service programs, industrial relations, public administration, and social work.

Career opportunities in the social sciences. University of Chicago, Office of Career Counseling and Placement. 1953. 20p. Free
Suggests vocational outlets for those trained in anthropology, economics, education, geography, history, political science, psychology, and sociology.

**Careers for social scientists. Chamberlin, Jo Hubbard. Henry Z. Walck, Inc. 1961. 108p. $3.50
Describes the work, opportunities, educational preparation, challenges, and rewards in each of the social sciences: anthropology, economics, history, political science, sociology. Reading list. Illustrated.

Careers in social science. Angel, Juvenal. World Trade Academy Press. 1963. 32p. $1.25
Includes description of the major fields of specialization, education required, opportunities, remuneration, future outlook, and methods of financing an education in this field.

Careers in social science. St. Francis College. 1957. 8p. Free
Includes a list of seventy-six careers and the nature of work in each. Bibliography.

Careers in the social sciences. Changing Times. 1960. 4p. 15c
Report on career opportunities in the social sciences.

**Employment outlook for social scientists. Bureau of Labor Statistics, U.S. Department of Labor. Supt. of Documents. 1964. 16p. 10c
Reprint from the *Occupational Outlook Handbook*.

**Employment outlook in the social sciences. Bureau of Labor Statistics, U.S. Department of Labor. Bulletin Number 1167. Supt. of Documents. 1954. 66p. 40c
Fields of employment, educational requirements, earnings, and outlook.

Faces of man. Milwaukee-Downer College. 1960. 16p. Free
A college bulletin describing opportunities open to students concentrating in the social sciences.

Guide to vocations in the social sciences. Ralya, Lynn and Ralya, Lillian. The Authors. 1957. 32p. $1
Information and reading lists on the numerous vocations in the seven social sciences: anthropology, economics, geography, history, political science, sociology, and statistics. Includes ten tables such as the distribution of social scientists by specialty, by type of employer, and by level of education.

**Social sciences. One chapter of *Occupational Outlook Handbook*.
Nature of work, where employed, training, other qualifications, and employment outlook for each of the following: economists, historians, political scientists, sociologists, and anthropologists.

Social sciences: earned degrees, by level, sex, and institution. One section of *Earned Degrees Conferred*.
Useful for judging the extent of a college's program in each of the following specialties: anthropology, basic social sciences, economics, history, international relations, political sciences, and sociology.

SOCIAL SCIENTIST—*Continued*

* Social scientists. Science Research Associates. 1961. 4p. 35c
Occupational brief describing nature of work, requirements, where work is obtained, earnings, advantages, disadvantages, and future outlook.

Social scientists. Chapter 12 of *The College Girl Looks Ahead.*
Characteristics of work, talents needed, trying out, entering the field, and kinds of work.

See also Scientist

SOCIAL WORKER 0-27.

Announcement of job opportunities for social workers. New Jersey State Department of Institutions and Agencies. 1962. 5p. Free
Description of work and requirements for positions in the state institutions.

Better human relations—the challenge of social work. Freeman, Lucy. Public Affairs Committee. 1956. 28p. 25c
Written for civic minded adults and parents who desire a better understanding of the nature of social work.

**Careers in social casework. B'nai B'rith Vocational Service. 1957. 16p. 35c
Outlook, nature of work, number of workers, earnings, training, qualifications, sources of employment, advantages, and disadvantages.

**Careers in social work. Angel, Juvenal L. World Trade Academy Press. 1962. 46p. $1.25
Description of work, training, opportunities, and remuneration for each of the following: caseworker, child welfare worker, community organizer, family social worker, group worker, medical social worker, psychiatric social worker, recreational leader, and research social worker. Also included is a list of colleges offering training, scholarships, and fellowships in social work.

Careers in social work. Changing Times. 1961. 3p. 15c
Facts on training, pay, and opportunities in social work.

**Careers in social work. Council on Social Work Education. 1956. 8p. 5c
An illustrated brochure describing the types of work, opportunities, salaries, unusual rewards, professional education, desirable qualitites, and next steps.

Careers in the profession of social work. Council on Social Work Education. No date. 17″ by 25″. 25c
Chart for bulletin board display providing information about the variety of social work positions, the kinds of social agencies in which social workers are employed, employment opportunities, requirements, outlook, and where to apply for social work positions.

A challenging career for you as a Veterans Administration clinical social worker. Veterans Administration, Department of Medicine and Surgery. 1963. 4p. Free
Description of work, training program, qualifications, and benefits.

Community development—opportunities for junior college graduates in the Peace Corps. Peace Corps. 1962. 6p. Free
Explanation of needs and qualifications.

**Counselor's kit for vocational guidance counselors and social workers. National Commission for Social Work Careers. 1963. Twenty booklets. $2
Career items that would cost $3.15 if purchased individually.

Could you take social work? Moss, Allyn and Small, Verna. Alumnae Advisory Center. 1955. 4p. 25c
Reprint from *Mademoiselle* describing experiences of two social workers, one of whom liked the work and the other did not.

Do you want a career helping people? Council on Social Work Education. 1957. 8p. 5c
Preparation, opportunities, and rewards.

**Employment outlook for social workers. Bureau of Labor Statistics, U.S. Department of Labor. Supt. of Documents. 1964. 8p. 5c
Reprint from the *Occupational Outlook Handbook.*

Financing your education for a social work career. National Commission for Social Work Careers. 1963. 4p. Single copy free
Includes brief list of sources of printed information.

A future for you . . . in social work. American National Red Cross. 1961. 12p. Free
Description of positions and qualifications for social workers and case aides assigned to Red Cross programs in military hospitals, with emphasis on the case aide position for college graduates.

Knock at the door, Emmy. Means, Florence C. Houghton Mifflin Company. 1956. 240p. $3.25
Career fiction. An itinerant basket seller succeeds against many odds in winning a scholarship to college and a promising career in social service. For grades 7 to 9.

Lillian Wald: angel of Henry Street. Beryl Williams. Julian Messner, Inc. 1948. 224p. $3.50. Library binding $3.34 net
Biography of a woman of wealth who chose to devote her services to New York's East Side, where she founded the Henry Street Settlement House.

List of accredited graduate professional schools of social work in Canada and the United States. Council on Social Work Education. 1963. 8p. 5c
List arranged by states designating whether approved programs are offered in group work, medical social work, psychiatric social work, and school social work.

Lorna Evans, social worker. McCarty, R. K. Julian Messner, Inc. 1961. 192p. $2.95
Career fiction. Utilizing authentic case histories, the author has written a career-romance about a girl dedicated to helping others.

Medical social worker. Pages 133-5 of *Health Careers Guidebook.*
Nature of work, training, personal qualifications, and prospects.

SOCIAL WORKER—*Continued*

Memo to college graduates. Council on Social Work Education. 1963. 6p. 5c

Job opportunities in social work for the college graduate without professional training.

Open letter to future social workers. National Commission for Social Work Careers. 1963. 3p. Single copy free

Brief information which may be sent in response to a request for information.

**Opportunities in social work. Anderson, Joseph P. Vocational Guidance Manuals. Revised 1963. 128p. $1.45 paper

Historical background and growth of social work, supply and demand, employment conditions, personal qualifications, educational preparation, typical jobs, how to get started, member schools of American Association of Schools of Social Work, organizations, and national social welfare agencies. Also, a chapter is included on scholarships, fellowships, and other student aids.

Out of focus . . . help the student, the class, the nation. National Commission on Social Work Careers. 1962. 6p. 5c

Stresses the need and importance of the school social worker.

Public social welfare personnel. Bureau of Family Services and Children's Bureau, U.S. Department of Health, Education, and Welfare. Supt. of Documents. 1962. 140p. 70c

A survey of characteristics of personnel in social welfare positions who are working in public assistance and child welfare programs. This is a statistical report of interest to research workers in this area.

The right job for Judith. Johnson, Enid. Julian Messner, Inc. 1951. 184p. $2.95

Career fiction. Disillusioned by her failure to become an opera singer, Judith finds a new outlet for her musical ability in settlement work.

Services in public assistance—the role of the caseworker. Foster, Helen B. Bureau of Public Assistance, U.S. Department of Health, Education, and Welfare. Report Number 30. Supt. of Documents. 1957. 34p. 20c

Includes the nature and the components of the basic job of the public assistance worker.

Should you be a social worker? Ballard, Russell W. New York Life Insurance Company. 1958. 12p. Free

Description of work, preparation, salaries, rewards, and drawbacks.

**So you want to be a social worker. Perlman, Helen Harris. Harper and Row. 1963. 192p. $3.50

Description of the various kinds of work, training, demands, and future outlook.

Social and religious workers and counselors. Chapter 7 of *The College Girl Looks Ahead.*

Characteristics of social work, talents needed, trying out and preparing for social work, entering, and kinds of work.

Social welfare as a career—a bibliography. National Social Welfare Assembly. 1963. 10p. 25c
 A bibliography of printed materials on the various fields of social welfare.

Social work. Adams, Margaret E. Bellman Publishing Company. 1958. 35p. $1
 Description of work in various types of social work agencies, qualifications, training, opportunities, and earnings. Includes list of accredited schools.

Social work as a career. Boston University. 1962. 12p. Free
 Recruiting booklet describing qualifications, opportunities, chances for advancement, and preparation. Discussion of the social service field, case work, group work, and community organization.

Social work as a career. Institute for Research. 1962. 24p. $1
 Typical day's work of a family welfare worker and a rural child welfare worker. Types of work in Federal positions, community organizations, and in local and state public welfare departments. Qualifications, preparation, salaries. List of schools approved by American Association of Schools of Social Work

**Social work as a profession. Council on Social Work Education. 1961. 40p. 25c
 Comprehensive information concerning nature of work, qualifications, training, and opportunities.

Social work: career in the headlines. Western Personnel Institute. 1956. 6p. 20c
 Information on training, salaries, and the need for social workers in juvenile delinquency, mental hygiene, and gerontology.

Social work fellowships and scholarships in Canada and the United States. Council on Social Work Education. 1962. 88p. $1
 A biennial compilation including grants from voluntary agencies, institutions, and government agencies.

Social worker. Splaver, Sarah. Personnel Services. 1961. 6p. 50c; 25c to students
 Occupational abstract. Nature of work, qualifications, preparation, entrance, advancement, earnings, supply and demand, and advantages.

* Social worker. Chronicle Guidance Publications. 1964. 4p. 35c
 Occupational brief summarizing work performed, working conditions, hours, earnings, personal qualifications, training requirements, opportunities, employment outlook, and entry into the job.

Social worker. The Guidance Centre. 1962. 4p. 15c in Canada; 20c elsewhere
 Importance and nature of work, qualifications, preparation, opportunities for advancement, remuneration, advantages, disadvantages, and related occupations.

Social worker. Simmons College. 1960. 4p. Free
 Nature of work, duties, qualifications, demand, and training.

Social workers. Careers. 1963. 8p. 25c
 Career brief describing work performed, training, personal qualifications, earnings, advancement prospects, and outlook.

SOCIAL WORKER—*Continued*

Social workers. Michigan Employment Security Commission. 1956. 18p. 25c

Introduction, nature of work, working conditions, location of jobs, employment outlook, earnings, qualifications for entry, organizations, advantages, and disadvantages.

* Social workers. Science Research Associates. 1960. 4p. 35c

Occupational brief describing several kinds of social work, requirements, earnings, advantages, disadvantages, and future outlook.

**Social workers. One section of *Occupational Outlook Handbook*.

Nature of work, where employed, training, other qualifications, advancement, employment outlook, earnings, and working conditions.

Student recruitment kit for the profession of social work. Council on Social Work Education. 1962. Twelve booklets. 50c

Brochures, folders, and bibliographies about special fields of social work.

Survey of salaries and working conditions of social welfare manpower. Bureau of Public Assistance, U.S. Department of Health, Education, and Welfare. 1961. 36p. National Social Welfare Assembly. $1.75

Highlights and statistical tables concerning social welfare employees and caseworkers in state and local agencies administering public assistance and public child welfare programs.

Their career: helping people help themselves. Family Service Association of America. 1956. 12p. 3c

Pictures of a day in the life of a young social worker with brief explanatory captions. Indicates the need to help families with problems of parent-child relationships, old age, mental illness, juvenile delinquency, and conflicts in marriage.

Undergraduate departments of colleges and universities in Canada and the United States. Council on Social Work Education. 1963. 8p. 5c

List, revised semiannually, of schools which offer an organized sequence of courses with social welfare content.

Your future in public welfare. American Public Welfare Association. No date. 6p. 5c

Brief statement of opportunities, nature of work, and advantages.

Your future in social work. Beck, Bertram. Richards Rosen Press. 1963. 158p. $2.95

Describes the necessary education and preparation, qualifications, outlook, and work in family counseling, psychiatric clinics, and institutions.

See also Group worker; Psychiatric social worker

SOCIOLOGIST   0-36.31

Careers in sociology. American Sociological Association. 1964. 4p. Free

Description of training and kinds of work in which sociologists are employed.

Sociologist. Careers. 1960. 7p. 25c
Career brief describing duties, working conditions, training, personal qualifications, earnings, advancement prospects, and outlook.

**Sociologists. One section of *Occupational Outlook Handbook*.
Nature of work, where employed, training, other qualifications, and employment outlook.

SOIL SCIENTIST 0-35.03

Careers in conservation. Soil Conservation Society of America. 1961. 12p. 4c. Single copy free
Discussion of kinds of work, places of employment, training, and opportunities. Illustrated.

Careers in soil conservation service. U.S. Department of Agriculture. Miscellaneous Publication Number 717. Supt. of Documents. 1960. 12p. 10c
Illustrated folder describing nature of work in twelve branches of the soil conservation service, qualifications, and how to apply for a Federal job.

Careers in soil science. California State Polytechnic College. 1962. 4p. Free
An illustrated brochure listing typical positions and outlining the course of study.

Conservation officer (Ontario). The Guidance Centre. 1962. 4p. 15c in Canada; 20c elsewhere
History and importance, nature of work, qualifications, working conditions, preparation, remuneration, outlook, related occupations, and how to get started.

Soil conservationist. Careers. 1961. 2p. 15c
Career summary for desk-top file. Duties, qualifications, and outlook.

* Soil conservationist. Chronicle Guidance Publications. 1960. 4p. 35c
Occupational brief summarizing work performed, working conditions, qualifications, training, earnings, opportunities, and outlook.

**Soil conservationists. One section of *Occupational Outlook Handbook*.
Nature of work, where employed, training, advancement, employment outlook, and earnings.

Soil savers. Colby, C. B. Coward-McCann, Inc. 1957. 48p. $2.50
Describes the work of the Soil Conservation Service of the U.S. Department of Agriculture. Describes jobs in crop rotation, contour plowing, strip cropping, and restricted grazing. Written for grades 4 to 8. Fifty illustrations.

A soil science career for you in Soil Conservation Service. U.S. Department of Agriculture. Miscellaneous Publication Number 716. Supt. of Documents. 1960. 8p. 5c
Illustrated folder describing nature of work in soil mapping, classification, correlation, laboratory research, soil investigation, and soil survey interpretation. Also contains employment facts such as work locations, advancement, and benefits.

SOIL SCIENTIST—*Continued*

* Soil scientists. Science Research Associates. 1963. 4p. 35c
Occupational brief describing nature of work, training, qualifications, opportunities, and outlook.

Students . . . start your career in Soil Conservation Service before you graduate. U.S. Department of Agriculture. Miscellaneous Publication Number 714. Supt. of Documents. 1960. 4p. 5c
An illustrated folder describing the work of a student trainee, qualifications, training, and how to apply.

See also Agricultural specialist; Agronomist

SOLDIER   2-68.10

The army. Daugherty, Charles M. Viking Press. Revised 1962. 192p. $3
Detailed regulations and opportunities. For grades 7 to 10.

Army careers (non-commissioned). Careers. 1961. 8p. 25c
Career brief describing ten career specialty areas.

**Army occupations and you. Army Careers, U.S. Continental Army Command. 1962. 160p. Free to counselors and librarians
A comprehensive reference handbook explaining job training opportunities in the Army. Includes fifty-five occupational briefs, an index, and pertinent information.

Careers in the U.S. Army. Institute for Research. 1959. 31p. $1
History of the Army and description of work in its several services. Qualifications for men in the various branches, attractive and unattractive features, and salaries and allowances of enlisted men and officers.

**Current career booklets. Army Careers, U.S. Continental Army Command. Ten booklets. Free
Frequently revised materials are available from local recruiting offices or the above. Examples of present titles are: Meet today's modern Army, Your son's future, The fork in the road, This is how it is, The secret of getting ahead, and An officer's career.

Let's go to West Point. Hamilton, Lee David. Putnam's Sons, Inc. 1962. 48p. $1.95
The reader is taken on a tour through the U.S. Military Academy and views cadets in their barracks, in classes, in the gym, and on parade. For younger boys.

Soldier. The Guidance Centre. 1959. 4p. 15c in Canada; 20c elsewhere
History and importance, nature of work, qualifications, working conditions, preparation, remuneration, advancement, outlook, related occupations, and how to get started.

Soldiers and what they do. Symons, Arthur. Franklin Watts, Inc. 1958. 243p. $3.95
Description of varied kinds of work, personal requirements, specialized training, outlook, and rewards. For ages 7 to 11.

Student's guide to military service. Channel Press. 1962. 313p. $5.95; $2.95 paper
Detailed information about the alternatives open to draft-age students.

This is West Point—a pictorial introduction to the United States Military Academy, West Point. The Academy, Office of Admissions and Registrar. 1962. 32p. Free
Description of cadet life, how to gain an appointment to West Point, the curriculum, and advantages of a service career.

United States Military Academy, West Point. The Academy, Office of the Registrar. 1963. 181p. Free
Information concerning the appointment, qualifications, admission, and the course of study available to young men at West Point. Thirty illustrations.

West Point: cadets, training, and equipment. Colby, C. B. Coward-McCann, Inc. 1963. 48p. Library edition $2.52 net
Photographs and brief text depict life at West Point. Written for grades 4 to 8.

West Point guidance information. U.S. Military Academy, Office of the Registrar. 1963. 18p. Free to counselors
Prepared for counselors to use in advising young men concerning admission to the academy. Other booklets available to counselors are: This is West Point, Steps to West Point, Books on West Point, Profile of the entering freshman class, and West Point . . . an opportunity, a career.

The West Point story. Reeder, Colonel Red and Campion, Nardi Reeder. Random House, Inc. 1956. 192p. $1.95
A stirring history of the great academy and picture of life at West Point. Nine boy scouts visiting the academy learn the history and traditions behind the school. For younger boys.

West Point; the life of a cadet. Engeman, Jack. Lothrop, Lee and Shepard Company. 1956. 151p. $3.50
Photographs and brief text depicting life at West Point from plebe year through graduation.

**Your future in the army. Walmsley, Harold. Richards Rosen Press. 1960. 159p. $2.95
Information and advice concerning life in the army, attitudes necessary for success, factors to consider, dividends of an army career, disadvantages, and preparation.

Your future in the army. Walmsley, Harold. Popular Library, Inc. 1962. 159p. 50c
A paperback edition of the book described above.

See also Military serviceman

SPECTROSCOPIST   0-50.44

Job description of spectroscopist. U.S. Employment Service, U.S. Department of Labor. Supt. of Documents. 1948. 6p. 5c
Occupational guide, Job summary, work performed, training, trainee-selection factors, related occupations, physical activities, working conditions, hazards, and employment variables.

SPEECH AND HEARING THERAPIST 0-32.09

Audiologist. Careers. 1961. 8p. 25c
 Career brief describing duties, working conditions, training, places of employment, earnings, and outlook. List of sixty-five colleges offering programs in audiology and speech pathology.

A career for you as a Veterans Administration audiologist and speech pathologist. Veterans Administration, Department of Medicine and Surgery. 1962. 4p. Free
 Description of work, training program, qualifications, and benefits.

Careers in speech and hearing. American Speech and Hearing Association. 1962. 5p. Free
 Description of careers in speech and hearing therapy.

Careers in speech and hearing . . . a rewarding profession. National Society for Crippled Children and Adults. No date. 6p. Single copy free
 Description of work, preparation, professional status, and opportunities.

Hearing clinician. Careers. 1961. 7p. 25c
 Career brief describing duties, working conditions, training, personal qualifications, certification, places of employment, earnings, and outlook.

The immediate gift. Pont, Clarice. David McKay Company. 1961. 224p. $3.25
 Career fiction. Story of a dedicated young teacher at work in her chosen field of speech therapy.

Speech and hearing clinicians. Science Research Associates. 1961. 4p. 35c
 Occupational brief describing nature of work, duties, qualifications, training, where employed, earnings, advantages, disadvantages, and future outlook.

Speech and hearing therapists. Pages 136-8 of *Health Careers Guidebook*.
 Nature of work, where therapists work, personal qualifications, training, certification, opportunities, and prospects.

Speech and hearing therapy. Chronicle Guidance Publications. 1960. 4p. 35c
 Occupational brief summarizing work performed, where employed, qualifications, training, and outlook.

Speech clinician. Careers. 1960. 8p. 25c
 Career brief desecribing duties, working conditions, training, personal qualifications, earnings, advancement prospects, and outlook.

Speech correctionists: the competencies they need for the work they do. U.S. Office of Education. Supt. of Documents. 1957. 77p. 45c
 Includes description of nature of work and procedures.

**Speech therapist. Robinson, H. Alan. Personnel Services. 1956. 6p. 50c; 25c to students
 Occupational abstract. Nature of work, future prospects, qualifications, preparation, entrance and advancement, earnings, advantages, and disadvantages.
 See also Physical therapist

SPORTS ANNOUNCER. *See* Radio and television announcer

STATIONARY ENGINEER 5-72.010

**Employment outlook for stationary engineers. Bureau of Labor Statistics, U.S. Department of Labor. Supt. of Documents. 1964. 4p. 5c
Reprint from the *Occupational Outlook Handbook*.

Stationary engineer. Careers. 1961. 7p. 25c
Career brief describing duties, working conditions, training, personal requirements, earnings, advancement, related careers, and outlook.

Stationary engineer. Chronicle Guidance Publications. 1963. 4p. 35c
Occupational brief summarizing work performed, wages, working conditions, qualifications, preparation, types of employment, and outlook.

**Stationary engineers. Science Research Associates. 1961. 4p. 35c
Occupational brief describing the work of the stationary fireman and the stationary engineer Includes requirements, methods of getting started, earnings, advantages, disadvantages, and future outlook.

**Stationary engineers. One section of *Occupational Outlook Handbook*.
Nature of work, where employed, training, employment outlook, earnings, and working conditions.

STATISTICIAN 0-35.75; 0-36.51

A career for you in agricultural statistics. U.S. Department of Agriculture. 1963. 4p. Free
Explanation of opportunities available through the student trainee program of the Federal Service Entrance Examinations.

**Careers in statistics. American Statistical Association and Institute of Mathematical Statistics. 1962. 23p. Free
Important concepts of statistics, where statistics may be applied, duties, qualifications, preparation, outlook, and rewards.

The educational qualifications of public health statisticians. American Public Health Association. 1963. 6p. Free

**Employment opportunities for women mathematicians and statisticians. Women's Bureau, U.S. Department of Labor. Bulletin Number 262. Supt. of Documents. 1956. 37p. 25c
Present and future supply and demand, preparation, personal characteristics needed, obtaining employment, advancement, earnings, and working conditions.

Health statistics. Pages 89-91 of *Health Careers Guidebook*.
Information about qualifications, training, and opportunitites for the public health statistician and the statisical clerk.

Statistical clerk. Chronicle Guidance Publications. 1963. 4p. 35c
Occupational brief summarizing work performed, where employed, qualifications, preparation, related jobs, methods of entry, and outlook.

STATISTICIAN—*Continued*

Statistical work as a career. Institute for Research. 1962. 24p. $1
Qualifications, preparation, and salaries of statistical work in business and in the Federal Government. Statement of U.S. Civil Service requirements. Includes description of statistical clerk, statistical draftsman, clerk coder, sorting machine operator, card punch operator, and tabulating machine operator.

* Statistical workers. Science Research Associates. 1963. 4p. 35c
Occupational brief describing the importance of statistics, nature of work, requirements, earnings, methods of getting started, advantages, disadvantages, and future outlook.

Statistician. California State Department of Employment. 1961. 6p. Free
Job duties, working conditions, salaries, hours, entrance requirements, promotion, training, and employment outlook.

Statistician. Careers. 1959. 2p. 15c
Career summary for desk-top file. Duties, qualifications, and outlook.

* Statistician. Chronicle Guidance Publications. 1963. 4p. 35c
Occupational brief summarizing work performed, earnings, personal qualifications, training, opportunities, where employed, related positions and employment outlook.

**Statisticians. One section of *Occupational Outlook Handbook*.
Nature of work, where employed, training, other qualifications, advancement, employment outlook, earnings, and working conditions.

See also Actuary; Mathematician

STEEL INDUSTRY WORKER   4, 6, 8-81. through 4, 6, 8-94.

Andrew Carnegie. Harlow, Alvin F. Julian Messner, Inc. 1953. 192p. $3.25. Library binding $3.19 net
Biography of an immigrant boy who became one of America's leading industrialists, founded a vast steel empire, and used his wealth to endow libraries and other institutions.

Careers for high school graduates in steel. American Iron and Steel Institute. 1964. 36p. 25c; single copy free
Describes a representative selection of beginning jobs, working conditions, and apprenticeships.

**Opportunities in the steel industry. Henkin, Shepard. Vocational Guidance Manuals. 1958. 76p. $1.45 paper
Scope of the industry, future outlook, employment opportunities, educational and personal requirements, remuneration, advantages, disadvantages, and how to get started. The processes by which steel is made are described in detail.

See also Iron and steel industry worker

STENOGRAPHER   1-37.00 through 1-37.29

**Career as a public stenographer. Institute for Research. 1962. 24p. $1
Description of work, duties, qualifications, typical day's work, specialization, earnings, attractive and unattractive features, outlook, and related fields.

Federal stenographer and typist examination—what it is and how it is given. U.S. Civil Service Commission. Form N-2400R. Supt. of Documents. 1961. 48p. 40c

Includes copies of actual tests that are no longer in use, instructions for scoring them, and forms used in taking the examination. Useful to give students familiarity with the timing of the tests and the manner in which they are conducted.

Secretaries, stenographers, and typists. One section of *Occupational Outlook Handbook.*

Nature of work, where employed, training, other qualifications, employment outlook, earnings, and working conditions.

Shorthand reporting as a career. National Shorthand Reporters Association. 1963. 16p. 25c

Information about the work, qualifications, and opportunities. Includes names of the state shorthand association secretaries.

Stenographer. Careers. 1963. 2p. 15c

Career summary for desk-top file. Duties, qualifications, and outlook.

* Stenographer. Chronicle Guidance Publications. 1964. 4p. 35c

Occupational brief summarizing work performed, working conditions, earnings, personal qualifications, training requirements, opportunities, employment outlook, and entry into the jobs.

Stenographer. The Guidance Centre. 1961. 4p. 15c in Canada; 20c elsewhere

Nature of work, qualifications. preparation, earnings, advancement opportunities, how to get started, advantages, and disadvantages.

Stenographic occupations. Michigan Employment Security Commission. 1963. 20p. 25c

Introduction, nature of work, location of jobs, employment prospects, earnings, working conditions, organizations, qualifications for entry, disadvantages, and advantages.

Wanted: stenographers . . . Far East assignments. American National Red Cross. 1955. 6p. Free

Description of qualifications for stenographers assigned to Red Cross offices in the Far East.

See also Court reporter; Legal secretary; Medical secretary; Secretary

STENOTYPIST 1-37.14

Stenotypist. Careers. 1961. 8p. 25c

Career brief describing duties, working conditions, training, personal qualifications, employment prospects, earnings, how to enter, and advancement prospects.

STOCK BROKER. *See* Securities salesman

STOCK CLERK   1-38.

Stock clerk. Careers. 1960. 2p. 15c
Career summary for desk-top file. Duties, qualifications, and outlook.

* Stock clerk. Chronicle Guidance Publications. 1961. 4p. 35c
Occupational brief summarizing work performed, working conditions, hours,
earnings, personal qualifications, training requirements, opportunities, employment outlook, and entry into the job.

**Stock clerks. Science Research Associates. 1964. 4p. 35c
Occupational brief describing work, qualifications, opportunities, and outlook.

STONEMASON   5-24.210

**Employment outlook for bricklayers, stonemasons, marble setters, tile
setters, and terrazzo workers. Bureau of Labor Statistics, U.S. Department of Labor. Supt. of Documents. 1964. 20p. 15c
Reprint from the *Occupational Outlook Handbook.*

Stonemason. Group, Vernard. Personnel Services. 1956. 6p. 50c; 25c to
students
Occupational abstract. Nature of work, future prospects, qualifications, preparation, entrance and advancement, earnings, advantages, and disadvantages.

Stonemason. Chronicle Guidance Publications. 1963. 4p. 35c
Occupational brief summarizing work performed, where employed, wages and
hours, qualifications, training, related occupations, opportunities, and outlook.

**Stonemasons. One section of *Occupational Outlook Handbook.*
Nature of work, where employed, training, other qualifications, employment
outlook, earnings, and working conditions.

SUBMARINE OFFICER   2-68.20

Captain Edward L. Beach: around the world under water. Becker, Beril.
Lippincott Company. 1961. 192p. $2.95
This story of the atomic submarine Triton's round-the-globe underwater
cruise in 1960 describes what it was like to live for three months under water.

Dive! Harris-Warren, Commander H.B. Harper and Row. 1960. 130p.
$2.95
Written for younger boys, this story explains how an atomic submarine works,
how torpedoes are handled, and the training, duties, and kinds of life aboard.

Nuclear submarine skippers and what they do. Steele, George and Gimpel,
H. J. Franklin Watts, Inc. 1962. 140p. $3.95
Description of typical background of a submarine captain, personal requirements, physical and mental qualifications, specialized training, nature of work,
and the role and exploits of a nuclear submarine. For grades 7 to 11.

Run silent, run deep. Beach, Edward L. Henry Holt and Company. 1955.
364p. $3.95
Career fiction. Account of the submarine training, patrolling, fighting, and
other activities in the Pacific during World War II.

Submarine: men and ships of the United States submarine fleet. Colby, Carroll B. Coward-McCann, Inc. 1953. 48p. $2.50
Brief text and photographs depict life and work aboard a submarine. For younger readers, grades 4 to 8.

Submariner. Lent, Henry. Macmillan Company. 1962. 182p. $3
Career fiction. Story of an eighteen-year-old boy and his shipmates during their tough eight-week training course at the U.S. Navy's submarine school. For ages 12 to 16.

SUPER MARKET MANAGER   0-72.21

Super market manager. Careers. 1963. 8p. 25c
Career brief describing duties, working conditions, training, personal qualifications, earnings, advancement prospects, and outlook. Additional readings.

See also Retail manager

SUPERINTENDENT, SCHOOLS   0-31.10

Public school administration as a career. Institute for Research. 1957. 24p. $1
General duties, typical day's work, typical week's work, types of positions, training, personal qualifications, attractive and unattractive features. Also brief information about the work of state supervisory officer.

School superintendents. Science Research Associates. 1961. 4p. 35c
Occupational brief describing work, qualifications, training, earnings, advantages, disadvantages, and outlook. Selected references.

SURGEON   0-26.10

Master surgeon: a biography of Joseph Lister. Farmer, Laurence. Harper and Row. 1962. 141p. $2.95
Biography of a leader in antiseptic surgery, containing his experiences as a surgeon.

Surgeon. Splaver, Sarah. Personnel Services. 1962. 6p. 50c; 25c to students
Nature of work, qualifications, preparation, certification, supply and demand, earnings, advantages, and disadvantages. References for further reading.

* Surgery as a career. Institute for Research. 1962. 24p. $1
Historical background, training, a typical day's work, personal qualifications, income, opportunities outside of private practice, attractive and unattractive features. Also distribution and description of surgical specialists, and minimum standards for graduate training and for certification in surgery.

See also Physician

SURVEYOR   0-64.10

**Employment outlook for technicians: engineering and science technicians, draftsmen, and surveyors. Bureau of Labor Statistics, U.S. Department of Labor. Supt. of Documents. 1964. 20p. 15c
Reprint from the Occupational Outlook Handbook.

SURVEYOR—*Continued*

**Pathfinders, U.S.A.: your career on land, sea, and air. Neal, Harry Edward. Julian Messner, Inc. Revised 1963. 192p. $3.95. Library binding $3.64 net
>An account of behind-the-scenes activities in a variety of jobs in the U.S. Merchant Marine, in weather forecasting and industrial meteorology, in highway building, in coastal surveying, geodetic work, and in the control of civil aviation. Includes names of colleges and schools for special training. Bibliography.

Rodman and chainman (surveying). Careers. 1963. 2p. 15c
>Career summary for desk-top file. Duties, qualifications, and outlook.

Snow surveyors: defenders against flood and drought. Colby, C. B. Coward-McCann, Inc. 1959. 48p. Library edition $2.52 net
>Photographs and brief text reveal how the U.S. Department of Agriculture's snow survey men go about the vital job of recording the annual snowfall. Written for grades 4 and up.

* Surveying. Chronicle Guidance Publications. 1961. 4p. 35c
>Occupational brief summarizing work performed, working conditions, qualifications, training, licensing, earnings, related occupations, and outlook.

Surveyor. Careers. 1963. 2p. 15c
>Career summary for desk-top file. Duties, qualifications, and outlook.

Surveyor. The Guidance Centre. 1963. 4p. 15c in Canada; 20c elsewhere
>Definition, history and importance, working conditions, qualifications, preparation, employment and advancement, earnings, advantages, disadvantages, how to get started, and related occupations.

* Surveyors. Science Research Associates. 1963. 4p. 35c
>Occupational brief describing nature of work, requirements, training, earnings, and future outlook.

**Surveyors. One section of *Occupational Outlook Handbook*.
>Nature of work, where employed, training, other qualifications, advancement, employment outlook, earnings, and working conditions.

SWIMMING POOL SERVICE TECHNICIAN 7-32.90

Swimming pool service technician. California State Department of Employment. 1962. 4p. Single copy free
>Job duties, working conditions, pay, hours, entrance requirements, promotion, training, and employment outlook in California.

Swimming pool service technician. Careers. 1962. 2p. 15c
>Career summary for desk-top file. Duties, qualifications, and outlook.

SYSTEMS ANALYST 0-69.985

Systems Analyst. Careers. 1960. 2p. 15c
>Career summary for desk-top file. Duties, qualifications, and outlook.

Systems analysts. Science Research Associates. 1963. 4p. 35c
>Occupational brief describing nature of work, training, qualifications, opportunities, and outlook. Selected references.

TAILOR   4-26.

Custom tailors and dressmakers. Science Research Associates. 1960. 4p. 35c
>   Occupational brief describing work, requirements, opportunities, earnings, things to consider, and outlook.

Job description for tailor I. U.S. Employment Service, U.S. Department of Labor. Supt. of Documents. 1947. 6p. 5c
>   Occupational guide. Job summary, work performed, training, related occupations, physical activities, and working conditions.

Tailor. Splaver, Sarah. Personnel Services. 1952. 6p. 50c; 25c to students
>   Occupational abstract. Nature of work, qualifications, preparation, entrance and advancement, distribution of workers, supply and demand, earnings, advantages, and disadvantages.

* Tailor. Chronicle Guidance Publications. 1962. 4p. 35c
>   Occupational brief summarizing work performed, employment conditions, qualifications, determination of aptitudes and interests, training, opportunities, outlook, and methods of entry.

Tailor. The Guidance Center. 1959. 4p. 15c in Canada; 20c elsewhere
>   Nature of work, qualifications, preparation, wages, opportunities for promotion, outlook, where employed, and methods of entry.

* Tailors. Careers. 1960. 8p. 25c
>   Career brief describing duties, working conditions, training, personal qualifications, earnings, unionization, and outlook.

* Tailors and dressmakers. Science Research Associates. 1960. 4p. 35c
>   Occupational brief describing nature of work, training, qualifications, opportunities, advantages, disadvantages, and future outlook.

TAX ATTORNEY   0-22.10

**Career as a tax lawyer. Institute for Research. 1958. 16p. $1
>   Description of work, historical sketch, typical week's work, attractive and unattractive features, qualifications, education and training, and the lawyer's code of ethics. Descriptions of jobs with the Treasury Department, Department of Justice, local and state governments, legal publishing house, trust office, corporation counsel, in private practice, and as a teacher.

**Careers in tax work. Internal Revenue Service. 1962. 14p. Free
>   Information about jobs in the tax field, employment outlook, location of jobs, personal qualifications, educational requirements, earnings, advancement, advantages, and disadvantages. Selected references.

TAXI DRIVER   7-36.040

Taxi driver. Careers. 1960. 2p. 15c
>   Career summary for desk-top file. Duties, qualifications, and outlook.

TAXI DRIVER—*Continued*

Taxi driver. The Guidance Centre. 1962. 4p. 15c in Canada; 20c elsewhere
    History and importance, nature of work, qualifications, preparation, outlook, remuneration, advantages, disadvantages, how to get started, and related occupations.

**Taxi drivers. One section of *Occupational Outlook Handbook*.
    Nature of work, where employed, qualifications, training, employment outlook, earnings, and working conditions.

* Taxicab drivers. Science Research Associates. 1961. 4p. 35c
    Occupational brief describing nature of work, requirements, earnings, getting started, advantages, disadvantages, and future outlook.

TAXIDERMIST 0-66.95

Big game hunter: Carl Akeley. Sutton, Feliz. Julian Messner, Inc. 1960. 192p. $3.25. Library binding $3.19 net
    Biography of a pioneer taxidermist who created many natural-history exhibits for the Chicago Natural History Museum.

TEACHER 0-30. through 0-32.

Adult education. Luke, Robert A. Bellmann Publishing Company. 1955. 19p. $1
    History and organization, educational requirements, remuneration and chance for advancement, and professional and trade associations.

The beginning teacher: status and career orientations. U.S. Office of Education. Supt. of Documents. 1961. 196p. $1.25
    Analysis of the social, professional, and economic status of beginning teachers; also their aspirations, values and attitudes concerning teaching.

Bulletin of information. National Teacher Examinations. Annual. 10p. Free
    Bulletin containing application for the examination, prepared and administered annually at more than two hundred testing centers. A candidate may take the common examinations, which include tests in professional information, general culture, English expression, and nonverbal reasoning; and one or two of the thirteen optional examinations designed to demonstrate mastery of subject matter to be taught.

Business teaching as a career. Delta Pi Epsilon. 1956. 16p. 35c
    Discussion of what business teaching offers, requirements, training, and a quiz to help one measure himself as a prospective teacher. Brochure is unusually attractive.

Career as a teacher of business and commercial subjects. Institute for Research. 1961. 24p. $1
    Description of duties, a typical day's work, qualifications, training, earnings, opportunities, and getting started. Includes a list of colleges offering degrees with majors in business education.

Careers for professional teachers. Angel, Juvenal L. World Trade Academy Press. 1957. 26p. $1.25

Career monograph describing the fields of specialization, opportunities, remuneration, advantages, and disadvantages. One list contains the names of colleges offering scholarships and fellowships in the field of teaching and another list contains the names of private organizations or foundations offering student aid.

Careers in education. Wynn, Richard. McGraw-Hill Book Company. 1960. 307p. $4.95

An introduction to careers in the field of education, this book is a discussion of some of the contemporary forces and issues affecting teaching.

Careers in the teaching field. Angel, Juvenal. World Trade Academy Press. 1960. 37p. $1.25

Includes description of the major fields of specialization, education required, opportunities, remuneration, and future outlook.

Classroom teacher salary schedules, 1962 63, districts having 6,000 or more pupils. National Education Association. 1962. 112p. $2.25

A tabulation of minimum and maximum salaries and annual increments for 557 of the largest urban school districts and 178 suburban districts. Also states the professional growth required for the maximum salary.

College and university programs for the preparation of teachers of exceptional children. Mackie, Romaine and Dunn, Lloyd. U.S. Office of Education. Bulletin 1954, Number 13. Supt. of Documents. 1954. 92p. 35c

Information on the need for, and the status of, college programs for the professional preparation of special education personnel. For each of the 122 institutions offering training, areas of specialties are indicated, such as teachers of the blind, crippled, deaf, speech handicapped, socially maladjusted, mentally retarded, and gifted.

College financial aid check list for prospective teachers. National Education Association. 1962. 8p. 35 copies $1

Describes the types of financial assistance available and lists sources of additional information.

College teaching as a career. American Council on Education. 1958. 28p. Free to counselors and librarians

A discussion of the pleasures and satisfactions in teaching in college.

College tips for future teachers. National Education Association. 1961. 8p. 35 copies $1

A leaflet on how to select and get into an accredited college of teacher education and what students can do while in high school to assure success in college.

Economic status of teachers in 1961-62. National Education Association. 1962. 54p. 75c

Annual report including certification and average salaries. Salaries are compared with earnings of other professional workers.

TEACHER—*Continued*

Education—an investment in people. Chamber of Commerce of the United States, Education Department. 1954. 46p. $1
Includes attractive charts in color on the value of education, our changing population, need for teachers, and current and predicted school conditions. Variations in regional and state conditions in education are presented in order to encourage local and state business and professional leaders to study the educational job ahead for them. Revision in preparation.

Education: earned degrees, by level, sex, and institution. One section of *Earned Degrees Conferred.*
Useful for judging the extent of a college's program in the specialized teaching fields, such as business education, speech correction, health education, and teaching of exceptional children.

The education of American teachers. Conant, James B. McGraw-Hill Book Company. 1963. 275p. $5
Contains many recommendations for changes in the preparation of teachers.

Education (teaching) as a career. Boston University. 1962. 18p. Free
Recruiting booklet describing qualifications, advantages, various kinds of teaching, and preparation.

Educators. Chapter 3 of *The College Girl Looks Ahead.*
Some characteristics of work in education, talents needed, trying out and preparing for work, entering, and kinds of work.

**Employment outlook for teachers. Bureau of Labor Statistics, U.S. Department of Labor. Supt. of Documents. 1964. 16p. 10c
Reprint from the *Occupational Outlook Handbook.*

The extra-special room. Hill, Margaret. Little, Brown and Company. 1962. 312p. $3.50
Career fiction. A story of a teacher's career. Written for junior high school girls.

Fair is the morning. Erdman, Loula Grace. David McKay Company. 1945. 186p. $3
Career fiction. Story of a rural school teacher and her experiences in making the school the center of community activities and in meeting problems in health, soil conservation, and social needs.

Financial aid for teacher education. National Commission on Teacher Education and Professional Standards. 1961. 4p. Single copy free
Explanation of aid available under the National Defense Education Act.

Find a career in education. Smith, Frances. Putnam's Sons. 1960. 160p. $2.95
Describes work in the elementary schools, junior and senior high schools, and colleges. Includes preparation, salaries, outlook, advantages, and disadvantages. Written for ages 11 to 15.

Future teachers of America. Future Teachers of America. 1961. 8p. Free
A leaflet about teaching and exploring teaching through membership in the Future Teachers of America.

Graduate study for future college teachers. American Council on Education. 1959. 114p. $1.50
Prepared for college administrators, this is a discussion of planning programs of graduate studies.

Hi! Teacher. McLelland, Isabel C. Henry Holt and Company. 1952. 212p. $2.96
Career novel of a teacher in a one-room school and her adjustment to the inconveniences of rural living.

High school teaching as a career. Institute for Research. 1958. 24p. $1
Requirements, demand, rewards, opportunities, and attractive and unattractive features.

I want to be a teacher. Greene, Carla. Childrens Press. 1957. 32p. $2
Prepared for beginning readers with a reading level of upper first grade. Illustrated in color.

An idea in action: new teachers for the nation's children. Women's Bureau, U.S. Department of Labor. Pamphlet Number 2. Supt. of Documents 1956. 37p. 20¢
Description of programs that prepare mature women college graduates to meet state certification requirements for teaching.

Industrial arts teaching as a career. Institute for Research. 1956. 24p. $1
History and types of positions, typical day's work, attractive and unattractive features, personal characteristics, education and training, earnings, chances of employment, and getting started. Also includes a list of colleges offering degrees with a major in industrial arts.

Introduction to teaching. Peters, Herman J.; Burnett, C. W.; and Farwell, Gail F. Macmillan Company. 1963. 389p. $6
Prepared as a college text to help the student evaluate the qualifications for a teaching career by introducing him to the requirements and rewards of teaching.

Invitation to teaching. Association for Childhood Education International. 1961. 6p. Single copy free
Includes the satisfactions of teaching and questions to consider in testing one's interest.

**Invitation to teaching. National Education Association. 1961. 21p. 25¢
Aimed at able youngsters considering a teaching career. Includes discussion of preparation, costs, employment outlook, and estimated earnings. Sources of information.

Jane Cameron: schoolmarm. Brady, Rita. Abelard-Schuman. 1954. 208p. $2.75
Career fiction. Story of a girl's first job in teaching, told with simplicity and sincerity.

Jobs in the education field. Changing Times. 1959. 3p. 15¢
Reprint discussing demand, pay, prestige, and benefits of careers in the education field.

TEACHER—*Continued*

Kathie: the new teacher. Rosenheim, Lucile G. Julian Messner, Inc. 1949. 195p. $2.95
Career fiction. A romance that tells of Kathie's first year of teaching.

A manual on certification requirements for school personnel in the United States. National Commission on Teacher Education and Professional Standards. 1962. 229p. $4
Contains specific requirements for all certificates in the fifty states and territories, a listing of all institutions approved for the preparation of teachers, and current trends in certification practices. Also includes information about teaching positions in the Overseas Dependents Schools and a list of teacher placement agencies in the respective states.

The national teacher examinations. Educational Testing Service. Published annually. Free
Bulletin of information for candidates. Includes application, list of examination centers, and representative questions.

* Opportunities in teaching. Fine, Benjamin. **Vocational Guidance Manuals.** 1963. 160p. $1.45 paper
The teaching profession today, need, outlook, satisfactions, what the educators think, the Indiana survey, personal attributes necessary for success, the changing role of the teaching profession, types of teachers, educational preparation, finding your job, salaries, paths to advancement, rural versus urban teaching, advantages, disadvantages, related fields, and educational associations.

Planning for teaching. Richey, Robert W. McGraw-Hill Book Company. 1963. 550p. $6.50
Prepared as a textbook for a college introductory course in education, this book includes the duties and responsibilities of teachers, salary, retirement benefits, professional training and growth, potential values in teaching, and problems one may face.

Rankings of the states, 1962. National Education Association. 1962. 60p. 75c
Research report showing rankings of the states by population, enrollment, number of teachers, educational attainment, and financial resources. Contains seventy-four tables.

Really, Miss Hillsboro! Hill, Margaret. Little, Brown and Company. 1960. 256p. $3
Career fiction. Story of a young teacher of the fifth grade.

Requirements for certification of teachers, counselors, librarians, administrators for elementary schools, secondary schools, and junior colleges. Woellner, Mrs. Robert C. and Wood, M. Aurilla. University of Chicago Press. 1962. 126p. $3.50
This is the twenty-seventh edition of an annual digest of certification requirements, by states, including elementary and secondary schools through junior colleges.

The road to teaching. Milwaukee-Downer College. 1960. 8p. Free
A college bulletin discussing teacher preparation and careers in education.

Salary incentives for teachers of industrial and distributive education. American Vocational Association. 1962. 42p. 10c
Reasons why salary schedules must be revised to attract competent instructors in these two fields. Includes selected examples of how this is being accomplished in vocational programs.

A school for Suzanne. Freer, Marjorie M. Julian Messner, Inc. 1959. 192p. $2.95
Career fiction. Includes the intangible rewards and satisfactions in teaching.

* School teaching as a career. Boylan, James R. Henry Z. Walck, Inc. 1962. 100p. $3.50
Discussion of preparation, opportunities, personal factors to be considered, and satisfactions. Reading list. Illustrated.

Secondary school teacher. Splaver, Sarah. Personnel Services. 1958. 6p. 50c; 25c to students
Occupational abstract. Nature of work, qualifications, preparation, entrance and advancement, opportunities for servicemen, supply and demand, advantages, and disadvantages. Bibliography.

**Secondary school teachers. One section of *Occupational Outlook Handbook.*
Nature of work, where employed, training, other qualifications, advancement, employment outlook, earnings, and working conditions.

Should you be a teacher? Russell, William F. New York Life Insurance Company. 1960. 12p. Free
Aimed to encourage parents to prepare for their children's future education. Includes advantages, qualifications, cost of training, prospects, and qualities one should possess.

**So you're going to be a teacher. Filbin, Robert L. and Vogel, Stefan. Barron's Educational Series, Inc. 1962. 141p. $2.95; $1.25 paper
Discussion of teaching as a career, rewards, hazards, and questions new teachers ask. Contains chart of certification requirements in the fifty states for elementary, junior high school, and senior high school teaching.

A special message—teachers and the Peace Corps. Peace Corps. 1962. 4p. Free
Illustrated leaflet describing needs, qualifications, and how to file application.

A study of the need for academic classroom teachers of the deaf. Volta Bureau. 1959. 4p. 25c
Survey of the need indicating shortage of trained teachers of the deaf.

Teach in New Jersey. New Jersey Education Association. 1963. 16p. Free
Advantages of teaching and a list of the seventeen colleges in New Jersey offering teacher-training courses.

Teacher. Careers. 1961-1963. 2p. 15c each
Career summaries for various subject areas:
Business teacher, high school
Elementary art teacher
English teacher

TEACHER—*Continued*

High school art teacher
High school teacher
Homemaking teacher
School nurse-teacher
Science teacher, high school
Teacher, high school foreign language
Teacher, high school social studies
Teacher, industrial arts
Teacher of handicapped children
Teacher of the deaf and hard of hearing

* Teacher. Chronicle Guidance Publications. 1964. 4p. 35c
Occupational brief summarizing work performed, working conditions, personal qualifications, training requirements, earnings, opportunities, employment outlook, and entry into the job.

The teacher and his work. Gould, G. and Yoakam, G. A. Ronald Press Company. 1954. 395p. $5
Includes discussion of the nature of work, qualifications, preparation, working conditions, and earnings.

The teacher and the law. National Education Association. 1959. 92p. $1
Summarizes the general legal status of the public school teacher as defined by state law and court decisions; includes admission to the profession, tenure, salaries, privileges, rights, and immunities.

Teacher (elementary and secondary). The Guidance Centre. 1963. 4p. 15c in Canada; 20c elsewhere
Nature of work, qualifications, preparation, advancement, outlook, remuneration, advantages, disadvantages, how to get started, and related occupations.

Teacher, public school. Careers. 1958. 7p. 25c
Career brief describing duties, advantages, disadvantages, earnings, advancement prospects, and outlook.

Teacher supply and demand in public schools. National Education Association. 1962. 55p. $1
This fifteenth annual study focuses upon the continuance of the national shortage of teachers.

Teachers. Michigan Employment Security Commission. 1962. 20p. 25c
Introduction, nature of work, working conditions, location of jobs, employment outlook, earnings, requirements for entry, disadvantages, and advantages.

Teachers. Science Research Associates. 1958. 4p. 35c
Occupational brief describing nature of work, qualifications, preparation, opportunities, advantages, disadvantages, and future outlook.

A teacher's guide to financial aid for postgraduate study. National Education Association. 1963. 4p. 35 copies $1
This leaflet was planned to help the teacher in service find financial assistance to make postgraduate study possible. Lists several programs and sources of information.

Teachers of exceptional children. Science Research Associates. 1961. 4p. 35c

Occupational brief describing nature of work, personal qualifications, training, earnings, pros and cons, and future outlook.

**Teaching. One chapter of *Occupational Outlook Handbook.*

Nature of work, training, other qualifications, employment outlook, advancement, earnings, and working conditions for each of the following: kindergarten and elementary school teachers, secondary school teachers, and college and university teachers.

Teaching: a second career. U.S. Department of Defense. 1961. 39p. Free

Information for the retired military personal to assist in identifying and attaining the qualifications prerequisite for successful teaching after retirement.

**Teaching as a career. Burton, William H. Bellman Publishing Company. 1963. 45p. $1

Number and types of positions available, supply and demand, advantages and disadvantages, rewards, activities and responsibilities of educational workers, training and certification, and methods of securing a position.

Teaching as a career. Institute for Research. 1955. 24p. $1

Qualifications, opportunities, and attractive and unattractive features.

**Teaching as a career. U.S. Office of Education. Supt. of Documents. 1963. 32p. 20c

Pamphlet designed to stimulate capable young people to become interested in careers in education. Headings are: What is teaching really like? Do I have what it takes? When do I start? What would be my best field? After college, what? Now as to the practical side. Sources of additional information.

**Teaching as a man's job. Lee, Edwin A., chairman. Phi Delta Kappa. Revised 1963. 64p. 50c

Presents the sacrifices and rewards of teaching. Prepared for use in senior high schools.

**Teaching career fact book. National Education Association. 1964. 58p. $1

Among the subjects covered are teacher supply and demand, teacher preparation, certification requirements, current salaries, conditions of work, professional responsibilities, and a list of colleges and universities accredited by the National Council for the Accreditation of Teacher Education. Good bibliography.

**Teaching career month packet. National Education Association. 1963. Thirty-five items. $2

An annual assortment of booklets for observance of a teaching career month.

Teaching in Europe. Callaway, Helen Lund. Alumnae Advisory Center. 1955. 9p. 25c

Reprint from *Mademoiselle* including a mimeographed insert containing a list of private or international schools in Europe that hire Americans with degrees in education.

Teaching is an attractive career. Anderson, Earl W. U.S. Office of Education. Supt. of Documents. 1954. 4p. 5c

Reprint from *School Life* useful for counseling students regarding vocational choices.

TEACHER—*Continued*

Teaching opportunities. U.S. Office of Education. Supt. of Documents. 1960. 39p. 30c
Contains information on securing teaching positions, summer positions, certification requirements, teacher supply and demand, and salaries.

Teaching salaries then and now—a second look. Fund for the Advancement of Education. 1961. 45p. Free
Statistical tables included which give a comparison with other occupations and industries.

They're waiting for you. Northeastern University. 1962. 28p. Free
An attractively illustrated booklet depicting the challenge of the elementary school teacher.

This booklet is for you IF. Tri-State Area School Study Council Office, University of Pittsburg. 1962. 20p. 15c
Written by teachers to stimulate interest in teaching as a career, the booklet summarizes information about demand, preparation, salaries, and types of positions open in the field.

Tomboy teacher. Betts, Miriam P. Julian Messner, Inc. 1961. 192p. $2.95
Career fiction. Shedding her tomboy ways, Nancy becomes a dedicated young teacher who tries to bring modern methods into an antiquated school system.

Vocational education for American youth. American Vocational Association. 1956. 16p. 10c
Statement of the aims, objectives, and accomplishments of vocational education. An authoritative account of this phase of American education.

What shall I teach? National Education Association. 1962. 8p. Thirty-five copies $1
Identifies the many different teaching positions for which a prospective teacher might want to prepare himself.

What you should know about new horizons. National Education Association. 1962. 42p. 25c
A condensed report of a study containing recommendations for improving the teaching profession in the decade ahead.

Why teach? Sharp, D. Louise, ed. Henry Holt and Company. 1957. 240p. $4
Opinions expressed by 120 people concerning the satisfactions of teaching.

Will you be my teacher? Volta Bureau. No date. 4p. Single copies free
Information concerning work as teacher of the deaf.

Wondering whether your child should be a teacher? National Education Association. 1960. 8p. Thirty-five copies $1
Describes some of the opportunities and advantages offered by careers in teaching.

Young man's view of the teaching profession. Future Teachers of America. 1961. 8p. 5c; Thirty-five for $1
An elementary school principal's opinion of teaching as a challenging career for young men.

**Your career in teaching. National Research Bureau. 1955. 30p. 20c
Need for teachers, opportunities, nature of work, qualities needed, training, how to get started, and future outlook. Eight illustrations.

Your career opportunities in teaching. Novak, Gail, ed. Rowman and Littlefield, Inc. 1962. 64p. 75c
One of the Visual Career Guides, about one half of the contents consists of photographs and charts. Includes description of the training, qualifications, earnings, and employment outlook.

See also College teacher; Elementary school teacher; Kindergarten teacher; Nursery school teacher

TECHNICAL WRITER. See Writer

TECHNICIAN   0-50.; 0-66.00 through 0-67.99

**Accredited technical institute programs in the United States. Engineers' Council for Professional Development. 1962. 8p. 25c
List of accredited programs of technical institute type in thirty-two institutions.

Aeronautical engineering technician. National Council of Technical Schools. 1953. 2p. 5c
Description of work, working conditions, opportunities, outlook, advantages, and methods of entering.

Can I be a technician? Let's find out. General Motors Corporation, Public Relations Staff. 1961. 20p. Free
Description of nature of work, preparation, opportunities, and typical course of study in a technical institute.

Career guidance information for engineering technicians. National Council of Technical Schools. 1958. 4p. 5c
Description of work, personal traits required, preparation, and training.

Career opportunities for the engineering technician. National Council of Technical Schools. 1961. 16p. 50c
Fifteen career monographs, each describing one of the engineering technical occupations.

Careers for technicians in the electrical field. Angel, Juvenal. World Trade Academy Press. 1960. 28p. $1.25
Includes information about each of several specialties within this field.

**Careers for women as technicians. Women's Bureau, U.S. Department of Labor. Supt. of Documents. 1961. 28p. 20c
This booklet presents the specializations of technicians as an emerging occupational field. It describes the basic requirements and characteristics of technicians, training, earnings, possibilities for advancement, outlook, and obstacles to women's employment.

Demand for engineers, 1962. Engineering Manpower Commission. 1962. 60p. $2
A special section is included on employment data for engineering technicians.

TECHNICIAN—*Continued*

Directory of technical institute courses. National Council of Technical Schools. 1961. 6p. Free
> Courses approved at each of seventeen technical schools for engineering technicians.

Employment outlook for technicians. VA Pamphlet 22-1. Veterans Administration. Supt. of Documents. 1958. 28p. 25c
> Report on technicians who work with engineers and physical scientists. Describes the nature of work, training required, employment outlook, earnings, and working conditions.

**Employment outlook for technicians: engineering and science technicians, draftsmen, and surveyors. Bureau of Labor Statistics, U.S. Department of Labor. Supt. of Documents. 1964. 20p. 15c
> Reprint from the *Occupational Outlook Handbook*.

**Engineering technician. American Society for Engineering Education. No date. 21p. 25c
> Nature of work, qualifications, preparation, training, typical courses of study, employment outlook, and areas of employment. Includes discussion of opportunities in twelve areas such as aeronautical technology, electronics technology, and instrumentation technology.

Engineering technician. Careers. 1961. 2p. 15c
> Career summary for desk-top file. Duties, qualifications, and outlook.

Engineering technician. Chronicle Guidance Publications. 1962. 4p. 35c
> Occupational brief summarizing work performed, working conditions, qualifications, determination of aptitudes and interests, selecting a technical institute, where employed, and employment outlook. Selected references.

Engineering technicians. Science Research Associates. 1960. 4p. 35c
> Occupational brief describing work, qualifications, training, earnings, and outlook. Selected references.

Industrial management and engineering technicians. Chronicle Guidance Publications. 1960. 8p. 50c
> Occupational brief summarizing work performed, qualifications, training, opportunities, salaries, location of work, and outlook.

**Jobs in technical work. Science Research Associates. 1959. 32p. $1
> Describes the variety of job prospects and opportunities within this field, especially for the air conditioning technician, draftsman, cartographer, instrument technician, electronics technician, medical technologist, and X-ray technician.

List of accredited programs of technical institute type. Engineers' Council for Professional Development. 1962. 6p. 25c
> Reprint from the Council's annual report listing thirty-two technical institutes with the names of the accredited programs such as electrical technology, electronic and radio technology, industrial chemistry, etc.

The mechanical technician. National Council of Technical Schools. 1953. 2p. 5c
> Describes work of the tool designer, qualifications, opportunities, outlook, and methods of entrance.

Technical occupations in research design and development considered directly supporting to engineers and physical scientists. U.S. Department of Labor. Supt. of Documents. 1961. 113p. 50c
Composite descriptions of twenty-nine technical occupations that provide direct support to engineers and physical scientists engaged in research, design, and development. Also included are estimates of worker trait requirements pertinent to each activity.

The technician and the engineer. National Council of Technical Schools. 1953. 2p. 5c
Explanation of how the technician and the engineer work together on industrial developmental problems.

Technicians. Chronicle Guidance Publications. 1962. 8p. 50c
Occupational brief summarizing work performed in a variety of classifications, working conditions, training, qualifications, earnings, opportunities, and outlook.

**Technicians: engineering and science technicians, draftsmen, and surveyors. One section of *Occupational Outlook Handbook*.
Nature of work, where employed, training, other qualifications, advancement, employment outlook, earnings, and working conditions.

Technicians, physical science and engineering. Careers. 1962. 8p. 25c
Career brief describing the growing importance of technicians, duties, working conditions, training, earnings, and outlook. Additional readings.

**Technicians who work with engineers and physical scientists. One section of *Occupational Outlook Handbook*, 1961 edition.
Nature of work, where employed, training, other qualifications, employment outlook, and earnings. Includes the following kinds of technicians: aeronautical, heating, air conditioning, refrigeration, chemical, civil engineering, electronics, industrial engineering, and mechanical engineering.

**Your opportunities in industry as a technician. National Research Bureau. 1957. 32p. 20c
Describes the wide range of career opportunities for technical specialists. Outlines the aptitudes, training required, and the challenging possibilities. Illustrated.

See also Laboratory technician; Medical technologist

TELEGRAPH OPERATOR   1-41.

Finding out about telegraph operators. Science Research Associates. 1964. 4p. 35c
Junior occupational brief containing some concise facts about the job and listing ways of finding out about the nature of the work.

See also Telephone operator

TELEPHONE AD TAKER   1-18.63

Magic in her voice. Panzer, Pauline. Julian Messner, Inc. 1953. 192p. $2.95
Career fiction. Story of a girl's experiences in the classified section of a newspaper as an ad taker and later in a department for the sale of used cars.

TELEPHONE AND TELEGRAPH INDUSTRY WORKER
5, 7-53.000 through 5, 7-53.999; 9-54.20

**Employment outlook in telephone occupations. Bureau of Labor Statistics, U.S. Department of Labor. Supt. of Documents. 1964. 20p. 15c
> Reprint from the *Occupational Outlook Handbook.*

Men against distance. Floherty, John J. J. B. Lippincott Company. 1954. 160p. $3.75
> The wonders of the telephone, telegraphy, radio, and television are reviewed with emphasis on the research programs responsible for their development. One chapter is a discussion of vocational opportunities in the field of communications.

**Telegraphers, telephoners, and towermen (railroad). One section of *Occupational Outlook Handbook.*
> Nature of work, training, other qualifications, advancement, employment outlook, earnings, and working conditions.

Teletype operator. Careers. 1961. 2p. 15c
> Career summary for desk-top file. Duties, qualifications, and outlook.

**Telephone occupations. One chapter of *Occupational Outlook Handbook.*
> Nature and location of the industry, kinds of work, employment outlook, earnings, and working conditions. Specific information is given for central office craftsmen, linemen, cable splicers, telephone and PBX installers and repairmen, telephone operators, and central office equipment installers. Six illustrations.

Women telephone workers and changing technology. Women's Bureau, U.S. Department of Labor. Supt. of Documents. 1963. 46p. 25c
> Information about employment opportunities, earnings, and training requirements. Includes discussion of employment implications of future technological changes.

TELEPHONE INSTALLATION AND MAINTENANCE WORKER
5, 7-53.000 through 5, 7-53.999

Central office craftsmen. One section of *Occupational Outlook Handbook.*
> Nature of work, training, other qualifications, advancement, employment outlook, earnings, and working conditions.

Central office equipment installers. One section of *Occupational Outlook Handbook.*
> Nature of work, training, other qualifications, advancement, employment outlook, earnings, and working conditions.

Finding out about telephone installers. Science Research Associates. 1963. 4p. 35c
> Junior occupational brief containing concise facts about the job.

Lineman. The Guidance Centre. 1961. 4p. 15c in Canada; 20c elsewhere
> History and importance, nature of work, qualifications, working conditions, preparation, remuneration, advancement, outlook, related occupations, and how to get started.

**Linemen and cable splicers. One section of *Occupational Outlook Handbook.*
> Nature of work, training, other qualifications, advancement, employment outlook, earnings, and working conditions.

Telephone and PBX installers and repairmen. One section of *Occupational Outlook Handbook.*
> Nature of work, training, other qualifications, advancement, employment outlook, earnings, and working conditions.

Telephone and telegraph linemen. Science Research Associates. 1960. 4p. 35c
> Occupational brief describing work, training, wage rates, and job prospects.

Telephone installer. Careers. 1960. 2p. 15c
> Career summary for desk-top file. Duties, qualifications, and outlook.

Telephone installers. Science Research Associates. 1963. 4p. 35c
> Occupational brief describing nature of work, training, qualifications, opportunities, and outlook. Selected references.

Telephone lineman and cable splicers. Careers. 1964. 8p. 25c
> Career brief describing duties, working conditions, training requirements, personal qualifications, earnings, advancement prospects, and outlook.

Telephone technician. The Guidance Centre. 1960. 4p. 15c in Canada; 20c elsewhere
> Development and growing importance of the work, duties, working conditions, qualifications, preparation, advancement opportunities, earnings, and how to get started.

TELEPHONE OPERATOR   1-42.

Careers for women in telephone work. Institute for Research. 1962. 24p. $1
> Types of jobs, typical day's work, attractive and unattractive features, personal qualifications, training, earnings, getting started, and related jobs.

Finding out about switchboard operators. Science Research Associates. 1963. 4p. 35c
> Junior occupational brief describing work and opportunities.

Finding out about telephone operators. Science Research Associates. 1964. 4p. 35c
> Junior occupational brief containing some concise facts about the job and listing ways of finding out about the nature of the work. Includes suggestions for reading and a list of other occupational briefs on related topics.

I want to be a telephone operator. Greene, Carla. Childrens Press. 1958. 32p. $2
> Prepared for beginning readers with a reading level of upper first grade. Illustrated in color.

TELEPHONE OPERATOR—*Continued*

Operator of telephone answering service. California State Department of Employment. 1960. 3p. Single copy free
Job duties, working conditions, pay, hours, entrance requirements, promotion, and employment outlook.

PBX operator. Careers. 1962. 2p. 15c
Career summary for desk-top file. Duties, qualifications, and outlook.

Private switchboard operators. Science Research Associates. 1963. 4p. 35c
Occupational brief describing nature of work, training, qualifications, training opportunities, and outlook. Two illustrations. Selected references.

* Telephone and telegraph operators. Science Research Associates. 1959. 4p. 35c
Occupational brief describing nature of work, qualifications, preparation, opportunities, advantages, disadvantages, and future outlook.

Telephone operator. Robinson, H. Alan. Personnel Services. 1954. 6p. 50c; 25c to students
Occupational abstract. Nature of work, future prospects, qualifications, preparation, entrance and advancement, earnings, advantages, and disadvantages.

Telephone operator. Careers. 1964. 2p. 15c
Career summary for desk-top file. Duties, qualifications, and outlook.

* Telephone operator. Chronicle Guidance Publications. 1962. 4p. 35c
Occupational brief summarizing work performed, employment conditions, qualifications, determination of aptitudes and interests, opportunities, outlook, methods of entry, and related jobs.

Telephone operator. The Guidance Centre. 1960. 4p. 15c in Canada; 20c elsewhere
Definition, importance of work, duties, qualifications, preparation, earnings, how to get started, advantages, and disadvantages.

**Telephone operators. One section of *Occupational Outlook Handbook*.
Nature of work, training, other qualifications, advancement, employment outlook, earnings, and working conditions.

TELETYPE OPERATOR. *See* Telephone and telegraph industry worker

TELEVISION ANNOUNCER. *See* Radio and television announcer

TELEVISION AND RADIO SERVICEMAN   5-83.416

**Employment outlook for television and radio servicemen. Bureau of Labor Statistics, U.S. Department of Labor. Supt. of Documents. 1964. 4p. 5c
Reprint from the *Occupational Outlook Handbook*.

Radio and television service and repairman. Careers. 1962. 2p. 15c
Career summary for desk-top file. Duties, qualifications, and outlook.

Radio and television servicemen. Michigan Employment Security Commission. 1958. 15p. 25c
Introduction, nature of work, location of jobs, working conditions, employment outlook, earnings, requirements for entry, disadvantages, and advantages.

* Radio and television servicemen. Science Research Associates. 1963. 4p. 35c

Occupational brief describing nature of work, qualifications, training, getting started, earnings, advantages, disadvantages, and future outlook.

Radio repairman. Group, Vernard. Personnel Services. 1961. 6p. 50c; 25c to students

Occupational abstract. Nature of work, future prospects, qualifications, preparation, entrance, advancement, earnings, number and distribution of workers, advantages, and disadvantages. References for further reading.

* Radio-TV repairman. Chronicle Guidance Publications. 1962. 4p. 35c

Occupational brief summarizing work performed, where employed, qualifications, training, and employment outlook.

Television and radio repairman. Florida State Employment Service. 1962. 7p. Single copy free to guidance personnel in Florida.

Example of a series prepared to provide information about occupations which offer employment opportunities in a specific state. Describes nature of work, qualifications, opportunities, advancement possibilities, working conditions, and wages.

** Television and radio servicemen. One section of *Occupational Outlook Handbook*.

Nature of work, where employed, training, other qualifications, advancement, employment outlook, earnings, and working conditions.

Television service and repairman. Robinson, H. Alan. Personnel Services. 1957. 6p. 50c; 25c to students.

Nature of the work, future prospects, opportunities for servicemen, qualifications, preparation, entrance and advancement, earnings, number and distribution, advantages, and disadvantages. Bibliography.

Television service and repairman and television installation man. California State Department of Employment. 1961. 5p. Single copy free

Duties, working conditions, how to find work, pay, hours, training, and employment prospects.

TELEVISION INDUSTRY WORKER
0-17.01; 0-61.; 0-97.70 through 0-97.79; 4, 6, 8-98.

Be on TV. Gardner, R. M. John Day Company. 1960. 128p. $3.50

Information ranging from running a television workshop to getting on the air. Written for ages 12 to 15.

Careers in television. Institute for Research. 1962. 24p. $1

History of the television industry; description of work in television manufacture, television station, technical and engineering jobs, and studio program production; typical week's work; attractive and unattractive features; and opportunities for women.

Careers in television. National Association of Broadcasters. 1963. 6p. Free

Brief history of the field, training, specific operations, getting a job, and opportunities for women.

TELEVISION INDUSTRY WORKER—*Continued*

Job opportunities in television. National Broadcasting Company, Department of Information. 1953. 5p. Mimeographed. Free
Description of duties and qualifications for eleven jobs in programming, eleven in technical operation, five in administration and sales, and one in research and development.

TV girl Friday. Milne, Ruth. Little, Brown and Company. 1957. 248p. $3
Career fiction. Story of a girl with her heart set on a career in front of the cameras who overcame her disappointment and discovered interesting work behind the scenes.

**Television and teamwork. Bell, Bob and Bell, Elise. Dodd, Mead and Company. 1962. 256p. $3.25
Career fiction. Interwoven in this story is description of many career opportunities, starting with reception clerk and ending with director-producer.

Television directors. Careers. 1962. 8p. 25c
Career brief describing duties, working conditions, training, personal qualifications, earnings, related careers, and outlook. Additional readings.

Television story. Floherty, John J. J. B. Lippincott Company. 1957. 160p. $3.95
The author reports on the history and development of the industry, the mechanics of television, how programs of various types are put on the air, and the duties of technicians, camera men, and actors. Good human interest anecdotes. Thirty-two illustrations.

* Television workers. Science Research Associates. 1959. 4p. 35c
Occupational brief describing various jobs, qualifications, opportunities, preparation, advantages, disadvantages, and future outlook.

**Your future in television. Deutscher, J. Noel. Richards Rosen Press. 1963. 158p. $2.95
This book presents the problems and opportunities in the broad field of television.

Your place in TV. Broderick, Edwin. David McKay Company. 1954. 142p. $3
Includes positions and qualifications in the administrative, technical and creative divisions. Also includes lists of colleges and technical schools offering courses in television.

See also Radio and television broadcasting industry worker

TELEVISION INSTALLATION MAN   5-83.417

Television installation man. California State Department of Employment. 1961. 5p. Single copy free
Occupational guide summarizing duties, working conditions, employment prospects, earnings, training, requirements for entry, and suggestions for locating a job.

TERRAZZO WORKERS. *See* Marble setter

TEXTILE INDUSTRY WORKER 4, 6, 8-14. through 4, 6, 8-27.

* Career as a home economist in the textile field. Institute for Research. 1958. 24p. $1

  Discussion of work in testing and research, fashion and styles, merchandising, public relations, and education.

Job descriptions for cotton textile industry. U.S. Employment Service. Supt. of Documents. 1939. 323p. $1.25

  One of a series of Volume Job Descriptions. Describes occupations concerned with manufacturing cotton yarn from raw cotton and with weaving all-cotton cloth of twelve inches or greater width. Illustrated.

Textile designer. Careers. 1964. 2p. 15c

  Career summary for desk-top file. Duties, qualifications, and outlook.

Textile engineering. Runton, Leslie A. Chapter 22 of *Engineering Enrollment in the United States.*

  Trends in enrollments and future requirements for specialists in this area.

**Textile industry workers. Science Research Associates. 1961. 4p. 35c

  Occupational brief describing work with cotton, woolen, and synthetic fibers. Also includes requirements, earnings, methods of getting started, advantages, disadvantages, and a look ahead.

Women have a place in textiles. Philadelphia College of Textiles and Science. 1951. 2p. Free

  Reprint from *The Textile Engineer* describing opportunities for women in the textile industry.

* Your career in textiles: an industry, a science, an art. American Textile Manufacturers Institute. 1962. 18p. 25c. Single copy free

  Attractive brochure, illustrated in color, presenting the varied career opportunities in each of three areas of textiles. The outlook is described in the industry for those with marketing, manufacturing, and management abilities; in science for those with engineering, science, and research skills; and in art for those with artistic and creative talents. Includes list of colleges offering degrees in this specialty.

THEATER MANAGER 0-98.54

Job description for theater manager. U.S. Employment Service. Supt. of Documents. 1948. 5p. 5c

  Occupational guide. Job summary, work performed, training, trainee-selection factors, related occupations, physical activities, working conditions, and employment variables.

Theater manager. Careers. 1963. 2p. 15c

  Career summary for desk-top file. Duties, qualifications, and outlook.

Theatre manager. The Guidance Centre. 1960. 4p. 15c in Canada; 20c elsewhere

  History and importance, nature of work, qualifications, working conditions, preparation, remuneration, advancement, outlook, related occupations, and how to get started.

THEATER MANAGER—*Continued*

**Theater managers. Science Research Associates. 1960. 4p. 35c
Occupational brief describing nature of work, duties, requirements, getting started, earnings and hours, advantages, disadvantages, and future outlook.

TICKET AGENT   1-44.12

Airline ticket agent. Careers. 1961. 2p. 15c
Career summary for desk-top file. Duties, qualifications, and outlook.

Job description for ticket agent. U.S. Employment Service. Supt. of Documents. 1948. 5p. 5c
Occupational guide. Job summary, work performed, training, trainee-selection factors, related occupations, physical activities, working conditions, hazards, and employment variables.

**Traffic agents and clerks (air transportation). One section of *Occupational Outlook Handbook.*
Nature of work, where employed, training, other qualifications, advancement, employment outlook, earnings, and working conditions.

TIME-STUDY MAN   0-68.73

Time-and-motion study man. Careers. 1962. 8p. 25c
Career brief describing duties, working conditions, training, personal qualifications, earnings, advancement prospects, and outlook.

Time study man. Group, Vernard F. Personnel Services. 1953. 6p. 50c; 25c to students
Occupational abstract. Summary of nature of the work, future prospects, opportunities for servicemen, opportunities for women, qualifications, preparation, entrance and advancement, earnings, number and distribution of workers, advantages, disadvantages, and related occupations.

See also Engineer

TOBACCO INDUSTRY WORKER   3-03.50; 4, 6, 8-12.

Tobacco manufacturing workers. Science Research Associates. 1961. 4p. 35c
Occupational brief describing nature of work, requirements, earnings, advantages, disadvantages, and future outlook.

TOOL AND DIE MAKER   4-76.

Finding out about tool and die makers. Science Research Associates. 1964. 4p. 35c
Junior occupational brief containing some facts about the job and listing ways of finding out about the nature of the work. Includes suggestions for reading and titles of other occupational briefs on related topics.

Tool and die industry. Bylander, Andrew E. Bellman Publishing Company. 1955. 26p. $1
History, definition of tools, organization of industry, opportunities, and professional and trade organizations.

Tool and die maker. Robinson, H. Alan. Personnel Services. 1956. 6p. 50c; 25c to students
Occupational abstract. Nature of work, future prospects, qualifications, preparation, entrance and advancement, earnings, number and distribution of workers, advantages, and disadvantages.

* Tool and die maker. Chronicle Guidance Publications. 1964. 4p. 35c
Occupational brief summarizing work performed, working conditions, hours, earnings, personal qualifications, training requirements, opportunities, employment outlook, and entry into the job.

Tool and die makers. Michigan Employment Security Commission. 1958. 16p. 25c
Introduction, nature of work, working conditions, location of jobs, employment outlook, earnings, requirements for entry, disadvantages, and advantages.

* Tool and die makers. Science Research Associates. 1963. 4p. 35c
Occupational brief describing nature of work, requirements, training, working conditions, earnings, and future outlook.

**Tool and die makers. One section of *Occupational Outlook Handbook*.
Nature of work, where employed, training, other qualifications, advancement, employment outlook, earnings, and working conditions.

Tool maker. Careers. 1963. 2p. 15c
Career summary for desk-top file. Duties, qualifications, and outlook.

Tool maker. The Guidance Centre. 1962. 4p. 15c in Canada; 20c elsewhere
Definition, qualifications necessary for entry and success, preparation, earnings, advantages, disadvantages, how to get started, and related occupations.

TOOL DESIGNER   0-48.41

Adventure into tomorrow through tool and manufacturing engineering. American Society of Tool and Manufacturing Engineers. 1963. 4p. Free
This booklet describes the work of the tool designer, opportunities available, education and training requirements, and future prospects.

Job description for tool designer. U.S. Employment Service. Supt. of Documents. 1948. 5p. 5c
Occupational guide. Job summary, work performed, training, trainee-selection factors, related occupations, physical activities, working conditions, hazards, and employment variables.

Tool designer. Careers. 1960. 2p. 15c
Career summary for desk-top file. Duties, qualifications, and outlook.

TRAFFIC AGENT. *See* Ticket agent; Traffic manager

TRAFFIC ENGINEER 0-39.94

**A career in traffic engineering. Institute of Traffic Engineers. 1962. 24p. Free
>Development of the work, duties, training, rewards, opportunities, and fields of employment.

Traffic engineer. Group, Vernard. Personnel Services. 1960. 6p. 50c; 25c to students
>Occupational abstract. Nature of work, future prospects, qualifications, preparation, entrance, advancement, and earnings.

Traffic engineer. Seburn, Thomas J. Research Publishing Company. 1959. 32p. $1
>Nature of work, history and importance, number engaged in the occupation, qualifications, working conditions, salaries and other returns, methods of securing jobs, and promotional opportunities.

Traffic engineer. Careers. 1964. 2p. 15c
>Career summary for desk-top file. Duties, qualifications, and outlook.

* Traffic engineers. Science Research Associates. 1963. 4p. 35c
>Occupational brief describing nature of work, training, qualifications, opportunities, and outlook. Selected references.

TRAFFIC MANAGER 0-97.66

Airline traffic agents and clerks. Science Research Associates. 1961. 4p. 35c
>Occupational brief describing nature of the work, requirements, getting started, earnings, working conditions, and future outlook. Selected references.

A career for you in traffic management. Academy of Advanced Traffic. No date. 8p. Free
>Description of work, qualifications, opportunities, and training.

The job of the traffic manager. Academy of Advanced Traffic. No date. 12p. Free
>Description of the work of the industrial traffic manager and the transportation traffic manager, qualifications, earnings, outlook, and related jobs.

**Employment outlook for purchasing agents and industrial traffic managers. Bureau of Labor Statistics, U.S. Department of Labor. Supt. of Documents. 1964. 8p. 5c
>Reprint from the *Occupational Outlook Handbook.*

Freight traffic management in transportation, industry, commerce, and government as a career. Institute for Research. 1957. 24p. $1
>History and development of work, description of types of jobs, attractive and unattractive features, qualifications, training, salaries, how to get started, and opportunities for women.

**Industrial traffic managers. One section of *Occupational Outlook Handbook.*
>Nature of work, where employed, training, other qualifications, advancement, employment outlook, earnings, and working conditions.

**Occupational guidance materials. American Society of Traffic and Transportation. 1964. Ten booklets. Free

Information concerning railroad, water carrier, motor, air, and pipe line transportation.

Should you be a traffic manager? Baker, George P. New York Life Insurance Company. 1959. 12p. Free

Description of duties, opportunities, qualifications, advantages, disadvantages, and training.

Traffic manager. Careers. 1964. 2p. 15c

Career summary for desk-top file. Duties, qualifications, and outlook.

Traffic manager. Chronicle Guidance Publications. 1960. 4p. 35c

Occupational brief summarizing work performed, working conditions, personal qualifications, training, opportunities, related jobs, methods of entry, and outlook.

Traffic manager. The Guidance Centre. 1050. 4p. 15c in Canada, 20c elsewhere

History and importance, nature of work, qualifications, working conditions, preparation, remuneration, advancement, outlook, related occupations, and how to get started.

Traffic manager. Michigan Employment Security Commission. 1960. 16p. 25c

Introduction, nature of work, location of jobs, employment outlook, working conditions, earnings, requirements for entry, disadvantages, and advantages.

**Traffic managers. Science Research Associates. 1961. 4p. 35c

Occupational brief describing duties, requirements, getting started and advancing, earnings, advantages, disadvantages, and future outlook.

TRANSPORTATION WORKER   5, 7, 9-35. through 5, 7, 9-49.

Occupations in transportation and communication. Chapter 15 of *Planning Your Future.*

Includes discussion of the importance of the industry, kinds of occupations, and information about a typical occupation in this group—the airplane pilot. Twelve illustrations.

Transportation and communication workers. Chapter 16 of *Vocations for Girls.*

Includes advantages and opportunities. Bibliography.

**Your future in the trucking industry. Eskow, Gerald W. Richards Rosen Press. 1964. 157p. $2.95; library edition $2.79 net

Includes information about a wide variety of jobs ranging from the semiskilled to the professional. The industry is presented as an expanding one which offers good opportunities for advancement.

See also Bus driver; Driver; Motor transportation worker; Truck driver

TRAVEL BUREAU SALESPERSON   1-18.42; 1-87.69

Careers in travel service. Institute for Research. 1962. 24p. $1
  Types of jobs, qualifications, earnings, opportunities, and methods of getting started.

Opportunities in travel. Short, Don. Vocational Guidance Manuals, Inc. 1953. 96p. $1.45 paper
  Discussion of work in commercial travel agency, automobile-club travel bureau, noncommercial travel bureau, governmental bureau, railroads, airlines, bus lines, sightseeing and tour companies, steamship lines, and hotels. Includes a discussion of salaries, opportunities, and how to get started. Includes lists of state and regional travel bureaus and travel promotion agencies, railroads, bus lines, steamship lines, and airlines.

Travel agent. California State Department of Employment. 1962. 4p. Single copy free
  Duties, working conditions, wages, hours, promotion, training, and employment outlook in California.

Travel agent. Careers. 1963. 2p. 15c
  Career summary for desk-top file. Duties, qualifications, and outlook.

Travel agent. Chronicle Guidance Publications. 1961. 4p. 35c
  Occupational brief summarizing work performed, related jobs, qualifications, training, earnings, methods of entry, advantages, disadvantages, and outlook.

Travel agent. The Guidance Centre. 1958. 4p. 15c in Canada; 20c elsewhere
  History and importance, nature of work, qualifications, working conditions, preparation, remuneration, advancement, outlook, related occupations and how to get started.

Tours by Terry. Freer, Marjorie Mueller. Julian Messner, Inc. 1958. 192p. $2.95
  Career fiction. Experiences of a graduate from business college at work in a travel agency.

* Travel agency workers. Science Research Associates. 1960. 4p. 35c
  Occupational brief describing nature of work, requirements, getting started and advancing, earnings and hours, advantages, disadvantages, and future outlook.

TREE SURGEON   0-68.13

Arborist. Chronicle Guidance Publications. 1963. 4p. 35c
  Occupational brief describing the care of trees and shrubs, importance of the work, training, wages, benefits, and employment outlook.

Orchard pruner. California State Department of Employment. 1959. 5p. Single copy free
  Job duties, working conditions, wages, hours, finding the work, promotion, training, and employment outlook.

Training and work of Davey tree experts. Davey Tree Expert Co. No date. 16p. Free

> Pictures and brief captions concerning training activities in tree surgery, pruning, tree feeding, spraying, tree trimming for public utilities, diagnosis, and tree moving.

The tree expert. Bartlett, F. A. Research Publishing Company. 1956. 32p. $1

> Description of general tree work and clearing for utility companies. Development of the work, skills needed, training, working conditions, advantages, and disadvantages are also given.

* Tree experts. Science Research Associates. 1963. 4p. 35c

> Occupational brief describing nature of work, requirements, methods of getting started, earnings, advantages, disadvantages, and future outlook.

Tree surgeon. Careers. 1960. 2p. 15c

> Career summary for desk-top file. Duties, qualifications, and outlook.

TRUCK DRIVER 5-36.099; 7-35.100; 7 36.200 through 7-36.299

The changing image of the truck driver. American Trucking Association. 1962. 5p. Free

> New insights into opportunities as a truck driver.

**Driving occupations. One chapter of *Occupational Outlook Handbook*.

> Nature of work, where employed, training, qualifications, employment outlook, earnings, and working conditions. Specific information is given for over-the-road truck driver, local truck driver, routeman, intercity bus driver, local transit bus driver, and taxi driver.

**Employment outlook in driving occupations. Bureau of Labor Statistics, U.S. Department of Labor. Supt. of Documents. 1964. 25p. 15c

> Reprint from the *Occupational Outlook Handbook*.

Heavy-truck driver. Careers. 1960. 2p. 15c

> Career summary for desk-top file. Duties, qualifications, and outlook.

I want to be a truck driver. Greene, Carla. Childrens Press. 1958. 32p. $2

> Prepared for beginning readers with a reading level of upper first grade. Illustrated in color.

Job description for electric-truck operator. U.S. Employment Service. Supt. of Documents. 1947. 4p. 5c

> Occupational guide. Job summary, work performed, training, related occupations, physical activities, and working conditions.

**Local truck drivers. One section of *Occupational Outlook Handbook*.

> Nature of work, where employed, qualifications, employment outlook, earnings, and working conditions.

Long haul truck driver, motor transport. California State Department of Employment. 1960. 6p. Single copy free

> Occupational guides summarizing duties, employment prospects, earnings, requirements for entry, and suggestions for locating a job.

TRUCK DRIVER—*Continued*

**Over-the-road truck drivers. One section of *Occupational Outlook Handbook*.

Nature of work, where employed, qualifications, training, advancement, employment outlook, earnings, and working conditions.

* Truck and bus drivers. Science Research Associates. 1959. 4p. 35c

Occupational brief describing the kinds of trucking, driver duties, qualifications, training, how to become a driver, opportunities, earnings, advantages, disadvantages, and future outlook.

* Truck driver. Chronicle Guidance Publications. 1963. 4p. 35c

Occupational brief containing definition, history, work performed, working conditions, personal requirements, determination of aptitudes and interests, training requirements, outlook, methods of entry, related jobs, and suggested activities.

Trucking industry careers—opportunities in the industry. American Trucking Associations. 1962. 13p. Free

Includes discussion of work in sales, traffic, operations, truck driving, maintenance engineering, and public relations.

See also Bus driver; Driver; Motor transportation industry worker; Transportation worker

TRUCK FARMER   3-09.10

About truck farming. Johnson, Irma B. Melmont Publishers. 1962. 32p. $2.50

Prepared to give younger readers in grades 1 to 4 an idea of the kinds of work on a truck farm and its importance. Illustrated in color.

Mushroom grower. The Guidance Centre. 1962. 4p. 15c in Canada; 20c elsewhere

History and importance, nature of work, qualifications, working conditions, preparation, remuneration, advancement, outlook, related occupations, and how to get started.

Truck farmer. Careers. 1960. 2p. 15c

Career summary for desk-top file. Duties, qualifications, and outlook.

Truck farmer. The Guidance Centre. 1962. 4p. 15c in Canada; 20c elsewhere

Definition, nature of work, working conditions, qualifications, earnings, employment and advancement, getting started, and related occupations.

Vegetable farmers. Science Research Associates. 1961. 4p. 35c

Occupational brief describing nature of work, preparation, opportunities, advantages, disadvantages, and future outlook.

Vegetable farming as a career. Institute for Research. 1954. 16p. $1

Kinds of work, earnings, attractive and unattractive features, and measures of success.

See also Farmer; Fruit and berry farmer

TYPIST 1-37.30 through 1-37.59

Clerk-typist. Robinson, H. Alan. Personnel Services. 1960. 6p. 50c; 25c to students

Occupational abstract. Nature of work, future prospects, qualifications, preparation, entrance, advancement, earnings, number and distribution, advantages, disadvantages, and related occupations.

Clerk-typist. California State Department of Employment. 1962. 4p. Single copy free

Duties, working conditions, wages, hours, finding the job, training, and employment outlook.

**Secretaries, stenographers, and typists. One section of *Occupational Outlook Handbook*.

Nature of work, where employed, employment outlook, earnings, and working conditions.

Typing occupations. Michigan Employment Security Commission. 1956. 20p. 25c

Introduction, nature of work, working conditions, location of jobs, employment outlook, earnings, organizations, qualifications for entry, disadvantages and advantages.

Typist. Careers. 1959. 8p. 25c

Career brief describing duties, working conditions, training, personal qualifications, earnings, advancement prospects, and outlook.

* Typist. Chronicle Guidance Publications. 1961. 4p. 35c

Occupational brief summarizing work performed, working conditions, qualifications, training, opportunities, methods of entry, related jobs, and outlook.

See also Clerical worker; Stenographer

UNDERTAKER. *See* Funeral manager

UNSKILLED WORKER 8-00. through 9-99.

Factory jobs—employment outlook for workers in jobs requiring little or no experience or specialized training. Bureau of Labor Statistics, U.S. Department of Labor. Supt. of Documents. 1961. 26p. 25c

Information about operative jobs in manufacturing industries, such as assemblers, inspectors, machine tool operators, and sewing machine operators.

Factory occupations not requiring specialized training. One section of *Occupational Outlook Handbook*.

Nature of work, employment outlook, earnings, and working conditions.

**Unskilled workers. Science Research Associates. 1960. 4p. 35c

Occupational brief listing some kinds of unskilled labor, earnings, advantages, disadvantages, and future outlook.

UPHOLSTERER 4, 6-35.

Furniture upholsterer. Careers. 1960. 8p. 25c
Career brief describing duties, working conditions, training, personal qualifications, earnings, outlook, and ways of measuring one's interest and ability.

Job description for upholsterer II. U.S. Employment Service. Supt. of Documents. 1947. 6p. 5c
Occupational guide. Job summary, work performed, training, related occupations, physical activities, and working conditions.

* Upholsterer. Chronicle Guidance Publications. 1961. 4p. 35c
Occupational brief summarizing work performed, training, working conditions, wages, personal requirements, and outlook.

* Upholsterers. Science Research Associates. 1961. 4p. 35c
Occupational brief describing nature of work, requirements, how to enter,
advancement, earnings and hours, advantages, disadvantages, and future outlook.

USHER 2-48.10

Usher. Careers. 1960. 2p. 15c
Career summary for desk-top file. Duties, qualifications, and outlook.

Usher. The Guidance Centre. 1960. 4p. 15c in Canada; 20c elsewhere
History and importance, nature of work, qualifications, working conditions,
preparation, remuneration, advancement, outlook, related occupations, and how
to get started.

VARI-TYPIST 1-37.38

Vari-typist. Careers. 1962. 2p. 15c
Career summary for desk-top file. Duties, qualifications, and outlook.

VENDING MACHINE OPERATOR 1-15.10

Vending machine operator. Chronicle Guidance Publications. 1961. 4p.
35c
Occupational brief summarizing work performed, where employed, working conditions, qualifications, training, earnings, advantages, disadvantages,
methods of entry, and outlook.

VETERINARIAN 0-34.10

Bird doctor. Tottenham, Katherine. Thomas Nelson and Sons. 1961. 160p.
$3
Career fiction. Relates experiences in caring for maimed and ailing wild
birds.

Career facts about veterinary medicine. American Veterinary Medical Association. 1962. 6p. Free
Brief description of opportunities in health services and science, qualifications, training, and list of twenty colleges of veterinary medicine.

Career opportunities for veterinarians in the Agricultural Research Service. U.S. Department of Agriculture. Supt. of Documents. 1963. 16p. 15c
Information about the opportunities that exist within the organization and the advantages of employment there.

**Employment outlook for veterinarians. Bureau of Labor Statistics, U.S. Department of Labor. Supt. of Documents. 1964. 4p. 5c
Reprint from the *Occupational Outlook Handbook*.

I want to be an animal doctor. Greene, Carla. Childrens Press. 1956. 32p. $2
Prepared for beginning readers with a reading level of upper first grade. Illustrated in color.

Lacy Edwards, veterinarian. Turner, Audrey. Lantern Press. 1957. 221p. $2.95
Career fiction. A girl's devotion to animals has inspired her to become a veterinary surgeon. For younger girls.

Park Avenue vet. Camuti, Louis and Alexander, Lloyd. Holt, Rinehart and Winston, Inc. 1962. 184p. $4
Biography including unusual experiences of a veterinarian who has specialized in the treatment of cats.

Report on educational qualifications of public health veterinarians. American Public Health Association. 1959. 4p. Free
General scope of the field, future outlook, educational qualifications, personal qualities, and lines of promotion.

* Should you be a veterinarian? Merchant, I. A. New York Life Insurance Company. 1961. 12p. Free
Description of opportunities, requirements for success, education, training, and future outlook.

* Specialized careers in veterinary medicine. Angel, Juvenal L. World Trade Academy Press. 1962. 26p. $1.25
Qualifications, training, opportunities, and remuneration for each of the following: general practitioner, small animal veterinarian, the veterinarian pathologist, poultry specialist, and food sanitarian veterinarian. Also included is a list of colleges and organizations offering scholarships in this field. Bibliography.

The vet is a girl. Dean, Nell M. Julian Messner, Inc. 1959. 192p. $2.95
Career fiction. A novel that contains authentic information about the work of the veterinarian and points out some opportunities for women.

Veterinarian. Jones, T. J. Research Publishing Company. 1954. 32p. $1
Nature of work, qualifications, preparation, earnings, opportunities, advantages, and disadvantages.

Veterinarian. Careers. 1963. 8p. 25c
Career brief describing nature of work, training, working conditions, personal qualifications, employment prospects, earnings, where employed, and related careers. Includes list of seventeen approved schools for training.

VETERINARIAN—*Continued*

**Veterinarian. Chronicle Guidance Publications. 1963. 4p. 35c

Occupational brief summarizing work performed, working conditions, earnings, personal qualifications, training requirements, opportunities, employment outlook, and entry into the job.

Veterinarian. The Guidance Centre. 1962. 4p. 15c in Canada; 20c elsewhere

Importance and growth of this profession, working conditions, qualifications, preparation, opportunities for promotion, earnings, advantages, disadvantages, how to get started, and related occupations.

Veterinarian. Michigan Employment Security Commission. 1961. 16p. 25c

Nature of work, location of jobs, working conditions, earnings, employment outlook, requirements for entry, advantages, and disadvantages.

Veterinarians. Science Research Associates. 1961. 4p. 35c

Occupational brief describing nature of work, requirements, training, getting started, earnings, advantages, disadvantages, and future outlook.

* Veterinarians. One section of *Occupational Outlook Handbook*.

Nature of work, where employed, training, other qualifications, advancement, employment outlook, earnings, and working conditions.

Veterinary doctor. Robinson, H. Alan. Personnel Services. 1960. 6p. 50c; 25c to students

Occupational abstract. Future prospects, nature of work, qualifications, preparation, licensing, entrance, earnings, number and distribution of workers, advantages, and disadvantages. References for further reading.

Veterinary medicine. Pages 138-41 of *Health Careers Guidebook*.

Nature of work, personal qualifications, training, licensing, opportunities, and prospects.

**Veterinary medicine as a career. American Veterinary Medical Association. 1954. 20p. Free

Nature of work, qualifications, college study required, opportunities, and rewards. List of twenty schools recognized by the American Veterinary Medical Association. Ten illustrations.

* Veterinary medicine as a career. Institute for Research. 1963. 24p. $1

Licensing requirements, opportunities, earnings, typical day's work, advantages, and disadvantages. Includes description of work in the Bureau of Animal Industry. List of schools recognized by the American Veterinary Medical Association.

What does a veterinarian do? Compton, Grant. Dodd, Mead and Company. 1964. 64p. $2.50; library edition $2.57 net

Photographs and brief text describe the work of the doctor to animals of all kinds from house pets and farm animals to circus performers. For grades 3 to 7.

**Your future in veterinary medicine. Riser, Wayne. Richards Rosen Press. 1963. 158p. $2.95

Presents career information concerning work on a governmental level as well as practice with small animals.

VOCATIONAL COUNSELOR. *See* Counselor; Personnel and employment manager

VOCATIONAL REHABILITATION COUNSELOR   0-36.23

List of colleges offering rehabilitation traineeships. Vocational Rehabilitation Administration. 1963. 2p. Free

List of schools that have received grants to provide traineeships on a graduate level.

Needed—rehabilitation counselors. Western Personnel Institute. 1956. 4p. 20c

Information about traineeship grants, training, and personal qualifications.

Rehabilitation counselor. Careers. 1963. 2p. 15c

Career summary for desk-top file. Duties, qualifications, and outlook.

**Rehabilitation counselor. One section of *Occupational Outlook Handbook*.

Nature of work, where employed, training, other qualifications, employment outlook, earnings, and working conditions.

Rehabilitation counselor preparation. National Vocational Guidance Association and National Rehabilitation Association. 1956. 78p. $1

Defines the functions and successful performance of the counselor in a rehabilitation setting. Prepared for use of those who are responsible for counselor preparation in colleges and rehabilitation agencies.

**Should you go into rehabilitation services? Rusk, Howard A. New York Life Insurance Company. 1959. 12p. Free

Description of services, need, preparation, and satisfactions.

Vocational rehabilitation counseling. Pages 141-3 of *Health Careers Guidebook*.

Duties, qualifications, and a description of a traineeship program.

Vocational rehabilitation counselors. Science Research Associates. 1961. 4p. 35c

Occupational briefs describing nature of work, requirements, getting started, earnings, advantages, disadvantages, and future outlook.

Your future: a career in rehabilitation. National Society for Crippled Children and Adults. No date. 8p. Free

Description of the work of rehabilitation specialists, training, places of employment, earnings, and sources of information.

VOCATIONAL REHABILITATION WORKER   0-27.99

A rewarding career for you as a Veterans Administration manual arts therapist. Veterans Administration, Department of Medicine and Surgery. 1963. 4p. Free

Description of work, training program, qualifications, and benefits.

VOCATIONAL REHABILITATION WORKER—*Continued*

Teaching and vocational rehabilitation of the physically handicapped—careers. Institute for Research. 1958. 24p. $1

> History and present extent of training of the handicapped, personal qualifications, training, certification, attractive and unattractive features, and how to secure a position. Included is a section on vocational rehabilitation for veterans.

VOCATIONAL TRAINING TEACHER   0-32.30

Trade and vocational teaching as a career. Institute for Research. 1957. 20p. $1

> Growth of vocational education, types of work, qualifications, training, attractive and unattractive features, earnings, and how to get started.

Training director. Group, Vernard. Personnel Services. 1955. 6p. 50c; 25c to students

> Occupational abstract. Nature of work, future prospects, qualifications, preparation, entrance and advancement, earnings, and number and distribution of workers.

Vocational education for American youth. American Vocational Association. 1956. 16p. 10c

> Includes qualifications of vocational teachers and administrators.

Vocational teacher. Chronicle Guidance Publications. 1963. 4p. 35c

> Occupational brief describing work performed, educational requirements, personal qualifications, working conditions, benefits, and employment outlook.

Vocational training teacher. Group, Vernard. Personnel Services. Revised 1956. 6p. 50c; 25c to students

> Occupational abstract. Nature of work, future prospects, qualifications, earnings, advantages and disadvantages.

WAC. *See* Military Servicewoman

WAITER AND WAITRESS   2-27.

Bus boy and bus girl. Careers. 1961. 2p. 15c

> Career summary for desk-top file. Duties, qualifications, and outlook.

Dining car waiters. One section of *Occupational Outlook Handbook*.

> Nature of work, training, other qualifications, advancement, earnings, and working conditions.

Railroad dining-car waiters. Science Research Associates. 1961. 4p. 35c

> Occupational brief describing work, qualifications, earnings, things to consider, and outlook.

Waiter or waitress. The Guidance Centre. 1962. 4p. 15c in Canada; 20c elsewhere

> History and nature of work, qualifications, preparation, working conditions, advancement, earnings, advantages, disadvantages, how to get started, and related occupations.

* Waiter-waitress. Careers. 1962. 7p. 25c

    Career brief describing duties, working conditions, training requirements, personal qualifications, employment prospects, advantages, disadvantages, earnings, measuring one's interest and ability, and suggested high school program.

* Waiter-waitress. Chronicle Guidance Publications. 1961. 4p. 35c

    Occupational brief summarizing work performed, working conditions, qualifications, training, opportunities, outlook, methods of entry, related jobs, and suggested activities.

Waiters and waitresses. Science Research Associates. 1958. 4p. 35c

    Occupational brief describing nature of work, qualifications, opportunities, advantages, disadvantages, and future outlook. Selected references.

**Waiters and waitresses. One section of *Occupational Outlook Handbook*.

    Nature of work, where employed, training, other qualifications, advancement, employment outlook, earnings, and working conditions.

WATCHMAKER AND WATCH REPAIRMAN 4-71.510

Careers in watch repairing. American Watchmakers Institute. No date. 8p. Free

    Description of work, qualifications, earnings, and outlook. List of forty schools for training for watchmaking.

**Employment outlook for watch repairmen, jewelers, and jewelry repairmen. Bureau of Labor Statistics, U.S. Department of Labor. Supt. of Documents. 1964. 12p. 10c

    Reprint from the *Occupational Outlook Handbook*.

Watch and clock repairmen. Michigan Employment Security Commission. 1955. 19p. 25c

    Introduction, nature of work, location of jobs, employment prospects, hiring qualifications, earnings, working conditions, organizations, and qualifications for entry.

Watch repairman. Robinson, H. Alan. Personnel Services. 1956. 6p. 50c; 25c to students

    Occupational abstract. Future prospects, nature of work, qualifications, preparation, entrance and advancement, earnings, number and distribution of workers, advantages, and disadvantages.

**Watch repairman. Careers. 1962. 8p. 25c

    Career brief describing duties, working conditions, training requirements, training opportunities, personal qualifications, employment prospects, advantages, disadvantages, earnings, related careers, measuring one's interest and ability, and suggested high school program.

Watch repairmen. Science Research Associates. 1961. 4p. 35c

    Occupational brief describing work, qualifications, training, earnings, and outlook.

**Watch repairmen. One section of *Occupational Outlook Handbook*.

    Nature of work, where employed, training, other qualifications, advancement, employment outlook, earnings, and working conditions.

WATCHMAKER AND WATCH REPAIRMAN—*Continued*

Watchmaker. Chronicle Guidance Publications. 1962. 4p. 35c
> Occupational brief summarizing work performed, qualifications, training, working conditions, wages, and opportunities.

Watchmaker. The Guidance Centre. 1959. 4p. 15c in Canada; 20c elsewhere
> Nature of work, qualifications, preparation, employment and advancement, earnings, advantages, disadvantages, how to get started, and related occupations.

Your future and our school—courses in watchmaking and repairing. Bowman Technical School. 1963. 16p. Free
> Illustrated recruiting bulletin describing careers and courses in watchmaking and repairing.

> *See also* Jeweler

WATER TRANSPORTATION INDUSTRY WORKER
5, 7, 9-49.100 through 5, 7, 9-49.199

Captain Thomas Fenlon: master mariner. Roark, Garland. Julian Messner, Inc. 1958. 192p. $3.25
> Biography of a pioneering merchant mariner, showing the dangers he encountered and the feats he accomplished during his fifty-four years of ship transportation.

I want to be a ship captain. Greene, Carla. Childrens Press. 1962. 32p. $2
> Prepared for beginning readers with a reading level of upper first grade. Illustrated in color.

Masters, mates, and pilots. Chronicle Guidance Publications. 1962. 4p. 35c
> Occupational brief summarizing duties, number employed, qualifications, preparation, formal maritime training, earnings, conditions of work, and methods of entering.

Shipboard occupations, Great Lakes area. Michigan Employment Security Commission. 1959. 23p. 25c
> Introduction, nature of work, location of jobs, working conditions, employment outlook, earnings, requirements for entry, disadvantages, and advantages.

WEATHER FORECASTER. *See* Meteorologist

WEAVER
4-15.

Job description for weaver IV. U.S. Employment Service. Supt. of Documents. 1947. 4p. 5c
> Occupational guide. Job summary, work performed, training, occupational tests, related occupations, physical activities, and working conditions.

WELDER 4, 6-85.

Electric welding machine operator. Careers. 1962. 2p. 15c
Career summary for desk-top file. Duties, qualifications, and outlook.

**Employment outlook for welders, oxygen and arc cutters, and boilermakers. Bureau of Labor Statistics, U.S. Department of Labor. Supt. of Documents. 1964. 12p. 10c
Reprint from the *Occupational Outlook Handbook.*

Opportunities in the welding industry. American Welding Society. 1962. 6p. Free
Discussion of the industry in general, educational requirements, wages, opportunities, and specific job descriptions.

Welder. The Guidance Centre. 1961. 4p. 15c in Canada; 20c elsewhere
History and importance, nature of work, qualifications, preparation, working conditions, advancement, earnings, advantages, disadvantages how to get started, and related occupations.

Welder (hand). Careers. 1959. 2p. 15c
Career summary for desk-top file. Duties, qualifications, and outlook.

**Welders. Chronicle Guidance Publications. 1962. 4p. 35c
Occupational brief describing work of arc, gas, and resistance welders. Includes description of working conditions, qualifications, training, outlook, where employed, unionization, and related jobs.

Welders. Science Research Associates. 1963. 4p. 35c
Occupational brief describing nature of work, requirements, training, earnings, and outlook.

**Welders and oxygen and arc cutters. One section of *Occupational Outlook Handbook.*
Nature of work, where employed, training, other qualifications, employment outlook, earnings, and working conditions.

Welders and oxygen cutters. Careers. 1960. 8p. 25c
Career brief describing duties, working conditions, training, personal characteristics, earnings, where employed, and outlook.

WHOLESALER 0-73.01

Career as a wholesale gasoline and oil distributor. Institute for Research. 1961. 24p. $1
Description of work, qualifications, training, earnings, attractive and unattractive features, outlook, and how to establish a distributorship.

Career opportunities in wholesaling. National Association of Wholesalers. 1963. 12p. Free
Function of wholesaling, kinds of jobs, training, advancement, working conditions, and trends.

Career with a future: wholesaling. Armstrong Cork Company. 1962. 6p. Free
One booklet is directed toward distributor opportunities in resilient flooring, another toward distributor activities in building products.

WHOLESALER—*Continued*

Careers in wholesale merchandising and distribution. Institute for Research. 1956. 24p. $1
> History and types of work, attractive and unattractive features, personal qualifications, training, earnings, and how to get started.

Occupations in wholesale and retail trade. Chapter 16 of *Planning Your Future.*
> Includes a discussion of the nature of wholesale and retail trade, how this group of occupations affects our way of life, the number and kinds of workers, and the work of a saleswoman.

* Wholesale salesman. Chronicle Guidance Publications. 1960. 4p. 35c
> Occupational brief summarizing work performed, qualifications, training, where employed, earnings, and outlook.

* Wholesale salesmen. Careers. 1961. 8p. 25c
> Career brief describing duties, working conditions, training, personal qualifications, earnings, and outlook.

WILDLIFE SPECIALIST   0-94.99; 3-96.; 3-97.

Careers in Federal and state fish and wildlife service. Institute for Research. 1960. 24p. $1
> Importance of fish and wildlife conservation, duties, typical day's work, attractive and unattractive features, qualifications, training, earnings, and outlook. Includes list of colleges offering training in wildlife management and conservation.

Employment opportunities in the Bureau of Sport Fisheries and Wildlife. Fish and Wildlife Service. 1960. 16p. Free
> Employment information, qualifications, how to apply, benefits, and preparation for a career in conservation work.

Fish and wildlife; the story of the work of the U.S. Fish and Wildlife Service. Colby, Carroll B. Coward-McCann, Inc. 1955. 48p. $2.50. Library binding $2.52
> Describes the work of protecting and conserving the wild birds, animals, and fish of our country. Written for grades 4 to 8.

Hunter. Hunter, John A. Harper and Row. 1952. 263p. $4.50; library binding $4.11 net
> Autobiographical account of big-game hunter's experiences in Africa. His job was to track down rogue elephants and to destroy disease-spreading buffaloes and cattle-killing leopards.

**Jobs in outdoor work. Science Research Associates. 1964. 48p. $1
> Describes the variety of job prospects and opportunities in outdoor work, including the wildlife manager, treeman, forester, surveyor, and nurseryman.

John Muir, protector of the wilds. Haines, Madge and Morrill, Leslie. Abingdon Press. 1957. 128p. $1.75
> Biography of the great naturalist who fought to preserve in national parks some of the wilderness he treasured.

Nature's guardians; your career in conservation. Neal, **Harry Edward. Julian Messner, Inc. 1963. 192p. $3.95, Library binding $3.64 net
Kinds of work, opportunities, and training in wildlife management, fishery work, forestry, or soil and water conservation. Bibliography.

Park naturalist. Careers. 1960. 2p. 15c
Career summary for desk-top file. Duties, qualifications, and outlook.

Scholarships and fellowships in conservation. National Wildlife Federation. 1963. 2p. Free
Description of program of student aid.

**Training and employment of wildlife biologists and fishery biologists. National Wildlife Federation. 1961. 12p. Single copy free
A statement of the general kinds of work done by fishery and wildlife biologists, the nature and amount of college training required, and where employment opportunities are found. Also appended are a list of institutions offering training with descriptions of degrees conferred and addresses of conservation agencies.

The United States Department of the Interior; a story of rangeland, wildlife, and dams. Duell, Sloan and Pearce. 1963. 117p. $2.95
Describes the activities of various agencies such as the Fish and Wildlife Service, the Bureau of Indian Affairs, the Bureau of Mines, the Bureau of Land Management, the Bureau of Reclamation, and the National Park Service.

Wildlife training and employment. U.S. Fish and Wildlife Service. 1960. 10p. Free
Preparation and employment opportunities for wildlife management. Also includes a partial list of colleges offering wildlife training.

Wildlife specialist. Careers. 1960. 8p. 25c
Career brief describing duties, working conditions, training, personal qualifications, earnings, advancement prospects, and outlook.

* Wildlife, fish, and game managers. Science Research Associates. 1961. 4p. 35c
Occupational brief describing nature of work, personal qualifications, educational requirements, earnings, advantages, disadvantages, and future outlook.

See also Fish and game warden; Conservation specialist

WINDOW TRIMMER. *See* Display Man

WINE MAKER   4-03.430

Enologist (wine maker). California State Department of Employment. 1960. 5p. Single copy free
Job duties, working conditions, pay, hours, training, and employment outlook in California.

WOODSMAN (LOGGING)   5-91.401

Woodsman. The Guidance Centre. 1957. 4p. 15c in Canada; 20c elsewhere
> Nature of work, history and importance, working conditions, qualifications necessary for entry and success, preparation, employment and advancement, remuneration, advantages, disadvantages, how to get started, and related occupations.

WRITER   0-06.

Career as a sports writer. Institute for Research. 1961. 23p. $1
> Description of duties, a typical day's work, qualifications, training, earnings, attractive and unattractive features, and outlook.

Careers in business publishing. National Business Publications. No date. 22p. 25c
> Includes description of careers available in the field of producing business publications.

Careers in technical writing. Angel, Juvenal. World Trade Academy Press. 1960. 22p. $1.25
> Includes description of work, opportunities, future outlook, rewards, advantages, and disadvantages.

Do young writers need agents? Alumnae Advisory Center. 1954. 6p. 25c
> Reprint from *Mademoiselle* describing what literary agents do for young writers. Illustrated.

Edna St. Vincent Millay: America's best-loved poet. Shafter, Toby. Julian Messner, Inc. 1957. 192p. $3.25. Library binding $3.19 net
> Biography of the well-known poet.

**Employment outlook for newspaper reporters and technical writers. Bureau of Labor Statistics, U.S. Department of Labor. Supt. of Documents. 1964. 12p. 10c
> Reprint from the *Occupational Outlook Handbook*.

Free-lance writer. Henderson, John. Research Publishing Company. 1962. 32p. $1
> Nature of work, history and importance, number engaged in occupation, qualifications, working conditions, trends, training, related occupations, methods of advancement, and promotional opportunities.

Free lance writer. Chronicle Guidance Publications. 1961. 4p. 35c
> Occupational brief summarizing work performed, where employed, working conditions, personal requirements, earnings, methods of entry, and outlook.

* Free-lance writers. Science Research Associates. 1958. 4p. 35c
> Occupational brief describing nature of work, training, qualifications, opportunities, advantages, disadvantages, and future outlook.

* Joan: free lance writer. Colver, Alice R. Julian Messner, Inc. 1948. 181p. $2.95
> Career fiction. Story containing practical advice about free-lance writing.

Literary and library prizes. Weber, Olga S. R. R. Bowker Company. Revised 1963. 280p. $8.50

This frequently-revised directory gives the description, requirements, means of selection, and names of winners for 250 international prizes from date of inception through the fall of 1962. Gives an idea of the rewards of literary work.

Literary market place—the business directory of American book publishing. R. R. Bowker Company. 1962. 565p. $7.45

Includes names and addresses of book publishers, advertising agents, author's agents, national associations, book clubs, columnists and commentators, and organizations marketing literary material. Also includes a list of courses given by twelve institutions and associations on phases of the book trade and graphic arts, list of writer's conferences with addresses and dates, and list of major awards given to books and authors. Revised annually.

A new profession—technical writing. Simmons College. 1957. 4p. Free

Description of work, qualifications, opportunities, and courses that should be taken in high school and college.

**Opportunities in free-lance writing. Maxon, Hazel C. Vocational Guidance Manuals. 1964. 128p. $1.45 paper

Discusses ability, expanding market, remuneration, opportunity, competition, education and experience desirable, how to keep in touch with the markets, how to begin, and how to prepare a manuscript. Description of a seamy day and a sunny day.

Pen to paper: a novelist's notebook. Frankau, Pamela. Doubleday and Company. 1962. 237p. $3.95

The author describes her experiences as a professional writer and discusses her techniques as a novelist.

Professional writing as a career. Institute for Research. 1961. 24p. $1

Qualifications, education and training, salary, outlook, and attractive and unattractive features. Also described are a day in the life of a free-lance writer and methods of selling the output.

Technical writer. Splaver, Sarah. Personnel Services. 1962. 6p. 50c; 25c to students

Occupational abstract. Nature of work, qualifications, preparation, entrance, advancement, outlook, advantages, and disadvantages. References for further reading.

Technical writer. Veon, Dorothy H. Research Publishing Company. 1957. 36p. $1

History and importance of the work, where needed, personal qualifications, educational background, promotional opportunities, compensation, and placement channels.

* Technical writer. Careers. 1963. 8p. 25c

Career brief summarizing duties, training, personal qualifications, earnings, advancement prospects, related careers, and outlook. Additional readings.

* Technical writer. Chronicle Guidance Publications. 1964. 4p. 35c

Occupational brief summarizing work performed, personal qualifications, training, opportunities, methods of entry, and outlook.

WRITER—*Continued*

Technical writer of technical publications. California State Department of Employment. 1961. 5p. Single copy free
Duties, working conditions, wages, promotion, training, and employment outlook.

Technical writers. Science Research Associates. 1960. 4p. 35c
Occupational brief describing work, qualifications, earnings, advantages, disadvantages, and outlook. Selected references.

**Technical writers. One section of *Occupational Outlook Handbook*.
Nature of work, where employed, training, other qualifications, advancement, employment outlook, earnings, and working conditions.

Technical writing as a career. Lytel, Allan. Bellman Publishing Company. 1961. 27p. $1
Description of work, types of technical writing, training, salaries, related occupations, and future outlook.

Twelve writing jobs. Alumnae Advisory Center. 1963. 7p. 25c
Reprint from *Mademoiselle* describing the work of twelve writers of non-fiction, employed in a variety of commercial writing fields.

Writer. Careers. 1962. 8p. 25c
Career brief describing duties, working conditions, training requirements, personal qualifications, employment outlook, salaries, related careers, measuring one's interest and ability, and suggested high school program.

Writers and editors. Pages 128-39 of *The College Girl Looks Ahead*.
Characteristics of the work, talents needed, trying out, preparation, and kinds of work.

**Writing as a career. Lobsenz, Norman M. Henry Z. Walck, Inc. 1963. 119p. $3.50
This book tells how to prepare for, where to find, and what to expect in eleven major career areas for writers: newspapers, consumer magazines, industrial magazines, business publications, free-lance writing, advertising, public relations, technical journalism, radio and television journalism, and creative writing. Reading list.

Writing for television and radio as a career. Institute for Research. 1958. 24p. $1
Description of work as a contract writer, staff writer, and free-lance writer. Includes education, training, personal qualifications, earnings, attractive and unattractive features, how to get started, and probable opportunities.

Why not write? Redgrave, William J., ed. Harian Publications. 1959. 61p. $1.50
Information about free-lance writing as a full or part-time career. Contains a guide to domestic and overseas literary markets.

Writers, newspaper workers, editors. Chapter 27 of *Vocations for Girls*.
Qualifications, opportunities, and kinds of work.

See also Playwright

X-RAY TECHNICIAN 0-50.04

Approved schools for X-ray technicians. Council on Medical Education and Hospitals of the American Medical Association. 1964. 15p. Free
Tabulated information concerning 680 approved schools.

**Career as an X-ray technician. Institute for Research. 1964. 24p. $1
Duties, qualifications, educational requirements, typical day's work, pleasant and unpleasant features. Describes work of the X-ray technician in hospital, industry, and in U.S. Civil Service. Requirements for registration with the American Registry of X-Ray Technicians.

**Careers in X-ray technology. American Society of X-ray Technicians. 1962. 6p. Free
Description of duties, qualifications, opportunities, types of employment, advantages, disadvantages, earnings, and employment outlook.

**Employment outlook for medical technologists, medical X-ray technicians, and medical record librarians. Bureau of Labor Statistics, U.S. Department of Labor. Supt. of Documents. 1964. 12p. 10c
Reprint from the *Occupational Outlook Handbook*.

Industrial X-ray technician. Careers. 1962. 2p. 15c
Career summary for desk-top file. Duties, qualifications, and outlook.

* Medical X-ray technicians. Careers. 1963. 8p. 25c
Career brief describing duties, working conditions, personal qualifications, training, places of employment, earnings, and outlook.

**Medical X-ray technicians. One section of *Occupational Outlook Handbook*.
Nature of work, where employed, training, other qualifications, advancement, employment outlook, earnings, and working conditions.

**Training of X ray technicians. American Registry of X-Ray Technicians. 1963. 8p. Free
General qualifications of trainees, training course curricula, classification of X-ray technicians, rules and regulations governing the registration, and qualifications of applicants for registration of X-ray technicians.

X-ray equipment operation. Pages 144-5 of *Health Careers Guidebook*.
Personal qualifications, training, status and standards, getting started, advancement, and future prospects.

X-ray technician. Splaver, Sarah. Personnel Services. 1949. 50c; 25c to students
Occupational abstract. Nature of work, qualifications, preparation, entrance and advancement, registration, supply and demand, and earnings.

X-ray technician. Widger, Jean. Research Publishing Company. 1959. 32p. $1
Nature of work, history and importance, number engaged in occupation, qualifications, working conditions, salaries and other returns, training, methods of securing jobs, and promotional opportunities.

X-RAY TECHNICIAN—*Continued*

X-ray technician. The Guidance Centre. 1961. 4p. 15c in Canada; 20c elsewhere
> Nature of work, qualifications, preparation, outlook, earnings, advantages, disadvantages, how to get started and related occupations.

X-ray technician (medical service). Chronicle Guidance Publications. 1962. 4p. 35c
> Occupational brief summarizing history and development, work performed, working conditions, qualifications, training, opportunities, related jobs, determination of aptitudes and interests, and suggested activities.

X-ray technicians. Science Research Associates. 1959. 4p. 35c
> Occupational brief describing nature of work, training, preparation, qualifications, opportunities, advantages, disadvantages, and future outlook.

X-ray the career for you? American Society of X-Ray Technicians. No date. 8p. Free
> Description of work, opportunities, qualifications, required training, earnings, and registration requirements.

YMCA SECRETARY   0-27.

The center for YMCA studies at Springfield College. No date. 6p. Free
> Includes qualifications for a YMCA career, career opportunities, and the curriculum at Springfield College.

Choose a YMCA career. National Council of the Young Men's Christian Association. No date. 8p. Free
> Ilustrated folder describing work for the YMCA.

Choose a YMCA career. Springfield College. No date. 8p. Free
> Folder describing duties, advantages, qualifications, and list of YMCA field offices.

Leaders of youth. Springfield College. No date. 12p. Free
> Brief information concerning admission and training.

Occupational brief. National Council of the Young Men's Christian Association. 1959. 2p. Free
> List of regional offices, number of employees, positions for college graduates, educational requirements, and methods of training.

**Professional opportunities in the YMCA today. National Council of Young Men's Christian Association. 1961. 2p. Free
> Duties, qualifications, education and training of secretaries, and methods of entering the profession.

YMCA secretary. Careers. 1960. 2p. 15c
> Career summary for desk-top file. Duties, qualifications, and outlook.

YWCA PROFESSIONAL WORKER   0-27.

**Basic booklet on YWCA job opportunities. Young Women's Christian Association, National Board. 1963. 12p. Free
> Information about professional work in the YWCA.

Fortunate you. Young Women's Christian Association, National Board. 1957. 24p. Free
Information about professional work in the YWCA, including requirements, opportunities for advancement, and personnel policies.

Open up a whole new world for yourself with a job in the YWCA. Young Women's Christian Association, National Board. 1963. 4p. Free
Recruitment brochure describing positions in this organization.

YWCA personnel administration manual. Young Women's Christian Association, National Board. 1958. 84p. $1.25
A manual on the responsibilities of the board, personnel committee, executive director and other supervisory staff; selection and employment; recommended policies and practices. Included are basic job descriptions, sample letter of employment, evaluation outline, and other related information for community and student YWCA's.

YWCA Professional workers. Careers. 1963. 2p. 15c
Career summary for desk-top file. Duties, qualifications, and outlook.

YOUTH ORGANIZATION WORKER. *See* Group worker

ZOOLOGIST   0-35.28

Careers in animal biology. American Society of Zoologists. 1961. 16p. 25c
This booklet describes the work of zoologists who specialize in the study of certain classes of animals. Includes the ornithologist's study of birds, the herpetologist's work with reptiles and amphibians, the ichthyologist's research with fishes, and the mammalogist's study of mammals.

I want to be a zoo keeper. Greene, Carla. Childrens Press. 1957. 32p. $2
Prepared for beginning readers with a reading level of upper first grade. Illustrated in color.

Ichthyologist. Careers. 1958. 2p. 15c
Career summary describing duties, qualifications, training, employment opportunities, earnings, and where employed. Selected references.

Zoologist. Careers. 1963. 2p. 15c
Career summary for desk-top file. Duties, qualifications, and outlook.

Zoologist. Chronicle Guidance Publications. 1962. 4p. 35c
Occupational brief summarizing work performed, where employed, earnings, personal qualifications, training, methods of entry, and employment outlook. Selected references.

**Zoologists. Science Research Associates. 1963. 4p. 35c
Occupational brief describing nature of work, requirements, preparation, opportunities, earnings, and outlook.

Zoologists. Brief section in *Occupational Outlook Handbook.*
Nature of work, training, and employment outlook.
See also Herpetologist

B. Books and Pamphlets Describing More than One Occupation

**American universities and colleges. Cartter, Allan M., ed. American Council on Education. 1964. 1212p. $15

Descriptive directory of 1,100 accredited universities and colleges, arranged by state. Lists of institutions offering professional instruction in each of twenty-three fields: agriculture, architecture, Bible, business administration, dentistry, engineering, forestry, home economics, journalism, law, librarianship, medicine, music, nursing education, optometry, osteopathy, pharmacy, religious education, social work, speech, teacher education, theology, and veterinary medicine. Several tables present the distribution of doctorates conferred by institution, subject, sex, and year.

American women who scored firsts. Forsee, Aylesa. Macrae Smith Company. 1958. 253p. $2.95

Biographies of ten American women who have achieved prominence in their fields. Includes Eleanor Roosevelt, Katharine Cornell, Marguerite Higgins, Marian Anderson, and Amelia Earhart.

Americans at work. Paradis, Adrian. David McKay Company. 1958. 224p. $3.95

Discussion of career opportunities in the American system as affected by rise of new industries and the development of old. Includes biographies of some of the men and women who have helped to fashion the American way of life.

Career fields for specialists in the humanities. St. Francis College. 1959. 8p. Free

Includes a list of 32 careers in the communication arts, 23 careers in social service, 19 in business and foreign trade, 10 in government service, 7 in research, and 7 in travel and shipping. The nature of work in each also is given.

Career: for the college man. Careers Incorporated. 1963. 108p. $2.95; paper $1.95

Aims to give college graduates information about openings in industry. Leading companies present descriptions of their policies and employment opportunities for highly qualified young men. Represented are areas of banking and finance, electronics, communications, manufacturing, insurance, public utilities, publishing, aviation, physics, and chemistry. Revised annually.

**Career guide for demand occupations. Bureau of Employment Security, U.S. Department of Labor. Supt. of Documents. 1959. 33p. 30c

For eighty-seven occupations for which workers are in demand, this guide presents information on training usually required, high school subjects of particular pertinence to the occupation, and special characteristics inherent in the job. Selected reference materials.

* Career guide for young people. Moore, Mary Furlong. Doubleday and Company. 1963. 262p. 95c paper

Arranged alphabetically under professions, arts, sciences, and business are brief job descriptions. Each explains the qualifications the job requires and the earnings, advancement, and opportunities one may expect.

* Career opportunities: a series of articles designed to help guide young people to a better future. New York Life Insurance Company. 1962. 384p. Free

A compilation of the fifty-four booklets on individual careers.

**Careers ahead for college women. Simmons College. 1959. 86p. $1.50. Free to counselors and librarians

Compilation of reprints of career leaflets describing the fields of work for which training is offered at Simmons College. Each one answers the questions a high school girl would ask about personal qualities needed for success, the beginning opportunities, prospects for advancement, and courses to take in high school and college to prepare for the work.

Careers for majors in English. Angel, Juvenal. World Trade Academy Press. 1959. 30p. $1.25

Includes description of the major fields of work requiring special skill in English, opportunities, remuneration, future outlook, and methods of financing a college education.

Careers for women. Texas Woman's University. 1962. 38p. Free

For each of twenty major fields there is a discussion of opportunities, positions held by graduates, and training. Illustrations of views and activities of the college.

* Careers outdoors. Joseph, James. Nelson and Sons. 1962. 320p. $5.95

Description of opportunities which combine life outdoors with profitable business careers. Includes case histories of about one hundred men and women who developed opportunities out of doors, many of them in the sports field and some in government jobs.

* Charting your course. Galus, Henry S. Macrae Smith Company. 1957. 310p. $3.75

Information about vocational opportunities for boys in fourteen broad fields of work and discussions of techniques of looking for work and applying for specific jobs.

College entrance guide. Murphy, Mark. Republic Book Company. 1959. 416p. $3.95 cloth; $1.95 paper

This book contains one section describing fifty leading occupations to which a college education may lead. These career capsules are about one half page in length.

**The college girl looks ahead to her career opportunities. Zapoleon, Marguerite W. Harper and Row. 1956. 272p. $4.50

Discussion of the characteristics of work in fifteen fields of work, talents needed, preparation, and methods of entering. Organization sources of further information are given for each chapter.

A counseling aid for high school counselors and deans of girls. University of Cincinnati, College of Business Administration. Annual. 42p. Free to counselors

Contains sixteen career articles written by women graduates of the degree program in business administration.

B. Books and Pamphlets Describing More Than
One Occupation—*Continued*

Cues for careers. Scott, Judith Unger. Macrae Smith Company. 1954.
251p. $3.50

Emphasizing the ideal of matching personal talents and interests to one's
job, this book examines requirements, routines, drawbacks, and compensations
of careers for girls in twenty fields of work.

Dictionary of occupational titles. U.S. Employment Service. Supt. of
Documents. Revised 1949. Volume I, 1518p. $5.50; Volume II, 743p.
$3; Part IV, 242p. $1; Supplement 1955, $1.25

Volume I, *Definitions of Titles,* contains definitions and code numbers of
22,028 jobs, Volume II, *Occupational Classification and Industry Index,* presents the structure of the occupational classification and lists the occupations in
numerical order according to the assigned code numbers. Part IV, *Entry
Occupational Classification,* presents an occupational classification of fields which
are open to beginning workers.

**Dictionary of occupational titles. Third edition. U.S. Employment Serv-
ice. Supt. of Documents. Volumes I and II. 1965. In preparation

Volume I contains job definitions and the functions performed by the worker,
the critical physical demands, working conditions, interests, temperaments, training time, and aptitudes involved. Volume II includes the occupational classification structure.

**Earned degrees conferred 1961-1962: bachelor's and higher degrees. Tol-
liver, Wayne. U.S. Office of Education. Supt. of Documents. 1963.
250p. $1.75

Analytic report of data relating to degrees conferred by major areas of study,
by type of institution, by region, and by institution. Degree data are summarized
at the bachelor's, master's, and doctor's level for each of 164 major fields of
study and for each of the 1,400 colleges conferring degrees.

Employment and earnings statistics for states and areas, 1939-62. Bureau
of Labor Statistics, U.S. Department of Labor. Supt. of Documents.
1963. 670p. $3.50

Basic information on payroll employment for each of the states and nearly
150 major metropolitan areas, providing a geographic profile of the industrial
complex.

Employment and earnings statistics for the United States, 1909-62. Bureau of Labor Statistics, U.S. Department of Labor. Supt. of Documents.
1963. 654p. $3.50

This volume presents statistics for over 350 industries, tracing the growth and
transformation of the nation's economy through the distribution of its employed
manpower. Data by industry are given on employment, weekly earnings, average hours, labor turnover rates, and employment of women.

Engineering, agriculture, arts and sciences. California State Polytechnic
College. 1961. 12p. Free

Brief statement of nature of work, training, and opportunities in each of
thirty fields of work.

**Estimates of worker trait requirements for 4,000 jobs. Bureau of Employment Security, U.S. Department of Labor. Supt. of Documents. 1956. 158p. $2.25

Alphabetical index of 4,000 jobs as defined in the Dictionary of Occupational Titles. In tabulated form, code numbers indicate the aptitudes, physical capacities, interests, working conditions, training time, and temperaments that contribute to successful performance in each of the jobs listed.

* Executive careers for women. Maule, Frances. Harper and Row. 1961. 240p. $3.95

Practical suggestions on advancing to executive positions. Includes opportunities in advertising, fashion, finance, government service, public relations, service industries, travel, and science and technology.

Famous American pioneering women. Yost, Edna. Dodd, Mead and Company. 1961. 158p. $3

Biographies of thirteen women who pioneered in their various fields, often in the face of prejudices against their doing so in a man's world.

**Federal career directory: a guide for college students. U.S. Civil Service Commission. Supt. of Documents. 1962. 84p. 60c

Includes ninety-two job briefs containing nature of work, qualifications required, and career opportunities. One index of job briefs is by position title and another by college major fields of study. For college graduates.

**From campus to career. New York State Employment Service. 1959. 90p. 60c

Factors to consider when choosing a job and advice to use one's abilities as an entry wedge to a long-range goal. Written especially for college graduates who majored in liberal arts or general business administration, this booklet includes a general outlook of opportunities in advertising, radio and television, education, market research, management, publishing, and social welfare.

**From college to career. Lewis, Adele and Bobroff, Edith. Bobbs-Merrill Company. 1963. 288p. $3.95

The directors of a New York employment agency offer practical advice to liberal arts graduates on the kinds of work available to beginners in publishing, advertising, market research, public relations, fashion, and television.

From high school to a job. Paradis, Adrian. David McKay Company. 1956. 249p. $3.50

For the student who does not plan to continue his education beyond high school. Discussion of fifteen careers including communications, construction, insurance, printing, selling, service, transportation, and travel. Also included are sections on finding the right job and preparing for a career.

* Future jobs for high school girls. Women's Bureau, U.S. Department of Labor. Supt. of Documents. 1959. 64p. 40c

Designed for high school graduates, this pamphlet provides information on a variety of occupations open to women, from the woman-dominated secretarial group to technical specialties where women are just beginning to make their marks.

B. Books and Pamphlets Describing More Than One Occupation—*Continued*

Futures for college women in New York. Alumnae Advisory Center. 1963. 56p. $1

Discussion of prospects for the beginner including secretarial work, publishing, programming, advertising, and fashion. Special advice on job seeking.

Great American Negroes. Richardson, Ben. Crowell Publishing Company. 1956. 352p. $3.95

Biographies of twenty-six Negro men and women who were successful in their occupations.

* Handbook of job facts. Third edition. Science Research Associates. 1963. 98p. $3.95

Compilation of information in tabular form, containing concise summaries of the basic facts about 237 major occupations. The ten headings include duties, number of workers, special qualifications, earnings, and supply and demand.

**Handbook on women workers. Women's Bureau, U.S. Department of Labor. Supt. of Documents. 1962. 202p. 55c

Biennial report on women's employment, the wide range of their occupations, age, earnings, income, their educational attainment, and marital status. Includes the twenty-five largest occupations for women. Good reading lists. Includes state laws affecting the employment and the civil and political status of women.

Hearts courageous; twelve who achieved. Herman, William. E. P. Dutton and Company. 1949. 254p. $3.75

Inspirational life stories of twelve men and women who overcame physical handicaps to achieve greatness.

How to get a job that takes you traveling. Ford, Norman. Harian Publications. 1961. 72p. $1.50

Describes the types of work and opportunities with the transportation lines, airlines, government agencies, commerce, and services such as the American National Red Cross.

How will I earn my living? Hess, Lawrence. Vantage Press. 1962. 139p. $2.75

Presents a picture of the occupational field in relation to changing job conditions. Includes interest check lists and exercises for use by parents, teachers, and teen-agers in the process of preparing for careers.

Industry wage surveys. Bureau of Labor Statistics, United States Department of Labor. Supt. of Documents. 1960-1964. 20c to 45c each

These bulletins summarize the results of surveys of wages and supplementary practices in the respective industries. Examples are: Basic iron and steel (30c), Footwear (45c), Hosiery (45c), Machinery manufacturing (40c), and Women's coats and suits (25c).

Is my job for you? Gardner, R. M. John Day Company. 1962. 128p. $3

The author interviewed men in fifteen careers and reports their opinions pertaining to preparation, duties, qualifications, earnings, and job satisfactions. The occupations selected were test pilot, professional baseball player, civil engineer, policeman, explorer, cowboy, lawyer, logger, missionary, medical doctor, Hollywood stunt man, archaeologist, wild-animal trainer, football player, and space scientist.

**Job guide for young workers. Bureau of Employment Security. Supt. of Documents. 1963. 78p. 45c

This booklet gives highlight information on 110 entry jobs frequently held by young beginners entering the labor market from high school. For each type of job, information is provided on employment prospects, qualifications for jobs and usual duties, opportunities for advancement, how and where jobs are obtained, and characteristics of jobs.

Job horizons for the college woman. Women's Bureau, U.S. Department of Labor. Pamphlet Number One. Supt. of Documents. 1956. 53p. 25c

About one page of suggestions is summarized for each of twenty careers which are expanding or for which industries are actively recruiting college women. The last section describes techniques for job finding.

The job outlook. Changing Times. 1962. 8p. 25c

A report on the most promising careers and industries in the years ahead and a discussion of where the jobs will be.

**Jobs in outdoor work. Science Research Associates. 1964. 48p. $1

Describes the variety of job prospects and opportunities in outdoor work, especially for the wildlife manager, treeman, oceanographer, forester, geologist, archaeologist, landscape nurseryman, and surveyor.

**Jobs in unusual occupations. Feingold, S. Norman and List, Harold. Science Research Associates. 1963. 48p. $1

Short descriptions of three jobs requiring each of the following: physical ability, manual dexterity, reasoning ability, handling detail, handling people, working with nature, and musical or dramatic ability.

Licensed occupations—Michigan. Michigan Employment Security Commission. 1961. 79p. 25c

Information about requirements, special education, experience, and written examinations for state licenses in forty two occupations licensed by the State of Michigan.

**Manpower report of the President and a report on manpower requirements, resources, utilization, and training by the U.S. Department of Labor. Supt. of Documents. 1963. 204p. $1.25

This report brings together the statistical data and information on the occupational and industrial employment patterns. Tables show the growth and change in the population and in the labor force, employment trends in major occupational groups, mobility of workers, etc. A useful table presents the total number employed in 1950 and in 1960 and the per cent change for each of 318 occupations.

Men at work in the mid-Atlantic states. Lent, Henry B. G. P. Putnam's Sons. 1961. 192p. $3.50

An overview of the occupations of those who work in the major industries and manufacturing plants in New York, New Jersey, Pennsylvania, West Virginia, Delaware, and Maryland. For younger readers, ages 8 to 12.

Other titles in the same series survey New England, the West Coast, Great Lakes States, Great Plains States, Mountain States, and the South.

B. Books and Pamphlets Describing More Than
One Occupation—*Continued*

Men who changed the world. Larsen, Egon. Roy Publishers. 1952. 224p.
$3
> Biographical sketches of twelve men whose inventions or discoveries have in
> some way contributed to the progress of civilization. Illustrated.

Modern vocational trends handbook. Glanvelle, J. L. World Trade Academy Press. 1964. 515p. $15
> Description of work, training, remuneration, and opportunities for each of
> thirty-four careers currently most popular among young men and women. A
> second section lists occupational titles for those who have special interests and
> aptitudes.

National survey of professional, administrative, technical and clerical pay.
Bureau of Labor Statistics, U.S. Department of Labor. Supt. of Documents. 1963. 55p. 40c
> Average monthly salaries for seventy-five jobs at various work levels in urban
> industry. Includes median salaries, middle ranges, distributions, and changes
> since 1961.

National survey of professional, administrative, technical, and clerical pay,
winter 1961-62. Bureau of Labor Statistics, U.S. Department of Labor.
Supt. of Documents. 1962. 57p. 40c
> Information on salary levels in the winter of 1961-1962 and on changes in
> average salaries since the previous survey a year earlier, for a wide range of
> white-collar occupations. The seventy-five job categories were selected from
> accounting, legal, engineering and chemistry, drafting and technical, personnel
> management, office services, and clerical.

Never too young to earn. Paradis, Adrian. David McKay Company. 1954.
179p. $3
> Suggests 101 part-time jobs for girls ages twelve to sixteen.

Night people. Colby, C. B. Coward-McCann, Inc. 1961. 48p. Library
edition $2.52 net
> Photographs and facts revealing the world of those who work after dark.
> Written for grades 4 and up.

**Occupational outlook handbook—employment information on major occupations for use in guidance. Bureau of Labor Statistics, U.S. Department
of Labor. Supt. of Documents. 1963. 792p. $4.75
> Brief reports on more than 650 occupations and 30 major industries including
> professions, skilled trades, clerical, sales, service occupations, and the major
> types of farming. Each report describes the employment trends and outlook,
> qualifications required for a beginning position, prospects for advancement,
> earnings, and working conditions. Introductory sections summarize the major
> trends in population and employment as background for an understanding of
> the individual occupations. 225 photographs; 46 charts.

Occupational wage surveys. Bureau of Labor Statistics, U.S. Department
of Labor. Supt. of Documents. 1963. 28p. 82 bulletins. 25c
> Surveys of occupational earnings and related benefits on an area-wide basis
> in the various important industrial centers. Recently issued surveys were con-
> ducted in San Diego, Kansas City, Baltimore, Indianapolis, Fort Worth, Colum-
> bus, and Trenton.

Occupations and industries regional series. Veterans Administration in cooperation with the Bureau of Labor Statistics. Supt. of Documents. 1954-1955.

Presents facts on the number of men and women employed in leading occupations and industries in each region, state, and metropolitan area. Also gives information for each region and state on changes in employment in major occupation groups, 1940-1950.

VA Pamphlet 7-7.1	New England States. 55c
VA Pamphlet 7-7.2	Middle Atlantic States. 50c
VA Pamphlet 7-7.3	East North Central States. 60c
VA Pamphlet 7-7.4	West North Central States. 60c
VA Pamphlet 7-7.5	South Atlantic States. 65c
VA Pamphlet 7-7.6	East South Central States. 40c
VA Pamphlet 7-7.7	West South Central States. 50c
VA Pamphlet 7-7.8	Mountain States. 50c

Occupations for men and women after 45. Angel, Juvenal L. World Trade Academy Press. 1963. 185p. $12.50

Suggestions are given for the mature worker. Topics include finding a position, jobs open to mature workers, make your own job by setting up a small business, part-time employment, and employment services for mature employees.

Occupations of Federal white-collar workers. U.S. Civil Service Commission. Supt. of Documents. 1963. 73p. 50c

Provides information on twenty-three occupational groups; a comparison of the distribution of employees by occupation; distribution of full-time employees by agency, grades, and average salaries on October 31, 1960.

1001 new job opportunities. Devaney, John. Popular Library, Inc. 1962. 160p. 35c

The author asserts there are opportunities in a large number of openings in sales, government jobs, technical work, armed services, Peace Corps, and going into business for oneself.

**Open letter to college graduates. Occupational Outlook Service, Bureau of Labor Statistics, U.S. Department of Labor. 1963. 21p. Free

Each year the Secretary of Labor reports on employment prospects and earnings in a number of fields: Civil service, business, engineering, physical sciences, mathematics, biological sciences, forestry, earth sciences, teaching, library work, law, journalism, social sciences, and health professions.

* Selecting an occupation. Sifferd, Calvin S. McKnight and McKnight. 1962. 237p. $3.50

Eleven chapters present significant facts about representative kinds of work, including educational requirements and future outlook. The book offers an analysis of jobs, factors that influence success, the procedures of studying occupations, and the methods of finding employment opportunities.

17 million jobs; the story of industry in action. Perry, John. McGraw-Hill Whittlesey House. 1958. 236p. $3.95

Designed to give an orientation to the vocational opportunities in industry, the book describes the work of unskilled labor, skilled craftsmen, foremen, and other specialized types of jobs.

Speaking of people. National Urban League. 1963. 32p. 10c
Pictures, brief biographical sketches, and description of work of fourteen successful Negro workers.

Three why's. General Electric Company. 1953. 12p. Free
Points out the need to study mathematics, science, and engineering.

Time of starting out. Ferris, Helen, ed. Franklin Watts, Inc. 1962. 203p. $3.95
Fourteen stories of girls on their first jobs provide high school girls an idea of the working world.

Undergraduate announcement and career guide. Lehigh University. 1963. 160p. Free
Discussions of factors which should influence a choice of a career and a college are followed by twenty career areas. These describe briefly major careers associated with courses of instruction at Lehigh. Revised annually.

**United States Census of Population: 1960. Detailed characteristics. U.S. Bureau of Census. Supt. of Documents. 1962. 687p. One for each state. $2.50 and $3 each
One table gives the number of men and women employed in each of 479 occupations and 149 industries.

* Unusual careers. Munzer, Martha A. Alfred A. Knopf, Inc. 1962. 142p. $3
Opportunities in careers necessary to conserve the country's natural resources, especially the city and regional planner, ecologist, geologist, meteorologist, oceanographer, research chemist, sanitary engineer, and solar scientist.

Vocations for boys. Kitson, Harry D. and Stover, Edgar M. Harcourt, Brace and World. 1955. 371p. $3.75
Forty-seven chapters are grouped under the following: skilled trades, vocations in business, professions, science and technology, government service, transportation, agriculture, hobbies with vocational potential, opportunities for the handicapped, and the look ahead.

Vocations for girls. Lingenfelter, Mary and Kitson, Harry D. Harcourt, Brace and World. 1951. 364p. $3.75
Steps to take in preparing for a vocation and over-all picture of the various occupations open to women. Vocations are grouped in eight sections: guardians of health, women who mean business, people are their business, scientists and engineers, literary and artistic workers, farm and home workers, workers for Uncle Sam, and new horizons for girls and women.

Wages and related benefits, part 1. Bureau of Labor Statistics, U.S. Department of Labor. Supt. of Documents. 1962. 188p. 75c
This annual report summarizes in tabular form the results of surveys conducted on an area-wide basis in eighty-two labor markets.

We have tomorrow. Bontemps, Arna Wendell. Houghton Mifflin Company. 1945. 131p. $2.75
Brief biographies of twelve young Negroes offer encouragement to other Negro youth. Includes a chemist, aeronautical engineer, milliner, radio technician, cartoonist, and others whose talent and perseverance brought them achievement.

What you can earn in 250 different careers. Puchaski, Ben. Chilton Company. 1959. 175p. $2.95

Salary ranges in a number of occupations, especially in civil service and military service.

What's new about women workers? A few facts. Women's Bureau, U.S. Department of Labor. Supt. of Documents. Revised 1963. 8p. 5c

Answers twelve questions frequently asked relating to the number, age, and marital status of women workers, their occupations, earnings, and education.

Where to find vocational training in New York City. Vocational Advisory Service. 1962. 312p. $7.50

Information about training in 600 vocations afforded by 607 schools in New York City. Arranged by occupation. Good indexes. Includes entrance requirements and tuition costs.

Who are the working mothers? Women's Bureau, U.S. Department of Labor. Supt. of Documents. 1962. 2p. 5c

Includes occupations in which employed mothers engage, trends in the employment of married women, reasons for working, ages of their children, and family income.

Womanpower. National Manpower Council. Columbia University Press. 1957. 395p. $5

Depicts the changing role of paid employment in the lives of American women, legislation affecting women workers, employer policies and practices involving women, the composition of the female labor force, and the problem of shortages of highly trained personnel.

A woman's guide to earning a good living. Winter, Elmer. Simon and Schuster, Inc. 1961. 401p. $4.75

Addressed to the older woman who wishes to return to work, this book offers many suggestions for finding jobs and describes opportunities including self-employment and work for the handicapped.

A woman's guide to part-time jobs. Cooper, Joseph D. Doubleday and Company. 1963. 312p. $5.95

Covers a wide variety of jobs.

Women in the Federal service, 1939-1959. Women's Bureau, U.S. Department of Labor. Supt. of Documents. 1962. 21p. 15c

This study covers the status of women working for the Federal Government— the types of positions, employment trends and standards, grades and salaries, and job locations. It reports number of employees in each of the Government agencies and the number in each of 125 occupations.

Women who made America great. Gersh, Harry. Lippincott Company. 1962. 224p. $4.50

Life stories of ten women whose interests carried them into fields previously open only to men. Illustrated.

Women who reached for tomorrow. Forsee, Aylesa. Macrae Smith Company. 1960. 203p. $2.95

Brief biographies of eight women who offered courageous solutions to baffling obstacles in their careers. Included are Ivy Baker Priest, U.S. Treasurer; Edith

B. Books and Pamphlets Describing More Than One Occupation—*Continued*

Head, fashion designer; Althea Gibson, tennis star; Audrey Hepburn, actress; Martha Berry, social worker; Wanda Landowska, musician; Martha Berry, educator; and Anne Carroll Moore, librarian.

Women's occupations through seven decades, 1870-1940. Women's Bureau, U.S. Department of Labor. Bulletin Number 218. Supt. of Documents. Reprinted 1951. 260p. 55c

>A study of trends in women's occupations from 1870 to 1940. One table presents the number of women engaged in each of 325 occupations in each of the eight Census reports. Considerable information not easily available.

**Your career—if you're not going to college. Splaver, Sarah. Julian Messner, Inc. 1963. 224p. $3.95. Library binding $3.64 net

>Discussion of the opportunities available to the high school graduate, ranging from the unskilled and semiskilled to the skilled, service, agricultural, clerical, sales, and technical occupations which may be entered without college training. The book also contains advice concerning techniques of searching for a job.

C. Apprenticeship

Apprentices. Careers. 1963. 8p. 25c

>Career brief describing training programs, outlook for apprenticeable occupations, and preparation. List of apprenticeable trades with number of years required for training.

Apprentices. Chronicle Guidance Publications. 1963. 4p. 35c

>Occupational brief summarizing need for apprenticeships, advantages, terms of usual agreements, a typical program, and list of trades for which apprenticeship is generally considered necessary.

Apprentices. Science Research Associates. 1958. 4p. 35c

>Occupational brief describing nature of training, opportunities, and outlook. Selected references.

Apprenticeship. Chapter 2 of *Vocations for Boys.*

>Explanation of apprentice training and its advantages.

Apprenticeship: an answer to training needs of business. U.S. Chamber of Commerce. 1963. 4p. Free

>Description of apprenticeship programs utilized by business firms. Other leaflets in the series on training and retraining programs describe on-the-job training, distributive education, vocational education, and accredited correspondence education.

Apprenticeship for me? Bureau of Apprenticeship and Training. 1961. 12p. Free

>Folder containing list of forty-seven skilled trades for which apprenticeships are usually available and list of the regional offices.

**Apprenticeship past and present—a story of apprentice training in the skilled trades since colonial days. Bureau of Apprenticeship, U.S. Department of Labor. Supt. of Documents. 1962. 28p. 20c

Description of the development of apprentice training procedures. Shows the work of Federal and state apprenticeship councils, labor unions, and employers in the training of skilled young workers. Illustrated.

Apprenticeships in America. Kursh, Harry. Norton and Company. 1958. 176p. $3.95

This book presents the advantages open to apprentice-trained skilled workers, the standard apprenticeship agreements and rates of pay, and the types of registered apprenticeship programs. An important feature of the book is the guide to thirty-four of the most popular crafts and the occupational outlook for each. Also given is a list of ninety-two of the apprenticeable occupations with the number of years of training required.

* Can I be a craftsman? Let's find out. General Motors, Public Relations Staff. 1961. 24p. Free

Includes an explanation of the apprentice program.

Learning a trade through apprenticeship. Chapter 8 in *Occupations and Careers.*

Explanation of training for the skilled crafts.

**The national apprenticeship program. Bureau of Apprenticeship and Training. 1962. 32p. Free

Explains in nontechnical language the national apprenticeship program, its aims and organization, and how it operates.

**Planned training . . . your future security. Bureau of Apprenticeship and Training. 1962. 8p. Free

An explanation of apprentice training and its advantages to young men in equipping them for careers as craftsmen in the skilled trades. Includes qualifications necessary for apprenticeship, list of forty-seven skilled trades in which apprentice training is given, and the usual number of years necessary to complete the training in each.

Research on apprenticeship. Busby, Walter A. Michigan State University, College of Education. 1962. 45p. $1.25

An annotated and classified list of ninety-five research studies dealing with apprenticeship completed during the period from 1930 to 1962. Of interest to persons concerned with the training of apprentices or those who are doing research in this area.

So you want to learn a trade? International Association of Machinists. 1961. 6p. Free

Information about the apprenticeable trades, including qualifications, earnings, length of apprenticeship, who supervises the training, and how to find apprenticeship openings.

D. Bibliographies and Indexes

Career guidance index. Careers. Monthly, September through May. $6 per year
   Each issue contains annotated references to selected free and inexpensive career materials.

Career index. Chronicle Guidance Publications. Monthly, September through April. $8 per year
   Each month the index contains from thirty to forty annotated references to free and inexpensive material. About half of the material listed is free and nothing is included which costs over fifty cents. Printed post cards are included so one can send for the free material by writing name and address only. Each issue contains an alphabetic list of titles included.

**Careers in engineering, mathematics, science, and related fields: a selected bibliography. U.S. Office of Education. Supt. of Documents. 1961. 39p. 25c
   Lists 385 free or inexpensive publications about careers in the sciences: agriculture, biological sciences, engineering, forestry, the health professions, mathematics, and the various physical sciences.

**Careers in fact and fiction. DiStefano, Corinna. New York State Education Department, Bureau of Guidance. 1961. 106p. 50c
   Annotated bibliography of over five hundred books which have pertinent information about specific or general careers.

**Careers in science: a selected bibliography for high school students. American Association for the Advancement of Science. 1961. 23p. 15c
   A useful guide to 236 books and pamphlets classified under 24 headings.

**Counselor's information service. B'nai B'rith Vocational Service. Quarterly. $6
   Annotated bibliography of recently published books, pamphlets, charts, and articles concerning occupations and vocational and educational guidance. Each issue lists from 160 to 170 publications.

Educator's guide to free guidance materials. Saterstrom, Mary H. and Steph, Joe A. Educators Progress Service. 1962. 253p. $6.50 paper
   This guide lists 992 free materials currently available from 309 sources. About two-thirds of the items are films. There are about 200 bulletins, magazines, pamphlets, and posters in addition to many filmstrips, tapes, scripts, and transcriptions. The guide is divided into four sections: career planning materials, social-personal materials, use of leisure time, and responsibility.

**Guidance exchange. Occu-Press. Four issues. $10 a year
   An annotated bibliography of guidance literature, edited by Sarah Splaver. Each issue contains from seventy-five to one hundred entries.

Guide to guidance. Hilton, M. Eunice, ed. Syracuse University Press. Issued annually. $1
   An annotated bibliography of current publications in guidance and student personnel work, prepared by a committee of student deans. This publication is still available through the 1960 bibliography.

Guide to local occupational information. U.S. Employment Service. 1962. 116p. Free to employment counselors
The booklet contains a listing of local occupational guides developed by state agencies under the Job Opportunities Information Program of the U.S. Employment Service. These labor market information materials provide data as to opportunities for employment. Publications from about thirty state employment security agencies are included.

**Implications of automation and other technological developments: a selected annotated bibliography. Bureau of Labor Statistics, U.S. Department of Labor. Supt. of Documents. 1963. 90p. 50c
Describes 307 books, pamphlets, articles, and reports published between the latter part of 1961 and early 1963. An earlier edition of this bibliography covers 500 publications issued from 1956 to 1961 and costs 65c.

List of occupational outlook publications. Occupational Outlook Service. 1962. 8p. Free
Career information for use in guidance.

NVGA bibliography of current occupational literature. National Vocational Guidance Association. 1963. 100p. $1
Compilation of lists which have appeared in the *Vocational Guidance Quarterly*. In addition to career materials, there are included booklets on occupational success, apprenticeship training, work in foreign countries, and scholarship aids.

Occupational index. Personnel Services. Quarterly. $7.50 a year
Annotated lists of current occupational books and pamphlets.

**Occupations—professions and job descriptions. Supt. of Documents. 1963. 20p. Free
Price list of publications available from the U.S. Government Printing Office, with catalog number, title, brief description, and price.

Patterns in reading: an annotated book list for young people. Roos, Jean C. American Library Association. 1961. 132p. $2.25
Approximately 1600 titles, both fiction and nonfiction are annotated and grouped in 75 broad patterns of reading interest. The arrangement within each pattern is progressive and books that are easy to read or simply presented are listed first. The reading interests include business, doctors, explorers, journalists, nursing, personal development, science fiction, scientific giants, space flight, and undersea adventure.

Publications of the Bureau of Labor Statistics. Bureau of Labor Statistics, U.S. Department of Labor. Monthly. Free
An annotated subject index lists all publications issued by the bureau during the month. The June and December issues include items published during the five preceding months. Also shows items in progress.

Publications of the National Science Foundation. National Science Foundation. 1962. 8p. Free
Price list of annual reports, brochures, bulletins, studies, and announcements.

D. Bibliographies and Indexes—*Continued*

Publications of the U.S. Department of Labor. U.S. Department of Labor. 1962. 20p. Free
> Subject listing, 1958 to June, 1962, prepared as a simplified guide for people interested in labor problems.

Publications on scientific and technical manpower. Bureau of Labor Statistics, U.S. Department of Labor. 1962. 8p. Free
> List of about forty publications on career opportunities, employment, and earnings.

**Selected aerospace career and scholarship information. Specialist for Aerospace Education, U.S. Office of Education. 1962. 16p. Single copy free
> Bibliography of sources of information in six parts: aerospace career books; military career information; career pamphlets; lists of schools offering certain aviation courses; scholarships, fellowships, and loan information sources; and guidance and counseling.

Vertical file index. H. W. Wilson Company. Monthly except August, with annual cumulation $8 a year, U.S. and Canada; $10, Foreign
> Look under subject heading "Occupations" for recently published pamphlets.

**Vocations in biography and fiction. Haebich, Kathryn A. American Library Association. 1962. 77p. $1.75
> Annotated listing of 1,070 currently available books, for grades 9 through 12, classified according to 200 careers. The author included books "which interpret vocations in terms of the lives and times of outstanding, interesting, and colorful personalities." Easy-reading titles below eighth-grade reading level have been designated by an asterisk.
>
> *See also* Periodicals

E. Charts, Posters, and Display Materials

Agricultural outlook charts. U.S. Department of Agriculture. Supt. of Documents. 1961. 66p. 45c
> Charts and maps dealing with the economic situation and trends affecting agriculture.

Announcement of the annual competitive examination. U.S. Coast Guard Academy. 1963. 9″ x 12″. Free
> Illustrated poster announcing the examination.

Are you dreaming of a career in medical science—be a medical technologist. American Society of Medical Technologists. 1963. 14″ x 24″. Free to counselors
> An arresting two-color poster pointing out the need for qualified laboratory workers.

Career adjustment posters. Chronicle Guidance Publications. Monthly. 17″ x 22″. $6 a year
> One poster is included each month in the Chronicle Guidance Service. Examples are: "Let's consider your future"; "The difference is in the planning"; "The more you learn the more you earn."

Career-brief posters. Careers. 11″ x 17″. 20c each

    The titles of these posters are the same as the thirty-two titles of the briefs published each year. Each poster is concerned with only one job and contains brief data on duties, outlook, and training. About half of the poster contains an illustration in two or three colors.

Career-data posters. Careers. 12 per year. 17″ x 22″. $3.50 per year. 35c each

    Illustrated posters designed to stimulate students to think about career planning and intelligent choices. Example: "Chart your course."

**A career in medicine. American Medical Association. 1963. 240-pound, 8-foot exhibit. Transportation costs, round-trip.

    An illuminated exhibit designed to interest high school and college students in becoming physicians. Emphasizes the range of opportunities and ways of preparing for medical study. The display features a literature rack for pamphlets which are shipped with the exhibit.

A career in two worlds. American Association of Medical Record Librarians. 1962. 16″ x 21″. 50c

    Prepared for recruitment purposes.

Career interest posters. Careers. 4 per year. 17″ x 22″. 35c each

    Illustrated posters designed to suggest careers related to special interests such as laboratory work, traveling, working out-of-doors, working with others, or working alone.

Career posters. American Physical Therapy Association. 1962. 11″ x 14″. Free to counselors

    Captions are: "What's a life worth? Make yours count!" and "Courage is catching . . . as a physical therapist you can give it and get it."

Career subject, interest, and data posters. Careers. 27 posters. 17″ x 22″. $10

    These posters relate school subjects and fields of interest to career opportunities and concern attitudes, personality, school planning, and looking ahead.

Career-subject posters. Careers. 8 per year. 17″ x 22″. 35c each

    Printed in two or three colors, each poster contains the titles of several related jobs which require ability in some school subject. Their purpose is to stimulate students to consider their abilities and interests in high school courses when selecting careers for further study.

Career with a future in the wonder world of medicine and science. Registry of Medical Technologists of the American Society of Clinical Pathologists. 1956. 13″ x 18″. Free

    Poster showing a medical technologist at work.

**Careers in business. South-Western Publishing Company. 1961. 18″ x 24″. Free

    Two-color chart listing beginning and top jobs and fields of opportunity in four types of business work: bookkeeping and accounting, stenographic and secretarial, general clerical, and merchandising. Also list of qualities to help one succeed. A border of illustrations across the top adds to its attractiveness.

E. Charts, Posters, and Display Materials—*Continued*

Careers in Jewish communal service kit. B'nai B'rith Vocational Service. 1961. Wall chart and 9 pamphlets. $3
> The kit includes an 18" x 24" wall chart describing nine fields of work and nine pamphlets, one for each major field of work: case work, cantorial work, community organization, community relations, group work, Jewish education, rabbinate, synagogue and temple administration, and vocational service.

Careers in the profession of social work. Council on Social Work Education. 1961. 17" x 25". 25c
> Chart for bulletin board display providing information about the variety of social work positions, the kinds of social agencies in which social workers are employed, employment opportunities, requirements, outlook, and where to apply for social work positions.

The Champaign guidance charts. Champaign Senior High School. 1950. 28p. 12" x 18". $2.00; on bristol board $3.75
> Twenty-five charts designed to show the relationship between school subjects and vocations. Good for bulletin board use. The last edition contains suggestions for using these charts.

Chart of airline hostess qualifications. Alumnae Advisory Center. Revised 1956. 3p. 25c
> Reprint from *Mademoiselle.* For each of twelve airlines, information is given concerning the requirements, training, salaries, and location of jobs.

**Chronicle college charts. Sabo, Alex, ed. Chronicle Guidance Publications. 1963. 134p. $3.50
> Current information summarized in chart form including units required for admission, average yearly costs, entrance exams required, enrollment, and related data. The 53 charts cover 2050 institutions of higher education.

Current Federal examination announcements. U.S. Civil Service Commission. Revised monthly. 16" x 21". Free
> List of civil service examinations currently open throughout the country, giving titles, salaries, location of positions, and brief information regarding each examination.

Educator's guide to free guidance materials. Saterstrom, Mary H. and Steph, Joe A. Educators Progress Service. 1962. 253p. $6.50 paper
> This guide lists 992 free materials currently available from 309 sources.. About two thirds of the items are films. There are also about 200 bulletins, magazines, pamphlets, and posters in addition to tapes, scripts, and transcriptions. The guide is divided into four sections: career planning materials, social-personal materials, responsibility, and use of leisure time.

Dietetics career posters. American Dietetic Association. 18" x 23". 3 posters. 5c
> Two-color posters for bulletin board use.

**Education: the more you learn, the more you earn. Occupational Outlook Service. 1963. 12" x 17". Free
> Wall chart portraying the importance of an education.

Exhibits on careers in dentistry. American Dental Association, Bureau of Dental Health Education. 1964. 4 exhibits. 8 and 10 feet wide. Transportation cost

Prepared to show high school and college students the various opportunities, requirements, and satisfactions of a career in dentistry. Good for career conferences or large exhibits.

Find your future in nursing. Committee on Careers in Nursing, National League for Nursing. 1955. 10″ x 20″. 3c

A four-color poster showing nurses and student nurses at work. Contributed by Bruck's Nurses Outfitting Company.

Find your future through the future nurses club. Committee on Careers, National League for Nursing. 1960. 11″ x 14″. 5c

Color poster for use on school bulletin boards.

General Electric progress posters. General Electric Company. Semimonthly. 14″ x 17″. Free to science and mathematics teachers and counselors

Drawings of current scientific developments, with description underneath, sent semimonthly during the school year.

Guidance posters. Science Research Associates. 14″ x 21½″. 25c each. 7 posters a year $1.50

Posters in color suggesting educational and vocational planning. Another series suggesting outlets of school subjects is available, 14 posters for $3.

Home economics bulletin board posters. American Home Economics Association. 1960. 12″ x 17″. $2

Sixteen posters depicting careers in nutrition, family economics, family relations, and home management.

Job opportunities for foreign language students. J. Weston Walch, Publisher. 1962. 8½″ x 11″. $1

Set consists of twelve pairs of posters. In each pair, one poster shows in cartoon form some of the vocational possibilities; its companion presents interesting facts about the same field. Other sets are available on opportunities in mathematics and science.

Look ahead to a career in nursing. Committee on Careers, National League for Nursing. 16″ x 20″. 1958. 2 copies 25c

A two-color picture of nurses in uniform. Contributed by Barco of California.

More schooling generally brings higher earnings. Chronicle Guidance Publications. 1963. 17″ x 22″. $1

A chart showing average lifetime earnings with various amounts of education is accompanied by the caption: "A cool quarter of a million more is earned by college graduates during their lifetime than by students dropping out before entering high school."

E. Charts, Posters, and Display Materials—*Continued*

National Forum Guidance Charts. National Forum, Inc. 1946. 6 sections. Easel size. $16.80

A section of thirty-three charts for each of six books: *Planning My Future, Our School Life, Discovering Myself, Toward Adult Living, About Growing Up* and *Being Teen-Agers.* Titles of charts follow closely the titles of chapters in the books.

NROTC offers you four years of college and a naval officer's career. U.S. Department of the Navy. Revised annually. 8½″ x 11″. Free

Colorful announcement of dates for applications and sources of additional information.

Occupational observation posters. Chronicle Guidance Publications. 2 posters per month. 11″ x 17″. $10 per year

Two of these posters are included each month in the Chronicle Guidance Service. They are printed in two colors and are illustrated. Usually contain information on duties, requirements, and employment outlook.

Occupations and subjects posters. Chronicle Guidance Publications. 17″ x 22″. Monthly. $6 a year

These posters include groups of occupations to which the various school subjects may lead. They are effective in pointing out the occupations related to mathematics, industrial arts, economics, etc.

Packet of literature, posters, and booklets for vocational guidance counselors. Graphic Arts Industry. 1962. $3.50

A selected set of career brochures and bulletin board posters.

Photo blowups and murals. Stites Portrait Company. Prices on request

Photographic enlargements of campus scenes, school buildings, or student activities. Supplied any size in hand colors, sepia, or black and white. Price list and information on request.

Pictorial desk calendar. Keystone Junior College. 1962. 24p. Free

A picture of a campus scene is on each monthly calendar, on the reverse side of which is a description of one of the curricula. Available after July 1 each year.

Posters for guidance bulletin board. Nancy Taylor Secretarial Finishing Schools. 1963. 11″ x 17″. Free

Several of the charts point out secretarial career opportunities. Other titles include: "You should complete your high school education." "What are the ten best-paying office jobs for girls," "What business careers offer the greatest job opportunities," and "Here's how to dress for an interview."

Posters on teaching. Future Teachers of America. 1962. 4 posters. Free to counselors and librarians

Teaching . . . Do you have what it takes?	17″ x 22″
Teaching . . . Do you measure up?	14″ x 18″
Teaching profession interests talented young men.	11″ x 17″
Teaching profession interests talented young women.	11″ x 17″

Products of the tree farm. American Forest Products Industries. 1958. 22″ x 34″. Free to schools

Wall display chart showing how man uses wood today. Useful in woodworking shops to show classification of forest products and ways wood is consumed.

S.R.A. wall charts. Science Research Associates. 1958-1963. 19″ x 24″. 16 charts. 35c each.

A chart is available for each of the Job Family Series booklets. Complete set of sixteen booklets and sixteen charts $16.

Space vehicles. Ford Motor Company. 1962. 9 Photographs. Free to counselors

A bulletin board kit of nine photographs, with captions, showing scale models and components of the Ranger spacecraft, built to carry an instrument package to the moon.

Teaching career month posters. National Education Association. Annual. 17¼″ x 22½″. Package of 5 for $1

Included in the Teaching Career Month packet each April or available separately. Full-color reproductions of oil paintings A package, however, contains only one type of poster.

There's a future for high school graduates in the restaurant industry. 1960. National Restaurant Association. 12″ x 17″. Free

Illustrated poster in color.

These CSS colleges can help you with scholarships, loans, jobs. College Scholarship Service. Annual. 16″ x 23″. Free

Poster listing the 450 colleges participating in the service.

Tree of knowledge and basic sciences. Museum of Science and Industry. 1938. 25″ x 38″. 95c

Chart from the Century of Progress Exposition in attractive colors, suitable for framing. Chart shows basic importance of mathematics to other fields of knowledge. At the base of the tree are listed mathematics, botany, chemistry, and seven other basic sciences. At the top of the tree are listed fourteen applied sciences such as architectural engineering, public health and hygiene, agronomy, and medicine.

**Wall chart series. Bureau of Labor Statistics, U.S. Department of Labor. 15 charts. 12½″ x 17″. Free

Charts which present occupational outlook data graphically. Available titles include building trades, electronic computer operation, driving occupations, performing arts, science, service, social science, television and radio broadcasting, and skilled occupations.

You are equipped for many careers when you specialize in dietetics. American Dietetic Association. 1956. 17″ x 21″. 5c

Three-color poster for bulletin board use.

You will like geometry. Museum of Science and Industry. 1962. 12p. 41c

Guide book published as an adjunct to the Illinois Institute of Technology's permanent geometry exhibit at the museum.

E. Charts, Posters, and Display Materials—*Continued*

Your high school record—does it count? (New Series). South Dakota Press. 1956. 18″ x 22″. Complete with glassed frame, $22.75; without frame, $21.25; book, $2.90
    Poster set, consisting of thirty-seven posters, adapted from book of same title is designed to prove to students that the records they are making in high school will count for or against them in later life.

F. Foreign Study or Employment

The American student abroad. Alumnae Advisory Center. 1962. 5p. 25c
    Reprint from *Mademoiselle* describing several study programs in foreign countries.

Careers in world affairs: at home and abroad. Doubleday and Company. 1961. 140p. $1.75
    This book is an enlargement of a special issue of *Intercom* compiled by the Foreign Policy Association-World Affairs Center. It tells what kind of jobs there are and what it takes to get them in government, business, church work, education, and with international organizations and voluntary agencies.

Careers in world affairs with a salute to the Peace Corps. Commission on World Mission. 1961. 64p. 75c
    An issue of *Intercom* listing available opportunities for work with organizations involved in world affairs overseas. There are references to government, business and industry, churches and missions, United Nations, and national governments.

Directory of American firms operating in foreign countries. World Trade Academy Press. 1964. 206p. $17.50
    List of 2,300 American corporations with addresses and names of executives in charge of foreign operations.

Education without boundaries. American Council on Education. 1959. 68p. $1
    A discussion of future goals of overseas university programs and the contribution of American universities to international understanding.

**Educational and cultural exchange opportunities. U.S. Department of State. Supt. of Documents. 1963. 27p. 15c
    Opportunities offered in the exchange of two thousand persons between the United States and seventy-two other countries sponsored by the International Educational Exchange Program. How exchange students are selected and where to apply for grants.

Employment abroad. Facts and fallacies. Foreign Commerce Department, Chamber of Commerce of the United States. 1961. 18p. 25c
    Suggestions about how to seek employment abroad and some of the problems to be faced.

Employment opportunities in binational centers abroad. U.S. Information Agency. 1963. 15p. Free
    A brief guide.

Federal jobs overseas. U.S. Civil Service Commission. Supt. of Documents. 1962. 10p. 10c

Types of positions, salaries, and minimum experience and training requirements. Also includes list of addresses to which inquiries may be sent.

Fellowships offered by foreign governments, universities, and private donors. Institute of International Education. 1963. 16p. Free

Fellowships and scholarships administered by the Institute of International Education for United States students to study abroad.

* Foreign study for United States undergraduates. Institute of International Education. 1958. 45p. 50c

A survey of undergraduate study abroad programs of American colleges and universities.

Foreign teaching opportunities. Advancement and Placement Institute. 1962. 13 guides. 50c each

Guide for opportunities in Alaska, Australia, Brazil, Canada, England, Greece, Hawaii, Japan, Nicaragua, Puerto Rico, Switzerland, Venezuela, and United States Government schools.

General memorandum for those interested in foreign study. Institute of International Education. 1961. 4p. Free

Discussion of factors involved in preparing for a period of foreign study.

Graduate study in the United States. Institute of International Education. 1958. 10p. 15c

A guide for foreign students who plan to do graduate work in the United States. Prepared in cooperation with the Association of Graduate Schools.

**A guide to study abroad, 1962-1963. Garraty, John A. and Adams, Walter. Channel Press. 1962. 352p. $5.95; paper $2.95

Includes university, summer school, tour, and work-and-study programs. Information is given on more than 400 programs from the secondary school to the graduate levels, including costs, credits, and kinds of classes. The authors have made regular surveys of twenty-six nations since 1958, when they were selected to undertake a Carnegie study of educational facilities abroad.

A guide to the admission and placement of foreign students. Institute of International Education. 1962. 170p. $2.50

Written to assist the admissions officers of an institution in developing effective procedures for admission and placement of foreign students to American colleges and universities. Includes discussion of evaluation of credentials, the use of health certificates, and the United States and foreign government regulations.

Handbook on international study: for foreign nationals. Institute of International Education. 1961. 304p. $3

A guide on study, training and other opportunities in the United States. Includes a discussion on education in the United States, a listing of scholarship and fellowship opportunities, organizations providing services to students and visitors, and pertinent United States Government regulations.

F. Foreign Study or Employment—*Continued*

Handbook on international study: for U.S. nationals. Institute of International Education. 1961. 303p. $3

A guide on study, training, and other opportunities abroad. Information is given concerning the government regulations which affect the American student abroad. Discussion of educational systems in ninety-one foreign countries and information on scholarship and fellowship programs.

If you'd like to study abroad. Science Research Associates. 1963. 48p. 50c

A look at foreign study and educational travel prepared by the Institute of International Education. Includes a list of programs for group study abroad.

International education. Western Personnel Institute. 1962. 20p. $1

Annotated bibliography of about fifty publications concerning study abroad, foreign students in the United States, handbooks, and other reference sources.

International educational exchange: a selected bibliography. U.S. Office of Education. Supt. of Documents. 1961. 117p. 50c

An extensive reference list of reports on exchange programs and international fellowships, scholarships, and the exchange of persons programs.

International educational exchange program. U.S. Dept. of State. Supt. of Documents. 1956. 56p. 25c

Discussion of cultural exchanges and the American foreign policy, scope of the program, and activities in various parts of the world. Includes numbers of exchange students to and from each of eighty-one countries.

Job opportunities abroad. Institute of International Education. 1962. 2p. Free

Mimeographed list of eighteen sources of information.

Jobs that take you places. Leeming, Joseph. David McKay Company. 1953. 244p. $3.50

Information for the young man or woman who wants to live in foreign lands or see the world and get paid for it. Lists of companies and organizations to write to follow each chapter. Partial contents: "Engineers really go places"; "Jobs with oil companies"; "Overseas work for scientists."

Laymen overseas. Commission on World Mission. 1962. 10p. Free

Includes names and addresses of several missionary, ecumenical, and government agencies with brief description of openings.

The liberal arts college in the United States. Institute of International Education. 1958. 32p. 15c

A guide to undergraduate study in the United States for foreign students. Prepared in cooperation with the American Association of Junior Colleges.

Looking for employment in foreign countries. Angel, Juvenal L. World Trade Academy Press. 1961. 165p. $8.50

Some topics included are where to look for employment, labor legislation in foreign countries affecting foreign employees, a directory of firms doing business abroad, and living conditions abroad.

National and international employment handbook for specialized personnel; practical handbook for those seeking employment here and abroad. Angel, Juvenal L. World Trade Academy Press. 1961. 309p. $17.50
Includes sections on employment possibilities in foreign countries, points to be considered when employed for overseas work, and employment legislation in foreign countries.

* New horizons in education; the benefits of study abroad. Pan American Airways. 1961. 526p. $2
Information concerning the study programs, costs, admission requirements, and other features of several universities in each of thirty-eight countries.

Opportunities for study in Latin America. Part I: Regular Academic Year. Part II: Summer. Pan American Union. 1962. 60p. 25c each part
A listing of academic sessions, study and vacation tours, and work projects and international living programs in Latin America.

Overseas opportunities for educators in Government dependent schools. Advancement and Placement Institute. 1962. 4p. 50c
Includes qualifications and salaries.

Overseas teacher. Gerard, Jane. Julian Messner, Inc. 1963. 192p. $2.95
Career fiction. Story of the challenges for the teacher in the overseas school system for Americans in the U.S. Air Force.

Research bulletin on overseas jobs for teachers. Changing Times. 1962. 2p. 15c
Description of teaching programs conducted overseas by private and government agencies.

Rising demand for international education. American Academy of Political and Social Science. 1961. 254p. $2
This issue of *The Annals* presents a series of articles on this subject. Includes a summary of the first fifteen years of the Fulbright program, the foreign student in the United States, the United States student abroad, and a look at the future.

Social work opportunities abroad: employment and education. National Association of Social Workers. 1958. 29p. $1
Prepared by the Committee on International Social Welfare.

Students abroad. Council on Student Travel. 1963. 32p. Free
A digest of international travel programs. In outline form, the handbook lists the overseas programs of about one hundred organizations and institutions, giving cost, age limit, countries visited, academic credit, and a brief description of each program.

**Study abroad: international handbook of fellowships, scholarships, and educational exchange. UNESCO. Columbia University Press. 1963. 721p. $3
A guide to opportunities for study throughout the world, this handbook includes information on fellowships, scholarships, and training grants. Gives an analysis of the world's foreign-student population and information on the programs for the international exchange of trainees.

F. Foreign Study or Employment—*Continued*

Summer study abroad. Institute of International Education. 1962. 8p. Free
> A listing of educational opportunities for summer study for United States students in foreign universities throughout the world.

Summer study abroad. Study Abroad, Inc. 1964. 8p. Free
> Brief announcement of study tours in education, fine arts, literature, music, social science, English, and French.

**Teacher exchange opportunities under the International Educational Exchange Program. Bureau of International Education, U.S. Office of Education. Published annually. Available August, September, and October. Free
> Information about the exchange program and when and where to apply for the teaching positions and summer seminar grants available to go abroad under the Mutual Educational and Cultural Exchange Act of 1961 (Fulbright-Hays Act).

Teaching abroad. Institute of International Education. 1962. 7p. Free
> Names and addresses of twenty-five administering agencies.

Teaching opportunities in Latin America for United States citizens. Pan American Union. 1962. 8p. Free
> Discussion of opportunities, how to prepare for the work, and how to make application.

Travel while you work or study. Western Personnel Institute. 1955. 4p. 20c
> Includes names of books and pamphlets containing information about exchange grants, scholarships, and study opportunities in foreign universities.

United States Government grants for graduate study abroad 1963-64 under the Fulbright-Hays Act. Institute of International Education. 1963. 10p. Free
> Explanation of the eligibility requirements and application procedures of the educational and cultural exchange programs of the Department of State.

Unusual teaching opportunities abroad. National Education Association. 1963. 2p. Single copy free
> List of some opportunities together with sources to which inquiries may be sent.

Vacations abroad. UNESCO. Columbia University Press. 1962. 161p. $1.25
> Details about 950 courses, study tours, and work camps for people interested in combining education with travel. UNESCO disseminates information on vacation courses and study tours in order to encourage students to gain a deeper insight into the cultural, social, and economic affairs of other lands.

* Work, study, travel abroad. United States National Student Association. 1963. 150p. $1.50
> An annual publication presenting information on opportunities available to students who desire to study, work, or travel abroad. Includes helpful advice, description of travel aids, and lists of travel programs.

World-wide graduate award directory. Advancement and Placement Institute. 1959. 56p. $3

> Description of assistantships, fellowships, scholarships, and research grants contributed by over one thousand universities and foundations in forty-four states and fifty-five foreign countries. Arranged by country or state.

The young American in Europe. Lynch, Nancy. Alumnae Advisory Center. 1956. 24p. 50c

> Reprint from *Mademoiselle* describing working or studying abroad. Presents ten ways to go such as tours, hosteling, and scholarships. A mimeographed insert contains list of leads for the internationally minded.

G. Gifted and Academically Talented

Academically talented boxed set. National Education Association. 1961. 14 publications. $9.75

> Fourteen publications on the academically talented student, valued at $17, attractively boxed for desk display. The publications cover administration, art, business, English, foreign languages, mathematics, music, research, science, and social studies. Includes an annotated bibliography and a conference report.

Administration procedures and school practices for the academically talented student in the secondary school. National Association of Secondary-School Principals. 1960. 223p. $1.25

> Suggestions for identification, motivation, and provision of enriched programs. Examples of varied school programs are described.

Annotated bibliography on the academically talented student. Gowan, John. National Education Association. 1961. 156p. $1

> The annotations indicate which entries report research. It also includes both a topical index and a subject index as well as the compiler's views of current emphases.

Building a program for superior and talented high school students. Bryan, J. N. North Central Association, STS Project. 1963. 90p. $1

> Description of a project designed to assist secondary schools in identifying, guiding, and motivating superior and talented students.

Creativity of gifted and talented children. Witty, Paul; Conant, James B.; and Strang, Ruth. Bureau of Publications. 1959. 51p. $1

> Ways of identifying these individuals and methods by which their creative powers can be developed.

Educating exceptional children. Kirk, S. A. Houghton Mifflin Company. 1962. 415p. $6

> This book describes the characteristics of the major types of exceptional children in physical, psychological, and social terms, and suggests educational programs adapted to their particular needs.

Educating gifted children. DeHaan, Robert and Havigurst, Robert. University of Chicago Press. 1961. 362p. $5

> Addressed to administrators who are setting up programs, one chapter is devoted to the motivation and guidance of the gifted.

G. Gifted and Academically Talented—*Continued*

Education for the gifted. 57th yearbook. National Society for the Study of Education. 1958. 427p. $4

The topics discussed include the importance of education for the gifted, motivation, creativity, social leadership, and characteristics and objectives of a program for the able student.

Education of the gifted. Educational Policies Commission. 1950. 88p. 35c

Includes a discussion of the identification and education of gifted students.

Encouraging the excellent. Paschal, Elizabeth. Fund for the Advancement of Education. 1960. 80p. Free

Report of experiments of efforts to improve the education of gifted students through a number of different programs, each of which attempted to break the educational lockstep and allow students to educate themselves as extensively and rapidly as their abilities would permit.

The gifted child: the yearbook of education 1962. Bereday, George and Lauwerys, Joseph, editors. Harcourt, Brace and World. 1962. 541p. $10.50

Examines the issues in the detection and selection of students having more than average ability, the methods used in various countries for recognizing and training those with special talent, and the ways in which the "pool of talent" can be increased.

The gifted: educational resources. Porter Sargent. 1961. 285p. $4

A directory of over eight hundred public and private school programs, nursery through college, which seek to realize the capabilities of mentally superior students. The programs are arranged by geographic regions and classified by types of programs offered.

**Guidance for the academically talented student. American Personnel and Guidance Association. 1961. 144p. $1

Report of a conference containing ideas for guidance work with the academically talented and methods by which these ideas may be implemented. Includes identification, motivation, counseling, and educational provisions. Selected bibliography.

**Guidance for the underachievers with superior ability. Miller, Leonard M., ed. U.S. Office of Education. Supt. of Documents. 1961. 85p. 35c

Discussion of identification of academic underachievers and methods of motivation. Selected references.

Guiding creative talent. Torrance, E. Paul. Prentice-Hall, Inc. 1962. 278p. $5

Discussions concerning the development and guidance of a wide range of creative talent at all age and educational levels.

Guiding superior and talented high school students. Endicott, Frank S. North Central Association of Colleges and Secondary Schools. 1961. 84p. $1

Suggestions for developing a guidance program for able youth, including identification, motivation, and helping them through guidance services.

Helping your gifted child. Strang, Ruth. Dutton and Company. 1960. 270p. $4.50

Aimed at helping parents recognize gifted children and cooperate with schools for the young person's optimum development. Selected references.

**The identification and education of the academically talented student in the American secondary school. National Education Association. 1958. 160p. $1.50

A conference report considering the identification, motivation, program organization, and curriculum considerations of the able student.

Planning for talented youth: considerations for public schools. Passow, A. Harry; Goldberg, Miriam; Tannenbaum, Abraham; and French, Will. Bureau of Publications. 1955. 84p. $1.25

Identifying the talented; administrative adaptations such as ability-grouping, acceleration, special provisions in regular classes; guidance services; community resources; and evaluation of the school's program for talented youngsters.

Research on the academically talented student. National Education Association. 1961. 92p. $1

A conference report describing illustrative research in this area. Good bibliography.

Talent and tomorrow's teachers: the honors approach. U.S. Office of Education. Supt. of Documents. 1963. 83p. 35c

A report of a conference on the superior student. Deals with developments of significance to colleges and universities with teacher training programs.

Teaching the bright and gifted. Cutts, Norma E. and Moseley, Nicholas. Prentice-Hall, Inc. 1957. 268p. $8.35; text edition $6.25

Procedures for identifying and instructing the gifted. One chapter is devoted to vocational guidance and one to educational guidance.

Working with superior students: theories and practices. Shertzer, Bruce, ed. Science Research Associates. 1960. 370p. $5.95

A collection of papers concerning the identification of talent, guidance services, motivation, and community participation in development programs for the gifted pupils.

H. Information about Colleges, Schools for Vocational Training, and Other Educational Institutions

Accredited curricula leading to first degrees in engineering in the United States. Engineers' Council for Professional Development. 1963. 18p. 25c

List of 162 engineering schools, arranged alphabetically, with the accredited curricula such as civil, mechanical, and chemical.

**Accredited higher institutions, 1960. Wilkins, Theresa Birch. U.S. Office of Education. Bulletin 1960 Number 24. Supt. of Documents. 1960. 156p. 60c

Quadrennial bulletin reporting institutions accredited by nationally recognized accrediting associations, state departments of education, and state universities.

H. Information about Colleges and Other Schools—*Continued*

Includes lists of professional and technical schools or departments accredited in thirty-three occupations such as architecture, dentistry, forestry, medical technology, music, podiatry, and public health.

Accredited technical institute programs. Engineers' Council for Professional Development. 1962. 8p. 25c
    List of accredited programs at thirty-two institutions.

Action under way to meet the rising tide of enrollment in American Colleges and Universities. American Council on Education. 1956. 36p. Free
    Reports of evidence of planning by institutions, by groups interested in statewide coordination, and by agencies promoting regional cooperation.

Admission requirements for approved technical institute programs of higher education. National Council of Technical Schools. 1958. 2p. 5c
    Entrance requirements of technical institutes and list of the fields of engineering technology available in approved technical institutes.

**Admission requirements of American medical colleges, including Canada. Association of American Medical Colleges. 1963. 252p. $3
    Information concerning the admission requirements, costs, and admission procedures of each of the eighty-eight medical schools in the United States, the twelve medical schools in Canada, and one in the Philippines. Recommendations on preparation for medical education and how to apply to medical schools. Good reading lists.

**Admissions schedules of the member colleges. College Entrance Examination Board. 1964. 42p. 50c
    Summarizes in tabular form the admissions requirements of the 543 College Board member colleges Shows test requirements, including the Writing Sample, with required, preferred, or acceptable testing dates. Includes the closing date for applications and indicates whether the college subscribes to the Candidates Reply Date agreement.

Advanced placement program: course descriptions. College Entrance Examination Board. 1962. 152p. $1.50
    Descriptions of the college-level courses to be given in high schools on which the examinations will be based for credit and advanced placement in colleges.

**American junior colleges. Gleazer, Edmund J., Jr. American Council on Education. 1963. 551p. $10
    Classified data for 655 two-year colleges recognized by regional or state accrediting agencies. Includes date organized, type of control, accreditation, enrollment, admission requirements, fees, curricula offered, size of campus, and table of transfer and terminal or occupational curricula.

American trade schools directory. Croner, Ulrich H. E. Croner Publications. Annually. 150p. With supplements, $9.95, for 1 year
    About 3,000 schools are classified according to trades taught and listed by states and cities. Loose-leaf edition permits use of supplements.

**American universities and colleges. Cartter, Allan M., ed. American Council on Education. 1964. 1212p. $15

Descriptive directory of 1,100 institutions accredited by the six regional accrediting associations. Data include their areas of instruction, number of faculty in each department, tuition and other fees, housing, student aid, areas of graduate work, and notable features. In addition, brief data are given on 2,016 accredited professional schools. A useful feature is the several tables giving the distribution of doctorates awarded by American universities and colleges by subject, year, sex, and institution. One section presents lists of institutions offering professional instruction in each of twenty-four professional fields.

**Answers to questions about college and you. General Motors Corporation, Public Relations Staff. 1962. 24p. Free

This booklet contains six articles on planning for college, including whether to go to college, how to choose and get into a college, how to finance a college education, and how to get along at college. Good reference lists at end of each section.

Baird's manual of American college fraternities. George Banta Company. 1963. 848p. $8

A directory of fraternities; sororities, and honor, professional, and recognition societies. This is the seventeenth edition.

Barron's guide to the two-year colleges. Eskow, Seymour. Barron's Educational Series, Inc. 1960. 320p. $4.95; $2.98 paper

A directory of more than 700 junior colleges, community two-year colleges, vocational, and technical institutes. Includes costs, control, enrollment, admission requirements, housing, certificates offered, and accreditation. A helpful section is a listing of 215 courses from accounting to welding, each followed by names and addresses of the colleges offering them.

Barron's profiles of American colleges. Fine, Benjamin S. Barron's Educational Series, Inc. 1963. 896p. $6.75; $3.95 paper

Information on each accredited American college and university including facilities, outstanding features and programs, admission requirements, costs, financial aid available, degrees awarded, enrollment, housing facilities, social or honorary societies, and religious or other regulations for student life.

The best college for you. Alumnae Advisory Center. 1954. 11p. 10c

Discussion of selection of a college including capsule profiles of sixteen colleges. Also includes some information on scholarships for practicing arts. Reprint from *Mademoiselle*.

A briefing for parents: your child and college. National Education Association. 1961. 16p. 35 for $1

This booklet offers advice on who should go to college, what college costs, and how parents can help.

Camp directory. New York State Camp Directors Association. 1963. 30p. Free

Information concerning 103 camps in New York State.

H. Information about Colleges and Other Schools—*Continued*

Campus, U.S.A. Boroff, David. Harper and Row. 1961. 210p. $4.50

Subtitled "Portraits of American colleges in action," this book describes the general atmosphere which prevails at ten varied schools: Harvard, University of Wisconsin, Claremont, Swarthmore, Brooklyn, Parsons, Birmingham-Southern, Smith, University of Michigan, and Sarah Lawrence.

Canadian universities and colleges. Canadian Universities Foundation. 1962. 284p. $3

Detailed information regarding forty-four universities and colleges in Canada, including enrollment, degrees conferred, fees and costs, admission requirements, and distinctive programs.

Career training guides. Careers. 1962-1963. $3 a year

Eighteen training guides per year, listing training opportunities for specific careers. Another set of fourteen college guides lists entrance requirements, costs, etc., on the liberal arts colleges. Included with the subscription services or separately at $3 per set.

Catholic colleges and universities. Catholic College Bureau. 1962. 168p. $1

Directory of 162 colleges. For each school there is given the enrollment, admission requirements, fees, housing, curriculum, accreditation, and significant aspects. There also is a directory of programs of study, listing the colleges offering training in music, dental hygiene, nursing, home economics, etc.

Choosing a camp for your child. American Camping Association. 1962. 60p. Free

Advantages of a summer camping experience and a directory of 350 camps.

Choosing an independent school for your child. National Association of Independent Schools. 1957. 20p. Free

This bulletin describes what the good independent school is and suggests a series of searching questions which parents might ask of the schools they visit.

Choosing the right college. Turngren, Annette. Harper and Row. 1952. 149p. $2.95

Addressed to prospective college students, this book explains what college has to offer and what it requires of the student. Included are discussions of job opportunities and scholarships; how to decide about type, size, and location of a college; how to rate a college; how to get admitted; and campus life.

Classrooms in the military. Clark, Harold F. and Sloan, Harold S. Bureau of Publications. 1964. 154p. $3.95

An over-all account of education in the Armed Forces of the United States.

College admissions. Volume IV. The student from school to college. College Entrance Examination Board. 1957. 128p. $3

Discussion of the interpretation by college admissions officers of the student's marks, rank in class, and test scores and the assessment of personality, character, and promise. Volume I of this series describes the collection, interpretation, and use of applicant data in college admissions procedures.

**College ahead! Revised Edition. Wilson, Eugene S. and Bucher, Charles A. Harcourt, Brace and World. 1961. 202p. $4.50

Includes discussion of requirements for college admission, how colleges differ, how to visit a college, how to apply, and how to make the first year a good one. Bibliography.

College and you. Sifferd, Calvin S. McKnight and McKnight. 1952. 111p. $3

Letters of a father to his twins, a boy and a girl, who are in their first year in college. The letters discuss what to expect during the first year, the difference between large and small schools, entrance requirements, expenses, time budgeting, sororities and fraternities, dating, part-time employment, and getting along with others. Two-color drawings illustrating some of the college experiences enliven the text.

The college blue book. Christian E. Burckel and Associates. 1962. Volume I. 802p. $20. Volume II. 727p. $20. Volume III. 450p. $10. Complete set $45

Information about 16,124 institutions of higher education in the United States. Data comprise names of administrative officers, accreditation, student enrollment, entrance requirements, degrees offered, capacity of dormitories, cost per term, tuition costs, and scholarships. Indexes are given to professional schools according to type of control and accreditation. Also includes lists of 3,000 organizations and 2,000 publications concerned with higher and secondary education.

College bound—planning for college. Brownstein, Samuel C. Barron's Educational Series. Revised 1962. 396p. $3.95 cloth; $1.98 paper

Contains descriptive data on 1,150 colleges as well as sections on preparing for college, life at college, and evaluating the professions. Also includes several lists of approved schools for training in specific fields.

College costs 1963-1964. Life Insurance Agency Management Association. 1963. 44p. Free

Tuition, basic fees, room and board costs, and the total undergraduate enrollment are listed for approximately 1,000 colleges and universities.

A college education: what is it worth and what does it cost? Fidelity Mutual Life Insurance Company. 1960. 36p. Free

Discussion of the values of a college education and methods of planning to meet the costs. Includes approximate minimum costs per year in 321 representative colleges and universities.

College entrance counselor. Wechsler, Louis K.; Blum, Martin; and Friedman, Sidney. Barnes and Noble, Inc. 1961. 413p. $5.95; $3.50 paper

Part I explores the reasons for going to college, how to plan for college, the kinds of colleges, finding the right college, the college entrance examinations, applying for admission, and the military obligation. Part II contains directories of both four-year and two-year colleges. Also given is a list of scholarships given by a variety of public and private agencies.

College entrance guide. Einstein, Bernice W. Grosset and Dunlap, Inc. 1963. 96p. $1.95 paperback

Includes data and suggestions on planning for college, entrance requirements, application and admission, and financing college expenses. Colleges are listed under specialized fields.

College entrance requirements and costs. Sabo, Alex, ed. Chronicle Guidance Publications. 1962. 84p. $2

Data on two thousand junior and senior colleges arranged alphabetically and indexed by state. Also data on enrollment, sex, and type of control.

College facts chart. National Beta Club. 1963. 42p. 50c

Information about colleges in fifty states in tabular form including degrees offered, enrollment, number of teachers, average tuition, cost of board and room, and average total cost for the school year. Compiled annually.

College for coeds. Muller, L. C. and Muller, O. G. Pitman Publishing Corporation. 1960. 221p. $3.95

This book covers many phases of life at college to give the prospective coed a clearer picture of what awaits her. Activities are explained from orientation ceremonies to the graduation dance and alumnae interests.

College for your child, why not? Michigan State University, School of Labor and Industrial Relations. 1963. 15p. 10c

Discussion of the nature and purpose of a college education and what parents can do to help their children get ready for it.

College freshmen speak out. Townsend, Agatha. Harper and Row. 1956. 136p. $5

Discussion of the need for high schools and colleges to prepare young people for the transition.

**College guide for Jewish youth. B'nai B'rith Vocational Service. 1963. 106p. $3

A directory of 430 selected colleges with facts about general enrollment, Jewish enrollment, B'nai B'rith Hillel Foundations and Counselorships, and type of school. Also contains general information about choosing a college and Jewish life on the campus.

**The college handbook, 1963-1965. College Entrance Examination Board. 1963. 614p. $2.50

Published biennially, the handbook comprises statements by 350 of the College Board member colleges. Each includes information on enrollment, location, courses of study, fees, financial aid program, and admission requirements. A tabular section summarizes test requirements, application closing dates, and other admissions information.

College know how. Dysinger, Wendell. McKnight and McKnight Publishing Company. 1957. 31p. 44c

Written to help young people succeed in college.

College: the life of a student. Engeman, Jack. Lothrop, Lee and Shepard Company. 1959. 128p. $3.50

More than 250 photographs, with informative text and captions, show many aspects of life in college and help prospective students know what lies in store for them during their college careers. Photographs were taken at fifty different colleges.

College tips for future teachers. National Education Association. No date. 8p. 35 copies $1

Advice on how to get into an accredited college and what to do to succeed in college.

College—whether to go, where to go. Alumnae Advisory Center. 1953. 15p. 25c

Illustrated in color. Partial contents: weighing what you can be, do, and have; can you afford not to go to college; can you afford to go to college; where do the top students go; sixteen students from different schools tell why they picked their alma maters; it's your move now. Reprint from *Mademoiselle*.

Colleges and universities in Pennsylvania. Department of Public Instruction, Commonwealth of Pennsylvania. 1962. 144p. $1

Information is compiled concerning 140 institutions, including entrance requirements, enrollment, costs, curriculum offered, living accommodations, accreditation, scholarships, and student loan funds.

Colleges classified—a guide for counselors, parents, and students. Nelson, A. Gordon. Chronicle Guidance Publications. 1963. 64p. $1

Colleges classified by various combinations of student body, enrollment, region, and cost. Useful in finding institutions which fit a student's expressed preferences.

Colleges with room for students. Changing Times. 1962. 22p. 75c

Fifth annual survey of openings in four-year accredited colleges, showing that 343 colleges could have accepted 41,200 freshmen in addition to those who actually registered in 1962. For each of the colleges, there is given the number of openings for the past two years and the number of transfer openings expected the following two years.

Commonwealth universities yearbook. Association of Universities of the British Commonwealth. Order from American Council on Education. 1963. 1826p. $15

Information on universities in the Commonwealth, including admission requirements, fees, academic year, libraries, and degrees and certificates offered.

**Complete planning for college: the Kiplinger guide to your education beyond high school. Sulkin, Sidney. McGraw-Hill Book Company. 1962. 268p. $5.95; $3.95 paper

Useful advice on preparing for college, choosing a suitable school, financing an education, and what to expect in college. Includes a list of accredited colleges with room for more students in 1962.

Continuing college after marriage. Alumnae Advisory Center. 1962. 4p. 25c

Reprint from *Mademoiselle* describing the plan of several women to continue study. Another publication, "The changing role of college women," lists about 125 titles of books and articles about women's changing roles and about practical approaches to going back to jobs or college. (50c)

Cost of attending college; a study of student expenditures and sources of income. U.S. Office of Education. Bulletin 1957, Number 9. Supt. of Documents. 1957. 91p. 45c

A report on what it costs students to attend college and where they get the money for this purpose. One of the conclusions is that scholarships accounted

H. Information about Colleges and Other Schools—*Continued*

for slightly less than 5 per cent of total income of all students, but they make a significant contribution to budgets of the 20 per cent of students who received them.

The cost of four years of college. New York Life Insurance Company. 1961. 48p. Free

The booklet shows the yearly fixed cost of tuition and room and board for most of the American colleges. Aimed to encourage parents to prepare for their children's future education.

**Counselor's manual for *How About College Financing?* American School Counselor Association. Order from American Personnel and Guidance Association. 1960. 43p. $1

Contains supplementary information for the counselor. Includes a chart showing the minimum amount of support expected from parents' income.

Directory for exceptional children. Fourth edition. Porter Sargent. 1962. 656p. $6

Descriptive listings of three thousand public and private schools, hospitals, clinics, and other facilities for the emotionally disturbed, the physically handicapped, and the mentally retarded. Included also are listings of associations and Federal and state agencies concerned with the education and welfare of the exceptional.

Directory issue. The Journalism Educator. 1963. 32p. $2

Bulletin of the American Society of Journalism School Administrators containing list of 140 schools and departments offering majors or degrees in journalism. Name of journalism unit is followed by year in which established, association affiliations, student organizations, facilities, and degrees offered.

Directory of accredited private home study schools. National Home Study Council. 1963. 12p. Free

List of sixty-three schools with addresses and dates founded. The leaflet also contains a partial list of the home study subjects.

Directory of business schools in the United States. United Business Schools Association. 1963. 24p. Free to counselors and librarians.

List of private business schools that have met membership requirements in the association.

Directory of private trade schools in New York State. Private Vocational Schools Association of New York. 1961. 23p. Free

Directory of 142 schools and the courses offered in each.

Directory of public secondary day schools. U.S. Office of Education. Supt. of Documents. 1961. 163p. $1.25

Lists secondary schools by name and location and gives for each the accreditation status, enrollment, classroom teachers, and other data.

Directory of small colleges. Council for the Advancement of Small Colleges. 1963. 68p. $1

The directory has three parts: (1) a general discussion of the features of this group of private liberal arts colleges with average enrollments of three hundred students; (2) a descriptive paragraph about each college with information about admissions requirements, specialized opportunities, and campus facilities; and (3) a table arranged alphabetically by states listing such items as size, costs, control, and academic programs.

**Directory of vocational training sources. Science Research Associates. 1964. 528p. $3

Information about training opportunities for those who do not plan to attend a four-year college. Lists more than 5,500 schools and the vocational courses they offer. Fifty major occupational areas range from accounting to welding. Part I includes information about courses, length of training, entrance requirements, and accrediting agencies. Part II is an alphabetical list of school names and addresses, arranged by state.

**Earned degrees conferred 1961-1962: bachelor's and higher degrees. U.S. Office of Education. Supt. of Documents. 1963. 250p. $1.75

Useful to students for judging the extent of a college's program in a particular field of study. Degree data are summarized at the bachelor's, master's, and doctor's level for each of 164 major fields of study and for each of the 1,400 colleges conferring degrees. Also includes an analytic report of data relating to degrees conferred by major areas of study, type of institution, region and institution. An annual report.

Education directory, 1962-63. Part 3: Higher education. U.S. Office of Education. Supt. of Documents. 1963. 221p. 75c

Annual directory, listing accredited colleges in the United States which offer at least a two-year program of college-level studies in residence, classified by highest level of offering and by type of program. Includes information on location, control, composition of student body, and enrollment.

Educational opportunities of Greater Boston for adults. Prospect Union Educational Exchange. Annual. 187p. $2.50

Description of Boston's day and evening courses for adults.

Engineering enrollments and degrees. Tolliver, Wayne and Armsby, Henry. U.S. Office of Education. Supt. of Documents. 1963. 45p. 35c

Annual analytic report of data relating to both undergraduate and graduate enrollment and degrees, classified in twenty-five fields. Degree data are summarized at the bachelor's, master's, and doctor's level, with indication as to Engineers' Council for Professional Development accreditation, for each of the 245 colleges conferring engineering degrees.

Enrollment for advanced degrees, fall 1960. U.S. Office of Education. 1963. 285p. $2.75

A second nation-wide survey of students enrolled in the various institutions for advanced degrees.

Enrollment projections for higher education, 1961-1978. Thompson, Ronald B. American Association of Collegiate Registrars and Admissions Officers. Order from American Council on Education. 1961. 10p. Free to college administrators

A projection of college-age youth and projections of enrollments in higher education based on the study of births from 1939 to 1960 and the Census data.

H. Information about Colleges and Other Schools—*Continued*

Estimates of school statistics, 1962-1963. National Education Association. 1962. 32p. $1
Annual report providing, on a state-by-state basis, up-to-date information on school districts, pupils enrolled, teachers' salaries, revenues and expenditures, and numbers of high school graduates.

**Facing facts about college admissions—a guide for pre-college students and their parents. Prudential Insurance Company. 1962. 27p. Free
Useful information to assist young people to make suitable decisions about college admission. Includes explanation of what colleges consider in connection with admission and what the student can do to make practical preparation for college.

**Facing facts about college costs—a guide for parents and pre-college students. Prudential Insurance Company. 1962. 28p. Free
Helpful information about college costs and ways of financing a college education.

Facing facts about the two-year college. Prudential Insurance Company. 1963. 32p. Free
The booklet traces the development of the two-year college and discusses the programs and courses of study available in them. It describes the junior college as a new college for a new society because four-year colleges will not be able to accommodate the millions who will be seeking entrance before the decade closes.

Fact sheet for guidance counselors. New York University, Office of the Registrar and Supervisor of Admissions. 1964. 6p. Free
A convenient reference brochure giving information about the six undergraduate divisions of the university, admission procedures, financial aid, and prospects of admission in 1964.

Facts about New England colleges and universities. New England Board of Higher Education. 1962. 20p. Free
Data about two hundred institutions authorized by their state legislatures to grant academic degrees. The information includes costs, enrollment, accreditation, and general type of curriculum.

Five thousand women college graduates report. B'nai B'rith Vocational Service. 1953. 66p. $2
Findings of a survey of the social and economic status of women graduates of liberal arts colleges. One table reports median earnings by occupation; another the degree of satisfaction with present occupation.

**The five W's of education. Colorado School of Mines. 1963. 8p. Free
Includes things to consider in the selection of a college. The five W's are: What makes success? Why go to college? Who should go to college? Where is my college? When do I apply?

Four big years: the importance of selecting the right college. Smith, Richard W. and Snethen, Howard P. Bobbs-Merrill Company. 1960. 189p. $3.50
The authors compare types of colleges and discuss admissions, financing, and other problems of college planning.

Freshman foresight. Upsala College. 1962. 6p. Free

Advice for young people now thinking of college. Discussion of ways to prepare for admission to college, beginning early in high school.

From high school to job. Gardner, John W. Carnegie Corporation of New York. 1960. 12p. Free

Reprint from the annual report suggesting that schools should provide continuing vocational and educational counseling for those who leave high school and those who do not go on to higher education.

The gifted: educational resources. Porter Sargent. 1961. 285p. $4

A nation-wide survey of over eight hundred public and private school programs, nursery through college, designed to challenge and develop academically talented students. The school programs are arranged by geographic regions and classified by types of programs offered.

The girl and the college 1957. Alumnae Advisory Center. 1957. 16p. 50c

Reprint from *Mademoiselle*. Subtitle: What you'll find at a state university (Indiana); Where to go to study for the professions; and Student opinions on fourteen colleges and the dollars you can earn there.

Go east to college. Seven College Conference. 1962. 8p. Free

Brief description of each college and the cooperative program whereby one may apply to three of the seven colleges with one application fee. Includes Barnard, Bryn Mawr, Mount Holyoke, Radcliffe, Smith, Vassar, and Wellesley.

Graduate study in the liberal arts college. Ness, Frederic W. and James, Benjamin D. Association of American Colleges. 1962. 182p. $2.50

The report provides advice for institutions contemplating inaugurating graduate programs.

Guide to American educational directories. B. Klein and Company. 1963. 336p. $20

Description of contents of 1,200 educational and related directories with price and address of publishers. Index lists such subjects as financial aid funds, grant programs, foundations, and employment guidance associations.

**Guide to college majors. Sabo, Alex, ed. Chronicle Guidance Publications. 1963. 162p. $5

Approved institutions which offer major programs of study in 310 subjects are arranged by subject and state.

Guide to correspondence study. National University Extension Association. 1963. 60p. 25c

Lists correspondence courses from more than fifty accredited universities and colleges, including those for college credit, self-interest, high school work, and vocational and technical interests. Key list indicates quarter or semester credits, cooperative contract with United States Armed Forces Institute, and Veterans Administration approval.

Guide to the evaluation of educational experiences in the armed services: formal service courses and schools. American Council on Education. 1954. 426p. $5

Designed to assist schools and colleges in evaluating, in terms of academic credit, educational experience which students may have had while in military service. This revision includes only the educational experiences of service personnel gained through formal service school training.

H. INFORMATION ABOUT COLLEGES AND OTHER SCHOOLS—*Continued*

A guide to graduate study: programs leading to the Ph.D. degree. American Council on Education. 1960. 457p. $6

> The directory includes the offerings of 174 institutions. For each there is given admission and residence requirements, fees, financial aid, and special facilities for study and research. For each area of specialization there is given the number of graduate students enrolled and the number of Ph.D.'s awarded in the period from 1955 to 1959.

Guide to summer camps and summer schools. Porter Sargent. 1962. 320p. $4.40; $2.20 paper

> This thirteenth edition describes a large number of summer camps for boys and girls.

**Handbook for college-bound students and their counselors. Association of College Admissions Counselors. 1963. 400p. $2

> In this handbook, published biannually, one page is devoted to each of four hundred colleges, setting forth the programs of study, admissions requirements, opening dates, costs and housing, financial aid, and name of admissions officer. All listed colleges are fully accredited by their regional accrediting associations.

Handbook of adult education in the United States. Knowles, Malcolm, ed. Adult Education Association of the United States. 1960. 624p. $7.50

> Includes institutional programs and resources.

**Handbook of private schools. 44th edition. Porter Sargent. 1963. 1370p. $10

> Information concerning 2,500 private schools. Includes tuition, faculty and enrollment data, graduate records, and some scholarship opportunities. Revised annually.

Helping your teenager choose a college. Klein, David. Child Study Association of America. 1963. 36p. 50c

> An aid to parents in clarifying the ways of looking at college choice. Provides suggestions on how to avoid common fallacies and pitfalls in selecting a college.

Higher education in the United States. American Council on Education. 1961. 189p. $2

> A reprint of Parts I and II of *American Universities and Colleges*. Part II has twenty-four sections on professional education and lists institutions offering programs. Helpful tables of earned degrees awarded by institutions and classified by subjects.

The home study blue book. National Home Study Council. 1961. 42p. Free

> Directory of fifty-eight accredited private home study schools and courses meeting standards of the Accrediting Commission of the National Home Study Council. Includes a section on how home study can help and schools offering approved courses in about three hundred occupations such as accountancy, advertising, air conditioning, and welding.

**How about college? A guide for parents of college-bound students. American School Counselor Association. Order from American Personnel and Guidance Association. 1960. 16p. 25c

Designed to help parents and high school students consider these topics: Why go to college? Who should go to college? What qualifications are necessary? Which college? How apply for admission? Can we afford it? Will the draft affect our planning? When must we decide?

**How about college financing? A guide for parents of college-bound students. American School Counselor Association. Order from American Personnel and Guidance Association. 1960. 20p. 30c

Designed to help parents and young people who are facing the problem of higher educational costs by suggesting the steps of systematic planning. Points out that a large percentage of parents want a college education for their children but are not realistic about financing it. Suggests ways to keep expenses down and explains planning through savings, loans, part-time work, scholarships, and grants.

How an Ivy League college decides on admissions. Kinkead, Katharine. Norton and Company. 1961. 94p. $2.95

Description of the painstaking procedures by which Yale University selected its freshman class of 1960. Parents and candidates facing college committee decisions can gain an idea of the process they will encounter. Written by a magazine reporter.

**How to be accepted by the college of your choice. Fine, Benjamin. Channel Press. Revised 1963. 332p. $4.95; $2.95 paper

Detailed advice and information on application procedures are followed by a tabulated report of the entrance criteria at each of the accredited colleges and the costs, enrollment, and time of year to apply.

**How to be accepted by the college of your choice. Fine, Benjamin. Popular Library, Inc. 1961. 439p. 75c

A paperback edition of book described above.

How to choose a college. Seventeen Magazine. 1962. 4p. 10c

Practical suggestions offered by twelve college girls.

How to choose a correspondence school. Kempfer, Homer. Bellman Publishing Company. 1959. 35p. $1

Information about correspondence courses and how to select a good school. Includes list of schools approved by the National Home Study Council.

How to choose a nursery school. Burgess, Helen S. Public Affairs Committee. 1961. 20p. 25c

Discussion of the elements that create a good nursery school experience for a preschool child and what to look for in the selection of a school.

How to choose your technical institute. Hartung, Walter and Brush, George. Bellman Publishing Company. 1960. 30p. $1

Information about engineering technician training and how to select a school for preparation for the work. Selected references.

H. Information about Colleges and Other Schools—*Continued*

How to finance a college education. Funds for Education, Inc. 1962. 8p. Free

Discussion of a college education as an investment and methods of securing loans.

**How to get into college. Third edition. Bowles, Frank H. Dutton and Company. 1963. 185p. $3.50

Provides information on many aspects of college selection, preparation, admission, financing, and succeeding during the first year. Material is presented in question and answer form.

How to get into college and stay there. Diamond, Esther. Science Research Associates. 1958. 80p. $1.25

Activity text which challenges students in grades 9 through 12 to consider plans for higher education.

**How to get into college in the sixties. Look Magazine. 1960. 4p. 10c

A five-year plan for college readiness, designed to minimize anxiety and match the desires of the young person with the aims of suitable colleges. Addressed to parents, this contains well-considered advice to students in grades 8 through 12.

How to pay for your child's college education. Margolius, Sidney. Public Affairs Committee. 1963. 22p. 25c

Description of various plans to utilize savings, student loans, jobs, work-study programs, and scholarships.

* How to prepare for college. Lass, Abraham. Washington Square Press. 1962. 466p. $2.95

Includes a wide variety of topics, including how to choose a college, how to conduct the college interview, and how to stay in college. A final chapter contains dos and don'ts for parents.

How to prepare for college. Lass, Abraham. Pocket Books, Inc. 1962. 466p. 95c paper

A paperback edition of the book described above.

How to select a school or college. Good Housekeeping. 1962. 21p. 25c

Addressed to parents, this booklet points out the problems to be considered in making this choice, suggests questions to be asked of oneself and of the schools under consideration, and presents some measures for comparison of colleges.

How to visit colleges. National Vocational Guidance Association. 1960. 32p. 30c

Practical suggestions concerning why and how to visit colleges as one step in making a wise choice. Also, some general suggestions on preparation for college admission.

International handbook of universities. International Association of Universities in Paris. Order from American Council on Education. 1962. 773p. $12

Descriptive entries in English for 560 universities in 84 countries outside of the United States and the British Commonwealth. Includes size of academic staff, enrollment, admission requirements, fees, language of instruction, degrees, and duration of studies.

Is college for me? Sterling Publishing Company. 1959. 176p. $1
Guide to what college offers, how to apply, facts on scholarships, relative merits of large and small schools, and how to enter and stay in school. Also contains classified lists of some low and free tuition colleges and junior colleges.

It's a wonderful college because it's small. Alumnae Advisory Center. 1955. 12p. 25c
Reprint from *Mademoiselle* containing some facts and impressions to help high school seniors make the choice between small and large colleges.

The Jewish college student: decennial census of Jewish college students. Shosteck, Robert. B'nai B'rith Vocational Service. 1957. 61p. $1.75
Data on general and Jewish enrollments in 1,610 colleges and universities in the period 1955 to 1956 by areas and states. Includes data on 21 major professions.

Jewish youth in college. B'nai B'rith Vocational Service. 1957. 16p. 35c
Summary report of the third decennial census of Jewish college students in the United States and Canada. Contains comparisons of data derived from the 1935, 1946, and 1955 studies.

Journal-American annual education guide. New York Journal-American. Annual. 24p. 8c in stamps
An annual compilation of the announcements which have appeared on the Display Education pages in the Sunday and Wednesday issues. Includes colleges, career schools, military academies, and boarding schools.

Junior college directory. Gleazer, Edmund J., Jr. American Association of Junior Colleges. Annual. 54p. $1
Information concerning both accredited and nonaccredited institutions, with symbols which indicate the type of accreditation or approval. Student enrollment, faculty size, type of control or affiliation, and type of school included.

Land-grant colleges and universities. U.S. Office of Education. Supt. of Documents. 1962. 86p. 35c
Presents the laws affecting resident instruction in the land-grant colleges and universities.

A listing of Catholic secondary schools in United States. National Catholic Welfare Conference. 1962. 87p. $1.50
Faculty and enrollment statistics on the 2,392 Catholic secondary schools in the United States and the 44 schools in Puerto Rico and the Virgin Islands.

Looking ahead through spare time study. International Correspondence Schools. 1963. 96p. Free
A description of the courses offered in many major career fields.

Looking at private trade and correspondence schools. National Vocational Guidance Association. 1963. 8p. 25c
This booklet is a guide for students who are considering continuing their education in private trade or correspondence schools. It provides information

H. Information about Colleges and Other Schools—*Continued*

on whether this is the kind of education suitable for the student, how to evaluate a school, things to watch out for, and how to make the best decision. Examples illustrate successful and unsuccessful selection of a school.

**Lovejoy's college guide. Lovejoy, Clarence E. Simon and Schuster, Inc. 1961. 336p. $5.95; $3.50 paper

Information concerning 2,356 colleges and universities, including tuition, typical living expenses, admission requirements, enrollment, and degrees offered.

Lovejoy's prep school guide. Lovejoy, Clarence E. Harper and Row. 1963. 136p. $5.95; paper $3.95

Presents facts on 1,830 nonpublic college preparatory schools, including independent, private, boarding, and day schools.

**Lovejoy's vocational school guide—a handbook of job training opportunities. Lovejoy, Clarence E. Simon and Schuster, Inc. 1963. 174p. $5.95; $3.95 paper

The schools are grouped according to major interests: business, nursing and medical technical, barbering and cosmetology, arts, home study, mechanical and technical, flying, public vocational schools, and schools for miscellaneous vocations. Under each of the above sections the schools are listed geographically, first by state and then under the cities and towns in which they are located. An index of occupational titles lists each school by number.

**Manual of freshman class profiles, 1963. College Entrance Examination Board. 1964. 584p. $7

Source book of information for secondary school guidance officers. Contains descriptions of the freshman class characteristics of 351 College Board member colleges. Tabular data include distribution of enrolled applicants according to College Board scores. Available only to school and college officers.

Michigan training directory. Michigan Employment Security Commission. 1962. 17p. Free to counselors

Directory of approved schools in Michigan offering training in aviation, barbering, cosmetology, medical technology, nursing, and X-ray technology. Also included are business schools and trade schools.

**National directory of schools and vocations. Miller, Adeline E. and Brown, Betty I. State Schools Publications. 1963. 703p. $12.95

For each of three hundred occupations the schools that offer training are listed alphabetically by states. Includes professional, technical, trade, and business schools. Many trades are included.

**The new American guide to colleges. Hawes, Gene R. Columbia University Press. 1962. 376p. $5.95

Information is compiled about 2,675 undergraduate institutions concerning admission requirements, costs, enrollment, degrees, and 41 kinds of factual data. Each school has been placed into one of 12 sections according to function, type of offering, and kind of control. Within each section the abbreviated entries are presented alphabetically by states.

The new American guide to colleges. Hawes, Gene R. New American Library of World Literature, Inc. 1962. 349p. 75c paper
Paperback edition of above-mentioned book.

A new social invention, the community college. Gleazer, Edmund J., Jr. American Association of Junior Colleges. 1962. 16p. 10c
Observations concerning the composition, objectives, and role of the two-year community college.

The 1963 official guide to Catholic educational institutions and religious communities in the United States. Catholic Institutional Directory Company. 1963. 182p. $2.95
Directory of 238 colleges and universities, 39 normal school training schools, 402 diocesan seminaries and religious houses of formation, and 305 boarding schools. Issued annually.

Occupational schools and junior colleges in Connecticut, Massachusetts, and Rhode Island. Research Publishing Company. 1963. 96p. $4
Alphabetically arranged indexes of over 1,750 courses and subjects in about 500 schools. Includes hospitals offering courses of training in medical technology, practical nursing, professional nursing, and X-ray technology.

Opening (fall) enrollments in higher education, 1962: institutional data. U.S. Office of Education. Supt. of Documents. 1962. 35p. 30c
Statistics on enrollments by institution, state, sex, and full-time and part-time attendance.

Parents' guide to college planning. Equitable Life Assurance Society. 1962. 64p. Free
Explanation of the advantages of a college education, what colleges consider in accepting students, and how to evaluate colleges. Also included is a list of representative colleges, their enrollment, and basic costs at each.

Patterson's American education. Educational Directories, Inc. 1963. 772p. $25
Most useful for the names and addresses of officials of colleges, universities, county and public school systems, and special, private, technical, and vocational schools. Also includes lists of schools, classified alphabetically, geographically, and by type of school.

Patterson's schools classified. Educational Directories, Inc. Published annually. 184p. $3.50. Paper
Includes a listing of 5,500 schools classified as to type, such as agriculture, architecture, art, fashion, and mechanical trades.

Plain talk about college. Ludden, Allen. Dodd, Mead and Company. 1961. 179p. $3
Discussion of pertinent aspects of life before and during college, such as selecting a college, choice of high school courses, methods of study, etiquette, fraternities, and making friends.

Planning for college. Keystone Junior College. No date. 8p. Free
Example of a recruiting brochure describing the advantages of a junior college and the application procedures. Applicable at many schools.

H. Information about Colleges and Other Schools—*Continued*

Policies of state departments of education for the accreditation of service experience of military personnel and of results on the tests of General Educational Development, seventh edition. Commission on Accreditation of Service Experience of the American Council on Education. 1963. 80p. Free to educational institutions
Reports the policies of the fifty state departments of education for accrediting the tests and service educational experiences. Not distributed to individuals.

Predicting college grades. College Entrance Examination Board. 1961. 124p. $6
A workbook for college admissions officers, presenting in detail methods of statistically forecasting the academic performance in a given college of applicants whose school rank in class and Scholastic Aptitude Test scores are known and can be compared with those of a previous freshman class.

Prep school guide for Jewish youth. Shosteck, Robert. B'nai B'rith Vocational Service. 1958. 32p. $1.75
An alphabetic guide of about 250 schools, by state, with tabulated data on enrollments, fees, faculty, program, control, and religious services.

Prep schools. Laney, Al. Doubleday and Company. 1961. 128p. $5.95
Characteristics, history, enrollment, curricula, and facilities are given for fifty-seven prep schools located on the East Coast. Photographic views included.

Preparatory trade and industrial training programs in public schools. U.S. Office of Education. Supt. of Documents. 1962. 278p. $1
A directory for 1961-1962. The training programs are listed by state and city, in alphabetical order. An appendix lists the occupational areas and the states in which training programs are available in each.

**Private independent schools, 17th Edition. Bunting and Lyon, Inc. 1964. 1498p. $12
One section is a directory of 270 private schools for boys and girls including boarding schools, day schools, and military schools with or without church affiliations. Contains statistical information, requirements for admission, costs, extracurricular activities, and a picture of each school. Another section is comprised of descriptive listings of 375 schools which hold membership in one of the 26 educational associations that compose the National Council of Independent Schools. Good index.

Private schools illustrated—a select directory of private boarding schools, day and country day schools in the United States. Porter Sargent. 1962. 352p. $1.10
A reprint of one section of the *Handbook of Private Schools.*

Programs in journalism. American Council on Education for Journalism. 1962. 12p. Free
The accredited list of forty-seven colleges.

Rankings of the states. National Education Association. 1963. 68p. $1
Eighty-eight different rankings.

Report of credit given by educational institutions. Kellogg, T. E., ed. American Association of Collegiate Registrars and Admissions Officers. Order from American Council on Education. 1962. 103p. $2

An annual report listing the acceptance of transfer credit for work done at colleges and universities within each state or territory. Based on a voluntary exchange of information among member institutions.

Sargent guide to private junior colleges and specialized schools and colleges. Porter Sargent. 1959. 448p. $5

Descriptive and statistical information on 1,700 schools, including two-year liberal arts programs and professional, business, and vocational post-secondary education.

Sargent guide to summer camps and summer schools. Porter Sargent. 1962. 320p. $4.40 cloth; $2.20 paper

Directory of about 750 foremost private resident camps and summer schools. Master listings give name and address, location, date of establishment, the director's name and his winter address, enrollment, fee, and special features.

School . . . or what else? Bureau of Labor Standards, U.S. Department of Labor. Supt. of Documents. 1962. 12p. 10c

Reasons why staying in school helps to prepare one for jobs that will bring lifetime rewards. Includes an interesting chart showing how much an education is worth in terms of actual income. Illustrates differences in earnings between eighth grade graduates, high school drop-outs, and high school graduates.

Schools of professional nursing in the United States. Committee on Careers, National League for Nursing. 1962. 40p. 10c

List of state-approved schools of professional nursing, coded for national accreditation, type of program, admission of men and nonwhite students, and other information.

Second report to the President. The President's Committee on Education Beyond the High School. Supt. of Documents. 1957. 114p. 55c

Prepared to stimulate local and state discussion and planning. Sections on the need for planning expansion and diversity of educational opportunities, the need for teachers, the need for assistance to students, and financing higher education.

Second semester. Swift, H. M. Longmans, Green and Company. 1961. 244p. $3.75

Career fiction. A picture of life in a small coeducational college, with overtones that will be of interest to young people embarking on their college careers.

Should you go to college? Warner, W. Lloyd and Havighurst, Robert J. Science Research Associates. 1961. 48p. 50c

Discussion of the importance of the decision and things to consider.

Should you go to college? New York University. 1957. 8p. 5c. Single copy free

Discussion of points to consider before going to college, costs, interests, requirements, and applying for admission.

H. Information about Colleges and Other Schools—*Continued*

Six Corning College Day speeches. Corning Glass Works Foundation. 1960. 40p. Free

    Addresses given on Corning College Day include Why go to college?; A college education is worth $500,000; A college education: the best investment for your future; Who should go to college? Excellent material.

The small college. Hill, Alfred T. Council for the Advancement of Small Colleges. 1963. 10p. Free

    Includes a list of fifty-eight small colleges of arts and sciences located in twenty-seven states, with enrollments, costs, and accreditation.

**State universities and colleges. Hoopes, Roy, ed. Robert B. Luce, Inc. 1962. 481p. $4.95; $3.95 paper

    Guide to 126 state institutions, with enrollments of 2,500 or more, that offer a full, four-year general liberal arts program. Arranged alphabetically by state, information is given on admission requirements, expenses, housing, financial help, undergraduate work, enrollment, calendar, library, organizations, and whether students are permitted to operate cars on campus. This is prefaced by a description of the school.

Statistics of higher education: faculty, students, and degrees. U.S. Office of Education. Supt. of Documents. 1962. 165p. $1.25

    Issued as one chapter of the Biennial Survey of Education, this report presents statistics on faculty, students, and degrees in institutions of higher education.

Statistics of land-grant colleges and universities. U.S. Office of Education. Supt. of Documents. 1962. 112p. 70c

    A statistical report issued annually containing information on faculty, students, degrees, income, expenditures, endowment, and plant facilities of the sixty-eight land-grant institutions.

Statistics of nonpublic secondary schools. U.S. Office of Education. Supt. of Documents. 1963. 53p. 40c

    Basic statistical information concerning 4,128 schools, including types of schools, enrollment, and size of teaching staff. Included are seventeen tables and charts.

Statistics of public secondary schools. U.S. Office of Education. Supt. of Documents. 1961. 52p. 40c

    Includes data on size of schools, enrollments, staff, and graduates.

Stay in high school. American School. 1964. 4p. Free

    Reasons why young people should stay in school and graduate. Available in sets for class or homeroom use.

Stay in school! U.S. Air Force. 1963. 6p. Free

    An attractive illustrated folder written for the teen-age group, discussing the advantages of getting as much education as possible. It points out the median income for men at various educational levels and the various jobs held by people with different educational backgrounds.

Study in Latin American universities. Pan American Union. 1960. 11p. Free

Discussion of Latin American universities to serve as preliminary and general orientation for the United States student interested in studying in Latin America.

Summary report of colleges interested in additional applications as of May, 1963. Chronicle Guidance Publications. 1963. 16p. $1

A clue to colleges which may accept applications, revised annually.

**Survey of state university admissions requirements. Brickell, Helen. Association of College Admissions Counselors. 1962. 34p. $1

In tabular form, information is given concerning the total number of units required and the number in English, social science, math, science, and foreign language. Data are also given concerning rank in class, minimum test scores, residence, and dates of preferred and final application.

The technical institute: its relation to engineering education and trade training. National Council of Technical Schools. 1952. 6p. 9c

Nature of the technical institute, present status, and strengths.

Technical training in the United States: Appendix I of *Education for a Changing World of Work.* Emerson, Lynn A. U.S. Office of Education. Supt. of Documents. 1963. 170p. $1.25

This report deals with technical education of semiprofessional level and the part it plays in providing trained technicians. It contains information about the technical occupations in industry, the need for workers to fill these jobs, the ways they are trained, and some recommendations.

Total enrollment in institutions of higher learning, first term, 1959-60. U.S. Office of Education. Supt. of Documents. 1962. 75p. 55c

A report on enrollment in the various colleges and universities.

Trade and industrial education for girls and women: a directory of training programs. U.S. Office of Education. Supt. of Documents. 1960. 65p. 30c

Lists courses in operation during the year 1958-1959 which deal with programs meeting requirements of the state plans for vocational education. Includes pre-employment and extension training for women.

Training opportunities for women and girls. Women's Bureau, U.S. Department of Labor. Supt. of Documents. 1960. 64p. 30c

A guide to types of training available in private and public schools and in initial and pre-employment programs offered by industry.

Training opportunities—non-college. Careers. 1962. 7p. 25c

Career brief describing on-the-job training, junior colleges, technical and trade schools, business schools, apprenticeship, correspondence schools, and company schools.

University entrance requirements to Nova Scotia colleges. Nova Scotia Guidance Newsletter. 1962. 4p. Free

Chart showing the requirements in English, math, languages, and electives for each of the ten institutions offering degrees.

H. INFORMATION ABOUT COLLEGES AND OTHER SCHOOLS—*Continued*

USAFI catalog. United States Armed Forces Institute. 1963. 178p. Free
    Description of courses available to young men and women on active duty
with the Armed Forces. Also information concerning individual study opportunities, testing service, applying for credit, special reference and resource
materials available from USAFI, and services available after discharge to
inactive duty.

Values in education series. Sun Life Assurance Company. 1960-63. 8 book-
    lets. 8p. each. Free from Branch Offices of the Company
    Titles include: Value of a college education, Why stay in school, Scholar-
ships and student loan programs, What about trade and industrial schools,
So you're going to college, and You can get higher marks.

Vocational training directory of the United States. Third edition. Cohen,
    Nathan M., compiler. Potomac Press. 1958. 228p. $2.95
    Compilation of information in tabular form about six thousand private
and public schools, offering over four hundred semiprofessional, technical,
and trade courses. Includes courses offered, entrance requirements, tuition
charges, and diploma or certificate upon completion. The schools have been
state-approved for veterans' training, or state-approved or -licensed, or approved by a responsible accrediting agency. They are listed by type of school,
geographically by state and city, and alphabetically by name of school; they
are indexed by type of course.

What about college? Lehigh University. 1962. 14p. Free
    Aimed to help and to encourage students to think about their abilities and
limitations, their career objectives, and their further educational plans. Good
advice about choice of a college and how to apply for admission. Revised
biannually.

What about junior college? National Education Association. 1961. 4p.
    35 copies $1
    Describes the junior college, explains some popular misconceptions, and
tells why one out of every four high school graduates who continue their
formal education does so in a junior college.

What you must know about getting into college. Rubinfeld, William A.
    Vocational Guidance Manuals. 1964. 160p. $1.45; library binding $2.65
    The chapter headings include: Preparation for college, Selection of a college,
Getting into college, Scholarships and financial aid, Visiting colleges, Tests for
admission to college, and Adjustment to college.

What's a good college. Changing Times. 1962. 5p. 15c
    Reprint describing the many factors that make up a good college.

Where to find vocational training in New York City. Vocational Advisory
    Service. 1962. 312p. $7.50
    Information about training in approximately 600 subjects afforded by 607
schools in New York City that give some form of training intended as
preparation for a specific kind of work. Arranged by occupation. Good indexes. Includes entrance requirements and tuition costs.

Which college for you? Hodnett, Edward. Harper and Row. 1961. 115p. $2.95

Includes several useful suggestions for comparing colleges.

Why finish high school? Elliott, C. M. American Personnel and Guidance Association. 1958. 4p. 100 copies $4

Facts cogently presented to encourage youth to graduate.

Work-study college programs. Wilson, James W. and Lyons, Edward H. Harper and Row. 1961. 240p. $3.50

An appraisal of the cooperative programs in liberal arts colleges and professional schools.

Worrying about college? Hechinger, Fred. Public Affairs Committee. 1960. 28p. 25c

Advice concerning seeking admission to college with a minimum of wasted effort. The summary paragraph is "Don't worry, but work!"

**Your child and college. National Education Association. 1962. 16p. 35 copies $1

Advice on who should go to college, which college, how colleges select students, what college costs, and how parents can help. Good reading list.

Your college choice. Careers. 1962. 8p. 25c

Things to consider in the selection of a college.

Your introduction to Oklahoma State University. Oklahoma State University. 1963. 48p. Free

An example of an illustrated college brochure containing courses and suggested high school preparation for each of the major fields of study.

Your life plans and the Armed Forces. National Association of Secondary-School Principals. 1958. 149p. $1.25

A unit of study to help high school youth fit service in the Armed Forces into their educational and vocational plans. Description of educational opportunities in the services. A good summary of the military obligations and options for young men.

I. Job Seeking

Agency, boss and you. Guitar, Mary Anne. Alumnae Advisory Center. 1954. 5p. 25c

Reprint from *Mademoiselle* describing the services of an employment agency.

**Can I get *the* job? Let's find out. General Motors Corporation, Public Relations Staff. 1954. 32p. Free

Suggestions to young people on preparation for the first job. Sections are entitled: What are my interests? What do I have to offer? What are employers looking for? How do I get an interview? Who does the talking? Available in classroom sets free of charge.

I. Job Seeking—*Continued*

Charm: the career girl's guide to business and personal success. Whitcomb, Helen and Lang, Rosalind. McGraw-Hill Book Company. 1964. 472p. $6.95

Includes practical suggestions on business etiquette, job finding techniques, and personal attributes which help the career girl achieve success.

**Choosing your occupation—career guidelines for high school students from your state employment service. Bureau of Employment Security. Supt. of Documents. 1961. 16p. 15c

Suggestions for a self-inventory of interests and ability, list of occupations for which there is a demand for more workers, and some advice about approaching occupational choice.

The college graduate and General Motors. General Motors Corporation, Salaried Personnel Placement Activity. 1961. 17p. Free

A pamphlet giving information concerning the types of work for which college students and graduates are employed in General Motors and the general procedure followed in their recruiting program.

College placement annual. College Placement Council. Annual. 472p. Available only through college placement offices or to subscribers to *Journal of College Placement.*

Articles written by experienced placement officers to give specific help to the job seeker in preparing for interviews. Contains a geographical and occupational index to aid students in determining where and with what companies they will be able to find opportunities in their chosen fields of interests.

College placement directory. Zimmerman, O. T. and Lavine, Irvin. Industrial Research Service. Second Edition, 1958. 577p. $10.75

Over one thousand employers who hire college graduates itemize their employment openings and the name of the personnel officer in charge. Another section lists the colleges with a description of type of institutions, size of enrollment, and the name of the placement officer. This directory acquaints the college graduate with the employment opportunities. Good indexes.

Directory of college placement officers. College Placement Council. Annual. 77p. $1.50

Listing of college placement officers including name and location of college; name, title, and telephone number of placement officer; date on which interviews begin for next school year; special requirements, if any, for scheduling of interviews; and months in which institution has graduating classes.

Dollars for you: 150 ways for boys to earn money. Paradis, Adrian. David McKay Company. 1957. 192p. $3

Discussion of a variety of jobs for vacation or after school. Sensible advice concerning choosing and obtaining a part-time job. Includes a list of contest opportunities, many of which offer cash and college scholarships.

Do's and don'ts for mature job seekers. National Association of Manufacturers. 1961. 6p. Free

A guide for employees. About twenty succinct statements of things to do and an equal number of reminders of things to avoid.

Eastman Kodak careers. Eastman Kodak Company. 1962. 36p. Free
Description of employment opportunities with the company. Copiously illustrated.

Eleven ways to lose a job. Changing Times. 1963. 2p. 15c
Some of the most common ways in which people lose their jobs.

The employment interview. Mandell, Milton. American Management Association. 1961. 110p. $4.50
Although the book is written for the employer, giving characteristics of successful interviews and suggesting methods, procedures, and administrative practices, an applicant also could benefit from reading it.

Facts you should know about employment agencies. Better Business Bureau. 1963. 6p. Free
Details concerning services, fees, etc., are discussed, as well as unethical practices which might be encountered.

Finding the right job. Part Two in *From High School to a Job.*
Chapter headings are: What the employer is seeking in you, Finding your job prospects, How to make an effective application, Interview, Employment agency, On the job, and You and the Armed Forces.

Finding your job. Wilson, Howard. Administrative Research Associates. 1963. 48p. $1
Prepared to aid the student in the job seeking process. Includes discussion of how to get leads, getting the interview, preparing for the interview, what to do during the interview, and the follow-up.

Finding your job. B'nai B'rith Vocational Service. 1946. 8p. 35c
Suggestions on the topic of choosing a career presented by means of line drawings and captions to appeal to the reader of cartoons.

* Fitting yourself for business: what the employer wants beyond skills. MacGibbon, Elizabeth Gregg. McGraw-Hill Book Company. 1961. 416p. $5.50
Practical instruction on applying for a job, adjusting to office work and personalities, managing one's income, and maintaining standards for correct dress and grooming.

Four why's. General Electric Company. 1954. 12p. Free
The four sections are entitled: Why stick to your studies? Why work? Why study English? Why read?

From college to career. Lewis, Adele and Bobroff, Edith. Bobbs-Merrill Company. 1963. 288p. $3.95
The directors of an employment agency give advice on how to hunt for the right job. Written for college graduates, the book includes discussion of realistic attitudes, how to be interviewed, and opportunities in many fields of work.

From high school to a job. Paradis, Adrian A. David McKay Company. 1956. 249p. $3.50
Job opportunities for young people who cannot pursue their studies beyond high school and those who are obliged to leave school before graduation.

I. JOB SEEKING—*Continued*

The fundamentals of college placement. College Placement Council. 1962. 242p. $3 to members of Regional Placement Associations; $5 to others

Textbook for college placement officers devoted to current practices in college placement and providing basic information on the planning and operation of a placement office. Of interest also to employers in the orientation of recruiters and as a check list for the development of a firm's college relations program.

**Futures for college women in New York. Alumnae Advisory Center. 1963. 56p. $1

Guidebook of informative material for college graduates who are seeking work in New York City. Contains advice on job seeking procedures, names of some employers who hire college women, employment agency fees, street address guide, list of reliable residences for women, nature of payroll deductions, and fringe benefits. Good bibliography on job seeking.

Getting your first job. Chapter 9 in *Occupations and Careers.*

Suggestions concerning the appointment, interview, application blank, letters of application, and other means of selling one's services.

Guide to preparing your résumé. New York State Department of Labor, Division of Employment. 1963. 39p. Single copies free to counselors and librarians.

Prepared to assist the job seeker in evaluating and formulating his assets in an organized and logical manner. Good suggestions for planning the résumé, suggested outline, sample résumés, and pointers on the covering letters.

Helping students find employment. Kirkpatrick, Forrest H. American Council on Education. 1949. 37p. 75c

A summary of various approaches to postcollege job placement.

How to find and apply for a job. Keily, Helen J. and Walters, R. G. South-Western Publishing Company. 1960. 91p. $1.20

This booklet has been prepared to help high school and college graduates to apply for positions in corporations and employment offices.

How to get a job. National Society for Crippled Children and Adults. 1955. 4p. 10c

How the job seeker with a crippling condition can increase the effectiveness of his search for employment.

How to get a raise. Alumnae Advisory Center. 1952. 5p. 25c

Gleanings on strategy of getting a raise from those who give them and those who get them.

How to get an executive job after forty. Miner, C. Harper and Row. 1963. 183p. $4.50

Practical suggestions on finding openings and marketing one's services.

How to get and hold the job you want. Larison, Ruth Hooper. David Mc-
Kay Company. 1950. 264p. $4.50

    Presents the ten consecutive steps for preparing an effective job-getting
campaign recommended by the Job-Finding Forum of the Advertising Club
of New York. One section is devoted to sample letters, résumés, and a
portfolio.

**How to get and hold the right job. New York State Department of Labor,
Division of Employment. 1961. 16p. Free to counselors and librarians

    Tips on getting and holding a job.

**How to get and hold the right job—facts from your employment service.
U.S. Employment Service. Supt. of Documents. 1962. 20p. 10c

    Clear and concise tips on getting and holding a job. Includes sections on
the following: What to look for in a job, Take stock of yourself, Consider
job requirements, Sources of job leads, Getting ready for the interview,
What to do during the interview, Your letter of application, Why people
sometimes fail to get the jobs they seek, Why workers lose their jobs, What
employers say they want, and Getting ahead in your field of work.

How to get that part-time job. Feingold, S. Norman and List, Harold. Arco
Publishing Company. 1958. 92p. $2.50 cloth; $1.50 paper

    Concise discussions of methods of seeking a part-time job in industry
and government, résumés, interviews, and applications. A glossary contains
a list of little-known and unusual part-time jobs and businesses. The book
concludes with a "bonus section" listing 1,005 free publications relating to
part-time jobs.

How to get *the* job. Dreese, Mitchell. Science Research Associates. 1960.
48p. 50c

    Discussion of steps necessary to plan and carry out a successful job cam-
paign, getting ahead on the job, and starting your own business.

How to get the job. Wilson, Howard. Administrative Research Associates.
1950. 48p. 50c

    Contents: The job of job finding, how to get your leads, getting the
interview, preparing for the interview, what to do during the interview, and
the follow-up. Contains a list of items on which the interviewer will rate
the applicant and a check list of questions to consider when preparing for the
interview.

**How to land the job you want; your key to a successful career. Willing,
Jules Z. New American Library of World Literature. 1954. 192p. 50c

    Practical advice on planning a job campaign, writing a résumé, using employ-
ment agencies, enlisting help of friends, and achieving successful interviews.

How to "sell yourself" to an employer. New York State Department of
Labor, Division of Employment. 1961. 4p. Free to counselors and librarians

    A checklist of fifteen proven points helpful in landing a job.

I. Job Seeking—*Continued*

How you can get a better job. Lasher, Willard K. and Richards, Edward A. American Technical Society. 1945. 221p. $2.50

Discussion of the basic personal factors that make for success and promotion in a job. One section includes suggestions on how high school graduates can partially offset their lack of actual working experience. Separate sections are available at 25c each.

**How you can get the job you want. Gardiner, Glenn L. Harper and Row. 1962. 178p. $3.95

This fourth edition offers a practical ten-step plan of action to help the prospective employee obtain the job he seeks. It also includes examples of data sheets and other tested techniques.

I want a job. Hudson, Margaret W. and Weaver, Ann A. Frank E. Richards, Publisher. 1963. 36p. $1

Workbook prepared for special education classes of slow learners, containing forms and procedures essential for job application. Includes simple directions about the birth certificate, social security card, work permits, application blanks, interview, and ways of holding a job.

Job education (finding and getting a job through planning). Benson, Warren E. Bellman Publishing Company. 1946. 32p. $1

Discussion of seven activities in the sales preliminaries, eight steps in the sales activities, and eighteen suggestions for interview procedure. Includes examples of a prospectus, portfolio, "lead," and "contact" chart.

**Job-finding techniques for the college woman. Women's Bureau, U.S. Department of Labor. Supt. of Documents. 1958. 10p. 10c

Advice and information about the following steps involved in finding a full-time job: Preparing a personal folder, Canvassing the possibilities, Submitting an application, Making the most of the interview, Choosing your job, and Reaching an agreement with the employer.

A job for you . . . sparetime, summer, Saturday. Peake, Miriam Morrison. Scholastic Book Services. 1964. 72p. 25c

Includes discussion of finding a job, making the most of an interview, behaving on the job, getting along with fellow employees, dealing with the public, and planning a budget.

**Job guide for young workers. Bureau of Employment Security. Supt. of Documents. 1963. 78p. 45c

This booklet gives highlight information on 110 entry jobs frequently held by young beginners entering the labor market from high school. For each type of job, information is provided on employment prospects, qualifications for jobs and usual duties, opportunities for advancement, how and where jobs are obtained, and characteristics of jobs.

Job hopping. Alumnae Advisory Center. 1951. 4p. 25c

Reprint from *Mademoiselle* containing the pros and cons of changing jobs frequently.

Job horizons for the college woman. Women's Bureau, U.S. Department of Labor. Pamphlet Number One. Supt. of Documents. 1956. 53p. 25c
    Includes sections on preparing a personal folder, canvassing the possibilities, submitting an application, making the most of the interview, choosing your job, and reaching an agreement with the employer.

Job hunting. Chronicle Guidance Publications. 1963. 4p. 35c
    A brief containing the following sections: Your first job, How to locate possible employers, Choosing your employer, How to find job openings, How to apply for a job, The application form, Interview, and After the interview.

Job strategy: preparing for effective placement in business and industry. Rood, Allen. McGraw-Hill Book Company. 1961. 281p. $4.95
    A guide to tested techniques for planning and conducting a successful job campaign.

Keys to etiquette for the business girl. French, Marilyn. Dartnell Corporation. 1953. 63p. 50c
    Includes suggestions for the first day on the job and for making progress.

Ma and Sue—on a job interview. Splaver, Sarah. Methods and Materials Press. 1955. 12p. 50c; Set of 6 copies, $2.40
    A skit followed by a discussion of a parent accompanying the applicant.

A manual for campus recruiters. College Placement Council. 1962. 39p. 50c
    Concise booklet covering the principles and practices of college recruitment. Includes the responsibilities of the employer, college, and student.

Memo on job-finding for the mature woman. Women's Bureau, U.S. Department of Labor. Leaflet Number 13. Supt. of Documents. Revised 1963. 8p. 5c
    Suggestions concerning the job hunt, and discussion of the job interview, social security, and the advantages of maturity.

Money in your pocket: a management guide for young adults. Patton, Price A. and Patton, Martha. David McKay Company. 1959. 192p. $3.50
    Discussion of the management of one's salary, budgeting, saving, installment buying, insurance, and business practices for the teen-ager.

National and international employment handbook for specialized personnel; practical handbook for those seeking employment here and abroad. Angel, Juvenal L. World Trade Academy Press. 1961. 309p. $17.50
    Instructions for the employable specialist on analyzing his abilities, factors to take into consideration before applying for work abroad, making a summary of his qualifications, how to find vacancies, agencies through which opportunities might be located, private industries offering foreign assignments, and making application by letter or interview.

National directory of employment services. Gale Research Company. 1962. 239p. $25
    Two sections on private employment agencies and college and university placement services are arranged alphabetically by state, followed by a smaller

I. Job Seeking—*Continued*

section on association employment services, arranged by name of association, and indexed by occupation. Information usually includes address, telephone number, executive, and type of personnel placed.

Ninety-nine ways for teen-agers to earn money during the summer. Advancement and Placement Institute. 1962. 24p. 50c

A compilation of ideas which have been tested money-makers in many parts of the country.

**Open letter to the college graduates of 1963. Secretary of Labor. Bureau of Labor Statistics, U.S. Department of Labor. 1963. 21p. Free

An annual report on the job outlook in biological sciences, business, civil service, earth sciences, engineering, forestry, health professions, journalism, law, library work, mathematics, performing arts, physical sciences, social sciences, and teaching.

The opportunities will be there. Eastman Kodak Company. 1962. 4p. Free

A radio program discussion pointing out that challenging new career opportunities will await those who get ready for them.

Part-time employment—employer attitudes on opportunities for the college-trained woman. Alumnae Advisory Center. 1964. 62p. $1

Intended as a guide to women seeking less than full-time employment.

Part-time employment for women. Women's Bureau, U.S. Department of Labor. Supt. of Documents. 1961. 53p. 30c

Describes part-time job opportunities in various industries, and future prospects for such work.

Personal data summary. New York Herald Tribune. 1956. 2p. 6 forms for 6c

A form to be filled out when applying for any position. Provides for a summary of personal data, education, employment record, and references.

Placement services for personnel in higher education. U.S. Office of Education. Supt. of Documents. 1961. 39p. 30c

Contains two lists of placement services: those offered by professional associations and those offered by colleges and universities.

**Planning your career. Calvert, Robert, Jr. and Steele, John E. McGraw-Hill Book Company. 1963. 152p. $3.75; paper $1.95

Includes model résumés, application letters, and other career-planning devices to help the reader develop skill in job-seeking techniques. Three phases of career development are presented: determination of career goals, location of suitable employment, and satisfactory progress in one's career.

Poise for the successful business girl. Parr, Mary. Dartnell Corporation. 1960. 61p. 50c

Ways of acquiring poise as an aid to success in business life.

The principles and practices of college recruiting. Chamber of Commerce of the United States. 1962. 8p. 10c

A statement of basic agreements developed by college placement directors and personnel recruiting officers on ethics of recruiting college graduates. Sets forth the responsibilities of students, employers, and colleges.

Principles and practices of college recruiting. College Placement Council. 1962. 6p. 10c

Compilation of accepted ethical concepts of college recruiting, providing a standard of conduct and procedure for the student, the college, and the employer.

Professional placement center. Professional Placement Center, New York State Employment Service. 1960. 18p. Free

Placement counselors find this booklet useful for its breakdown of positions in various professional fields.

Rate yourself. Rhodes, R. M. Executive Development Press. 1951. 14p. 30c

A number of self-rating check lists designed to point out personal strengths and weaknesses in attitudes, working characteristics, self-management, and taking it on the chin. Also included are suggestions for discovering their strong points and "what to do about yourself."

Seasonal employment in the National Park Service. National Park Service, U.S. Department of the Interior. 1963. 22p. Free

Information concerning seasonal employment in the National Park Service and with concessioners in the parks. Description of types of positions, qualifications needed, and pay. Includes names and addresses of concessioners to whom applications for summer employment should be made.

Small-town Jewry tell their story. B'nai B'rith Vocational Service. 1953. 57p. $2

A socio-economic report based on 2,400 questionnaires returned by Jewish people living in 200 small towns, used for the purpose of giving guidance to those interested in moving to small communities.

Sterling guide to summer jobs. Sterling Publishing Company. 1961. 128p. $2.50

Advice concerning finding vacation or week-end jobs. Some are discussed in the light of maximum earnings over a short period of time, others as stepping-stones to lifetime employment.

Successful job hunting. Costello, Eileen. Vocational Guidance Manuals. 1958. 58p. $1.45 paper

Suggestions on the use of the résumé, employment agencies, newspaper advertisements, and personal contacts. Also hints to be followed before and during the employment interview.

Suggestions to women and girls on training for future employment. Women's Bureau, U.S. Department of Labor. Supt. of Documents. 1962. 12p. 10c

Brief description of types of training available in schools and industry.

I. Job Seeking—*Continued*

Summer employment directory. National Directory Service. 1964. 144p. $4

> Contains a list of organizations throughout the United States that expect to hire high school seniors, college students, and teachers.

Summer job directory. Advancement and Placement Institute. 1963. 68p. $4

> Annual listing of summer jobs, compensated projects, apprenticeships, and permanent jobs; those for high school students are so indicated. Includes a sampling of 25,000 opportunities in the United States and 24 foreign countries. Entries include job descriptions, openings, salaries, names and addresses of personnel directors, and employers.

Summer jobs for students. Bureau of Employment Security. Supt. of Documents. 1962. 6p. 5c

> Suggestions for obtaining summer jobs and tips on selling one's services.

Summer jobs for teen-agers. Chronicle Guidance Publications. 1963. 4p. 35c

> Some general suggestions for getting a job with specific information about resort jobs, work in children's camps, national parks, direct selling, and making one's own job.

Summer opportunities for teenagers. Advancement and Placement Institute. 1963. 72p. $3

> An annual compilation of opportunities in camping, hobbies, hosteling, farming, travel, reading, and volunteer service projects. Also features some job leads and ways by which the teenager can make his own job.

Teen-age summer guide. Reinhold, Meyer. Barron's Educational Series, Inc. 1963. 192p. $2.25

> Information about study, travel, jobs, sports, and fun for young people from age 12 to 18, suggested as worthwhile summer activities.

Thinking about your first job? Remember Uncle Sam when it comes to choosing an employer. U.S. Civil Service Commission. 1961. 8p. Free

> A recruiting leaflet pointing out the advantages and opportunities of work for the Government.

Training for a career. Caterpillar Tractor Company. 1956. 12p. Free

> Description of four types of training offered for employment with this company: apprentice, trainee, cooperative, and orientation programs.

Transition from school to work. U.S. Office of Education. Supt. of Documents. 1957. 12p. 10c

> A series of questions for community leaders to use to evaluate their efforts to help young people make wise occupational choices, prepare for work, obtain appropriate employment, and make satisfactory occupational adjustments.

Today's woman in tomorrow's world. Women's Bureau, U.S. Department of Labor. Supt. of Documents. 1960. 138p. 50c
A report of the conference discussions and speeches upon the occasion of the fortieth anniversary of the Women's Bureau. Includes job preparation, employment opportunities, and problems to be faced in the future world of work.

Twelve pointers that lead to promotion. Moulton, Richard H. Executive Development Press. No date. 16p. 30c.
Practical suggestions for a man with managerial aspirations to improve his relationships with those above him.

The way to a job in government. U.S. Civil Service Commission. Pamphlet 47. Supt. of Documents. 1963. 6p. 5c
Brief comments on finding out about examinations, applying for them, and taking them.

Ways to improve your personality. Bailard, Virginia and Strang, Ruth. McGraw-Hill Book Company. 1951. 250p. $3.36
Helps teen-agers build desirable qualities of personality.

What industry looks for in the high school graduate. McMillan, John E. Eastman Kodak Company, Public Relations Department. No date. 7p. Free
Discussion of character traits considered important for success in industry.

Why and how to prepare an effective résumé. Angel, Juvenal L. World Trade Academy Press. 1961. 105p. $8
Information for persons planning to look for work or change positions. Some topics included are the necessity of a good résumé; the analytical, functional, and chronological résumé; work-sheet; and examples.

Why young people fail to get and hold jobs. New York State Department of Labor, Division of Employment, New York State Employment Service. 1963. 12p. Single copies free to counselors and librarians
These cases illustrating why young people fail to get and hold jobs are examples of actual problems faced by young people in adjusting to their vocations after they leave school.

A woman's guide to part-time jobs. Cooper, Joseph D. Doubleday and Company. 1963. 312p. $4.50
Includes basic approaches to job finding, special opportunities in part-time work, new challenges for employers and communities, and ways of managing both a job and home.

Working for the U.S.A. U.S. Civil Service Commission. Supt. of Documents. 1962. 23p. 15c
Contains general information about Federal employment, what the Government expects of Federal workers, and applying for a civil service job.

World-wide summer placement directory. Advancement and Placement Directory. 1962. 68p. $3
An annual compilation of summer employment opportunities, projects, and awards available to college students, teachers, and librarians. Information includes opportunities listed by all states and many foreign countries.

I. Job Seeking—*Continued*

The young woman in business. McLean, Beth B. and Paris, Jeanne. Iowa
State University Press. 1962. 304p. $5
> Information concerning procedures in job seeking, planning for the future,
> advancement, and combining marriage with career.

Your first job. Kiwanis Club. 1949. 4p. 3c
> Hints to young job seekers summarizing first steps, arranging for the
> interview, getting ready for the interview, selling one's self in the interview,
> and what to do after the interview.

Your first job. National Research Bureau. 1960. 32p. 20c
> Important things one should know about the business system in which
> one will be making a living.

* Your job and your future. Changing Times. 1963. 32p. 35c
> Reprint of eight articles that give helpful information on the best job
> opportunities, job interviews, use of employment agencies, writing résumés,
> and getting a raise.

Your job campaign. Weaver, Polly. Alumnae Advisory Center. 1957. 4p.
25c
> Advice on job hunting strategy, application letters, résumés, and inter-
> views.

J. Legislation and Social Security

American labor unions—what they are and how they work. Peterson, Florence. Harper and Row. 1963. 271p. $5.50
> An objective description of the mechanism and activities of the labor
> union movement. Includes details of trade union structure, government, in-
> ternal rules of procedure, and activities.

American women, report of the President's Commission on the Status of
Women. Supt. of Documents. 1963. 86p. $1.25
> Presents findings and recommendations regarding the opportunities of
> American women in seven categories: education, employment, labor standards,
> security of basic income, equality of rights under the law, participation in
> government, and home and community.

The American workers' fact book. U.S. Department of Labor. Supt. of
Documents. Revised 1960. 355p. $1.50
> Includes many tables and statistics on the labor force growth and char-
> acteristics, shifts in occupational distribution, mobility of the labor force,
> demand for labor, unemployment, economic security, and labor-management
> relations.

Compilation of the social security laws. Supt. of Documents. 1961. 504p.
$1.25
> Contains the Social Security Act, as amended, as in effect on December 31,
> 1960, plus all sections of the amending acts having a current effect on the
> act, but which are not part of the act, and the provisions of the act repealed
> by the Social Security Amendments of 1960 and all prior amending acts.
> Compiled solely for reference purposes.

Economic indicators relating to equal pay. Women's Bureau. Supt. of Documents. 1962. 20p. 15c

Analysis of economic data concerning occupational earnings of selected groups, annual wage and salary income, and pay practices of employers.

Employment and economic status of older men and women. Bureau of Labor Statistics, U.S. Department of Labor. Bulletin Number 1213. Supt. of Documents. 1956. 41p. 20c

Presents current and historical data on the employment and economic status of older men and women. Designed to contribute to informed understanding of the effect of population, employment, and economic trends on the older age groups in the population, and especially in the labor force.

Employment certificates. Bureau of Labor Standards, U.S. Department of Labor. 1963. 6p. Free

Explanation of the usefulness of employment certificates, how and where they may be obtained, and what papers are necessary to get them.

An explanation of the Manpower Development and Training Act. U.S. Department of Labor. 1962. 15p. Free

Description of the provisions of the law and the training and skill development programs.

Federal benefits for veterans and dependents. VA Fact Sheet IS-1. Veterans Administration. Supt. of Documents. 1962. 44p. 20c

Information concerning benefits for veterans, their dependents, and beneficiaries.

For the job you choose—will you need a license? *Occupational Outlook Quarterly*, May, 1963. 6p. 30c

Contains the license requirements of many occupations.

Good news for household workers. Social Security Administration. Supt. of Documents. 1962. 24p. 10c

Explains how the law affects cooks, maids, laundresses, chauffeurs, gardeners, and others who are employed in private homes. Available free from local social security offices.

Growth of labor law in the United States. U.S. Department of Labor. Supt. of Documents. 1962. 316p. $1

Gives history of major state labor laws in the United States. Examines and compares current state provisions. Includes chapters on child labor, hours and minimum wage, occupational health and safety, unemployment insurance, workmen's compensation, anti-discrimination, and other laws. Twenty-three tables. Twenty-seven maps.

**Handbook on women workers. Women's Bureau, U.S. Department of Labor. Supt. of Documents. 1962. 202p. 55c

Includes recommended standards for employment of women, state labor laws, and information concerning the civil and political status of women.

How to begin working. New York State Department of Labor, Division of Employment. 1961. 10p. Free to counselors and librarians

The legal requirements for the protection of young workers; working papers; tips on jobs and salaries; minimum wages; unemployment insurance.

J. LEGISLATION AND SOCIAL SECURITY—*Continued*

If you become disabled. Social Security Administration. Supt. of Documents. 1962. 32p. 10c

Describes the disability provisions of the social security law and lists the requirements for disability insurance benefits. Available free from local social security offices.

If you work while you get social security payments. Social Security Administration. Supt. of Documents. 1963. 30p. 10c

Explains the benefits for any month or year and points out that investment income will not affect the payment of social security benefits but can be used as a foundation to which one can add through private savings, pensions, and investments.

Industry wage surveys. Bureau of Labor Statistics, U.S. Department of Labor. Supt. of Documents. 1960-63. 34p. 30c each

Information on the average straight-time earnings of workers in about seventy-five fields of work, such as communications, department stores, and machinery manufacturing.

Labor laws and their administration. Bureau of Labor Standards, U.S. Department of Labor. Supt. of Documents. 1962. 164p. 50c

Proceedings of the Forty-fourth Convention of the International Association of Governmental Labor Officials, held in Portland, Oregon, August 28-31, 1961.

Now that you are retiring. Social Security Administration. Supt. of Documents. 1963. 32p. 15c

Suggestions for making one's retirement years more satisfying. Includes suggestions for part-time work, maintaining one's health, deciding where to live, sources of supplemental income, and how to get help with special problems.

Occupational wage surveys. Bureau of Labor Statistics, U.S. Department of Labor. Supt. of Documents. 1961-1963. 82 bulletins. 25c and 30c each

A series of studies in eighty-two labor markets of average earnings for sixty occupations by area and broad industry divisions. Includes the occupational wage structure and wage practices. Surveys are available for major labor market areas.

Reemployment rights of Federal employees who perform duty in the Armed Forces. Civil Service Commission. Supt. of Documents. 1963. 7p. 5c

Up-to-date information about regulations.

Security for you. Segal, Martin. Associated Press Newsfeatures. 1961. 20p. 25c

Sixty-two answers to help get the most out of social security.

Social security benefits—a replacement of lost earnings. Social Security Administration. Supt. of Documents. 1962. 8p. 5c

Explanation of the retirement test under which benefits are withheld for those who earn over a certain amount. Available free from local social security offices.

**Social security benefits—how you earn them, how to estimate them. Social Security Administration. Supt. of Documents. 1962. 10p. 10c
This leaflet gives a simple explanation of what social security credits are, how one earns them, and how many are needed. It also contains a step-by-step explanation of how to estimate the amount of one's benefit. Available free from local social security offices.

Social security handbook on old-age, survivors, and disability insurance. Social Security Administration. Supt. of Documents. 1963. 314p. $1.25
A detailed explanation of who is entitled to benefits and how to get them. Helpful information on coverage provisions, figuring the benefit rate, filing a claim, and establishing rights to benefits. Designed for professional people who help others with social security matters.

Social security information for self-employed farmers. Social Security Administration. Supt. of Documents. 1961. 8p. 5c
Specific information concerning how the self-employed farmer may earn social security credits and how to figure and report net earnings. Available free from local social security offices.

Social security information for the self-employed. Social Security Administration. Supt. of Documents. 1962. 10p. 5c
Explanation of how the law affects those who are in business for themselves or who engage in professional work.

State minimum-wage laws and other provisions affecting working conditions. Women's Bureau, U.S. Department of Labor. Supt. of Documents. 1961. 147p. 75c
Historical development and statutory provisions.

Summer jobs for teen-agers. Chronicle Guidance Publications. 1963. 4p. 35c
A brief containing the following sections: Why work summers, Choosing your summer job, When to look for a summer job, What summer jobs are available, Earnings, Laws governing the employment of minors, How to locate jobs, and Things to consider.

Teaching high school students about labor unions. American Federation of Labor and Congress of Industrial Organizations. 1960. 8p. Free
A report of a unit of study on collective bargaining.

Union wages and hours, by trade or occupation. Bureau of Labor Statistics, U.S. Department of Labor. Supt. of Documents. 1960-63. 42p. 35c each
Surveys made in the building trades, local transit operation, motor truck driving, and printing trades.

Wages and related benefits. Bureau of Labor Statistics, U.S. Department of Labor. Supt. of Documents. 1961. 137p. 70c
Survey of earnings in eighty-two labor markets. Includes supplementary practices and labor-management agreement coverage.

Woman at work, the autobiography of Mary Anderson as told to Mary N. Winslow. Anderson, Mary. University of Minnesota Press. 1951. 266p. $3.50
Account of her experiences as head of the Women's Bureau of the U.S. Department of Labor for twenty-five years and other work as a labor leader. Illustrated.

J. Legislation and Social Security—*Continued*

You don't have to retire completely to get social security benefits. Social Security Administration. Supt. of Documents. 1963. 8p. 5c. Free from local social security offices

Explains how earnings of over $1,200 affect the social security benefit payments for the year.

Your retirement system. U.S. Civil Service Commission. Pamphlet 18. Supt. of Documents. 1961. 44p. 20c

Questions and answers concerning the Federal civil service retirement law.

**Your social security. Social Security Administration. Supt. of Documents. 1963. 26p. 10c

Describing social security rights and responsibilities, this booklet provides details on retirement, survivors, and disability payments; amount of work required; events that stop payments; kinds of work covered; and procedure for checking one's account. Includes changes made in the law effective January 1963. Available free from local social security offices.

Your social security check. Social Security Administration. Supt. of Documents. 1963. 6p. 5c

Information on when you may expect your check; what to do if you lose your check; if it doesn't come when expected; if you change address; and how to protect against the theft and forgery of the check.

Your social security earnings record. Social Security Administration. Supt. of Documents. 1961. 22p. 5c

Gives in a nutshell what every person should know about the program and should do to keep his social security account straight. Available free from local social security offices.

K. Occupations for the Handicapped

Assessing the hearing handicapped for vocational placement. Troop, Harry W. American Hearing Society. 1962. 6p. 20c

Methods of appraising the individuals.

The blind person as a college teacher. McCauley, W. Alfred. American Foundation for the Blind. 1961. 88p. $1

A report aimed to give an understanding of the opportunities and problems of blind persons in the teaching role.

Books about the blind. Lende, Helga. American Foundation for the Blind. 1953. 357p. $2.50

Annotated bibliography of references on various subjects relating to the blind. Includes sections on vocations and economic adjustment, education of the young blind, and biographies.

Careers in hearing. American Hearing Society. No date. 4p. Free

Opportunities and need for specialists working with the hard of hearing.

Casework performance in vocational rehabilitation. U.S. Office of Vocational Rehabilitation. Supt. of Documents. 1959. 59p. 25c
Information contained in several workshop proceedings compiled for in-service training of rehabilitation counselors.

Counseling the handicapped in the rehabilitation process. Hamilton, Kenneth W. Ronald Press Company. 1950. 296p. $6
Discussion of methods.

Counselors guide: how to analyze the rehabilitation needs of blind persons on the farm. U.S. Office of Vocational Rehabilitation. 1954. 30p. Free
Suggested procedures for the counselor, an example of rehabilitating a blind person as a farm operator, and examples of rural occupations in which blind and partially sighted persons have successfully engaged.

Counselors guide: how to find employment and place blind persons on jobs of an industrial character in nonindustrial areas. U.S. Office of Vocational Rehabilitation. 1953. 28p. Free
Suggested procedures for the counselor and examples of jobs of an industrial character on which blind persons have worked successfully.

**Directory for exceptional children. Fourth edition. Porter Sargent. 1962. 656p. $6
Descriptive listings of three thousand public and private schools, hospitals, clinics, and other facilities for the emotionally disturbed, the physically handicapped, and the mentally retarded. Included also are listings of associations and Federal and state agencies concerned with the education and welfare of the exceptional.

Education of the severely retarded child. U.S. Office of Education. Supt. of Documents. 1960. 25p. 15c
A bibliography of more than three hundred titles on the training and education of severely retarded children.

Eligibility requirements for vocational rehabilitation. Hartley, L. B. American Hearing Society. 1961. 4p. 10c
Discussion of employment handicap of the hard of hearing.

Employability of the multiple-handicapped. National Society for Crippled Children and Adults. 1959. 9p. 25c
Description of work adjustment in the sheltered shop under counselor supervision.

Employment of blind workers in industry. Clunk, Joseph F. U.S. Office of Vocational Rehabilitation. 1948. 4p. Free
Reprint from *Personnel* containing discussion of the variety of jobs held by blind workers.

Employment of the physically handicapped—a bibliography. The President's Committee on Employment of the Physically Handicapped. Supt. of Documents. 1957. 93p. 35c
A bibliography of recent literature pertaining to employment and rehabilitation of physically handicapped persons. Included is a section on specific disabilities such as amputation, blindness, cerebral palsy, heart disease, and tuberculosis.

K. Occupations for the Handicapped—*Continued*

Facts about employment and heart disease. American Heart Association. 1958. 12p. Single copy free from local Heart Associations
> Leaflet giving information in the form of questions and answers aimed to remove some of the obstacles which prevent employment of persons known to have heart disease.

* Guidance and the physically handicapped child. Ratchick, Irving and Koenig, Frances. Science Research Associates. 1963. 64p. $1.50
> Includes sections on vocational planning for the handicapped and where to get help. Selected references.

**Guide to job placement of mentally retarded. The President's Committee on Employment of the Handicapped. 1963. 16p. Free to counselors
> A guide to assist in job placement of the mentally retarded.

* Guiding the physically handicapped college student. Rusalem, Herbert. Bureau of Publications. 1962. 151p. $2.75
> Includes a survey of the programs available to the physically handicapped college student and the resources available to personnel workers. There is a bibliography of sixty-eight books and pamphlets concerning the topic.

Handbook of job descriptions in rural activities suitable for the employment of blind persons. U.S. Office of Vocational Rehabilitation. 1948. 50p. Free
> Series of job descriptions prepared for the use of employment counselors engaged in the rehabilitation of blind persons into rural employment.

Handbook of representative industrial jobs for blind workers. U.S. Office of Vocational Rehabilitation. 1948. Mimeographed. 26p. Free
> Prepared for the use of industrial employment counselors.

Help for handicapped women. U.S. Office of Vocational Rehabilitation. Supt. of Documents. 1958. 52p. 40c
> Discussion of the vocational rehabilitation program, community resources for the handicapped, and careers in rehabilitation.

Help for the disabled through vocational rehabilitation. U.S. Office of Vocational Rehabilitation. Revised 1961. 11p. Free
> General information concerning the service of restoring the disabled to paid jobs through medical service, counsel and guidance, and training.

Instructional guide for use in vocational schools providing training for blind persons. U.S. Office of Vocational Rehabilitation. 1950. 45p. Free
> Assistance to teachers in the shops in the best method of training blind students in the use and manipulation of both hand and power tools as well as informing them of methods used by blind persons in achieving their objectives.

An introduction to the vocational rehabilitation process. U.S. Office of Vocational Rehabilitation. Supt. of Documents. 1960. 201p. $1
> A manual for orientation and in-service training of rehabilitation counselors.

Jobs for the hard of hearing. The Volta Bureau. 1939. 4p. 15c

> Suggestions for the job seeker and brief biographical sketches of hard of hearing individuals who are earning their living as employees of the Federal Government as office manager, librarian, statistician, accountant, plant physiologist, and a chart corrector.

Law as a profession for the blind. American Foundation for the Blind, Inc. 1950. 45p. 35c

> Discussion of problems and compensations. Sections on the law student, city lawyer, small town lawyer, suburban lawyer, judge, law professor, and the lawyer in public life.

Materials relating to employment of properly qualified handicapped persons. President's Committee on Employment of the Handicapped. 1963. 8p. Free

> The current announcement of the "ability counts" contest contains a reading list of biographies of persons who have overcome handicaps.

Mental health and guidance for exceptional children. Frampton, Merle E. and Gall, Elena D., ed. Porter Sargent. 1956. 80p. $1.25

> Includes eight articles, bibliography, and list of state mental health societies.

New hope for the disabled. U.S. Office of Vocational Rehabilitation. Revised 1961. 23p. Free

> Contains essentials of the vocational rehabilitation amendments of 1954 and related legislation. Includes services available to the disabled and training programs.

Occupations of epileptic veterans of World War II and Korean Conflict. VA Pamphlet 22-6. Veterans Administration. Supt. of Documents. 1960. 62p. 40c

> Report of the employment experiences of veterans with epilepsy.

Occupations of paraplegic veterans of World War II and Korea. VA Pamphlet 7-12. Veterans Administration. Supt. of Documents. 1957. 52p. 35c

> Report of the employment experience of paraplegics.

Occupations of totally blinded veterans of World War II and Korea. VA Pamphlet 7-10. Veterans Administration. Supt. of Documents. 1956. 28p. 25c

> A report for use in the vocational rehabilitation of the totally blind.

Opportunities for blind persons and the visually impaired. U.S. Office of Vocational Rehabilitation. Revised 1959. 24p. Free

> General information concerning the vocational rehabilitation program.

Opportunities for blind teachers in public schools. American Foundation for the Blind. 1961. 39p. 50c

> A report on legal aspects, policies, and practices affecting employment.

Opportunities for the deaf and the hard of hearing. U.S. Office of Vocatonal Rehabilitation. 1961. 14p. Free

> One section contains a report on kinds of jobs obtained.

K. Occupations for the Handicapped—*Continued*

Opportunities for the tuberculous through vocational rehabilitation. U.S. Office of Vocational Rehabilitation. Revised 1961. 20p. Free
Contains a discussion of suitable and unsuitable jobs.

The placement process in vocational rehabilitation counseling. United States Office of Vocational Rehabilitation. Supt. of Documents. 1960. 104p. 35c
Prepared as a guide for use in training programs for the placement of the disabled into suitable employment.

Preparation of mentally retarded youth for gainful employment. U.S. Office of Vocational Rehabilitation. Supt. of Documents. 1959. 86p. 35c
Includes reports from several localities where special efforts are put forth.

Psychological aspects of physical disability. U.S. Office of Vocational Rehabilitation. Supt. of Documents. 1952. 195p. 60c
Assistance to rehabilitation counselors in planning better rehabilitation programs.

Rehabilitation literature, 1950-1955. Graham, Earl and Mullen, Marjorie. Blakiston Division. 1956. 632p. $13
A bibliographic review of the medical care, education, employment, welfare and psychology of handicapped children and adults. Index and review of 5,214 periodical articles, pamphlets and books, by subject.

Rehabilitation of the physically handicapped. Second edition. Kessler, Henry H. Columbia University Press. 1953. 293p. $5.50
Comprehensive reference book on rehabilitation for the professional worker. Includes a directory of national agencies serving the handicapped and a chapter on legislation for the handicapped.

Resources for special education. Frampton, Merle E. and Gall, Elena D., ed. Porter Sargent. 1956. 250p. $2.20 paper; $3.30 cloth
Bibliographies, lists of agencies, and references of resource materials concerning special education for the exceptional. Includes vocational guidance and employment references for the blind, deaf, hard of hearing, speech defective, orthopedically handicapped, etc.

Resources for the orthopedically disabled in New York City. Federation of the Handicapped. 1963. 163p. $1.65
A directory of facilities adapted to the needs of the handicapped, including agencies, special equipment, housing, recreation, and transportation.

Safe work for the aurally handicapped and industrial hearing conservation. American Hearing Society. Yantis, Phillip. 1962. 6p. 20c
Discussion of safe employment of the hard of hearing.

Scholarships for specialized training in cerebral palsy. National Society for Crippled Children and Adults. Revised annually. 4p. Free
Terms of eligibility.

Selected references on the vocational rehabilitation, placement, and employment of handicapped workers. National Society for Crippled Children and Adults. 1962. 15p. Single copy free
An annotated bibliography of publications for counselors and employment professional workers.

Self-employment. U.S. Office of Vocational Rehabilitation. 1948. 54p. Free
A follow-up study of disabled persons who were rehabilitated in self-employment.

Services for children with orthopedic handicaps. American Public Health Association. 1962. 128p. $2.50
A handbook whose seven sections outline approved practices in the field, describe types of services and facilities, and list national organizations and qualifications for professional personnel.

Small business enterprises for the severely handicapped. U.S. Office of Vocational Rehabilitation. Supt. of Documents. 1955. 152p. 45c
A catalog of small business experiences of the homebound and severely handicapped in the State-Federal Vocational Rehabilitation Program. Reports of about fifty successful small businesses carried on by severely handicapped persons.

Small business enterprises in vocational rehabilitation. U.S. Office of Education. Supt. of Documents. 1963. 42p. 20c
Designed for use of rehabilitation workers who are interested in placement opportunities in small business enterprises and other self-employment for handicapped persons.

Some do's and don'ts when applying for work—tips for handicapped job seekers. President's Committee on Employment of the Handicapped. 1962. 6p. Free
Some succinct reminders to an applicant.

They return to work—the job adjustment of psychiatrically disabled veterans of World War II and Korean Conflict. Veterans Administration. Supt. of Documents. 1963. 210p. 70c
A study of the employment records of veterans with histories of mental illness showing the growing possibilities of rehabilitation. Includes 337 case briefs which illustrate the variety of occupations in which those studied were employed.

Total rehabilitation of epileptics—gateway to employment. U.S. Office of Vocational Rehabilitation. Supt. of Documents. 1962. 207p. $1.25
A resource handbook for individuals and organizations concerned with rehabilitation services to epileptics.

Vocational counseling for children with heart disease or a history of rheumatic fever: a pilot study. American Heart Association. 1961. 258p. $3; $1.50 paper
An account of a community project designed to study and serve a selected number of individuals with a specific handicap. Early and intensive vocational counseling for these handicapped children is indicated.

K. Occupations for the Handicapped—*Continued*

Vocational counseling of blind students. Raskin, Nathaniel J. American Foundation for the Blind. 1955. 24p. 30c

A study sponsored by the committee on relationships between rehabilitation agencies and schools for the blind. For counselors and administrators.

Vocational rehabilitation of the mentally retarded. U.S. Office of Vocational Rehabilitation. Supt. of Documents. 1958. 184p. 65c

Written as a guide for vocational rehabilitation counselors.

Vocational schools as training facilities for blind workers. McAulay, John H. American Foundation for the Blind. 1954. 95p. $1.25

Written for administrators with the aim of improving services for blind individuals.

Workshops for the disabled—a vocational rehabilitation resource. U.S. Office of Vocational Rehabilitation. Supt. of Documents. 1956. 167p. 60c

Discussion of services provided in the several different kinds of workshops for the vocational rehabilitation of persons having substantial employment handicaps.

L. Package Purchases

Careers exploratory kit for counselors' desk-top use and students' library table-top use. Careers. $50

This kit contains 245 summaries and 160 career briefs plus a file box and a set of alphabetical tab cards.

Careers junior high desk-top kit. Careers. $89.50

A metal desk-top file containing 329 career summaries, 430 career reprints, 176 career briefs, posters, and monthly career guidance index.

Careers junior high guidance service. Careers. Monthly, September through May. $25 per year

Each year this service includes 75 career summaries, 40 career briefs, 90 reprints, 9 career indexes, 27 posters, and monthly career guidance index.

Careers senior high desk-top kit. Careers. $97.50

Collection of 329 career summaries, 430 reprints, 176 career briefs, 16 college guides, 9 career indexes, and 27 posters in a metal file 6" x 9" x 16". For use on top of desk or table.

Careers senior high guidance service. Careers. Monthly, September through May. $30 a year

Each year this service includes 75 career summaries, 40 career briefs, 90 reprints, 9 career indexes, 32 educational materials, 27 posters, and 9 book reviews. The bonus items include a desk-top file, 40 printed tab cards, and a calendar.

Chronicle career kit, number 670 F. Chronicle Guidance Publications. $155 F.O.B. Moravia, N.Y.

File drawer of treated fiber containing 350 letter-size folders with job titles printed in color and arranged numerically according to the symbols in the *Dictionary of Occupational Titles.* The folders are stocked with Chronicle briefs, reprints, and posters. The cost includes a year's advance subscription to the Chronicle "3-in-1" Guidance Service.

Chronicle career kit, number 670 PSH. Chronicle Guidance Publications. $267.50 F.O.B. Moravia, N.Y.

"Tudror" mobile steel file cabinet in tan or gray; occupational filing plan of 350 letter-size folders inserted in 120 "Pendaflex" hanging folders, tabbed with codes and titles of the *Dictionary of Occupational Titles.* The folders are stocked with Chronicle briefs, reprints, and posters. The cost includes a year's advance subscription to the Chronicle "3-in-1" Guidance Service.

Chronicle educational service. Chronicle Guidance Publications. $15 per year

Service for one year includes: *Student Aid Annual* ($5); *Guide to College Majors* ($5); *College Entrance Requirements and Costs* ($2); *Colleges Classified* ($1); four *Student Aid Bulletins* ($3.50). Booklets and bulletins available separately or on a subscription basis at $15.

Chronicle professional file. Chronicle Guidance Publications.

Number 700. 176 printed manila folders. $24.50

Number 700P. 176 printed manila folders inserted in "Pendaflex" hanging folders. $49.50

Number 700TU. Above 700P file in a "Tudror" mobile steel file cabinet. $103

Purchase price of above forms includes a year's subscription to the Chronicle Professional Service, plus a packet of professional articles in print at time of purchase.

Chronicle professional service. Chronicle Guidance Publications. $10 per year

Mailed monthly September through April. Consists of two or more four- and eight-page articles of interest to counselors relative to guidance practices, successful guidance programs, data gathering, and in-service training.

Chronicle "3-in-1" guidance service. Chronicle Guidance Publications. Monthly September through April. $42.50 per year

Subscribers receive all materials contained in the occupational, educational, and professional services plans.

College admissions data service. Educational Research Corporation. 1962. $50 annual subscription

This service includes a loose-leaf handbook with facts on 350 colleges, plus monthly bulletins to keep the information current. Annual revisions are issued.

College kit. American Personnel and Guidance Association. 1963. 4 booklets. $1

Contained in this kit are three booklets on college and one on vocational planning.

Combination offer. Personnel Services, Inc. $37.50

One set of about 130 *Occupational Abstracts* currently available, plus an annual subscription to the *Occupational Index,* and an annual subscription to the ten new titles of *Occupational Abstracts.* Without the *Occupational Index,* the combination price is $33.

L. Package Purchases—*Continued*

Guidance kit. B'nai B'rith Vocational Service. 57 publications. $30

Set of all publications produced by B'nai B'rith Vocational Service. The cost, if purchased separately, would amount to $34.15. Includes the occupational brief series, one year's subscription to the *Counselor's Information Service,* and other booklets listed in the 1963 catalog.

Guideposts kit. B'nai B'rith Vocational Service. $10

A package of pamphlets and material designed to meet the needs of the Jewish organization, parent, or student.

Mademoiselle college and career information: two loose-leaf binders. *Mademoiselle,* College and Careers. $6 each

Over sixty reprints in each: File A for college students; File B for high school use. Only prepaid orders are accepted. Reprints are from *Mademoiselle* and are distributed individually by the Alumnae Advisory Center for 25c a single copy.

S.R.A. career information kit. Science Research Associates. $165

This information kit consists of over 500 occupational pamphlets, selected from many sources. The materials are assembled in a transfer case of metal-reinforced cardboard and filed in 199 file folders. The contents of the file drawer may be inserted in a regular filing cabinet if desired. A manual and guide accompany the kit. In two-drawer metal file cabinet on wheels $225.

S.R.A. careers in science and math. Science Research Associates. $25

A selection of 80 occupational briefs, 8 job family booklets, and 4 posters.

S.R.A. guidance service subscription plan. Science Research Associates. $34.50 per year

Includes 28 occupational briefs, 50 job briefs, 7 guidance newsletters, 7 research reports, 7 posters, 7 booklets, 1 full-length book, and special bonus material. A condensed subscription plan is offered for those specifically interested in occupational information at $28.

S.R.A. higher education planning kit. Science Research Associates. $79.50

A selection of bookets for use with students from grades 7 through 12.

S.R.A. occupational exploration kit. Science Research Associates. $75

Includes 300 occupational briefs, 7 guidance series booklets, 50 student worksheets, and 21 coding cards.

S.R.A. professional guidance books. Science Research Associates. $40

A selection of fourteen reference books.

S.R.A. widening occupational roles kit. Science Research Associates. 1963. $114.50

Teaching material for grades 6 to 9. Includes 300 junior occupational briefs, 5 guidance filmstrips, 5 junior guidance booklets, 50 student workbooks, and a teacher's manual. May be used in the homeroom, for group guidance, or with English and social studies classes. Referred to as WORK.

The Sextant series for exploring your future. American Liberty Press. Set of 12 volumes, hard cover, $60; soft cover, $48. Complete set with wall charts and profile forms $75

Ten books have been released, each combining job descriptions with a method of personal profiling. Each book contains job descriptions of the range of occupations in that industry, organizational charts, and a set of personal profile forms for individual pupil use.

3-in-1 occupational outlook service. Bureau of Labor Statistics, U.S. Department of Labor. Supt. of Documents. 1964. $26.35

For one check every two years the following services are offered: The 1963-1964 *Occupational Outlook Handbook,* a two-year subscription to the *Occupational Outlook Quarterly,* and two complete sets of the 109 reprints.

M. Periodicals

Basic facts about military service. High School News Service. Monthly. Free

Two publications, a magazine (High School News Service Report) and a single page news and picture clipsheet, are distributed to participating schools once each month during the school year. The September issue is a comprehensive survey designed primarily as a yearlong reference source for counselors.

Career guidance digest. Career Guidance Digest, Inc. 9 issues. $4 per school year

A monthly digest of current articles and statistics concerning business careers for young women, extracted from Government publications, guidance journals, and business periodicals.

Career guidance index. Careers. Monthly, September through May. $6 per year

Each issue contains from thirty to forty annotated references to free and inexpensive materials.

Career index. Chronicle Guidance Publications. Monthly, September through April. $8 per year

Annotated references to free and inexpensive materials.

College Board review. College Entrance Examination Board. 3 issues per year. $1

Current reports on the activities of the College Entrance Examination Board, research developments, the College Scholarship Service, and Advanced Placement Program. Articles of fact and opinion offer new insights on important aspects of college admissions and guidance.

Counselor education and supervision. Association for Counselor Education and Supervision. Order from American Personnel and Guidance Association. 4 issues. $4

Deals with issues and topics of interest to those in counselor education and supervisory positions, especially in state departments of education and in colleges.

M. Periodicals—*Continued*

**Counselor's information service. B'nai B'rith Vocational Service. Quarterly. $6
Annotated bibliography of recently published books, pamphlets, charts, and articles concerning occupations and vocational and educational guidance. Each issue lists from 160 to 170 publications.

Crusade for education. Advancement and Placement Institute. Monthly. $6 individual membership, $12 institutional
Placement journal describing professional openings in the United States and abroad for teachers, librarians, administrators, and scientists. Also contains information on scholarships, awards, summer opportunities, and some part-time work.

Employment and earnings. Bureau of Labor Statistics, U.S. Department of Labor. Supt. of Documents. Monthly. $3.50 a year
Detailed national statistics on employment, unemployment, labor force, weekly hours, hourly and weekly earnings, payroll and man-hour indexes, labor turnover rates, and industry data for states and areas. Subscription includes an annual supplement which provides annual averages for the series.

Employment security review. Bureau of Employment Security, U.S. Department of Labor. Supt. of Documents. Monthly. $2 per year
This publication is the principal medium for the exchange of experience among local and state offices of the employment security system. Of interest to placement counselors.

**Guidance exchange. Occu-Press. 4 issues. $10 a year
An annotated bibliography of guidance literature and a section devoted to counselors' exchange of noteworthy experiences. Published in October, December, February, and April.

Information bulletin. Vocational Advisory Service. Weekly, September to June. $1.50
Mimeographed bulletin describing new educational and occupational materials and giving information to supplement *Where to Find Vocational Training in New York City.*

Journal of college placement. College Placement Council. Quarterly. $5
Articles of interest to college placement officers who help students and graduates find employment. Also of interest to the industrial personnel representatives.

Journal of college student personnel. American College Personnel Association. Order from American Personnel and Guidance Association. 4 issues. $4
Covers topics of interest to counselors and student personnel workers in higher education.

Journal of the Association of College Admissions Counselors. Association of College Admissions Counselors. Quarterly. $2 in U.S.; $2.50 in Canada
Professional publication devoted to articles in the field of counseling, admissions, and financial aid.

The labor market and employment security. Bureau of Employment Security, U.S. Department of Labor. Supt. of Documents. Monthly. $3 per year

This publication provides information on current, economic, and labor market developments and trends. Useful for employment counselors.

* Lovejoy's guidance digest. Lovejoy, Clarence E., editor. The editor. Monthly. $10 per year

Current information about college entrance requirements, scholarships, draft news, etc.

Monthly labor review. Bureau of Labor Statistics, U.S. Department of Labor. Supt. of Documents. Monthly. $7.50 per year; $9 outside the United States

This publication includes information on trends and levels of the labor force, employment, earnings, wages, hours, and related employer practices. Much of this information is available for particular industries, occupations, and localities. Also covers other aspects of labor economics and industrial relations, such as prices and cost of living, labor laws, trade union activities, collective bargaining agreement provisions, work stoppages, and labor turnover.

Occupational index. Personnel Services. Quarterly. $7.50 a year

Annotated lists of current occupational literature.

**The occupational outlook quarterly. Bureau of Labor Statistics, U.S. Department of Labor. Supt. of Documents. Published in February, May, September, and December. 36p. $1.25 a year; 35c a copy

Supplements the *Occupational Outlook Handbook* and reports on current occupational outlook and trends. Information is based primarily on the continuous research and statistical program of the Bureau of Labor Statistics.

**The personnel and guidance journal. American Personnel and Guidance Association. Monthly, September through May. $10

The official publication distributed to all members of APGA. Includes professional articles for counselors, book reviews, and notes on current publications.

Placement service bulletin. American Personnel and Guidance Association. Seven issues. $4 per year

A publication of the Placement Service, listing position openings in the field of guidance and personnel and availability notices of APGA member-candidates.

Rehabilitation counseling bulletin. American Rehabilitation Counselors Association. Order from the American Personnel and Guidance Association. 4 issues. $2

Covers topics of interest to the counselor working in the area of rehabilitation.

**Scholarships, fellowships and loans news service. Subscription service. Bellman Publishing Company. $35 per year

There are two types of subscriptions. Four newsletters a year, annual index, and binder cost $20. With the addition of two scholarship search problems and a special technical report on student aid, $35. Each issue contains information about new funds and foundations, scholarships, and loans. Publications of particular merit are recommended.

M. Periodicals—*Continued*

The school counselor. American School Counselor Association. Order from American Personnel and Guidance Association. 4 issues. $2

> Articles of interest to counselors in elementary, junior and senior high school.

* Student aid bulletin. Chronicle Guidance Publications. 4 issues per year. $1.50

> These bulletins provide information on scholarships available from sources other than colleges.

Student personnel association for teacher education journal. Student Personnel Association for Teacher Education. Order from American Personnel and Guidance Association. 3 issues. $2

> Articles of interest to personnel workers in teacher training institutions.

The vocational guidance quarterly. National Vocational Guidance Association. Quarterly. 75p. each issue. $3 per year

> The professional publication for the Association, carrying reports of current studies and conferences.

Your future occupation. Randall Publishing Company. Semimonthly, September through June. 4p. $2 per year

> Edited by Max Baer, a former president of the American Personnel and Guidance Association, this publication contains stimulating articles, on expanding fields of work, news items on scholarship opportunities, and information about colleges. Teacher guides for lesson planning available. A cumulative service and index are also published at a cost of $15 per set.

N. Planning a Career

After college, what? Wilson, Eugene S. Amherst College. Revised 1956. 15p. 25c

> An illustrated pamphlet urging beginning college freshmen to start vocational planning early. Includes a plan of action and a timetable for the four college years.

B'nai B'rith cartoon series. B'nai B'rith Vocational Service. 1947. 5 booklets. 35c each

> Information presented by means of line drawings and captions to appeal to the reader of cartoons. Titles: Choosing your life work, Finding your job, Getting ahead on your job, Planning your college career, and Meeting your college expenses.

Career experts can help chart your future. Seventeen Magaine. 1956. 4p. 10c

> Includes the role of the counselor in helping a person plan his career.

Career planning for high school students. Reilly, William J. Harper and Row. 1953. 110p. $2.95

> Suggestions for analyzing one's aptitudes and interests and planning for the job or college training which is most suitable.

A career-planning guide: prepared for the World Book Encyclopedia. Edgerton, A. H. Field Enterprises. 1960. 48p. $1
Discussion and check lists for parents and their sons or daughters to work together on career selection. Includes material for estimating abilities and career interests.

Career planning in college. Plummer, Robert and Blocker, Clyde. Science Research Associates. 1963. 48p. 50c
Suggestions for planning ahead.

* Careers. Lifton, Walter M. United Educators, Inc. 1961. 10p. 20c
A reprint from the American Educator Encyclopedia, containing information about planning a career. Includes a list of the 150 leading occupations in which the greater number of people engage.

Careers for you. Ferrari, Erma Paul. Abingdon Press. 1953. 160p. $1 paper
Information about opportunities and suggestions on self-evaluation. Also suggestions for acquiring the necessary training and experience.

**Careers—opportunities and preparation. General Electric Company. 1960. 5p. Free
Information about opportunities and preparation for careers, especially science and engineering. Answers questions frequently asked about choice of a college, ways of financing higher education, and the most important college subjects to take.

Charting your job future. Giles, Lambert. Science Research Associates. 1957. 72p. $1.50
Activity text aimed to help high school students make career plans, find out about job qualifications, and learn how to seek employment. Includes charts, self-quizzes, and checklists to help students analyze their interest and ability.

Choosing a career. Humphreys, J. Anthony. Science Research Associates. 1961. 48p. 50c
Shows how to analyze one's interests and abilities, how to find out the essential items about a great variety of jobs, and how to relate your knowledge of yourself to your knowledge of jobs.

Choosing a career in a changing world. Westervelt, Virginia V. Putnam's Sons. 1960. 192p. $2.95
A guide to help teen-agers plan suitable careers. Written for ages 12 to 16.

**Choosing a career—the economic framework. Bureau of Labor Statistics, U.S. Department of Labor. Supt. of Documents. 1963. 24p. 15c
A reprint from the introduction to the Occupational Outlook Handbook, 1963-64 Edition, explaining how occupational trends affect career planning and presenting the outlook for occupational change.

Choosing an occupation: a guide for high school students. Bail, Joe P. and Nelson, A. Gordon. Cooperative Education Service, New York State College of Agriculture. 1963. 12p. 15c
Discussion of the following topics: Planning for the future, What people do for a living, Understanding yourself, Self-inventory worksheet, Exploring an occupation, and Worksheet for studying an occupation.

N. Planning a Career—*Continued*

Choosing your career. Wilson, Howard. Administrative Research Associates. 1963. 45p. $1

>Prepared as an aid for analysis of one's self, the world of work, and a specific career. Topics include self-appraisal scales, the major occupations, and college and training institutions.

Choosing your life work. B'nai B'rith Vocational Service. 1946. 8p. 35c

>Nine cartoon-like illustrations on a page grouped according to the topics: discovering yourself, discovering occupations, and discrimination.

**Choosing your occupation—career guidelines for high school students from your state employment service. Bureau of Employment Security. Supt. of Documents. 1961. 16p. 15c

>Advice about approaching occupational choice, suggestions for a self-inventory of interests and ability, and a list of occupations for which there is a demand for more workers.

Choosing your occupation. Chapter 6 in *Occupations and Careers.*

>Other chapters in the same book are entitled: How to study occupations, Learning a trade through apprenticeship, Preparing for an occupation, and Getting your first job.

College, careers, and you. Plummer, Robert and Blocker, Clyde. Science Research Associates. 1963. 48p. 50c

>Discussion of career plans in a changing world, planning on graduate school, and what employers will consider.

**Complete planning for college: the Kiplinger Guide to your education beyond high school. Sulkin, Sidney. McGraw-Hill Book Company. 1962. 268p. $5.95; $3.95 paper

>Emphasis is on planning. Includes planning the most appropriate high school courses, planning for the right college for the right student, planning for college financing, and planning for the most suitable career.

Directory of approved counseling agencies. American Personnel and Guidance Association. 1963. 185p. $2

>List of counseling agencies approved by the American Board on Counseling Services with pertinent information about each.

Getting the most out of college. Bennett, Margaret. McGraw-Hill Book Company. 1957. 219p. $4.75 cloth; $3.50 paper

>Suggestions to help students make the most of their opportunities throughout their college years. Chapter headings are: Getting acquainted with your college, What are you looking for, Learning to learn, Learning self-direction, Learning about yourself, Charting a life span, and Developing a life philosophy. A list of films is appended.

* Girls and their futures. Zapoleon, Marguerite W. Science Research Associates. 1962. 48p. 50c

>Chapter headings are: Will you drift or steer into your future? For what work should you plan? How your schooling affects your future, Planning for employment, and Planning with a total view. Selected readings.

A guide for parents and students. American Legion. 1963. 8p. $2.50 for 500 copies
Some succinct suggestions for preparing for college or vocational training.

Helping rural youth choose careers. U.S. Department of Agriculture. Supt. of Documents. 1963. 8p. 5c
Points up some of the shifts in the employment picture with special concern for the effects of recent social and economic trends.

How to be happy though young. Lawton, George. Vanguard Press. 1949. 300p. $3.50
One chapter is devoted to planning a career and one to streamlining one's study habits.

How to choose that career: civilian and military. Feingold, S. Norman. Bellman Publishing Company. 1954. 52p. $1
Suggestions on choosing a career, planning a high school and college program, and making a choice of a military service.

**How to express yourself vocationally. National Vocational Guidance Association. 1961. 32p. 30c
Discussion of vocational planning so as to achieve personal satisfaction, social usefulness, and the realization of one's highest self-potential. Chapter headings are: Realize the promise of the 1960's, Consider your vocational future, Figure out the real you, Watch the changing world of work, and Use the help all around you.

**How to visit colleges. National Vocational Guidance Association. 1960. 32p. 30c
Practical suggestions concerning why and how to visit colleges as one step in making a wise choice. Also, some general suggestions on preparation for college admission.

How will you ever pay for college? Changing Times. 1964. 6p. 25c
A reprint with an emphasis on planning ahead. Includes ways to cut the cost of college.

**Investing in yourself. Strang, Ruth. National Association of Secondary-School Principals. 1945. 90p. 50c
Encouragement to the young person to use his resources effectively in securing an education, investing in personal development, and getting a start in his career. Bibliography at end of each section.

It's your future. Dubois, Ethel. Educational Era Publishers. 1960. 50p. $1
Information to assist high school students with decisions concerning future work and education. The author has used this material in mimeographed form with guidance classes and group meetings.

Looking ahead. Chapters 15 of The College Girl Looks Ahead.
Sections on knowing one's self, work experience, fitting into the pattern of what is wanted, knowing what is wanted, and relating your occupation to homemaking.

N. Planning a Career—*Continued*

**Looking ahead to earning a living. Bureau of Labor Statistics, U.S. Department of Labor. Supt. of Documents. 1962. 18p. 15c

A reprint from the introduction to the *Occupational Outlook Handbook, 1961 Edition*, explaining how occupational trends affect career planning, the outlook for occupational change, the kinds of jobs there will be, and the implications of the outlook for education and training.

Looking ahead—to go or not to go to college. Smith, Ira M. National Research Bureau. 1956. 24p. 30c

Information to help the high school senior plan for college realistically and to help the college freshman make the most of his opportunity. Explains some of the reasons why many who enter college never graduate.

Planning your career. Calvert, Robert, Jr. and Steele, John E. McGraw-Hill Book Company. 1963. 152p. $3.75; paper $1.95

Three phases of career development are presented: selecting a goal, organizing a job campaign, and evaluating one's progress.

Prepare for the future at Albright College. Albright College. 1960. 8p. Free

Leaflet containing pictures of student activities and list of representative courses. Typical of college brochures which lend atmosphere to a counseling office.

Preparing for your career. Part Three in *From High School to a Job*.

Chapter headings are: Selecting your occupation, Getting business experience, Junior achievement, Apprenticeship, What you should know about business; What about college, and Occupational literature.

Prudential's pocket guide to college costs. Prudential Insurance Company. 1963. 28p. Free

Includes a list of two hundred colleges with costs of tuition, other fees, room and board, and total expenses per year. Encourages parents to plan for their children's college expenses.

School subjects and jobs. Brochard, John. Science Research Associates. 1961. 48p. 50c

In chart form, this booklet shows how the different subjects taken in high school are related to different jobs.

The scientific approach to career planning. Cobb, M. C. Lantern Press. 1961. 142p. $3.95

Descriptions of general occupational fields are given, suggestions for career planning, and methods of seeking the chosen job in a businesslike manner.

Selecting a career—decision based on information. Institute for Research. 1963. 24p. $1

Introduction to series of career monographs. Youth is advised to look over the fields of work and become acquainted with their scope and variety.

**Selecting an occupation. Sifferd, Calvin S. McKnight and McKnight. 1962. 237p. $3.50

Eleven chapters present significant facts about representative types of work. Eight additional chapters provide suggestions and directions for finding the demands and opportunitites of occupations, for checking individual assets against such demands, for selecting a suitable occupation, and for finding employment.

**Start planning now for your career. General Electric Company. 1956. 7p. Free

Encourages early planning, solid subject matter courses, and good grades in high school as three basic steps to college admission. Available in classroom sets.

Stay in school. U.S. Department of the Navy. 1960. 32p. Free

Illustrated booklet written for the teen-age group, discussing the advantages of remaining in high school until graduation. It points out that the high school graduate has a better chance at the better jobs and is most likely to succeed and advance on the job.

Successful adjustment in college. Revised edition. Chandler, John R. and others. Prentice-Hall, Inc. 1958. 202p. $3.75

Prepared to assist the entering college student in making an adjustment to his new environment. Although personal growth is the major area considered, some sections are devoted to making a wise vocational choice, exploring vocations, and discovering vocational interests.

Time on your hands—choosing and using recreation. National Association of Secondary-School Principals. 1945. 122p. 50c

Includes some suggestions for choosing an avocation which would be helpful to young persons in planning a career.

The twenty-minute lifetime: a guide to career planning. Pitt, Gavin. Prentice-Hall, Inc. 1959. 178p. $2.95; $1.95 paper

Stressing the importance of the twenty-minute employment interview to the college undergraduate and recent alumni, the author points out the need for career planning. Suggests what a young man can expect and what will be expected of him in the first few years of work in a variety of fields.

**Vocational planning for college students. Borow, Henry and Lindsey, Robert. Prentice-Hall, Inc. 1959. 186p. $2.95 paper

By means of a developmental series of written projects, laboratory exercises, discussion units, and reading assignments, the student is taught a systematic method for evolving a suitable career plan.

What good is high school? Mowrer, George and Clark, Glynn. Science Research Associates. 1961. 48p. 50c

Discussion of the importance of education, where high school leads, and the importance of choosing electives and cocurricular activities.

What's ahead? National Urban League. 1963. 12p. 5c; $4 per 100

A pocket-sized booklet for parents and other adults published as a guide to helping youngsters choose worthwhile careers.

N. Planning a Career—*Continued*

What's ahead for your own boy or girl? National Urban League. No date. 9p. 5c

Booklet written for parents to help them understand how they can help their boy or girl choose a satisfying and profitable career.

Why finish high school? Elliott, C. M. American Personnel and Guidance Association. 1958. 4p. 5c; 100 copies $4

Facts cogently presented to encourage youth to graduate.

**You and your career. Collier's Encyclopedia. Crowell-Collier Publishing Company. 1962. 28p. 50c

A reprint containing suggestions for planning a career, followed by a chart giving information about 121 careers in tabular form. Headings include nature of work, employment trends, preparation, entrance requirements, and earnings.

Your future is what you make it. National Research Bureau. 1954. 32p. 20c

Suggestions for a young person to take stock of his interests and abilities, choose and prepare for a vocation, get a job, and earn advancement. The importance of personal attitudes and actions is emphasized. Illustrated.

Your interests and your career. B'nai B'rith Vocational Service. 1952. 6p. 35c

Includes a discussion of the relationship between interests and careers and between interests and school planning. The importance of leisure-time interests in the choice of a career is stressed.

**Your life plans and the Armed Forces. National Association of Secondary-School Principals. 1958. 149p. $1.25

Prepared by the Defense Committee of the North Central Association of Colleges and Secondary Schools. Units of study for secondary-school pupils prepared to help them make realistic life plans, to inform them of military obligations and options, and to describe opportunities for continuing their education while in service. Includes the various types of educational and vocational offerings in the Air Force, Army, Coast Guard, Marine Corps, and Navy.

Your life work. Kiwanis Club. 1949. 4p. 3c

Practical suggestions are grouped under the following headings: You should have a vocation; Decide on your vocation early; Study yourself first; Study the occupational fields; Make your choice on a sound basis; Plan your preparation carefully; Plan for your first job; Make good in your life work.

Your vocational adventure. Burt, Jesse C. Abingdon Press. 1959. 203p. $2.95; $1.65 paper

Suggestions for choosing the vocation which will be suitable and will open the doors of opportunities.

O. Preparing for Examinations

Advanced placement program: course descriptions. College Entrance Examination Board. 1962. 152p. $1.50

An explanation of the program, descriptions of advanced course objectives, and illustrative examination questions in each of the eleven advanced placement subjects.

**Barron's how to prepare for college entrance examinations. Brownstein, S. C. and Weiner, Mitchel. Barron's Educational Series, Inc. Revised 1963. 448p. $5.25; paper $2.50

Part I consists of a general discussion on selecting a college, filing application, conducting oneself during the personal interview, and taking entrance examinations. Part II stresses what to study in preparing for scholastic aptitude tests and includes exercises in vocabulary and arithmetic fundamentals. Part III contains specimen exams and answers.

Barron's how to prepare for high school entrance examinations. Barron's Educational Series, Inc. 1962. 512p. $4.95; $2.98 paper

Contains two sets of model private secondary school tests and model Catholic high school admission tests with answers, suitable for review for a high school admission test.

Bulletin of information, scholastic aptitude test, achievement tests, writing sample. College Entrance Examination Board. 1963. 90p. Free

Explains how the student should arrange to take the tests and includes application form and list of examination centers.

Civil service exam books. Arco Publishing Company. 1954-1964. 180 books. $1 to $4 each

For each of 190 jobs there is given study material and illustrative exam questions and answers. Examples of titles are accountant, employment interviewer, fireman, post office clerk-carrier, patrolman, parole officer, and toll collector.

**College entrance examinations. Wechsler, Louis; Blum, Martin; and Friedman, Sidney. Barnes and Noble, Inc. 1960. 305p. $1.95; $2.15 in Canada

For verbal and mathematical aptitude tests and for achievement tests in fourteen subjects, there are given practice tests with explanations, sample questions with solutions, review exercises, and study materials. Very comprehensive.

College entrance guide. Murphy, Mark. Republic Book Company. 1959. 416p. $3.95 cloth; $1.95 paper

Includes 30 practice examinations with answers, a directory of 1,900 American colleges, and 50 career capsules to which a college education may lead.

College entrance practice book for the Scholastic Aptitude Test and the Preliminary Scholastic Aptitude Test. College Entrance Publications Corporation. 1960. 182p. $1.25

In addition to specimen tests and answers, there is a discussion of several questions. Stresses the types of questions which have been used in the verbal and mathematics sections of the College Entrance Examination Board tests.

College entrance reviews. Educators Publishing Service. 1961-1963. 124p. $2 each.

Aimed to provide practice exercises and many typical questions and answers to familiarize students with the form and content of objective tests. In mathematics, the exercises are graded according to progressive difficulty. Titles are English aptitude, English composition, Mathematics aptitude, and Intermediate mathematics.

O. Preparing for Examinations—*Continued*

**A description of the College Board Achievement Tests. College Entrance Examination Board. 1963. 120p. Free

Suggestions for preparing for the test, filling out the answer sheet, and taking the test. Illustrative questions and answer key are provided.

**A description of the College Board Scholastic Aptitude Test. College Entrance Examination Board. 1963. 54p. Free

A booklet discussing the abilities the test is designed to measure, how it is prepared, the kinds of questions used, and the use of test scores. Written primarily for the student, it includes many illustrative sample questions, answer key, and sample answer sheet.

A description of the supplementary achievement tests. College Entrance Examination Board. 1963. 64p. Free

Information concerning the thirty-minute listening comprehension tests in French, German, Italian, Russian, and Spanish and the ninety-minute achievement tests in Greek and Italian. Specimen tests and answers for each.

Effective study. Robinson, Francis P. Harper and Row. 1961. 278p. $4.50

The author urges the student to develop better study habits by learning to survey, question, read, recite, and review.

**End-of-year examinations in English for college-bound students, grades 9-12. College Entrance Examination Board. 1963. 193p. $2

The purpose of the book is to demonstrate some of the skills and understandings which the Commission on English believes a college preparatory student ought to have acquired by the end of each year of secondary school. The book contains four experimental examinations designed for end-of-the-course use in grades 9-12. Each examination question is followed by actual student answers, ranging from excellent to poor, with detailed analysis and evaluation of each answer.

English review series. Educators Publishing Service. 1958-1962. 5 books. $1.15 each

Review exercises and test questions. The books have accompanying teachers' keys. Also available is a series of language review exercises and a vocabulary builder series.

Exams and answers. Barron's Educational Series, Inc. 1956. 160p. 75c and 95c each

Review questions and answers in 35 subjects, including American history, English, algebra, geometry, trigonometry, biology, physics, chemistry, economics, business subjects, and languages. Serves as refresher material when preparing for college entrance, final, or civil service examinations.

General information bulletin. American College Testing Program. 1963. 32p. Free

A summary statement of the conduct of the testing program, use of score reports, test dates, and research service. Other booklets available contain information for the student.

Getting the most out of high school. Scott, J. I. E. Oceana Publications. 1957. 144p. $2.50

Includes self-tests to help the reader to measure the effectiveness of his study and work habits and to improve them.

High school diploma tests. Arco Publishing Company. 1960. 310p. $4

Prepared for survey study material for review before taking the equivalency diploma test.

How to be a better student. Wrightstone, J. Wayne. Science Research Associates. 1956. 96p. $1.75

Activity text or workbook designed to aid pupils in junior high schools to develop academic skills and improve study habits. Includes charts and self-quizzes to enable one to evaluate and improve his study skills.

**How to be accepted by the college of your choice. Fine, Benjamin. Channel Press. 1963-1964 edition. 320p. $2.95

Includes discussion on the significance of grades and class rank, the growing reliance on College Board scores, how to improve your College Board score, writing the five hundred-word autobiography and how these are judged by the colleges, interviewing procedures, and how to file an application. Also included is a college fact-finder which given in tabulated form the entrance criteria at each of the accredited colleges plus pertinent facts on costs, enrollment, and time to apply.

How to become a successful student. Froe, Otis and Lee, Maurice. Arco Publishing Company. 1960. 310p. $2.50; $1.25 paper

Urges arrangement of the study environment, building reading skills, developing study and learning techniques, and other ways of forming sound study habits.

How to get higher marks in school. Shefter, Harry. Washington Square Press. 1961. 264p. 60c

Suggestions to develop better study and work habits. Designed to help both the slower and the more advanced student make the most of the educational opportunities offered them.

How to improve your reading. Witty, Paul. Science Research Associates. 1963. 380p. $4.95

Aimed to help junior high school students to develop better reading skills through reading exercises, a progress folder, and a reading list arranged by interest areas. A similar book prepared for persons above the ninth grade is entitled *How To Become a Better Reader.*

**How to pass Annapolis and West Point entrance exams. Arco Publishing Company. 1959. 222p. $3.50

Samples of examinations, questions and answers, and study material inform candidates of the nature and difficulty of the tests. In addition to practice sections in mathematics, vocabulary, spelling, grammar, literature, and United States history achievement tests, there are study materials for artificial language, judgment, form and space analysis, and graph reading.

How to pass dental aptitude test. College Publishing Corporation. 1962. 301p. $3.95

Typical questions and answers.

O. Preparing for Examinations—*Continued*

How to pass employment tests. Liebers, Arthur. Arco Publishing Company. 1960. 220p. $3.50

Sample tests and answers followed by study sections.

**How to pass high on college entrance tests. Turner, David and Peters, Alison. Arco Publishing Company. 1961. 256p. $3.50 cloth; $2 paper

Section one consists of a directory of colleges and universities, the tests each of them gives, and whether the tests are used for entrance, placement, or aptitude. Section two describes various college entrance tests and gives specimen tests. These descriptions are followed by study material and additional practice tests.

How to pass high on high school entrance and scholarship tests. Turner, David. Arco Publishing Company. 1962. 272p. $2.50

Practice questions and answers, study material, and analysis of test material designed for preparation of seventh, eighth, and ninth grade students.

How to pass high on reading tests. Arco Publishing Company. 1960. 236p. $3

Questions and answers on reading comprehension, interpretation, paragraph meaning, sentence completion, literary materials, and judgment and reasoning.

How to pass high on the American College Testing Program exams. Arco Publishing Company. 1959. 310p. $3

Specimen test questions in each phase of the examination: English usage, mathematics, literature and reading interpretation, art and music, social studies, and the natural sciences. Many supplementary test questions and answers.

How to pass high on the graduate record examination. Gruber, Edward. Arco Publishing Company. 1962. 278p. $4

Specimen tests in biology, education, history, literature, and mathematics.

How to pass high on the nursing school entrance examination. Gruber, Edward. Arco Publishing Company. 1964. 300p. $4

Sample tests are included covering psychological exams, English, grammar, vocabulary, numerical relations, and other aptitudes.

How to pass law school admission test. College Publishing Corporation. 1963. 294p. $3.95

Typical questions and answers on legal principles, graphs, charts, tables, verbal and quantitative ability, and general background information.

How to pass medical college admission test. College Publishing Corporation. 1963. 304p. $3.95

Typical questions and answers on general background information as well as tests of verbal and quantitative ability.

How to pass National Merit Scholarship Tests. Tarr, H. A. and Van Treese, I. Arco Publishing Company. 1956. 316p. $3

Contains instructions in test materials, study materials on the usual exam subjects, and specimen test questions and answers for practice.

How to pass National Teacher Examinations. Technical Extension Service. 1961. 25 books. $3.50 and $3.95 each
> Questions and answers for five of the common examinations and for twenty optional subject matter exams.

How to pass the Graduate Record Examination Series. Technical Extension Service. 1962. 72p. $3.50
> Typical questions and answers. One book pertains to the common (basic) examination and other books are available for the individual subject areas.

How to prepare for College Board Achievement Tests. Barron's Educational Series, Inc. 1960-62. 6 books
> Review books designed to provide practice drill material, model achievement tests, and answers. Titles available are:

Biology. 1962. $2.25   German. 1961. $2.25
Chemistry. 1961. $2.25   Physics. 1962. $2.25
French. 1960. $1.50   Spanish. 1960. $1.75

How to qualify for the United States Air Force Academy. Arco Publishing Company. 1959. 214p. $3
> Study material for the entrance examination.

How to score high on science scholarship examinations. Gruber, Edward C. Arco Publishing Company. 1962. 240p. $3
> Suggested preparation for Westinghouse Scholarship and similar examinations. Typical exam questions and answers, recent winning entries, and help in planning report.

How to score high on the Catholic high school entrance examination. Gruber, Edward. Arco Publishing Company. 1963. 320p. $4; $2.50 paper
> Examples of tests and answers, with suggestions for study.

How to score high on the National Teacher Examination. Arco Publishing Company. 1962. 240p. $4
> Specimen tests and supplementary practice questions in professional information, English, social studies, fine arts, literature, science, mathematics, and nonverbal reasoning.

**How to score high on the Scholastic Aptitude Test and other college entrance tests. Genua, A. J. John F. Rider, Publisher. 1962. 220p. $2.10
> Each section contains material for study and review, practice exercises, and answers. A special feature is the section on word building and the study guide on prefixes, roots, and suffixes. A list of colleges with the entrance tests required by each is arranged alphabetically by states.

How to study. Morgan, Clifford and Deese, James. McGraw-Hill Book Company. 1957. 127p. $1.50
> Suggestions for college students on the art of studying efficiently, the value of a schedule, improving one's reading, taking notes, taking examinations, writing themes, studying foreign languages, and solving mathematical problems.

O. Preparing for Examinations—*Continued*

How to study. Preston, Ralph and Botel, Morton. Science Research Associates. 1956. 128p. $1.95
> Activity text or workbook designed to help the high school and college student evaluate and improve his study habits. Includes a section on getting ready for and taking examinations.

How to study and be successful in school. Narramore, Clyde. Zondervan Publishing House. 1961. 45p. 50c
> Discussion of budgeting one's time, where to study, note taking and keeping, use of library, report writing, and preparation for tests.

How to study and prepare for exams. Woodley, Colin E. New American Library of World Literature. 1961. 127p. 50c
> Suggestions concerning the development of habits and skills to enable one to get maximum returns from his study-time investment. Includes environment, planning, note taking, and aids to concentration.

How to study and take exams. Pettit, Lincoln. John F. Rider, Publisher. 1960. $1
> In addition to the mechanics of studying, this book aims to provide motivation for learning.

**How to study better and get higher marks. Ehrlich, Eugene H. Thomas Y. Crowell Company. 1961. 287p. $4.95
> Includes discussions of improving one's memory, writing papers, studying effectively, and getting higher marks on examinations.

How to study in college. Pauk, Walter. Houghton Mifflin Company. 1962. 132p. $1.95 paper
> Basic methods of study such as time scheduling, note taking, efficient reading, vocabulary improvement, ability to concentrate, preparation for examinations, and writing themes.

How to win a college scholarship. Tarr, Harry A. Arco Publishing Company. 1060. 520p. $3
> Provides study material, examination-type questions and answers for the subjects normally encountered on tests given to scholarship candidates.

How to win Regents Scholarships. Technical Extension Service. 1962. 480p. $3
> Typical questions and answers for each of the sections.

How to win Westinghouse Science Scholarships. Technical Extension Service. 1957. 256p. $3
> Suggestions for preparing for the written science aptitude examination, typical questions and answers, and aids in writing the project report.

**How to write the college entrance examination "writing sample." Blau, Harold. Chilton Company. 1961. 100p. $1.95
> Suggestions concerning the preparation of the outline, development of the idea, use of good vocabulary, and the importance of good handwriting. Some practice exercises are given at the end of chapters.

How you can be a better student. Flesch, Rudolf; Witty, Paul; and others. Sterling Publishing Company. 1957. 192p. $3.95

A compilation of material contained in booklets published by the Science Research Associates entitled: You and your mental abilities, How to take a test, How to write better, Streamline your reading, and Study your way through school.

The improvement of study habits and skills. Traxler, Arthur E. Educational Records Bureau. 1954. 39p. $1

Summary of procedures to help pupils to learn to study more effectively and evaluate their study habits and skills. Bibliography.

Learn how to study. Kelner, Bernard. Science Research Associates. 1961. 66p. 85c

An easy-to-read workbook for grades 4 to 7 stressing the importance of good study habits, setting up good conditions for study, and how to organize and report information.

Learning is your business. National Education Association. 1963. 8p. 35 copies $1

Tells how the junior or senior high school student can get the most out of his in-school and at-home studying.

Mathematics workbook for college entrance examinations. Brownstein, Samuel C. and Weiner, Mitchel. Barron's Educational Series. 1961. 128p. $3.95; $1.75 paper

Additional practice material to supplement textbooks. Includes ten tests of thirty problems each.

Meeting the test. Anderson, Scarvia; Katz, Martin; and Shimberg, Benjamin. Scholastic Book Services. 1963. 185p. 45c

Designed to help high school students succeed with tests by relieving their anxieties about them. Emphasizes the constructive use of the variety of tests used in education and industry.

New York State Regents Scholarship Exams. Tarr, Harry A. Arco Publishing Company. 1956. 325p. $3

Includes study and practice material in literature, composition, reading interpretation, vocabulary, spelling, social studies, mathematics, sciences, music, and art. Specimen test questions from previous examinations are given.

On being a student. Oklahoma State University. 1962. 8p. Free

Some suggestions on learning how to study.

Practice for the Armed Forces tests. Arco Publishing Company. 1959. 292p. $3

Description of 33 Armed Forces tests, sample questions and answers, and instruction for study.

Prepare for the official U.S. Army-Navy-Air Force tests. Capitol Publishing Company. 1951. 165p. $2

Includes details of the induction procedure, the four basic subjects of the Army General Classification Test, and securing a rating or commission. Sample examinations and practice material with answers are presented. Special attention is given to questions in arithmetic, cube counting, vocabulary, and questions designed to determine mechanical and clerical aptitude.

O. Preparing for Examinations—*Continued*

Preparing for college study. Fedde, Norman A. Readers Press. 1962. 156p. 95c

Suggestions to help the student develop self-discipline under the new circumstances that college presents. Includes discussion of scheduling, concentration, note-making, methods of reading, use of the library, academic writing, and preparing for examinations.

Preparing for the American College Testing Program. Orgel, Joseph R. Educators Publishing Service. 1962. 120p. $2

Suggestions and specimen test questions of the type previously used in this test program.

Republic study guide for Regents scholarship preparation. Harris, Brother Philip. Republic Book Company. 1959. 160p. $1.25

Five sets of Regents' Scholarship Examination questions and answers. Some study materials also are included.

Reviewing mathematics for college entrance examinations. Cohen, Martin. Republic Book Company. 1957. 60p. 90c

Review materials and a series of test questions with answers. A companion volume is entitled *Reviewing English*.

Science scholarship exams. Gruber, Edward. Arco Publishing Company. 1963. 235p. $3

Includes suggestions for the Westinghouse Scholarship competition.

Study and succeed. Tussing, Lyle. Wiley and Sons. 1962. 170p. $2.95

Discussion of methods that a student can use to help increase his learning efficiency and utilize the information he acquires to the best advantage.

Study is hard work. Armstrong, William H. Harper and Row. 1957. 167p. $3.50

Helpful chapters on putting ideas in order, acquiring skill in study, interest and motivation in study, and reviewing for tests and examinations.

Study successfully; 18 keys to better work. Orchard, Norris Ely. McGraw-Hill Book Company. 1953. 80p. $1.95

Includes discussion of methods of planning compositions and term papers, taking lecture notes from different types of teachers, how to find information when the subject is not listed in the library catalog, and independent study.

Studying for success. B'nai B'rith Vocational Service. 1961. 16p. 35c

Discussion of good study practices such as planning one's time, scheduling one's work, and giving careful attention to directions. Selected references.

Taking a test: how to do your best. Manuel, Herschel T. Harcourt, Brace and World. 1956. 77p. $1

Discussion of good test-taking practices and exercises to give experience in taking a variety of tests. Factors which may affect test scores are pointed out to the reader and suggestions made.

Teacher's license examination series. Technical Extension Service. 1960-1963. About 25 books. $3.50 and $3.95 each

Typical questions and answers in individual subjects and for various parts of the National Teacher Examinations.

This is the way to study. Brown, Howard Elmer. J. B. Lippincott Company. 1955. 109p. $2.75
> Discussion of the mechanical and psychological factors affecting concentration and study habits.

Tips on taking tests. National Education Association. 1963. 8p. 35 for $1
> This leaflet gives pointers on how a student can do his best on any test.

U.S. Merchant Marine Academy tests. Arco Publishing Company. 1956. 230p. $3
> Contains a specimen entrance examination and study material in spatial relations, cube counting, mechanical aptitude, analogies, mathematics, vocabulary, reading, graph and table interpretation, and symbol series.

War service scholarships. Arco Publishing Company. 1955. 225p. $3
> Study material, practice questions, and answers for exams given veterans for some state scholarships.

**You can win a scholarship. Brownstein, S. C.; Weiner, Mitchel; and Kaplan, Stanley. Barron's Educational Series, Inc. Revised 1963. 429p. $2.98 paper; $4.95 cloth
> Contains a large section of information about sources of scholarships. The rest of book contains specimen exams, including questions from previous New York State scholarship exams. Also, there is a chapter on preparation for scholarship exams in each specific subject field. Answers are given for some specimen sets. Useful to give students some practice in answering questions comparable to those they may encounter in the college entrance exams or other competitive tests.

Your College Board scores: Preliminary Scholastic Aptitude Test. College Entrance Examination Board. 1963. 12p. Free
> A leaflet for students explaining the meaning of scores and their use in college planning.

Your College Board scores: Scholastic Aptitude Test, Achievement Tests. College Entrance Examination Board. 1963. 18p. Free
> A leaflet for students briefly explaining the meaning of scores. Intended as a basis for conferring with school counselors concerning the use of scores in college admissions.

P. Professional Counseling Services

Catholic College Admissions and Information Center, 3805 McKinley St., N.W., Washington 15, D.C. $10
> This national admissions center has been established to help prospective freshmen find unfilled places in the country's 240 Catholic colleges and universities. For a $10 fee this center will make applications available to Catholic colleges seeking students. Catholic University, Washington, D.C. will operate a separate informational service on the programs of Catholic colleges.

College Admissions Assistance Center, 41 E. 65th St., New York 21. $15
> This is a clearinghouse service designed to assist prospective college students find colleges with room for more students. It is sponsored by the Council of

Higher Educational Institutions in New York City and serves students over a wide geographical area. Authorized college officials review student records and contact those students in whom they are interested. A service for those students experiencing difficulty in gaining admission to college through normal channels.

College Admissions Center, 610 Church Street, Evanston, Ill. $15

Students register with this nonprofit admissions clearinghouse by filling out and returning its registration form with a fee. Representatives of colleges review the records of unplaced students and communicate directly with those who interest them for their colleges. The center is open on a year-round basis; students can thus be considered for admission at any semester or quarter of the year.

Directory of approved counseling agencies. American Board on Counseling Agencies. Order from American Personnel and Guidance Association. 1963. 167p. $2

The directory contains relevant information on 168 agencies in the United States, Canada, and Puerto Rico which have met the standards of the association. Includes address, telephone number, hours and fees for each agency, as well as a description of the clientele served and the professional staff.

Independent School Admissions Advisory Center, 12 North Main St., Wallingford, Conn.

The authors of *Private Independent Schools* conduct an advisory center for parents of children in the primary, elementary, or high school grades. They advise parents of the enrollment situations in various schools where it might be to their advantage to make application. The expense of the consultations is covered by fees paid by the families.

National Scholarship Service and Fund for Negro Students, 6 E. 82nd St., New York 28

To enable Negro students to attend college in a nonsegregated environment, this organization assists them in obtaining admission and winning scholarship aid at a wide variety of colleges. Students are required to submit their scores on the National Merit Scholarship Test or the Preliminary Scholastic Aptitude Test.

Q. Scholarships

American foundations and their fields. Rich, Wilmer S. American Foundations Information Service. 1955. 744p. $35. Out of print but available in large libraries.

A full description of the foundations and their purposes.

Announcement of activities, awards, contests, loans, and scholarships available nationally to high school students. Sabo, Alex, ed. Chronicle Guidance Publications. 1962. 88p. $1

Information on 230 student aids from 160 sponsoring sources.

Announcement of award. The Amy Loveman National Award. Annual. 5p. Free

Interesting offer of an award of $1,000 to the college senior with the best personal library of thirty-five or more books. Applications must be submitted before April 30 of each year.

Announcement of scholarships offered by labor unions to entering college freshmen. Sabo, Alex, ed. Chronicle Guidance Publications. 1962. 28p. 50c
One of the *Student Aid Bulletins* in the Chronicle Educational Service.

Announcement of state scholarships available to entering college freshmen. Sabo, Alex, ed. Chronicle Guidance Publications. 1962. 28p. $1
One of the *Student Aid Bulletins* included in the Chronicle Educational Service.

Awards for singers. Central Opera Service. 1963. 4p. 25c
Information, compiled by states, concerning financial aid and scholarships.

Awards for study abroad. Rotary Foundation of Rotary International. Annual. 2p. Free
Students with B.A. degrees may apply through local Rotary Clubs for awards consisting of tuition, transportation, and expenses for study abroad. For graduate students only.

Background for a national scholarship policy. American Council on Education. 1956. 160p. $1.50
Prepared for administrators of a scholarship program. Sections include the problem, sources of funds, motivational factors relating to college attendance, the administration of scholarship programs, and studies needed. Bibliography.

Bausch and Lomb awards. Bausch and Lomb, Incorporated. 1963. 20p. Free
Description of plan whereby the Bausch and Lomb science award winner in each high school may compete for scholarship aid at the University of Rochester.

Blueprint for talent searching. Plaut, Richard. National Scholarship Service and Fund for Negro Students. 1957. 42p. 50c
Suggestions for administrators of scholarship programs.

College entrance counselor. Wechsler, Louis; Blum, Martin; and Friedman, Sidney. Barnes and Noble, Inc. 1961. 413p. $5.95; $3.50 paper
This book on preparation for college includes a list of scholarships given by a variety of public and private agencies.

College financial aid check list. National Education Association. 1962. 4p. 35 copies $1
Kinds and sources of financial aid for college undergraduates.

Commercial loans for college. Changing Times. 1962. 5p. 15c
Survey of commercial college loans made by 1,500 banks and financial institutions.

Commercial loans for college. Changing Times. 1962. 112p. $1.50
Report of a study of commercial educational loan programs in 1962.

Designing and building a model car. Fisher Body Craftsman's Guild. 1963. 4p. Free
An annual publication for boys interested in the model car competition.

Q. Scholarships—*Continued*

Directory of international scholarships in the arts. Institute of International Education. 1958. 120p. 50c
> A survey of awards and scholarships available to persons who wish to study or train in foreign countries in the fields of the creative arts.

Do you want to go to college? National Scholarship Service and Fund for Negro Students. 1962. 14p. Free
> Description of what the student should do to help himself and how he can take advantage of opportunities offered by the organization.

Educational grants and awards in the field of music. Music Educators National Conference. 1957. 45p. 50c
> A directory of assistance awards, commissions, fellowships, and scholarships.

Fellowships and loans for study abroad of the Organization of American States and its Specialized Organizations. Pan American Union. 1962. 8p. Free
> Of interest to those who wish to travel and study in Latin America.

Fellowships for specialized training for counselors in work with cerebral palsied and other severely handicapped workers. National Society for Crippled Children and Adults. Revised annually. 4p. Free
> Description of training course for qualified counselors and other professional persons who are working with the crippled or physically impaired. Includes eligibility requirements and procedures for application.

Fellowships in counseling. National Society for Crippled Children and Adults. 1963. 4p. Free
> Includes eligibility requirements and procedures for application.

Fellowships in the arts and sciences. Quick, Robert, ed. American Council on Education. 1963. 95p. $2.25
> Prepared for prospective graduate students. Catalog of financial aid programs available from over one hundred private foundations, government agencies, professional associations, industries, and other sources outside the universities. Information about each fellowship program includes qualifications of candidates, stipends, conditions, type of application, and deadline for application.

Fellowships, scholarships, grants-in-aid, loan funds, and other assistance for library education in the United States and Canada. American Library Association. 1964. 104p. 50c
> Includes funds available from library schools and other funds available to residents of specific states or cities. Information on 1,550 scholarships.

Financial aid for college students: graduate. Mattingly, Richard C. U.S. Office of Education. Bulletin 1957, Number 17. Supt. of Documents. 1957. 151p. 50c
> Contains summary of institutional financial aid, such as fellowships, loans, and employment for graduate students. The report includes 330 colleges, arranged by states, awarding 24,885 fellowships having a total value of over $9 million.

Financial aid for students: scholarships, loans, and employment. Indiana University. 1963. 32p. Free
An example of a college brochure listing the names of scholarships, number available, amount, and eligibility requirements.

Financial aid for teacher education. Future Teachers of America. 1962. 4p. Free
Information about student loans available under the National Defense Education Act as extended in 1961.

Financial aid manual, 1962-64. College Entrance Examination Board. 1962. 134p. $4
Available only to school and college officers, this is a guide to administering student aid programs at colleges and to analyzing the financial need of applicants. Explains the method of computing the financial need of students from the Parents' Confidential Statement of the College Scholarship Service.

Financial aid to the undergraduate: issues and implications. West, Elmer D. American Council on Education. 1963. 153p. $2
A report for the Council's Commission on Federal Relations on the need for scholarships, the portion of the college-age population presently reached by scholarship assistance, and the implications for college admissions. For administrators. Good bibliography.

Financial aids for undergraduate students: sources of information. U.S. Office of Education. Supt. of Documents. 1962. 9p. 10c
Sources of information and a list of publications about financial assistance.

Financial assistance for college students: undergraduate. Mattingly, Richard C. U.S. Office of Education. Bulletin 1962, Number 11. Supt. of Documents. 1962. 360p. $1.25
This bulletin reports information about scholarships, loans, and opportunities for employment available to undergraduate students at 1,677 colleges and universities. Closing dates for applications for scholarships are included. Individual scholarships are not named, but there is a summary of the total number of students receiving scholarship, loans, and part-time employment. The average value of scholarships and loans is also given.

**Financing a college education: a guide for counselors. College Scholarship Service. 1963. 19p. 25c
A summary of suggestions for counselors, college financial aid principles, description of the College Scholarship Service, explanation of the parents' confidential statement, and how financial need is determined. Good list of references.

**Financing an undergraduate education. Office of Education, U.S. Department of Health, Education, and Welfare. Supt. of Documents. 1964. 22p. 15c
A brief summary of total college costs, types of financial assistance, and sources of financial assistance. List of fourteen references.

Foundation directory. Russell Sage Foundation. 1964. 1,000p. $10
Describes over 6,000 foundations, their purposes, and current areas of interest. Includes information on scholarships or fellowships offered.

Q. SCHOLARSHIPS—*Continued*

Foundation news. Foundation Library Center. Bimonthly bulletin. $3 per year

Current information about foundations and their activities. The Foundation Library Center maintains files of materials indexed by major fields, available to the public on business days, and periodically prepares the *Foundation Directory* which is published by Russell Sage Foundation.

The General Henry H. Arnold Educational Fund. Air Force Aid Society. No date. 7p. Free

Information about loans and grants available through this fund for the college education of children of Air Force personnel.

Guide to scholarships, fellowships and loans in the mental health field. National Association for Mental Health. 1963. 20p. 50c

Types and sources of financial aid available to potential mental health workers interested in training for careers in psychiatry, psychology, nursing, social work, occupational therapy, and recreation.

Handbook on baking schools and scholarships. Allied Trades of the Baking Industry. 1962. 24p. Free

Contains discussion of the need for more and better trained young bakers, advantages of work in the industry, and information about specific scholarships at various schools of baking.

How about college financing? A guide for parents of college-bound students. American School Counselor Association. Order from American Personnel and Guidance Association. 1960. 20p. 30c

Suggests ways to keep expenses down and explains methods of systematic planning through savings, loans, part-time work, scholarships, and grants.

* How and where to get scholarships and loans. Angel, Juvenal L. World Trade Academy Press. 1964. 225p. $2.95 paper

Sources are listed alphabetically, by specialized fields, and by states.

How to finance a college education. Craig, W. Bradford. Henry Holt and Company. 1959. 79p. $1.95

Many practical suggestions.

How to finance a college education. Funds for Education, Inc. 1962. 8p. Free

Description of several plans.

How to get into college. Third edition. Bowles, Frank H. Dutton and Company. 1963. 185p. $3.50

The president of the College Entrance Examination Board gives detailed answers to over 350 questions on college preparation, admission, and financing. Special suggestions are included on earning scholarships.

**How to get money for college. Fine, Benjamin and Eisenberg, Sidney. Doubleday and Company. 1964. 227p. $4.95; paper $2.50

A compilation of sources of scholarships, loans, and grants.

How to get money for college. Fine, Benjamin and Eisenberg, Sidney. Dollars for Scholars. 1962. 8 bulletins. $1

The bulletins may be ordered separately at prices given below, if accompanied with a self-addressed, long, stamped envelope.
1. Major sources of scholarship aid. 15c
2. Fellowships and grants. 10c
3. Where to get loans. 10c
4. Scholarships for children of veterans. 10c
5. The National Merit Scholarship Program and how to qualify. 10c
6. Scholarships and loans for medical students. 10c
7. Scholarships, fellowships and loans for nursing students. 10c
8. Union scholarships in the United States (2 parts) 15c each

How to look for scholarships. Angel, Juvenal L. World Trade Academy Press. 1960. 37p. $1.25

Helpful discussions are included on the following topics: How to follow through on scholarship possibilities, Analysis of the scholarship application, Typical letters of recommendation, The scholarship résumé, Points to be considered before accepting a scholarship, and Supplementary means of financing one's education.

How to pay for your child's college education. Margolius, Sidney. Public Affairs Committee. 1963. 22p. 25c

Discussion of the practical ways of planning for college expenses including jobs, loans, savings plans, and scholarships. Includes sources and comparative costs of National Defense Act loans, state-sponsored loans, United Student Aid funds, college loan funds, installment loans, bank loans, and others.

Information on science scholarships and student loans. National Science Foundation. 1960. 9p. 15c

Information on aids for study of science.

The John Hay fellowship program. John Hay Fellows Program. 1963. 4p. Free

Description of year fellowships in the humanities for teachers in public senior high schools. Includes qualifications for candidacy and how to apply.

Journalism scholarship guide. Sigma Delta Chi. 1964. 65p. Free

A listing of journalism scholarships, fellowships, assistantships, and loans in about one hundred universities.

Latest information on scholarships in the space age. Feingold, S. N. Bellman Publishing Company. 1962. 6p. 50c

Reprint of an article in the *Occupational Outlook Quarterly*.

List of foundations, public trusts, and funds. World Almanac. Annually. 3p. $1.50

Names and addresses of sixty-four major funds with their stated purpose, amounts of assets, and annual expenditures.

**Lovejoy's scholarship guide. Second edition. Lovejoy, Clarence E. Simon and Schuster. 1964. 91p. $2.95 paper

A useful reference book giving information about scholarships, fellowships, grants-in-aid, loan funds, assistantships, workshops, contests, and awards. In-

Q. Scholarships—*Continued*

cludes scholarships sponsored by industry; labor unions; welfare groups; professional associations; foundations; and fraternal, educational, religious, and patriotic groups.

Low-cost loans for college. United Student Aid Funds, Inc. 1962. 6p. Free

Explanation of the plan and how to participate.

Medical education loan guarantee program. American Medical Association. 1963. 6p. Free

Explanation of the loan program for medical students sponsored by the American Medical Association Education and Research Foundation.

Merit scholarships. National Merit Scholarship Corporation. Published annually. 30p. Free to counselors

Written primarily for the use of scholarship sponsors, this is a report of the number of awards and some statistics concerning the award winners.

Million dollar giveaway. Seventeen Magazine. 1956. 4p. 10c

Includes twenty-seven representative sources of scholarship aid and eligibility requirements.

National defense graduate fellowship program: a report on the first two years. U.S. Office of Education. Supt. of Documents. 1961. 12p. 15c

Report of the accomplishments of the Title IV program, awarding 2,500 fellowships and $9 million to support graduate programs.

National defense student loan program: a 2-year report. U.S. Office of Education. Supt. of Documents. 1961. 44p. 35c

Discussion of the basic policy and summary of statistical data reported by colleges and universities.

The national defense student loan program: basic facts. U.S. Office of Education. Supt. of Documents. 1960. 11p. 10c

Answers questions most frequently asked about the general purposes and operations of the program of loan funds established at institutions of higher education.

National defense student loan program, including participating institutions 1963-1964. U.S. Office of Education. 1963. 41p. Free

This booklet describes aid to undergraduates; another is available concerning graduate study.

National Foundation health scholarships. National Foundation. Annual. 6p. Free

Announcements of awards offered annually to students who plan careers in medicine, nursing, physical therapy, occupational therapy, or medical social work. Selection of winners is based on scholastic achievement, personal qualifications, professional promise, and financial need.

**National register of scholarships and fellowships. Volume I: scholarships and loans. 4th Edition. Angel, Juvenal L. World Trade Academy Press. 1964. 494p. $15

The first part contains a description, three to eight lines in length, of the 193 national scholarships offered without geographical restriction, giving name of sponsor, number of scholarships, amount, and brief statement of qualifications. In the second part, the scholarship descriptions are arranged by states and subdivided into three categories: those sponsored by organizations and corporations, educational institutions, and government agencies.

National register of scholarships and fellowships. Volume II: fellowships and grants. 4th Edition. Angel, Juvenal L. World Trade Academy Press. 1963. 208p. $15

Arranged by states, the student aid on the graduate level is presented as in Volume I.

National Science Foundation graduate fellowships. National Academy of Sciences. 1963. 4p. Free

Conditions of appointment, eligibility, stipends, and application dates. For graduate study.

**Need a lift to educational opportunities? American Legion. 1963. 100p. 25c

Sources of scholarships and financial aid. Also information, tabulated by states, concerning state educational benefits to children of deceased veterans. Good sources of career information are included. Revised annually.

Need financial aid for college? Engineers' Council for Professional Development. No date. 8p. 3c

Advice to students to make college plans early and some suggestions concerning financial aid.

**New American guide to scholarships, fellowships and loans. Bradley, John. New American Library of World Literature. 1961. 235p. 75c. Paperback

An inexpensive guide to financial assistance offered by nonacademic organizations. Names and addresses of sponsors include business firms, civic groups, fraternal organizations, labor unions, professional associations, and veterans groups.

The P. D'Agostino memorial scholarships. National Association of Retail Grocers. 1963. 4p. Free

Announcement of annual awards of $1,000. Applicants are eligible who have worked part-time for at least five months in a retail food store, or who are sons or daughters of a foodstore owner, operator, executive, or staff member. Announcements are made by November 1 of each year and applications must be filed before February 1,

A program for basic research in the physical sciences. Alfred P. Sloan Foundation. 1960. 42p. Free

Description of program which provides grants to selected young scientists for basic research. Candidates do not apply but are nominated by department chairmen or other scientists.

Q.　Scholarships—*Continued*

RCA aid to education—scholarships and fellowships.　Radio Corporation of America.　1963.　14p.　Free

This booklet presents information on the various plans under which the Radio Corporation of America assists college and university students through scholarships and fellowships.

Report of the National Defense Education Act: fiscal year ending June 30, 1960.　U.S. Office of Education.　Supt. of Documents.　1961.　93p.　55c

Reports for each of the ten titles of the 1958 NDEA the amounts authorized and appropriated, whether or not on a matching basis; the need, purpose, provisions, and accomplishments of grants.　Includes information on student loan funds.

Rules and regulations.　General Electric Scholarship Contest.　Annual.　6p.　Free

Entry blank for the ten scholarship awards of $6,000 each.　The 1963 topic for a five hundred-word entry was "My most unforgettable teacher."

Scholarship hunt, begin here.　Treichler, Jessie.　Alumnae Advisory Center.　1958.　4p.　50c

Reprint from *Mademoiselle* containing the above mentioned article, a profile of Oberlin College, and "dating maps" showing women's colleges and the nearby men's colleges for areas where separate schools for men and women prevail.

Scholarship information.　Boys' Clubs of America.　1963.　4p.　Free

A general description of the various scholarship programs available for education and training to men planning a professional career in Boys' Club work.

Scholarship programs of motor carriers.　American Trucking Associations.　1962.　11p.　Free

List of scholarships offered by motor carriers and allied companies.　Includes contributors, eligibility, number, value, field of study, and source of additional information.

Scholarship tests.　Committee on Careers, National League for Nursing.　1964.　6p.　Two lists, 5c each

One list consists of sources of scholarships and loans for students entering schools of nursing; the other for graduate nurses.

Scholarships.　Union Carbide Corporation.　1960.　4p.　Free

Information concerning engineering scholarships established at thirty-five colleges and universities by Union Carbide Corporation.

Scholarships and educational loans.　Board of Christian Education, United Presbyterian Church.　1962.　12p.　Free

Includes description of the graduate and undergraduate National Presbyterian college scholarships.

Scholarships and fellowships—a selected bibliography.　Mattingly, Richard C.　U.S. Office of Education.　Bulletin Number 7.　Supt. of Documents.　1957.　28p.　15c

A bibliography of articles and other material describing research studies in the field of financial aid to students and in related areas.　These areas cover plans of high school seniors, academic performance of scholarship holders, problems of administration of scholarship programs, and proposals for more student financial aid.

Scholarships and loans for rehabilitation careers. National Society for Crippled Children and Adults. 1960. 50p. 50c

Representative sources of assistance for training in many of the careers in rehabilitation such as medicine, nursing, occupational therapy, special education, speech and hearing therapy, social work, and others.

**Scholarships, fellowships and loans. Feingold, S. Norman. Bellman Publishing Company. Volume III. 1955. 471p. $10. Volume IV. 1962. 368p. $10. Volume V scheduled for 1964

These volumes list scholarships, fellowships, and loans alphabetically by administering agency, with name and address, qualifications, funds available, special fields of interest, and where to apply for information and application. All volumes contain an index of scholarships listed under vocations, such as agriculture, dietetics, journalism, and music. Includes student assistance awarded by fraternal organizations, labor unions, management, religious groups, and philanthropic foundations. Volume IV contains an index to Volumes III and IV.

Scholarships, fellowships and loans news service. Subscription service. Bellman Publishing Company. $35 per year

There are two types of subscriptions. Four newsletters a year, annual index, and binder cost $20. With the addition of two scholarship search problems and a special technical report on student aid, $35,

Scholarships, fellowships, and work-study plans for graduate social work education for individuals interested in Jewish community center work as a career. National Jewish Welfare Board. 1963. 8p. Free

Annual listing of plans which help a potential social work student to prepare for work in a Jewish community center.

Scholarships, fellowships, educational grants, and loans available on a national or regional basis to graduate nurses. Committee on Careers, National League for Nursing. 1961. 6p. 5c

Sources of student aid for graduate nurses.

Scholarships, fellowships, loans, grants-in-aid for school librarianship. American Association of School Librarians. Available from Office for Recruitment, American Library Association. 1963. 40p. $1

This provides a state-by-state compilation of scholarships and other forms of student aid, in four categories: parent teacher associations, state school library associations, state departments of education and state teachers associations, and student assistant organizations.

Scholarships for children of deceased veterans. Amvets National Service Foundation. 1957. 4p. Free

Scholarships available to high school seniors who are children of deceased or totally disabled veterans of World War II or the Korean conflict.

Scholarships, loans, and self-help opportunities in West Virginia colleges. Brannon, Paul. West Virginia State Department of Education. 1962. 152p. $1 paper

Prepared for high school students in West Virginia, the information has value to counselors and students in other states.

Q. SCHOLARSHIPS—*Continued*

Scholarships offered by the graphic arts industry. Graphic Arts Industry, Inc. 1962. 15p. Free
List of scholarships arranged by states.

**Selected aerospace career and scholarship information. Specialist for Aerospace Education, U.S. Office of Education. 1962. 16p. Single copy free
Bibliography of sources of information in six parts: aerospace career books; military career information; career pamphlets; lists of schools offering certain aviation courses; scholarships, fellowships, and loan information sources; and guidance and counseling.

A selected list of major fellowship opportunities and aids to advanced education. National Academy of Sciences. 1963. 8p. Free
Sources of graduate fellowships and loans.

Seven College Conference scholarship program. Seven College Conference. 1962. 6p. Free
Instructions for applying to three of the seven colleges with one application fee. Includes Barnard, Bryn Mawr, Mount Holyoke, Radcliffe, Smith, Vassar, and Wellesley.

Sloan national scholarships. Alfred P. Sloan Foundation. 1963. 23p. Free
Discussion of the concept and objectives of the scholarship program, names of institutions awarding the scholarships, and procedures for applying.

Social work fellowships and scholarships in Canada and the United States. Council on Social Work Education. 1962. 88p. $1
A biennial compilation of information about social work fellowships, scholarships, assistantships, loan funds, and work-study plans.

Sources of financial assistance for physical therapy students. American Physical Therapy Association. 1963. 8p. 5c. Single copy free
Includes sources available to prospective students, arranged by states.

Sponsored scholarship programs using College Board services—a partial listing for student guidance. College Entrance Examination Board. 1963. 24p. Free to counselors
Information about forty-two sponsored scholarship programs which use services provided by the Board, including nature of the aid, application procedures, tests used in selection, and eligibility requirements.

**Student aid annual. Sabo, Alex, ed. Chronicle Guidance Publications. 1963. 192p. $3.50
Financial assistance programs available to entering freshmen in 1,325 colleges, arranged by institution. An annual survey.

Student financial aid. Western Personnel Institute. 1963. 10p. 75c
Annotated bibliography of about thirty-five publications on this subject.

Student financial aid and national purpose. College Entrance Examination Board. 1962. 103p. $2.50
Twelve papers explore the ways financial aid to college students can help to meet the nation's economic, social, and educational needs. The papers cover

the traditions of student aid in America, the national stake in conserving talent, the cost of an ideal student aid program, and the appropriate roles of Federal, state, and private support of student aid.

Student financial aid in higher education: an annotated bibliography. Eells, Walter C. and Hollis, Ernest V. U.S. Office of Education. Supt. of Documents. 1960. 87p. 35c

References on financial aid problems and issues, including published materials on scholarships, fellowships, loan funds, assistantships, and other part-time employment.

Student financial aid in the United States: administration and resources. Moon, Rexford, Jr. College Entrance Examination Board. 1963. 47p. $1.50

A study of the number of awards and the total value of financial aid activities by colleges, states, Federal Government, private corporations, and civic groups. The report concludes that the total annual expenditure is over $700 million a year.

**Student financial aid: manual for colleges and universities. Babbidge, Homer D., Jr. American College Personnel Association. Order from American Personnel and Guidance Association. 1960. 56p. $1.50

Designed to help in the effective administration of measuring student need, scholarships, loan assistance, student employment, and miscellaneous forms of financial aid.

Student financial assistance selected references. Weary, Bettina. Chronicle Guidance Publications. 1963. 4p. 35c

List of thirty-six books and pamphlets. Prices and length of publications are not given.

Student information bulletin. National Merit Scholarship Corporation. Published annually. 32p. Free

Provides information of particular interest to high school students planning to participate in the annual National Merit Scholarship competition. It includes eligibility rules and requirements and a descriptive list of currently available scholarships awarded by the 150 cooperating companies, foundations, unions, professional associations, and other sponsors of Merit Scholarships.

Summer science training programs for high-ability secondary school students. National Science Foundation. Published annually. 20p. Free

Explanation of the types of training offered, qualifications, and financial aid for participants. List of colleges which offer these programs and the number of students accepted in each.

Talent bank: U.S.A. National Urban League. 1961. 24p. 25c. Free to counselors

Report of activity to provide incentives to Negro youth to prepare to become tomorrow's scientists and technicians.

The tuition plan. The Tuition Plan of New Hampshire. 1963. 8p. Free

Description of a method of paying college fees in monthly installments and a parent work sheet for computing costs.

Q. SCHOLARSHIPS—*Continued*

United States Government grants. Institute of International Education. 1962. 8p. Free
Graduate study awards under the Fulbright-Hays Act.

War orphans education. VA Pamphlet 22-3. Veterans Administration. 1961. 6p. Free
Description of program of financial aid for the education of sons and daughters of deceased war veterans.

What a counselor should know about financial aids for college students. Michigan State University, College of Education. 1958. 12p. 20c
Discussion of the counselor's responsibility in helping students with financial aids and description of the kinds of financial assistance available. Recommended source materials.

What kind of educational expense plan? Mullins, John M. College Entrance Examination Board. 1962. 2p. Free
Questions to ask about commercial plans for financing an education before selecting the one with the most desirable features.

World-wide graduate award directory. Advancement and Placement Institute. 1959. 56p. $3
Description of assistantships, fellowships, scholarships, and research grants contributed by over one thousand universities and foundations in forty-four states and fifty-five foreign countries. Arranged by country or state.

**You can win a scholarship. Brownstein, S. C.; Weiner, Mitchel; and Kaplan, Stanley. Barron's Educational Series, Inc. Revised 1963. 429p. $4.95; $2.98 paper
One section contains information about sources of scholarships. Other sections present illustrative exams, including questions from previous New York State scholarship examinations.

R. TEXTBOOKS FOR PUPILS

Building your life. Landis, Judson T. and Landis, Mary G. Prentice-Hall, Inc. 1959. 350p. $3.80
Written for young people in their early teens. Sections are devoted to the following topics: You and your personality, Learning to understand others, Obligations to self and society, Family understanding, Physical and mental health, and Growing up economically. Self-evaluation tests have been included with each chapter to help the student understand his present development and social adjustment.

Career planning. Smith, Leonard J. Harper and Row. 1959. 263p. $3.50
Textbook for a college course in career planning. Includes sections on studying an occupation, securing a job, self-employment, on-the-job relationships, and personal growth and advancement.

Educational and vocational planning. Martinson, William D. Scott, Foresman and Company. 1959. 84p. $1.50
Textbook for a college course. Includes units on the need for planning, learning about jobs, reaching a decision, learning to know yourself, planning your education, and locating a job.

Growing up. Second edition. Billett, Roy O. and Yeo, J. Wendell, D. C. Heath and Company. 1958. 374p. $4.96

Suitable for grades 8 to 10. Two of the twelve sections are devoted to educational planning and preparation for vocational choice. A teacher's manual for use with the text is available. $1.40.

**I find my vocation. Kitson, Harry D. McGraw-Hill Book Company. 1954. 282p. $3.96

Emphasis on the project method of giving the pupil projects and exercises which provide practice in consulting original sources of occupational information and developing ability to solve occupational problems. Includes list of biographies and autobiographies grouped according to occupations.

**If you're not going to college. Spiegler, Charles and Hamburger, Martin. Science Research Associates. 1959. 80p. $1.50

An activity-textbook for high school students who are not planning on four-year college training. Includes range of possibilities from semiprofessional and technical to trade and business education and on-the-job training opportunities.

The insight series—It's your education; It's your personality; It's your life; It's your future. Cribbin, James J.; McMahon, William J.; and Harris, Brother Philip. Harcourt, Brace and World. 1959-1962. 4 books. $2.64 each

This four-book series is designed for group guidance in Catholic high schools. The first book provides insight into the high school experience, the second insight into one's personality and relations with others, the third encourages planning for the future, and the fourth concerns the immediate job horizon, part-time work in college, military obligations, and a lifetime career. Teachers' handbooks are available.

It's your life—a group guidance program for Catholic high schools. Cribbin, James J.; Harris, Brother Philip; and McMahon, William J. Harcourt, Brace and World. 1958. 348p. $2.64

Includes topics for group guidance, including choosing a career and planning one's education. The chapters on colleges contain information about the Catholic colleges only. A teacher's handbook is available for use with the text.

Making the most of school and life. Robinson, Clark. Macmillan Company. 1952. 491p. $4.64

Contents: The part you play in your own growth, Improving your learning ability, Learning about people, Setting your goals, Your relations with others, Living well, and Choosing your life work. Teaching aids are presented for each chapter.

My career guidebook. Belman, Harry S. and Shertzer, Bruce. Bruce Publishing Company. 1963. 48p. 60c

A workbook for making future educational and vocational plans. Prepared for students at the junior high school level.

Occupational guidance. Chapman, Paul. Turner E. Smith and Company. 1950. 635p. $3.39

Textbook for ninth-grade course in occupations containing twenty-two chapters on representative occupations. Aids the student in analyzing his abilities, personality traits, and interests. A student's workbook, priced at $1, is available for use with the text.

R. Textbooks for Pupils—*Continued*

**Occupations and careers. Greenleaf, Walter. McGraw-Hill Book Company. 1955. 605p. $6.64
  Ten chapters on choosing and preparing for a job are followed by twelve chapters devoted to the major groups of occupations and twelve chapters containing information about the major industries. Bibliography.

Occupations text-notebooks. McKnight and McKnight Publishing Company. 1955. 6 units. $1 each
  A series of six text-notebooks designed for use with a course in occupations. Titles of booklets are: The Bobby G., Growing up, You and your future, Exploring occupations, Success in the world of work, and You and your work ways.

The opportunity series. McKnight and McKnight. 1962. 3 books. $1 each
  These books provide the framework for systematic instruction in group guidance. Individual titles are described below: Planning your school life, Planning your life's work, and Planning your future.

**Our world of work. Wolfbein, Seymour and Goldstein, Harold. Science Research Associates. 1961. 48p. 50c
  Presents a panoramic view of what our work force is like today and of the various trends that forecast its future. Includes discussion of how the world of work has changed in the past fifty years, what industries employ over sixty million workers, the major occupational fields, and other data about the rapidly growing labor market.

Planning my future. National Forum Foundation. 1963. 368p. $3.12
  One of a series of six books designed for homeroom or group guidance purposes. Written and illustrated to appeal to teen-agers. The titles are:

About Growing Up	1963 ed. $2.34	7th Grade
Being Teen-agers	1962 ed. $2.46	8th Grade
Our School Life	1961 ed. $2.46	9th Grade
Discovering Myself	1961 ed. $2.64	10th Grade
Planning My Future	1963 ed. $3.12	9-12 Grades
Toward Adult Living	1961 ed. $2.94	12th Grade

Planning your future. Hatch, Raymond; Parmenter, Morgan; and Stefflre, Buford. McKnight and McKnight Publishing Company. 1962. 80p. $1
  Prepared for use in grades 11 or 12, this book stresses job seeking, military service, and college admission.

Planning your future. Myers, George; Little, Gladys; and Robinson, Sarah. McGraw-Hill Book Company. 1953. 526p. $4.96
  The fourth edition of a textbook for courses in Occupations. Fourteen chapters are devoted to groups of occupations; for example, agriculture, mining, construction, transportation, and personal services. List of visual aids. Illustrated.

Planning your life's work. Hatch, Raymond; Parmenter, Morgan; and Stefflre, Buford. McKnight and McKnight Publishing Company. 1962. 104p. $1.20
  Intended for use in grades 9 or 10, this book stresses the developmental task of career choice. The student is urged to weigh the values and limitations of a variety of occupations and his relationship to them.

Planning your school life. Hatch, Raymond; Parmenter, Morgan; and Stefflre, Buford. McKnight and McKnight Publishing Company. 1962. 80p. $1

Guidebook prepared especially for grades 7 and 8. Chapter headings are: Self-discovery, Getting along with others, You and your school, Preparing for your career choice, Studying your way through school, and Your next steps.

Points for decision—a guide to help youth solve their problems. Mahoney, Harold and Engle, T. L. Revised edition. Harcourt, Brace and World. 1961. 566p. $4.96

Five of the fourteen chapters are entitled: Choosing a vocation, Learning about jobs, Getting and holding a job, Continuing education after high school, and Entering the Armed Forces. A teacher's supplement is available.

Selecting an occupation. Sifferd, Calvin S. McKnight and McKnight. 1962. 237p. $3.50

Eight chapters provide suggestions and directions for finding the demands and opportunities of occupations, for checking individual assets against such demands, for selecting a suitable occupation, and for finding employment. Eleven additional chapters present significant facts about representative types of work.

Success in the world of work. Cromwell, Floyd; Hatch, Raymond; and Parmenter, Morgan. McKnight and McKnight. 1953. 57p. $1

One of a series of text-notebooks containing illustrations, assignment pages, and discussion of the following topics: Deciding what one has to offer, finding the vacancy, letters of application, application forms and special tests, the employment interview, making progress, and what employers want.

**Vocational planning for college students. Borow, Henry and Lindsey, Robert. Prentice-Hall, Inc. 1959. 186p. $2.95 paper

Prepared as a textbook for a college course in orientation. Includes discussion of learning to explore occupations, delimiting the range of occupational choices, comparative study of two occupations, and understanding the world of work.

You and your career. Parmenter, Morgan. Guidance Centre, University of Toronto. Revised 1962. 128p. $1.32

A text-workbook for group guidance in secondary schools. Includes material on self-appraisal, occupations and industry, opportunities for education, and find a job. Other books in this series are:

Exploring occupations. 1962. $1.16
Growing up. 1962. 94c
Your further education. 1962. 80c
Success in the world of work. 1961. 75c
Teacher's manual. 1960. 37c

You and your lifework: a Christian choice for youth. Science Research Associates. Developed in cooperation with the Department of the Ministry, Commission on Higher Education, National Council of the Churches of Christ in the U.S.A. 1963. 72p. $1.25

A study-notebook prepared for use under the direction of a church leader. A *Local Church Leader's Guide* is available for $1.50.

You: today and tomorrow. Katz, Martin R. Cooperative Test Division, Educational Testing Service. 1959. 102p. $1

A work-text prepared for the eighth or ninth grade group guidance program, focusing on students' self-appraisal for educational and vocational planning. A teacher's guide is available at a cost of $1.

Your future job, a guide to personal and occupational orientation of youth in the Atomic Age. Bedford, J. H. Society for Occupational Research. 1956. 412p. $3.50

Contains sixteen chapters on the main occupational groups such as building and construction, clerical, health, personal service, and transportation. Within each chapter about two pages are devoted to each of eight or ten representative kinds of work. Illustrated. Bibliography.

Your high school days. Detjen, Mary Ford and Detjen, Ervin W. McGraw-Hill Book Company. 1958. 246p. $3.96

Discussion of topics important to a young person during his high school years: becoming adjusted to a new school, choosing the right subjects, knowing how to study, conducting meetings and organizing groups, getting along with teachers, making friends, engaging in part-time work, making the best use of leisure time, and becoming a mature individual.

S. USE OF OCCUPATIONAL INFORMATION
AND
THE COUNSELOR'S PROFESSIONAL BOOKSHELF

The adolescent views himself. Strang, Ruth. McGraw-Hill Book Company. 1958. 581p. $6.95

Two chapters contain discussions of progress toward educational and vocational goals and achieving scholastic success.

The American high school today. Conant, James B. McGraw-Hill Book Company. 1959. 140p. $2.95; paper $1.50

Contains specific recommendations for guidance in the secondary schools.

The American occupations finder. Benson, Warren E. Research Publishing Company. 1960. 470p. $7.50

A device to assist pupils in planning a job objective keyed to their academic courses taken in high school.

**America's resources of specialized talent. Wolfle, Dael. Harper and Row. 1954. 332p. Out of print but available in many libraries

Report of the Commission on Human Resources and Advanced Training. An appraisal of current resources and a look ahead.

Answers to questions about guidance. National Education Association. 1963. 4p. 35 copies $1

Provides answers to twelve questions about objectives, methods, and results of modern school guidance programs. Prepared to use with parent meetings.

Appraising vocational fitness by means of psychological tests. Revised edition. Super, Donald E. and Crites, John C. Harper and Row. 1962. 704p. $12

Revision of earlier book containing discussion of tests for educational and vocational appraisal. It analyzes many aspects of the most useful tests under the headings of intelligence, proficiency, clerical aptitude, manual dexterities, mechanical aptitude, spatial visualization, aesthetic judgment and artistic ability, musical talent, custom-built batteries for specific occupations, interest, and personality and temperament.

Basic concepts in vocational guidance. Sanderson, Herbert. McGraw-Hill Book Company. 1954. 338p. $6.25

Presents a discussion of the theoretical aspects of counseling adolescents. Includes a section on the relationship of vocational guidance to other helping professions.

Bennett occupations filing plan. Bennett, Wilma. Distributed by Careers, Largo, Florida. 1958. $16

A set of gummed printed labels for about three hundred fields of work and five hundred cross references which may be pasted on file folders and arranged alphabetically. Also includes a booklet outlining the filing plan.

Cardinal principles of secondary education. U.S. Office of Education. Supt. of Documents. 1918. Reprinted 1958. 32p. 15c

Stresses the right of every boy and girl in the country to a high school education, the worth of the individual, and the exploration of individual talents; underlines the importance of developing common ideals and knowledge for a rich, democratic life.

Career development: choice and adjustment. Tiedeman, David V.; O'Hara, Robert P.; and Baruch, Rhoda W. College Entrance Examination Board. 1963. 108p. $2.50

Career development is described as a evolutionary process in which the individual chooses a vocation according to his personality traits and then adjusts himself to the demands of that vocation. Includes an analysis of three tape-recorded case histories to illustrate the interrelationship of personality and career choice.

Career development: self-concept theory. Super, Donald; Starishevsky, Reuben; Matlin, Norman; and Jordaan, Jean Pierre. College Entrance Examination Board. 1963. 95p. $2.50

Second of two volumes on the subject of career development. Explains the self-concept theory, which divides an individual's life into five stages: growth, exploration, establishment, maintenance, and decline. Shows how knowledge of a person's behavior patterns during the earlier stages can be used to predict his behavior during the later ones.

Career exploration: a guide for extension workers. U.S. Department of Agriculture. Supt. of Documents. 1963. 19p. 15c

Explains how the county agent can interest youth and the community in career problems.

S. Use of Occupational Information and the Counselor's Professional Bookshelf—*Continued*

Chart of occupational titles and related high school subjects. Hansson, Andrew and Ida, Alfred. Research Publishing Company. 1954. 22p. $2

> A chart suggests the subjects a high school student should take to prepare for each of 175 occupations and trades. Prepared for help in making out student programs.

College Board score reports: a guide for counselors. College Entrance Examination Board. 1963. 45p. 25c. Free to counselors

> Detailed information about the use and interpretation of scores on the Scholastic Aptitude Test, the achievement tests, and the Preliminary Scholastic Aptitude Test.

**Complete planning for college: the Kiplinger guide to your education beyond high school. Sulkin, Sidney. McGraw-Hill Book Company. 1962. 268p. $5.95; $3.95 paper

> Includes planning the high school courses, planning for the right college for the right student, financing, and planning for a suitable career.

Counseling and employment service for youth. Bureau of Employment Security, U.S. Department of Labor. Supt. of Documents. 1962. 84p. 40c

> Description of the procedures used by the state employment services in the placement of youth in suitable jobs. Sample forms are appended.

Counseling and guidance: an exploration. Moser, L. E. and Moser, R. S. Prentice-Hall, Inc. 1963. 446p. $6.95

> An introduction to current concepts, theories, and practices.

Counseling and guidance in schools. Patterson, C. H. Harper and Row. 1961. 382p. $4.75

> Part three contains a discussion of the presentation of occupational information and educational-vocational counseling.

Counseling psychology. Hahn, Milton and MacLean, Malcolm. McGraw-Hill Book Company. 1955. 302p. $5.95

> This revised edition presents the basic theories and concepts of clinical counseling. Especially helpful chapters on a systematic case study and the techniques of counseling.

**The counselor in a changing world. Wrenn, C. Gilbert. American Personnel and Guidance Association. 1962. 195p. $2.50

> Report of the Commission on Guidance in American Schools, containing discussion of major elements in the school counselor's task, the nature of changes in the next decade, new social forces that are influencing young people, and personal and professional recommendations to the school counselor. Selected references.

Cross references for Careers desk-top kit. Careers. 1962. 16p. Free to users of the kit.

> List of about eight hundred cross references, including the titles used in an occupational file and the "see also" references to related or alternate careers. Useful in setting up an extensive filing plan.

Design for community action. Supt. of Documents. 1962. 36p. 20c
Suggestions for mobilizing community resources to help youth enter the world of work.

Dolan guide to student preparation of occupational materials. Dolan, Robert A. Research Publishing Company. 1960. 8p. $15 per 100 copies
Enables a teacher to assign to a group of pupils the project of compiling a set of occupational facts about many careers which can be incorporated into a class career book. Chart contains headings that designate the types of information and provides blank spaces for pupils to fill in the assembled information.

Education and manpower. David, Henry, ed. Columbia University Press. 1960. 326p. $5
Includes discussion of manpower shortage and ways in which individual abilities can best be developed and utilized.

Education for a changing world of work. Willis, Benjamin C. et al. U.S. Office of Education. Supt. of Documents. 1963. 296p. $1.25
Report of President's panel of consultants on vocational education containing analysis of implications of automation, technological advance, population mobility, discrimination, and urbanization. Concludes that vocational education is not sufficiently sensitive to supply and-demand factors in the labor force and that service to the urban population is meager.

Education, manpower and economic growth: strategies of human resource development. Harbison, Frederick and Myers, Charles A. McGraw-Hill Book Company. 1964. 229p. $7.50
The authors stress that the development of human resources is a more reliable indicator today of the growth of nations than any other measure. Methods of greater investment in people through education and training are suggested.

Educational Testing Service annual report. 1962. 132p. Free to counselors
Review of activities for the year and comments on various aspects of testing. A summary of current projects is included.

Elementary school guidance. Detjen, Ervin W. and Detjen, Mary F. McGraw-Hill Book Company. 1963. 240p. $5.95
Provides an introduction to the guidance services of the elementary school, the functions of guidance personnel, and some of the techniques and methods which can be used by teachers.

The faculty in college counseling. Hardee, Melvene D. McGraw-Hill Book Company. 1959. 391p. $6.95
Describes the functions of the faculty member as an adviser to students and relates faculty advising to the program of total college counseling.

Gathering and filing occupational information. Christensen, Thomas E. Research Publishing Company. 1957. 32p. $1.50
Sources of occupational materials are followed by a discussion of the mechanics of occupational file arrangement.

S. Use of Occupational Information and the Counselor's
Professional Bookshelf—*Continued*

Guidance—an examination. Harvard Educational Review. Fall 1962
issue. 159p. $1.50
Special issue with the stated purpose of subjecting guidance to critical and
scholarly review. Includes an interesting article by Carl Rogers.

Guidance and counseling in groups. 2nd edition. Bennett, Margaret E.
McGraw-Hill Book Company. 1963. 421p. $7.75
Includes developments in research and practice with respect to group guidance work. One chapter is devoted to vocational planning and one to educational planning.

Guidance for children in elementary schools. U.S. Office of Education.
Supt. of Documents. 1963. 22p. 15c
Outlines some current educational practices which are common to a selected
number of elementary school programs and suggests new approaches for further
research.

Guidance for the underachiever with superior ability. Miller, Leonard
M. U.S. Office of Education. Supt. of Documents. 1961. 85p. 35c
Contains suggestions for identification of the guidance needs and problems of
the underachiever and meeting those needs at the various levels of education.

Guidance in business education. Dame, J. Frank and Brinkman, Albert
R. South-Western Publishing Company. 1961. 330p. $4
Several chapters are devoted to methods of imparting occupational informa-
tion.

**Guidance in the junior high school. Cottingham, Harold F. and
Hopke, William. McKnight and McKnight Publishing Company.
1961. 390p. $6
A philosophical framework is followed by details of an organized guidance
program with examples from specific junior high schools. The authors have
summarized information from more than three hundred junior high schools
recommended for their successful guidance programs.

Guidance in the modern school. McDaniel, Henry B. with Shaftel,
G. A. Holt, Rinehart and Winston. 1956. 526p. $5.75 Revision in
process
One section is a discussion of the informational program.

Guidance policy and practice. Mathewson, Robert H. Harper and
Row. 1962. 397p. $6
This third edition contains a discussion of future directions and changing
trends.

Guidance: program development and management. Peters, Herman J.
and Schertzer, Bruce. Merrill Books, Inc. 1963. 592p. $10
This book presents plans for initiating, developing, and appraising a modern
school guidance program. One chapter is devoted to developing a vocational
guidance service and one to educational guidance.

**Guidance services. Humphreys, J. Anthony; Traxler, Arthur E; and North, Robert D. Science Research Associates. 1960. 414p. $5.25
Discussion of principles and techniques. Includes chapters on making vocational choices, solving educational problems, and finding jobs.

Guidance services. Stoops, Emery, ed. McGraw-Hill Book Company. 1959. 302p. $6.25
Provides basic principles and techniques for organizing and administering a pupil guidance program.

Guidance services in schools. Froehlich, Clifford P. McGraw-Hill Book Company. 1958. 383p. $6.50
Two chapters are entitled: Disseminating occupational information by group methods; Aids in the dissemination of occupational information.

Guidance services in the modern school. Ohlsen, Merle M. Harcourt, Brace and World. 1964. 515p. $6.95
One section focuses attention on educational and vocational planning.

Guidance services in the secondary school. Hatch, Ray; Dressel, Paul; and Costar, James. Wm. C. Brown Company. 1963. 206p. $3.75
This revision of an earlier book identifies the functions of a guidance service and presents many practical methods.

**Guidance services, Section G, evaluative criteria. National Study of Secondary School Evaluation. 1960. 16p. 25c
Statement of guiding principles, check lists, and criteria for evaluations.

Guiding today's youth. Los Angeles County Supt. of Schools. California Test Bureau. 1962. 411p. $5.95
Contains many practical suggestions for assisting youth to make realistic plans.

Guidelines for preparing and evaluating occupational materials. National Vocational Guidance Association. Revised 1964. 11p. 10c
Includes a guide for preparing industrial careers brochures and standards for use in preparing and evaluating occupational literature.

Handbook on women workers. Women's Bureau, U.S. Department of Labor. Supt. of Documents. 1962. 202p. 55c
This handbook of facts on women workers, published biennially, brings together basic information on trends in women's employment and occupations; the age and marital status of women workers; earnings and income; educational status; and state laws affecting the employment of women. Includes a directory of national organizations of interest to women.

Helping counselors grow professionally. Evraiff, William. Prentice-Hall, Inc. 1963. 376p. $5.95
Many helpful suggestions for personal and professional growth.

High school personnel work today. Warters, Jane. McGraw-Hill Book Company. 1956. 358p. $5.50
One chapter is entitled, "Helping the individual to learn about the world of work."

How to set up a guidance unit. Munson, Harold L. Science Research
Associates. 1957. 48p. $1.25
Suggestions for a unit in a course in English and social studies.

How to set up a semester or year course in guidance. Hill, Wendell.
Science Research Associates. 1958. 48p. $1.25
Designed for a group guidance course in planning for future education and
work.

How, when, and where to provide occupational information. Weaver,
Glen. Science Research Associates. 1954. 48p. $1.25
Suggestions for providing a continuous program of giving information about
occupations.

**The information service in guidance: occupational, educational, social.
Norris, Willa; Zeran, F. R.; and Hatch, R. N. Rand McNally and
Company. 1960. 598p. $7
The nature, scope, types, and sources of information are outlined, followed
by chapters on the presentation of the information and programming the
services.

Interest check list. U.S. Employment Service. Supt. of Documents.
1946. 4p. 5c each; $1.50 per 100 copies
Items in the check list are based on the grouping of jobs as found in Part IV
of the *Dictionary of Occupational Titles*. Useful as an interviewing aid when
working with persons who have no definite stated work interest or who have
limited knowledge of the wide variety of tasks and activities in various occupational fields. A manual of instruction is available for five cents additional
cost.

Introduction to counseling. Tolbert, E. L. McGraw-Hill Book Company. 1959. 322p. $6.25
Prepared as a text for a beginning course in counseling techniques for pre-
service and in-service training of teachers. Two chapters pertain to the use of
occupational and educational information in counseling.

Junior high-school guidance. Johnson, Mauritz; Busacker, William; and
Bowman, Fred. Harper and Row. 1961. 275p. $4.50
One chapter contains description of information services; several suggest
homeroom, classroom, and student activities.

Keep them in school. Bureau of Labor Standards, U.S. Department of
Labor. Supt. of Documents. 1963. 10p. 10c
Leaflet addressed to parents of school-age children. Presents information on
the value of education and gives hints on how parents may help their children
stay in school and graduate. Stresses that a good education helps provide a
better job, more pay, and greater job security.

Labor in America 1913-1963. Bureau of Labor Statistics, U.S. Department of Labor. 1963. 23p. Free
This pamphlet contains twenty-six charts depicting fifty years of increasing
human welfare, such as per cent of population enrolled in school, changes in

skill distribution of labor force, average hours in work week, life expectancy at birth, personal consumption expenditures per capita, and current expenditures per pupil in public schools.

Librarians and counselors work together for an effective guidance program in the school. American Association of School Librarians. 1960. 8p. Free to counselors and librarians
  Suggestions for cooperation and a short list of source materials.

Man in a world at work. Borow, Henry, ed. Houghton Mifflin Company. 1963. 606p. $8.25
  Written to commemorate the fiftieth anniversary of the National Vocational Guidance Association, the twenty-four writings are grouped under the following headings: Roots of vocational guidance, the occupational kaleidoscope, research horizons, and the professional practice of vocational guidance.

Man, work, and society. Nosow, Sigmund and Form, William H. Basic Books, Inc. 1962. 612p. $8.50
  A collection of writings of men in the field of sociology about man's relationship to work and the society he lives in. Good bibliography on the psychology of work.

Manpower and training: trends, outlook, program. Office of Manpower, Automation, and Training, U.S. Department of Labor. 1963. 26p. Free
  This bulletin reviews the status of employment, unemployment, and the programs developed to solve problems faced by displaced workers as a result of changes in the structure of the economy. Many charts predict the labor force growth.

Manpower: challenge of the 1960's. U.S. Department of Labor. Supt. of Documents. 1960. 24p. 25c
  Shows by text, graphs, tables, and charts the many changes in our population and labor force which are expected to take place between 1960 and 1970.

Meeting the manpower challenge of the sixties. U.S. Department of Labor. Supt. of Documents. 1960. 76p. $1
  A guide for leaders for conducting discussions on labor trends and occupational growth.

Methods of vocational guidance. Revised edition. Forrester, Gertrude. D. C. Heath and Company. 1951. 463p. $6.75
  Twenty chapters are devoted to methods of presenting information about occupations. Source materials and selected references are recommended for each topic.

Military guidance in secondary schools. Army Careers, U.S. Continental Army Command. 1962. 40p. Free to counselors
  Guide for counselors to assist students and parents with military obligation problems.

The motivation to work. Herzbert, Frederick; Mausner, Bernard; and Snyderman, Barbara. Wiley and Sons. 1959. 157p. $4.50
  A study of job attitude, job motivation, and job satisfaction of over two hundred management persons who reported major changes in their feelings to-

ward their jobs. The authors conclude that the most profound motivation to
work comes from the recognition of individual achievement and from the sense
of personal growth in responsibility.

**Occupational information. Hoppock, Robert. McGraw-Hill Book Company. 1963. 546p. $7.95

Revision of the author's *Group Guidance*. Includes discussions of basic
theories of occupational choice, the use of occupational information in counseling, principles and methods of teaching courses in occupations, and suggestions
for college instructors of courses in occupations.

Occupational information for counselors. Mahoney, Harold J. Harcourt,
Brace, and World. 1952. 70p. $1

Survey as to the contents that ought to comprise the area of training in occupational information for secondary school counselors. A jury of experts checked
a list of 203 items in the area of occupational information, classified under nine
appropriate categories.

**Occupational information in the elementary school. Norris, Wilma.
Science Research Associates. 1963. 243p. $4.95

Includes theory and methods of presenting occupational information from
kindergarten through sixth grade. The last half of the book contains lists of
books, pamphlets, films, filmstrips, songs, and recordings suitable for use.

**Occupational information; its development and application. Shartle,
Carroll L. Prentice-Hall, Inc. Revised 1959. 384p. $8.65

Needs and uses of occupational information, methods of classification of
occupations, and discussion of patterns of occupations, entry fields of work, and
occupational families. Lists of sources of occupational information materials.

**Occupational information: its nature and use. Baer, Max F. and Roeber,
Edward C. Science Research Associates. 1959. 495p. $5.95

Includes discussion of the use of occupational information in counseling interviews and with groups of students.

Occupational information reference file. Wellington, A. M. Counselor
Education Press. 1962. 23p. $1

List of about one thousand titles for folder labels, listed both numerically by
code number and alphabetically by title. Titles are the base titles to which
code numbers have been assigned in Volume II of the *Dictionary of Occupational Titles*.

Occupational planning for women. Zapoleon, Marguerite. Harper and
Row. 1961. 276p. $5

Addressed to those whose function it is to help girls and women in their occupational planning. Includes description of what is being done in schools, public employment offices, and other settings to provide vocational guidance.

Organization and administration of guidance services. Roeber, Edward;
Smith, Glenn; and Erickson, Clifford. McGraw-Hill Book Company.
1955. 294p. $6.25

Includes discussion of initiating, administering, and evaluating a program of
guidance services. Many procedures are recommended. Includes chapters on
counseling, individual inventory, information, placement and follow-up, certification of counselors, and evaluation of the guidance services.

Organization and administration of guidance services. Zeran, Franklin and Riccio, Anthony. Rand McNally and Company. 1962. 302p. $6
Includes sections on informational services, analysis of the individual, counseling services, placement and follow-up, evaluation of existing services, and organizational practices. Two chapters are devoted to informational services and the dissemination of information.

Organization and administration of pupil personnel service programs in selected school systems. U.S. Office of Education. Supt. of Documents. 1961. 73p. 30c
Presents description of illustrative program in eight urban school districts.

Physical facilities for school guidance services. Twiford, Don, ed. U.S. Office of Education. 1960. 22p. Free to counselors
A statement of educational specifications to assist in planning and improving physical facilities for guidance. Includes a bibliography and sample floor plan layouts.

Planned group guidance. Wrenn, C. Gilbert; Hein, Reinhard G.; and Schwarzrock, Shirley P. American Guidance Services. 1961. 82p. $2.50
A manual for the sponsor of various types of planned group guidance activities in four basic orientation areas: to school, to others, to self, and to the future. Includes thirty-eight discussion projects with suggested procedures.

A policy for skilled manpower. National Manpower Council. Columbia University Press. 1954. 250p. $4.50
This book examines the nature of the manpower situation in the United States, shows the major effects and implications for American schools and colleges, and presents suggestions for educational policy. States that effort must be devoted to improving the training, guidance, distribution, and utilization of manpower resources because of the present shortage in fields in which exceptional talent and special training are necessary.

Principles and practices in guidance. Stoops, Emery and Wahlquist, Gunnar. McGraw-Hill Book Company. 1958. 369p. $6.25
Chapter five is devoted to group methods of presenting vocational information.

Principles and practices of the guidance program. Smith, Glenn E. Macmillan Company. 1951. 379p. $5.75
Two of twelve chapters contain discussion of the information service.

Principles of guidance. Fifth edition. Jones, Arthur J. McGraw-Hill Book Company. 1963. 305p. $6.50
Discussion of the meaning and function of guidance, the organization in schools, information essential for effective guidance, methods, new areas, and present status.

The psychology of careers. Super, Donald E. Harper and Row. 1957. 362p. $6.50
One section on the dynamics of vocational development is a discussion of the influence of aptitude, interest, personality, family, economics, disabilities, and chance on vocational development.

The psychology of occupations. Roe, Anne. John Wiley and Sons. 1956. 340p. $6.75
Includes analysis of research studies pertaining to vocations as affected by personality, intelligence, and life histories. Psychological aspects of jobs are stressed. A two-dimensional classification of occupations is presented.

Pupil personnel and guidance services. Johnson, Walter; Stefflre, Buford; and Edelfelt, Roy. McGraw-Hill Book Company. 1961. 407p. $6.50
This book delineates the areas best served by guidance specialist, administrator, and teacher. Also describes trends and changing values which are changing the form of school guidance practices.

Pupil personnel services in American schools. Arbuckle, Dugald, S. Allyn and Bacon, Inc. 1962. 419p. $6.75
One section is devoted to the informational service and another to a discussion of teachers and counselors in action.

Readings in guidance: principles, practices, organization, administration. Crow, L. D. and Crow, Alice, editors. McKay Company. 1962. 640p. $3.95
Ninety-five articles have been selected to present the responsibilities of counselors, teachers, parents, and administrators. Six are concerned with occupational information and vocational guidance.

Remedial reading—teaching and treatment. Woolf, Maurice D. and Woolf, Jeanne A. McGraw-Hill Book Company. 1957. 424p. $6.75
Includes a section on counseling the retarded reader and a ten-page list of easy books which have interested retarded readers and non-readers.

School guidance and personnel services. Rosecrance, Francis C. and Hayden, Velma. Allyn and Bacon. 1960. 373p. $6
Several chapters contain discussions of methods of imparting information about occupations.

Selecting an occupation. Sifferd, Calvin. McKnight and McKnight Publishing Company. 1962. 237p. $3.50
This book includes procedures of studying occupations, methods of finding employment opportunities, and factors that influence success.

Selection and use of occupational-information materials. Michigan State University, College of Education. 1955. 20p. 60c
Designed to aid teachers of agriculture in the identification and use of related occupational information.

Socio-guidramas. Splaver, Sarah, editor. Methods and Materials Press. 1954-1963. 12p. 30 titles. 50c each
Ten-minute playlets designed to promote discussion of teen-age problems, some of which are occupational.

The sociology of work. Caplow, Theodore. University of Minnesota Press. 1954. 330p. $5
A treatise on the subject of occupational sociology. Has two indexes, occupational and general. Bibliography.

Standard industrial classification manual. Technical Committee on Industrial Classification, Division of Statistical Standards, Bureau of the Budget. Supt. of Documents. 1957. 433p. $2.50. Supplement 1963. 71p. 30c

A classification structure with descriptions of the industries to be included in each category. This system consists of nine major classifications, divided into seventy-nine major groups which are further subdivided into five hundred closely related industries.

Student personnel services in colleges and universities. Williamson, E. G. McGraw-Hill Book Company. 1961. 474p. $7.50

Defines the educational role of personnel services and the efforts of colleges to assist students in solving their own problems in connection with their intellectual and personal development.

Student personnel services in higher education. Arbuckle, Dugald S. McGraw-Hill Book Company. 1953. 268p. $6.50

Discussion of techniques and procedures used in institutions of higher learning.

Teacher's guide to You; Today and Tomorrow, Cooperative Test Division, Educational Testing Service. 1959. 32p. $1

Suggestions for using the textbook in a group guidance program.

The teacher's handbook for your life plans and the Armed Forces. 1955. 60p. 60c

Teaching methods to be used with the manual, Your Life Plans and the Armed Forces. Contains a series of thirty instructional units which may be incorporated into a high school curriculum, providing information concerning military obligations, options, and vocational and educational opportunities in the military service.

Techniques of counseling. Warters, Jane. McGraw-Hill Book Company. 1964. 478p. $7.95

Discussion of tests, inventories, observation reports, self-reports, cumulative personnel records, case studies, and case conferences.

Techniques of guidance. Traxler, Arthur E. Harper and Row. 1957. 374p. $6.50

Especially helpful chapters on testing and analysis of the individual.

10,000 careers. Thorndike, Robert L. and Hagen, Elizabeth. Wiley and Sons. 1959. 346p. $8.50

Report of the comparison of the results of aptitude tests taken by 10,000 men in military service in World War II with their progress in postwar careers. Discussion of the use of aptitude tests to predict a person's ability to prepare for, obtain, and hold a job.

Testing in guidance and counseling. Berdie, Ralph F.; Swanson, Edward C.; Hagenah, Theda; and Layton, W. F. McGraw-Hill Book Company. 1963. 288p. $6.75

Discussion of tests in counseling and other methods of personality evaluation, such as occupational and educational planning, responsibilities of the counselor, and research in counseling.

S. Use of Occupational Information and the Counselor's
Professional Bookshelf—*Continued*

Testing; its place in education today. Chauncey, Henry and Dobbin, John
E. Harper and Row. 1964. 223p. $4.96

The president and project director of the Educational Testing Service discuss
testing techniques, the strengths and limitations of testing, uses, and characer-
istics of specific tests.

Training activities under the Manpower Development and Training Act.
U.S. Office of Education. Supt. of Documents. 1963. 87p. 55c

A report of the administrative structure, analysis of operations, criteria for
assessing training, and evaluation of trainees and training programs.

**United States census of population: 1960. Detailed characteristics. U.S.
Bureau of Census. Supt. of Documents. 1962. 687p. One for each
state. PC (1) 32D. $2.50 and $3 each

This report gives statistical information concerning jobs in the economy,
employment data, detailed occupation, and detailed industry. Includes number
of men and women in each of 479 occupations and 149 industries. Another
table presents earnings in each of 8 brackets for each of the occupations.
Good statistical reports for counselors and research workers.

Use of occupational information materials. Ross, Roland G. Research
Publishing Company. 1949. 24p. $1

Includes discussion of use by classroom teachers, counselors, pupils, industry,
and the community.

Vocational counseling: a reappraisal in honor of Donald G. Paterson.
Viteles, Morris S., Brayfield, Arthur H. and Tyler, Leona E. University of Minnesota Press. 1962. 70p. $1.50

Papers concerning the past, present, and future of vocational guidance.

Vocational development: a framework for research. Super, Donald, and
others. Bureau of Publications. 1957. 142p. $4.25; $2.75 paper

Review of various approaches to vocational choice and behavior and indications for further research.

The vocational maturity of ninth-grade boys. Super, Donald and Over-
street, Phoebe. Bureau of Publications. 1960. 212p. $5.25

Study of the vocational maturity of a group of ninth grade boys, ascertain-
ing relationships between vocational maturity measures and other personal
and background variables.

Why people work: changing incentives in a troubled world. Levenstein,
Aaron. Crowell-Collier Press. 1962. 320p. $3.95

After a discussion of the reasons for changing attitudes toward work, the
author points out that the job satisfaction factors begin with security, interest,
opportunity for advancement, and authority for making decisions. He notes
that wages are far from the first incentive in the list.

Worker security in a changing economy. Monthly Labor Review. June 1963. 153p. 75c

A special issue in honor of the 50th anniversary of the U.S. Department of Labor. Reviews the structure of worker security that underlies American employment and raises questions as to its future adequacy. Includes the workers' search for security, the dynamic nature of workers' goals, and the response to change.

**Your college education—how to pay for it. Splaver, Sarah. Julian Messner, Inc. 1964. 288p. $4.95; library binding $4.64 net

Discussion of methods of increasing a student's financial resources, decreasing his college costs, and securing financial aid when need exists. Two sections of special interest to the counselor are the financial aid programs and informational materials provided by states and those available in the major fields of study.

Publishers' Directory

Abelard-Schuman, Limited, 6 W. 57th St., New York 19

Abingdon Press, 201 Eighth Ave. S., Nashville 3, Tenn.

Academy of Advanced Traffic, 63 Vesey St., New York 7

Acoustical Society of America, 335 E. 45th St., New York 17

Administrative Research Associates, Box 3, Deerfield, Ill.

Adult Education Association of the United States, 743 N. Wabash Ave., Chicago 11, Ill.

Advancement and Placement Institute, 169 N. 9th St., Brooklyn 11, N.Y.

Advertising Federation of America, 655 Madison Ave., New York 21

Aero Publishers, Inc., 2162 Sunset Blvd., Los Angeles 26, Calif.

Air-Conditioning and Refrigeration Institute, 1815 N. Fort Myer Drive, Arlington 9, Va.

Air Force Aid Society, National Headquarters, Washington 25, D.C.

Air Transport Association of America, 1000 Connecticut Ave., N.W., Washington 6, D.C.

Albright College, Reading, Pa.

Allied Trades of the Baking Industry, 625 Madison Ave., New York 22

Allis-Chalmers Manufacturing Company, Public Relations Division, Box 512, Milwaukee 1, Wis.

Allyn and Bacon, Inc., 150 Tremont St., Boston 11, Mass.

Alpha Kappa Psi, 111 E. 38th St., Indianapolis 5, Ind.

Aluminum Company of America, 1501 Alcoa Bldg., Pittsburgh 19, Pa.

Alumnae Advisory Center, Inc., 541 Madison Ave., New York 22

American Academy of Political and Social Science, 3937 Chestnut Street, Philadelphia 4, Pa.

American Accounting Association, School of Commerce, University of Wisconsin, Madison 6, Wis.

American Anthropological Association, 1530 P St., N.W., Washington 5, D.C.

American Association for Health, Physical Education, and Recreation, 1201 16th St., N.W., Washington 6, D.C.

American Association for Rehabilitation Therapy, Box 34, Lemay Branch, St. Louis 25, Mo.

American Association for the Advancement of Science, 1515 Massachusetts Ave., N.W., Washington 5, D.C.

American Association of Advertising Agencies, 200 Park Ave., New York 17

American Association of Anatomists, Department of Anatomy, School of Medicine, University of Pennsylvania, Philadelphia 4, Pa.

American Association of Dental Schools, 840 N. Lake Shore Drive, Chicago 11, Ill.

American Association of Industrial Nurses, 170 E. 61st St., New York 21

American Association of Junior Colleges, 1777 Massachusetts Ave., N.W., Washington 6, D.C.

American Association of Land-Grant Colleges and State Universities, Division of Agriculture, Care of Chester S. Hutchison, Ohio State University, College of Agriculture, Columbus 10, Ohio

American Association of Medical Record Librarians, 840 N. Lake Shore Drive, Chicago 11, Ill.

American Association of Nurse Anesthetists, Prudential Bldg., Prudential Plaza, Chicago 1, Ill.

American Association of Nurserymen, 835 Southern Bldg., Washington 5, D.C.

American Association of School Librarians, 50 E. Huron St., Chicago 11, Ill.

American Association of Theological Schools, 934 Third National Bldg., Dayton 3, Ohio

American Astronomical Society, Care of Paul M. Routly, 265 FitzRandolph Road, Princeton, N.J.

American Bakers Association, 20 N. Wacker Drive, Chicago 6, Ill.

American Bankers Association, 12 E. 36th St., New York 16

American Bar Association, Information Service, 1155 E. 60th St., Chicago 37, Ill.

American Book-Stratford Press, Inc., 75 Varick St., New York 13

American Camping Association, 342 Madison Ave., New York 17

American Cemetery Association, 329 E. Broad St., Columbus 15, Ohio

American Ceramic Society, 4055 N. High St., Columbus 14, Ohio

American Chamber of Commerce Executives, Education Committee, 1627 K St., N.W., Washington 6, D.C.

American Chemical Society, 1155 16th St., N.W., Washington 6, D.C.

American Collectors Association, Inc., 5011 Ewing Ave., South, Minneapolis 10, Minn.

American College of Hospital Administrators, 840 N. Lake Shore Drive, Chicago 11, Ill.

American College Testing Program, 519 W. Sheridan Road, McHenry, Ill.

American Collegiate Retailing Association, 24 Waverly Place, New York 3

American Council on Education, 1785 Massachusetts Ave., N.W., Washington 6, D.C.

American Council on Education for Journalism, Ernie Pyle Hall, Indiana University, Bloomington, Ind.

American Council on Pharmaceutical Education, 77 W. Washington St., Chicago 2, Ill.

American Dental Assistants Association, 410 First National Bank Bldg., La Porte, Ind.

American Dental Association, 222 E. Superior St., Chicago 11, Ill.

American Dental Association, Council on Dental Education, 222 E. Superior St., Chicago 11, Ill.

American Dental Hygientists' Association, 100 E. Ohio St., Chicago 11, Ill.

American Dietetic Association, 620 N. Michigan Ave., Chicago 11, Ill.

American Economic Association, Northwestern University, 629 Noyes St., Evanston, Ill.

American Educational Theatre Association, Northwestern University, 1925 Orrington Ave., Evanston, Ill.

American Federation of Labor and Congress of Industrial Organizations, Department of Education, 815 16th St., N.W., Washington 6, D.C.

American Federation of Technical Engineers, 900 F St., N.W., Washington 4, D.C.

American Fisheries Society, 1404 New York Ave., N.W., Washington 5, D.C.

American Forest Products Industries, Inc., 1816 N St., N.W., Washington 6, D.C.

American Foundation for the Blind, 15 W. 16th St., New York 11

American Foundations Information Service. See Foundation Library Center

American Geological Institute, 1444 N St., N.W., Washington 5, D.C.

American Geophysical Union, 1515 Massachusetts Ave., N.W., Washington 5, D.C.

American Guidance Services, Inc., 720 Washington Ave., S.E., Minneapolis 14, Minn.

American Guild of Organists, 630 Fifth Ave., New York 20

American Hearing Society, 919 18th St., N.W., Washington 6, D.C.

American Heart Association, 44 E. 23d St., New York 10

American Historical Association, 400 A St., S.E., Washington 3, D.C.

American Home Economics Association, 1600 20th St., N.W., Washington 9, D.C.

American Hospital Association, 840 N. Lake Shore Drive, Chicago 11, Ill.

American Hotel and Motel Association, 221 W. 57th St., New York 19

American Institute for Design and Drafting, 18465 James Couzens, Detroit 35, Mich.

American Institute of Accountants, 666 Fifth Ave., New York 19

American Institute of Aeronautics and Astronautics, 1290 Ave. of the Americas, New York 19

American Institute of Architects, 1735 New York Ave., N.W., Washington 6, D.C.

American Institute of Biological Sciences, 2000 P St., N.W., Washington 6, D.C.

American Institute of Certified Public Accountants, 666 Fifth Ave., New York 19

American Institute of Industrial Engineers, 345 E. 47th St., New York 17

American Institute of Mining, Metallurgical, and Petroleum Engineers, 345 E. 47th St., New York 17

American Institute of Nutrition, 9650 Wisconsin Ave., N.W., Washington 6, D.C.

American Institute of Physics, 335 E. 45th St., New York 17

American Institute of Planners, 917 15th St., N.W., Room 800, Washington 5, D.C.

American Iron and Steel Institute, 150 E. 42nd St., New York 17

American Legion, Education and Scholarship Program, 700 N. Pennsylvania St., Indianapolis 6, Ind.

American Liberty Press, 746 W. Winnebago St., Milwaukee 5, Wis.

American Library Association, 50 E. Huron St., Chicago 11, Ill.

American Library Association, Office for Recruitment, 50 E. Huron St., Chicago 11, Ill.

American Management Association, 135 W. 50th St., New York 20

American Marketing Association, 230 N. Michigan Ave., Chicago 1, Ill.

American Mathematical Society, 190 Hope St., Providence 6, R.I.

American Meat Institute, Department of Membership and Personnel Development, 59 E. Van Buren St., Chicago 5, Ill.

American Medical Association, 535 N. Dearborn St., Chicago 10, Ill.

American Meteorological Society, 45 Beacon St., Boston 8, Mass.

American National Red Cross, National Headquarters, Personnel Services, Washington 6, D.C.

American Newspaper Publishers Association Foundation, 750 Third Ave., New York 17

American Nurses' Association, 10 Columbus Circle, New York 19

American Nurses' Association, Occupational Health Nurses Section, 10 Columbus Circle, New York 19

American Occupational Therapy Association, 250 W. 57th St., New York 19

American Optometric Association, 4030 Chouteau Ave., St. Louis 10, Mo.

American Orthoptic Council, 4200 N. Woodward Ave., Royal Oak, Mich.

American Osteopathic Association, 212 E. Ohio St., Chicago 11, Ill.

American Paper and Pulp Association, 122 E. 42nd St., New York 17

American Personnel and Guidance Association, 1605 New Hampshire Ave., N.W., Washington 9, D.C.

American Petroleum Institute, Committee on Public Affairs, 1271 Avenue of the Americas, New York 20

American Pharmaceutical Association, 2215 Constitution Ave., N.W., Washington 7, D.C.

American Physical Therapy Association, 1790 Broadway, New York 19

American Physiological Society, 9650 Wisconsin Ave., Washington 14, D.C.

American Phytopathological Society, Care of Thomas Theis, Public Relations Committee, Plant Industry Station, Beltsville, Md.

American Podiatry Association, 3301 16th St., N.W., Washington 10, D.C.

American Press, Stanton, N.J.

American Psychiatric Association and National Association for Mental Health, Joint Information Service, 1700 18th St., N.W., Washington 9, D.C.

American Psychological Association, 1333 16th St., N.W., Washington 6, D.C.

American Public Health Association, 1790 Broadway, New York 19

American Public Welfare Association, 1313 E. 16th St., Chicago 37, Ill.

American Registry of X-Ray Technicians, Executive Director, Alfred B. Greene, 2600 Wayzata Blvd., Minneapolis 5, Minn.

American School, Drexel Avenue at 58th St., Chicago 37, Ill.

American Society for Engineering Education, Technical Institute Division, Care of W. Leighton Collins, University of Illinois, Urbana, Ill.

American Society for Horticultural Science, Department of Horticulture, Michigan State University, East Lansing, Mich.

American Society for Microbiology, 115 Huron View Blvd., Ann Arbor, Mich.

American Society for Personnel Administration, 16 Kellogg Center, East Lansing, Mich.

American Society for Pharmacology and Experimental Therapeutics, 9650 Wisconsin Ave., Washington 14, D.C.

American Society for Public Administration, 6042 Kimbark Ave., Chicago 37, Ill.

American Society of Agricultural Engineers, 420 Main St., St. Joseph, Mich.

American Society of Agronomy, 677 S. Segoe Road, Madison 11, Wis.

American Society of Biological Chemists, 9650 Wisconsin Ave., Washington 14, D.C.

American Society of Civil Engineers, 345 E. 47th St., New York 17

American Society of Industrial Designers, 15 E. 48th St., New York 17

American Society of Internal Medicine, 3410 Geary Blvd., San Francisco 10, Calif.

American Society of Landscape Architects, 2000 K St., N.W., Washington 6, D.C.

American Society of Limnology and Oceanography, Sapelo Island Research Foundation, Sapelo Island, Ga.

American Society of Mechanical Engineers, 345 E. 47th St., New York 17

American Society of Medical Technologists, Suite 25, Hermann Professional Bldg., Houston 25, Tex.

American Society of Photogrammetry, 44 Leesburg Pike, Falls Church, Va.

American Society of Planning Officials, 1313 E. 60th St., Chicago 37, Ill.

American Society of Plant Physiologists, Division of R and O, Smithsonian Institution, Washington 25, D.C.

American Society of Safety Engineers, 5 N. Wabash Ave., Suite 1705, Chicago 2, Ill.

American Society of Tool and Manufacturing Engineers, 10700 Puritan Ave., Detroit 38, Mich.

American Society of Traffic and Transportation, 22 W. Madison St., Chicago 2, Ill.

American Society of X-Ray Technicians, 537 S. Main St., Fond du Lac, Wis.

American Society of Zoologists, Department of Biology, Goucher College, Baltimore 4, Md.

American Sociological Association, 1755 Massachusetts Ave., N.W., Washington 36, D.C.

American Speech and Hearing Association, 1001 Connecticut Ave., N.W., Washington 6, D.C.

American Statistical Association, 810 18th St., N.W., Washington 6, D.C.

American Technical Society, 848 E. 58th St., Chicago 37, Ill.

American Textile Manufacturers Institute, Inc., 1501 Johnston Bldg., Charlotte 2, N.C.

American Trucking Associations, Education Section, Public Relations Dept., 1616 P St., N.W., Washington 6, D.C.

American Veterinary Medical Association, 600 S. Michigan Ave., Chicago 5, Ill.

American Vocational Association, 1010 Vermont Ave., N.W., Washington 5, D.C.

American Watchmakers Institute, 18465 James Couzens, Detroit 35, Mich.

American Welding Society, 345 E. 47th St., New York 17

American Woman's Society of Certified Public Accountants, 327 S. LaSalle St., Chicago 4, Ill.

Amherst College, Office of Admission, Amherst, Mass.

Amvets National Service Foundation, 1710 Rhode Island Ave., N.W., Washington 6, D.C.

The Amy Loveman National Award, Box 553, Times Square Post Office, New York 36

Antioch College, Yellow Springs, Ohio

Appleton-Century-Crofts, Inc., 60 E. 42nd St., New York 17

Arco Publishing Company, 219 Park Ave. S., New York 3

Armstrong Cork Company, Public Relations, Lancaster, Pa.

Army Careers, United States Continental Army Command, Fort Monroe, Va.

Associated General Contractors of America, 1957 E St., N.W., Washington 6, D.C.

Associated Master Barbers and Beauticians of America, 537 S. Dearborn St., Chicago 5, Ill.

Associated Press Newsfeatures, 50 Rockefeller Plaza, New York 20

Association for Childhood Education International, 3615 Wisconsin Ave., N.W., Washington 16, D.C.

Association for Computing Machinery, 211 E. 43rd St., New York 17

Association of American Colleges, 1818 R St., N.W., Washington 9, D.C.

Association of American Geographers, 1201 16th St., N.W., Washington 6, D.C.

Association of American Medical Colleges, 2530 Ridge Ave., Evanston, Ill.

Association of American Railroads, Public Relations Department, Transportation Bldg., Washington 6, D.C.

Association of College Admissions Counselors, 610 Church St., Evanston, Ill.

Association of Collegiate Schools of Architecture, 521 18th St., N.W., Washington 6, D.C.

Association of Industrial Advertisers, 271 Madison Ave., New York 16

Association of Medical Illustrators, Care of Rose Reynolds, College of Medicine, University of Nebraska, Omaha 5, Neb.

Atchinson, Topeka and Santa Fe Railway System. *See* Santa Fe System Lines

Atheneum Publishers, 162 E. 38th St., New York 16

Atlantic-Little, Brown and Company, 34 Beacon St., Boston 6, Mass.

Automobile Manufacturers Association, 320 New Center Building, Detroit 2, Mich.

Bankers Publishing Company, 89 Beach St., Boston 11, Mass.

George Banta Company, Menasha, Wis.

Barbizon School of Modeling, 576 Fifth Ave., New York 36

A. S. Barnes and Company. Order from Thomas Yoseloff, Publisher, 8 E. 36th St., New York 16

Barnes and Noble, Inc., 105 Fifth Ave., New York 3

Barron's Educational Series, Inc., 343 Great Neck Road, Great Neck 2, N.Y.

Basic Books, Inc., 404 Park Ave. S., New York 16

Battelle Memorial Institute, 505 King Ave., Columbus 1, Ohio

Bausch and Lomb, Incorporated, Science Award Committee, Rochester 2, N.Y.

Bellman Publishing Company, P.O. Box 172, Cambridge 38, Mass.

Beneficial Management Corporation, Beneficial Building, 200 South St., Morristown, N.J.

Benton and Bowles, Inc., 666 Fifth Ave., New York 19

Bethany Press, Box 179, 2640 Pine Blvd., St. Louis 66, Mo.

Better Business Bureau, 220 Church Street, New York 13

Biophysical Society, Box 3054, University Station, Columbus 10, Ohio

Blakiston Division, McGraw-Hill Book Company, 330 W. 42nd St., New York 36

B'nai B'rith Vocational Service, 1640 Rhode Island Ave., N.W., Washington 6, D.C.

Board of Christian Education, United Presbyterian Church in the U.S.A., Division of Vocation, 808 Witherspoon Bldg., Philadelphia 7, Pa.

Board of Missions of The Methodist Church, 475 Riverside Drive, New York 27

Bobbs-Merrill Company, 4300 W. 62nd St., Indianapolis 6, Ind.

Book Publishing Company, Law Books and City Codes, Seattle, Wash.

Boston University, Director of Admissions, 705 Commonwealth Ave., Boston 15, Mass.

Botanical Society of America, Inc., Department of Botany, University of Texas, Austin 12, Tex.

Bowker, R. R., Company, 1180 Avenue of the Americas, New York 36

Bowman Technical School, Lancaster, Pa.

Boy Scouts of America, National Council, New Brunswick, N.J.

Boys' Clubs of America, 771 First Ave., New York 17

Mrs. F. G. Brooks, Box 515, Ansonia Station, New York 23

Brotherhood of Painters, Decorators, and Paperhangers of America, Painters and Decorators Bldg., Lafayette, Ind.

William C. Brown Company, 135 S. Locust St., Dubuque, Iowa

Bruce Publishing Company, 400 N. Broadway, Milwaukee 1, Wis.

Bryant College, Providence, R.I.

Bunting and Lyon, Inc., 12 N. Main St., Wallingford, Conn.

Burckel, Christian E., and Associates, P.O. Box 311, Yonkers, N.Y.

Bureau of Apprenticeship and Training, U.S. Department of Labor, Washington 25, D.C.

Bureau of Employment Security, U.S. Department of Labor, Washington 25, D.C.

Bureau of Family Services, U.S. Department of Health, Education, and Welfare, Washington 25, D.C.

Bureau of International Education, Office of Education, U.S. Department of Health, Education, and Welfare, Washington 25, D.C.

Bureau of Labor Standards, U.S. Department of Labor, Washington 25, D.C.

Bureau of Labor Statistics, U.S. Department of Labor, Washington 25, D.C.

Bureau of Public Assistance, Social Security Administration, U.S. Department of Health, Education, and Welfare, Washington 25, D.C.

Bureau of Publications, Teachers College, Columbia University, 525 W. 120th St., New York 27

Burroughs Williams and Company, Inc., Tuckahoe, N.Y.

California State Department of Employment, 800 Capitol Ave., Sacramento 14, Calif.

California State Polytechnic College, San Luis Obispo, Calif.

California Test Bureau, Monterey, Calif.

Camp Fire Girls, Inc., 65 Worth St., New York 13

Canadian Library Association, Recruitment Committee, Care of Mrs. Margaret Mavins, 63 Sparks St., Ottawa 4, Onario, Canada

Canadian Universities Foundation, 75 Albert St., Ottawa 4, Ontario, Canada

Capitol Publishing Company, 215 E. 22nd St., New York 10

Career Guidance Digest, Inc., 1406 G St., N.W., Washington 5, D.C.

Careers, P.O. Box 135, Largo, Fla.

Careers Incorporated, 770 Lexington Ave., New York 21

Carnegie Corporation of New York, 589 Fifth Ave., New York 17

Casualty Actuarial Society, 200 E. 42nd St., New York 17

Caterpillar Tractor Company, Peoria 8, Ill.

Catholic College Admissions Center, 3805 McKinley St., N.W., Washington 15, D.C.

Catholic College Bureau, 25 E. Jackson Blvd., Chicago 4, Ill.

Catholic Institutional Directory Company, 9 N. Village Ave., Rockville Centre, N.Y.

Central Committee for Conscientious Objectors, 2006 Walnut St., Philadelphia 3, Pa.

Central Opera Service, National Council of Metropolitan Opera Association, 147 W. 39th St., New York 18

Chamber of Commerce of the United States, Education Department, 1615 H St., N.W., Washington 6, D.C.

Champaign Senior High School, 610 W. University Ave., Champaign, Ill.

Changing Times, The Kiplinger Magazine, 1729 H St., N.W., Washington 6, D.C.

Channel Press, 60 E. 42nd St., New York 17

Child Study Association of America, 9 E. 89th St., New York 28

Children's Bureau. Order from Superintendent of Documents

Childrens Press, Inc., Jackson Blvd. and Racine Ave., Chicago 7, Ill.

Chilton Company, Book Division, Chestnut and 56th Sts., Philadelphia 39, Pa.

Chronicle Guidance Publications, Inc., Moravia, N.Y.

Church of the Brethren, General Offices, Elgin, Ill.

Cincinnati College of Embalming, 3202 Reading Road, Cincinnati 29, Ohio

Citadel Press, 222 Park Ave S., New York 3

Clairol Institute of Haircoloring, 666 Fifth Ave., New York 19

College Admissions Assistance Center, 41 E. 65th St., New York 21

College Admissions Center, 610 Church St., Evanston, Ill.

College Entrance Examination Board, Box 592, Princeton, N.J.

College Entrance Publications Corporation, 104 Fifth Ave., New York 11

College of Agriculture, Department of Dairy Technology, Ohio State University, 122 Vivian Hall, Columbus 10, Ohio

College Placement Council, 35 E. Elizabeth Ave., Bethlehem, Pa.

College Publishing Corporation, 132 Livingston St., Brooklyn 1, N.Y.

College Scholarship Service, Box 176, Princeton, N.J., or Box 27896, Los Angeles 27, Calif.

Collier's Encyclopedia, Library and Educational Division, 640 Fifth Ave., New York 19

Colorado School of Mines, Golden, Colo.

Columbia University Press, 2960 Broadway, New York 27

Columbia University, School of Dental and Oral Surgery, Courses for Dental Hygiene, 630 W. 168th St., New York 32

Commercial Chemical Development Association, 100 Church St., New York 17

Commission on World Mission of the National Student Christian Federation, 475 Riverside Drive, New York 27

Committee on Careers, National League for Nursing, 10 Columbus Circle, New York 19

Conference of Catholic Schools of Nursing, 1438 S. Grand Blvd., St. Louis 4, Mo.

Cooper Union, School of Art and Architecture, Cooper Square, New York 3

Cooperative Extension Service, New York State College of Agriculture, Cornell University, Ithaca, N.Y.

Cooperative Test Division, Educational Testing Service, 20 Nassau St., Princeton, N.J., or 4640 Hollywood Blvd., Los Angeles 27, Calif.

Corning Glass Works Foundation, Corning, N.Y.

Council for Professional Education for Business, 101 N. Skinker Blvd., St. Louis 30, Mo.

Council for the Advancement of Small Colleges, 1327 18th St., N.W., Washington 36, D.C.

Council on Hotel, Restaurant and Institutional Education, Statler Hall, Cornell University, Ithaca, N.Y.

Council on Medical Education and Hospitals of the American Medical Association, 535 N. Dearborn St., Chicago 10, Ill.

Council on Opportunities in Selling, Inc., 630 Third Ave., New York 17

Council on Rural Health, American Medical Association, 535 N. Dearborn St., Chicago 11, Ill.

Council on Social Work Education, 345 E. 46th St., New York 17

Council on Student Travel, Information Department, 179 Broadway, New York 7

Counselor Education Press, 924 W. Beaver Ave., State College, Pa.

Coward-McCann, Inc., 200 Madison Ave., New York 16

Criterion Books, Inc., 6 W. 57th Street, New York 19

Croner Publications, 211 Jamaica Ave., Queens Village, N.Y.

Thomas Y. Crowell Company, 201 Park Ave. S., New York 3

Crowell-Collier Press, 60 Fifth Ave., New York 11

Crowell-Collier Publishing Company, 640 Fifth Ave., New York 19

Crucible Manufacturers' Association, 271 North Ave., New Rochelle, N.Y.

Dartnell Corporation, 4660 Ravenswood Ave., Chicago 40, Ill.

Davey Tree Expert Company, Kent, Ohio

John Day Company, 62 W. 45th St., New York 36

Delta Pi Epsilon, Executive Secretary, John E. Binnion, University of Denver, 1445 Cleveland Place, Denver 2, Colo.

Dental Hygienists Alumnae Association, Columbia University, School of Dental and Oral Surgery, 630 W. 168th St., New York 32

Department of Public Instruction, Commonwealth of Pennsylvania, Box 911, Education Bldg., Harrisburg, Pa.

DeVry Technical Institute, 4141 Belmont Ave., Chicago 41, Ill.

Dial Press, 750 Third Ave., New York 17

Diesel Engine Manufacturers Association, 122 E. 42nd St., New York 17

Direct Mail Advertising Association, 230 Park Ave., New York 17

Division of Vocational and Technical Education, U.S. Office of Education, Department of Health, Education, and Welfare, Washington 25, D.C.

Dodd, Mead and Company, 432 Park Ave. S., New York 16

Dollars for Scholars, Bell Syndicate Research Office, Box 725, Cleveland 22, Ohio

Domestic Distribution Department, Chamber of Commerce of the United States, Washington 6, D.C.

Doubleday and Company, 277 Park Ave., New York 17

Duell, Sloan and Pearce, Inc., 60 E. 42nd St., New York 17

E. I. du Pont de Nemours and Company, Public Relations Department, 1007 Market St., Wilmington 98, Del.

E. P. Dutton and Company, 201 Park Ave. S., New York 3

Eastman Kodak Company, 343 State St., Rochester 4, N.Y.

Educational Directories, Inc., P.O. Box 199, Mount Prospect, Ill.

Educational Era Publishers, 651 Stowe Ave., Baldwin, N.Y.

Educational Policies Commission, 1201 16th St., N.W., Washington 6, D.C.

Educational Records Bureau, 21 Audubon Ave., New York 32

Educational Research Corporation, 10 Craigie St., Cambridge 38, Mass.

Educational Testing Service, 20 Nassau St., Princeton, N.J.

Educators Progress Service, Randolph, Wis.

Educators Publishing Service, 301 Vassar St., Cambridge 39, Mass.

Electronic Computer Programming Institute, 116 W. 14th St., New York 11

Electronic Industries Association, 1721 De Sales St., N.W., Washington 6, D.C.

Engineering Manpower Commission of Engineers Joint Council, 345 E. 47th St., New York 17

Engineers' Council for Professional Development, 345 E. 47th St., New York 17

Entomological Society of America, 4603 Calvert Road, College Park, Md.

Equitable Life Assurance Society of the United States, 1285 Avenue of the Americas, New York 19

Evangelical United Brethren Church, Board of Christian Education, 601 W. Riverview, Dayton 6, Ohio

Executive Development Press, Littleton, N.H.

Fairchild Publications, Inc., 7 East 12th St., New York 3

Family Service Association of America, 44 E. 23rd St., New York 10

Federal Aviation Agency, Washington 25, D.C.

Federal Bureau of Investigation, U.S. Department of Justice, Washington 25, D.C.

Federation of the Handicapped, 211 W. 14th St., New York 11

Fibre Box Association, 1145 19th St., N.W., Washington 6, D.C.

Fidelity Mutual Life Insurance Company, Parkway at Fairmount Ave., Philadelphia 1, Pa.

Field Enterprises Educational Corporation, Merchandise Mart Plaza, Chicago 54, Ill.

Financial Executives Institute, 50 W. 44th St., New York 36

Finney Company, 3350 Gorham Ave., Minneapolis 26, Minn.

Fish and Wildlife Service, U.S. Department of the Interior, Washington 25, D.C.

Fisher Body Craftsman's Guild, General Motors, Warren, Mich.

Florida State Employment Service, Florida Industrial Commission, Tallahassee, Fla.

Ford Motor Company, Educational Affairs Department, The American Road, Dearborn, Mich.

Foreign Commerce Department, Chamber of Commerce of the United States, 1615 H St., N.W., Washington 6, D.C.

Foundation Library Center, 444 Madison Ave., New York 22

Friendship Press, 475 Riverside Drive, New York 27

Fund for the Advancement of Education, 477 Madison Ave., New York 22

Funds for Education, Inc., 319 Lincoln St., Manchester, N.H.

Funk and Wagnalls Company, 360 Lexington Ave., New York 17

Future Scientists of America, Foundation of the National Science Teachers Association, National Education Association, 1201 16th St., N.W., Washington 6, D.C.

Future Teachers of America, 1201 16th St., N.W., Washington 6, D.C.

Gale Research Company, 2200 Book Tower, Detroit 26, Mich.

General Electric Company, Educational Relations Service, 1 River Road, Schenectady 5, N.Y.

General Electric Scholarship Contest, Box 4448, Chicago, Ill.

General Motors Corporation, Public Relations Staff, General Motors Bldg., Detroit 2, Mich.

General Motors Corporation, Salaried Personnel Placement Activity, 3044 W. Grand Blvd., Detroit 2, Mich.

General Motors Institute, Flint 2, Mich.

Geographical Research Institute, 5235 Ravenswood Ave., Chicago 40, Ill.

Georgia Institute of Technology, 225 North Ave., Atlanta 13, Ga.

Girl Scouts of the U.S.A., 830 Third Ave., New York 22

Golden Press, Inc., 630 Fifth Ave., New York 20

Good Housekeeping School Department, 57th St. at Eighth Ave., New York 19

Graduate Library School, University of Chicago, Chicago 37, Ill.

Graphic Arts Industry, Inc., Education Council, 1411 K St., N.W., Washington 5, D.C.

Gregg Publishing Division, McGraw-Hill Book Company, 330 W. 42nd St., New York 36

Grosset and Dunlap, Inc., 1107 Broadway, New York 10

The Guidance Centre, Ontario College of Education, University of Toronto, 371 Bloor St. W., Toronto 5, Ontario, Canada

Watson Guptill Publications, Inc., 111 Fourth Ave., New York 3

Hammond Organ Company, 4200 W. Diversey Ave., Chicago 39, Ill.

Harcourt, Brace and World, Inc., 757 Third Ave., New York 17

Harian Publications, Greenlawn, N.Y.

Harper and Brothers. *See* Harper and Row

Harper and Row, Publishers, 49 E. 33rd St., New York 16

Harvard Educational Review, 13 Appian Way, Cambridge, Mass.

Harvard-Radcliffe Program in Business Administration, Radcliffe College, Cambridge 38, Mass.

Hawthorn Books, Inc., 70 Fifth Ave., New York 11

D. C. Heath and Company, 285 Columbus Ave., Boston 16, Mass.

Hebrew Union College and Jewish Institute of Religion, 3101 Clifton Ave., Cincinnati 20, Ohio

High School News Service, U.S. Department of Defense, Building 3109, Great Lakes, Ill.

Holiday House, 8 W. 13th St., New York 11

Henry Holt and Company. Order from Holt, Rinehart and Winston, Inc.

Holt, Rinehart and Winston, Inc., 383 Madison Ave., New York 17

Houghton Mifflin Company, 2 Park St., Boston 7, Mass.

Huebner Foundation for Insurance Education, The University of Pennsylvania, 3620 Locust St., Philadelphia 4, Pa.

Illinois Institute of Technology, Technology Center, 3300 Federal St., Chicago 16, Ill.

Immigration and Naturalization Service, Board of Civil Service Examiners, 119 D St., N.E., Washington 25, D.C.

Independent School Admissions Advisory Center, 12 N. Main St., Wallingford, Conn.

Indiana University, Bloomington, Ind.

Industrial Design Education Association, College of Design, Architecture and Art, University of Cincinnati, Cincinnati 21, Ohio

Industrial Designers Institute, 441 Madison Ave., New York 22

Industrial Research Service, Masonic Bldg., Dover, N.H.

Institute for Research, 537 S. Dearborn St., Chicago 5, Ill.

Institute of Distribution, Inc., 1441 Broadway, New York 18

Institute of Internal Auditors, 120 Wall St., New York 5

Institute of International Education, 800 Second Ave., New York 17

Institute of Life Insurance, 488 Madison Ave., New York 22

Institute of Meat Packing, American Meat Institute, 59 E. Van Buren St., Chicago 5, Ill.

Institute of Radio Engineers, Inc., 1 E. 79th St., New York 21

Institute of the Aerospace Sciences. *See* American Institute of Aeronautics and Astronautics.

Institute of Traffic Engineers, 1725 DeSales St., N.W., Washington 6, D.C.

Insurance Information Institute, 110 William St., New York 38

Interagency Committee on Oceanography, Room 1714, Bldg. T-3, 17th St. and Constitution Ave., N.W., Washington 25, D.C.

Interboard Committee on Christian Vocations, The Methodist Church, Box 871, Nashville 2, Tenn.

Internal Revenue Service, U.S. Treasury Department, Washington 25, D.C.

International Accountants Society, 209 W. Jackson Blvd., Chicago 6, Ill.

International Association of Chiefs of Police, 1319 18th St., N.W., Washington 6, D.C.

International Association of Fire Chiefs, 232 Madison Ave., New York 16

International Association of Fire Fighters, 815 16th St., N.W., Washington 6, D.C.

International Association of Machinists, 1300 Connecticut Ave., N.W., Washington 6, D.C.

International Business Machines Corporation, Department of Employment, 590 Madison Ave., New York 22

International Chiropractors Association, 741 Brady St., Davenport, Iowa

International Correspondence Schools, Scranton 15, Pa.

International Graphic Arts Education Association, 1411 K St., N.W., Washington 5, D.C.

Intersociety Committee for Research Potential in Pathology, Inc., Care of Milan Herzog, 922 Oakwood, Wilmette, Ill.

Interstate Printers and Publishers, 19 N. Jackson St., Danville, Ill.

Investment Bankers Association of America, 425 13th St., N.W., Washington 4, D.C.

Iowa State University Press, Press Bldg., Ames, Iowa

Jewish Statistical Bureau, 320 Broadway, New York 7

John Hay Fellows Program, 9 Rockefeller Plaza, New York 20

Journalism Educator, Duquesne University, Department of Journalism, Pittsburgh 19, Pa.

Kappa Epsilon Career Guidance Committee, 1539 N. 51st St., Milwaukee 8, Wis.

Keystone Junior College, Public Relations Department, La Plume, Pa.

Kiwanis Club of Long Beach, California, Committee on Vocational Guidance, 255 E. 8th St., Long Beach 13, Calif.

B. Klein and Company, 27 E. 22nd St., New York 10

Alfred A. Knopf, Inc., 501 Madison Ave., New York 22

Lantern Press, 257 Park Ave. S., New York 10

Lehigh University, Bethlehem, Pa.

Life Insurance Agency Management Association, 170 Sigourney St., Hartford 5, Conn.

J. B. Lippincott Company, E. Washington Square, Philadelphia 5, Pa.

Liquefied Petroleum Gas Association, 11 S. LaSalle St., Chicago 3, Ill.

Little, Brown and Company, 34 Beacon St., Boston 6, Mass.

Longmans, Green and Company. Order from David McKay Company, 119 W. 40th St., New York 18

Long's College Book Company, 1836 N. High St., Columbus 1, Ohio

Look Magazine, Educational Consultants, 488 Madison Ave., New York 22

Lothrop, Lee and Shepard Company, 419 Park Ave. S., New York 16

Lovejoy, Clarence E., 443 Broad St., Red Bank, N.J.

Robert B. Luce, Inc., 1244 19th St., N.W., Washington 6, D.C.

Lutheran Church in America, Board of College Education and Church Vocations, 231 Madison Ave., New York 16

McGraw-Hill Book Company, 330 W. 42nd St., New York 36

McGraw-Hill Whittlesey House, 330 W. 42nd St., New York 36

David McKay Company, 750 Third Ave., New York 17

McKnight and McKnight Publishing Company, Towanda Ave. and Route 66, Bloomington, Ill.

Macmillan Company, 60 Fifth Ave., New York 11

Macrae Smith Company, 225 S. 15th St., Philadelphia 2, Pa.

Mademoiselle, College and Careers, 420 Lexington Ave., New York 17

Manhattan College, Riverdale, 71 N.Y.

Manufacturing Chemists' Association, 1825 Connecticut Ave., N.W., Washington 9, D.C.

Massachusetts Institute of Technology, Office of Publications, Cambridge 39, Mass.

Material Handling Institute, Suite 759, 1 Gateway Center, Pittsburgh 22, Pa.

Mathematical Association of America, University of Buffalo, Buffalo 14, N.Y.

Medical Library Association, 919 N. Michigan Ave., Chicago 11, Ill.

Melmont Publishers, Childrens Press, Inc., Jackson Blvd. and Racine Ave., Chicago 7, Ill.

Meredith Press, 1716 Locust St., Des Moines 3, Iowa

Merrill Books, Inc., 1300 Alum Creek Drive, Columbus 16, Ohio

Julian Messner, Inc., 8 W. 40th St., New York 18

Methods and Materials Press, 6 S. Derby Road, Springfield, N.J.

Metropolitan Life Insurance Company, School Health Bureau, 1 Madison Ave., New York 10

Michigan College of Mining and Technology, Department of College Relations, Houghton, Mich.

Michigan Employment Security Commission, 7310 Woodward Ave., Detroit 2, Mich.

Michigan State University, College of Education, Office of Publications, 252 College of Education Bldg., East Lansing, Mich.

Michigan State University, Department of Forestry, East Lansing, Mich.

Michigan State University, Department of Urban Planning and Landscape Architecture, South Campus, East Lansing, Mich.

Michigan State University, School of Labor and Industrial Relations, East Lansing, Mich.

Milk Industry Foundation, 1145 19th St., N.W., Washington 6, D.C.

Miller, Ray A. York Junior College, Country Club Road, York, Pa.

Milwaukee-Downer College, 2812 E. Hartford Ave., Milwaukee 11, Wis.

Milwaukee Journal, 333 W. State St., Milwaukee 1, Wis.

Missouri School of Mines and Metallurgy, Rolla, Mo.

Modern Language Journal, 7144 Washington Ave., St. Louis 30, Mo.

Modern Library, Random House, Inc., 457 Madison Ave., New York 22

Monthly Labor Review, Supt. of Documents, Washington 25, D.C.

William Morrow and Company, 425 Park Ave. S., New York 16

Museum of Science and Industry, Jackson Park, Chicago 37, Ill.

Music Educators National Conference, 1201 16th St., N.W., Washington 6, D.C.

National Academy of Sciences, National Research Council, Fellowship Office, 2101 Constitution Ave., N.W., Washington 25, D.C.

National Advisory Commission on Careers in Pharmacy, 2215 Constitution Ave., N.W., Washington 7, D.C.

National Aeronautics and Space Administration, Educational Publications Branch, Code AFEE, Washington 25, D.C.

National Aerospace Education Council, 1025 Connecticut Ave., N.W., Washington 6, D.C.

National Architectural Accrediting Board, Secretary, Robert H. Dietz, 521 18th St., N.W., Washington 6, D.C.

National Art Education Association, 1201 16th St., N.W., Washington 6, D.C.

National Association for Mental Health, 10 Columbus Circle, New York 19

National Association for Practical Nurse Education and Service, Inc., 475 Riverside Drive, New York 27

National Association of Broadcasters, 1771 N St., N.W., Washington 36, D.C.

National Association of Chain Drug Stores, 1625 Eye St., N.W., Washington 6, D.C.

National Association of Cosmetology Schools, 3839 White Plains Road, Bronx 67, N.Y.

National Association of Dental Laboratories, 201 Mills Bldg., Washington 6, D.C.

National Association of Direct Selling Companies, 165 Center St., Winona, Minn.

National Association of Home Builders, 1625 L St., N.W., Washington 6, D.C.

National Association of Independent Schools, 4 Liberty Square, Boston 9, Mass.

National Association of Manufacturers, Industrial Relations Division, 2 E. 48th St., New York 17

National Association of Motor Bus Owners, 839 17th St., N.W., Washington 6, D.C.

National Association of Printing Ink Makers, 39 W. 55th St., New York 19

National Association of Purchasing Agents, 11 Park Place, New York 7

National Association of Real Estate Boards, 36 S. Wabash Ave., Chicago 3, Ill.

National Association of Retail Grocers, 360 N. Michigan Ave., Chicago 1, Ill.

National Association of Schools of Art, 50 Astor Place, New York 3

National Association of Schools of Design, 50 Astor Place, New York 3

National Association of Secondary-School Principals, 1201 16th St., N.W., Washington 6, D.C.

National Association of Social Workers, 2 Park Ave., New York 16

National Association of Wholesalers, 1725 K St., N.W., Washington 6, D.C.

National Beta Club, Box 730, Spartanburg, S.C.

National Broadcasting Company, Department of Information, 30 Rockefeller Plaza, New York 20

National Bureau of Standards, U.S. Department of Commerce, Washington 25, D.C.

National Business Publications, 1913 Eye St., N.W., Washington 6, D.C.

National Cartoonists Society, 152 Colonial Parkway, Manhasset, N.Y.

National Cash Register Company, Merchants' Service, Main and K Sts., Dayton 9, Ohio

National Catholic Welfare Conference, 1312 Massachusetts Ave., N.W., Washington 5, D.C.

National Chiropractic Association, Department of Education, National Bldg., Webster City, Iowa

National Coal Association, 1130 17th St., N.W., Washington 6, D.C.

National Commission for Social Work Careers, Jointly Sponsored by Council on Social Work Education and National Association of Social Workers, 345 46th St., New York 17

National Commission on Teacher Education and Professional Standards, National Education Association, 1201 16th St., N.W., Washington 6, D.C.

National Consumer Finance Association, 1000 16th St., N.W., Washington 6, D.C.

National Council of Churches, Department of Ministry, 475 Riverside Drive, New York 27

National Council of Teachers of Mathematics, 1201 16th St., N.W., Washington 6, D.C.

National Council of Technical Schools, 1507 M St., N.W., Washington 5, D.C.

National Council of the Churches of Christ, Office of Publication and Distribution, 475 Riverside Drive, New York 27

National Council of Young Men's Christian Association, Personnel Services, 291 Broadway, New York 7

National Council on Crime and Delinquency, 44 E. 23rd St., New York 10

National Dairy Council, 111 N. Canal St., Chicago 6, Ill.

National Directory Service, Box 32065, Cincinnati 32, Ohio

National Education Association, 1201 16th St., N.W., Washington 6. D.C.

National Executive Housekeepers Association, Holzer Hospital and Clinic, Gallipolis, Ohio

National Forum, Inc., 407 S. Dearborn St., Chicago 5, Ill.

National Foundation, 800 Second Ave., New York 17

National Funeral Directors Association, 135 W. Wells St., Milwaukee 3, Wis.

National Hairdressers and Cosmetologists Association, 175 Fifth Ave., New York 22

National Health Council, 1790 Broadway, New York 19

National Home Study Council, 1601 18th St., N.W., Washington 9, D.C.

National Housing Center, 1625 L St., N.W., Washington 6, D.C.

National Institute of Drycleaning, Silver Spring, Md.

National Jewish Welfare Board, Bureau of Personnel and Training, 145 E. 32nd St., New York 16

National Landscape Nurserymen's Association, P.O. Drawer 281, Leesburg, Fla.

National League for Nursing, Committee on Careers, 10 Columbus Circle, New York 19

National League for Nursing, Division of Nursing Education, 10 Columbus Circle, New York 19

National Lumber Manufacturers Association, Technical Education Department, 1619 Massachusetts Ave., N.W., Washington 6, D.C.

National Merit Scholarship Corporation, 1580 Sherman Ave., Evanston, Ill.

National Paint, Varnish and Lacquer Association, 1500 Rhode Island Ave., N.W., Washington 5, D.C.

National Park Service, U.S. Department of the Interior, Washington 25, D.C.

National Recreation Association, 8 W. 8th St., New York 11

National Research Bureau, Inc., 221 N. LaSalle St., Chicago 10, Ill.

National Restaurant Association, 1530 N. Lake Shore Drive, Chicago 10, Ill.

National Retail Dry Goods Association. See National Retail Merchants Association

National Retail Hardware Association, 964 N. Pennsylvania St., Indianapolis 4, Ind.

National Retail Merchants Association, 100 W. 31st St., New York 1

National Scholarship Service and Fund for Negro Students, 6 E. 82nd St., New York 28

National Science Foundation, 1951 Constitution Ave., N.W., Washington 25, D.C.

National Science Teachers Association, Project on Information Processing, Dr. Hugh Allen, Director, Box 201, Montclair State College, Upper Montclair, N.J.

National Secretaries Association, Suite 410, 1103 Grand Ave., Kansas City 6, Mo.

National Selected Morticians, 1616 Central St., Evanston, Ill.

National Service Board for Religious Objectors, 401 Third St., N.W., Washington 1, D.C.

National Shorthand Reporters Association, Care of Mrs. Louise Williams, 3054 U.S. Court House, Philadelphia 7, Pa.

National Social Welfare Assembly, 345 E. 46th St., New York 17

National Society for Crippled Children and Adults, 2023 W. Ogden Ave., Chicago 12, Ill.

National Society for the Study of Education. Yearbooks distributed by the Chicago University Press

National Society of Art Directors, 115 E. 40th St., New York 16

National Society of Professional Engineers, 2029 K St., N.W., Washington 6, D.C.

National Study of Secondary School Evaluation, 1785 Massachusetts Ave., Washington 6, D.C.

National Teacher Examinations, Educational Testing Service, Princeton, N.J.

National University Extension Association, Business Office, Bldg., TSMc, Room 112, University of Minnesota, Minneapolis 14, Minn.

National Urban League, 14 E. 48th St., New York 17

National Vocational Guidance Association, 1605 New Hampshire Ave., N.W., Washington 9, D.C.

National Wildlife Federation, 1412 16th St., N.W., Washington 6, D.C.

Thomas Nelson and Sons, 18 E. 41st St., New York 17

New American Library of World Literature, Inc., 501 Madison Ave., New York 22

New Brunswick Secretarial, Accounting and Prep School, 110 Albany St., New Brunswick, N.J.

New England Board of Higher Education, 31 Church St., Winchester, Mass.

New Jersey Education Association, 180 W. State St., Trenton 8, N.J.

New Jersey State Department of Institutions and Agencies, 135 Hanover St., Trenton 25, N.J.

New Mexico Institute of Mining and Technology, Campus Station, Socorro, N.M.

New York Central System, 466 Lexington Ave., New York 17

New York Herald Tribune, Classified Advertising Department, 230 W. 41st St., New York 36

New York Journal-American, Display Education Department, 220 South St., New York 15

New York Life Insurance Company, Career Information Service, Box 51, Madison Square Station, New York 10

New York Mergenthaler Linotype School, 244 W. 23rd St., New York 11

New York State Camp Directors Association, 2112 Broadway, P.O. Box 723, Ansonia Station, New York 23

New York State Department of Civil Service, 1220 Washington Ave., Albany 1, N.Y.

New York State Department of Commerce, 230 Park Ave., New York 17

New York State Department of Labor, Division of Employment, New York State Employment Service, 444 Madison Ave., New York 22

New York State Education Department, Bureau of Guidance, Albany 1, N.Y.

New York State Employment Service, Public Information Office, 370 Seventh Ave., New York 1

New York University, Director of Admissions, University Heights, New York 53

New York University, Office of the Registrar and Supervisor of Admissions, Washington Square, New York 3

New York University Press, 32 Washington Place, New York 3

New York University, School of Education, Prosthetics and Orthotics Curriculum, 342 E. 26th St., New York 10

Newark College of Engineering, Public Relations Office, 323 High St., Newark 2, N.J.

Newspaper Fund, Inc., 44 Broad Street, New York 4

North Central Association of Colleges and Secondary Schools, 5835 Kimbark Ave., Chicago 37, Ill.

North Central Association, STS Project, 5454 S. Shore Drive, Chicago 15, Ill.

Northeastern University, College of Education, Department of Admissions, 360 Huntington Ave., Boston 15, Mass.

W. W. Norton and Company, 55 Fifth Ave., New York 3

Nova Scotia Guidance Newsletter, Pupil Personnel Services, Box 578, Halifax, Nova Scotia

Oak Ridge Institute of Nuclear Studies, P.O. Box 117, Oak Ridge, Tenn.

Occupational Outlook Quarterly. Order from Superintendent of Documents, Washington 25, D.C.

Occupational Outlook Service, Bureau of Labor Statistics, U.S. Department of Labor, Washington 25, D.C.

Occu-Press, P.O. Box 1464, Grand Central Post Office, New York 17

Oceana Publications, 40 Cedar St., Dobbs Ferry, N.Y.

Office for Recruitment, American Library Association, 50 E. Huron St., Chicago 11, Ill.

Office of Education. See U.S. Office of Education

Office of Manpower, Automation, and Training, U.S. Department of Labor, Washington 25, D.C.

Ohio Department of Health, Columbus 15, Ohio

Ohio Leather Company, 1052 N. State St., Girard, Ohio

Ohio State School of Cosmetology, 199½ S. High St., Columbus 15, Ohio

Oklahoma State University of Agriculture and Applied Science, Stillwater, Okla.

Olin Mathieson Chemical Corporation, 460 Park Ave., New York 22

Pan American Airways, Educational Director, 28-19 Bridge Plaza N., Long Island City 1, N.Y.

Pan American Union, Division of Education, Washington 6, D.C.

Park Publishing House, 4141 W. Vliet St., Milwaukee 8, Wis.

Peace Corps, Office of Public Affairs, Washington 25, D.C.

Pennsylvania State University, College of Mineral Industries Experiment Station, University Park, Pa.

Personnel Services, Inc., P.O. Box 306, Jaffrey, N.H.

Charles Pfizer and Company, 235 E. 42nd St., New York 17

Phi Delta Kappa, Eighth and Union, Bloomington, Ind.

Philadelphia College of Pharmacy and Science, 43rd St., Kingsessing and Woodland Aves., Philadelphia 4, Pa.

Philadelphia College of Textiles and Science, School House Lane, Philadelphia 44, Pa.

Philadelphia Museum College of Art, Broad and Pine Sts., Philadelphia 2, Pa.

Pitman Publishing Corporation, 20 E. 46th St., New York 17

Platt and Munk Company, 200 Fifth Ave., New York 10

Pocket Books, Inc., 1 W. 39th St., New York 18

Popular Library, Inc., 355 Lexington Ave., New York 17

Popular Mechanics Press. Distributed by Hawthorn Books, Inc., 70 Fifth Ave., New York 11

Potomac Press, 121 N. Oakland St., Arlington 3, Va.

Pratt Institute, Publications Office, Brooklyn 5, N.Y.

Prentice-Hall, Inc., Englewood Cliffs, N.J.

President's Committee on Employment of the Handicapped, U.S. Employment Service, Bureau of Employment Security, U.S. Department of Labor, Washington 25. D.C.

Theodore Presser Company, Presser Place, Bryn Mawr, Pa.

Printing Industries of Metropolitan New York, Inc., 461 Eighth Ave., New York 1

Private Vocational Schools Association of New York, 154 W. 14th St., New York 11

Professional Photographers of America, 152 W. Wisconsin Ave., Milwaukee 3, Wis.

Professional Placement Center, New York State Employment Service, 444 Madison Ave., New York 22

Project on Information Processing, National Science Teachers Association, Box 201, Montclair State College, Upper Montclair, N.J.

Prospect Union Educational Exchange, 18 Brattle St., Cambridge 38, Mass.

Prudential Insurance Company of America, Education Department, Box 36, Prudential Plaza, Newark 1, N.J.

Public Affairs Committee, Inc., 22 E. 38th St., New York 16

Public Health Service, U.S. Department of Health, Education, and Welfare, Washington 25, D.C.

Public Personnel Association, 1313 E. 60th St., Chicago 37, Ill.

Public Relations Society of America, 375 Park Ave., New York 22

Purdue University, Office of University Editor, Lafayette, Ind.

G. P. Putnam's Sons, 200 Madison Ave., New York 16

Quill and Scroll, International Honor Society for High School Journalists, State University of Iowa, Iowa City, Iowa

Radio Corporation of America, Department of Information, 30 Rockefeller Plaza, New York 20

Lynn and Lillian Ralya, 907 14th St., Santa Monica, Calif.

Rand McNally and Company, College Department, P.O. Box 7600, Chicago 80, Ill.

Randall Publishing Company, Benjamin Franklin Post Office, P.O. Box 7408, Washington 4, D.C.

Random House, Inc., 457 Madison Ave., New York 22

Readers Press, 282 York Street, New Haven, Conn.

Registry of Medical Technologists of the American Society of Clinical Pathologists, Box 44, Muncie, Ind.

Republic Book Company, 104-16 Roosevelt Ave., Flushing 68, N.Y.

Research Publishing Company, P.O. Box 245, Boston 1, Mass.

Reynolds Tobacco Company, Youth Education Department, Sales and Marketing Executives International, 630 Third Ave., New York 17

Frank E. Richards, Publisher, 215 Church St., Phoenix, N.Y.

John F. Rider, Publisher, Inc., 116 W. 14th St., New York 11

Rinehart and Company. Order from Holt, Rinehart and Winston, Inc., 383 Madison Ave., New York 17

Ritter Company, 400 West Ave., Rochester 3, N.Y.

Rittners School, 345 Marlborough St., Boston 15, Mass.

Rochester Institute of Technology, Department of Public Relations, 65 S. Plymouth Ave., Rochester 8, N.Y.

Ronald Press Company, 15 E. 26th St., New York 10

Richards Rosen Press, 29 E. 21st St., New York 10

Rotary Foundation of Rotary International, 1600 Ridge Ave., Evanston, Ill.

Rowman and Littlefield, Inc., 84 Fifth Ave., New York 11

Roy Publishers, Inc., 30 E. 74th St., New York 21

Royal McBee Corporation, School Department, 850 Third Ave., New York 22

Russell Sage Foundation, 505 Park Ave., New York 22

Saint Francis College, Guidance Center, 35 Butler St., Brooklyn 31, N.Y.

Sales and Marketing Executives-International, Youth Education Department, 630 Third Ave., New York 17

Santa Fe System Lines, Public Relations Department, 80 E. Jackson Blvd., Chicago 4, Ill.

Porter Sargent, 11 Beacon St., Boston 8, Mass.

Scholastic Book Services, Englewood, N.J.

School of Commerce, Accounts, and Finance, New York University, Washington Square, New York 3

Science Clubs of America, 1719 N St., N.W., Washington 6, D.C.
Science Research Associates, 259 E. Erie St., Chicago 11, Ill.
Science Service, 1719 N St., N.W., Washington 6, D.C.
Scott, Foresman and Company, 433 E. Erie St., Chicago 11, Ill.
Charles Scribner's Sons, 597 Fifth Ave., New York 17
Seven College Conference, Scholarship Program, Vassar College, Poughkeepsie, N.Y.
Seventeen, America's Teen-Age Magazine, 320 Park Ave., New York 22
Sigma Delta Chi, National Journalistic Society, 35 E. Wacker Drive, Chicago 1, Ill.
Simmons College, Registrar, 300 The Fenway, Boston 15, Mass.
Simon and Schuster, Inc., 630 Fifth Ave., New York 20
Alfred P. Sloan Foundation, 630 Fifth Ave., New York 20
Small Business Administration, Washington 25, D.C.
Turner E. Smith and Company, 680 Forrest Road, N.E., Atlanta 12, Ga.
Smithsonian Institution, Washington 25, D.C.
Social Security Administration. Order from Superintendent of Documents.
Society for Occupational Research, 518 Solway St., Glendale 6, Calif.
Society of Actuaries, 208 S. LaSalle St., Chicago 4, Ill.
Society of American Florists and Ornamental Horticulturists, Sheraton-Park Hotel, Washington 8, D.C.
Society of American Foresters, 425 Mills Bldg., 704 17th St., N.W., Washington 6, D.C.
Society of Exploration Geophysicists, 913 Shell Bldg., Tulsa 19, Okla.
Society of Fire Protection Engineers, 60 Batterymarch St., Boston 10, Mass.
Society of Mining Engineers, 345 E. 47th St., New York 17
Society of Plastics Engineers, Inc., 65 Prospect St., Stamford, Conn.
Society of Reproduction Engineers, 18465 James Couzens, Detroit 35, Mich.
Society of the Plastics Industry, Inc., 250 Park Ave., New York 17
Society of Women Engineers, 345 E. 47th St., New York 17
Soil Conservation Society of America, 7515 N. E. Ankeny Road, Ankeny, Iowa
South Dakota Press, Vermillion, S. D.
Southern Regional Education Board, 130 Sixth St., N.W., Atlantic 13, Ga.
Southern Technical Institute, Marietta, Ga.
South-Western Publishing Company, 5101 Madison Road, Cincinnati 27, Ohio
Special Libraries Association, 31 E. 10th St., New York 3
Specialist for Aerospace Education, U.S. Office of Education, Department of Health, Education, and Welfare, Washington 25, D.C.
Springfield College, Center for YMCA Studies, Springfield 9, Mass.
Squibb and Sons Division, Olin Mathieson Chemical Corporation, 745 Fifth Ave., New York 22
Standard Oil Company of New Jersey, 30 Rockefeller Plaza, New York 20

State of California Department of Employment. See California State Department of Employment

State Schools Publications, North Springfield, Erie County, Pennsylvania

State University of Iowa, Department of Botany, Iowa City, Iowa

State University of New York, College of Forestry, Syracuse 10, N.Y.

State University of New York, Maritime College, Fort Schuyler, Bronx 65, N.Y.

Sterling Publishing Company, 419 Park Ave. S., New York 16

Stites Portrait Company, Shelbyville, Ind.

Structural Clay Products Institute, Mason Relations Department, 1520 18th St., N.W., Washington 6, D.C.

Study Abroad, Inc., P.O. Box 1505, Escondido, Calif.

Sun Life Assurance Company of Canada, Box 6075, Montreal, Canada

Superintendent of Documents, U.S. Government Printing Office, Washington 25, D.C.

Syracuse Pulp and Paper Foundation, State University College of Forestry at Syracuse University, Syracuse 10, N.Y.

Syracuse University Press, University Station, Syracuse 10, N.Y.

Nancy Taylor Secretarial Finishing Schools, 55 W. 42nd St., New York 36

Technical Association of the Pulp and Paper Industry, 360 Lexington Ave., New York 17

Technical Extension Service, 132 Livingston St., Brooklyn 1, N.Y.

Texas Woman's University, Admissions Office, University Hill Station, Denton, Tex.

Tri-State Area School Study Council, University of Pittsburgh, Pittsburgh 13, Pa.

Tri-State College, Director of Admissions, College Hill, Angola, Ind.

Tuition Plan of New Hampshire, Inc., 18 School St., Concord, N.H.

Tupper and Love, Inc., 3030 Peachtree Road, N.W., Atlanta 5, Ga.

Underwood Corporation, Education Department, 1 Park Ave., New York 16

Union Carbide Corporation, Public Relations Department, 270 Park Ave., New York 17

Union College, Schenectady 8, N.Y.

United Air Lines, Personnel Department, New York International Airprot, Jamaica 30, N.Y.

United Air Lines, School and College Service, P.O. Box 8800, Chicago 66, Ill.

United Business Schools Association, 1518 K St., N.W., Washington 5, D.C.

United Christian Missionary Society, Church Vocations Office, 222 S. Downey Ave., Indianapolis 7, Ind.

United Church of Christ, Council for Church and Ministry, Church Vocations Office, 2969 W. 25th St., Cleveland 13, Ohio

United Educators, Inc., Tangley Oaks Educational Center, Lake Bluff, Ill.

United Presbyterian Church, Board of Christian Education, 830 Witherspoon Bldg., Walnut and Juniper Sts., Philadelphia 7, Pa.

U.S. Air Force Academy, USAF Academy, Colorado

U.S. Air Force, Recruiting Service, Wright-Patterson Air Force Base, Ohio

U.S. Armed Forces Institute, Department of Defense, Madison 3, Wis.

U.S. Army Medical Service, Department of the Army, Washington 25, D.C.

U.S. Atomic Energy Commission, Division of Organization and Personnel, 1901 Constitution Ave., N.W., Washington 25, D.C.

U.S. Atomic Energy Commission, Division of Technical Information Extension, P.O. Box 62, Oak Ridge, Tenn.

U.S. Atomic Energy Commission, Office of Technical Services, Department of Commerce, Washington 25, D.C.

U.S. Bureau of Census. Order from Superintendent of Documents

U.S. Chamber of Commerce. See Chamber of Commerce of the United States

U.S. Civil Service Commission, Washington 25, D.C.

U.S. Coast Guard Academy, New London, Conn.

U.S. Coast Guard, Public Information Division, Washington 25, D.C.

U.S. Department of Agriculture, Washington 25, D.C.

U.S. Department of Commerce. Order from Superintendent of Documents

U.S. Department of Defense, The Pentagon, Washington 25, D.C.

U.S. Department of Defense, Defense Advisory Committee on Women in the Services, The Pentagon, Washington 25, D.C.

U.S. Department of Health, Education, and Welfare, Washington 25, D.C.

U.S. Department of Labor, Washington 25, D.C.

U.S. Department of State, Employment Division, Washington 25, D.C.

U.S. Department of the Army. See Army Careers

U.S. Department of the Interior. Order from Superintendent of Documents

U.S. Department of the Navy, Bureau of Medicine and Surgery, Washington 25, D.C.

U.S. Department of the Navy, Bureau of Ships, Washington 25, D.C.

U.S. Department of the Navy, Recruiting Service, Bureau of Naval Personnel, Washington 25, D.C.

U.S. Employment Service, U.S. Department of Labor, Washington 25, D.C.

U.S. Information Agency, Washington 25, D.C.

U.S. Marine Corps, Department of the Navy, Washington 25, D.C.

U.S. Merchant Marine Academy, Kings Point, N.Y.

U.S. Military Academy, Department of the Army, West Point, N.Y.

The U.S. National Student Association, Educational Travel, Inc., 20 West 38th St., New York 18

U.S. Naval Academy, Department of the Navy, Annapolis, Md.

U.S. Naval Institute, Annapolis, Maryland

U.S. Office of Education, Department of Health, Education, and Welfare, Washington 25, D.C.

U.S. Office of Vocational Rehabilitation, Department of Health, Education, and Welfare, Washington 25, D.C.

U.S. Securities and Exchange Commission, Director of Personnel, Washington 25, D.C.

United Student Aid Funds, Inc., College Square, Indianapolis 5, Ind.

UNIVAC Division of Remington Rand, Inc., UNIVAC Park, St. Paul 16, Minn.

University of Chicago, Office of Career Counseling and Placement, Chicago 37, Ill.

University of Chicago Press, 5750 Ellis Ave., Chicago 37, Ill.

University of Cincinnati, College of Business Administration, Cincinnati 21, Ohio

University of Michigan, Publications Distribution Service, 3519 Administration Bldg., Ann Arbor, Mich.

University of Minnesota Press, 2037 University Ave., S.E., Minneapolis 14, Minn.

University of Missouri, School of Forestry, Columbia, Mo.

University of Notre Dame Press, Notre Dame, Ind.

Upjohn Company, Employment Office, Kalamazoo, Mich.

Upsala College, East Orange, N.J.

Vanguard Press, 424 Madison Ave., New York 17

Vantage Press, 120 W. 31st St., New York 1

Veterans Administration, Washington 25, D.C.

Veterans Administration, Department of Medicine and Surgery, Code 135D2, Washington 25, D.C.

Viking Press, Inc., 625 Madison Ave., New York 22

Virginia Polytechnic Institute, Blacksburg, Va.

Vocational Advisory Service, 23 E. 26th St., New York 10

Vocational and Technical Education Division, Office of Education, U.S. Department of Health, Education, and Welfare, Washington 25, D.C.

Vocational Guidance Manuals, Division of Universal Publishing and Distributing Corporation, 800 Second Ave., New York 17

Vocational Rehabilitation Administration, U.S. Department of Health, Education, and Welfare, Washington 25, D.C.

Volta Bureau, 1537 35th St., N.W., Washington 7, D.C.

J. Weston Walch, Publisher, Box 1075, Portland, Me.

Henry Z. Walck, Inc., 19 Union Square W., New York 3

Walker and Company, 10 W. 56th St., New York 19

Ives Washburn, Inc., 750 Third Ave., New York 17

Washington Square Press, Pocket Books, Inc., 630 Fifth Ave., New York 20

Washington University, Admissions Office, St. Louis 5, Mo.

Watson-Guptill Publications, Inc., 165 W. 46th St., New York 36

Franklin Watts, Inc., 575 Lexington Ave., New York 22

West Virginia State Department of Education, State Capitol, Charleston, W. Va.

Western Personnel Institute, Tenth and Dartmouth St., Claremont, Calif.

Westminster Book Store, Witherspoon Bldg., Philadelphia 7, Pa.

Wiley and Sons, 605 Third Ave., New York 16

H. W. Wilson Company, 950 University Ave., Bronx 52, N.Y.

John C. Winston Company. Order from Holt, Rinehart and Winston, Inc., 383 Madison Ave., New York 17

Women's Bureau, U.S. Department of Labor, Washington 25, D. C.

The World Almanac, 125 Barclay St., New York 15

World Trade Academy Press, 50 E. 42nd St., New York 17

Young Men's Christian Association, National Council, 291 Broadway, New York 7

Young Women's Christian Association, National Board, 600 Lexington Ave., New York 22

Zondervan Publishing House, 1415 Lake Drive, S.E., Grand Rapids 6, Mich.

Index